Abridged
Dewey Decimal Classification
and Relative Index

Forest Press OCLC
85 Watervliet Avenue
Albany, New York 12206-2082
USA

Abridged Dewey Decimal Classification and Relative Index

Devised by Melvil Dewey

EDITION 12

Edited by

John P. Comaromi, Editor

Julianne Beall, Assistant Editor

Winton E. Matthews, Jr., Assistant Editor

Gregory R. New, Assistant Editor

FOREST PRESS

A Division of

OCLC Online Computer Library Center, Inc.

ALBANY, NEW YORK

1990

Library of Congress Cataloging-in-Publication Data
Dewey, Melvil, 1851-1931
Abridged Dewey decimal classification and relative index / devised by Melvil Dewey. -- Ed. 12 / edited by John P. Comaromi, Julianne Beall, Winton E. Matthews, Jr., Gregory R. New.
ISBN: 0-910608-42-3 (alk. paper)
1. Classification, Dewey decimal. I. Comaromi, John P. (John Phillip), 1937- . II. Beall, Julianne, 1946- . III. Matthews, Winton E. IV. New, Gregory R. V. Forest Press. VI. Title.
Z696.D5192 1990 025.4′31--dc20 90-31428

The paper used in this publication meets the minimum requirements of American National Standard for Information Sciences-Permanence of Paper for Printed Library Materials, ANSI Z39.48-1984.

Recycled paper

Contents

Publisher's Foreword

The present Abridged Edition 12 is based on the four-volume Edition 20 of the Dewey Decimal Classification (DDC 20) published in January 1989. Abridged Edition 12 is recommended for use in smaller public and school libraries (up to twenty thousand volumes) which do not anticipate significant collection growth.

Abridged Edition 12 is a true abridgment of DDC 20. Numbers in this abridgment conform to Unabridged Edition 20, so that if a library outgrows the Abridged, its staff can easily move to the Unabridged Edition.

This Abridged Edition contains all of the user-convenient features of DDC 20: a completely new introduction, more explanatory notes and summaries, and a manual to help users interpret and apply the schedules. All of this material has been rewritten, to the extent necessary, to insure accuracy and relevance to the Abridged Edition.

This is the first abridged edition to be published since Forest Press became a part of OCLC Online Computer Library Center, a not-for-profit organization which provides computer products and services to more than 10,000 libraries through a network which now extends to Europe and Asia. This edition was printed from a database prepared at the Library of Congress using a computer-based editorial support system. Joining the DDC database with the resources of OCLC will allow the development of computer products needed by DDC users.

Editing of this volume was done by the staff of the Decimal Classification Division of the Library of Congress, under a contract between the Library and Forest Press. The Division is the largest user of the Dewey Decimal Classification in the world, applying Dewey numbers to over 100,000 bibliographic records annually. In this way, classification theory and practice are combined, allowing for continuous and thorough review of the content of the Classification.

The editor of this edition is John P. Comaromi, assisted by Julianne Beall, Winton E. Matthews, Jr., and Gregory R. New. Many other persons contributed to the preparation of this edition; their names are noted in the DCEPC Preface and the Editor's Acknowledgments in the pages which follow.

I would also like to thank the staff of Forest Press for their dedicated support and assistance, particularly Judith Kramer-Greene, who had responsibility for the preparation and production of this edition, and Judith Pisarski and Mildred Dugan, who provided effective help and support throughout.

Peter J. Paulson
Executive Director, Forest Press
A division of OCLC Online Computer
Library Center, Inc.

30 January 1990

Preface by the Decimal Classification Editorial Policy Committee

The Decimal Classification Editorial Policy Committee was established in 1937 to serve as an advisory body in determining the general direction and policies of the Dewey Decimal Classification (DDC). It was reconstituted as a joint committee of the Lake Placid Education Foundation and the American Library Association in 1955; and was continued by OCLC Online Computer Library Center after OCLC purchased Forest Press in 1988. Its constituency consists of libraries, information agencies, and users of the Classification in the United States and abroad.

The current membership of the Committee consists of a diverse group of library and information professionals and is international in scope. Its membership of ten includes persons with experience in public, special, and academic libraries; library educators; representatives of the American Library Association, the Library of Congress, and Forest Press OCLC (publisher of the DDC); a representative of the (British) Library Association; and a Canadian librarian. The main functions of the Committee are to work with the editors of the DDC and advise Forest Press in matters relating to changes, innovations, and the general development of the Classification.

The intention of the abridged edition is to provide a scheme for users who do not require the extensive detail set forth in the unabridged edition. The twelfth abridged edition represents an abridgment of the twentieth unabridged edition. In both, the areas of the scheme that have undergone substantial revision include 780 (Music), a completely revised schedule which replaces the outdated version in the earlier editions; 004-006 (Data Processing and Computer Science); and 301-307 (Sociology), schedules developed to accommodate the literature of these fields. There are also major revisions of the area notations in Table 2 for Southern Africa (—68) and Papua New Guinea (—95), and almost every country now has its own number. A manual has been included in this edition to offer advice on classifying in difficult areas, and to explain how to choose between related numbers.

In addition to these changes, the entire scheme was carefully examined. When determining which revisions were to be made, the extent of their effect on library service was always considered.

In creating new schedules and revising existing ones, the Editorial Policy Committee called upon the expertise of outside groups. Such groups included various committees of the American Library Association, library associations of other countries, the African Section of the Library of Congress, working classifiers, and experts in various subjects (such as computer science and music). The completely revised schedule for 780 Music, for instance, which took over fifteen years to develop, involved classification and music experts in the United States, United Kingdom,

Canada, and Australia. The music schedule was also reviewed by a special subcommittee of the Association for Library Collections & Technical Services (then the Resources and Technical Services Division) Subject Analysis Committee (SAC) of the American Library Association. For the abridged edition, the SAC Subcommittee on Dewey Abridged Edition 12 was established specifically to advise the Editorial Policy Committee and the editors with regard to the extent of abridgment and the coverage of subject areas in the abridged edition.

Since the publication of Edition 19, many individuals have served on the Editorial Policy Committee, each making unique contributions to its deliberations. Following is a list of the members who contributed to the preparation of Abridged Edition 12, with the positions they held or hold during their tenure on the Committee: Joanne S. Anderson, Coordinator of Reference Services, San Diego Public Library; Henriette D. Avram, Associate Librarian for Collections Services, Library of Congress; David Balatti, Chief, Subject Analysis Division, National Library of Canada; Lizbeth J. Bishoff, formerly Principal Librarian for Support Services, Pasadena (California) Public Library, now Manager, Cataloging and Database Services, OCLC; Barbara Branson, Principal Cataloger, Perkins Library, Duke University; Lois Mai Chan, Professor, College of Library and Information Science, University of Kentucky; Margaret E. Cockshutt, Professor, Faculty of Library and Information Science, University of Toronto (Canada); John P. Comaromi, formerly Associate Professor, Graduate School of Library and Information Science, UCLA, now Editor of the Dewey Decimal Classification; Betty M. E. Croft, Technical Services Librarian, Northwestern Missouri State University; Joel C. Downing, Director of Copyright and English Language Services, The British Library; Joseph H. Howard, Assistant Librarian for Processing Services, Library of Congress; John A. Humphry, Executive Director, Forest Press; Donald J. Lehnus, Associate Professor, Graduate School of Library and Information Science, University of Mississippi; Joan S. Mitchell, formerly Library Network Support Manager, AT&T Bell Laboratories, now Director, Instructional Technology and Academic Computing, Carnegie Mellon University; Peter J. Paulson, formerly Director of the New York State Library, now Executive Director, Forest Press OCLC; Lucia J. Rather, Director for Cataloging, Library of Congress; Clare E. Ryan, Head, Technical Services, New Hampshire State Library; Marietta D. Shepard, Chief of the Library Development Program of the Organization of American States; Russell Sweeney, Head of Department of Library and Information Studies, Leeds Polytechnic, England; Patricia M. Thomas, Head Cataloger, Stockton-San Joaquin County Public Library; and Arnold S. Wajenberg, Principal Cataloguer, University of Illinois at Urbana-Champaign.

The Editorial Policy Committee acknowledges the assistance provided by many groups and individuals in the preparation of Abridged Edition 12, including those groups mentioned earlier and individuals too numerous to name here. The Committee recommends to you this new abridged edition of the Dewey Decimal Classification, with a sense of pride that this edition represents the best efforts of many individuals and the awareness that it is still far from being perfect. The continuing development and viability of the Dewey Decimal Classification will rely on the interest and concern of all users around the world. Your comments, advice, and suggestions are ever welcome.

Lois Mai Chan
Chairperson (1986-)
Margaret E. Cockshutt
Chairperson (1980-1985)
Decimal Classification
Editorial Policy Committee

1 March 1990

DEWEY DECIMAL CLASSIFICATION, ADDITIONS, NOTES AND DECISIONS

Dewey Decimal Classification Additions, Notes and Decisions, popularly known as *DC&*, is published regularly to keep users up to date on developments regarding the Classification. All purchasers of Edition 12 are entitled to a subscription to *DC&*. Your library may be placed on the mailing list for this publication by either returning the enclosed card or by writing to Forest Press OCLC, 85 Watervliet Avenue, Albany, New York 12206-2082, U.S.A.

Acknowledgments

Developing and maintaining the Dewey Decimal Classification involves a cast of hundreds. I acknowledge the assistance of the members of the cast whose number does not permit me to name them all here; acknowledge the debt to those who have gone before us and upon whose shoulders we stand; acknowledge the work of the staff of Forest Press who bring our efforts to final and published form; acknowledge the advice and assistance of the Decimal Classification Editorial Policy Committee, our sure guide; acknowledge the extensive assistance of the Subject Analysis Committee of the American Library Association, especially its Subcommittee on the Abridged Edition whose members were Susan Koch Gegenhuber, Principal Librarian for Support Services, Pasadena (California) Public Library; Joycelyn Brand, Head of Cataloging, Cataloging Card Corporation of America; Lois Winkle, Editor, *Elementary School Library Collections;* and Sharon Zuiderveld, Cataloger, Bound to Stay Bound Books, Inc.; and acknowledge the work of the present and former staff of the Decimal Classification Division who worked upon Abridged Edition 12 in various capacities and to varying degrees: Benjamin A. Custer, Editor; Julianne Beall, Winton E. Matthews, Jr., Gregory R. New, and Margaret J. Warren, assistant editors; and Melba D. Adams, Kenneth Austin, Frances A. Bold, Michael B. Cantlon, Carletta Cartledge, Della M. Chase, Rosalee Connor, Eve M. Dickey, Darlene Foster, Idalia V. Fuentes, Glenna Sue Garner, Tina Golden, Valexia Hall, William S. Hwang, Irma Lashley, Nobuko Ohashi, Letitia J. Reigle, Virginia Anne Schoepf, Ruth Ann Sievers, David A. Smith, Emily K. Spears, Cosmo D. Tassone, Marcellus S. Todd, Marisa C. Vandenbosch.

John P. Comaromi
Editor
Dewey Decimal Classification
Library of Congress

4 April 1990

New Features in Abridged Edition 12

The aim of Abridged Edition 12 is user convenience, through clearer instructions, more explanations, elimination of duplicate provisions for classifying single subjects, and a Manual to guide the classifier.

Manual

The most striking change in Abridged Edition 12 is the presence of a Manual to assist in its application. The Manual describes policies and practices of the Decimal Classification Division of the Library of Congress, offers advice on classifying in difficult areas, and explains how to choose between related numbers. It should help classifiers resolve problems and apply the DDC with greater consistency.

Complete revision (780) and new schedule (004-006)

The only completely revised schedule in Abridged Edition 12 is 780 Music, originally developed in Great Britain by Russell Sweeney and John Clews. A detailed description of the changes in 780 is found under the heading 780 in the Manual. Tables comparing topics (comparative table) and equivalent numbers for the 780 class in Editions 11 and 12 (equivalence tables) are found on pages 171–179.

The schedule for 004–006 Data processing and computer science, which replaces 001.6 Data processing, is new.

Important Areas of Revision in the Tables

Table 1. Standard Subdivisions

−028	*Auxiliary* techniques and procedures; apparatus, equipment, materials Use of this number for basic techniques and procedures of the subject discontinued; class in 001–999 without adding notation from Table 1.
−0285	Data processing and computer application is new.
−071	Schools and courses is new.
−08	History and description of a field with respect to kinds of persons is new.

Table 2. Geographic Areas, and Persons

(1) Countries with an individual number in Unabridged Edition 20 have an individual number in Abridged Edition 12.

(2) Turkey in Europe relocated from −563 to −4961.

(3) The countries of −681 (Botswana, Lesotho, Swaziland) relocated to −688.

(4) Melanesia −93 relocated to −95.

(5) New Zealand's number reduced from −931 to −93.

Important Areas of Revision in the Schedules

001–006	The span of numbers covering knowledge, systems, and data processing has been extensively revised. An abridgment of the relocation and expansion of data processing and computer science that appeared in the 1985 publication *004–006 Data Processing and Computer Science and Changes in Related Disciplines* has been incorporated in Abridged Edition 12 with a few changes. The corresponding standard subdivision —0285 provides for computer application to a specific subject.
207	Christian education and religious instruction relocated to 268 Religious education in order to distinguish Christianity as an academic subject (207) from instruction in Christianity as a way of life (268).
232	The Second Coming and Judgment of Christ relocated to 236 Eschatology.
248.4	Guides to Christian life for specific classes of persons (e.g., the young) of specific denominations relocated from the denomination to the class of persons in 248.8
267	The Salvation Army, a Christian movement, relocated to 287.9.
288	The Unitarian Church relocated to 289.1 with the Universalist Church.
305	The effect of media (e.g., television) on social groups (e.g., children) now classed with the medium in 302.23, not with the group affected.
312	Demographic statistics relocated to 304.6 and to the specific subject, e.g., statistics on deaths by crimes of violence 364.1.
323.4	Comprehensive works on civil rights moved from 323.4 to 323.
327.3–.9	Espionage and subversion by specific countries now classed at 327.12 rather than at foreign relations in 327.3–.9.
362–363	Specific social problems and services expanded, e.g., 362.29 Substance abuse.
380.3	Comprehensive works on communications relocated to 384 in order to bring together general works and works on specific topics.
380.5	Comprehensive works on transportation relocated to 388 in order to bring together general works and works on specific topics.
529	Time systems relocated from 529 to 389, time instruments from 529 to 681.1.
604.6	Waste technology relocated to 628.4.
612	Human physiology expanded.
621.3819	Computer engineering relocated to 621.39.
720–724, 730	Geographical treatment of architecture and sculpture, especially with respect to Oriental art, extensively revised.

780	Music has been completely revised. The new development is described in the 780 section of the Manual.
796.4	Weightlifting, track and field, gymnastics revised and expanded; athletic exercise relocated to 613.71 Physical fitness.
940–990	The number for the most recent period in a nation's history, if it appeared in Unabridged Edition 20, is always given.

Lists of relocations and reductions and also comparative and equivalence tables for 780 Music are found on pages 165-179.

Relative Index

See references have been eliminated from the Index since nearly all terms now have a number. See also references lead to broader or related terms.

Proper names are indexed under their AACR2 form, and under commonly used forms of the name.

The four Tables are identified by T1, T2, T3, and T4, e.g., the area number for the United States is T2—73.

Suggestions from Users

Suggestions for improving the Dewey Decimal Classification are always given serious consideration and effected if found to be reasonable and feasible. We welcome any suggestions for improving Edition 12 and developing Abridged Edition 13. Suggestions and questions should be directed to the following parties:

(1) For editorial policy (such as areas needing extensive revision or expansion, and indexing policy), format, workshops, aids for the classifier, and copyright questions:

Executive Director
Forest Press OCLC
85 Watervliet Ave.
Albany, New York 12206-2082 U.S.A.

(2) For corrections and questions on how to apply the Classification:

Editor
Dewey Decimal Classification
Decimal Classification Division
Library of Congress
Washington, DC 20540 U.S.A

Introduction to the Dewey Decimal Classification

About the Introduction

1.1 This Introduction is written primarily for students and beginning classifiers. It may be used in conjunction with the Manual, which contains additional and more detailed information about the use of the Classification, offers advice on classifying in difficult areas, and explains how to choose between related numbers.

1.2 A Glossary (to which references appear throughout the Introduction) follows the Introduction.

How Abridged Edition 12 Is Arranged

2.1 Abridged Edition 12 is composed of six major parts:

(A) Introduction: Introduces the user to the Dewey Decimal Classification system (DDC) and provides instructions on its use.
(B) Manual: Provides advice for classifying in difficult areas, and describes policies and practices followed by the Decimal Classification Division at the Library of Congress. Information in the Manual is arranged in the order in which the numbers appear in the Tables and Schedules.
(C) Lists which compare Abridged Editions 11 and 12.
(D) Tables: The four numbered Tables provide notation that can be added to the class numbers in the Schedules to provide greater subject specificity.
(E) Schedules: Knowledge organized from 001–999.
(F) Relative Index: An alphabetical list of subjects found in the Schedules and Tables, including synonyms and selected terms in common use.

Classification: What It Is and What It Does

3.1 *Classification* provides a system for organizing a universe of items, be they objects, concepts, or records.

3.2 *Notation* is the system of symbols used to represent the classes in a classification system. In the Dewey Decimal Classification system, the notation is expressed in Arabic numerals. The notation gives at once both the unique meaning of the class and its relation to other classes. It permits the searcher to find a specific item within the class to which it belongs and near related classes. No matter how words describing subjects may differ, the notation identifying the subject is always the same, e.g., dog or hound, Hund or chien, Doberman or poodle are all found at 636.7.

3.3 Libraries usually arrange their collections according to the systematic structure of a library classification. Each item is assigned a *call number* (see **Glossary**), usually consisting of the notation for its class, accompanied by a book number or some other device to subarrange the items of a class. The call number provides a unique identifying code that is used as an "address" on the shelf, and as a tag for library record-keeping in circulation and inventory control.

3.4 The *subject catalog* is the index to the contents of a library collection. It lists works, parts of works, and important essays or literary works in collections by topic. If arranged alphabetically by words, it is called an *alphabetical subject catalog* (the pre-eminent form in North America). If arranged by the notation of a library classification system, it is called a *classified catalog* (the pre-eminent form in Europe). In addition to providing the class number at which the item is shelved, classified catalogs provide numbers for other subjects in the work.

History and Current Use of the Dewey Decimal Classification

4.1 The Dewey Decimal Classification is the most widely used library classification system in the world. It is used in more than 135 countries, and has been translated into over 30 languages. In the United States, 95% of all public and school libraries, 25% of all college and university libraries, and 20% of special libraries use the DDC.

4.2 The DDC was conceived by Melvil Dewey in 1873 and first published in 1876. The first edition was 44 pages long: 14 pages of front and back matter, 12 pages of summaries and schedules, and 18 pages of index. The first edition of the Abridged DDC appeared in 1894.

4.3 The DDC is developed, maintained, and applied in the Decimal Classification Division of the Library of Congress (LC), where over 100,000 DDC numbers are assigned annually to works acquired by the Library. In the United States, DDC numbers are incorporated into machine readable catalog (MARC) records, and distributed to libraries by way of computer tapes, Cataloging-in-Publication (CIP) data, and LC cards. DDC numbers also appear in MARC records in 12 other countries and are used in the national bibliographies of Australia, Canada, India, Indonesia, Italy, Jordan, Kenya, Pakistan, the United Kingdom, Zimbabwe, and other countries. Various bibliographic utilities and services in the United States and elsewhere make DDC numbers available to libraries through online access, publications, and production of catalog cards.

Overview of the Dewey Decimal Classification

Conceptual Framework

5.1 In the DDC, basic classes are defined by traditional academic disciplines or fields of study. No principle is more basic to the DDC than this: the parts of the Classification are arranged by discipline, not by subject.

5.2 The consequence of this principle is that there is likely to be no one single place for a given subject. "Women" as a subject, for example, has aspects which fall under several disciplines, such as civil rights, education, and law. The civil rights of women belong in 323.3 as part of the discipline of political science; the education of women in 376 as part of the discipline of education; and the legal status of women in 346.01 as part of the discipline of law. The Relative Index assembles many of the disciplinary aspects of a subject in one place:

Women	305.4
	T1—082
biography	920.72
civil rights	323.3
education of	376
government programs for	350.81
central government	351.81
local government	352.94
legal status	346.01
constitutional law	342
psychology	155.6
religion	291.082
Christianity	208.2
guides to life	248.8
social theology	261.8
comparative religion	291.082
social theology	291.1
Judaism	296.082
social theology	296.3
social aspects	305.4
social theology	291.1
social welfare	362.83

Notation

5.3 At the broadest level, the DDC is divided into ten *main classes*, which together cover the entire world of knowledge. These classes are divided into ten *divisions* and each division into ten *sections*, although not all the numbers for the divisions and sections have been used. (The word "class" is used generally to indicate divisions, sections, and any other notational level in the hierarchy.)

5.4 The ten main classes are:

000	Generalities
100	Philosophy, parapsychology and occultism, psychology
200	Religion
300	Social sciences
400	Language
500	Natural sciences and mathematics
600	Technology (Applied sciences)
700	The arts Fine and decorative arts
800	Literature (Belles-lettres) and rhetoric
900	Geography, history, and auxiliary disciplines

5.5 Main class 000 is the most general class, and is used for works not limited to any one specific discipline, such as encyclopedias, newspapers, and general periodicals. This class is also used for certain specialized disciplines that deal with knowledge and information generally, such as information science, library science, computer science, journalism, and bibliography. The content of the other nine classes is self-explanatory.

5.6 The first digit in the numbers listed above indicates the *main class.* Although each number contains three digits, only the first digit is significant in this list. The remaining zeros fill out the notation to the required three digits.

5.7 Each main class consists of ten *divisions,* also numbered 0 through 9. The number of significant digits here is two, the second digit indicating the division. 600 is used for general works on the applied sciences, 610 for the medical sciences, 620 for engineering, 630 for agriculture.

5.8 Each division has ten *sections,* again numbered 0 through 9. The third digit in each three-digit number indicates the section. Thus, 630 is used for general works on agriculture, 631 for specific techniques, 632 for plant injuries, 633 for field and plantation crops.

5.9 A decimal point (see **Glossary**) follows the third digit, after which division by ten continues on down to as specific a degree of classification as may be desired.

PRINCIPLE OF HIERARCHY

5.10 Hierarchy in the DDC is expressed through both notation and structure.

5.11 *Notational hierarchy* is expressed by length of notation. As the following example shows, numbers at any given level are subordinate to a class whose notation is one digit shorter; coordinate with a class whose notation has the same number of significant digits; and superordinate to a class with numbers one or more digits longer. The underlined digits in the example below demonstrate this notational hierarchy:

600	Technology (Applied sciences)
630	Agriculture and related technologies
636	Animal husbandry
636.7	Dogs
636.8	Cats

5.12 "Dogs" and "Cats" are more specific than (or subordinate to) "Animal husbandry"; they are equally specific as (or coordinate with) each other; and "Animal husbandry" is less specific than (or superordinate to) "Dogs" and "Cats."

5.13 Relationships among topics that violate notational hierarchy are indicated by notes and other devices. A *centered entry* often constitutes a major departure from notational hierarchy. A centered entry (so called because its numbers, heading, and notes appear in the center of the page) occurs when a span of numbers rather than a single number is used for a subject. In the DDC, centered entries are always flagged typographically by the symbol > in the number column.

5.14 *Structural hierarchy* means that aside from the ten main classes every topic is subordinate to and part of all the broader topics above it. The corollary is also true: whatever is true of the whole is true of its parts. This important concept is sometimes called *hierarchical force* (see **Glossary**). Any note regarding the nature of a class holds true for all the subordinate classes (including logically subordinate topics classed at coordinate numbers). Because of this, such notes are given only once—at the highest level of application. For example, the scope note at 700 applies to 730 and 736. The words "Description, critical appraisal . . ." found in the scope note also govern 736 Carving and carvings, which thus includes the critical appraisal of carving.

Classifying with the DDC

Determining the Subject of a Work

6.1 Classifying a work properly depends upon determining the subject of the work in hand. Judicious use of the following sources is suggested:

(A) The *title* is sometimes a succinct abstract of the subject of a work, but it must always be regarded with suspicion; *Zen and the Art of Motorcycle Maintenance* does not sound like a work on values, but it is.

(B) The *table of contents,* if genuinely descriptive, should display the main topics discussed.

(C) *Chapter headings* may make up for the lack of a table of contents. Chapter subheadings often prove useful.

(D) If an *introduction* (by someone other than the author) is provided, it should be perused. Such introductions are intended to assist the reader by indicating the subject of the work and suggesting the place of the work in the development of thought on the subject.

(E) A *preface* (or introduction by the author) usually provides original purposes and afterthoughts.

(F) A *bibliography, bibliographic footnotes,* and *references* are all valuable sources of information.

(G) *Cataloging copy* from centralized cataloging services is often helpful by providing subject headings, classification numbers, and notes. Such copy appears on the verso of U.S. and British books as part of Cataloging-in-Publication (CIP) data.

(H) The *text of the work* and *book reviews* can verify the conclusions reached by using the sources listed above.

(I) *Reference tools* or *knowledgeable people* often help define terms.

The steps above are necessary for works on technical, scientific, and historical matters; they are seldom necessary when classifying literary works of the imagination. In the DDC, works of the imagination are generally classified by literary form rather than by subject.

Determining the Discipline for a Work

6.2 The classifier must then select the proper discipline, or field of study, of the work. Because discipline is the primary consideration in classifying a work, works that are used together are found together.

6.3 The guiding principle of the DDC is that a work is classed in the discipline for which it is intended, rather than the discipline from which the work derives. For example, a work by a zoologist on agricultural pest control should be classed in agriculture unless it concentrates on background biological data, in which case it should be classed in biology.

6.4 Once the subject has been determined, and information on the discipline has been found, the experienced classifier will turn to the Schedules. The Summaries beginning on page 239 are a good means of mental navigation for beginners. The *Relative Index* may help by suggesting the disciplines in which a subject is normally treated (for a discussion of the Relative Index, see paragraphs 10.1-10.14).

6.5 Whether or not the Relative Index is used, the classifier must rely on the structure of the Classification, and various aids throughout, to arrive at the proper place to classify a work. Even the most promising Relative Index citations must be verified in the Schedules; the Schedules are the only place where all the information about coverage and use of the numbers may be found.

More Than One Subject

6.6 When two or more subjects are treated in a work, use the following guidelines:

(A) Class a work dealing with interrelated subjects with the subject that is being acted upon. This is called the "rule of application," and takes precedence over any other rule. For instance, class an analytical work dealing with Shakespeare's influence on Keats with Keats.

(B) Class a work on two subjects with the subject receiving fuller treatment.

(C) If two subjects receive equal treatment, and are not used to introduce or explain one another, class the work with the subject whose number comes first in the DDC Schedules. This is called the "first-of-two rule." For example, a history dealing equally with the United States and Japan, in which the United States is discussed first and is given first in the title, is classed with the history of Japan because 952 precedes 973.

Occasionally, specific instructions are given to use numbers which do not come first in the Schedules, e.g., to class birds (598) and mammals (599) in 599, which is the comprehensive number for warm-blooded vertebrates. Also disregard the "first-of-two rule" when the two topics are the two major subdivisions of a subject. For example, water supply (628.1) and waste technology (628.4) taken together constitute most of 628 Sanitary engineering; works on these topics are classed in 628 (not 628.1).

(D) Class a work on three or more subjects that are all subdivisions of a broader subject in the first higher number that includes them all (unless one subject is treated more fully than the others). This is called the "rule of three." For example, a history of Portugal (946.9), Sweden (948.5), and Greece (949.5) is classed with the history of Europe (940).

More Than One Discipline

6.7 Treating a subject from the point of view of more than one discipline is different from treating several subjects in one discipline. Use the guidelines in paragraphs 6.8-6.11.

6.8 Use the interdisciplinary number provided in the Schedules or Relative Index if one is given. An important consideration in using such an interdisciplinary number is that the work must contain significant material on the discipline in which the interdisciplinary number is found. For example, 305.23 (a sociology number) is provided for interdisciplinary works on children. However, if a work that is interdisciplinary with respect to children gives little emphasis to their social aspects and a great deal of emphasis to their psychological and physical aspects

(155.4 and 612.6, respectively), class it in 155.4 (the first number in the Schedules of the next two obvious choices). In short, interdisciplinary numbers are not absolute; they are to be used only when applicable.

6.9 Class works not given an interdisciplinary number in the discipline that gives the subject fullest treatment. For example, a work dealing with both the scientific and the engineering principles of electrodynamics is classed in 537.6 if the engineering aspects are introduced primarily for illustrative purposes, but in 621.31 if the basic scientific theories are only preliminary to the author's exposition of engineering principles and practices.

6.10 When classifying interdisciplinary works, do not overlook the possibilities of main class 000 Generalities, e.g., 080 for a collection of interviews of famous people from various fields.

6.11 Any other situation is treated in the same fashion as those found above in the instructions at More Than One Subject (paragraph 6.6).

When All Else Fails

6.12 When several numbers have been found for the work in hand, and each seems as good as the next, the following may prove useful:

6.13 *Rule of Zero.* Subdivisions beginning with zero should be avoided if there is a choice between 0 and 1-9 at the same point in the hierarchy of the notation. Similarly, subdivisions beginning with 00 should be avoided when there is a choice between 00 and 0.

6.14 *Table of last resort.* In the absence of any other rule, the following table (in order of preference) may be used with caution:

(1) Kinds of things
(2) Parts of things
(3) Materials from which things, kinds, or parts are made
(4) Properties of things, kinds, parts, or materials
(5) Processes within things, kinds, parts, or materials
(6) Operations upon things, kinds, parts, or materials
(7) Instrumentalities for performing such operations

Key Features of the Schedules and Tables

Summaries

7.1 Summaries provide an overview of the structure of classes. Two types of summaries appear in the Classification:

(A) The summaries of the Schedules as a whole are found just before the Schedules, on pages 239-250.

(B) Summaries in the Schedules and Tables provide an overview of classes that have subdivisions extending over more than two pages. For example:

SUMMARY

660.01–.09	**Standard subdivisions**
661	**Technology of industrial chemicals**
662	**Technology of explosives, fuels, related products**
663	**Beverage technology**
664	**Food technology**
665	**Technology of industrial oils, fats, waxes, gases**
666	**Ceramic and allied technologies**
667	**Cleaning, color, related technologies**
668	**Technology of other organic products**
669	**Metallurgy**

ENTRIES

7.2 Schedule and Table entries are composed of a DDC number in the number column (the column at the left margin), a heading describing the class that the number represents, and often one or more notes.

7.3 The first three digits of Schedule numbers (main classes, divisions, sections) appear only once in the number column (when first used). They are repeated at the top of each page where their subdivisions continue. Subordinate numbers (beginning with a decimal point) appear in the number column, with the initial three digits understood. For example:

371 School organization and management; special education

Including student services

.6 Physical plant

Including buildings, grounds; noninstructional facilities, e.g., dormitories

.602 8 Auxiliary techniques and procedures; apparatus, equipment, materials

Class maintenance and repair in 371.6

7.4 Table numbers are given in full in the number column of the Tables, and are never used alone. They may be used only when appended or added to numbers from the Schedules. There are four numbered Tables in Abridged Edition 12, as follows:

T1	Standard Subdivisions
T2	Geographic Areas, and Persons
T3	Subdivisions for Individual Literatures, for Specific Literary Forms
T4	Subdivisions of Individual Languages

Except for notation from Table 1 (which may be added to any number unless there is an instruction in the Schedules to the contrary), Table notations may be added only as instructed in the Schedules (for a detailed discussion of the use of the four Tables, see paragraphs 8.3-8.8).

7.5 When a subordinate topic is a major part of a number, it is sometimes given as a part of the heading. For example:

—72	Middle America	Mexico
610	Medical sciences	Medicine

7.6 Some numbers in the Schedules and Tables are in brackets or parentheses. Numbers in brackets ([ ]) represent topics which have been relocated elsewhere or are unassigned. Bracketed numbers should never be used. Numbers and notes in parentheses provide options to standard practice (for a discussion of options, see paragraphs 11.1-11.3).

NOTES

7.7 Notes are important because they supply information that is not obvious in the notational hierarchy or in the heading with regard to order, structure, subordination, and other matters. The notes described below (A) define what is found in the class and its subdivisions; (B) identify topics in "standing room," i.e., topics with insufficient literature to have their own number; (C) describe what is found in other classes; and (D) explain changes in the Schedules and Tables. Other notes are described in the sections on number building (paragraphs 8.1-8.10), citation and precedence order (paragraphs 9.1-9.5), and options (paragraphs 11.1-11.3).

7.8 Notes in categories (A) and (C) have hierarchical force (i.e., are applicable to all the subdivisions of a particular number). Those in category (B) do not have hierarchical force except where noted.

(A) Notes That Describe What Is Found in a Class

7.9 *Definition and scope notes* indicate the meaning and scope of the class. For example:

004.7 Peripherals

Input, output, storage devices that work with a computer but are not part of its central processing unit or internal storage

7.10 *Variant name notes* are used for synonyms or near synonyms. For example:

531 Mechanics Solid mechanics

Variant names for mechanics: classical mechanics, continuum mechanics

7.11 *General aspects notes* enumerate aspects that are not found in the standard subdivisions of Table 1 but are applicable to all the subdivisions of a particular number. For example:

690 Buildings

General aspects: planning, analysis, engineering design, construction, destruction of habitable structures and their utilities

7.12 *Class-here notes* list major topics that are included in a class even though they may be broader or narrower than the heading, overlap it, or define another way of looking at essentially the same material. For example:

363.7 Environmental problems and services

Class here environmental protection

Environmental protection overlaps 363.7 and is a large part of it.

7.13 Class-here notes are also used to indicate where interdisciplinary and comprehensive works are classed. In the DDC, "interdisciplinary works" treat a subject from the perspective of more than one discipline. "Comprehensive works" treat a subject from various points of view within a single discipline. For example:

391 Costume and personal appearance

Class here interdisciplinary works on costume, clothing, fashion

636.5 Poultry

Class here comprehensive works on raising birds

(B) Notes That Identify Topics in Standing Room

7.14 Standing room notes identify topics that have "standing room" in the number where the note is found. Standing room numbers provide a location for topics with relatively few works written about them, but whose literature may grow in the future, at which time they may be assigned their own number. These notes are introduced by one of the following terms: "Including," "Contains," or "Example(s)". Standard subdivisions cannot be added to topics in standing room, nor are other number-building techniques allowed.

7.15 *Including notes* list topics that are not obviously a part of the number. For example:

005.7 Data in computer systems

Including data communications, interfacing; conversion to machine-readable form, data entry

7.16 *Contains notes* list all of the major components of the number that do not have their own subdivisions. For example:

—419 Munster

Contains Clare, Cork, Kerry, Limerick, Tipperary, Waterford counties

7.17 *Example notes* describe the contents of a category when the specific contents may not be apparent. For example:

303.48 Causes of change

Examples: contact between cultures, development of science and technology, disasters, social reform

(C) Notes on What Is Found in Other Classes

7.18 *Class-elsewhere notes* indicate where to class parts of a subject or topics related to it, if they do not class in subdivisions of the number at hand. All notes that begin with the word "class" are class-elsewhere notes, except when they begin with "class here" (*class-here notes* are described in paragraphs 7.12 and 7.13). For example:

—028 Auxiliary techniques and procedures; apparatus, equipment, materials

Class interdisciplinary works on safety in 363.1, on personal safety in 613.6, on technology of safety in 620.8, on measurement in 530.8, on testing in 620, on technology of testing and measuring instruments in 681, on maintenance and repair in 620; educational testing in —076; use of apparatus and equipment in study and teaching in —078

7.19 *See references* begin with the word "For." A see reference in the DDC signifies that the subject referred to is a part of the class from which the reference is made. For example:

027 General libraries, archives, information centers

For libraries, archives, information centers devoted to specific disciplines and subjects, see 026

7.20 *See-also references* refer to subjects tangentially related to the class in hand. They are reminders that minor differences in wording and context often imply major differences in classification. For example:

630 Agriculture and related technologies

See also 306.3 for agricultural sociology, 307.72 for rural sociology, 333.76 for agricultural land economics, 338.1 for agricultural economics, 900 for rural conditions and civilization

(D) Notes Explaining Changes in the Schedules and Tables

7.21 *Discontinued notes* indicate that a number from an earlier edition is no longer used, or that some part of the subject of a number has been moved to a shorter number. For example:

523 Specific celestial bodies and phenomena

Use of this number for comprehensive works on descriptive astronomy discontinued; class in 520

7.22 *Relocation notes* state that all or part of the contents of a number have been moved to a different number. For example:

513 Arithmetic

Business arithmetic relocated to 650.01

The relocation note is usually restated at the new number, either in the heading or in the appropriate note:

650.01 Philosophy and theory [of business]

Including business arithmetic [*formerly* 513]

Number Building

8.1 The classifier will sometimes find that to arrive at a precise number for a work it is necessary to build or synthesize a number that is not specifically printed in the Schedules. Such built numbers allow for greater depth of content analysis. They are used only when instructions in the Schedules make them possible (except for standard subdivisions which are discussed in paragraphs 8.3-8.4). Building numbers begins with a base number (always stated in the instruction note) to which another number is added.

8.2 Basically there are four ways to build numbers: (A) from standard subdivisions (Table 1); (B) from Tables 2-4 when specifically instructed to do so; (C) from other parts of the Classification; and (D) from "add tables" (see *Glossary*) in the Schedules.

(A) Adding Standard Subdivisions from Table 1

8.3 Notation from Table 1 Standard Subdivisions may be added to any number in the Schedules unless there is a specific instruction to the contrary. A *standard subdivision* represents a recurring bibliographic form (such as a dictionary, periodical, or index) or approach (such as history or research) and thus is applicable to any subject or discipline. Here are a few examples:

150.5	Periodical on psychology
203	Dictionary of Christianity
507.8	Use of apparatus and equipment in the study and teaching of science, e.g., science fair projects
622.0285	Use of computers in mining

The number of zeros is always indicated in the Schedules; the classifier should never use more than one zero in applying a standard subdivision unless instructed to do so.

8.4 The most important caveat with respect to standard subdivisions is that in most cases they are added only for works that cover or *approximate the whole of the subject* of the number. For example, literacy policy in Ohio should be classed in 379.2, the number for public education and the state, which includes literacy policy, not in 379.209771, the number for public education and the state in Ohio. The classifier should not attempt to specify Ohio because literacy policy does not approximate the whole universe of public education in Ohio. Further instructions on using Table 1 are found at the beginning of Table 1 and in the Table 1 section of the Manual.

(B) Adding from Tables 2–4

8.5 The classifier may be instructed to add a number from Tables 2–4 to a base number from the Schedules or to a number from a Table:

8.6 *Table 2 Geographic Areas, and Persons.* Table 2 numbers are added through the use of standard subdivision —09 from Table 1, e.g., education in Australia 370.994, or directly when instructed to do so by a note. For example:

373.3–373.9	Secondary education and schools by specific continents, countries, localities

> Add to base number 373 notation 3–9 from Table 2, e.g., secondary schools of Canada 373.71

8.7 *Table 3 Subdivisions for Individual Literatures, for Specific Literary Forms.* These subdivisions are used only in class 800 as instructed, usually following numbers for specific languages in 810–890.

8.8 *Table 4 Subdivisions of Individual Languages.* These subdivisions are used only in class 400 as instructed, following numbers for specific languages in 420–490.

(C) Adding from Other Parts of the Schedules

8.9 There are a few instructions to make a direct addition to a number from another part of the Schedules. For example:

016 Bibliographies and catalogs of works on specific subjects or in specific disciplines

Add to base number 016 notation 001–999, e.g., general bibliographies of works about serials 016.05 [*formerly* 011], general catalogs of works about serials 016.05 [*formerly* 017–019], bibliographies of philosophy 016.1

351.07–.08 Other [executive] departments

Add to base number 351.0 the numbers following 351 in 351.7–351.8, e.g., departments of labor 351.083

(D) Adding from Tables Found in the Schedules

8.10 The add tables in the Schedules provide numbers to be added to designated schedule numbers (identified by a footnote); these tables must be used only as instructed. An example of an add table can be found at 380.

Number Building: Citation and Precedence Order

9.1 Precedence and citation order come into play when multiple aspects or characteristics of a subject (such as age, area, gender, historical periods, national origin) are provided for in the Classification, and a single work treats more than one of them.

Citation Order

9.2 Citation order allows the classifier to build, or synthesize, a number using two or more aspects or characteristics as specified in instruction notes. Success in building a DDC number requires determining which characteristics apply to a specific work, and determining from the DDC the sequence in which the characteristics will be ordered.

9.3 The notes at the beginning of Table 3 are an example of number-building instructions which specify the sequence in which characteristics of literature will be shown: first language, then literary form, then (if applicable) collections or history and criticism.

PRECEDENCE ORDER

9.4 If there is no provision to show more than one of the aspects or characteristics, it is a matter of *precedence* (because one choice must be made among several characteristics). Precedence notes come with or without tables. An example of a precedence note without a table follows:

302–307 Specific topics in sociology and anthropology

Unless other instructions are given, class complex subjects with aspects in two or more subdivisions of 302–307 in the one coming last in the schedule, e.g., social decay during civil wars 303.6 (*not* 303.45); however, class the effect of one factor on another with the factor affected, e.g., the effect of climate on social change 303.4 (*not* 304.2)

See the Glossary for a definition of "complex subject."

9.5 An example of a table indicating precedence order is found at 800:

800 Literature (Belles-lettres) and rhetoric

Unless other instructions are given, observe the following table of precedence, e.g., collections of drama written in poetry from more than one literature 808.82 (*not* 808.81)

Drama
Poetry
Fiction
Essays
Speeches
Letters
Miscellaneous writings
Satire and humor

This list means that fiction written as poetry is classed in poetry, but humorous fiction is classed in fiction.

The Relative Index

10.1 The Relative Index is so called because it relates subjects to disciplines. In the Schedules, subjects are distributed among disciplines; in the Relative Index subjects are arranged alphabetically, with terms identifying the disciplines in which they are treated subarranged alphabetically under them. For example:

Censored books	098
Censorship	363.3
law	344
libraries	025.2
public administration	350.75
central government	351.75
local government	352.93
social control	303.3
Census	
public administration	351.81
statistical reports	310
Census records	
genealogy	929

How to Use the Relative Index

10.2 Once the subject of the work in hand is determined and located in the Relative Index, the classifier may find it helpful to review the disciplines and DDC numbers listed in the Index under the subject term. In all cases, however, the discipline and number must be checked in the Schedules or Tables, where complete information about the number and what it includes can be found.

10.3 The Relative Index is primarily an index to the terminology of the DDC. If the term sought is not found, the classifier should try a broader term, e.g., Automobile insurance if No-fault insurance is not found.

Format and Arrangement of the Relative Index

10.4 Index entries are arranged alphabetically word by word, e.g., Birth order precedes Birthday, New Zealand precedes Newfoundland. Hyphenated words are filed as two words, e.g., Cro-Magnon files before Crocheting. All abbreviations are spelled both with and without periods, e.g., D.N.A. and DNA. With periods, they are placed at the head of their letter; without periods, they are filed as if they constitute a single word. Terms indented below the main headings are alphabetized in one group even though they may be a mixture of disciplines, topical subheadings, and words that, when combined with the main heading, form phrases or inverted phrases. Terms qualified by words in parentheses file following words that are not so qualified, e.g., Bridges (Dentistry) files after Bridges.

10.5 Class numbers are printed in groups of three for ease of reading and copying. The spaces are not part of the numbers and *do not represent convenient places to abridge the number.*

10.6 Virtually all entries in the Abridged Index are direct. For example:

Adult education
Special libraries
Television programs

10.7 See-also references are used for synonyms, for references to broader terms (but only when two or more new numbers will be found at the broader term), and for references to related terms (which may provide only one new number).

10.8 Numbers drawn from Tables 1-4 are indicated by T1 through T4:

T1 Standard Subdivisions
T2 Geographic Areas, and Persons
T3 Subdivisions for Individual Literatures, for Specific Literary Forms (for use in 800)
T4 Subdivisions of Individual Languages (for use in 400)

Order in Which Numbers Are Displayed

10.9 The first class number displayed in an Index entry (the unindented term) is the number for interdisciplinary works (for a discussion of interdisciplinary numbers, see paragraphs 6.7-6.11). If the term also appears in the Tables, the Table numbers are listed next, followed by other aspects of the term. For example:

Babies	305.23
	T1—083
home care	649
pediatrics	618.92
see also Diseases (Human)	
psychology	155.42
social welfare	362.7

Terms Included in the Relative Index

10.10 The Relative Index contains terms found in the headings and notes of the Schedules and Tables, synonyms, and selected terms in common use.

10.11 The following types of names from Table 2 Geographic Areas are included in the Index: (A) names of countries; (B) names of the states and provinces of the United States, Canada, and Australia; (C) names of the counties and regions of the United Kingdom; and (D) names of certain important geographic features.

10.12 Also included in the Relative Index are a few heads of state used to identify historical periods, e.g., Juan Carlos I; and founders of religions, e.g., Muhammad.

10.13 Place names and other proper names are generally given in the form specified by the second edition of the *Anglo-American Cataloguing Rules* (AACR2), based on the names established in the Library of Congress authority files. Where an established form of the name was not available, an AACR2 form was provided by the editors. Diacritics have been provided for the following languages: Amharic, Chinese, Czech, Dutch, Finnish, French, German, Greek, Italian, Japanese, Portuguese, Spanish, and Urdu.

TERMS NOT INCLUDED IN THE RELATIVE INDEX

10.14 Terms usually not included in the Index are:

(A) Phrases (mostly in the arts) beginning with the adjective form of languages and countries, e.g., *American* poetry, *French* cooking, *Italian* architecture

(B) Phrases which contain general concepts represented by standard subdivisions such as education, statistics, laboratories, and management, e.g., Art *education*, Educational *statistics*, Medical *laboratories*, and Bank *management*.

Options

11.1 The recommended standard notation for English-language users of the DDC is provided in this Edition. At a number of places in the Schedules, options are provided for libraries whose needs are not met by the standard provisions.

11.2 Options are found in parentheses and, when they apply to a specific note, are indented under the note. International users find options particularly helpful. Some important options for these users include inserting letters in the notation or using briefer notation to give prominence to the religion, literature, and language of a particular country. An example of an option follows:

340 Law

(Option: Class the law of a specific discipline or subject with the discipline or subject, using notation 026 from Table 1, e.g., education law 370.26)

11.3 While options are printed in the DDC, they are not used in the centralized classification service supplied by the Library of Congress (except for a second number in law 340 and for biography), and are only occasionally supplied by other centralized services.

Close and Broad Classification

12.1 One of the valuable features of the DDC notation is its adaptability to both close and broad classification. *Close classification* means that the content of a work is specified by notation to the fullest extent possible. *Broad classification* means that the notation places the work only in a broad class by the use of shorter notation. For instance, a work on French cooking is classed closely at 641.5944 (641.59 cooking by place + 44 France from Table 2), broadly at 641.5 Cooking. Close classification is recommended for classes in which many works are found. How close or how broad the classification of a specific library should be depends on the size and diversity of the collection.

12.2 The classifier should never reduce the notation to less than the most specific three-digit number (no matter how small the library's collection). A number also must never be reduced so that it ends in a 0 anywhere to the right of the decimal point.

Book Numbers

13.1 Most libraries find that some sort of subarrangement of the classes of the DDC is necessary for the efficient shelving and retrieval of specific works.

13.2 A common filing device for small libraries is to give the first three letters of the main entry (usually the author) on the spine. For example:

937 Gibbon's *Decline and Fall of the Roman Empire*
Gib

Such libraries often class all biography in a "B" collection, and all fiction in an "F" collection, still using three-letter book numbers for the subject and author, respectively. In the latter case a single letter may indicate a title by an author. For example:

B A biography of Lincoln
Lin

F *David Copperfield* by Dickens
DICd

13.3 For larger libraries and those expecting to grow, the Cutter-Sanborn tables (available from Libraries Unlimited, P.O. Box 3988, Englewood, Colorado 80155) may be preferred over letters alone. Numbers from these tables provide the greater specificity needed to overcome the inevitable conflicts arising when several authors with the same last name write about the same topic, several biographies on the same person are acquired, several people with the same name write about an author, or the same person writes about an author more than once.

Selected Bibliography

14.1 Richard Hyman's *Shelf Access in Libraries* (Chicago: American Library Association, 1982) provides a full discussion of the role of library classification in accessing books. For an introductory discussion of classification in general, see Eric J. Hunter's *Classification Made Simple* (Aldershot, Eng.: Gower Publishing Co., Ltd., 1988). A good introduction to the nature and characteristics of specific classifications can be found in the most recent edition of A.C. Foskett's *The Subject Approach to Information* (Hamden, Conn.: Linnet Books, 1982) and in Lois M. Chan's *Cataloging and Classification* (New York: McGraw-Hill, 1981). For the history of the DDC, see John P. Comaromi's *The Eighteen Editions of the Dewey Decimal Classification* (Albany, N.Y.: Forest Press, 1976); a digested version appeared in *The Quarterly Journal of the Library of Congress* (33:311-331, October 1976), and was included in Bill Katz's *Library Lit. 8- ; the Best of 1977* (Metuchen: Scarecrow, 1978). For development of the Classification through Edition 20, see Jeanne Osborn's and John P. Comaromi's account in *Dewey Decimal Classification, 20th Edition: A Study Manual* (Littleton, Colo.: Libraries Unlimited, 1990). Their work is valuable as a study guide to the structure of the DDC and as an introduction to the Classification, to the editorial practices that govern it, and to the publishing practices regarding it. For works on book numbers, see John P. Comaromi's *Book Numbers: A Historical Study and Practical Guide to Their Use* (Littleton, Colo.: Libraries Unlimited, 1981) and Donald Lehnus's *Book Numbers: History, Principles, and Applications* (Chicago: American Library Association, 1980).

Glossary

Add table. *See* **Table (2).**

Approximate the whole. When the topic of a work is approximately coextensive with the topic of a DDC heading, the work is said to "approximate the whole." The term is also used to characterize works that cover more than half the content of the heading, and works that cover representative examples from three or more subdivisions of a class. When a work approximates the whole of a subject, standard subdivisions may be added for it. Approximating the whole is the opposite of having standing room. *See also* **Standing room.**

Aspects. Those approaches to a subject that belong to different disciplines, e.g., the *technical* or *economic* aspects of the manufacture of television sets. *See also* **Discipline; Facet; Subject.**

Author number. *See* **Book number.**

Base number. A number to which other numbers are appended or added.

Book number. That part of a call number that designates a specific item within its class. A library using the Cutter-Sanborn system can have D548d indicate *David Copperfield* by Dickens (where D stands for the D of Dickens, 548 for "ickens", and d for *David Copperfield*). *See also* **Call number.**

Broad classification. The classification of works in broad categories even when more specific numbers are available, e.g., classing a cookbook of Mexican recipes in 641.5 Cooking (instead of in 641.5972 Mexican cooking).

Built number. *See* **Number building.**

Call number. A set of letters, numerals, or other symbols (in combination or alone) used by a library to identify a specific copy of a work. A call number consists of the class number, book number, and sometimes such other data as date, volume number, copy number, and location symbol. *See also* **Book number; Class number.**

Centered entry. An entry representing a subject covered by a span of numbers, e.g., 372–374 Levels of education. The entry is called "centered" because the span of numbers is printed in the center of the page rather than in the number column on the left side of the page. Centered entries are identified by the symbol > in the number column.

Citation order. The order in which the facets or characteristics of a class are to be combined in number building. When number building is not permitted or possible, an order of precedence with respect to the choice of facets or characteristics is provided. *See also* **Precedence order.**

Class. *(Noun)* (1) A group of objects exhibiting one or more common characteristics, usually identified by a specific notation. (2) One of the ten major groups numbered 0–9 of the DDC. Also known as **Main class.** (3) A subdivision of the DDC of any degree of specificity. *(Verb)* To assign a class number to an individual work. Also called **Classify.**

Class-elsewhere note. A note instructing the classifier to class parts of a class or topics related to it in numbers that are not subdivisions of the number at hand.

Class-here note. An instruction identifying subjects (both broader and narrower than the number) that are to be classed in the given number and in its subdivisions. The narrower subjects identified in class-here notes are said to "approximate the whole." *See also* **Approximate the whole.**

Class number. Notation that designates the class to which a given item belongs. *See also* **Call number.**

Classification. A logical system for the arrangement of knowledge.

Classification by attraction. The classification of a specific aspect of a subject in an inappropriate discipline, usually because the appropriate discipline contains no explicit provision for the subject in question. For example, in the 18th and earlier editions of the DDC, social services related to water pollution were not provided for in 363, so works on this subject were attracted to the engineering numbers in 628.1.

Classified catalog. A catalog arranged according to the notational order of a classification system (rather than alphabetically).

Classify. (1) To arrange a collection of items according to a classification system. (2) To assign a class number to an individual item. Also called *Class (Verb).*

Close classification. (1) A classification providing for minute subdivision of topics. (2) Arrangement of works in conformity with the provisions of such a scheme.

Comparative table. When complete or extensive revision has taken place, a comparative table lists in alphabetical order selected topics with their current number and the number used in the previous edition. Found in this edition on pages 171-175. *See also* **Equivalence table; Revision.**

Complete revision. *See* **Revision.**

Complex subject. A complex subject as used in the DDC is a subject that has more than one characteristic. For example, the subject "unemployed bibliographers" has more than one characteristic (employment status and occupation) and is therefore a complex subject. *See also* **Precedence order.**

Comprehensive number. A number (often identified by a comprehensive works note) that covers all the components of the subject treated within that discipline. The components may be in a span of consecutive numbers, e.g., Sociology 301–307 (comprehensive number 301); or distributed in the Classification, e.g., automated retrieval in 025.04, with kinds of automated retrieval with the kind in 025.06–025.6 *See also* **Interdisciplinary number.**

Cross reference. *See* **Class-elsewhere note; See-also references; See references.**

DDC. Dewey Decimal Classification.

Decimal point. The dot that follows the third digit in a DDC number. In strict usage the word "decimal" is not accurate since the point following the third digit is a separating point, and the three-digit number preceding it is not to be regarded as an integer; however, common usage is followed in this edition's explanatory material.

Discipline. An organized field of study or branch of learning, e.g., 200 Religion, 530 Physics, 364 Criminology. In the DDC, subjects are arranged by disciplines. *See also* **Subject.**

Discontinued number. A number from the preceding edition that is no longer used because the subject represented by the number is now classed in a more general number. Numbers are usually discontinued because they identify a topic with negligible current literature or represent a distinction no longer valid in the literature or common perception of the field.

Division. The first level of subdivision of the ten main classes, represented by the first two digits in the notation, e.g., 53 in 530. More often than not the division is a discipline, e.g., 530 Physics. *See also* **Main class; Section.**

Entry. (1) In the Schedules and Tables: a self-contained unit consisting of a number or span of numbers, a heading, and often one or more notes. (2) In the Relative Index: a term or phrase followed by a DDC number.

Equivalence table. When a complete revision has taken place, an equivalence table lists in numerical order the classes of the current edition with the equivalent number in the former edition (and vice versa). Found in this edition on pages 176-179. *See also* **Comparative table; Revision.**

Facet. Any of the various categories into which a given class may be divided, e.g., division of the class "people" by the categories race, age, education, language spoken, and so on. Each category contains terms based on a single characteristic of division, e.g., children, adolescents, and adults are characteristics of division of the "ages" category. *See also* **Citation order.**

First-of-two rule. The rule instructing that works on two mutually exclusive subjects, whether in adjacent or widely separated numbers, are to be classed in the number coming first in the Schedules or Tables.

Heading. The word or phrase used as the caption of a given class.

Hierarchical force. The principle that the attributes of a class that are defined in the heading and in certain basic notes apply to all the subdivisions of the class and to all other classes to which reference is made.

Hierarchy. The arrangement of a classification system from general to specific. In the Dewey Decimal Classification, the degree of specificity of a class is usually indicated by the length of the notation and the corresponding depth of indention of the heading.

Including note. An enumeration of topics that are not obviously a part of the class and that have not been given separate provision. Standard subdivisions may not be added to the numbers for these topics. *See also* **Standing room.**

Interdisciplinary number. A number (often identified by an interdisciplinary works note) used for works covering a subject from the perspective of more than one discipline, e.g., the interdisciplinary number for marriage is 306.81 in Sociology. *See also* **Comprehensive number.**

Main class. One of the ten major subdivisions of the Dewey Decimal Classification, represented by the first digit in the notation, e.g., the 3 in 300. *See also* **Division; Section.**

Manual. A guide to the use of the DDC that is made up primarily of extended discussions of problem areas in the application of the Classification. In the Schedules and Tables, see-Manual notes indicate that relevant information is available in the Manual.

Notation. Numerals, letters, and/or other symbols used to represent the main and subordinate divisions of a classification scheme. In the DDC, Arabic numerals are used to represent the classes, e.g., notation —07 from Table 1 and 511.3 from the Schedules.

Number building. Making a given Schedule number appropriately specific by adding notation from the Tables or other parts of the Schedules. *See also* **Citation order.**

Number column. The column of numbers printed in the left margin of the Schedules and Tables, and to the right of the alphabetical entries in the Relative Index.

Precedence order. The order indicating which one of two or more numbers is to be chosen when the numbers represent different characteristics of a subject that cannot be shown in full by number building. A note (sometimes containing a table of precedence) always indicates which characteristic is to be selected for works covering more than one characteristic. When the notation can be synthesized to show two or more characteristics, it is a matter of citation order. *See also* **Citation order.**

Relative Index. The index to the DDC, called "Relative" because it relates subjects to disciplines. In the Schedules, subjects are arranged by disciplines. In the Relative Index, subjects are listed alphabetically; indented under them is an alphabetical list of the disciplines in which they are found.

Relocation. The shifting of a topic in a new edition of the DDC from one number to another number which differs from the old number in respects other than length, e.g., the relocation of the Salvation Army from 267 to 287.9.

Revision. The result of editorial work that alters the text of any class of the DDC. There are four degrees of revision: *Routine revision* is limited to updating terminology, clarifying notes, and providing modest expansions. *Substantial revision* involves a class that requires major redefinitions and significant relocations. In this edition, the revision of 720–724 Geographic treatment of architecture is an example of substantial revision. *Extensive revision* involves a major reworking of subdivisions but leaves the main outline of the schedule as it was. The changes are shown only through a comparative table rather than through relocation notes in the schedule or table affected. There are no extensive revisions in Edition 12. *Complete revision* (formerly called a *phoenix*) is a new development; the base number remains as in the previous edition, but virtually all subdivisions are changed. In this edition, only 780 Music is a complete revision. *See also* **Comparative table.**

Rule of application. The rule instructing that works about the application of one subject to a second subject are classified with the second subject.

Rule of three. The rule instructing that works that give equal treatment to three or more subjects that are all subdivisions of a broader subject are classified in the first higher number that includes all of them.

Schedules. The series of DDC numbers 001–999, their headings, and notes.

Section. The third level of subdivision in the Classification, represented by a three-digit notation not ending in zero, e.g., 629. *See also* **Division; Main class.**

See-also references. Notes in the Schedules and Tables to classes that are tangentially related to the number and that therefore might be confused with it. See-also references in the Relative Index may be to a broader term, or simply to any related term.

See references. A note in the Schedules and Tables introduced by the word "for" that leads from the number in which a subject is classed to component parts of the subject located elsewhere. *See also* **Class-elsewhere note.**

Separates. Extensive segments of the DDC that are published between editions.

Standard subdivisions. Subdivisions found in Table 1 that represent frequently recurring physical forms (dictionaries, periodicals) or approaches (history, research) applicable to any subject or discipline. They may be added to any number in the Schedules unless there are instructions to the contrary.

Standing room. A term which characterizes topics that are considerably less extensive in scope than their class numbers; standard subdivisions cannot be added to these topics nor are other number-building techniques allowed. Topics listed in notes beginning with "contains," "examples," and "including" have standing room in the class number, as do other minor topics which are not named. To have standing room is the opposite of approximating the whole. *See also* **Approximate the whole.**

Subject. An object of study. It may be a person or a group of persons, a thing, place, process, activity, abstraction, or any combination of these. It is often studied in more than one discipline, e.g., gold is studied in prospecting, mineralogy, jewelry-making, minting coins, economics, and dentistry. In the DDC subject is contrasted with **Discipline.** Also called *topic.*

Summary. A listing of the chief subdivisions of a class. Summaries provide a brief overview of the structure of the class, and are printed immediately under the entry for the class. For the whole Classification, the first, second, and third summaries (of main classes, divisions, and sections) appear before the Schedules.

Table. In the DDC, a table of numbers that may be added to other numbers in the Schedules to make a class number appropriately specific to the work being classified. The numbers found in a table are never used alone. There are two kinds: (1) Tables 1–4 (always referred to with a capital T) representing such concepts as geographical area and standard subdivisions. (2) Sets of tabulated numbers found in add notes under specific numbers throughout the Schedules and occasionally in Tables 1–4. These tabulated numbers are called *add tables.*

Table of precedence. *See* **Precedence order.**

Topic. *See* **Subject.**

Index to the Introduction and Glossary

References to the Introduction are identified by paragraph numbers. References to the alphabetically arranged Glossary are identified by G.

Manual

Use of the Manual

The Manual for the Abridged Dewey Decimal Classification is intended to serve practicing classifiers and students. It describes the policies and practices of the Decimal Classification Division of the Library of Congress. Outline maps provide a display of key area numbers from Table 2. Users are led from the Schedules and Tables to the Manual by see-Manual notes.

The Manual is arranged in the numerical order of the Tables and Schedules. For certain classes there are several notes which are subarranged in the following sequence:

(A) Notes on problems common to more than one number (the notes for numbers linked by "-" or "and," e.g., 580-590 or 658 and T1—068).

(B) Notes on problems involving only one number (or a single number and its subdivisions).

(C) Notes on differentiating numbers (the notes linked by "vs.," e.g., 300 vs. 600).

These notes may contain sections on specific problems, e.g., the treatment of adaptations in 800 literature.

There is an unusually full note on 780 Music to explain the complete revision of the class introduced in this edition.

A section at the end of the Manual describes the policies and procedures of the Decimal Classification Division of the Library of Congress in respect to the following: Segmentation in centrally cataloged records, bracketed DDC numbers on LC bibliographic records, and classifying children's books in the Decimal Classification Division.

Notes on Table Numbers

Table 1. Standard Subdivisions

Standard subdivisions are so called because they are applicable to virtually all classes. There are several kinds of standard subdivisions:

1. Subdivisions which indicate the bibliographic form that the information may take, e.g., encyclopedias, periodicals.

2. Subdivisions which treat the whole subject, but in a restricted situation, e.g., by areas, kinds of persons.

3. Subdivisions which identify a specific kind of information about the subject, e.g., illustrations, directories, product lists.

4. Subdivisions which bring the methods of other disciplines to bear on the subject, e.g., management, education, auxiliary techniques.

5. Subdivisions which relate the subject to its users, e.g., the subject as a profession.

6. Miscellaneous subdivisions, e.g., biography.

The common feature of standard subdivisions is that they identify limited treatment of the subject that may be wanted by users not immediately concerned with the rest of the subject. This feature leads to the first general rule in applying them: in doubtful cases do not use standard subdivisions, since they serve to segregate specialized material from works of general interest. For example, avoid using the historical treatment subdivision T1—09 for recent developments in a subject because most readers will expect to find such works in the main number.

Use whether or not supplied in the schedules

Standard subdivisions can be used anywhere in the schedules unless there are instructions to the contrary. They are not normally supplied in the number column except where needed to fill out three-digit numbers under the main classes. However, under certain numbers a few standard subdivisions are supplied when these subdivisions have special meanings or when extended notation is required for the subject in question. The rest of the standard subdivisions (those not supplied) are to be used with their normal meanings as given in this table. For example, in the standard subdivision position under 370 Education the schedule lists several numbers, including three subdivisions of 370.1 not found in Table 1, four subdivisions of 370.7 to show that concepts covered by these standard subdivisions are not found in their usual places, and 370.28 to show that one aspect of this standard subdivision is classed elsewhere. (If the entire concept is classed elsewhere, the number is enclosed in brackets.) The subdivisions of notation 02–09 that are not printed in 370.2–.9 are to be used with their normal meanings as though they were printed.

Whenever the base digits of a normal standard subdivision are supplied, all further subdivisions found in Table 1 are implied. For example, the regular heading for notation 07 from Table 1, "Education and related topics," is supplied at 507, implying that 507.1 is to be used for schools and courses in the natural sciences, 507.6 for review and exercises in the natural sciences, etc. The entry for 507.8 is given only to introduce the note on science projects.

Approximating the whole

Standard subdivisions should be added only when the work in hand applies to the whole, or approximately the whole, of the subject of the number. For example, there is no number for spiders under 595.4, the number for arachnids. Do not, therefore, assume that spiders of Mexico should be classed in the number for arachnids (595.4) plus the standard subdivision for Mexico (0972), i.e., in 595.40972. Stop at 595.4. (There is a number for spiders in the unabridged edition of DDC, to which the standard subdivision for Mexico could be added, but such detailed numbers are not available in the abridged edition.)

The approximate-the-whole restriction need not be applied to the individual elements of a unitary term. Many headings contain two or more parts joined by the word "and." Sometimes the words thus joined are so close in meaning that they are unlikely ever to be separated. These headings (and similar phrases in class-here notes) constitute unitary terms. (See discussion of class-here notes below.) When a unitary term is at issue, standard subdivisions are added even when the work in hand uses only one of the terms and attempts to draw a distinction between the two.

Examples of unitary terms are:

255	Religious congregations and orders
301	Sociology and anthropology
338.9	Economic development and growth
341.5	Disputes and conflicts between states
362.2	Mental and emotional illnesses and disturbances

These are not to be confused with related terms which commonly go together to form a larger whole. Such terms could each have its own subdivision (and usually do in the unabridged edition):

306.8	Marriage and family
332.8	Interest and discount
347	Civil procedure and courts

The normal rule for determining what subject or combination of subjects approximates the whole of a larger subject is that a work covering three subdivisions approximates the whole. If there are only three subdivisions, then normally two subdivisions approximate the whole. However, if a subject consists of several distinct subclasses, a work on representatives of three or more subdivisions is counted as approximating the whole. For example, a work on a cathedral, a museum, and a chateau in France will be classed in 720.944, i.e., as representative architecture (720) in the area (9) of France (44).

Class here notes and approximating the whole

The class-here note, i.e., the instruction note beginning with the words "Class here," is a reliable guide that standard subdivisions may be added to the notation for the term or terms listed. The terms that refer to subjects larger than the one indicated by the heading clearly justify the use of applicable standard subdivisions. However, the terms in a class-here note for concepts smaller than the subject for the heading are regarded as approximating the whole, and thus also justify use of applicable standard subdivisions.

Use of two standard subdivisions in a single number

Do not add one standard subdivision to another standard subdivision unless specifically instructed. In the following cases, addition of a second standard subdivision is allowed:

1. With standard subdivision T1—04, which is actually not a *standard* subdivision, but a special topic subdivision available to permit introduction of new development where there is no suitable vacant notation in direct 1–9 subdivisions.

2. With standard subdivisions that have specially changed or extended meanings, e.g., periodicals on educational psychology 370.1505. (In contrast, the periodicals subdivision is not added to true standard subdivisions, e.g., not to educational organizations 370.6, or the history of political science 320.09.)

3. With standard subdivision concepts displaced to nonzero numbers (usually for geographical treatment), the full range of standard subdivisions is available, e.g., museums of North American geology 557.074.

T1—01 **Philosophy and theory**

Notation 01 is not used in this abridged edition for classification, communication, or language (terminology), even though these topics are found in subdivisions of T1—01 in the unabridged edition of the Dewey Decimal Classification. Class these topics in 001–999 without adding notation from Table 1.

T1—01 vs. 302–307 **Philosophy and theory vs. Specific topics in sociology and anthropology**

While application of psychology to any subject is classed in with the subject with use of notation 01, application of social psychology to a subject is classed in the social sciences (most often in 302–307) without use of notation 01. For example, class individual psychology of religion in 200.1, social psychology of religion in 306.6.

T1—02 **Miscellany**

Notation 02 is not used in this abridged edition for audiovisual and humorous treatment, identification marks, manuals, patents, standards, statistics, other tabulated material, or works for specific types of users, even though these kinds of material are found in subdivisions of T1—02 in the unabridged edition of the Dewey Decimal Classification. Class such material in 001–999 without adding notation from Table 1.

T1—022 vs. 912 **Illustrations vs. Graphic representations of surface of earth and extraterrestrial worlds**

Geographic atlases and maps, i.e., atlases and maps which either do not emphasize a subject, or are devoted to any subject in 910 (general geography and travel) are classed in 912. Road atlases and maps, being primarily intended for travelers, are also classed in 912, but railroad atlases are normally devoted to transportation, so are classed in 385.022 or (if limited to a specific place) in 385.09, e.g., a railroad atlas of Brazil 385.0981.

T1—028 **Auxiliary techniques and procedures; apparatus, equipment, materials**

Class maintenance and repair in numbers denoting fabrication, manufacture, construction, not in numbers denoting use, operation or application when these are different, even if it means that notation 028 will not be used, e.g., repair of mining machinery 681 (not 622.028).

T1—0285 **Data processing Computer applications**

Do not use T1—0285 to indicate that a work is in machine-readable form, e.g., use 317.3 (not 317.30285) for a compilation of general statistics of the United States on a hard disc. A program, however, may be regarded as a kind of apparatus (a device to make a computer work properly or to accomplish a particular task) while works about programs typically discuss techniques and procedures. Hence T1—0285 should be used for programs themselves and for works about programs, regardless of form, e.g., for programs in machine-readable form or printed program listings bound into books.

Do not use T1—0285 for items that include both programs and data files, unless the data files are clearly of minor importance, e.g., small files intended merely to help beginners learn to use the programs.

If in doubt, do not use T1—0285.

T1—06 **Organizations and management**

Organizations in T1—06 primarily refer to membership organizations and associations, but also to certain nonmembership institutions, foundations, and agencies. However, before using T1—06 for nonmembership organizations, determine that the concept of organization is not inherent in the subject. For example, do not use T1—06 for nonmembership organizations with most subdivisions in 250–280 Christian church, in 355–359 military science, or in 360 social service. Under such numbers, use T1—09 for the basic organizations in specific areas, e.g., organizations providing health services in China 362.10951. However, use T1—06 for associations whose members are the basic operating organizations, e.g., an association of health institutions and agencies in China 362.106.

T1—06 vs. T1—025 **Organizations and management vs. Directories of persons and organizations**

Be alert for certain works covering several or many organizations that in fact constitute directories, even if not so called, i.e., works that supply addresses, key officers or contact people, phone numbers, and brief statements of purpose. There may be directory information about component parts of individual organizations, and/or a limited amount of general information on structure and component parts. These works are classed in T1—025. However, if there is more than about a page of general information per organization, consider T1—06. The chief thrust of material intended for T1—06 is indicated by the terms in the including note: administrative proceedings and reports, charters, history, membership lists, and regulations, but also includes conference programs and organizational handbooks.

Normally a combined organizational handbook and membership directory is classed in T1—06, even if the membership portion predominates. However, if the organizational part consists of only a few preliminary pages followed by an extensive directory of members, then the work may be more useful classed as a directory of the organization in T1—025.

A membership list that includes addresses is counted as a directory, and is classed in T1—025.

If in doubt, prefer T1—025.

T1—07 Education and related topics

Notation 07 is not used in this abridged edition for works about research, even though research is found in a subdivision of T1—07 in the unabridged edition of the Dewey Decimal Classification. Class interdisciplinary works on research in 001.4, research in a specific subject in 001–999 without adding notation from Table 1.

T1—07 vs. 016, 026 Education and related topics vs. Bibliographies and catalogs of works on specific subjects or in specific disciplines vs. Libraries, archives, information centers devoted to specific disciplines and subjects

Notation 07 from Table 1 is used for comprehensive works on resources for study and teaching. Many of the resources are encompassed by subdivisions of T1—07, e.g., schools, collections of objects (such as botanical collections), and financial support. Books, manuscripts, recordings, and the like are also resources, but works that describe such resources will normally be classed in 016 or 026 unless the work (a) also describes kinds or resources not found in 016 or 026 or (b) emphasizes how to use the library or archival resources for study and teaching. If in doubt between the subject plus T1—07 from Table 1 and 016 or 026, prefer 016 or 026.

To be classed in 016, a work about resources in a field should describe individual works, such as books and articles. A work about kinds of material not traditionally described in detail, however, is also classed in 016 if small units are described, e.g., five shelf feet of correspondence of a particular person on a particular subject. Inventories and calendars of archives are typically classed in 016. Works about resources in a field that give broad descriptions of whole collections held by libraries, archives, and other information organizations are classed in 026. Such works often include directory information about the institutions and organizations. In case of doubt between 016 and 026, prefer 016.

Notation 07 may be used in 016 if the resources being described treat study and teaching, e.g., a bibliography of material on the study and teaching of mathematics 016.5107.

T1—089 vs. T1—09 **Racial, ethnic, national groups vs. Historical, geographic, persons treatment**

Subdivision T1—089 takes precedence over notation in T1—09 except for groups which predominate in an area, e.g., French people in Australia T1—089, but French people in France T1—0944; Arabs generally or Arabs in France T1—089, but Arabs in Egypt T1—0962. Notation 0917 is not used for groups of persons treatment since such use would practically duplicate the group treatment numbers, e.g., Arabs who are residents of all areas where they predominate taken together constitute the overwhelming majority of all Arabs, so T1—089 is used for them, not T1—0917.

Use T1—09 to identify distinguishing characteristics of a subject rather than T1—089, e.g., Arab architecture 720.917, not 720.89; French agriculture 630.944, not 630.089.

T1—09 **Historical, geographic, persons treatment**

Be alert for the distinction occasionally made between the historical and geographic treatment of a subject and the historical and geographic treatment of the discipline within which the subject is studied. For example, 591.9 is provided for historical and geographic treatment of animals, while 591.09 is given for historical and geographic treatment of zoology, which is the study of animals. Use 591.97 for a description of animals found in North America, 591.097 for a work on how the study of animals grew or is carried out in North America. Where the distinction is not made between the subject and the discipline, use T1—09 for either or both aspects.

T1—092 **Persons**

These instructions apply also to notation 2 from Table 2 when numbers from Table 2 are added directly without the interposition of T1—09.

In the notes below, the word "biography" is used for stylistic convenience; however, the instructions apply fully to description and critical appraisal as well as other "persons" aspects.

T1—092 is not used for the actual works of a person except where so instructed at certain numbers in 700–770.

Comprehensive biography: General

Class a comprehensive biography of a person with the subject of the person's most noted contribution. If the person made approximately equal contributions to a number of fields, class in the subject which provides the best common denominator, giving some extra consideration to the person's occupational commitment. For example, a physicist who became a science teacher, then head of a school of science, but went on to become a university president would be classed in the university's area number under 378. The biography of a person who made significant contributions in political science, in university education, and in the study of administrative and economic aspects of utility regulation will be classed in 300.92, since social science is the common denominator for the person's work. However, a famous woman doctor who also served as a feminist leader, wrote novels, and often served as a delegate to political conventions will normally be classed in 610.92 unless there is an obvious emphasis on her avocations. Give weight to designations listed first in biographical dictionaries, but make allowances for the tendency to list occupation first even when a career transcends occupation.

If in doubt between a number for a discipline and a number for a specific subject within the discipline, prefer the number for the discipline, e.g., a mechanical engineer who also did important work in transportation and construction engineering 620.0092 rather than 621.092.

Comprehensive biography: Public figures

Biographies of public figures frequently present difficulties because the figures may have filled several positions which are given varying emphasis by different authors, or may have filled one position which had many facets. For persons who held such positions, prefer history numbers in 930–990 for comprehensive works. However, for biographies that emphasize one position or interest of a person's career, e.g., a biography emphasizing Wayne Morse's promotion of the National Institutes of Health 362.1092, even though he was a U.S. Senator. (See also Biography of part of a person's life, below.)

There are a number of offices a public figure may hold that afford an opportunity to exert a wide-ranging impact upon the history of the jurisdiction served. For example, Daniel Webster is most famous as a U.S. Senator, although he served twice as Secretary of State. In both positions, as well as in his position as lawyer and orator, he influenced the history of his time, so the best number for his biography is 973.5092, not 328.73 for his senatorial service, 327.730092 for his foreign relations service, or 342.73 for his contributions to constitutional law.

For public figures who served in several capacities, give greatest weight to the highest office reached, normally the one in the highest category in the following table. When there is no clear reason to the contrary, use the following table of precedence:

1. 930–990 for kings, presidents, other heads of state, prime ministers, vice presidents, regents using the number for the period during which they held office. Also class here public figures of any position or combination of positions who had a significant impact upon general history, including the king makers and the powers behind the throne, using the period numbers which best approximate their period of influence. Candidates of major political parties for the highest office of a country are also assigned history numbers, generally using the period for which they ran for office, e.g., 973.6 for Stephen Douglas who ran against Lincoln.

2. The number for the field of service for cabinet members, e.g., a finance minister of France 336.44092.

3. 327.3–.9 for ambassadors and pre-World War 2 ministers plenipotentiary.

4. 328.4–.9 for legislators not warranting a specific subject number, e.g., a floor leader, party whip, or member noted for promoting legislative work. Consider, however, that biographers tend to concentrate upon legislators who left their mark on general history, so always weigh the number in 900 for the area the legislature served before assigning another. Only occasionally will a work focus on a legislator's own constituency.

5. 327.3–.9 for diplomats below the level of ambassador, unless associated with notable events, then with the events.

6. The number for field of service for public administrators not holding cabinet positions, if their contribution to the service was significant, otherwise 353–354.

Give comparable precedence to public figures of state, provincial, and local jurisdictions. Normally national office takes precedence over other levels, but the weight of contributions must be considered. For example, DeWitt Clinton, the famous governor of New York, was briefly U.S. Senator, and was a minor party candidate for President, but his comprehensive biography should be classed in 974.7 for the history of the state.

Families and close associates of the famous

Class a history of the immediate or extended family of a famous person with the biography of that person if the work strongly emphasizes the famous person. The same rule applies to the biography of a single relative or close associate of a famous person. However, if the relative or associate is important in his or her own right, or if the famous person is not strongly featured, class the life of the relative in the subject warranted by his or her own work, e.g., a biography of evangelist Ruth Carter Stapleton, sister of President Jimmy Carter, that treats the president only incidentally 269. If in doubt, do not use the number for a famous person for a relative or close friend; prefer a number warranted by the biographee's own activities. Class a general family history in 929.

Biography of part of a person's life

Each biography featuring a specific contribution of a person is classed with the contribution. However, a biography of the portions of a person's life that preceded the activity with which he is chiefly associated is classed in his comprehensive biography number when there is no significant alternative subject emphasis. For example, Justice Byron White's life as an All-American football player 796.332092; but the childhood of Elizabeth II of Great Britain 941.085092, not 941.084092.

Table 2. Geographic Areas, and Persons

T2—1 **Areas, regions, places in general**

Subdivisions of T2—1 are used only for areas, regions, and places that overlap more than one continent (considering Pacific Ocean islands as a continent), e.g., urban regions of the United States, Europe, and Japan T2—173. Such regions within one continent but covering several countries are classed with the number for the continent, e.g., urban regions of Europe T2—4.

Within a single country or place these general regions are classed in the general number for the country or place, e.g., a history of the urban regions of England 942, geography of the urban regions of England 914.2.

See also T2—2 vs. T2—1, T2—3-9.

T2—163 and T2—164, T2—165 **Atlantic Ocean [and] Pacific Ocean [and] Indian Ocean**

This table divides the world ocean in three parts—Atlantic, Indian, and Pacific Oceans. The "Arctic Ocean" is considered a sea of Atlantic. There is no Antarctic Ocean, but provision is made in T2—167 for the extreme southern portions of the three oceans.

Notes and references throughout show where to class connecting bodies of water, e.g., Bering Strait T2—164, not T2—163.

T2—19 vs. T2—99 **Space vs. Extraterrestrial worlds**

Class in T2—19 only space itself. The various bodies of the universe moving through space are classed in T2—99, e.g., moon rocks 552.0999. The anticipated use of T2—19 is not great.

T2—2 vs. T2—1, T2—3-9 **Persons vs. Areas, regions, places in general [and] Specific continents, countries, localities**

Observe that T2—2 covers persons "regardless of area, region, place," which means that persons are classed here, not in T2—1 or T2—3-9, e.g., a Brazilian is classed in T2—2, not T2—81. There are similar instructions in Table 1 for preferring notation 092 over notation 091 and T1—093-099.

T2—3-9 **Specific continents, countries, localities; extraterrestrial worlds**

Parts of oceans and non-inland seas limited by either country or locality are classed in T2—16. For example, Chesapeake Bay, an arm of the Atlantic Ocean that is almost surrounded by Maryland and Virginia, is classed in T2—163, not in either T2—752 or T2—755. Be alert that estuaries are sometimes named rivers. Estuaries that are parts of oceans and non-inland seas are classed in T2—16. For example, the York River, an estuary of the Chesapeake Bay, is classed in T2—163 (not T2—755).

See also T2—2 vs. T2—1, T2—3-9.

T2—3 vs. T2—4-9 **The ancient world vs. The modern world; extraterrestrial worlds**

Under T2—3 "The ancient world" are gathered those parts of the world more or less known to people of classical antiquity, and considered only during the period of "ancient history." The same areas in later times, as well as other areas such as America in both ancient and later times, are classed in T2—4-9. Examples: ancient China T2—31, later China T2—51; ancient Palestine T2—33, later Palestine T2—5694; ancient Gaul T2—364, France T2—44; Guatemala, both ancient and later, T2—7281. The approximate date of demarcation between "ancient" and "later" varies from place to place and may be determined by examination of the terminal dates in the Schedules in 931-939, e.g., 931 China to 420, 933 Palestine to 70.

T2—4-9 **The modern world; extraterrestrial worlds**

Physiographic regions and features

Class features not named in the area table and that are wholly or mostly contained within a political or administrative unit with the unit, e.g., the Everglades, Florida T2—759; Lake Tahoe, which is mainly in California, T2—794. Class a river with the unit where its mouth is located, e.g., Arkansas River T2—767. However, if the upper part of the stream is more important politically, economically, or culturally, class the river with that part, e.g., Rhine River T2—43 rather than T2—492.

Changes in geographical concepts

Note that some geographical concepts of an earlier day have been divided by whims of history. Many such concepts are given special notes to show where comprehensive works are to be classed, e.g., Armenia as a whole and Turkish Armenia at T2—566, Soviet Armenia at T2—47.

However, in many cases adjustments have been made between recent editions of the DDC to conform to historical changes. For example, Finland, which before World War I was part of the Russian empire, was placed by Melvil Dewey in T2—471, as the first subdivision of Russia. It was not until recently that the DDC relocated works on Finland to T2—4897.

On the other hand, Hawaii, which is not part of North America, is classed in T2—969 under Oceania, separated from the rest of the United States in T2—73-79; and the Asian parts of the U.S.S.R. are classed in T2—57-58, quite apart from the European portion of the U.S.S.R. in T2—47.

Table 3. Subdivisions for Individual Literatures, for Specific Literary Forms

To determine the comprehensive number for collected works, critical evaluation, or biography of an author, follow the criteria given below on language and form.

Language

Class an author with the language in which he writes.

For an author who continues to write in the same language, but who changes his place of residence or national affiliation to a country with a different language, use the language in which he writes. For example, class a novel in Russian by Solzhenitsyn in 891.73, even if the novel was written while the author was living in the United States.

For an author who changes his national affiliation to a country with the same language as that in which he has been writing, use the literature number for the country of which he is now a citizen. Thus T.S. Eliot is classed as a British author.

For an author who changes his place of residence, but not his national affiliation, to another country with the same language as that in which he has been writing, continue to use the literature number of his original country. Thus, a New Zealand author living in London, but still retaining New Zealand citizenship, is classed as a New Zealand author.

If information about an author's national affiliation is not readily available in the work being classed or in standard reference books, use the literature number of the author's country of origin, if known; or the literature number of the country in which his earlier works were published.

Class an author who writes in more than one language with the language that he used last, e.g., Samuel Beckett 840. However, if another language is predominant, class with that language. (Individual works of such an author are classed with the language in which they were originally written.)

Literary form

Use the form with which an author is chiefly identified, e.g., Jane Austen 823. If the author is not chiefly identified with one form, use form T3—8 Miscellaneous writings. Thus, class a late-20th-century English author who is equally famous as a novelist, dramatist, and poet in 828. (An individual work of such an author, of course, is classed with the form exemplified by the work.)

Biography

Do not use notation 092 from Table 1 for biography. Class literary reminiscences in T3—8, e.g., Hemingway's *A Moveable Feast* 818.

Examples of number building

Here are examples of basic number building for works in an individual language by or about individual authors and by or about more than one author. The following elements are used to build the numbers: base number; form; notation 08 Collections of literary texts or notation 09 History, description, critical appraisal (plus additional 0s in some cases).

Note: notation 08 and 09 are not used for works by or about single authors, e.g., a collection of poetry by Walt Whitman 811; nor are notation 08 and 09 used for works consisting equally of literary texts and history, description, critical appraisal, e.g., a collection of texts and criticism of literary works in German 830.

More than one form: works by or about more than one author

Base no. + notation 08 or 09

81 + 08 = 810.8 (an anthology of American literature)

83 + 09 = 830.9 (criticism of 18th-century German literature)

Forms T3—1–7

1. Works by or about more than one author, limited to a specific form but not limited to a specific period nor to a specific kind, scope, or medium

Base no. + form + notation 08 or 09

82 + 3 + 09 = 823.09 (criticism of English fiction)

2. Works by or about an individual author or more than one author: restricted to a specific form and to a specific period

Base no. + form

82 + 1 = 821 (Spenser's *Faerie Queene*)

83 + 2 = 832 (criticism of German drama of the second half of the 20th century)

3. Works by or about more than one author: restricted to a specific form and to a specific kind, scope, or medium

Base no. + form

84 + 3 = 843 (a collection of French short stories)

Form T3—8 Miscellaneous writings

Works by or about an individual author or more than one author: restricted to a specific form, period, and subform

Base no. + form

81 + 8 = 818 (a collection of epigrams of an individual American author of the later 19th century)

84 + 8 = 848 (a collection of jokes of several French authors of the later 20th century)

T3—1 vs. T3—2 **Poetry vs. Drama**

Dramatic poetry in T3—1 is poetry that employs dramatic form or some element of dramatic technique as a means of achieving poetic ends. Poetic plays intended for theatrical presentation, such as the plays of Shakespeare and Marlowe, are classed in T3—2. Poetic plays designed to be read rather than acted, such as Milton's *Samson Agonistes*, are also classed in T3—2.

The dramatic monologues classed in T3—1 are poems in which the speaker is a fictional or historical character speaking to an identifiable but silent listener at a dramatic moment in the speaker's life, for example, Robert Browning's "My Last Duchess." The monologues classed in

T3—2 are typically intended for use in theatrical presentations featuring only one actor.

T3—6 **Letters**

Class in T3—6 letters compiled from several authors to be read for their literary value. Class collections of the letters of an individual author that are biographical in the comprehensive works number for the author. (See also Table 3: Language; Literary Form; Biography.) Class the letters of an individual author in T3—6 only if they have been published for a literary purpose, e.g., to exhibit the style of the writer.

T3—7 vs. T3—8, 001–999 **Satire and humor vs. Miscellaneous writings vs. [Specific subject or discipline]**

Jokes and humorous literary works without identifiable literary form are classed in T3—8. In T3—7 are classed *only* collections of satire or humor in more than one literary form. (Works in a particular form, e.g., poetry or fiction, are classed with the form.)

Any subject may be dealt with in a humorous or satirical manner. Works dealing with a subject in such a manner fall in one of the following categories:

1. The humor involved is entirely incidental to the serious treatment of the subject, e.g., a joke injected in a lecture to provide respite from a serious mood;

2. A subject is dealt with in a serious way, but the humorous or satiric treatment of the subject is vital to the author's intent, e.g., political satire grounded in genuine political criticism;

3. The subject merely provides the occasion for humor, the author's primary concern being to amuse, e.g., a collection of jokes about cats.

Only works falling in the third category are classed in literature, usually at T3—8. Works in the first and second category are classed with the subject.

T3—8 **Miscellaneous writings**

Class in T3—8 diaries of literary authors not identified with a specific form of literature, in which the life of the author or authors as such is of key interest. If the author or authors are identified with a specific form, class the diary or diaries with that form. However, class the diaries of literary authors that emphasize some other subject besides the general life of the author with the subject emphasized. For example, class the diary of an author compiled while in a prisoner-of-war camp during World War II in 940.54.

Table 4. Subdivisions of Individual Languages

T4—3 **Dictionaries of the standard form of the language**

The Decimal Classification Division classes a bilingual dictionary with entry words in both languages with the language coming later in the sequence 420–490.

T4—3 vs. T4—81 **Dictionaries of the standard form of the language vs. [Standard usage of] Words**

Works classed in T4—3 are intended for ready-reference use. While specialized dictionaries may be arranged in other ways besides alphabetically (e.g., picture dictionaries in subject order, thesauri in classified order), the order must be appropriate for ready reference.

Works classed in T4—81 are intended to be read or studied in full in order to learn vocabulary. They may be informal and entertaining, e.g., narratives for small children, or they may be formally organized into lessons with quizzes.

T4—7 **Historical and geographic variations, modern nongeographic variations**

Remember that a language may have multiple standard forms. A work on standard Australian English pronunciation, for example, is classed in 421, not 427. A work on Australian English pronunciation is classed in 427 only if it stresses the distinctive characteristics that make Australian pronunciation different from British or American pronunciation.

T4—86 vs. 001–999 **Readers vs. [Specific subject or discipline]**

Class in T4—86 readers for nonnative speakers intended to instill a knowledge of the special vocabulary of a specific subject or discipline, e.g., German science readers for Spanish-speaking people 438.6. Class works on the vocabulary of a specific subject or discipline without regard to the language status of the user with the subject or discipline.

Notes on Schedule Numbers

000 Generalities

Two categories of works fall within the Generalities class:

(1) Works in "umbrella" or "tool" disciplines, that is, disciplines relating to or applied to many other disciplines, e.g., systems analysis and computer science (003–006), bibliography (010 and 090), library and information sciences (020), museum science (069), journalism and publishing (070). In the case of bibliography, the link between it and other disciplines may be shown by attachment of a number from the 001–999 span, e.g., 016.54 bibliographies of chemistry. In other cases the links may be shown by the use of standard subdivisions notation from Table 1, e.g., computer applications in business 650.0285.

(2) Multidisciplinary works, e.g., general encyclopedias (030), general periodicals (050), works on general organizations (060), general collections (080). There is parallel notation in Table 1 for three of these types of works, so that they may be shown in connection with specific subjects:

030 General encyclopedic works

T1—03 Dictionaries, encyclopedias, concordances

050 General serial publications and their indexes

T1—05 Serial publications

060 General organizations ...

T1—06 Organizations ...

001.9 and 130 **Controversial knowledge [and] Paranormal phenomena**

001.9 and 130 both pertain to topics in the twilight realms of half-knowledge, topics that refuse either to be disproved or to be brought into the realm of certain and verifiable knowledge. Certain characteristics of a work are good indicators that it belongs in either 001.9 or 130:

1. A claim of access to secret or occult sources;

2. A rejection of established authority;

3. A pronounced reverence for iconoclasts, for laymen-become-experts;

4. An uncritical acceptance of lay observation of striking phenomena;

5. A fixation on the unexplained, the enigmatic, the mysterious;

6. A confidence verging on certainty in the existence of conspiracies and the working of malevolent forces;

7. An acknowledgment of the powers of extraterrestrial beings or intelligences (other than religious beings).

Phenomena classed in 130 are closely linked to human beings—the human mind, human capabilities and powers, human happiness. Phenomena classed in 001.9 are not closely linked to humans. In case of doubt, and for interdisciplinary works, prefer 001.9.

003 Systems

Class works treating systems in related disciplines in the appropriate broad number for those disciplines, using notation 01 from Table 1, e.g., systems in medicine, engineering, management, and manufacturing 601. To be classed in 003 a work must be applicable to at least three main classes (e.g., 300, 500, 600).

Most works on forecasting and forecasts treat primarily social forecasting; such works are classed in 303.49. Works classed in 003 treat forecasting as applied in a variety of social and nonsocial disciplines. Such works typically focus on methods of forecasting.

004–006 vs. 621.39 [Data processing Computer science] vs. [Engineering of] Computers

Works classed in 004–006 treat (a) computer hardware from the user's viewpoint and/or (b) software. Works classed in 621.39 (a) treat computer hardware solely from the viewpoint of engineering or manufacturing and (b) do not treat software. Comprehensive works on the computer science and computer engineering aspects of a computer topic are classed in 004–006.

004 vs. 005 Data processing Computer science vs. Computer programming, programs, data

Class in 004 works on computer hardware and works treating both computer hardware and the "soft" aspects of computer systems—programs, programming, and data. Class works treating only these "soft" aspects in 005.

004.1 General works on specific types of computers

In this number, its subdivisions, and analogous numbers elsewhere in 004–006, computers and processors (central processing units) are treated for classification purposes as if they were the same. In fact they are not, but few works about processors can avoid discussing the other parts of the computer with which the processor must interact; hence works about specific types of computers and processors are typically not different enough to justify separate numbers.

004.165 **Specific digital microcomputers**

Do not class here or in any other number for specific microcomputers a work treating more than one microcomputer or microprocessor unless:

1. The work treats a single series of very closely related microcomputers or microprocessors (e.g., the Intel 8080® and 8080A® microprocessors 004.165); or

2. The work treats primarily one specific computer or processor but adds that it is also applicable to other similar machines (e.g., a work about programming the IBM PC® that says it can also be used as a guide to programming "IBM-compatible" computers 005.265).

Note: A work that discusses a computer and its processor is in effect a work about the computer and should be treated as such (e.g., a work about the Apple II® microcomputer and the 6502® microprocessor 004.165).

004.2 vs. 003 **Systems analysis and design, computer architecture vs. Systems**

In addition to the analysis and design of computer-based systems, class in 004.2 systems analysis of a user's problem in order to design a computer-based system to solve it. Class a work on systems analysis and design that is not concerned primarily with computer-based systems in 003 or with the specific system.

004.6 and 005.7 **Interfacing and communications [and] Data in computer systems**

Class in 004.6 selection and use of computer interfacing and communications equipment—the "hard" aspects. Class in 005.7 comprehensive works on the "soft" aspects of computer interfacing and communications—programming, programs, and data in interfacing and communications. Class comprehensive works on both the "hard" and "soft" aspects of computer interfacing and communications in 004.6.

005 **Computer programming, programs, data**

Text processing as classed here is broader than word processing; it includes all computer processing of information coded as characters or sequences of characters (as contrasted with information coded as numbers), e.g., counting word frequency, making concordances, storing and retrieving text, sorting lists alphabetically. Class specific applications of text processing with the application, e.g., alphabetic sorting 005.74, word processing 652.5.

005.1 vs. 005.3 **Programming vs. Programs**

Class a work devoted equally to programming and programs in 005.1 Programming or 005.2 Programming for specific types of computers.

Class in 005.1 testing and measurement as part of program development. Class in 005.3028 and other numbers for programs works that discuss ways for users to test or measure programs as an aid in selection.

005.1 vs. 510 [Computer] Programming vs. Mathematics

Certain terms may be used for both a computer science concept and a mathematics concept. *Algorithm*, for example, may be used for processes to solve mathematical problems—with or without the aid of a computer; general works on algorithms in this sense are classed in 511. *Algorithm* may also be used in the context of computer programming for processes to solve many different kinds of problems—information-retrieval and word-processing problems, for example, as well as mathematical problems; general works on algorithms in this sense are classed in 005.1.

Similarly, *programming* may refer to a branch of applied mathematics that has no necessary connection with computers, though computations necessary for this branch are commonly accomplished with the aid of a computer; programming in this sense is classed in 519.7. *Programming* may also refer to writing instructions to direct the operation of a computer or its peripheral equipment; programming in this sense is classed in 005.1.

005.13 Programming languages

Most machine and assembly languages are limited to a specific computer or processor (or at least to a specific type); and most works about specific machine and assembly languages emphasize programming with these languages; hence most works about specific machine and assembly languages are classed in 005.2 Programming for specific types of computers.

005.3 Programs

Class programs for a specific application in computer science with the application in 005–006, but never in 004. Among the numbers most frequently used for software besides 005.3 and its subdivisions are 005.4 for systems software and operating systems, 005.7 for interfacing and data communications programs, 005.74 for database management systems, and 006.6 for computer graphics programs.

005.362 [Programs] In specific programming languages

Class here programs and works about programs only if the material being classified emphasizes the programming language. For much off-the-shelf software, the user does not need to know in what programming language it was written; such software is classed in subdivisions of 005.3 not devoted to specific programming languages.

005.369 Specific programs

Class here specific programs having interdisciplinary applications, such as electronic spreadsheets (which can be used in research, business, personal finance, indeed any time a matrix format is useful) and statistics packages that are used more widely than just in research and that have report formatting or other features beyond statistical capabilities. If a work discussing how to use such a program is a guide that would be helpful to users applying the program in many fields, class it in 005.369 even if most of the examples come from one field. If a work truly focuses on how to use such a program in a particular field, however, class it with that field, using notation 0285 from Table 1, e.g., use of a particular electronic spreadsheet in financial administration 658.150285. In case of doubt, prefer 005.369.

005.6 Microprogramming and microprograms

Microprogramming does not mean programming for microcomputers, nor does *microprogram* mean a program for a microcomputer. *Microprogramming* means writing programs in which each instruction specifies a minute operation of the computer. Such programs are microprograms. Class programming for microcomputers in 005.26, programs for microcomputers in 005.36.

005.74 Data files and databases

Although there are technical differences between data files and databases, they are treated as the same for classification.

Class in 005.74 computer science aspects of databases, that is, the narrowly technical issues of designing, programming, and installing databases and database management systems—the kinds of things that system designers and programmers need to know but that users generally do not need to know unless they are installing a database on their own computer. Class the subject content of databases (and works discussing that content) as if the databases were books, e.g., encyclopedic databases 030, bibliographic databases 010, nonbibliographic chemistry databases 540. Do not add notation 0285 from Table 1 except for works that focus on the computer science aspects of the databases rather than the subject content. Class in 025.04 the information science aspects of the automated storage and retrieval systems that make databases available—the kinds of things that users need to know about the systems in order to benefit fully from them. Class in 025.06 the information science aspects of the automated systems that make databases on specific subjects available to users. Class interdisciplinary works on databases in 025.04.

011 vs. 005.3029 **Bibliographies vs. [Commercial miscellany about computer programs]**

Class general bibliographies of machine-readable works and general lists of software in 011. Class annotated lists of software in 011 if the annotations are relatively brief; but class lists with lengthy reviews as buyers' guides in 005.3029, e.g., a collection of reviews of microcomputer software 005.36029.

020 Library and information sciences

The order of precedence in the schedule for library and information science is complex. The following table shows precedence among 022, 023, 025, 026, and 027:

025 Operations, such as technical services, e.g., acquisitions, cataloging; readers' services, e.g., reference, circulation

Exceptions: (a) Administration (025.1) has a lower precedence than other operations. (b) Readers' services for special groups and organizations are classed with libraries for special groups and organizations in 027.6, not in 025.5. (c) Comprehensive works on operations in a specific kind of institution are classed with the kind of institution in 026–027, not in 025.

022, 023, 025.1 Administration

026 Institutions devoted to specific disciplines and subjects

027 General institutions

Examples follow:

1. Administration of cataloging

   Operation (cataloging) + administration

   025.3 + T1—068 (notation from Table 1) = 025.3068

2. Administration of school libraries

   Administration + institution (school library)

   025.1

   (Note that type of institution [027.8] cannot be shown in the number.)

3. Book selection in special libraries

   Operation (book selection) + institution (special library)

   025.2

   (Note that type of institution [026] cannot be expressed in the number.)

4. Reference services in prison libraries

   Library for a special group (prisoners) + operation (reference services)

   027.6

   (Note that the usual facet order of operation + institution is reversed here because of the exception listed above under 025. Note also that the operation [025.5] cannot be indicated in the number.)

026–027 Specific kinds of institutions

Libraries, archives, information centers devoted to specific kinds of special materials are classed in 026–027. Those limited to a specific subject or discipline are classed in 026, e.g., libraries devoted to music scores, to maps.

A general library (1) devoted to a kind of special material and (2) not serving special groups and organizations may be loosely regarded as devoted to a subject and classed in 026, e.g., a rare book library. A general library devoted to a kind of special material and serving special groups and organizations is classed in 027.6, e.g., a braille library.

027 General libraries, archives, information centers

Few archives are sufficiently general to be classed here; most are classed in 026 because they contain primarily material on specific disciplines and subjects, e.g., archives of religious organizations 026 (not 027.6).

027.5 Government libraries

General government archives for a specific jurisdiction usually contain primarily material reflecting the history and civilization of the place; works on such archives are classed in 026, e.g., United States National Archives 026.

080 General collections

To be classed here a work must contain a collection of writings, statements, or quotations on a variety of topics. Examples: selected articles of a general nature from one or more periodicals, such as highlights from *The Atlantic*; a collection of quotations by Winston Churchill on various topics.

100 Philosophy, parapsychology and occultism, psychology

Ethics is an exception to the rule that the philosophy of a discipline or subject is classed with the discipline or subject. Class the ethics of a discipline or subject in 172–179. Class ethics within or based on a religious tradition with the religion in 200. For example, class philosophy and theory of international relations in 327.101; the ethics of relations between states in 172; the ethics of those relations treated as part of Christian moral theology in 241.

100, 109 vs. 190 **Philosophy, parapsychology and occultism, psychology [and] Historical and collected persons treatment of philosophy vs. Modern Western philosophy**

190 is the comprehensive number for (a) Christian philosophy; (b) Western philosophy from ancient Greece to the present; (c) modern philosophy, even when both modern Western and modern Oriental philosophies are treated; and (d) European philosophy. For this reason, 190 is used more often than 100 or 109 for what appear to be general works on philosophy.

To be classed in 100 or 109, works must include (a) discussion of the discipline of philosophy itself or several of philosophy's major questions and branches, as is common in introductory works; or (b) discussion of philosophy broad enough to include non-Western and ancient or medieval as well as modern Western philosophy.

100 vs. 200 **Philosophy, parapsychology and occultism, psychology vs. Religion**

Both philosophy and religion deal with the ultimate nature of existence and relationships, but religion treats them within the context of revelation, deity, worship. Natural theology (210) does not involve revelation or worship but does examine questions within the context of deity.

Any work that emphasizes revelation, deity, or worship is classed in 200, even if it uses philosophical methods, e.g., a philosophical proof of the existence of God 212. Sometimes the thought of a religious tradition is used to examine the questions of philosophy without reference to deity or religious topics, e.g., Jewish philosophy 181, Christian philosophy 190. However, class ethics based on a religion in 200. If in doubt, prefer 200.

130 vs. 133 **Paranormal phenomena vs. Parapsychology and occultism**

Note that 130 by itself is seldom used; most general works on paranormal phenomena in fact focus on parapsychology and occultism and thus are classed in 133, not 130.

133 vs. 200 **Parapsychology and occultism vs. Religion**

If the author of a work about parapsychological or occult phenomena describes them as religious, or the believers and practitioners consider them to be religious, the work is classed in 200. If parapsychological and occult phenomena are not presented as religious, or if in doubt as to whether they have been so presented, prefer 133.

Class knowledge reputedly derived from secret and ancient religious texts but not applied for religious purposes in 133; however, class editions of the texts in 200, even if annotated from an occultist viewpoint, e.g., discussion of occult traditions derived from the Zohar, a cabalistic text, 135; but the text of the Zohar 296.1.

133.9 vs. 129 Spiritualism vs. Origin and destiny of individual souls

Class in 133.9 accounts of life after death from personal sources or from within the occult tradition. Class in 129 philosophical discussions of personal survival and life after death. If in doubt, prefer 133.9.

140 Specific philosophical schools and viewpoints

Viewpoints or schools of philosophy are sets of attitudes or presuppositions that a given philosopher or group of philosophers brings to the study of various topics. Topics are the questions studied by philosophy, such as the self 126. Only general works that discuss how a viewpoint or school treats a wide variety of topics are classed in 140, e.g., existentialism 142, but existentialist views of the self 126.

140 vs. 180–190 Specific philosophical schools and viewpoints vs. Historical, geographic, persons treatment of philosophy

Unless other instructions are given, class in 140 specific modern Western schools and viewpoints and comprehensive works on specific schools and viewpoints, but class in 180 ancient, medieval, and Oriental schools and viewpoints, e.g., modern Western idealism, comprehensive works on ancient and modern idealism or on Indian and Western idealism 141, but Indian idealism 181. Class in 190 historical and geographic treatment of modern Western philosophy not limited to a specific viewpoint, but class a specific school or viewpoint with the school or viewpoint regardless of time or place, e.g., French philosophy 194, but existentialism in France 142.

Class collected works of an individual philosopher and criticism of his work as a whole in 180–190, even if his work falls entirely within one philosophical viewpoint or serves as the foundation of a school, e.g., the works of Immanuel Kant 193, but Kantianism as a viewpoint espoused by philosophers 142.

146 vs. 335.4 Naturalism and related systems and doctrines vs. Marxian systems

Class in 335.4 dialectical materialism applied to the economic and political aspects of Marxian systems. Class in 146 dialectical materialism as a philosophical viewpoint either not applied to topics outside philosophy or else applied to many different disciplines. If in doubt, prefer 335.4.

150 vs. 302–307 **Psychology vs. Specific topics in sociology and anthropology**

Class in 150 works that focus on the individual, including those that discuss the influence of group behavior on the individual. Class in 302–307 works that focus on group behavior, including those that discuss the role of the individual in group behavior. If in doubt, prefer 302–307.

150.19 vs. 616.89 **Systems, schools, viewpoints [of psychology] vs. Mental disorders**

The psychoanalytic systems classed in 150.19 are the foundation of much of the writing on psychiatric disorders (616.89), and are also the bases of several schools of psychology. Most of the founders of psychoanalytic systems were physicians, so material from psychiatry is heavily used to illustrate the principles of the various psychoanalytic systems. Class comprehensive works on a system or its founder in 150.19. Class applications of a system to specific topics or branches of normal psychology or of both normal and abnormal psychology in the appropriate subdivision of 150. Class applications of a system to psychiatry in 616.89 and related numbers, e.g., psychoanalytic treatment of mental illness 616.89. If in doubt, prefer 616.89.

152 vs. 612.8 **[Psychology of] Sensory perception, movement, emotions, physiological drives vs. [Physiology of] Nervous functions Sensory functions**

Class in 152 works that emphasize awareness, sensation, intentions, meanings, and actions as experienced by the individual or observed and described without reference to the physics or chemistry of the nervous system, e.g., seeing colors, feeling anger. Class in 612.8 works that emphasize the physical and chemical mechanisms and pathways of sensations, emotions, movements, e.g., studies using electrodes to determine what parts of the brain process different kinds of stimuli. Class comprehensive works in 152. If in doubt, prefer 612.8.

152.1 vs. 153.7 **Sensory perception vs. Perceptual processes**

153.7 is more comprehensive because it includes works that focus on the active, interpretative mental processes associated with perception in general; sensory perception is a part of these processes. Also, class in 153.7 types of perception that involve more than one sense, e.g., spatial perception which includes vision and touch. Class in 152.1 works that focus on the receptive aspects of sensory perception and comprehensive works on perception by a specific sense, e.g., visual perception 152.14. If in doubt, prefer 153.7.

152.3 vs. 153.6 **Movements and motor functions vs. Communication**

Use of 152.3 is limited to noncognitive aspects of expressive movements, e.g., habituation, emotional content. Class the meaning of movements (as in body language) and the cognitive processes involved in interpreting movements in 153.6. If in doubt, prefer 153.6.

153.1 vs. 155.4–.6 **Memory and learning vs. Psychology of specific ages**

Class a work on the learning psychology of people of a specific age bracket in 155.4–.6 when age isactually the focus of the work. If the reference to age is vague or incidental, class the work in 153.1. If in doubt, prefer 155.4–.6.

153.1 vs. 370.15 **Memory and learning vs. Educational psychology**

Be careful to distinguish between studies that use students as subjects for research into the fundamental processes of learning, which are classed in 153.1 and related numbers, and studies on the application of learning psychology to education, which are classed in 370.15 and related numbers. In case of doubt, prefer 153.1.

153.4 vs. 153 **Knowledge (Cognition) vs. Conscious mental processes and intelligence**

The terminology in this field is used in a variety of overlapping senses. Many works that claim to be about cognition, thought and thinking, or reasoning also cover such subjects as memory, communication, perception, motivation, and intelligence. These broader works are classed in 153, not 153.4. A book about "cognitive psychology" is more apt to belong at 153 than 153.4.

153.4 vs. 160 **Knowledge (Cognition) vs. Logic**

Class the psychology of reasoning and problem solving in 153.4. Class the science of reasoning and problem solving, that is, the logical processes considered apart from internal mental operations, in 160. If in doubt, prefer 153.4.

153.9 **Intelligence and aptitudes**

Note that 153.9, when it is used to refer to aptitude or vocational interest tests, has priority over other psychology numbers, as shown in the table of precedence at 150. Class in 153.9 tests to determine aptitude in specific fields even if drawn from other branches of psychology, e.g., color matching tests for interior decorators 153.9 (not 152.14), personality tests for social workers 153.9 (not 155.2). Also class in 153.9 aptitude and vocational interest tests and testing limited to categories of persons defined in 155.3–.6, e.g., vocational interest tests for young adults 153.9 (not 155.5).

154.6 vs. 612.8 **[Psychology of] Sleep phenomena vs. [Physiology of] Nervous functions Sensory functions**

Class sleep phenomena in 154.6 if the emphasis is on the overall state of sleep, on the effect of sleep on other psychological activity, or on dreams as phenomena that have meaning in themselves or in the life of the dreamer. Class sleep phenomena in 612.8 if the emphasis is on the chain of bodily activities or on other physiological activity accompanying sleep or dreams, e.g., eye movements, breathing, brain waves. If in doubt, prefer 612.8.

155 Differential and developmental psychology

Some works on the psychology of sensory perception, movement, emotions, physiological drives (152) and conscious mental processes (153) analyze research based on persons belonging to one or several differential categories or subject to one or several environmental influences that are provided for in 155.3–.9. If there is clearly little or no interest in the distinctiveness of the category or influence, class the work in 152–153. This guideline is particularly applicable to ethnic and national groups (155.8), adults (155.6), and social environment (155.9) where the researcher has simply reached out for convenient samples.

Similarly, a study on sex psychology, drawing almost exclusively upon adult middle-class whites, but showing only marginal interest in the class, age, or race of the respondents, is classed in 155.3. Discussion of the class, national, or ethnic bias of such research is classed with the research in 155.3 since the interest is in the validity of the findings about sex psychology.

155.3 vs. 306.7 Sex psychology and psychology of the sexes vs. Institutions pertaining to sexual relations

Most works on the psychology of sexual relations treat social psychological aspects—the interaction between the partners. Such works are classed in 306.7. Only an occasional work emphasizes the psychology of the individual and is therefore classed in 155.3, e.g., a work that focuses on the anxieties of the individual with regard to sexual relations. In case of doubt, prefer 306.7.

155.9 vs. 158, 302–307 Environmental psychology vs. Applied psychology vs. Specific topics in sociology and anthropology

Class in 155.9 the influence of family, friends, and other people upon the individual. Class in 158 the art of getting along with people. Class in 302–307 social interaction regarded as group behavior.

When a work treats both the psychology of social influences (155.9) and social interaction (302–307), prefer 302–307, e.g., the influence of a rural community on individuals and interactions within a rural community 307.72 (not 155.9).

171 [Ethical] Systems and doctrines

Class collected works, biography, and critical appraisal of the work of an individual moral philosopher in 171, if the ethical system represented can be determined (e.g., critical appraisal of the ethics of Jeremy

Bentham, who is associated with utilitarianism, 171). Otherwise, class such works in 170.92.

174 Economic, professional, occupational ethics

Class in 174 a discussion of occupational ethics for clergy from a secular or philosophical viewpoint. If the subject is treated as part of the moral theology or ethics of a particular religion, class it with the religion, e.g., a discussion of the occupational ethics of clergy as part of Christian morality 241.

180–190 Historical, geographic, persons treatment of philosophy

Class single works by individual philosophers with the topic in philosophy. If there is no focus on a specific topic, class a work expressing primarily the philosopher's own viewpoint with the collected works of the philosopher in 180–190. For example, a general work by Hegel, such as *Phenomenology of Spirit*, is classed in 193.

Class a work by an individual philosopher that is primarily a discussion of other philosophers' writings with the other philosophers' writings.

200 Religion

200 is the comprehensive number for religion in general and for Christianity. 200 and standard subdivisions 200.1–.9 are used for religious thought and the general religious situation and conditions. 201–209 are the standard subdivisions of Christianity in general. 210 is for natural religion and religion based on reason alone. 220 is for the Bible. 230–280 are used for various topics in Christianity. 291 is used for comparative religion and for individual religious topics treated with respect to religions based on revelation or authority. 292–299 are for religions other than Christianity. For any specific topic in religion, the classifier must consider whether the topic is treated within one religion and should be classed in 201–209, 230–280 or 292–299; or whether it is treated from the viewpoint of comparative religion or of various religions and should be classed in 291; or whether it is treated using reason alone and should be classed in 210.

200.1 vs. 210, 291 Philosophy and theory of religion vs. Natural theology vs. Comparative religion

Comprehensive works on the philosophy of religion are classed in 200.1, but the study of specific topics in religion by use of philosophic methods may be provided for elsewhere, especially in 210 and 291. Natural theology (210) is an older term for the study of religion that excludes divine revelation but uses the methods of philosophy heavily. Hence, abstract questions are nearly always classed in 210, e.g., a philosophical treatment of the existence of God 212. Discussions of religious practice and experience nearly always involve the outlook of religions based on revelation, authority, or traditions; these are usually classed in 291 when treated in a philosophical manner, even if the methods of comparative religion are not emphasized. For example, a philosophical treatment of religious rituals would nearly always be classed in 291.3. Some topics may be treated equally well from the point of view of natural theology or world religions. The reconciliation of science and religion, for example, is classed in 215 if no appeal to revelation, sacred scriptures, or authority is apparent, or in 291.1 if the work assumes revelation. Works comparing or describing three or more religions are classed in 291, e.g., a comparison of the concept of God in Christianity, Islam, and Hinduism 291.2.

207 vs. 268 Education and related topics of Christianity vs. [Christian] Religious education

Class education in and teaching of Christianity as an academic subject in 207, e.g., a course on Christianity in secular secondary schools 207. Class in 268 religious education for the purpose of confirming believers in Christian faith and life. It is assumed that this is the purpose of any religious education sponsored by a church, so comprehensive works on religious education are classed in 268. The only exception is that education at the university level is classed in 207, including education in universities sponsored by churches.

Study and teaching with regard to any specific topic in 200 is classed with the topic using notation 07 from Table 1, e.g., study and teaching of church history 270.07.

209.2 [Biography of persons associated with Christianity and Christian thought]

Use the following table of precedence for comprehensive biographies:

Jesus Christ, Mary, Joseph, Joachim, Anne, John the Baptist	232.9
Other persons in the Bible	220
Founders of denominations	280
Founders of religious orders	271
Higher clergy (e.g., popes, metropolitans, archbishops, bishops) prior to 1054	270.1–.3
Higher clergy subsequent to 1054	280
Theologians	230
Moral theologians	241
Missionaries	266
Evangelists	269
Persons noted for participation in associations for religious work	267
Martyrs	272
Heretics	273
Saints	270
Saints prior to 1054	270.1–.3
Saints subsequent to 1054	280
Mystics	248.2
Hymn writers	264
Religious educators	268
Members of religious orders	271
Clergy prior to 1054	270.1–.3
Clergy subsequent to 1054	280
Members of the early church to 1054	270.1–.3
Members of denominations	280

This number (209.2) is the last resort for Christian biography. Class here only biographies of persons known not to be members of any church. This number may also be used when it has not been possible to determine whether there is church membership or not. Class in 280 without subdivision church members whose affiliation is not known and members of nondenominational and interdenominational churches.

Except for religious mysticism, do not use 248.2 Religious experience for comprehensive biographies, e.g., a biography of Teresa of Avila's religious life 282.092, not 248.2092. However, biographical accounts written for devotional purposes, not as comprehensive accounts of a person's life, may be classed in 248.2.

253, 255, and 262 are no longer used for biographies of the kinds of persons listed above in the table of precedence.

Certain numbers in the range 220–269 other than those listed in the table of precedence above may be used for comprehensive biographies of persons with specialized religious careers, but are more commonly used for books treating only one aspect of a person's life and work, e.g., 220.092 for a Biblical scholar.

Examples:

270.092	(Collected biography of saints)
225.9	(New Testament biography) Paul the Apostle
230	(Catholic theology) Saint Thomas Aquinas
232.9	(John the Baptist) John the Baptist
266	(Catholic missions) Saint Francis Xavier
269	(Evangelism) Billy Graham
271	(Trappist order in church history) Thomas Merton
270.2092	(Church history, 325–787) Pope Gregory the Great
283.092	(Anglican churches) Thomas Cranmer
287.092	(Methodist churches) John Wesley

See 291 for non-Christian and comparative religious biographies.

See also 220.9; 232.

212 vs. 231 Existence, knowability, attributes of God [in natural theology] vs. God [in Christian theology]

Class in 212 any discussion of proofs of the existence of God based on reason alone, including discussions by Christian theologians, e.g., by Thomas Aquinas. Class proofs of God's existence in 231 only if they are treated as part of Christian theology.

220 Bible

Biblical theology usually means using the Bible for the basis of Christian or Judaic doctrine and is classed as directed at 220. But if a book on Biblical theology does no more than interpret the text of the Bible, it is classed in 220.6 or with the specific part in 221–229. The key difference is whether the author adheres to the Biblical text and its meaning (220 numbers), or whether he uses the Biblical text as a springboard to the interpretation of theological concepts (230 or 296 numbers).

220.9 **Geography, history, chronology, persons of Bible lands in Bible times**

Class a comprehensive biography of a Biblical character with the book or books with which the character is most closely associated. In many cases this is the historical part of the Bible in which persons' lives are narrated, e.g., Solomon, King of Israel, in 1st Kings 222. Solomon's association with 223 Poetic books is weaker. However, some Biblical characters are more closely associated with nonhistorical books. For example, class Isaiah and Timothy with the books that bear their names. They appear briefly in historical narratives, but their lives are not narrated in full there. Class the apostles John, Peter, and Paul at 225.9 since each is associated with a number of books in the New Testament, but class the rest of the original Apostles, associated primarily with Gospels and Acts, in 226.

See also 209.2

231.7 vs. 213, 575 **[God's] Relation to the world [in Christian theology] vs. Creation [in natural theology] vs. [Organic] Evolution and genetics**

Most works on creation science or creationism are classed in 231.7 because they are written by Christians who assume that the Bible provides a chronology of natural history and who attempt to support this interpretation by using arguments from the natural sciences. Works by creationist authors that are limited to criticizing the methods or conclusions of the natural sciences are classed in 500 with the branch of science criticized, even if the criticism is considered unorthodox by most scientists. Works refuting creationism are usually classed in 231.7, unless they take the writings of creationists as a starting point from which to demonstrate the case for evolution. The latter works are classed in 575 or other appropriate numbers in 500.

Other 500 numbers that must sometimes be considered for works of a limited scope concerning evolution are 523.8 (stellar evolution), 551.7 (historical geology), and 560 (paleontology).

Works that consider the relation between divine creation and evolution as a philosophical problem, without appealing to a particular religion or scripture, are classed in 213.

232 **Jesus Christ and his family Christology**

Class doctrine and theories about Jesus Christ in 232, events in the life of Jesus in 232.9, e.g., the doctrine of the resurrection 232, historicity and narration of events surrounding the resurrection 232.9.

Use notation 092 from Table 1 for criticism, biography of Christologists (232.092) and Mariologists (232.91092). Class biography of Jesus, Joseph, Joachim, Anne, and John the Baptist in 232.9; of Mary in 232.91.

251–254, 259 vs. 260 Local church [and] Activities of the local church vs. Christian social and ecclesiastical theology

The local church is the group in which individual believers can meet regularly face to face for worship, fellowship, and church activities—for example, a congregation, a college church group.

Among the more recent forms of the local church are the small groups called basic Christian communities or basic ecclesial communities. These are smaller than parishes or congregations, but, like other forms of the local church, are organized for the general religious welfare of their members, not just for special projects or functions. They are classed in the same way as parishes, i.e., comprehensive works are classed in 250 (or in 262 when treated as part of ecclesiology) and specific aspects are classed with the aspect in the subdivisions of 250.

Activities undertaken by the church may be classed in 250 or 260, depending on the context. Most of the works in 250 are intended for the individual practitioner in the local setting. The local setting may be as small as a parish youth group or as large as a counseling program that serves a metropolitan area. Class the church's attitude to cultural and social problems, and its activities regarding them in 261 unless the context is limited to the local church, e.g., a practical work for the prison chaplain 259, but the church's attitude to the treatment of criminals 261.8.

Some activities that can be conducted by the local church are classed in 260, e.g., public worship (264–265), religious education (268), spiritual renewal and evangelism (269). The context of works on these subjects is often broader than that of the local church.

Class church organization in 262, unless the scope is limited to administration of the local church (254).

261.5 Christianity and secular disciplines

Class here personal Christian views and church teachings about secular disciplines as a whole, their value, how seriously a Christian should take them, how far the disciplines should affect faith. Class Christian philosophy of a secular discipline or Christian theories within a discipline with the discipline, e.g., a Christian philosophy of psychology 150.1. Be alert for specific uses of secular disciplines for religious purposes, e.g., use of drama 246. If in doubt, class with the secular discipline.

Class here works treating generally antagonism between and reconciliation of Christian belief and another discipline. Class antagonism of a specific Christian doctrine and another discipline with the doctrine in 231–239. For example, class the relation between Christian doctrines in general and science in 261.5; but class the relation between Christian doctrine on the soul and modern biology in 233.

261.8 vs. 241 Christianity and socioeconomic problems vs. [Christian] Moral theology

Some topics, such as family relationships, are covered in both moral and social theology. Class in 241 works that focus on what conduct is right or wrong. Works classed in 261.8 may discuss right and wrong, but they treat the topic in a broader context as a problem in society and discuss Christian attitudes toward and influence on the problem. Class in 241 works that emphasize what the individual should do; class in 261.8 works that stress what the church's stance should be, or the church's view on problems transcending individual conduct. If in doubt, prefer 241.

280 vs. 270.8, 262.001 Denominations and sects of the Christian church vs. Modern period, 1789– [in church history] vs. Philosophy and theory [of ecclesiology]

Class in 270.8 the ecumenical movement as part of general church history. Class in 280 relations between two or more specific denominations having notation that differs in the first three digits, e.g., relations between Roman Catholics (282) and Lutherans (284.1). Class works about relations among denominations having the same notation in the first three digits in the most specific number that includes them all, e.g., relations among the various Baptist denominations, between Baptists and Disciples of Christ 286. Class works about relations between one denomination and several others with the denomination emphasized, e.g., relations of Baptists with other denominations 286. Class theoretical works on ecumenism at 262.001. Class discussions among denominations with respect to a specific subject with the subject, e.g., the Eucharist 234.

281 Early church and Eastern churches

The early church is considered to be undivided by denominations until the schism of 1054. So the history of the Church prior to 1054 is classed in 270.1–.3, not here. The history of specific churches prior to 1054 is classed in 274–279.

290 Comparative religion and religions other than Christianity

290 by itself will never be used, since 291 has been designated as the number for comprehensive works on the non-Christian religions, on Christian and non-Christian religions, and for works on comparative religion.

Note that 200 and standard subdivisions 200.1–.9 are used for religion and religious thought in general, not for the description and analysis of various religions.

291 Comparative religion

The subdivisions of the various religions in 292–299 are based on the subdivisions of 291. The order is sometimes different, but all topics in 291 are provided for either explicitly, by synthesis, or by implication under the separate religions included in 292–299. What is said about 291, therefore, will also be true of 292–299.

A comparison of the topics in 291 with the subdivisions of Christianity can sometimes be helpful in determining what goes where. A comparative list follows:

Social theologies	291.1	261
Doctrinal theologies	291.2	230
Public worship	291.3	246–247, 263–265
Religious experience, life, practice	291.4	242, 245, 248
Moral theology	291.5	241
Leaders and organizations	291.6	250, 262, 267
Pastoral theology and work	291.6	253
Missions, religious education	291.7	266, 268
Sources	291.8	220
Denominations, sects, reform movements	291.9	280

291.2 includes the topics listed at 231 that are not limited to Christianity: goodness, justice, love, omnipotence, omnipresence, omniscience, providence, wisdom of God; ways of knowing God; relation to human experience.

Treat the early history of a specific religion before its division into sects as general history of the religion, but class a comprehensive survey of the various sects in the number for the sects of the religion, e.g., the sects and reform movements of Judaism 296.8. A work dealing with both early history and sects is classed in the general number for history of the religion.

Class the history of a specific congregation in the number for the sect to which it belongs, if this can be determined. ("Congregation" here refers to organizations in other religions analogous to the local church in Christianity, e.g., synagogues, mosques.) If the sect cannot be determined, class the work in the broadest number for the sects of the religion. For example, the history of a Jewish synagogue and its congregation, which may have changed sects over the years or whose sect cannot be determined, is classed in 296.8. In such a case do not add standard subdivisions.

Class religious orders in 291.6 and cognate numbers in 292–299, and not with any sect within the religion to which they may belong.

Biography

Persons associated with the religions in 292–299 are often identified with a number of religious functions and activities. A Hindu guru, for example, may be thought of as a theologian, a teacher, a missionary or a clergyman. If a religious leader cannot be identified primarily with one function, activity, or sect, class his biography in the base number for the religion and add notation 092 from Table 1. For comprehensive biographies of persons of an identifiable function, activity, or sect, use the following table of precedence.

Divinely inspired persons, founders of religions	291.6
Founders of sects	291.9092
Founders of religious orders	291.6
Religious leaders	291.092
Of specific sects	291.9092
Theologians	291.2092
Moral theologians	291.5092
Missionaries	291.7092
Martyrs, heretics, saints	291.092
Of specific sects	291.9092
Teachers	291.7092
Members of religious orders	291.6
Clergy	291.9092
Members of sects and movements	291.9092

Except for founders of religions and of religious orders, 291.6 is not used for biography, but for the nature, role, and function of religious leaders.

Works dealing with only one specialized aspect of a person's career are classed with the aspect.

291.09 vs. 294, 299 Historical, geographic, persons treatment [of comparative religion] vs. Religions of Indic origin vs. Other religions

The religions in 294 and some of the religions in 299 originated in particular geographic areas. Most of these religions have spread beyond the area where they originated. For example, Taoism is considered a religion of Chinese origin and would be classed in 299, but it is present in other countries as well. If a work covers various religious traditions in an area, not just the religions that originated there, class it in 291 and use notation 09 from Table 1. For example, the religions of India (including Christianity and Islam besides those listed under 294) 291.0954, of China (including Christianity and Buddhism) 291.0951.

300 Social sciences

Sociology 301–307 is the study of the processes, interactions, groups, culture, and cultural institutions that give form and purpose to every society. Part of the subject matter of sociology is found in 390 Customs, etiquette, folklore.

Some of the raw data for the study of human society is found in 310 General statistics. The statistics of a particular subject are classed with the subject throughout the Classification, e.g., crime statistics of the United States 364.973.

In order to maintain internal peace and safety from external threat, societies devise political processes and institutions, such as the state, government, elections, monarchy. These are dealt with in 320 Political science and in 350–354, the latter span of numbers dealing with the executive branch of government and public administration. The legislative branch is classed in 328, the judicial branch in 347. The military arm of government is found in 355–359.

The production, distribution, and consumption of the goods and services needed to maintain society are dealt with in 330 Economics. That part of economics that deals with commerce, communications, and transportation is classed in 380.

Law 340 treats the codified social, political, and economic rules that society requires and by which its members agree to live.

No social structure, however good, is perfect. Social problems are inevitable. They and society's solutions to overcome them are classed in the 360s, where are found social welfare, criminology, penology, insurance, police and fire protection services, and so on.

Education 370 is the major means through which society attempts to socialize the young and to prepare them for a useful role in the life of the society.

The last of the manifestations of a society's activities is language, which is classed in 400.

300 vs. 600 Social sciences vs. Technology (Applied sciences)

Many topics are discussed from both the technological and the social points of view. If a work discusses how to make, operate, maintain, or repair something, it is normally classed in technology. If, on the other hand, it discusses the social implications of a technological operation, it falls in the social sciences, e.g., the economics of agriculture 338.1, not 630 (where the technology of agriculture is found).

Class the social use, social control, and social effects of technology in 300.

The following criteria will be useful in determining what material should be classed in 300 rather than 600:

1. When the emphasis is on the social use or effect of the topic rather than on operating or processing it, e.g., how the automobile has affected modern society 303.48, how to drive an automobile 629.28.
2. When the emphasis is on the overall perspective, e.g., the value of solar heating 333.792, not 621.47.
3. When the emphasis is on social control as opposed to the control exercised during the manufacturing process, e.g., standards imposed by the government for the quality of medicine 363.19, not 615 (where making the medicine is found).
4. When raw statistics are cited, e.g., crop production 338.1, not 631.

Interdisciplinary works

Generally speaking, the 300 number is the interdisciplinary number for a phenomenon of social significance; it is used as the place of last resort for general works on a subject lacking disciplinary focus, e.g., a work on the history of clothing that does not emphasize how the clothing was made 391, not 646 or 687. However, works that emphasize descriptions of products or structures, such as clocks, locomotives, and windmills, are classed in technology.

Biography and company history

Biographies of artisans, engineers, and inventors are normally classed in technology, unless they come to be regarded as entrepreneurs and are classed in 338.7. Descriptions of the products of a company, such as Ford trucks, are classed in technology (which includes the 700s when the products under examination are not found in the 600s). However, when the organization or history of the company receives significant attention, class the works in 338.7, e.g., Ford trucks 629.223, the Ford Motor Company 338.7.

Technical reports

Many technical and research reports actually emphasize procedural technicalities and may refer to economic, legal, administrative, or regulatory complexities. Such reports should be classed in the social sciences. In determining the classification of a report series, and of individual reports in a series, consider the purpose of the writer and the mission of the agency authorizing the reports. If the emphasis is on the exercise of social control over a process, the report is classed in 300, not with the process in technology which is being controlled. For example, water quality monitoring systems are more likely to be 363.73 than 628.1.

It cannot be stressed too strongly that most of the social sciences are involved in technological processes, but are quite distinct from them. The classifier must go behind the technological vocabulary that often dominates title pages and tables of contents and analyze what is being described. A book on trains is not classed in 625.2 if it describes how railroads serve Great Britain, but in 385.0941; and a report on fertilizer and rice is not classed in 633.1 if it is studying production efficiency in developing countries, but in 338.1.

301–307 vs. 361–365 **[Sociology and anthropology] vs. Social problems and services**

To be classed in 301–307 works on a social phenomenon must deal with its social background, its role in the social structure, its effects on society, its innate characteristics and inner structure.

Social problems apart from remedial measures are often found in 301–307, but are more likely to be considered in connection with actual and potential remedies found in the 361–365 span. For example, the family as a social phenomenon is classed in 306.85. The dissolution of the family can be classed in either 306.88 or 362.82, depending on the focus of the work. A work discussing the effect of the changing social role of women in contributing to family dissolution is classed at 306.88. Once this topic begins to be considered as a problem about which something should be done, the work is classed in 362.82. If in doubt, prefer 361–365 over 301–307 for social problems.

301 **Sociology and anthropology**

Sociology and anthropology describe and analyze social phenomena, and physical phenomena that have social significance. The distinction that sociology studies the social phenomena of complex societies while anthropology studies the social phenomena of simple societies is not made in the DDC.

A work on social phenomena is classed in 301–307 even if it is being studied in a special context, e.g., in a political or economic institution. For instance, the sexual behavior of legislators is classed in 306.77, not in 328.

302–307 **Specific topics in sociology and anthropology**

Topics in sociology and anthropology are arranged in a sequence that moves from the general to the specific. The most general topics and those most applied to other topics come first, followed in order by the less general and less applied, ending with the ones most often subject to analysis by the preceding topics. Social interaction, covering the basic forms of behavior in groups and between groups is found in 302; social processes that are needed so that society can function, in 303; consideration of factors that affect social behavior, such as the environment, genetic makeup, and weather, in 304; social stratification and the social groups, classes, and kinds of persons that every society forms, in 305; the culture and institutions that are the framework within which groups carry on the processes, in 306; and geographically restricted communities studied in various ways but always considered as whole communities, in 307.

305 vs. 306, 909, 930–990 **Social groups vs. Culture and institutions vs. World history [and] History of ancient world, of specific continents, countries, localities; of extraterrestrial worlds**

305 is the comprehensive number for social groups that interact more or less freely with the rest of society, and is used for the totality of the culture and institutions of specific groups except as provided in 306.08 (which is the number for anthropological works about societies that have generally existed apart from the modern world, e.g., the social life of North American Indians 306.089). The role of social groups in specific institutions of society, however, is classed with the institution in 306, using notation 08 from Table 1 if appropriate, e.g., women as a social category 305.4, women's roles in the family 306.85082. The role of social groups in history is classed in 900. The history of specific social groups, particularly that part of their history which is called their civilization can cause difficulty. Class in 900 only accounts of the major events shaping the history and civilization of a group. If in doubt between 305 and 900, prefer 305. If in doubt between 305 and 306, prefer 306.

The following table indicates the general relation among these numbers and other related ones:

Anthropology	301
Cultural and social anthropology	306
Of specific groups	305
Unassimilated indigenous ethnic groups	306.08
Physical anthropology	573
Criminal anthropology	364.2
Ethnology, cultural ethnology	305.8
Of unassimilated indigenous ethnic groups	306.08
History of specific ethnic groups	909
In specific countries	930–990
Social situation and conditions	306
In specific areas	306.09
Of specific groups	305
Specific unassimilated indigenous ethnic groups	306.08

305.81 North Americans

Use this number for (a) comprehensive works on all the peoples of North America, (b) the people of Canada (305.811) and the United States (305.813) as national groups, (c) North Americans of British origin, and (d) Canadians of French origin (305.811). Works on noncitizens of British origin in either Canada or the United States are classed in 305.82; on noncitizens of French origin in Canada, in 305.84. Works focusing on other national or ethnic groups in North America are also classed elsewhere in 305.8, e.g., people of French origin in the United States 305.84, Mexicans as a national group 305.868, the Inuit 305.897.

307 Communities

This section includes works on the community in a relatively restricted area as a social phenomenon and works on community planning, development, and redevelopment. These terms are used here in their ordinary meaning to imply to matters relating to the community as a whole.

320 [The state and government]

The concepts of "the state" and "government" are emphasized in varying proportions in the subdivisions in 320–323. The state refers to the politically organized body of people occupying a more or less definite territory, while government (in the sense relevant here) is the organization through which the state exercises its authority and function. The state may be considered an abstraction, the government its concrete embodiment. Comprehensive works on the abstraction are classed in 320.1; specific kinds of states in 321; and the relation of the state to people (and *vice versa*) in 322–323, e.g., political rights 323.5.

In contrast to "the state," the concept of "government" is more central to political science, and the word is often used loosely as an approximate equivalent of political science, so it has no separate number. However, specific aspects do have separate numbers, notably comparative government in 320.3, structure and functions of government in 320.4, and kinds of government in 321.4–.9.

320 vs. 302–307 Political science (Politics and government) vs. Specific topics in sociology and anthropology

Some works on major social institutions, processes, and phenomena may have a decidedly political cast, but if they emphasize how the social topics are related to and manifested in political ones, they are classed in 302–307. For example, a work on the relation between the women's liberation movement and progress in women's political rights is classed in 305.42, not 323.5.

320 vs. 306.2 Political science (Politics and government) vs. [Sociology of] Political institutions

Be alert for works that discuss not politics and government but the dynamics of political institutions. The basic thrust of 306.2 is to find out the social sources (e.g., race, class, family) and the social processes of political institutions, or the impact of these institutions and their activity on the social environment. In addition, it is used for works dealing with political institutions and processes as models for social institutions and processes. In contrast, the objective in 320 is the descriptive, comparative, historical, and theoretical study of political institutions and processes. In these political studies, the social environment is considered only as a background. While 306.2 is the comprehensive number, use 320 if in doubt.

320 vs. 909, 930–990 Political science (Politics and government) vs. World history [and] History of ancient world; of specific continents, countries, localities; of extraterrestrial worlds

Politics

In the subheading "Politics and government" the word "politics" adds to "government" the ideas of adjusting relationships among individuals and groups in a political community, guiding and influencing the policy of government, and winning and holding control of society. More of the subdivisions of 320 are used for politics in the broad sense than are used for state and government. While the number 320 is used for comprehensive works on politics in the broad sense, most works on politics in the sense of party politics fall in 324.

Political history

Political history with an emphasis on major political events typified by the "battles, kings, and dates" school of history is clearly 900. Political history with an emphasis on the mechanics of give and take of political forces and movements and on their internal development is usually classed in 320.9, but if the forces and movements come to power or bring about major changes in society, their successes or failures become general history, and should be classed in 900.

Political activities

The sum total of political activity of a specific period or place is also considered general history, and is classed in 909 or 930–990. Various subdivisions of 320 include material on important political activities when considered in terms of the discipline "political science;" but when the activity is discussed in a manner which highlights the influence on general events, 900 must be considered. The general rule is: Important events and leaders with wide-ranging responsibilities are classed in general history, unless considered primarily in the context of a specific subject. The chief problems concern three numbers: 320.9, 324, and 328:

320.9: Under political situation and conditions there can be works on habitual activities and styles of leading political figures as a group, and on activities reflecting the adjustment of political forces or on the status of political parties and movements. But when the activities are analyzed in terms of their effect on general events, use 900.

324: Party histories are classed in 324.2; and histories of nomination and election campaigns, in 324.5 and 324.9, respectively, but only when they concern largely internal events of the parties and campaigns, or report winners, losers, and votes. A history of how a party or candidate came to power (or almost did), or a discussion of how party and campaign events move nations (or other areas) in certain directions is classed in 900.

328: Histories of specific legislative bodies are classed in 328.4–.9 or 328.3093, but only when they are largely limited to what happened within or to the bodies, without significant consideration of what the legislative body did for the political unit it served. The accomplishments of a given legislative session are normally a matter of general history, and are classed in 900, but if a work concentrates on the body's internal history it is classed in 328. While the report of proceedings of a legislature (i.e., its motions, debates, actions) may constitute the raw material of history, it is not in itself general history, and remains in 328.

Politics of specific subjects

Political activities relating to specific problems, issues, and organizations are classed with the subject in social science, e.g., the politics of immigration 325, of the banking system 332.1, of welfare policy 361.6. However, the politics of an administrative agency is classed in the subject which it administers, not with the subject in public administration (unless there is no alternative), e.g., the politics of the U.S. Federal Aviation Administration 387.7068, not 353.0087.

320.5 vs. 320.9, 324 Political ideologies vs. Political situation and conditions vs. The political process

The noun "movement" is used in various senses in each of these numbers, and a given ideological movement may be treated in any one of them, depending upon the emphasis of the work. Use 320.5 for works concerning the thought and internal history or dynamics of such movements, 324 for their attempts to achieve power by nonviolent means and their ventures into electoral politics (even as splinter parties with scant chance of success), and 320.9 for the impact of the movements upon the political system and their interaction with other political forces. Class comprehensive works on specific ideological movements in 320.5, but if in doubt, give preference first to 324, then to 320.9. However, also consider history numbers for movements which come to power or directly affect the major events of history.

See also 320 vs. 909, 930–990.

322 vs. 261.7, 291.1 **Relation of state to organized groups and their members vs. Christianity and political affairs [and] Religious mythology, social theology, interreligious relations and attitudes**

Religion and the state

The difference lies in the perspective. 261.7, 291.1 and similar numbers in 292–299 are in social theology, and are used for works on the position that religious people and organizations take or should take toward political affairs (including the state). 322 is used for works with a secular perspective, discussing the relationships between religious organizations or movements and states or governments. If in doubt, prefer 322.

324.24–.29 and 324.209 **Parties in specific countries in modern world [and] Historical, geographic, persons treatment [of political parties]**

For political parties, the three kinds of areas that are usually treated in a single span (continents, countries, localities) are treated in three different ways. They are differentiated because the country (nation) is the main effective unit of political activity, and thus of party life and power. In most countries the local party is a branch of the national party, or, at most, a local organization of persons who regard themselves as members of a national party. Treatment by locality within a country is classed in the country number, with use of standard subdivision 009 (under country notation) or T1—09 (after party notation) at the appropriate point, e.g., the parties of Scotland 324.241009411, the Liberal party in London 324.2410609421. However, for Australia, Canada, and the United States, each of which has strong traditions of autonomy for state and provincial parties, the states and their parties are treated like "countries" rather than like "localities."

Treatment of parties in general by continent and by region larger than a specific country is classed in 324.209, while treatment of specific kinds of parties (e.g., socialist parties) in such regions is classed in 324.2 without further subdivision.

324.6 vs. 342 **Election systems and procedures; suffrage vs. Constitutional and administrative law**

Use 324.6 for manuals outlining procedures for the conduct of elections. However, if laws or administrative regulations for elections, or legal discussions of them, are brought in to any significant extent, use 342. If in doubt, prefer 342.

331 vs. 331.8 Labor economics vs. Labor unions (Trade unions), labor-management (collective) bargaining and disputes

Industrial relations in the broad sense of all relations between management and individual employees or employee groups are classed in 331. Industrial relations in the narrow sense of relations between management and labor unions are classed in 331.8.

332 vs. 338, 658.15 Financial economics vs. Production vs. Financial management

The choice among 332, 338, and 658.15 depends upon the point of view from which the topics are treated. Class in 332 works treating financial topics from the viewpoint of people or organizations with money to invest and those who serve them—investors, bankers, stockbrokers, and the like. Class in 338 works that treat financial topics from the viewpoint of people concerned with the production of goods and services, people who are interested in capital because it is necessary for production. Class in 658.15 (or with the subject, using notation 068 from Table 1) works that treat financial topics from the viewpoint of an executive responsible for the financial management of an organization, works that focus narrowly on managerial concerns. In case of doubt, prefer 332.

332.024 vs. 640 Personal finance vs. Home economics and family living

Class in 640 works that deal only with everyday household finance, e.g., how to control day-to-day expenditures, how to budget for rent and groceries. Class in 332.024 works that are broader in scope, e.g., how to plan for one's financial future, including such topics as insurance and investing for retirement income. Class interdisciplinary works in 332.024.

332.7 vs. 332.1 Credit vs. Banks and banking

Some works on credit are classed in 332.7, some in 332.1. At 332.7 the focus is on type of credit, e.g., agricultural credit, home finance, personal loans, credit cards. At 332.1 (including 332.2 and 332.3, which are logically subordinate to 332.1), the focus is on the type of financial institution offering credit as a service, e.g., commercial banks, savings and loan associations, consumer finance institutions, insurance companies. Comprehensive works on a particular type of credit are classed in 332.7, e.g., a work discussing home mortgages as issued by commercial banks, mutual savings banks, savings and loan associations, and insurance companies. Comprehensive works on the credit offered by a particular type of institution and works discussing only one type of credit offered by a particular type of institution are both classed with the institution in 332.1–.3. For example, a work discussing all the kinds of loans and debit cards available from savings and loan associations and a work discussing the home mortgages available from savings and loan associations are both classed in 332.3. Similarly, comprehensive works on credit cards offered by commercial banks, department stores, oil companies, and travel agencies are classed in 332.7, but works about credit cards issued by commercial banks are classed in 332.1.

333.1–.5 vs. 333.73–.78 **Ownership and control of land and other natural resources vs. [Land]**

Land as property is classed in 333.1–.5, where the central issues are the right to possession and use, and the right to transfer possession and use. The only control of land and resources that belongs in 333.1–.5 is the control that stems from ownership.

Land as a natural resource, as a source of economic goods (chiefly agricultural and mineral), is classed in 333.73–.78. The uses to which land and its resources are or could be put (as distinct from the right to use) are classed in 333.73–.78, as are controls of usage that hold regardless of who owns the land, e.g., zoning.

Comprehensive works on concepts from both spans are classed in 333.

333.1–.5 vs. 346.04 **Ownership and control of land and natural resources vs. Property law**

Class economic aspects of the various forms of ownership, use and transfer of land in 333.1–.5. Class legal aspects in 346.04. If in doubt, prefer 346.04.

333.7–.9 **[Natural resources and energy]**

Consumption, development, and control of usage of natural resources are classed in 333.7–.9. Consequently, some works discussing natural resources that are no longer in their natural state are properly classed in 333.7–.9, e.g., works about controlling usage of urban lands 333.77.

333.8 vs. 338.2, 553 **Subsurface resources vs. Extraction of minerals vs. Economic geology**

For subsurface resources, class reserves in nature in appropriate subdivisions of 553, e.g., reserves of oil that have never been pumped out of the ground 553.2. The only kind of reserves that may be classed in 333.8 are reserves in storage, e.g., crude oil stored in salt caves as a strategic reserve and crude oil in tanks awaiting refinement both 333.8. Class works treating equally reserves in nature and in storage in 553. Do not class any sort of reserves in 338.2.

Class requirements (need, demand) for subsurface resources in 333.8. Do not class demand in 338.2 or 553.

335 vs. 320.5 Socialism and related systems [of economics] vs. Political ideologies

Since socialism and related systems are based upon theories of how the economy does or should work, interdisciplinary works and works on their philosophical foundations are classed in 335. The number is also used for wide-ranging works that do not fit within normal disciplinary boundaries but are clearly about socialism and related systems.

Use 320.5 only for works clearly limited to political science—works that emphasize how political movements intend to introduce socialism and what political forces they expect to harness to attain and keep power, or that discuss political movements and forces without in-depth discussion of the economic dynamics or theory.

336 vs. 351.72 Public finance vs. [Public] Financial administration

Class in 351.72 works focusing on the practical aspects and details of financial management and accounting in the public sector. For example, class budget estimates of expenditures, administrative reports of actual expenditures, and works on how to prepare them in 351.72. Class in 336 works on the economics of public finance, e.g., economic analyses of government spending policy 336.3. Class works treating both public finance and public financial administration in 336.

336.2 vs. 343.04 Taxes and taxation vs. Tax law

Most works on taxes, especially popular ones, are classed in law, because they explain what the law allows and prohibits. For example, a work for taxpayers about U.S. income tax deductions is classed in 343.7305. Works on the economics of taxes and interdisciplinary works on taxes are classed in 336.2, e.g., an economic and political analysis of U.S. tax policy 336.200973.

337.1 vs. 337.3–.9 Multilateral economic cooperation vs. Foreign economic policies and relations of specific jurisdictions and groups of jurisdictions

Class cooperative relations among the states of multistate groups, e.g., cooperation within the European Common Market, in 337.1; but class relations between a cooperative group treated as a whole and other countries or groups in 337.3–.9, e.g., economic relations of the Common Market with Japan 337.4052 (not 337.1), economic relations of the Common Market with the rest of the world 337.4 (not 337.1).

338.7 Business enterprises and their structure

Use 338.7 for directories of companies in specific industries or groups of industries, e.g., directories of manufacturing companies 338.7. However, class works called directories that include lists of products and services offered for sale or free distribution (even if the works are arranged by company rather than product or service) with the subject, using notation 029, e.g., lists of manufactured products for sale 670.29.

Biographies of people associated with the development and operation of specific types of enterprises but not confined to a specific industry or group of industries are classed in 338.6–.8, e.g., persons associated with trusts 338.8. Company directors on the boards of companies in several industries or groups of industries are classed in 338.7092.

339 vs. 332, 336 **Macroeconomics and related topics vs. Financial economics [and] Public finance**

Macroeconomics is the study of the economy as a whole, especially with reference to its general level of output and income and the interrelationships among sectors of the economy. Some topics appearing in 332 and 336 are considered in macroeconomics (339). These topics, however, will be classed in 339 only when they are clearly discussed in relation to the total economic picture of a country or region. For example, monetary policy, normally 332.4, is classed in 339.5 when used to stabilize the economy as a whole. In case of doubt, prefer 332 and 336.

340 Law

Law, one of the chief instruments of social control, consists of the whole body of customs, practices, and rules recognized in a society as binding, and promulgated or enforced by a central authority.

Three general forms of literature may be distinguished in this field:

1. the laws themselves as promulgated by a body officially authorized to do so;
2. decisions of the courts or other adjudicative bodies on matters of dispute that arise under these laws;
3. treatises written on various aspects of the laws.

The first two of these, laws and decisions, are considered to be original materials. Treatises are derivative in nature and are considered to be secondary. A special section (348) has been provided for original materials and guides to them when such materials are not confined to any specific branch or topic in law. Original materials that are confined to a specific branch or topic are to be classed with that branch or topic. Treatises have no special place or designation, but are classed in 349 if dealing with the total law of a jurisdiction, or in the number for the specific branch or topic without further indication.

Civil law

Civil law has two meanings that must be distinguished. In one sense it is the name of a system of law derived from Roman law and in use to a greater or lesser extent in most countries in the modern world, e.g.,

Germany, France, Japan, Brazil, and even in some subordinate jurisdictions of countries that otherwise use another system, e.g., the province of Quebec in Canada and the state of Louisiana in the United States. It is frequently used in contrast to the other great systems of law, though they are all classed in the same number 340.5. The more common meaning of the term is all law that is not criminal law, i.e., 342–344 and 346–347.

Law enforcement

Law enforcement is not necessarily a police matter. Any government agency may enforce the law. A department of education, for instance, is enforcing the law when it sees to it that the requirements of the law are being met by the schools. Enforcement of law in this sense is classed with the subject outside law. A work about the law enforcement activities of a department of education is classed in 350.85 or in cognate numbers in 352–354. Law enforcement by the police is classed in 363.2.

Laws of countries with federal governments

Countries with federal governments present special problems as there are several sets of laws at work: those of the central jurisdiction (national laws) and those of subordinate jurisdictions (laws of provinces, states, counties, cities, etc.). Laws of a lesser jurisdiction than the national are classed using the area number for the jurisdiction in question, e.g., criminal law of the state of California 345.794, of New South Wales 345.944. However, the laws of the lesser jurisdictions taken as a whole are classed in the same numbers as the laws of the nation, e.g., criminal laws of the states of the United States 345.73, of the states of Australia 345.94.

340.9 Conflict of laws

This topic is usually called private international law, which is something of a misnomer, since it is not the law governing the interrelationships of nations, but is the law governing the conflicts and disputes between private citizens of different nations. Its matter is drawn from private law. The chief point at issue is usually which jurisdiction's laws are to govern the case, hence the term conflict of laws. For example, whose laws will govern in the case of a Canadian citizen married in France to a citizen of Germany and later divorced in Mexico when a dispute arises as to the disposition of jointly owned personal property?

341 International law

International law lacks two of the features that commonly characterize law: genuine enforceability and promulgation by a central authority. The validity of international law depends on the good faith of nations, national self-interest, the pressure of world opinion, fear of reprisal, and sanctions imposed by international bodies and other nations. International law is embodied in treaties, protocols, conventions, and other international agreements (analogous to statutes); decisions of international courts; and writings (treatises) by recognized legal scholars (publicists).

341 vs. 327 **International law vs. International relations**

Distinguishing between international law and international relations is no easy matter at times. To some extent it might be considered as the difference between what actually is (327) and what ought to be (341). Works on international relations will discuss what is actually transpiring (including the theory as to why things happen as they do), and the effects of what has happened. Works on international law will discuss those standards and principles which it is commonly felt should govern international relations, and will also discuss concrete events from the standpoint of the problems that they pose to this system of order. Included in international law, of course, will also be works on treaties and the cases of international courts. If in doubt, prefer 341.

341.2 **The world community**

Interdisciplinary works on international organizations and works dealing with the structure and overall functions of such organizations are classed in 341.2, even when no substantial discussion of the law establishing such organizations appears in the work under consideration. A specific aspect of one of these organizations is classed with the subject outside of law, e.g., economic aspects of the European Community 337.1.

342 **Constitutional and administrative law**

Administrative law involves the exercise by the executive branch of certain judicial functions, e.g., settling disputes, imposing fines, specifying certain remedies. When a work deals with such functions, it is classed here. Class administrative law on a specific subject with the subject in law, e.g., the role of the United States federal government in settling a dispute with air traffic controllers 343.7309. Standards set by an agency are classed where the standards are applied outside law, e.g., elementary school learning standards 372.

345 vs. 346.03 **Criminal law vs. Torts (Delicts)**

Criminal law deals with acts so damaging that the interests of society are considered to be directly at stake. For this reason, cases in criminal law are always between the state acting for society and the individual charged with a crime. In contrast, there are many acts (called torts) which may be damaging to members of society, but are not considered to be direct threats to society. Torts are settled in civil suits. Sometimes an act (such as damage to property) may be treated as either a crime or a tort. If action is taken by the state seeking to punish the alledged perpetrator, class the matter as criminal law in 345; if action is taken by an individual seeking redress, class it as a tort case in 346.03.

350 Public administration and military science

The two halves of the 350s are distinct except for one narrow field where they overlap: the administration of defense forces and departments. Apart from works on departments of defense in 351.06 and related numbers in 353–354, administration of military and defense matters is classed in 355–359. Comprehensive works on military administration are classed in 355.6. Administration of a specific branch or service is classed with the branch or service. Administration of a specific military topic is classed with the topic without the use of standard subdivision T1—068 from Table 1.

350–354 [Public administration]

Basis of arrangement

Two basic distinctions are made in the public administration schedule: first between administration in general and administration of specific jurisdictions, and second between administration of central and administration of local jurisdictions.

350 is used for public administration in general, when works refer to matters relating to both central and local administration. Its subdivisions may be divided by area, using notation 09 from Table 1 when discussion refers primarily to principles and practices in a country or region, but does not refer predominately to the central administration of any one country, state, or large province, e.g., local, state, and federal welfare administration in the United States 350.840973.

351 is used for central administration in general, but not for the administration of any specific jurisdiction. Its subdivisions are divided by area only for treatment covering two or more countries. Central administration of specific countries and of their states or state-like provinces is found in 354, except for the United States, which is found in 353.

352 is used for local administration irrespective of jurisdiction, i.e., for local administration in general, in specific countries or regions, or in specific localities.

State and provincial administration

Central administration in 351 and 353–354 includes public administration of states and of provinces in countries that have large provinces encompassing a large number of separate local governments, e.g., Canada and China.

There is specific provision for administration of states of the United States in 353.9. For any other country, administration of states and of provinces of size equal to states is classed under the country's area notation in 354, e.g., central administration of Brazil, of Minas Gerais 354.81.

Citation order of jurisdiction vs. topic

The basic citation order for administration of specific central governments is Level + Jurisdiction + Topic. It is switched for local governments to Level + Topic + Jurisdiction. *(See 353–354 for examples with central administration, 352 for an example with local administration.)*

Public policy

Public policy in specific fields of social concern is normally classed with the specific field in the social sciences, regardless of whether the policy is formulated by legislation, administrative decision, or informal public consensus. For example, economic development and growth policies are classed in 338.9, welfare policies in 361.6. Public policy in matters outside the social sciences generally is classed with the subject in public administration, e.g., art policy 351.85, not 700. However, a policy with civil rights implications will be classed with civil rights in 323, e.g., religious policy 323.44, not 200, 351.81, or 351.85.

Certain policies that have names suggesting one discipline actually concern another. For example, technology policy, technology transfer policy, research and development (R&D) policy, and even science policy are often formulated in terms of promoting economic growth and development. In each case, where the policies are metaphors for growth policies, they should be classed in 338.9.

These remarks refer only to the policies themselves and arguments for and against them, not to policy execution or formulation. How to carry out policy, or how to set up procedures for resolving policy issues is administration. For example, class a work about what civil rights policies are or should be in 323, but a work on how to administer civil rights policies in 351.81.

350–354 vs. 320.4, 320.9 **[Public administration] vs. Structure and functions of government [and] Political situation and conditions**

The terms "government" and "public administration" can be easily confused and are sometimes used interchangeably. In the Dewey Decimal Classification, however, they are kept quite distinct. Government is limited to top-level considerations: the nature, role, goals, structure of states; their political direction and control; and the critical matter of forms by which central controls are exercised and balanced against each other. Public administration concentrates on public agencies and the procedures used to carry out their goals, policies, and actions in various fields.

Of the several numbers in 320 concerning different aspects of government, 320.4 is the one often confused with public administration. It includes works on the overall structure of governments, emphasizing their chief legislative, judicial, and executive organs. It may be used for works that discuss typical activities of the different branches, e.g., patrolling streets as an illustration of the police function. However, it should not be used for works emphasizing the kind of work that executive agencies perform.

Some works that seem to cover the activities of government are simply discussing the habitual conduct and methods of people in high office, and should be classed in 320.9.

Most works that should be classed in 350–354 will clearly emphasize agencies of the executive branch, or the usual components of administration: planning, organizing, staffing, financing, and equipping agencies to do a job or perform a function. Works on these components will be classed in 350–354 when they apply to any two of the three branches of government. For example, financial administration of the legislative and judicial branches taken together is classed in 351.72 and related numbers.

350–354 vs. 658, T1—068 **[Public administration] vs. General management [and Standard subdivision for] Management**

In the Dewey Decimal Classification "public administration" refers primarily to running government agencies that regulate and exercise control of various fields, while "management" refers to running organizations, public or private, that are directly performing the work within their scope. The former is classed in 350–354, the latter with the subject outside 350–354. In some agencies the operational management is called administration, as in library or hospital administration, but is, nevertheless, classed outside 350–354.

For certain activities performed by government that have not been provided for outside public administration, the actual operation is classed in 350–354, e.g., licensing, taxing, and gathering census information. In addition, the administrative management of foreign affairs is classed in 351.89 and cognate numbers in 353–354, not in 327.

There is often both public administration and management in the same field. For example, managing railroads is classed in 385.068, while running agencies that regulate railroads is found in 351.87; administering library systems is classed in 025.1, while administering agencies that regulate and support libraries is found in 351.85. If in doubt, prefer the number outside public administration.

350.003–.9 vs. 351 **Specific aspects of public administration vs. Administration of central governments**

Class comprehensive works on specific topics in public administration in 350.003–.9, unless the topic either pertains to a field that is seldom or never assigned to local governments, e.g., foreign affairs (351.89), foreign trade and financial institutions (351.82); or has little relevance in local administration, e.g., cabinets (351.004) and cabinet departments (351.01–.08). In case of doubt, check the topic in the index: if no 350 number is given, use the cited 351 number for comprehensive works.

352 **Administration of local governments**

The basic citation order for local administration is Level + Topic + Jurisdiction. Jurisdiction is supplied by notation 09 from Table 1. For example:

> A periodical on local financial and property administration in Texas is analyzed as Level (local, 352) + Topic (financial and property administration, 1) + Jurisdiction (Texas, 09764). The notation for periodicals (05) yields precedent to treatment by specific area (093–099) and is thus not shown. The number is built 352 + 1 + 09764 = 352.109764.

352.2–.9 **Local administration of specific fields**

The instruction at 350–354 vs. 658, T1—068 concerning management of public organizations that are directly delivering the services within their field of activity apply with particular force for many agencies of local government. Management of agencies actually delivering services is classed with the subject outside public administration, e.g., managing school systems is classed in 371.2 (school administration and management); library systems, in 025.1 (library administration). However, managing local police departments is classed in 352.2, not 363.2068 (which is not used).

Numbers in 352.3–.9 should be used only for two kinds of material:

1. Works on regulation and support in specific fields where the work is not performed by the government, e.g., control of private waste collection 352.6, issuance of construction permits 352.92.

2. Works emphasizing external managerial relations of specific agencies and kinds of agencies, e.g., the position of the New York Fire Department in the New York City government 352.309747. The internal management of the Department is classed in 363.37068, as is comprehensive treatment of management of fire departments.

If in doubt between numbers in 352 and numbers outside public administration, prefer the outside numbers.

353–354 [Administration of specific central governments]

The basic citation order for administration of central governments is Level + Jurisdiction + Topic + Standard subdivision. For example:

1. A discussion of personnel management in the government of Spain is analyzed as Level (national, 354) + Jurisdiction (Spain, 46) + Topic (personnel management, 001) + Standard subdivisions (none). The number is built 354 + 36 + 001 = 354.46001.

2. The duties of the governor of California are analyzed as Level (state, 353.9) + Jurisdiction (California, 794) + Topic (governor, 03) + Standard subdivision (none). The number is built 353.9 + 794 + 03 = 353.979403.

355 vs. 623 Military science vs. Military and nautical engineering

Use 623 for physical description, design, manufacture, operation, and repair of ordnance; use 355–359 for procurement, deployment, and control of units and services which use ordnance. Histories of the development of weapons emphasizing the interplay of human and social factors are regarded as procurement history, and are classed in 355.8 or with specific services in 356–359.

355.0071 Military schools

Military schools that are not official training academies, most of whose students (except in wartime) enter civilian occupations, are treated like other educational institutions and classed in 373 or 378 plus notation for the area where they are located, e.g., Virginia Military Institute (Lexington, Virginia) 378.755, The Citadel (Charleston, South Carolina) 378.757.

355.0092 vs. 930–990 [Persons treatment in military science] vs. History of ancient world; of specific continents, countries, localities; of extraterrestrial worlds

Use 930–990 for comprehensive works on soldiers chiefly associated with a specific war, e.g., William Tecumseh Sherman 973.7; use 355.0092 for comprehensive works on soldiers associated with more than one war, or who had long and varied careers, e.g., Douglas MacArthur. If in doubt, prefer 355.0092.

355.4 vs. 355.02 Military operations vs. War and warfare

Use 355.02 for works on strategy that consider the overall problems and objectives of national policy; use 355.4 for works on strategy that emphasize military operations. If in doubt, prefer 355.02.

361–365 Social problems and services

Problems and services in this section of the schedules are often linked terms. When only one is spelled out, the other is normally implied. Thus, Mental retardation at 362.3 implies services to mentally retarded persons, while Public safety programs at 363.1 implies the problems that require such programs.

See also 300 vs. 600.

Political, economic, and legal considerations

Many publications give considerable emphasis to the political and legal considerations related to social services. So long as the focus is on the problem or the service, class such publications here. Thus, a discussion of political obstacles to effective poverty programs is classed in 362.5, of the political maneuvering behind the adoption of an act of the United States Congress spelling out a new housing program in 363.5.

361–365 vs. 350–354 Social problems and services vs. [Public administration]

Much of the material on social problems and services consists of government reports. Reports about welfare programs and institutions are classed in 361–365. Reports concentrating on the administrative activities of agencies supporting and regulating the programs and institutions are classed in 350–354. If in doubt, class in 361–365; however, prefer 350–354 for administrative annual reports of agencies not actually providing the services.

361 vs. 362 Social problems and social welfare in general vs. Social welfare problems and services

361 is used for two kinds of material: comprehensive works on the whole range of problems and services found in 362–363, and works on principles and methods of assessing and solving the problems. The second kind of material normally does not address specific problems but may refer to welfare problems, usually found in 362. Material on the principles and methods of welfare work in general is classed in 361. Application of the principles and methods to a specific problem is classed with the problem.

A helpful guide in deciding between 361 and 362 is the table of contents. If it reads like a summary of the subdivisions of 362, class the work in 362; if like a summary of the subdivisions of 361, class the work in 361. In the absence of a table of contents or summary, the arrangement of topics is a useful guide. If topics in both 361 and 362 are covered, class in 361. If in doubt, class in 361.

361.1 vs. 362, 301 **Social problems vs. Social welfare problems and services vs. Sociology and anthropology**

Social welfare problems at 362 is a narrower concept than 361.1. 361.1 encompasses any and all kinds of social problems from providing child care to supplying water. Class in 362 social problems that apply to individuals as such and the remedial measures for these problems. 361.1 comprises social problems as a background to social action, and should be used sparingly. If in doubt, prefer 361.1.

301 is used for social problems primarily when they are discussed as social phenomena, rather than as matters that society should take action to solve. Usually the emphasis in works on social problems is clearly towards problems to be solved and thus indicates 361.1. If the emphasis is not clear or if in doubt between 301 and 361.1 or 362, prefer 301.

361.2 vs. 322.4 **Social action vs. Political action groups**

General discussions about social protest, dissent, and reform movements are classed in 322.4. If the discussion is limited to social action as an aspect of social welfare, it is classed in 361.2. If the discussion is limited to a specific problem, it is classed with the problem.

361.6 vs. 361.7, 361.8 **Governmental action vs. Private action vs. Community action**

Organizations are classed in 361.6, 361.7, and 361.8 depending upon who has financial control. For example, the Peace Corps, a governmentally funded organization of overseas volunteers, is classed in 361.6; Canadian University Service Overseas, a privately funded organization of overseas volunteers, is classed in 361.7; a combined public and private organization of volunteers is classed in 361.8.

362.1–.4 vs. 610 **Problems of and services to sick and disabled people vs. Medical sciences Medicine**

Class health services from the social viewpoint in 362.1–.4, from the technological viewpoint in 610. For example, class social measures for the provision of dental care through clinics in 362.1, but how dentists actually use their skill in 617.6. Class works treating both the medical sciences and the medical social services in 362.1–.4. If in doubt, prefer 362.1–.4.

Biographies

Class in 362.1–.4, using notation 092 from Table 1, biographies and memoirs of the sick, the handicapped, and the dying that lack any other disciplinary focus. The rationale behind this rule is that these biographies illustrate the way society addresses itself to fundamental health problems and their solution. Be alert, however, for significant disciplinary emphasis, e.g., a work offering guidance in the Christian life with respect to health misfortunes is classed in 248.8, Christian meditations in 242. Class studies of individual cases designed for the use of researchers, practitioners, and students in the field in the number for the field, without adding notation 092 from Table 1. Class in 616–618 studies of patients describing their illnesses in medical terms rather than their lives in social terms, e.g., case studies of heart disease 616.1. If in doubt, prefer 362; however, prefer 616.89 and related numbers for psychiatric disorders, since the consideration of external circumstances is generally subordinated to the discussion of the state of mind of the patient.

While most personal and biographical treatment of medical personnel is classed in 610, works on public health doctors or nurses emphasizing their influences on public health services and awareness are classed in 362, e.g., a biography of a doctor noted chiefly for promoting nursing homes 362.1.

363 **Other social problems and services**

Several subdivisions involve the control of technology, particularly under safety (363.1) and environment (363.7). Class in 363 works addressing what must be done, regulating how it is to be done, inspecting to see whether or not it has been done, and investigating when it was not done. Only works dealing with the technological procedures for carrying out a given operation are classed in technology. Finding out what broke is 600; finding out who let it break is 363. Machinery breakdown is 600; institutional breakdown is 363.

A useful clue in choosing the appropriate discipline is the perspective of the author or publishing agency. If the author is interested in social service and social need, the work is classed in 363; in the economics of what we have to live on, 333.7; in how the environment works, 304.2; in how to make things, 620–690; in how organisms survive, 570–590; in how crops survive, 632–635; in physical techniques for controlling pollution, 628.5. In general, commercial publishers and environmental or safety advocacy groups tend to produce works that are classed in the social sciences, e.g., 304.2, 333.7, or 363.

To summarize: class comprehensive works and works oriented toward problems and their solution in 363, resource-oriented material in 333.7, works giving significant consideration to the social dynamics of the problem in 302–307, those emphasizing technology in 600.

See also 300 vs. 600; 301–307 vs. 361–365.

363 vs. 340, 350–354 **Other social problems and services vs. Law vs. [Public administration]**

Class the work of agencies by which the government carries out the detailed intent of the law in matters of population, safety, the environment, and provision of basic necessities in 363. Class the internal administration of agencies concerned with these fields, including their administrative annual reports, in 350–354. The law itself, draft laws, and enforcement of the law in courts are classed in 341–346. But most of the discussion of policy and most detailed procedures for enforcing law, policy, or regulation are classed in 363. If in doubt, class in 363.

363.1 Public safety programs

The word "safety" is used loosely and equivocally in many instances. It may be so broad as to cover most of the social services. In this case the work is classed at 363, or even at 361 if sufficient 362 material is included. On the other hand, it may be so narrow as to comprise only the work of the police and fire departments, in which case the work is classed at 363.2.

Safety regulations

Class safety regulations that spell out operating and construction techniques in explicit detail with the technology involved even if they are in the form of an officially promulgated regulation by a safety authority. In some cases such regulations may not even warrant the addition of notation 028 from Table 1 for safety measures because they cover more or less the whole construction picture. On the other hand, manuals written by or for safety agencies may discuss, among other things, various technical details useful as background for regulation and inspection of various operations while still focusing primarily on safety services. These are classed in 363.1.

Priority of safety

Class those aspects of safety that society must deal with through investigations and programs in 363.1 or 363.3 rather than with the subject elsewhere in the social sciences, e.g., railroad safety 363.12, not 385.028. However, the public administration of safety is classed as instructed at 351.78 and 352.3 in the schedule.

Investigation of specific incidents

Prefer 363.1 and other numbers in 363 to numbers in 600 for accident investigations when the investigation implicates large, impersonal agencies (companies or governments) that should have prevented the accident by proper supervision, inspection, or regulation. For example, class a technical description of what went wrong at Three Mile Island in 621.48, but an investigation of why it took so long to find out what went wrong in 363.1.

363.17 Hazardous materials

Note that many works on hazardous materials are not classed in 363. The material as an environmental factor affecting the natural ecology is classed in 574.5, as a cause of disease or injury in an organism in 574.2, and as a cause of injury to persons in 615.9 (for chemicals) and 616.9 (for radiation hazards).

363.17 vs. 604.7 **[Social programs and services relating to] Hazardous materials vs. Hazardous materials technology**

While the technology of handling hazardous materials is classed in 604.7, be alert for works on "handling" that are addressed to those responsible for monitoring or inspecting the handling, and that may be devoid of engineering considerations. Class such works in 363.17. If in doubt, prefer 363.17.

363.5, 363.6, 363.8 vs. 338 **Housing [and] Public utilities and related services [and] Food supply vs. Production**

363.5, 363.6, and 363.8 deal with the problems of providing the basic necessities of life. Each has economic implications; thus, a careful distinction must be made between these numbers and the economics of industries under 338. If the work deals with the effect of these topics on the economic aspects of society, or the impact of economic conditions on the availability of housing, water, fuel, or food, it is classed in 338. If it deals with broader social factors affecting these commodities, or with social measures to insure an adequate supply, class it in 363.5, 363.6, or 363.8. For example, a study of the effect of a drop in farm prices on the food supply is classed in 338.1; a study of the mismatch between the expected growth of the food supply and of the population is classed in 363.8. If in doubt, prefer 363.5, 363.6, or 363.8.

363.6 **Public utilities and related services**

Water supply reports concentrating on the supply of water on hand are classed in 553.7; on water used, or needed in the future, in 333.91; on the problem of treating and delivering water to consumers in 363.6; on assuring that waste waters are properly treated and on protection of natural waters in 363.7.

Water quality monitoring reports serve several purposes. As tools for assuring compliance with water supply standards they are classed in 363.6, for assuring compliance with waste water pollution standards in 363.7, for determining plant loads and technical difficulties in water treatment in 628.1, and for checking the effectiveness of sewage treatment works in 628.3. Those reporting the present chemical and biological status of available water, but not focusing on a specific objective, are classed as economic geology in 553.7. The most general works on monitoring "to protect water quality" are classed in 333.91, e.g., an environmentalist's alert "we must monitor our water supply."

363.6 vs. 333.7 **Public utilities and related services vs. Natural resources and energy**

Use care in distinguishing between the resources and energy (333.7–.9) and the utilities delivering the resources to customers (363.6). For instance, class in 333.7 comprehensive works on resources, projection of needs and supplies, development, conservation, protection of resources. Class in 363.6 problems and services related to distributing the resources to users. A useful device in distinguishing the two is to consider that "supply" as a noun is classed in 333.7, while "supply" as a verb is classed in 363.6. If in doubt, class in 333.7.

An exception is made for electrical power companies. Works about these utilities almost always emphasize the problems of developing the "supply" as a noun, saying little about the problems of distributing the electricity to customers, and seldom discuss prices without reference to production costs. A work about electrical power utilities focusing on distribution should be classed in 333.79 with the bulk of works about electrical power companies.

Class the rationing of natural resources still in their natural state at 333.7 and related numbers in 333.7–.9, but of final products in 363, e.g., wellhead allocation of natural gas for companies or jurisdictions 333.8, but rationing of natural gas among consumers or classes of consumers at the other end of the line 363.6.

363.7 vs. 333.7, 304.2 **Environmental problems and services vs. Natural resources and energy vs. Human ecology**

"Environmentalism" refers to two different sets of issues. Use 363.7 when the issues are preserving and restoring the quality of the social living space, i.e., taking care of waste, pollution, noise, the dead, and pests. Use 333.7 for the broader concept of preserving and protecting the supply as well as the quality of natural resources. Works about the environmental movement that focus on the concerns it shares with the long established conservation movement are classed in 333.7. Use 304.2 for works that emphasize the effect upon society of overuse, misuse, or pollution of the environment. If in doubt between 333.7 and either 363.7 or 304.2, prefer 333.7. If in doubt between 304.2 and 363.7, prefer 304.2.

363.8 vs. 338.1 **[Social problems and services relating to] Food supply vs. [Economics of] Agriculture**

The whole problem of supplying food to society is classed in 363.8, while the routine economic aspects are classed in 338.1. Economic problems like poverty and maldistribution are at the root of most food supply and nutrition problems, but most works concerning such problems focus on the resulting social problems and on the social services needed to overcome them, and therefore are classed in 363.8. Requirements of specific segments of the population are also classed in 363.8.

For example, total economic demand for food in Nigeria is classed in 338.1, food requirements of the urban poor in Nigeria in 363.8, normal food trade in Nigeria in 381, distribution of food during a famine in Nigeria in 363.8. If in doubt, prefer 363.8.

364.1 vs. 362–363 **Criminal offenses vs. Specific social problems and services**

Some human activities can be considered either as social problems or as crimes. An activity as a social problem is classed in 362–363. The activity treated as a crime is classed in 364.1. For example, drug addiction as a social problem is classed in 362.29, but illegal use of drugs is classed in 364.1. Suicide as a social problem is classed in 362.2, but suicide treated as a crime is classed in 364.1. If in doubt, prefer 362–363.

368.3 vs. 362.1 **Insurance against death, old age, illness, injury vs. Physical illness**

Works on health insurance plans that focus on their insurance features, such as prepaid health care rates, are classed in 368.3. Works that focus on their health services features are classed in 362.1. If in doubt, class in 362.1.

368.4 vs. 362 **Government-sponsored insurance vs. Social welfare problems and services**

Social security as a government-sponsored insurance scheme is classed in 368.4. Social security that is not insurance is classed in 362, e.g., social security in the United Kingdom 362.0941. If in doubt, class in 362.

371.2 vs. 379 **School administration and management vs. Government regulation, control, support of education**

In 371.2 are found the operations and activities of schools and school systems: how a school is administered, its students bused and taught, its buildings maintained. In 379 are found the activities of the state (government at any level) regarding the regulation, supervision, and support of the schools and school systems under its control or purview: the finance of public and private schools, their standards, evaluation, and accreditation. If in doubt, class in 371.2.

375 **Curriculums**

Works on the curriculum of a specific subject will be classed here infrequently inasmuch as two or more levels of education must be treated; works on curriculum usually consider only one level. If the curriculum is discussed at the elementary level, the work is classed in 372; if discussed at any other level, the work is classed with the subject, using notation 071 from Table 1. For example, a mathematics curriculum for the elementary level 372.7, for the secondary level 510.71, for elementary and secondary levels considered together 375.

380 Commerce, communications, transportation

Commerce deals with the distribution of goods and services, and is a part of the discipline of economics. So too is transportation, an activity that adds to the value of the goods moved. Both communication and transportation developed primarily in response to commercial needs and practices, i.e., to trade, banking, accounting, and so on; therefore, they have been placed in 380 with commerce. The technical aspects of commerce, transportation, and communication are classed in 600.

In order of precedence of subjects under 330, commerce and transportation take the same position as production, i.e., 380 has precedence above 335, 337, and 339 (Socialism and related systems, International economics, and Macroeconomics and related topics) but below 331–333, 334, and 336 (Factors of production, Cooperatives, and Public finance).

Add Table

06 vs. 09 Organization and management vs. Historical, geographic, persons treatment

Use notation 06 when the work discusses the corporate history of the organization, e.g., the corporate history of the Union Pacific Railroad 385.06.

Use notation 09 when the work discusses the system (facilities, activities, services) maintained by the company in a specific area, e.g., railroad transportation provided by the Union Pacific Railroad 385.0978.

If in doubt, prefer 09.

380.1 vs. 658.8 Commerce (Trade) vs. Management of distribution (Marketing)

Class in 380.1 the economic aspects of trading and selling goods, what is, in fact, traded and in what amounts. Class managerial techniques for successfully disposing of the products and services of enterprises in 658. If in doubt, prefer 380.1.

384 vs. 791.4 Communications Telecommunication vs. [Performing arts aspects of] Motion pictures, radio, television

Class in 791.4 the various aspects of producing an individual program, e.g., arranging the various acts of a television variety show 791.45. Class in 384 the various aspects of presenting the finished program to the general public, e.g., selecting the correct day and time to broadcast a television variety show 384.55.

The history of a radio, television, or motion picture company is classed using the following criteria:

1. Class in 384, using notation 09 from Table 1, a general history of the organization, e.g., a history of NBC (National Broadcasting Company) Radio Network 384.540973.

2. Class in 384, using notation 06 from the add table under 380, the corporate history of the organization, e.g., the corporate history of the NBC Radio Network 384.5406.

3. Class in 384 without use of either notation 06 or 09, the history of the system (facilities, activities, services) maintained by the organization, e.g., stations broadcasting NBC radio programs 384.54.

4. Class in 791.4, using notation 09 from Table 1, the history and critical appraisal of the products of the organization, e.g., the history of the radio programs provided by NBC 791.440973.

Class works combining aspects of 384 and 791.4 in 384

384.3 vs. 004.6 **Computer communication vs. Interfacing and communications**

Class economic and related aspects of providing computer communication services to the public in 384.3. Class computer communication and its hardware in office and private use, computer science applied to the technological aspects of computer communication, and interdisciplinary works in 004.6. If in doubt, prefer 004.6.

386 vs. 387.1 **Inland waterway and ferry transportation vs. Ports**

The distinction is based on whether the port is on tidal waters (387.1) or on nontidal waters (386), not upon either the distance from the sea or the ability to handle ocean-going ships. For example, class the port of New Orleans (110 miles from the mouth of the Mississippi River but on tidal waters) in 387.109763, the port of Chicago (which can handle ocean-going vessels but is on nontidal waters) in 386.

390 Customs, etiquette, folklore

Customs, etiquette, and folklore are among the raw material of the social sciences, particularly of anthropology and sociology—the descriptive and analytical aspects of the study of the behavior of humankind in general social groups. Melvil Dewey considered customs to be a summary of social activity and classed them in 390, just before language, the last of the social sciences and a main class requiring a whole digit (4) to itself.

391 vs. 646, 746.9 **Costume and personal appearance vs. Sewing, clothing and accessories, management of personal and family living vs. [Artistic aspects of] Costume**

Costume, clothing, and fashion can be treated in terms of customs, home economics, or art. Customs, such as what was worn, what is fashionable, national costumes, are classed in 391. Home economics aspects, such as how to dress on a limited budget, select the best quality clothing, dress correctly for the business world, are classed in 646. Artistic aspects, such as clothing as a product of the textile arts, fashion design, are classed in 746.9. If in doubt between 391 and 646 or 746.9, prefer 391; between 646 and 746.9, prefer 746.9.

394 vs. 791.6 **General customs vs. Pageantry**

Class in 394 works that discuss traditions of pageants, processions, or parades and works that describe the event. Class in 791.6 works that discuss planning, promoting, and staging the event, including such topics as publicity and float construction. If in doubt, prefer 394.

394.2 vs. 263, 290 **Special occasions vs. Days, times, places of [Christian] religious observance [and] Comparative religion and religions other than Christianity**

Class in 394.2 the secular customs associated with religious holidays, e.g., Easter egg hunts. Class in 263 and related numbers in 290 the religious customs associated with religious holidays, e.g., sunrise Easter services 263. If in doubt, prefer 263 and related numbers in 290.

395 **Etiquette (Manners)**

Etiquette includes prescriptive works on rules of conduct designed to make life more pleasant and seemly and to eliminate the causes of friction in the numerous inevitable minor opportunities for conflict or offense that arise in daily life. More important matters of conduct are classed in 170 Ethics.

398.2 **Folk literature**

There is no notation available for folk literature in 398.2 to distinguish literary forms, collections, or criticism as there is for general literature in 800. In each case, disregard these aspects in classifying, using the most specific number available.

Standard subdivisions may be added to subdivisions of this number even if the subject of the work does not approximate the whole, e.g., French folk tales about fairies 398.210944. However, do not add standard subdivisions for individual folk tales, e.g., Sleeping beauty 398.21, not 398.210944.

398.2 vs. 291.1 **Folk literature vs. Religious mythology, social theology, interreligious relations and attitudes**

Class in 398.2 mythology having a real, legendary, or nonreligious basis. Myths populated by gods, goddesses, quasi-gods, or quasi-goddesses are classed either in 398.2 or 291.1 according to content, mode of presentation, or author's or editor's intention. Thus, mythology presented from a strictly theological point of view or presented as an embodiment of the religion of a people would be classed in 291.1. However, myths or mythology presented in terms of cultural entertainment or, especially, as representatives of the early literary expression of a society are classed in 398.2. Often the literary or religious focus is clear (e.g., almost all myths retold for a juvenile audience are classed in 398.2); if in doubt, prefer 398.2.

Specific myths and legends presented as examples of a people's religion are classed with the subject in religion, e.g., legends of Jesus' coming to Britain 232.9.

398.21 vs. 398.22 **Tales and lore of paranatural and legendary beings of human and semihuman form vs. Tales and lore of historical and quasi-historical persons and events**

Folktales about quasi-historical persons (who may have actually existed), e.g., King Arthur, are classed in 398.22. Tales about purely legendary persons, e.g., Paul Bunyan, are classed in 398.21. If in doubt, prefer 398.21.

Certain types of persons, such as giants, kings, witches, can either be historical or nonhistorical. The listing of such a type in the example notes at either 398.21 or 398.22 does not preclude tales about that type of person from classing in the other number. For example, "Hansel and Gretel" is classed in 398.21 even though "witches" is given in the note at 398.22.

400 Language

Class examples and collections of "text" whose purpose is to display and study a language with the language, even if limited to a particular subject, e.g., a grammar of scientific English 425. Language analysis of a specific work is criticism and is classed with the work.

400 vs. 800 **Language vs. Literature (Belles-lettres) and rhetoric**

Many works treating both language and literature are predominantly about literature; such works are classed in 800. Comprehensive works on language and literature, giving equal attention to both, are classed in 400.

400 vs. 909, 930–990 **Language vs. World history [and] History of ancient world; of specific continents, countries, localities; of extraterrestrial worlds**

Class in 400 studies that emphasize language and literature, even though some material on culture and history is included; but class in 900 studies in history and culture that include but do not emphasize language and literature.

401 vs. 412, 415, 306.4 **Philosophy and theory [of language] vs. Etymology vs. Structural systems (Grammar) vs. Specific aspects of culture**

Semantics at 401 is the branch of linguistics that deals with meaning in language. In trying to answer the question of what meaning is, semantics deals with such subtopics as synonymy, ambiguity, semantic truth (metalinguistic truth), and entailment. Closely linked with philosophy, semantics is particularly concerned with the underlying logical structure of natural language, i.e., what elements are necessary beyond correct grammar for statements to make sense.

Etymology at 412 has only a narrow interest in meaning; it studies the history of the meanings of words.

Grammar at 415 also has only a narrow interest in meaning; it is concerned with meaning only in relation to morphology and syntax.

The sociology of language at 306.4 is concerned with meaning as it is affected by its sociocultural context. Most works on linguistic pragmatics deal with language in its sociocultural context and are classed in 306.4. The exception would be works on pragmatics that focus on the individual psychological context; such works are classed in 401 with psycholinguistics.

407, T1—07 vs. 410.7, 418.007, T4—8007, 401 **[Education and related topics in language and Table 1 notation for] Education and related topics [under individual languages] vs. [Education and related topics in linguistics] vs. [Education and related topics in standard usage of language] and [Table 4 notation for education and related topics under individual languages] vs. Philosophy and theory [of language]**

The basic distinction between prescriptive and nonprescriptive linguistics is explained in the Manual note at 410. Class in 418.007 works on how to study or teach language using a prescriptive approach.

Class in 407 broad works on language education not limited to the prescriptive approach and comprehensive works on the study and teaching of both language and literature.

Class in 410.7 works on the study and teaching of linguistics.

Class in notation 8007 from Table 4 works on how to study or teach a specific language using a prescriptive approach, e.g., how to teach basic French 448.007. In Table 4 there is no analogue to 410.7. Class with the specific language, using notation 07 from Table 1 (which is incorporated in Table 4), works on studying and teaching the linguistics of the language, broad works on studying and teaching the language that are not limited to the prescriptive approach, and comprehensive works on studying and teaching both the language and its literature.

Class in 401 works on the psychology of learning language informally, as a child learns from its parents, and comprehensive works on the psychology of informal and formal language learning. Class works on the psychology of formal study and teaching of language in the study-and-teaching numbers discussed above, primarily 418.007 and T4—8007. Since notation 01 Philosophy and theory, which includes psychological principles, from Table 1 cannot be added to notation 07 from Table 1, the numbers for works on the psychology of study and teaching of language do not express the psychological aspect.

410 Linguistics

Prescriptive linguistics is concerned with promoting standard or correct usage of language. Anyone trying to learn to speak or write like educated native users of a standard form of a language is involved with prescriptive linguistics. The various nonprescriptive approaches to linguistics (e.g., descriptive, theoretical, comparative linguistics) are concerned with describing or explaining language usage as it does or did exist, without regard to an ideal of correct usage. Most works of prescriptive linguistics are classed in 418 or with the specific language, using notation 8 from Table 4; works of nonprescriptive linguistics are classed elsewhere in 410–490. For example, descriptive works about grammar are classed in 415 and with the specific language, using notation 5 from Table 4; but prescriptive works about grammar are classed in 418 or with the specific language, using notation 8 from Table 4. Dictionaries, however, are classed in 413 or with the specific language, using notation 3 from Table 4, regardless of whether they are prescriptive or descriptive.

General historical (diachronic) linguistics is classed in 417. Under some languages, specific early forms of the language are classed in notation 7 from Table 4, e.g., 427 Middle English. For general historical linguistics of a specific language, or for historical linguistics of a specific topic, use notation 09 from Table 1 if the work gives a history, but not if the work merely discusses the processes of change in a general way. For example, class a general discussion of grammatical change in 415, a history of grammatical changes in the English language in

425.09, a history of all kinds of changes in the English language in 420.9.

Class a comparison of two languages with the language requiring local emphasis (usually the language that is less common in the particular setting). For example, a work comparing English and Japanese is classed in 495.6 in English-speaking countries, but in 420 in Japan. If no emphasis is required, class the work with the language coming later in 420–490.

Class a comparison of three or more languages in the most specific number that will contain them all; e.g., class a comparison of Dutch, German, and English at 430 since all are Germanic languages.

If there is no number that will contain them all (e.g., a comparison of French, Hebrew, and Japanese), class the work in 410.

For comparisons of just one feature of various languages, apply the criteria given above, except do not add notation from Table 4 to the number for language families. A comparison of French, Hebrew, and Spanish grammar is classed in 415; a comparison of Dutch, German, and English grammar at 430.

411–418 [Specific elements of linguistics]

Note that most of these topics correspond to those listed in Table 4, although there is not a complete correspondence in the extent to which the notation is developed or applied. For example, a general bibliographic guide to foreign-language texts is classed in 016.418, but a bibliographic guide to English texts for non-English-speaking students is classed in 016.4282.

420–490 Specific languages

The citation order of 420–490 is straightforward and without exception: Language + language subdivision from Table 4 + standard subdivision from Table 1.

1. Russian grammar:

   491.7 + T4—5 = 491.75

2. History of the Korean language:

   495.7 + T1—09 = 495.709

3. Etymological dictionary of the English language

   42 + T4—2 + T1—03 = 422.03

It frequently happens that one source calls a particular tongue a language, and another calls it a dialect. Consequently, it is common for a tongue to be treated as a dialect in the Dewey Decimal Classification and as a language in the work being classified, or vice versa.

470 Italic languages Latin

The dates of the Classical Age of Latin are 80 B.C. to 130 A.D. (the Ciceronian Age 80 B.C. to 43 B.C., the Golden Age of Augustan literature 43 B.C. to 18 A.D., the Silver Age 18 A.D. to 130 A.D.). The formal or literary Latin written at any time thereafter that conforms to the standards of that age is classed in 471–475 and 478. However, works on Vulgar Latin, on Old Latin (80 B.C. or earlier), or on Postclassical Latin are classed in 477. The phrase "Postclassical Latin" refers to the nonclassical or vulgarized Latin used from the death of Juvenal (140 A.D.) until the period of renewed interest in the "pure" Latin of the Classical Age in the eleventh and twelfth centuries, and from the fourteenth century onward. Classical Latin did not die out during the interim, however; and a linguistic study written on, say, Latin manuscripts of the monks of Iona is properly classed with classical Latin.

500 vs. 001 Natural sciences and mathematics vs. Knowledge

Be careful about equating the word "science" with the natural sciences and mathematics in 500. Quite often the word is used to cover the social sciences and the analytical aspects of other disciplines. Class a work in 001 when "science" is used without implying emphasis on natural science, in 001.2 (scholarship and learning) when used to cover disciplines outside 500, and in 500 only when clearly used to imply emphasis on the natural sciences. Works on scientific method and scientific research are particularly apt to belong in 001.4 (the interdisciplinary number for research) rather than 500. However, there is often literary warrant for equating the word "science" with the natural sciences in certain terms, e.g., history of science, which usually relates to the history of the discipline of natural sciences, and is thus classed in 509.

500 vs. 600 Natural sciences and mathematics vs. Technology (Applied sciences)

The natural sciences (500) describe and explain the world and the universe. Technology (600) uses science and whatever else it can to manipulate matter for the benefit of the human race. Be alert, however, for certain subdivisions of 500 that are actually technology, e.g., surveying and cartography in 526, and certain subdivisions of 600 that are actually science, e.g., 611–612 human anatomy and physiology.

Class in 500 interdisciplinary works on any science and its applications in technology. For example, a work on space science (500.5), engineering in other worlds (620), and astronautics (629.4) is classed in 500.5.

508 vs. 574, 910, 304.2 **Natural history vs. Biology vs. Geography and travel vs. Human ecology**

Use 508 if a work on natural history has significant emphasis on earth sciences phenomena (e.g., climate, land and water features), but use 574 if the work concentrates on various living things and their settings. If a work covers the description of human settlement as well as natural phenomena, class it in 910. If the emphasis is upon the relationship between the natural phenomena and human institutions, class it in 304.2. Class interdisciplinary works on natural history and its human setting in 304.2. If in doubt between science and nonscience numbers, prefer science numbers; if in doubt between 508 and 574, prefer 574.

510 Mathematics

The units of mathematics presently taught in elementary and secondary schools are not broad enough to warrant three digit numbers except for Arithmetic 513. The following is a list of the units taught:

Arithmetic	513
Algebra	512.9
Geometry	516.2
Trigonometry	516.24

520 vs. 523.1 **Astronomy and allied sciences vs. The universe; space, galaxies, quasars**

Use 520 for works describing the universe in its several distinct components, e.g., as individual planets, stars, galaxies. Use 523.1 for works treating the universe as a single unit. If in doubt, prefer 520.

523.8 vs. 523.1 **Stars vs. The universe; space, galaxies, quasars**

Use 523.8 for comprehensive works on stars and galaxies when they are treated as individual astronomical bodies. However, use 523.1 when stars are considered primarily as components of galaxies.

530 vs. 500.2 **Physics vs. Physical sciences**

Physics deals with the ultimate nature and behavior of matter and energy. As originally formulated in what is now called classical physics (exemplified in most of the span 531–538), it deals largely with matter on a visible or palpable scale. Thus it fit logically between astronomy (520) which deals with matter and energy on an extremely large scale, and chemistry (540) which deals with matter and energy on an extremely small scale. However, modern physics has outflanked chemistry by developing fundamental theories based on the behavior of components of atoms, phenomena much smaller than chemistry usually deals with. Chemistry has borrowed the part of this new physics that explains chemical reactions in both the inorganic world and the phenomena of life, leaving most other physical relationships and reactions to the physicists. By now, physics has grown to the point that it can be said that chemistry is but a part of physics.

Modern physics has been accommodated at the two ends of Dewey's original development for classical physics, i.e., in 530.1–.4 and 539. Notation 539 is used for comprehensive works on modern physics while 530 and its standard subdivisions are used for comprehensive works on classical physics, on classical and modern physics, and on physics and chemistry. If mathematics *per se* or astronomy, or both, are added to the mix, the result is classed in 500.2.

530 vs. 540 Physics vs. Chemistry, crystallography, mineralogy

Class works on specific topics common to both physics and chemistry with chemistry 540 when they relate to chemical composition, or to reactions affecting the combination of atoms in chemical processes. Class other works in physics 530. Clues more useful here than in most DDC disciplines are the occupations of the authors or the fields of the sponsoring organizations, the presumption being that chemists are writing about chemistry and physicists about physics. In cases where these clues give no indication, class with the topic in physics 530.

544–545 vs. 543 [Qualitative and quantitative analysis] vs. Analytical chemistry

The distinction between qualitative and quantitative analysis has been rendered largely obsolete by the growing sophistication of techniques. Therefore, prefer 543 over 544 or 545 for specific techniques unless qualitative or quantitative use is specifically emphasized.

546 vs. 541 Inorganic chemistry vs. Physical and theoretical chemistry

The rule that physical and theoretical chemistry of specific elements or compounds is classed in 546 does not apply when one or two examples drawn from large groupings like metals or nonmetals are used primarily to study a certain topic in physical or theoretical chemistry. In such cases, use the number in 541, e.g., oxidation reactions 541.3, not 546.

546 vs. 549 Inorganic chemistry vs. Mineralogy

Chemistry and mineralogy are considered to be coordinate subjects. As a result, many topics of physical and theoretical chemistry pertaining to structure and behavior of homogeneous crystalline solids will not be classed in 546. Use 546 for comprehensive works on the chemistry and mineralogy of specific chemical types, but if in doubt, prefer 549.

548 vs. 549 Crystallography vs. Mineralogy

The relation between crystallography and mineralogy is approximately the same as between physical and theoretical chemistry (541) and inorganic chemistry (546). The crystallography of specific minerals is classed in 549 unless used to study or explain a topic in 548, e.g. quartz and feldspar 549, but the study of crystal lattices using quartz and feldspar 548.

550 vs. 910 **Earth sciences vs. Geography and travel**

Geophysics (550) is the analysis of the structure of the earth and the forces shaping it; physical geography (part of geography and travel in 910) is the description of the resulting landscape. Descriptions of the results of a specific force or process is classed with the subject in 551; the operation of all forces and processes which combine to create a specific topographic land form is classed in 551.4; the operation of all the forces and processes taken as a whole in a specific area, especially if emphasizing solid geology, is classed with the area in 554–559. However, if the work treats the whole geographic landscape with only minor consideration of the geophysical processes, it is classed in 910 or under the specific area number in 913–919. For example, physical description of surface features in Burma 915.91, geophysical processes operating in Burma or the geology of Burma 555.91, earthquakes in Burma 551.2, mountains in Burma 551.4. If in doubt, prefer 550.

Description of surface features for travelers, which usually covers resort accommodations and the ambience as well as the features, is also classed in 910, with use of notation 04 from the table under 913–919 as appropriate, e.g., tourist beaches in Burma 915.9104.

551.46 vs. 574.92 **Hydrosphere Oceanography vs. Aquatic biology Marine biology**

While 551.46 is the comprehensive number for physical oceanography and marine biology, works on marine biology (574.92) that include significant consideration of ocean waters as part of the environment of marine organisms should, nevertheless, be classed in 574.92. If in doubt, prefer 574.92.

551.6 vs. 551.5 **Climatology and weather vs. Meteorology**

Meteorology analyzes and describes the properties and phenomena of the atmosphere, and thus explains climate and weather. Meteorology is also the comprehensive subject, encompassing consideration of climatology and weather. Unfortunately, however, some works on the larger subject (meteorology) may be called "climatology," "climate and weather," or simply "climate" or "weather," but must be classed in 551.5 in spite of the words used in the titles. Books so titled are classed in 551.6 only when the words are limited to four senses:

1. The description of phenomena of the atmosphere taken as a whole, weather usually being the short-range description, and climate the long-range description.

2. The prediction of weather, climate, or specific meteorological phenomena, i.e., weather forecasting and forecasts.

3. The study of climate or meteorology in small areas, i.e., microclimatology or micrometeorology.

4. The attempt to modify weather or any meteorological phenomena (551.68), which is actually a technology.

All other elements, including description (weather reports) of specific phenomena, remain in 551.5, regardless of the terms used in the works in hand. For example, reports of rainfall are classed in 551.57, forecasts of rainfall in 551.6, a description of rain belts of Asia in 551.6, a description of how weather works in 551.5.

551.7 vs. 560 Historical geology vs. Paleontology

Paleontology is the study of life in former geologic ages through the interpretation of fossils. It utilizes the same material as historical geology (i.e., the geologic record) but only as a record of life and the environment in which life evolved. Historical geology emphasizes the rocks and their strata, using paleontological facts to help date and interpret deposition, movement, erosion. If in doubt, prefer 551.7.

552 vs. 549 Petrology vs. Mineralogy

Rocks can be defined as aggregates of minerals, the minerals being homogeneous, usually crystalline grains (large and small) that give rocks their texture. Petrology encompasses the study of rocks and minerals, or of rocks alone. The homogeneous minerals studied by themselves are classed in 549. If in doubt, prefer 552.

560 vs. 575 Paleontology Paleozoology vs. Evolution and genetics

Paleontology provides a major part of the evidence for evolution, and many works cover both fields. Class in 575 works that cite paleontological evidence for evolution and works that add significant nonpaleontological evidence to the picture. Prefer 560 for works emphasizing the description of extinct organisms and environments as the history of life, and for works on the evolution of extinct forms of life. If in doubt, prefer 575.

573 vs. 611 Physical anthropology vs. Human anatomy, cytology (cell biology), histology (tissue biology)

Anthropometry is concerned with measuring human beings to determine variation and presumed evolutionary development. The emphasis is generally on external variation and bone structure, in contrast to anatomy (611), which is more concerned with norms of structure, internal as well as external. Prefer 573 for external features and shapes, and gross bone structure (e.g., the comparison of heavy- and thin-boned people, indexes of length and breadth of skeletal features); 611 for all other features.

573.2 **Evolution and genetics of humankind**

Be alert for misleading and equivocal phrases like "evolution of man." They may refer to the whole field of evolution (575), review all of paleontology or paleozoology (560), or concentrate on the immediate forebears of modern humankind (573.3).

574.5 vs. 574.909–.92 **Ecology vs. [Biology of specific kinds of environments]**

Kinds of environment are important both in ecology (574.5) and biogeography (574.9). Class in 574.5 works emphasizing the interrelationships among various organisms and environmental factors in a specific kind of area, in 574.909–.92 descriptive accounts of organisms characteristic of a kind of area. The latter span may be used for works describing characteristic life cycles and behavior of particular kinds of organisms, but stops short of discussing interrelationships. In case of doubt, prefer 574.5.

580–590 **[Botanical and zoological sciences]**

The sequence of taxonomic groups of plants and animals can be described as following the course of the letter U. It begins at one tip of the U with the most highly developed and complex plants (dicotyledons among the flowering plants) and moves down the base of the U for fungi, algae, and bacteria. The sequence skips over to 590 to begin up the other arm of the U with protozoa. After moving up through increasingly complex invertebrates, it reaches the vertebrates, and finally humankind, the most highly developed animal.

580–590 vs. 630, 641.3 **[Botanical and zoological sciences] vs. Agriculture and related technologies vs. Food**

Interdisciplinary numbers

Numbers in 580–590 are used for interdisciplinary works on plants and animals. However, many works on species known primarily in agriculture emphasize growing and harvesting while giving some biological information as background. Class these works in 630, e.g., a work on cotton that gives enough about the physiology of cotton to explain why it should be cultivated in a certain way 633.5, a work on aquarium fish that tells where they are found in nature but concentrates on how to grow them 639.3.

A complicating consideration is that the interdisciplinary number for food is 641.3. Thus works on the utilization and food value as well as the agriculture and biology of edible plants and animals are classed in 641.3, not in 580–590.

Physiology and pathology

The classification of physiology and anatomy differs between agricultural plants and animals. Physiology and anatomy of plants are classed in botany (581.1, 581.4, and related numbers); that of animals, in agriculture (636.089 and related numbers).

The classification of pathology and diseases is the same for agricultural plants and animals; they are classed in agriculture. The number for plant pathology and diseases (and for comprehensive works on plant and animal pathology and diseases) is 632; for animal pathology and diseases is 636.089 *(However, see also 591 vs. 610 for experimental work in medicine.)*

581 **Botany**

Use 581 with caution, since many works on "plants" are in fact limited to seed-bearing plants (582), flowering plants (582.13), or dicotyledons (583). Substantial treatment of nonseed-bearing plants, e.g., ferns, mosses, algae, must be present to justify the use of 581.

591 vs. 599 **Zoology vs. Mammals**

Consider 599 for works on "animals" when warm-blooded animals predominate, even if there is a sprinkling of material on other animals. However, note that diseases of useful animals are classed in 636–639, e.g., diseases of silkworms 638.

See also 591 vs. 610

591 vs. 610 **Zoology vs. Medical sciences Medicine**

Results of anatomical and physiological research with animal models are classed in zoology (591–599), but results of pharmacological, therapeutic, and pathological research with animals and plants are classed in 615–619 if the medical relevance for humans is stated or implied.

591.2 vs. 616.07 **Pathology of animals vs. Pathology [in medicine]**

Class in 616.07 and other numbers in 616–618 works emphasizing immunology in relation to diseases and problems in human beings. If in doubt between a 590 number and a 616–618 number, prefer 616–618.

608 vs. 609 **Inventions and patents vs. Historical, geographic, persons treatment [of technology]**

Use 608 for works on inventions that are primarily descriptive (and usually arranged topically); 609 for works that emphasize historic factors that stimulated inventions, or that arrange inventions chronologically. If in doubt, prefer 608.

610.69 Medical personnel

Be careful not to confuse the nature of the duties performed by the personnel with the technology of the operations used to discharge the duties, e.g., the technology of the services of medical technicians 610.73, not 610.69.

610.73 Nursing and services of medical technicians and assistants

Class here only works that emphasize what the nurse does. As the nursing profession continues to expand its responsibilities and gain recognition for those it already has, more and more works by and for nurses are about the subjects of medical science in a larger context than intended here. Class such works in other medical numbers, e.g., a survey of medical sciences for nurses 610, not 610.73; a work treating the problems and techniques of surgery written to help nurses understand the context of their duties 617, not 610.73, even if called surgical nursing.

610.9 Historical, geographic, persons treatment [of medical sciences, of medicine]

Class in 610.9 the history of three or more medical sciences. Class the history of a particular medical science with the science, e.g., the history of nursing 610.7309, of surgery 617.09, of internal medicine 616.009. Class histories of major diseases and their distribution in 614.4, and histories of medical service and medical welfare in 362.109. If in doubt, prefer 362.109.

Class works on former medical practices emphasizing therapy, e.g., folk remedies, in 615.8.

611 vs. 612 Human anatomy, cytology (cell biology), histology (tissue biology) vs. Human physiology

Anatomy concerns the form and structure of organs in contrast to their physiology, which deals with how they work. Sometimes works bearing the names of organs emphasize their physiology or treat physiology as well as anatomy; class these works in 612, unless they are limited to the cytological and histological level. Class treatment of anatomy, physiology, and pathology at the cytological and histological level in 611.

612 vs. 616 Human physiology vs. Diseases

Class in 612 comprehensive works on physiology and pathological physiology (612 plus 616.07). Class in 616 comprehensive works on diseases that move from a discussion of physiology to a more general consideration of causes of disease, complications, prevention, and therapy. For example, class the normal and pathological conditions of the circulatory system in 612.1, but the physiology, pathology, and therapeutics of the circulatory system in 616.1. If in doubt, prefer 616.

613 vs. 615.8 Promotion of health vs. Specific therapies and kinds of therapies

Note that many of the topics in 613 appear also in 615.8, e.g., breathing, diet, exercise. In each case the 613 number refers to the preventive or "staying healthy" aspects, while 615.8 refers to the therapeutic or "regaining health" aspects. Class comprehensive works in 613.

613.2 vs. 641.3, 363.8 Dietetics vs. Food vs. Food supply

Class comprehensive works on personal aspects of nutrition in 613.2. However, class interdisciplinary works on food in 641.3, on nutrition in 363.8. The thrust of 613.2 is to help individuals meet dietary requirements and maintain optimal balanced intake without gaining or losing weight. Also included is material for dietitians in planning diets for individuals. In contrast, the emphasis in 641.3 is on the food itself, and in 363.8 it is on meeting and maintaining the needs of society in general and of various social groups.

613.6 vs. 363.11 Special topics [in promotion of health] vs. Occupational and industrial hazards

Use 613.6 for works that emphasize technical measures to be taken for promotion of industrial and occupational health. Use 363.11 for works that emphasize social and institutional arrangements. In case of doubt, prefer 363.11.

613.7 vs. 646.7, 796 Physical fitness vs. Management of personal and family living Grooming vs. Athletic and outdoor sports and games [as recreation]

Exercise and sports activities as means of improving physical fitness are classed in 613.7, as means of improving the appearance of the body in 646.7, as recreation in 796. For example, lifting weights for physical fitness is classed in 613.7, bodybuilding contests in 646.7, weight lifting as a sport (i.e., contests to determine who can lift the most weight) in 796.41. If in doubt among 613.7, 646.7, and 796, prefer 613.7.

614.4–.5 vs. 362.1–.4 [Incidence of and public measures to prevent disease] vs. Problems of and services to sick and disabled people

Studies of epidemics and of the incidence of physical disease (including mental retardation and physical handicaps) are classed in 614 when treated solely from the medical standpoint. Works emphasizing diseases as social problems are classed in 362.1.

Works on the social provision of services to the physically ill are classed in 362.1. Works on preventive measures, however, are classed in 614.4–.5, regardless of whether the emphasis is medical or social. Thus works on social provision of immunization services are classed in 614.4, as are works on the medical aspects of immunization. Note that the public measures classed in 614.4–.5 are strictly limited to preventive ones. For example, class fluoridation and programs advising people how to avoid cavities in 614.5, but class programs to identify and treat people with cavities in 362.1.

Works about the incidence and prevention of mental illness, mental illness as a social problem, and social provision of services to the mentally ill, are all classed in 362.2.

614.4 Incidence of and public measures to prevent disease

The term "epidemiology" sometimes refers to a research technique with application outside 614, e.g., in determining etiologies, such as smoking as a cause of cancer 616.99; in determining the dimensions of social service requirements, such as the boundaries of the mental retardation problem 362.3; in exploring the possible effectiveness of proposed preventive measures, such as in reducing traffic accidents 363.12.

614.5 vs. 363.8 Incidence of and public measures to prevent specific diseases and kinds of diseases vs. Food supply

Class nutrition surveys in 363.8. These surveys sometimes mention prevalence of malnutrition as an indicator of nutrition levels. Only if the emphasis is on the malnutrition problem *per se* should a survey be classed in 614.5.

615 vs. 616–618 Pharmacology and therapeutics vs. Diseases, surgery, other branches of medicine

Class in 615 only general works on the pharmacodynamic action of drugs and their effects on the human body. Class the use of a drug in treatment in 616–618. If in doubt, prefer 616–618.

615.5 Therapeutics

Use 615.5 when the discussion of general therapeutic systems is historical or theoretical, e.g., a discussion of the theory of chiropractic 615.5. When these systems are discussed in their application to therapy, class them in a therapy number, e.g., the application of chiropractic 615.8. When the therapies are applied to specific conditions, class in 616–618, e.g., chiropractic in musculoskeletal diseases 616.7.

Be careful about biography. Founders of systems are usually classed with the respective systems, e.g., a biography of Andrew Taylor Still, the founder of osteopathy, 615.5. Other practitioners of a specific system are usually classed in 610.92. Many chiropractors limit their practice to therapeutic manipulation (615.8) or to manipulation for diseases of the musculoskeletal system (616.7). For these people, the best biography number is one that emphasizes their special therapeutic system—615.5. For chiropractors who do not limit their practice, use 610.92 for biographies.

615.8 Specific therapies and kinds of therapies

Several therapies listed in 615.8 are usually applied only to certain specific types of disorders, and works on the therapies take such application for granted without highlighting it in the title. Note the unstated emphasis and class accordingly, e.g., radiotherapy emphasizing cancer treatment 616.99, music therapy emphasizing psychiatric uses 616.89.

Use 615.8 with caution for diet therapy; when a single food element is heavily emphasized, dietotheraphy may amount to therapy with a specific drug, which is classed in 615, e.g., a diet distinctive largely by its use of enzymes or by its use of royal jelly.

Folk medicine

Class a work of medical folk literature in 398.27 if the emphasis is on the story told; a work on the sociology of medical folklore in 398 if the emphasis is on the tales as cultural and social phenomena. Class in 615.8 only if the emphasis is on the medical practice.

Note that folk medicine is under therapy. If a work gives more than token consideration to folk theories on the causes of disease, it must be classed in 610, e.g., folk etiologies and therapies of India 610.954 (or 616.00954 when the material is arranged by class of disease as in 616.1–.9).

616 vs. 576 Diseases vs. Microbes

Do not confuse medical microbiology in 616 with deleterious microorganisms in 576 and cognate numbers for the biology of microorganisms in 589 and 593.1. For example, a general study of toxic, pathogenic, obnoxious microorganisms found in food and water is classed in 576, but a study of their role in causing human diseases is classed in 616. If in doubt between 576 and 616, prefer 576.

616 vs. 610 Diseases vs. Medical sciences Medicine

Class in 616 comprehensive works on the diseases listed in 616–618. However, if a work contains separate treatment of health, pharmacology, and therapeutics, as well as of diseases, class it in 610.

When the whole of medicine is brought to bear on the concept of diseases in a single treatise that discusses group after group of diseases, class the work in 616. The table of contents usually offers guidance. If it reads like a summary of topics in 610.73–619, class the work in 610; if it reads like a summary of topics in 616.02–.99 or in 616–618, class the work in 616.

Use notation from Table 1 with caution under 616 except for internal medicine or works clearly limited to the concept of diseases. Prefer 610.3 for medical dictionaries, 610.71 for medical schools, 610.92 for doctors not having a distinct specialty.

616 vs. 616.07 **Diseases vs. Pathology**

"Clinical medicine" has two meanings. In one sense it approximates 616, i.e., the application of all branches of medicine to treatment of various diseases. However, just as often it is shorthand for the work of a clinical diagnostic laboratory, and is properly classed at 616.07.

616 vs. 616.9 **Diseases vs. Other diseases**

Do not confuse medical microbiology in 616 with the classes of communicable disease in 616.9 caused by various types of microorganisms. The emphasis in 616 is on the organism, usually as the cause of disease, while in 616.9 it is on the whole disease and its course, cure, and prevention. Each is comprehensive in its own way, 616 as the interdisciplinary number for pathogenic organisms affecting humans and domestic animals, and 616.9 for the resulting diseases. If in doubt, prefer 616.9.

616.1–.8 **Diseases of specific systems and organs**

When a disease of one system affects another system so strongly that it is the second system that must be the focus of concern and treatment, class the work with the affected system, e.g., retinal complications of diabetes 617.7 Ophthalmology, not 616.4.

616.9 vs. 616.3 **Other diseases vs. Diseases of the digestive system**

"Cholera" was formerly a nonspecific term for a variety of gastrointestinal disturbances. Cholera morbus and other choleras using the former meaning of "cholera" are classed in 616.3. Today, "cholera" is limited to the type of viral disease formerly called Asiatic cholera and is classed in 616.9. If in doubt, class in 616.9.

617 vs. 616 **Miscellaneous branches of medicine Surgery vs. Diseases**

617 contains a mixed set of nonsurgical and surgical specialties. If there is a provision in both 616 and 617 for an organ that defines a specialty, use the 617 number only for surgery. *See also 617.5.*

Class comprehensive works on medical treatment of the handicapped in 617 unless the term is clearly used to cover all disabling diseases, in which case, class in 616. If in doubt whether to class a work on the handicapped in 616 or 617, prefer 617.

617.3 vs. 616.7, 617.5 **Orthopedics vs. Diseases of the musculoskeletal system vs. Regional medicine Regional surgery**

Use 617.3 only for works covering orthopedics in general, and its subdivisions only for works that emphasize deformities. If in doubt whether to class a work on orthopedics in 617.3 or in 616.7 Diseases of the musculoskeletal system, prefer 616.7. If in doubt between 617.3 and 617.5 regional medicine, prefer 617.5.

617.3 vs. 617 **Orthopedics vs. Miscellaneous branches of medicine Surgery**

If in doubt whether to class a work on appliances with orthopedic appliances in 617.3 or with prosthetic equipment or surgical appliances, both in 617, prefer 617.

617.4 vs. 616 **Surgery by systems vs. Diseases**

617.4 is primarily limited to operative surgery of systems. Nonoperative therapies are usually classed in 616, e.g., therapeutic manipulation of muscles 616.7, not 617.4. Nonoperative therapies are classed in 617.4 only if they have some connection with operative surgery, e.g., electrotherapy by heart pacer 617.4, since the pacer must be surgically implanted.

617.5 **Regional medicine Regional surgery**

Two quite different concepts are spliced together here: (1) regions, which incorporate parts of several physiological systems, e.g., the abdominal region; and (2) organs, which are parts of single systems, e.g., the stomach. In the case of regions, resolve doubts in favor of 617.5 numbers. In the case of organs, resolve doubts in favor of 616 numbers or numbers in 617.6–.8 for teeth, eyes, and ears.

617.5 vs. 617.6 **Regional medicine Regional surgery vs. Dentistry**

"Oral surgery" is a term much used in the dental profession. Do not class a work so identified in 617.5 unless it covers substantially more than procedures for which one would go to a dentist (617.6).

618.92 vs. 616, 618.3 **Pediatrics vs. Diseases vs. Diseases and complications of pregnancy**

Use caution in classing in 618.92 certain diseases that are most often treated in children, but that remain lifetime problems or threats, e.g., congenital diseases, mumps. Class these in 616 unless actually limited to their occurrence in children.

Works on diagnosing genetic diseases in the fetus, e.g., by amniocentesis, typically focus on immediate measures, not lifetime treatment; class such works in 618.3.

618.92 vs. 617 **Pediatrics vs. Miscellaneous branches of medicine Surgery**

Class in 618.92 nonsurgical specialties provided for in 617.5 and 617.7–.8 when applied to children (regional medicine, ophthalmology, otology, audiology). Class surgical specialties applied to children in 617—comprehensive works in 617.9, surgery of a specific organ, system, disorder with the subject. For example, class medicine of the back for children in 618.92, but surgery of the back in 617.5.

Class both medical and surgical aspects of dentistry for children in 617.6. Also class both nonsurgical and surgical aspects of topics provided for in 617.1–.3 in 617 when applied to children, e.g., pediatric sports medicine 617.1, pediatric orthopedics 617.3.

618.97 vs. 617 **Geriatrics vs. Miscellaneous branches of medicine Surgery**

Class in 618.97 nonsurgical specialties provided for in 617.5–.8 when applied to persons in late adulthood (regional medicine, dentistry, ophthalmology, otology, audiology). Class surgical specialties applied to persons in late adulthood in 617—comprehensive works in 617.9, surgery of a specific organ, system, disorder with the subject. For example, class medicine of the back for persons in late adulthood in 618.97, but surgery of the back in 617.5; class diseases of the teeth and gums in 618.97, but dental surgery in 617.6.

Class both nonsurgical and surgical aspects of topics provided for in 617.1–.3 in 617 when applied to persons in late adulthood, e.g., injuries in late adulthood 617.10084, geriatric orthopedics 617.30084.

621 vs. 530 **Applied physics vs. Physics**

When the heading of an applied physics subdivision corresponds to one in physics, use the 621 number when the focus is on technology, even though much of the work is scientific background; use the 530 number when the focus is equally on science and technology. If in doubt, prefer 530.

621.382 vs. 003 **Communications engineering vs. Systems**

Information theory was originally developed in the context of communications engineering, then applied as well in other disciplines. Class in 003 only interdisciplinary works. Class information theory in communications engineering in 621.382 or with the specific kind of communication, e.g., radio 621.384 (without using notation 01 from Table 1 in either case). Class information theory in any other specific subject with the subject, using notation 01 from Table 1, e.g., information theory in economics 330.01.

621.382 vs. 621.39, 004.6, 384 **Communications engineering vs. [Engineering of] Computers vs. Interfacing and communications [in computer science] vs. Communications [services] Telecommunication**

Exercise caution in classifying works on digital communication. If they emphasize engineering, they may be either computer data communications (621.39), digital telecommunications (621.382), or digital aspects of both telecommunications and data communications (also 621.382). If in doubt between the engineering numbers, prefer 621.382.

In works that do not emphasize engineering, "digital communications" is apt to refer to communications in computer science 004.6. This number is used for works dealing with telecommunications and data communications engineering plus interfacing and communications in computer science. However, works covering economic and public service aspects of data communications are classed in 384. If in doubt between engineering and nonengineering numbers, prefer nonengineering ones; if in doubt between 004.6 and 384, prefer 384.

For other choices for works not emphasizing engineering, see 004.3 and 005.7; 384.3 vs. 004.6.

621.3841 vs. 621.3845 **Amateur (Ham) radio vs. Radiotelephone**

Both ham and CB are two-way systems for nonprofessionals involving reserved bandwidths not available to commercial stations. However, the word "amateur" has by tradition been reserved for long-distance (usually shortwave) communication regulated by international treaties, with stiff licensing requirements for operators. In contrast, citizens band is local (ca. 10 miles or 15 kilometers), with easier or no licensing requirements. If in doubt, prefer 621.3841.

622 vs. 669, 662 **Mining engineering and related processes vs. Metallurgy [and] Technology of explosives, fuels, related products**

Ore dressing, which refers to physical means of separating more usable ore from what has been dug out of the ground, is classed in 622. When means that effect substantial chemical change are applied, the process normally becomes chemical engineering (usually metallurgy, 669). For example, magnetic separation of iron ore is classed in 622, but electrodeposition of iron from ores is classed in 669.

Since use of high temperatures causes drastic chemical changes, it is counted as chemical engineering, e.g., pyrometallurgy 669.028.

In-situ processing involves using chemical techniques to get the target materials (or compounds containing the target materials) out of the ground. It is, therefore, usually considered as mining, and is classed in 622. However, in situ processing of a fossil fuel usually transforms the fuel into another form. When there is such a transformation, class the processing in the chemical engineering number for the material produced, e.g., coal gasification 665.7.

624.1 vs. 624 Structural engineering and underground construction vs. Civil engineering

Structural engineering may be considered the "general topics" heading for civil engineering. It comprises the specific subdisciplines of civil engineering that have general applicability to all kinds of structures. Basic texts on civil engineering often emphasize the subject, but should be classed in 624 if they also discuss the various types of structures to which it is applied. Use 624.1 only for works that take a narrow view of structural engineering, and do not discuss the various types of structures. If in doubt, prefer 624.

628 Sanitary and municipal engineering Environmental protection engineering

Note that sanitary engineering for rural and sparsely populated areas is classed at 628 without subdivision, even if limited to topics found in 628.1–.4. While the goals in rural areas are the same as in urban areas, the population served is so scattered that it is usually difficult to use all of the methods applied in urban settings. (In the unabridged edition of DDC, a number is provided for sanitary engineering in rural and sparsely populated areas.)

628.4 vs. 363.72 Waste technology, public toilets, street cleaning vs. Sanitation problems and services

Use 628.4 with caution for works on specific kinds of solid wastes, since most of these works emphasize the social context of waste and pollution problems, or programs with incentives to recycle materials, and are classed in 363.72. If in doubt, prefer 363.72.

Of the technological works on specific kinds of solid wastes, many will concentrate on the specific technology which creates or utilizes the waste, and should be classed with that technology, e.g., technology of recycling glass bottles 666. Class in 628.4 works on the technology of treatment and disposal that do not concentrate on products of a specific manufacturing technology, and works that emphasize technology of collection (which is usually not handled within the specific manufacturing industry).

629.04 vs. 388 Transportation engineering vs. Transportation [services] Ground transportation

The following guidelines help to distinguish between the vehicle numbers in 385–388 and those in 623.7, 623.8, 625.2, 629, and 688.6.

Class in 385–388:

1. Services provided by the vehicle, e.g., transportation of passengers by trains 385.

2. Operation (general) of the vehicle, e.g., duties of the ship's captain 387.5.

3. Economic and social aspects of the vehicle, e.g., a register of the airplanes owned by a company 387.7.

Class in 629.04 and related numbers in the 600s:

1. Description of the vehicle, e.g., steam locomotives of the 1930s 625.2.

2. Technology of the vehicle, e.g., design tests for ships 623.8.

3. Operation (technical) of the vehicle, e.g., piloting spacecraft 629.45.

4. Maintenance and repair of the vehicle, e.g., repairing motorcycles 629.28.

If in doubt, prefer 629.04 and related numbers in the 600s.

629.226 vs. 643, 690, 728.7 **Motorized homes, campers, trailers (caravans) vs. Housing and household equipment [and Construction of] Buildings [and Architecture of] Vacation houses, cabins, hunting lodges, houseboats, mobile homes**

Use the housing numbers (not 629.226) for what are essentially houses on wheels, i.e., mobile homes that must be towed. Use 629.226 (which is listed under types of motor land vehicles) for what are essentially either automobiles with living accommodations, collapsible living accommodations to be used with trucks or trailers, or trailers with such limited living accommodations that they could not (even when hooked up) serve as permanent homes. Use the housing numbers if in doubt, and use 643 for interdisciplinary works on movable homes.

631.5 vs. 338.1 **Cultivation and harvesting vs. [Economics of] Agriculture**

Usually works on crop yields are compilations giving the total production of an area, and are classed in 338.1. Works on yield per acre are also classed in 338.1 if they are taken as indicators of agricultural efficiency. If yield studies per unit of area are used in technical tests, class them with the subject in agriculture, e.g., yield tests of fertilizer use 631.8028. Use 631.5 for tests of cultivation and harvesting techniques, and for works having little or no economic or testing implications, e.g., lists of record yields of various crops. If in doubt, class in 338.1.

633–635 Specific plant crops

Certain plants are important for two or more quite different crops, and may be classed in different numbers for each. Some of the more important distinctions are:

Cereal grains versus cereal grasses (633.1 vs. 633.2)

Class in 633.1 if grown for grain (even if the fodder is an important by-product), in 633.2 if the whole plant is to be consumed (even if the grain is allowed to ripen).

Legumes (633.3 vs. 635)

Class in 633.3 if grown for either the ripened fruit or forage, in 635 if the pod is to be picked green or unripened for human consumption.

Other crops

When the difference in the crop produced by the farmer is minor, class the crop in the category which best fits the predominant use, e.g., potatoes grown for food, feed, or starch all look about the same, so class in 635. However, hemlock grown for lumber looks quite different from hemlock grown for landscaping, so the first is classed in 634.9, the latter in 635.9. If the crop described does not fit existing numbers where the plant is named or implied, class the work in the closest suitable number, e.g., a legume grown for fiber 633.5. If in doubt, prefer the first number in the schedule where the plant is named or implied.

643 vs. 363.5 Housing and household equipment [in home economics] vs. Housing [in social services]

A distinction is often made between "housing" and "houses." The term "housing" normally refers to the provision of shelter considered in the abstract, while the term "houses" normally refers to the buildings considered as concrete objects. Class the home economics aspects of either housing or houses, and interdisciplinary works on *houses* and their use in 643. However, class interdisciplinary works on *housing* in 363.5, since they usually emphasize or imply the social aspects of shelter.

643 vs. 690 Housing and household equipment [in home economics] vs. [Construction of] Buildings

The scope note at 643 reading "works for owner-occupants and renters covering activities by members of household" indicates that 643 is used for a broad range of material intended for the do-it-yourself enthusiast. Only works on home renovation and remodeling for professional builders are classed in 690. If in doubt, prefer 690.

647 vs. 647.068, 658.2, T1—068 **Management of public households (Institutional housekeeping) vs. Management [in institutional housekeeping] vs. Plant management [and Table 1 notation for] Management**

Use the management notation from Table 1 with caution in 647.068 and in subdivisions of 647.9, because the term "management" often refers to the basic techniques of operating an establishment, i.e., to the topics found in 641–646 and 648 taken as a whole, when they apply to public facilities. Use 647.068 (or 647.94068 and 647.95068) only when the reference is to the kind of management topics found in 658.1–.2 and 658.4–.8, e.g., financial management and marketing. (Personnel management is not a part of T1—068 in 647.)

Plant management covers some of the same topics as institutional housekeeping, e.g. utilities, equipment, maintenance. The emphasis in 647 (or in other 640 numbers for specific aspects) is on doing the actual work, while the emphasis in 658.2 is on making sure that the work is done. For example, class a how-to work on running utilities for restaurants in 644, on hospital sanitation in 648; but class a work on managing restaurant utilities in 647.95068, on managing a hospital sanitary service in 362.1.

650 vs. 330 **Management and auxiliary services vs. Economics**

Works about business can be classed in several places. Most often the choice is between 330 and 650. Use 330 if the work presents general information, economic conditions, financial information (such as interest rates), and reports on what certain companies are doing. Use 650 when the work presents only practical managerial information that covers 651 Office services as well as 658 General management. If the work is limited to general management, use 658. Class comprehensive works on 330 and 650 in 330.

651.7 vs. 808, 658.4 **Communication Creation and transmission of records [as an office service] vs. Rhetoric and collections of literary texts from more than one literature vs. Executive management**

Class in 651.7 such topics as the use of the telephone, techniques of dictation, how to use microcomputer software for form letters, mail-handling techniques—in short, the mechanics of communication. Do not class in 651.7 works that emphasize effective business writing style.

Class in 808 style manuals for business writing and works on how to do effective business writing, whether aimed at secretaries or executives. Class in 808 works on how to write a specific type of communication (e.g., business letters) and model collections of a specific type intended to illustrate good writing style. In case of doubt between 651.7 and 808, prefer 808.

Class in 658.4 works that focus on use of communication to achieve management goals. Often these works emphasize the personal relations aspects of management communication.

657 vs. 658.15 Accounting vs. Financial management

Accounting and bookkeeping are not included in the numbers for financial management, 658.15 and notation 068 from Table 1. Financial management deals with money from the managerial viewpoint: how to raise funds to initiate or expand an organization, how to invest capital in capital goods or in the securities of other organizations, how to allocate funds to various operations (budgeting), and how to control expenses and costs.

How to do accounting is classed in 657, use of accounting information by management in 658.15. How to prepare a financial statement is classed in 657, use of a financial statement by management to improve business performance in 658.15. Design of accounting systems in general and for outside reporting is classed in 657. Design of accounting systems with specific emphasis on increasing the internal flow of information to management is classed in 658.15. If in doubt, prefer 657.

658 and T1—068 General management [and Table 1 notation for] Management [in specific fields]

Management comprises the conduct of all types of enterprises except government agencies that do not themselves provide direct services. *(See 350–354 vs. 658, T1—068.)* Management is not confined to "business enterprises."

Organizations to be managed may be divided in three ways. First is division by size or scope of the enterprise, which is classed in 658 for big business and 658.02 for small business. Second is division by the legal form of the enterprise, e.g., corporations, partnerships, etc., which is classed in 658. Third, and most important, is division by the kind of work the organization does: selling books, manufacturing light bulbs, carrying freight, caring for the sick, etc. Management of enterprises doing specific kinds of work is classed with the kind of work being done, with use of notation 068 from Table 1, e.g., management of airlines 387.7068. If there is no specific number for the kind of work, notation 068 cannot be used, e.g., management of savings and loan institutions 332.2. In some cases there is a special provision for management of organizations in a specific field, e.g., 025.1 for management of libraries, 371.2 for school administration and management. 658 and its subdivisions are reserved for discussions of management applicable to any type of enterprise. Comprehensive works on management of government corporations are classed in 351.009.

For an enterprise's field of work, select if possible a straightforward number for making a product or performing a service. For example, class works on the management of automobile manufacturing in 629.222068, not 338.7, because 338.7 is for the economics of automobile manufacturing.

For management of a particular kind of retail store, use 658.8 if there is no emphasis on a specific kind of product. For example, class management of retail chain stores in 658.8, not 381, since chain stores are a form of management organization. 381 is for the economic aspects of such an organization. However, class management of a retail store marketing a specific product in 381, e.g., a bookstore.

See also 363.1; 658, T1—068 vs. 302.3.

658, T1—068 vs. 302.3 General management [and Table 1 notation for] Management [in specific fields] vs. Social interaction within groups

Class in 658 and T1—068 works that emphasize how to manage. Class in 302.3 works that analyze and describe the social dynamics of how people behave and work in organizations. If in doubt, prefer 302.3.

658.15 and T1—068 Financial management [and Table 1 notation for] Management [in specific fields]

Financial management deals with money: how to raise funds to initiate or expand an organization, how to invest capital in capital goods or in the securities of other organizations, how to allocate funds to various operations (budgeting), and how to control expenses and costs. These aspects of financial management do not vary greatly from enterprise to enterprise, except with respect to sources of funds.

658.15 and notation 068 do not include bookkeeping or accounting. Class works on these subjects in 657.

Examples of numbers for financial management in various fields follow:

Financial management of airlines: 387.7068.

Financial management of banks: 332.1068.

Financial management of automobile manufacturing firms: 629.222068.

Financial management of schools: 371.2.

Financial management of libraries: 025.1.

658.2 and T1—068 **Plant management [and Table 1 notation for] Management [in specific fields]**

Plant management deals with the physical environment and tools requisite to the performance of the organization's work. It includes land, buildings, utilities (light, heat, etc.), and the specific equipment (such as vehicles, machinery, furnishings) necessary to do the work. Acquisition of grounds, buildings, and major equipment is classed in 658.15, since these are considered to be capital goods. Their maintenance is classed with plant management, as is the use of land, buildings, and utilities. Use of production equipment is classed with production management in 658.5.

Examples of numbers for plant management in various fields follow:

Plant management for airlines: 387.7.

The note under 068 in the table at 380 forbids use of notation 068 for plant management here.

Plant management for banks: 332.1068.

Plant management for automobile manufacturing firms: 629.222068.

Plant management for schools: 371.6.

Plant management for libraries: 022.

658.3 and T1—068 **Personnel management [and Table 1 notation for] Management [in specific fields]**

Personnel management deals with people: how to recruit, select, place, train, develop, and motivate them in performing the work of the organization. It also includes pay, hours, leave, retirement, and pensions, as well as subjects like discipline and discharge, all from the management perspective.

Examples of numbers for personnel management in various fields follow:

Personnel management in airlines: 387.7068.

Personnel management in banks: 332.1068.

Personnel management in automobile manufacturing firms: 629.222068.

Personnel management in schools: 371.2.

Personnel management in libraries: 023.

658.3 vs. 331 Personnel management vs. Labor economics

Many of the topics in 658.3 are paralleled in 331. Class in 658.3 works written from the viewpoint of management, in 331 works written from the viewpoint of the employee (the worker). Also class in 331 works written from a neutral standpoint, simply describing the phenomena, and comprehensive works including both management and employee views.

658.4 vs. 658, 658.1 Executive management vs. General management [and] Organization and finance

In 658.4 "organization" means the internal managerial organization of an enterprise, not the form of legal or ownership organization. Internal organization is concerned with the way that authority and responsibility are apportioned. For example, in line organization a single manager exercises final authority, either directly over production workers or over several supervisors who in turn supervise workers. Class forms of legal and ownership organization (e.g., corporations, partnerships) in 658, and initiation of business enterprises of specific forms of legal and ownership organization in 658.1.

658.5 and T1—068 Management of production [and Table 1 notation for] Management [in specific fields]

Production management is the management of the work that the organization exists to perform. It concerns itself with the organization of the work flow and the methods to be used in performing individual operations. It also deals with insuring the quality and accuracy of the operations and of their results. It is related to, but not the same as, the technology involved in the operations. It differs radically from one organization to another.

Management of factory production is the organization and direction of the processes by which raw materials, parts, and subassemblies are combined and processed through the operation of people and machines to produce such concrete objects as automobiles, bread, toys, etc. This is also known as logistics.

658.5 fits the nature of factory operations better than production management of other kinds of enterprises because it reflects an earlier state of the management art when books of management were chiefly concerned with industrial management. Accordingly, 658.5 is used for production management in factories in general rather than 670.

Examples of numbers for production management in various fields follow:

Production management for airlines: 387.7068.

Production management for banks: 332.1068.

Production management for automobile manufacturing firms: 629.222068.

Production management for schools: 371.2.

Production management for libraries: 025.1.

658.7 and T1—068 **Management of materials [and Table 1 notation for] Management [in specific fields]**

Management of materials involves the raw materials, parts, and subassemblies used in creating the final product or service; the supplies necessary for conducting the business, e.g., ink, pens, paper; and other small pieces of equipment, e.g., typewriters, filing cabinets.

The activities dealing with these materials fall into three distinct categories: acquisition, internal management, and physical distribution.

Acquisition, or procurement, involves contracts and their negotiation, vendor selection, order work, receiving and unloading shipments, and expediting and tracing when done by the purchaser.

Internal management involves storage and the maintenance of inventory, checking materials out of inventory for use in the work process, their movement from work station to work station, checking them into storage and storing them prior to sale, and maintaining the inventory at this point. In service organizations, where there is no sale of a final product, the process is complete when materials and supplies are issued for and used in the work process.

Physical distribution involves processing orders received, matching the orders to items in inventory, checking the items out of inventory, packing them, loading them, selecting carrier and routing, and expediting and tracing when done by the shipper. Note that major equipment is considered to be capital, and its acquisition is classed in 658.15. Physical distribution is not a factor in most service organizations.

Examples of numbers for materials management in various fields follow:

Materials management for airlines: 387.7068.

Materials management in banks: 332.1068.

Materials management in automobile manufacturing firms: 629.222068.

Materials management in schools: 371.2

Materials management in libraries: 025.1.

However, class management of the acquisition of books and other information media in 025.2068, their internal management in 025.8, their circulation (analogous to physical distribution) in 025.6.

658.8 and T1—068 **Management of distribution (Marketing) [and Table 1 notation for] Management [in specific fields]**

Marketing management deals with the sale of the product or service of the organization. This concept also includes credit management.

Examples of numbers for marketing management in various fields follow:

Marketing management for airlines: 387.7068.

This number is used chiefly for sales promotion and credit management. Most sales effort for such an organization is concentrated in advertising, which is classed in 659.1.

Marketing management for banks: chiefly advertising, which is classed in 659.1.

Marketing management for automobile manufacturing firms: 629.222068.

Marketing management for schools: not applicable.

Private schools do some advertising and public relations, but these are classed in 659.

Marketing management for libraries: class public relations of libraries in 021.7.

658.8, T1—068 vs. 659 **Management of distribution (Marketing) [and Table 1 notation for] Management [in specific fields] vs. Advertising and public relations**

Marketing (658.8) is the broader concept; it includes sales management, marketing research, channels of distribution, and customer credit management, which are classed in 658.8; it also includes the advertising and public relations that have been drawn off to 659. What belongs in 659 is the publicity used by an organization to present itself and its goods and services to the public. Research focused on advertising or public relations is the only kind of marketing research classed in 659; broader research is classed in 658.8. If in doubt, prefer 658.8.

660 vs. 604.7 Chemical engineering and related technologies vs. Hazardous materials technology

Use 660 for consideration of hazardous chemicals during chemical engineering; prefer 604.7 for comprehensive consideration of hazardous chemicals that includes handling, transporting, and utilization outside the chemical industry.

However, for specific hazardous chemicals, the comprehensive technology number is usually found in 660, e.g., processing, transportation, utilization of natural gas 665.7.

Class interdisciplinary works on hazardous chemicals in 363.17.

670.285 vs. 670.42 Data processing Computer applications [in manufacturing] vs. Factory operations engineering

Works on flexible manufacturing systems are classed in 670.42 if limited to computer-aided manufacture; in 670.285 if including also other computer applications in manufacturing, such as computer-aided design or computer applications in management of manufacturing.

671–679 vs. 680 Manufacture of products from specific materials vs. Manufacture of products for specific uses

The distinction between 671–679 and 680 cannot be drawn consistently because some manufacture by material appears in 680, e.g., leather and fur goods 685; and some products for specific uses appear in 671–679, e.g., paper plates and cups 676. In general 671–679 has primary products in contrast to the final products from a given material in 680, e.g., textiles 677, clothing 687; but that distinction is not relevant in many specific cases, e.g., brushes 679, combs 688. In case of doubt, prefer 671–679.

680 Manufacture of products for specific uses

The order of the subdivisions of 680 is drawn from that of 670; the 680 numbers usually represent a type of final product related in some general way to the material in the comparable 670 number:

672	682	Ferrous metals [vs.] Small forge work
673	683	Nonferrous metals [vs.] Hardware and household appliances
674	684	Lumber, cork, wood [vs.] Furnishings and home workshops
675	685	Leather and fur [vs.] Leather and fur goods
676	686	Pulp and paper [vs.] Printing
677	687	Textiles [vs.] Clothing

690 vs. 624 **Buildings vs. Civil engineering**

To be classed in 690, the work must limit its discussion to habitable structures (buildings). If other structures are discussed, the work is classed in 624. Works about "building" in the sense of constructing all types of structures are classed in 624, not 690. If in doubt, prefer 624.

The word "construction" in the title usually implies that a work covers more than habitable structures. However, it is sometimes used loosely for construction of 690–type buildings.

700 The arts Fine and decorative arts

Generally the word "arts," used without a qualifier, is a signal that the area covered is broader than the fine and decorative arts. Literature, music, and the performing arts are the other kinds of arts most often included. A quick check each time that "art" or "arts" is used should establish the area covered.

"Computer art" usually refers to two different uses of computers in the arts. The computer can be a device employed in creating the final art work, as when the computer serves as an aid in composing music to be played on traditional instruments or as an aid in designing or engraving the plates for otherwise traditional prints. Alternatively, the computer can serve as the instrument on which music is performed, as in computer music, or as the display medium for visual art, as when computer graphics works are intended for display on a computer monitor. The computer as a device is classed with other devices using either notation 0285 from Table 1 or specific provisions in the schedule, e.g., computers and the arts 700.285, computers in the graphic arts 760.0285, computer composition of music 781.3. The computer as an instrument or display medium is classed with the type of art, e.g., history of computer art 709.04, computer graphic art 760, computer music 786.7.

700.92 **Persons [in the arts]**

The instructions at each major area for the classification of artists vary. Even within one division, the 730s, the treatment varies: 730.92 for a sculptor, 739.2 for a goldsmith, 730.092 for a sculptor who has also worked in one or more of the other plastic arts.

Works of an artist or artists are designated in one of two ways, either by notation 092 from Table 1 as in sculpture, or by notation for period or place as in drawing 741.93–.99.

704.9 **Iconography**

Iconography takes precedence over historical and geographical treatment, e.g., a general work on Romanesque art 709.02, Romanesque art of Normandy 709.44, but the Virgin Mary and Child in Romanesque art of Normandy 704.9. However, care should be taken in classifying schools and styles that usually are limited in subject matter, such as early Christian, Byzantine, and Romanesque schools, which usually treat religious themes. Class in 704.9 only if a point is made that iconography or one of its aspects is the focus of the work.

709.01–.05 vs. 709.3–.9 Periods of development [of fine and decorative arts] vs. Treatment by specific continents, countries, localities [of fine and decorative arts]

Class the works produced by an artistic school or in a particular style as follows:

1. From two countries, with the country coming first in Table 2 in 709.3–.9.

2. From three or more European countries, with the period when the school or style flourished in 709.01–.05.

3. From three or more non-European countries within the same continent, with the continent in 709.3–.9.

4. From three or more countries not within the same continent, with the period when the school or style flourished in 709.01–.05.

If in doubt, prefer 709.01–.05.

711 vs. 307.1 Area planning (Civic art) vs. Community planning and development

Works that focus on the presentation and analysis of the physical plans, even if some historical and social material is included, are classed in 711. Works that focus on the historical or social aspects are classed in 307.1. If in doubt, class in 307.1.

721 vs. 690 Architectural structure vs. Buildings

Descriptive details of buildings erected in the past or planned for the future are classed in 721. Principles of engineering design and construction or actual instruction (e.g., for the builder) on how to put structural elements, shapes, and materials together are classed in 690. If in doubt, prefer 721.

729 Design and decoration of structures and accessories

More material is taken out of 729 by notes than is left in. Class in 729 only those general works in which the focus is specifically architectural design. Design and construction treated together are classed in 721. Construction alone is classed in 690. Decoration is classed in 729 only when the subject is being treated as an aspect of architectural decoration rather than as an art object in itself. For example, comprehensive works on murals are classed in 751.7; however, the use of murals as architectural decoration is classed in 729.

736–739 vs. 731–735 **Other plastic arts vs. Sculpture**

The products and techniques of the plastic arts in 736–739 are often difficult to separate from those of sculpture; if in doubt, prefer 731–735. For example, bronze figures are usually classed in sculpture, but a bronze figure is classed in 739.5 if it was a part (such as a finial or handle) of a larger decorative work.

745.1 **Antiques**

Class a specific type of antique with the subject in art if a number is provided, e.g., gold coins 737.4, antique New England furniture 749.214.

If there is no available number in 700–799, use the appropriate number in 600–699, e.g., antique passenger automobiles 629.222. If there is a separate technology number for the use of the object in question as opposed to the number for the manufacture of the object, prefer the use number, e.g., thimbles 646 rather than 687.

If antiques and collectibles fit in neither the art nor the technology numbers, class with the subject with which they are most closely associated, e.g., Shirley Temple collectibles 791.43.

745.5 vs. 680 **[Artistic] Handicrafts vs. Manufacture of products for specific uses**

Handicraft when limited to artistic work is classed in 745.5. In general usage the term "crafts" may be used for country crafts, and cottage industries and trades, such as those of the farrier, the cooper, and the thatcher. Crafts in this sense and handicrafts as the routine way of manufacturing secondary and final products are classed in 680. If in doubt, prefer 680.

745.592 **Toys, models, miniatures, related objects**

Class handcrafted miniatures and models as follows:

Class in 700:

1. If there is a specific number for the model, e.g., paper airplanes 745.592.

2. If there is a specific number for the subject illustrated by the model, e.g., handcrafted miniature furniture 749.

3. If there is no number in 600 for the model or the subject illustrated. In this case the most specific number possible is chosen.

Class in 600 if there is no specific number in 700–779 *and* either of the following conditions is met:

1. If there is a specific number in 600–699 for the model, e.g., handcrafted model airplanes 629.133.

2. If there is a specific number for the subject illustrated by the model, e.g., handcrafted miniature reciprocating steam engines 621.1.

745.6 Calligraphy, illumination, heraldic design

Illumination includes not only the manuscripts and books produced in medieval Europe, but Egyptian and Roman survivals from antiquity. In addition, Persian, Mogul, and Indian illuminations often labeled "miniatures" are considered painted illustrations or illuminations and are classed here rather than in 751.7.

753–758 Iconography

Iconography takes precedence over historical and geographic treatment, e.g., a general work on Romanesque painting 759.02, Romanesque painting of France 759.409, but the Virgin Mary and Child in Romanesque painting of France 755. However, care should be taken in classifying schools and styles that usually are limited in subject matter, such as early Christian, Byzantine, and Romanesque schools, which usually treat religious themes. Class in 753–758 only if a point is made that iconography or one of its aspects is the focus of the work.

Notation 09 from Table 1 plus notation 3–9 from Table 2 is added to show the nationality or locality of the artists rather than the location of the subject, e.g., Canadian portraits of British royalty 757.0971.

769.92 [Printmakers]

Printmakers who copy other artists or the artists being copied (if only prints are being discussed) are classed here, e.g., prints after Gainsborough 769.92. Prints produced by either a print workshop or studio are classed in 769.93–.99.

778.3 vs. 621.36 Special kinds of photography vs. Applied optics and paraphotic engineering

The techniques of producing the picture as an end unto itself are classed in 778.3. The engineering technology underlying the photography and the scientific applications are classed in 621.36. Applications to a specific field of science are classed with the field, e.g., to astronomy 522. If in doubt, prefer 778.3.

780 Music

Overall structure

780.1–.9	Standard subdivisions, regular and modified
781	General principles and musical forms
781.1	Aesthetics, appreciation, taste
781.2	Elements of music
781.3	Composition
781.4	Techniques of music
781.5	Kinds of music (e.g., for specific occasions)
781.6	Traditions of music (e.g., folk, popular)
781.7	Sacred music
781.8	[General] musical forms
782–788	Voices and instruments
782–783	Voices and vocal music
782	Vocal music
783	Music for single voice The voice
784–788	Instruments and their music
784	Instruments and instrumental ensembles and their music
785	Ensembles with only one instrument per part
786–788	Specific instruments and their music
786	Keyboard, mechanical, electrophonic, percussion instruments
787	Stringed instruments
788	Wind instruments

Citation order

The citation order is:

Voices and instruments	782–788
Musical forms	781.8
Sacred music	781.7
Traditions of music	781.6
Kinds of music	781.5
Techniques of music	781.4
Composition	781.3
Elements of music	781.2
Aesthetics, appreciation, taste	781.1
Standard subdivisions	780.1–.9

Note that a major facet, the composer, is not indicated in the class number (unless the option at 789 is used for literature about music). A cutter number or other alphabetizing device will perform the role of indicating composer. Notation 092 from Table 1 is used to indicate a biography, a general criticism of the composer, an analysis of a composer's contribution to the development of some aspect of music (such as Haydn's role in the development of the concerto form), and critical works on the body of a composer's work (such as a critique of the piano music of Ravel). Criticism of an individual work by a composer does not receive notation 092 in order that a piece of music and criticism of it will fall at the same class number. Similarly, for a composer who composed in more than one form, criticism of a specific form, e.g., symphonies, does not receive T1—092.

Literature about music vs. scores and recordings

The major difference between music and other subjects is the need to distinguish literature about music from music as bibliographic objects in the form of scores and recordings.

Edition 11 provided separate class numbers for literature about music and for music itself. Edition 12 does not provide separate numbers, but libraries may make the distinction by using other devices in the call number (*see the option note at 780 in the Schedules*).

Standard subdivision 026

Extended standard subdivision 026 Treatises on music scores, recordings, texts, may cause difficulty. Note that the meaning of 026 is applied differently when used within 780–788 and when used with 780–788 numbers added to other numbers in the Classification. Within 780, 026 is used only for treatises about scores and recordings. The Classification does not distinguish among scores, recordings, and treatises about the music. A library using the DDC has to make the distinction either by applying the optional provision or by some other notational device if it wishes to separate the material on music. When used with numbers from 780–788 added to other numbers in the Classification, 026 is used for scores and recordings and treatises about them. This distinction is made in order to separate scores, recordings, and treatises about them from treatises about the music. For example:

Number	Used for
787.2	A treatise on violin music, AND
787.2	Violin scores, AND
787.2	Recordings of violin music
787.2026	A treatise on violin scores
BUT	
016.7872	A bibliography of treatises on violin music
016.7872026	A bibliography of violin scores, AND
016.7872026	A bibliography of treatises on violin scores, AND
016.7872026	A discography of recordings of violin music.

Unlike Edition 11, Edition 12 makes no distinction between the music of a place and music in a place, e.g., Parisian opera and the opera in Paris are both classed in 782.10944, Viennese music and music played in Vienna are both 780.9436.

782–783 Voices and vocal music

The primary characteristic of arrangement in Edition 11 was that of *character*. That is, vocal music was either dramatic (782) or nondramatic (783 and 784); nondramatic was either sacred (783) or secular (784). The distinctions are maintained in Edition 12: Vocal music is either dramatic (782.1) or nondramatic (782.2–.4); nondramatic is either sacred (782.2–.3) or secular (782.4). There similarity between the two editions ceases.

In vocal music 782–783 whether an item is a score, a treatise, or a recording determines how the work is to be classed. The following flowchart is offered as an aid in determining the correct section of vocal music.

Flow chart for vocal music

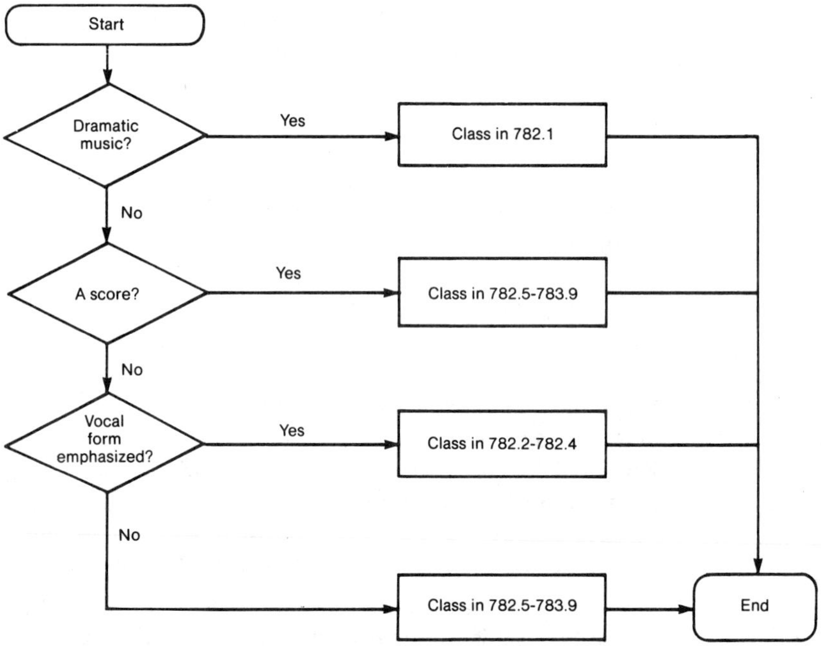

Examples (from applying the flow chart):

Soprano arias from opera [scores]	782.1
Soprano airs not from opera [scores]	783.6
Sacred songs by sopranos [recordings]	782.25
Women's soprano voice [treatise]	783.6

Vocal scores

When dealing with scores, kind of voice, and size of vocal ensemble must be considered. The distinction between 782.5–.9 and 783 is made upon the number of voices per part. That is, in 782.5–.9 go works that treat music having several voices per part (what is usually meant by choral music). In 783 go works that treat music having one voice per part (part songs and solos). The citation order for scores and parts of nondramatic vocal music is:

Size of vocal ensemble (including solos)

Type of voice, e.g., male, high, soprano, child's

Vocal forms

784–788 Instruments and their music

Instruments and their music are allotted the span 784–788, which proceeds from orchestral ensembles (more than one instrument to a part) through chamber music (only one instrument per part) to single instruments.

789 Composers and traditions of music

The optional number 789 may be used for both composers and traditions of music. The citation orders and instructions provided in 780–788 are applicable here when the option is followed.

780.26 **Treatises on music scores, recordings, texts**

Use this subdivision for texts only for building other numbers; never use it by itself. In most instances it will be used in 782–783, e.g., plots of operas 782.1026, lyrics of songs 782.42026.

780.89 vs. 781.62 **Music with respect to specific racial, ethnic, national groups vs. Folk music**

Works discussing a racial, ethnic, or national group in relation to music in general are classed in 780.89, e.g., a work about Afro-American composers, opera singers, and jazz conductors. Works discussing music indigenous to the group, e.g., Afro-American music, is classed in 781.62. If in doubt, class in 781.62.

781.62009 vs. 781.62 **Historical, geographic, persons treatment [of folk music] vs. Folk music**

The folk music of an area is usually the folk music of the racial, ethnic, or national group living in that area. Thus, 781.62 is usually used instead of 781.620093–.620099. 781.62 is used both for groups that predominate in an area and for groups that predominate in an area and for groups that do not, and it is used for national groups that may include multiple ethnic groups, e.g., people of the United States. However, when there is no one specific ethnic group, 781.620093–.620099 is used. For example, folk music of Germany is classed in 781.62, while folk music of Europe is classed in 781.620094.

790 Recreational and performing arts

The original heading for 790 was Amusements. There are two ways of being amused: One can be entertained by others (791 and 792) or one can amuse oneself (793–799). The settings where one can be amused are two: indoors (793–795) and outdoors (796–799). As Dewey made the first number of each span the general number for the activity (i.e., 791, 793, 796), the classifier can usually expect to find in these numbers a broader spectrum of forms of entertainment or amusement.

During the past century participatory amusements have become entertainments as well. Where once golfers were accompanied by only a few individuals who wished to witness this novel recreation, now millions watch them in person or on television. The same is true of most sports. And some outdoor amusements, such as American football, are now played indoors occasionally. Consequently, technology and social values have so altered over the past century that while the location of a subject within the 790s is predictable and reasonable with respect to the original structure of the class, it is neither predictable nor reasonable in the light of modern practices and concepts.

791.092 Persons [associated with public performances]

Class the biography of a performer with the activity with which the person's career is chiefly identified, e.g., the biography of an opera singer 782.1092. If the person's career involves more than one kind of public performance with no particular predominance, class the biography with the activity that comes first in the following table of precedence:

music	780
dancing	792.8
stage	792
motion pictures	791.43
television	791.45
radio	791.44

For example, class the biography of a stage actor who has also done considerable work in television in 792. Activities listed in the table above take precedence over all other other activities listed in 791.

791.43 and 791.44, 791.45, 792.9 Motion pictures [and] Radio [and] Television [and] Stage productions

The text of a play is classed in the appropriate number in literature, e.g., the text of Thornton Wilder's *Our Town* 812. A production script is classed in either 791 or 792, e.g., the production script for a staged production of *Our Town* 792.9. A production script is distinguished from a literary text in that it contains a variety of directions, e.g., where the furniture is to be placed, where the actors are to stand.

A production recorded in a different medium than the original production is classed with the recording, not with the production. For example, a staged opera recorded for television would class with television in 791.45, not with staged opera in 792.5.

792.5 vs. 782.1 [Stage presentations of] Opera vs. [Musical aspects of] Dramatic vocal forms Operas

Class in 782.1 works that discuss dramatic vocal forms as a type of vocal music, including such topics as tempos, plots, singers, conducting. Class in 792.5 works that discuss dramatic vocal forms as a type of stage presentation, including such topics as costumes, sets, direction. Works about an opera house and its productions are classed in 792.509, e.g., a history of La Scala, Milan 792.50945. If in doubt, class in 782.1.

792.8 vs. 793.3 **Ballet and modern dance vs. Social, folk, national dancing**

A social, folk, or national dance can be given in the theater, just as a theatrical dance can become a social dance. A dance is classed in either 792.8 or 793.3 depending upon the focus of the work. For example, the waltz is usually treated as a ballroom dance and is classed in 793.3; but waltzes as an integral part of Balanchine's *Vienna Waltzes,* a ballet, are classed in 792.8.

800 Literature (Belles-lettres) and rhetoric

In the following discussion, whenever application of principles to various literatures is being discussed, notation from Table 3 is mentioned. For example, "T3—1" is used to discuss poetry in specific literatures rather than "811, 841, etc."

Choice between literature and nonliterary subject

The aims of literature, according to Horace, are twofold: to teach and delight. The Dewey Decimal Classification holds to this precept. Works of the imagination intended to delight are classed in 800, but works that are essentially informational are classed according to subject in other parts of the schedule. The discipline of literature is restricted to: (1) works of the imagination that are written in the various literary forms, e.g., fiction, poetry; (2) literary criticism and description; (3) literary history and biography. The exclusion of informational works from the realm of belles-lettres holds regardless of the literary form of a work. Jonathan Swift's *The Drapier's Letters*, therefore, is not classed as a collection of the author's letters, rather as a work on monetary policy in 332.4.

Essays, speeches, letters, and diaries are commonly used for nonliterary purposes. If in doubt whether a work in one of these forms should be classed as literature in 800 or with a subject elsewhere in the schedule, class with the subject.

The nonfiction novel is a problem for classifiers. This kind of novel uses the techniques of fiction writing to tell the story of actual people and actual events. Class an account of a true event or series of events using the names of the people involved, not inventing characters or distorting facts to enhance an intended artistic effect, not going beyond the information available to the author from investigation and interviews, in the discipline appropriate to the facts described. Truman Capote's *In Cold Blood*, a true account of a multiple murder, has not been assigned a fiction number, but is classed in 364.1, the criminology number for murder. If, however, the author goes beyond what he learned from investigation and interviews in describing conversations, feelings, thoughts, or states of mind of the people he is writing about, then he is treating them as fictional persons, and the work should be classed as fiction, e.g., Norman Mailer's *The Executioner's Song* 813. In case of doubt, class as fiction.

Other kinds of fiction, and poetry and drama are sometimes used as vehicles for conveying factual information. Biographies have been written in verse, and fiction has been employed to teach the fundamentals of mathematics. Prefer 800 for poetry, drama, and fiction unless the form is purely incidental to the explanation of a specific subject, e.g., Harvey's *Circulation of the Blood* (written in Latin verse) 612.1, not 871.

An exception to the general rule is made for certain ancient works that have long been classed as literature regardless of the content of the work. For example, Hesiod's *Works and Days* is classed in 881, not 631, even though it deals with practical agriculture. These ancient works continue to be classed as literature, but new works whose major purpose is to inform are classed with the subject treated.

A literary study of nonliterary works is classed in 809, e.g., the Bible as literature 809.

Language

Literature always involves the use of language, and language is the basic facet for building numbers in 800.

Class literary works by language, not by country of origin. A major exception to this rule is that works in English originating in countries of the Western Hemisphere are classed in 810, not in 820 with English literature from the Eastern Hemisphere and comprehensive works on English literature.

Class literary works in the language in which they were originally written. An English translation of a work originally written in Spanish is classed with Spanish literature in 860, not with English literature in 820.

Literature of two or more languages. Works treating literature of two or more languages are usually collections or works of criticism. If two languages are involved, class the work in the number coming first in 820–890, except class Greek and Latin in 880, not 870. If more than two languages are involved, class the work in the most specific number that will contain them all. For instance, class a work including English, German, and Dutch in 830 since these are all Germanic languages. Class a work involving English, French, and Russian in 808 for collections or 809 for criticism. If any one language is predominant, class with that language.

Literary form

The second facet to be applied in literature is form. In literature there are two basic modes of expression: poetry and prose. Drama, whether in poetry or prose, is classed with drama in T3—2. The epigram is classed with miscellaneous writings in T3—8, regardless of mode. Works in other forms are classed with poetry in T3—1 if written in verse. Only prose works are classed in T3—3 Fiction, T3—4 Essays, T3—5 Speeches, T3—6 Letters, and (except for verse epigrams) T3—8 Miscellaneous writings. Prose literature in T3—8 is used only for prose works in more than one literary form; prose works in a specific form are classed with the form.

Though satire and humor have the number T3—7 in the span for specific forms, they are neither form nor mode; rather, they are categories of writing marked in the case of satire by ridicule and derision, in the case of humor by a manner of expression that makes a point amusingly. Literary works in a particular form (T3—1-6 and T3—8) exhibiting satire and humor are classed with the form. A collection of works by an individual author in more than one form exhibiting satire and humor is classed in T3—8.

Literary criticism

As used here the term "literary criticism" includes textual criticism.

The chief rule to be observed in classing criticism is that it is always classed with the literature being criticized.

Criticism of a specific work is classed with the work, e.g., a critical analysis of Hemingway's *For Whom the Bell Tolls* is classed in 813, the same number as the work itself. Criticism of the work of an author in general is classed in the comprehensive number for the author in question, e.g., criticism of Hemingway 813.

809 and notation 09 and cognate numbers under specific forms of literature are used for criticism of all kinds of literature except the works of individual authors. Criticism of several literatures as a whole is classed in 809, criticism of fiction from several literatures in 809.3. Criticism of the literature of the United States in general is classed in 810.9, criticism of fiction of the United States in general in 813.009, criticism of early 20th-century American fiction in 813.

Class criticism of literature in a specific form from more than one literature in 809.1-.7. Class in 801 the theory and technique of literary criticism. Class in these numbers also critical works in which the emphasis is on the various forms of literature as such, not on the various authors and literatures that may be used as examples. If in doubt between 801 and 809.1–.7, prefer 809.1–.7.

Appreciation of literature is classed in the same manner as other criticism.

Criticism of criticism is classed with the criticism being criticized and hence with the original subject of criticism. Criticism of Hemingway is classed in 813. If a third person writes a criticism of the criticism of Hemingway, this also is classed in 813.

Works about critics are treated in the same manner as works about other authors, i.e., the critic is classed with the kind of literature that he chiefly criticizes. Thus, a man who devoted the major part of his life to criticizing the works of Hemingway is classed in 813. A critic of Spanish literature is classed in 860.9.

It should be noted that criticism and critics are classed with the language of the literature they are criticizing, not with the language in which the criticism is written. For example, a French critic writing in French but criticizing American literature is classed in 810.9.

Adaptations

An adaptation may alter the form of a work or modify the content to such an extent in language, scope, or level of presentation that it can no longer be considered a version of the original. An adaptation is classed in the number appropriate to the adaptation, e.g., Lamb's *Tales from Shakespeare* 823. *For translations, see 800: Language.*

Note, however, that a prose translation of poetry (which is merely a change in mode) is not treated as an adaptation, e.g., Dante's *Divine Comedy* translated into German prose 851.

Excerpts

Treat a collection of excerpts as a collection. However, if the collection is meant to serve as a model for studying another discipline, class with the discipline illustrated. For instance, class in 307 a collection meant to explain what a community is.

800 vs. 398.2 Literature (Belles-lettres) and rhetoric vs. Folk literature

Folk literature consists of brief works in the oral tradition and is classed in 398.2. Whatever literary individuality the folk literature may once have had has been lost to the anonymity that the passage of time brings. Anonymous classics, however, are not considered to be folk literature. Despite the fact that their authorship is unknown, such works have a recognized literary merit, are almost always lengthy, and form a part of the literary canon. Therefore, they are classed in 800, e.g., *Chanson de Roland* 841, *Cantar de mio Cid* 861, *Kalevala* 894.

Some legendary or historical events or themes, such as the search for the Holy Grail or the battle of Roland with the Saracens, appear as the basis for original works in many literatures, periods, and forms, the medieval works involving them often being anonymous. Although the theme rather than the literature is the binding thread, what is read is a literary work. Consequently, class each retelling of the event or theme with the literature, form, and period in which it was written, e.g., Mary Stewart's Merlin trilogy 823. Class works about a specific theme treated in several literatures in 809.

If in doubt, prefer 800.

800 vs. 591, 636, 398.24 **Literature (Belles-lettres) and rhetoric vs. Zoology vs. Animal husbandry vs. Tales and lore of plants and animals**

Works about animals intended to contribute to some discipline other than literature are classed in the relevant discipline. Class narratives about animals in which the author's emphasis is on the habits and behavior of the animal in 591, on the care and training of the animal in 636. Class folk literature about animals in 398.24.

Literary accounts of animals are classed with the appropriate form in literature, e.g., poetry. Such accounts may be either fictional or true. A book about animals is certainly fiction if it contains conversations or thoughts of animals. Literary accounts of actual animals are often in the form of anecdotes or personal reminiscences. Such accounts are usually accommodated in T3—8 Miscellaneous writings.

800 vs. 741.6 **Literature (Belles-lettres) and rhetoric vs. Graphic design, illustration, commercial art**

Class illustration in general in 741.6. Class a specific type of illustration with the art form represented if the type is emphasized, e.g., etchings. If the illustrations merely accompany or enhance the literary text, class with the text in literature.

808 **Rhetoric and collections of literary texts from more than one literature**

Readers used in the study of composition are classed here. Readers limited to a particular literary form are classed in the rhetoric number for the form, e.g., short stories 808.3. Academic readers in a subject are classed with the subject.

808.001–.7 vs. 070.5 **[Rhetoric] vs. Publishing**

Three elements combine to produce the finished piece of writing: composition, preparation of the manuscript, and publishing:

1. Composition

   General 808

   How to write for newspapers 808

   How to write about law 808

   How to write plays 808.2

2. Preparation of the manuscript

   General 808

   For newspapers 808

   For works about law 808

   For plays 808.2

3. Publishing 070.5

   Class in 070.5 works limited to securing agents, submitting manuscripts, the relations of authors and publishers.

Works combining (2) and (3) are classed in the numbers for preparation of the manuscript (808, etc.) unless heavily weighted toward the publishing end:

How to make money in free-lance writing 808

Where to market your manuscript 070.5

808.1 vs. 414, T4—1 **Rhetoric of poetry vs. Phonology [and] Writing systems and phonology of the standard form of the language**

Because many studies of prosody are concerned with how to write poetry, general studies of literary prosody are classed in 808.1. However, works on the prosody of a specific literature are classed as criticism of the literature, e.g., a study of the use of language by American poets 811.009, a study of the prose rhythms of a later-19th-century French essayist 844.

Prosodic studies of a particular language as a whole from the linguist's viewpoint are classed with intonation for the specific language, using notation 1 from Table 4, e.g., 451 for prosodic studies of the Italian language. Linguistic studies of prosody across several languages and from the linguist's viewpoint are classed in 414.

900 Geography, history, and auxiliary disciplines

History is a record of events, their causes and effects, and of the contemporary conditions that clarify and enrich these events. When a work is the story of events that have transpired or an account of the conditions that have prevailed in a particular place or region, it is classed in 900. When it is the history of a specific subject, it is classed in the appropriate discipline, e.g., a history of political developments (such as internal developments in government) without respect to their effect upon the larger society and place where they occur 320.9; of economic events in France 330.944; of warfare 355.0209.

Political history is a strong component of history because it affects the whole of a particular society. But the history of political developments as they affect the internal activity of parties or other political groups is classed in 320.9 or in the 324 numbers for parties, campaigns, and election history.

History includes the present (situation and conditions), but not the future (projected events). Class projected events at 303.4.

Note that position on the map rather than political affiliation usually determines the number assigned to the history or the geography of a particular place, for while political affiliation may change, position on the earth's surface does not.

Historical events vs. nonhistorical events

Depending upon their impact, specific events are classed either in 900 or in specific disciplines in 001–899. Events that are important enough to affect the general social life and history of the place are classed with the history of the place regardless of any discipline involved. For example, the sinking of the Lusitania is classed in 940.4, the assassination of Abraham Lincoln in 973.7092, the San Francisco earthquake in 979.4.

Other specific events are classed with the history of the discipline to which they relate. For example, the history of a crime is classed in 364, e.g., the Whitechapel murders committed by Jack the Ripper 364.1. A sporting accident is classed in 796–799, e.g., a fatal accident during an automobile race 796.7.

In applying the above, the classifier should take into account the author's purpose or point of view. For instance, a work about the assassination of John F. Kennedy that is focused on the modus operandi of the crime, the detective work involved in solving it, or both, is classed in 364.1, not in 973.922092.

Works about events are more apt to emphasize social aspects than technological aspects and are usually classed in 300 rather than 600. If safety factors are stressed, the work is classed in 363, not with any other discipline involved. For example, a study of the wreck of the Andrea Doria to determine what the causes of the accident were, what preventive measures might be mandated as a result of the incident, is classed at 363.12.

Collected accounts of events are treated in the same manner, provided that they all pertain to one discipline, e.g., scientific travel 508. Class collected events without such focus in 904.

910 vs. 909, 930–990 **Geography and travel vs. World history [and] History of ancient world; of specific continents, countries, localities**

If a work deals with geography and civilization or travel and civilization, class it in 909 or 930–990; however, if the treatment of geography or travel is predominant, class the work in 910. If in doubt, prefer 909 or 930–990.

If the work deals with the description of the physical earth only, class it in 910 or in 913–919.

913–919 **Geography of and travel in ancient world and specific continents, countries, localities in modern world; extraterrestrial worlds**

Historic sites and buildings

Except as discussed below, class here works describing historic sites and buildings (and parts thereof) designed for the use of visitors to the sites whether or not the works are designated specifically as guides. For example, a contemporary guide to the historic houses of England is classed in 914.2.

Class historic buildings that have become museums or monuments in one of the following ways:

1. If the museum or monument is associated with the life of an individual, class with the biography number for that person, e.g., the home of Thomas Wolfe in Asheville, North Carolina 813.

2. If the museum or monument is associated with the history of a place, class with the appropriate number in 930–990, using notation 074 from Table 1 if applicable, e.g., a museum of Canadian history 971.0074.

3. If the building is still in use for a specific purpose, class with the purpose, e.g., a guide to the New York Stock Exchange building 332.64. Buildings for religious and related purposes do not follow this rule but are classed in 726.

Class histories of historical buildings and houses in 930–990, architecture in 720, interior decoration in 747.

Add table

The following flow chart is offered as an aid to building numbers and as a supplement to the detailed directions at 913–919.

Flow chart for geography and travel

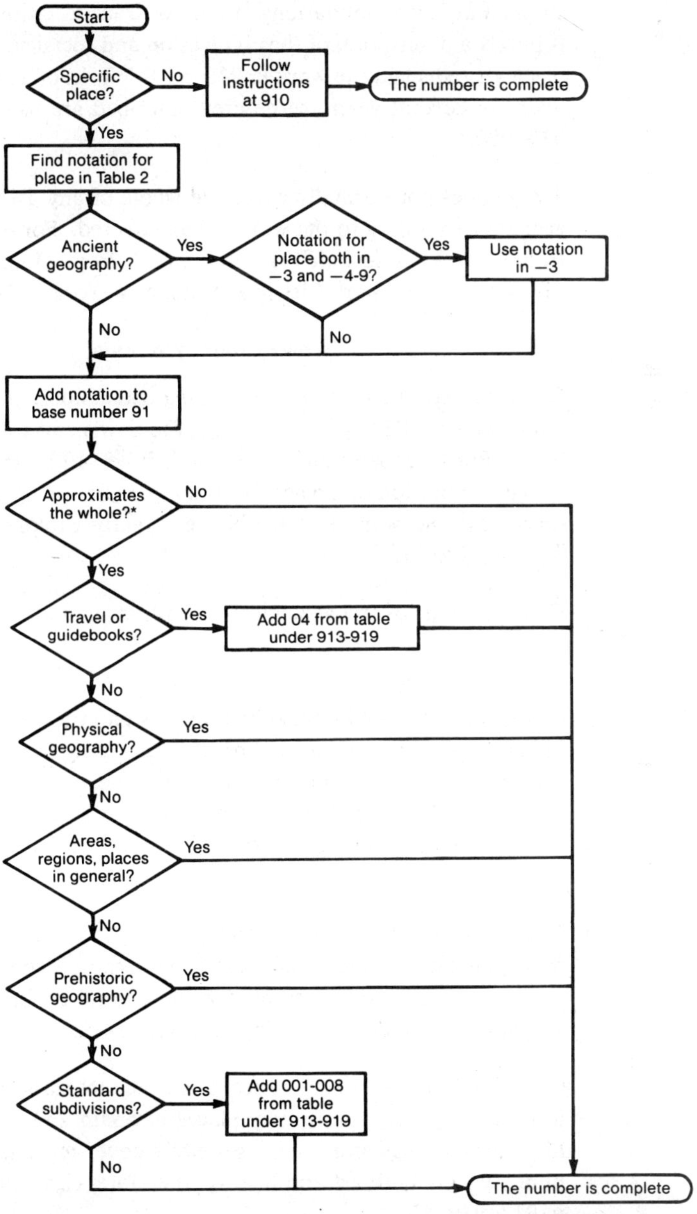

*See also "Approximates the whole" section of Manual notes on Table 1

04 Travel

Accounts of travel should emphasize events of the trip, places stopped at, accommodations, modes of transportation. If the work is purely a description of the civilization and social conditions of the place visited, class the work in 930–990. Works of a person who has lived for several years in the area described are usually classed in 930–990.

Travel does not normally cover the whole of any given area. Class accounts according to the widest span covered. For example, travel from New York to San Francisco 917.3, from Marseilles to Paris 914.4, from New York City to Buffalo, New York 917.47.

Discovery and exploration

Class in 913–919 works describing excursions into previously unknown or little known areas, e.g., the Lewis and Clark expedition 917.8, Byrd's expedition to the South Pole 919.8. However, if the initial exploration of a place forms an important part of its early history, class the work in 930–990, e.g., early exploration of North America 970.01.

Class accounts of archaeological expeditions in 930.1.

Guidebooks

Guidebooks are books providing tourists and travelers with detailed information about the area through which they travel, telling them what to see, where to stay, and where to dine, e.g., guidebooks to the national parks of the United States 917.3. However, if lodging and dining are the only topics treated in the guidebook, class it in 647.94–.95.

Class contemporary guidebooks to ancient areas in 913, e.g., Pausanias' guide to Attica 913.8. Class modern guidebooks to ancient areas in the corresponding modern area numbers in 914–919, e.g., 1982 Fodor's guide to the ruins of Rome 914.5.

Guidebooks emphasizing a specific subject are classed with the subject, e.g., a guidebook to holy places in Spain 263. Guidebooks to historic buildings and houses generally cover more than one discipline, usually both art and history; therefore, class such guidebooks in 913–919.

Class a guide for persons moving to another country on a permanent basis in 940–990.

See also 913–919: Historic sites and buildings.

930–990 History of ancient world; of specific continents, countries, localities; of extraterrestrial worlds

Wars

In most instances, the history of a war is classed with the history of the country or region in which most of the fighting took place, e.g., the Vietnamese War 959.704, the Napoleonic wars 940.2. However, some wars are arbitrarily assigned to either the history of one of the principle participants or to the region where the war began. For example, the Spanish-American War is classed with United States history in 973.8. World War II is classed in European history (the area where the war began) at 940.53, and not in world history at 909.82.

Regardless of the area to which a war is assigned, specific battles or actions of a war are classed in the number for the war, not with the number of the place where the action occurred. For example, a battle occurring in the Philippines during the Spanish-American War is classed in 973.8, not 959.9; air raids on Tokyo in World War II 940.54, not 952.

There are two kinds of wartime history that are not classed in the war numbers (unless the area covered coincides with the area used for the war). Routine history of the everyday events of an area, even if during wartime, and the effect of military action on the everyday life and civilization of a place is classed with the history of the place, not with the war, e.g., the effect of Civil War military actions on Maryland 975.2, not 973.709752. These two kinds of history must be carefully distinguished from the participation of an area in the war because the area's participation in the war is classed with the war, e.g., Maryland's participation in the Civil War 973.709752, not 975.2. Usually, national histories covering a time of war will emphasize the country's participation and will be classed with the war; if there is no such emphasis, the history will be classed in the appropriate national history number. For example, British participation in World War II 940.53, history of Britain during George VI's reign 941.084.

See also 355.0092 vs. 930–990.

Occupied countries

The history of the occupation of a country during time of war is classed with the war, e.g., occupation of countries in World War II 940.53. Military administration of the government of an occupied country during or following the war is classed in 355.4. International law with respect to occupation is classed in 341.6.

Specific units in a war

The history of specific military units in a war is classed with the history of the particular war, e.g., military units in World War I 940.4.

Class comprehensive works on specific military units and military units in peacetime in 355.3 or cognate numbers in 355–359.

Personal narratives

The narrative of a person's experiences during time of war, if it does not focus on the war as such, is classed as biography and not in the number for the war. For example, an actor's personal experiences of performing in Scotland during 1940–1942 is classed in 792.092, not 940.53

Historic preservation

Class comprehensive works on historic preservation and lists of preservation projects to be undertaken in 363.6. However, if such a list is primarily devoted to inventorying or describing the sites, class the list in the appropriate number in 930–990, or, if primarily a description of buildings at the site, class in 720.

Class administrative annual reports of agencies promoting the preservation of historical sites in 351.85 and cognate numbers in 352–354.

Class historic preservation in an architectural context in 720.28 and cognate numbers in 721–729.

Add table

The following flow chart is offered as an aid to building numbers and as a supplement to the detailed instructions at 930–990.

Flow chart for history

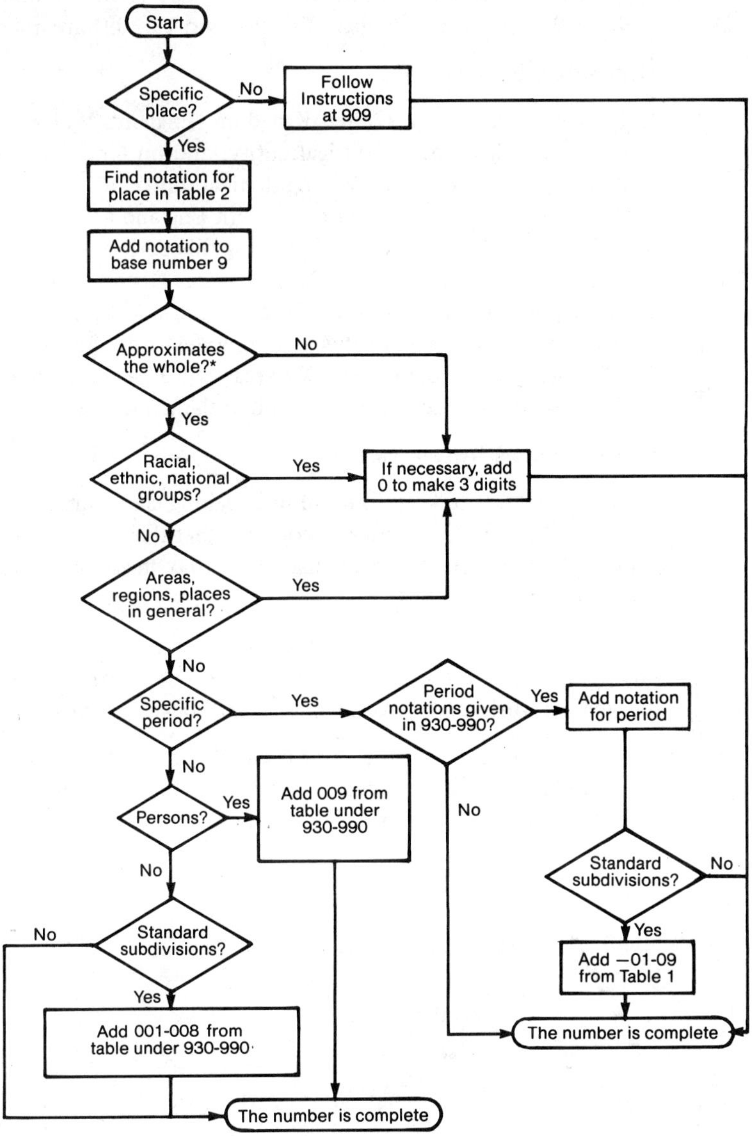

*See also "Approximates the whole" section of Manual notes on Table 1

01–09 Historical periods

When adding standard subdivisions to the historical periods, use notation 01–09 from Table 1, not 001–009 from the table under 930–990. However, numbers T1—089 and T1—091 are not used.

941 [History of the] British Isles

Class here works on the United Kingdom (England, Wales, Scotland, and Northern Ireland), a political entity, and on Great Britain (England, Wales, and Scotland), a geographical entity. Class in 942 only works dealing with England alone, or with England and Wales. Histories of the period since 1603 (or including this period) will seldom deal with England or England and Wales alone. Histories of the period before 1603 may deal with England or England and Wales alone. Books on the civilization of this area may deal with any combination. The following combinations of two areas will be classed in 941: England and Scotland, England and Ireland, Ireland and Wales.

970.004 North American native peoples

The principal fact to keep in mind in assigning class numbers to works of the various native American peoples is that they have moved in the course of time from place to place and that these places are often widely scattered.

Therefore, in general, a work on specific peoples is classed in 970.004, no attempt being made to assign a more specific location. For example, general works on Cherokees class in 970.004.

If, however, the focus of the work is clearly on the native peoples in a specific place, use the number for the place. For example, native peoples of Canada, 971, Cherokees in North Carolina 975.6.

Policies and Procedures of the Library of Congress Decimal Classification Division

Segmentation in Centrally Cataloged Records

One aid to reduction of the full DDC number is the segmentation provided in DDC numbers by centralized cataloging services, such as the Decimal Classification Division of the Library of Congress, the British Library, and the National Library of Canada. The segmentation is indicated by a prime mark (′), a slash mark (/), or other comparable indicators.

The segmentation provided by the Decimal Classification Division is applied according to two different principles. A segmentation mark can indicate the end of an abridged number (as found in the Abridged Edition of the DDC), or the beginning of a standard subdivision. Thus, a DDC number can consist of one, two, or three segments. For example:

324.6′23′092 — A biography of Susan B. Anthony

324.6 — Election systems and procedures; suffrage (the number found in the Abridged Edition)

23 — Women's suffrage (the remainder of the number from the Schedules of the Unabridged Edition)

092 — Persons (from Unabridged Table 1)

323′.025′73 — Directory of civil rights leaders and organizations in the United States

323 — Civil and political rights (the number found in the Abridged Edition)

.025 — Directories (applicable standard subdivision from Abridged Table 1)

73 — United States (area notation from Table 2 that can be added to the directories number [025] in Unabridged Table 1)

Bracketed DDC Numbers on LC Bibliographic Records

Libraries using cataloging data provided by the Library of Congress will notice that there are sometimes two or more DDC numbers or non-numeric notation in the DDC field. On LC printed cards, all but the first DDC number is given in brackets ([ ]). The following examples (omitting segmentation marks described above) explain the practices of the Decimal Classification Division with respect to bracketed DDC numbers:

Nonjuvenile Works

A. For works belonging to a monographic series classed as a set but analyzed in full or in part according to the decisions of the Subject Cataloging Division of the Library of Congress, the Decimal Classification Division assigns two numbers:

081 s	the number for the item if the series is kept together at one class number
[327.7]	the number for the specific item in the series

B. For biography and works primarily biographical, the Division assigns a number and the letter [B]:

780.92	the number if the item is added to the classified collection
[B]	the letter if the item is added to the biography collection

C. Brackets for a monograph in a series and for biography may both be present:

780.92 s	the number for the series
[787.66092] [B]	the number and the letter for a monograph in a series

D. For law, the Division makes the only exception to its practice of eschewing optional numbers. It supplies both the preferred number and the Option B number:

345.7308	the preferred number
[347.3058]	the Option B number

E. When works on law belong to analyzed monographic sets, four numbers are supplied. On Library of Congress catalog cards, they are usually printed two by two, with the DDC preferred numbers on the top line and the optional numbers on the bottom line:

343.41052 s	[343.410523]
344.10352 s	[344.103523]

Juvenile Works

For juvenile works, bracketed numbers and alphabetical codes (other than [B]) are assigned by the Children's Literature Section of the Library of Congress.

A. Easy books

1. Easy books without a clearly defined topic in a recognized field of study are assigned [E], e.g., Tommy takes his first trip to the store [E].
2. Easy books with a discernible topic in a recognized field of study are assigned both an [E] and a DDC number, e.g., Tommy takes his first trip to London 914.2 [E].
3. Easy fiction, for children K-3 (through eight years old) is assigned [E].

B. Fiction intended for grades 4–6, or ages 9–11, is assigned [Fic]. Adult fiction that has been deemed appropriate for a juvenile and classes of children's literature that have a continuing adult audience will be assigned [Fic] as well as a class number, e.g., *Treasure Island* 823.8 [Fic].

C. Biography

1. Without subject or disciplinary associations

One person	[92]
Several persons	[920]

2. With subject or disciplinary association

One person	509.2	[B]	[92]
Several persons	509.22	[B]	[920]

Classifying Children's Books in the DCD

The Decimal Classification Division classifies most children's literature processed by the Children's Literature Section of the Library of Congress, except that works designated by [Fic] or [E] are normally sent on without further classification.

Relocations and Reductions

Here are brought together in two lists all the relocations and reductions since Edition 11, except the 780 Music schedule—which has been completely revised.

The column headed *Edition 11* indicates in numerical order each number in that edition from which a topic or group of topics has been shifted; the column headed *Edition 12* indicates each corresponding number in the present edition to which those topics or groups of topics have been shifted. If two or more topics have been shifted from one number to two or more numbers, each separate shift is shown.

Numbers in the *Edition 11* column printed in square brackets are no longer in use; those not printed in brackets have lost part of their meaning through relocation or reduction, but still retain some of their original meaning.

Relocations

In a relocation one or more topics are shifted to a number differing from the old in respects other than length. If the relocation is partial, the original number remains valid; but if it is total, the original number is no longer used. Relocations are described and explained in the Introduction.

Relocations that have appeared previously in *Dewey Decimal Classification Additions, Notes and Decisions* volume 4 are indicated by * next to the Edition 11 number. Relocations that eliminate dual provision for the same topic or topics are indicated by † next to the Edition 11 number.

"Scatter" means that a topic has been split and relocated to so many numbers that it is not feasible to name them all.

For example, part of what was in 011 has been relocated to 016.05; all that was in 001[.54] has been relocated to 652; all that was in 001[.53] has been relocated, some to 006.3 and some to 511.3 to eliminate dual provision.

An indented number is an element of an add table. The number or span under which it is indented shows the location of the add table. For example, the 003 under 913–919 indicates that the 003 is an element of the add table at 913–919.

For details of the specific relocated topics the classifier should consult the appropriate entries in the tables and schedules.

Edition 11	*Edition 12*	*Edition 11*	*Edition 12*
T1—028†	T1—078	T2—66	T2—671
T1—029	T1—05	[T2—681]	T2—688
T1—029†	332.6	T2—755 †	T2—163
T1—076†	T1—078	T2—769	T2—77
T2—431	T2—432	T2—93	T2—95
T2—563	T2—496 1	T3—3†	741.5
T2—629	T2—625	T4—2	T4—01

†Eliminates dual provision

Edition 11	*Edition 12*	*Edition 11*	*Edition 12*
000–999†	016	[332.024 01–.024 07]	332.024 001–.024 007
001.4	003	[332.024 09]	332.024 009
[001.5]	302.2	[332.5]	332.4
[001.53]	003	332.64	332.63
[001.53]	006.3	333.1	333.7
[001.53]†	511.3	333.1†	333.73
[001.54]	652	333.3†	333.7
[001.6]	004	333.5*†	333.33
001.9†	030	338.2*†	333.8
001.9*	573.3	338.4	333.79
011	016.05	338.6†	338.1–.4
017–019	015	348	340
017–019	016.05	351	T1—025
025.1	070.5	351†	324.025
069	T1—074	351.72*	351.003–.9
069	T1—075	355.1	331.25
069	070.5	355.1†	362.86
069	659.2	355.3†	355.6
069	686.2	355.4†	363.3
070.502 9†	015	361	362.9
153.4	155.2	362–363†	363.1
[157]†	616.89	362.82	Scattered within 362–363
174	179	363.6	333.79
197	198	364.4	363.2
207	268	372.8	372.3
232†	236	[380.3]	384
233	231.7	[380.5]	388
248.4	248.8	384†	363.1
259†	253.7	[384.4]	384.1
265	264	384.6	384.3
267	287.9	387.5	387.2
[288]	289.1	[391.8]	Scattered within 392–394
291.07	291.7	401	306.4
296.06	296.6	409†	417
296.07	296.6	412	401
302.2	306.4	417	411
304.6†	363.9	513	650.01
305	302.230 8	519.4	003
306†	305	519.4	004.01
306	305.8	521	520.1
306.7	306.85	521	523
306.77	306.877	525†	551.47
[312]†	304.6	[526.8]	526.022
[312]	Scattered	531†	621.8
320.092	320.5	535	502.8
[320.2]	320.01	535.5†	621.36
320.4	320.8	535.8†	621.36
323.42	323.1	537.5†	621.381
323.5†	324.6	537.6†	621.31
324.24–.29	324.209		
324.9*	324.609		
327.3–.9	327.123–.129		

*Previously published
†Eliminates dual provision

Edition 11	*Edition 12*	*Edition 11*	*Edition 12*
538†	621.34	658.3	651.306 8
547.8	547.7	658.5†	624.068
547.8†	668.4	658.8†	T1—068
547.8†	677	693.8	628.9
550.1†	551.9	704.9†	709.04
551.01†	551.9	722	720.9
551.69	551.65	722	720.95
553.6†	631.4	722	723
572*	305.8	722	724
575.2	575.1	722†	720.97
[604.6]†	628.4	722†	720.98
[606.8]†	658	724†	720.942
616.07	616.97	724†	720.946
[620.7]	620.001	729†	721
620.8†	628	729†	726
621.31	621.48	732	730.9
621.37†	681	732	730.95
621.380 28	621.382	732	734
621.381	621.389	732	735
[621.381 9]	621.39	741.092	741.5—.7
621.382 †	621.383	741.9*	741.5—.7
621.384 1	621.384 5	[750.28]	751
[621.384 6]	621.384 5	[756]	758
621.389	621.382	769.5†	741.6
621.39	333.79	[770.28]†	771
621.39*	621.319	782.1	792.5
621.39*	621.402	791.43	070.1
621.6	621.5	791.44†	070.1
621.9	681	791.44†	070.4
622*†	628.1	791.45†	070.1
627†	628.1	791.45†	070.4
628.1†	333.91	793.3	792.7
628.1	628.4	793.3	792.8
628.5	628.4	796.4†	613.7
629.8†	511	796.41†	613.7
630.2†	631.5	796.41	796.44
631	630.2	797.1*	797.3
631.2†	633.1	808.81—.87	808.81—.87
631.2†	633.2	[01—08]	001—008
631.3†	631.5	[09]	009
631.7†	631.5	909	306.09
633	630.2	912.09	912.3—.9
633	631	913—919	913—919
633	632	[01—02]	001—002
633†	635	[03]	003
636.001	636.08	[05—07]	005—007
641.6	641.5	930—990	306.09
645†	747	958.1†	939
646	648	[968.1]	968.8
649†	248.8	970.004*	971—979
649†	291.4	993†	995
651.7	808	[993.101—.103]	993.01—.03

*Previously published
†Eliminates dual provision

Reductions

A reduction is the result of shifting one or more topics to a number shorter than the old number but otherwise not differing from it. If all topics in a given number are thus shifted, the number is no longer valid.

In addition, 808.59 has been dropped because its content in Edition 11 was meaningless within the context.

Reductions that have appeared previously in *Dewey Decimal Classification Additions, Notes and Decisions* volume 4 are indicated by * next to the Edition 11 number.

"Main number" means that the provision for the topic within a table has been discontinued to the schedule numbers to which the table number would previously have been added.

An indented number is an element of an add table. The number span under which it is indented shows the location of the add table.

For example, 332[.9] has been discontinued and all of its content moved up to the broader number 332, while only part of the content of 333.3 has been moved up to 333. Part of the content of 03, an element of the add table at 354.3–.9, has been discontinued from the add table to the schedule numbers to which the table number would previously have been added.

For details of the specific reduced topics the classifier should consult the appropriate entries in the tables and schedules.

Edition 11	*Edition 12*	*Edition 11*	*Edition 12*
T1—02	Main number	281.909	281.9
T1—028	Main number	282.09	282
T2—931	T2—93	283.09	283
T3—08	Main number	284.109	284.1
T3—1-8		285.709	285.7
8	Main number	285.809	285.8
[069.1–.5]	069	286.609	286.6
152.8	152	286.709	286.7
[159]*	150	289.109	289.1
[204.01–.09]	204	289.309	289.3
[207.4–.6]	207	289.409	289.4
[219]	210	289.509	289.5
[222.01–.09]	222	289.609	289.6
[223.01–.09]	223	289.709	289.7
[224.01–.09]	224	291.7	291
[226.01–.09]	226	293.06	293
[227.01–.09]	227	293.07	293
[228.01–.09]	228	294.306	294.3
[253.7]	253	294.307	294.3
[254.3–.4]	254	294.406	294.4
[261.1]	261	294.407	294.4
[268.068]	268	294.506	294.5

*Previously published

Edition 11	*Edition 12*
294.507	294.5
294.606	294.6
294.607	294.6
295.06	295
295.07	295
297.06	297
297.07	297
305.5	305
[320.2]	320
[320.901−.909]	320.9
[321.03−.08]	321
[321.1−.3]	321
321.5	321
[321.6]	321
323.1	323
323.4	323
[332.024 08]	332.024
[332.5]	332
[332.9]	332
333.3	333
335.5	335
351.003	351
354.3−.9	354.3−.9
03	Main number
[382.1−.9]	382
499	490
[515.3−.9]	515
523	520
[523.02]	523
[526.8]	526
616.07	616
616.86	616.8
618.028	618
[620.7]	620
621.381 5	621.381
621.384 1	621.384
621.39*	621.3
623.7	623
[623.74]	623.7
629.202 8	629.2
631	630
639.091 62	639
[640.68]	640
641.3	641
646.202 8	646
[646.708]	646.7
659.2	659
[660.2]	660
[724.9]	724
728.3	728
738.2	738
[739.270 28]	739.27
[741.64−.68]	741.6
[743.028]	743
751.7	750
794.2	794
[808.59]	Without meaning
808.8	800
808.81−.87	808.81−.87
[09]	Main number
899	890
911.09	911
912.09	912
913–919	913–919
[09]	Main number
945.09	945
946.08	946
993.1	993

*Previously published

Comparative Table for 780 Music

As noted in the schedules, the development for 780 Music is new. The following list, arranged alphabetically by topic, shows the number changes from Edition 11 to Edition 12 for a substantial number of topics. Usually only numbers for comprehensive works are given; however, some numbers are combinations, e.g.:

Topic	*Edition 11*	*Edition 12*
Rock	780.42	781.66
songs	784.5	782.421 66

This indicates that the comprehensive works number for rock has been changed from 780.42 to 781.66, and also that the number for rock songs has been changed from 784.5 to 782.42166. The abbreviation *T1* in these lists means Table 1 Standard Subdivisions.

Topic	*Edition 19*	*Edition 20*
Accompaniment	781.6	781.47
Accordion	786.9	788.8
Anthems	783.4	782.2
Appreciation	780.1	781.1
Arrangement	781.6	781.3
Art music	780.43	781.6
songs	784.3	782.421 68
Bagpipe	788	788.4
Ballads	784.3	782.4
Ballet music	782.9	781.5
Band music	785.1	784.18
Bands	785.06	784
Banjo	787	787.8
Bassoon	788	788.5
Bells	789	786.8
Bluegrass	780.42	781.642
Blues	781	781.643
songs	784.5	782.421 64
Brass band	785.06	784.9
Brass instruments	788	788.9
Bugle	788	788.9
Cantatas	782.8	782.2
sacred	783.4	782.2
secular	782.8	782.4
Carillon	789	786.6
Carols	783.6	782.28
Castanets	789	786.8
Celesta	789	786.8
Cello	787	787.4
Chamber music	785.7	785
ensembles	785.06	785
Chamber orchestra	785.06	784.3
Chants	783.5	782.2
Anglican	783.5	782.32
Gregorian	783.5	782.32
Children's voices	784	782.7

Topic	*Edition 11*	*Edition 12*
Chimes	789	786.8
Choirs	784.1	782.506
sacred	783.8	782.5
Choral music	784.1	782.5
Christian sacred music	783	781.71
liturgical	783.2	782.32
Christmas music	783	781.723
carols	783.6	782.28
liturgical	783.2	782.2
Classical music	780.43	781.6
Clavichord	786.2	786.3
Composition	781.6	781.3
Concerti grossi	785.6	784.2
Concertina	786.9	788.8
Concerto	785.6	784.2
Concerts	T1—073	T1—078
Conducting	781.6	781.45
Cornet	788	788.9
Counterpoint	781.4	781.2
Country music	780.42	781.642
songs	784.5	782.421 64
Cymbals	789	786.8
Dance band	785.06	784.4
Dance music (Form)	781	784.18
orchestral	785.4	784.8
Dance orchestra	785.06	784.4
Double bass	787	787.5
Double-reed instruments	788	788.5
Dramatic music	782	781.5
incidental	782.8	781.5
vocal	782	782.1
Drum	789	786.9
Easter music	783	781.727
liturgical	783.2	782.2
Electronic instruments	789.9	786.7
organs	786.9	786.5
Electronic music	789.9	786.7
Embellishments	781.6	781.2
English horn	788	788.5
Ethnic music	781.7	781.62
Ethnomusicology	781.7	780.89
Film music	782.8	781.5
Flute	788	788.3
Folk music	781.7	781.62
songs	784.4	782.421 62
Forms of music	781	781.8
French horn	788	788.9
Fugue	781.4	784.18
Gregorian chants	783.5	782.32
Guitar	787.6	787.87
Harmonica (Mouth organ)	788	788.8
Harmony	781.3	781.2
Harp	787	787.9
Harpsichord	786.2	786.4

Topic	*Edition 11*	*Edition 12*
Horn	788	788.9
Hymns	783.9	782.27
Improvisation	781.6	781.3
Instrumental ensembles	785	784
Instruments	781.91	784.19
Jazz	781	781.65
band music	785.42	784.165
bands	785.06	784.165
orchestras	785.06	784.4
Librettos	781.9	782.002 6
Liturgical music	783.2	782.2
Lute	787	787.8
Madrigals	784.1	782.4
Mandolin	787	787.8
March	781	784.18
band music	785.1	784.8
Marching band	785.06	784.8
Mass	783.2	782.32
Melody	781.4	781.2
Men's voices	784	782.8
Military band	785.06	784.8
Motets	783.4	782.2
Mouth organ	788	788.8
Movie music	782.8	781.5
Music box	789	786.6
Musical forms	781	781.8
Musical plays	782.81	782.1
National songs	784.7	782.42
Nomenclature	781	780
Notations	781	780
Oboe	788	788.5
Operettas	782.81	782.1
Oratorios	782.8	782.23
sacred	783.3	782.23
secular	782.8	782.4
Orchestras	785.06	784.2
Organ	786.5–.8	786.5
Overtures	781	784.18
orchestra music	785.5	784.2
Part songs	784.1	783.1
Passions	783.3	782.23
Patriotic songs	784.7	782.42
Percussion		
bands	785.06	784.6
instruments	789	786.8
Performance techniques	781.6	781.4
Performances	T1—073	T1—078
Piano	786.2	786.2
Piccolo	788	788.3
Player piano	789	786.6
Plectral instruments	787	787.7
Popular Western music	780.42	781.64
songs	784.5	782.421 64

Topic	*Edition 11*	*Edition 12*
Program music		
orchestral	785.3	784.2
Radio music	782.8	781.5
Recitals	T1—073	T1—078
Recorder (Wind instrument)	788	788.3
Recording music	789.9	781.49
Recordings	789.9	780
treatises on	789.9	780.26
Reed instruments	788	788.4
organs	786.9	786.5
Rhythm (Musical element)	781.6	781.2
Rhythm band	785.06	784.6
Rock	780.42	781.66
songs	784.5	782.421 66
Sacred music	783	781.7
instrumental	783.1	784.17
vocal	783.2—.9	782.2
Saxophone	788	788.7
Scores	780.8	780
reading	781.6	781.4
treatises on	780.8	780.26
Serenades	781	784.18
orchestra music	785.3	784.2
Sonata	781	784.18
Songs	784.3	782.42
blues	784.5	782.421 64
country music	784.5	782.421 64
folk	784.4	782.421 62
for children	784.6	782.420 83
for home	784.6	782.42
for students	784.6	782.420 8
national	784.7	782.42
patriotic	784.7	782.42
popular (Western)	784.5	782.421 64
rock	784.5	782.421 66
sacred	783.6	782.25
secular	784.3	782.42
soul	784.5	782.421 64
Soul music	780.42	781.644
songs	784.5	782.421 64
Spirituals	783.6	782.25
String orchestras	785.06	784.7
Stringed instruments		
bowed	787	787
keyboard	786.1—.4	786
plectral	787	787.7
Students' songs	784.6	782.420 8
Suite	781	784.18
orchestra music	785.8	784.2
Symphony	781	784.18
orchestra music	785.1	784.2
Symphony orchestras	785.06	784.2
Television music	782.8	781.5
Triangle	789	786.8

Topic	*Edition 11*	*Edition 12*
Trombone	788	788.9
Trumpet	788	788.9
Tuba	788	788.9
Twelve-tone system	781.3	781.2
Ukulele	787	787.8
Viola	787	787.3
Violin	787.1	787.2
Violoncello	787	787.4
Vocal music	784	782
dramatic	782	782.1
sacred	783.2–.9	782.2
secular	784	782.4
Voice	784.9	783
Whistling	784.9	782.9
Wind band	785.06	784.8
Wind instruments		
brass	788	788.9
woodwind	788	788.2
Women's voices	784	782.6
Woodwind instruments	788	788.2
Xylophone	789	786.8
Zither	787	787.7

Equivalence Tables for 780 Music

The equivalence tables that follow lead in Table A from Edition 11 numbers to Edition 12 numbers for use by persons familiar with the music numbers from Edition 11, in Table B from Edition 12 numbers to Edition 11 numbers for classifiers whose libraries are remaining on Edition 11.

In most cases, the contents of an Edition 11 number will be assigned to the same Edition 12 number (and vice versa). If the topics are assigned to a different number, the topics will be listed separately in the Note column.

Table A

Edition 11	*Edition 12*	*Notes*
780.1	781.1	Music appreciation
780.42	781.63	
780.43	781.6	
780.7	781.4	Techniques for acquiring musical skills and learning a repertoire
780.73	780.78	
780.8	780	Music scores
780.8	780.26	Treatises on music scores
781	780	Nomenclature, Notation, System of terms
781	784.18	Sonata
781.3	781.2	
781.4	781.2	
781.4	784.18	Canon, Fugue
781.6	781.2	Embellishment, Meter, Rhythm
781.6	781.3	Arrangement, Composition, Improvisation
781.6	781.4	Performance
781.6	781.45	Conducting
781.6	781.46	Interpretation
781.6	781.47	Accompaniment
781.7	780.089	Music of racial, ethnic, national groups
781.7	781.62	Folk music
781.73–.79	780.93–.99	
781.9	782.002 6	Words to be sung or recited
781.91	784.19	
782	782.1	
782.8	781.5	Incidental dramatic music
782.8	782.2	Cantatas
782.8	782.23	Oratorios
782.8	782.4	Secular cantatas, Secular oratorios
782.81	782.1	
782.9	781.5	Ballet music
782.9	782.1	Masques
783	781.7	
783.1	784.17	
783.2	782.2	Liturgical forms
783.2	782.3	Services
783.3	782.23	
783.4	782.2	

Topic	*Edition 11*	*Edition 12*
783.5	782.3	Jewish chants
783.5	782.32	Ambrosian chant, Anglican chant, Gregorian chant
783.6	782.25	
783.6	782.28	Carols
783.8	782.5	
783.9	782.27	
784	782–783	
784.1	782.5	Choruses
784.1	783.1	Part songs
784.2	782.5	
784.3	782.42	
784.4	782.421 62	
784.5	782.421 64	
784.5	782.421 66	Rock songs
784.6	782.42	
784.7	782.42	Patriotic songs
784.7	782.420 89	Songs of ethnic and cultural groups
784.9	783	
785	784	
785.06	784.2	Symphony orchestra
785.06	784.3	Chamber orchestra
785.06	784.4	Dance orchestra, Salon orchestra
785.06	784.7	String orchestra
785.06	784.8	Wind band
785.06	784.9	Brass band
785.1	784	Band music
785.1	784.18	Symphony form
785.2	784.2	
785.3	781.5	Program music
785.3	784.18	Romantic music, Symphonic poems, Variations
785.4	784.18	Dance music
785.4	784.6	Music for rhythm and percussion bands
785.42	784.165	
785.5	784.18	
785.6	784.2	
785.7	785	
785.8	784.18	
786.1–.4	786.2–.4	
786.5–.8	786.5	
786.9	786.5	Electronic organ, Reed organ
786.9	788.8	Accordions, Concertinas
787.1	787.2	
787.6	787.87	
789	786.8	Percussion instruments
789	786.9	Drums
789.9	780	Recordings
789.9	780.26	Treatises on recordings
789.9	781.49	Recording music
789.9	786.7	Electronic instruments

Table B

Edition 12	*Edition 11*	*Notes*
780	780.8	Music scores
780	781.2	Nomenclature
780	789.9	Recordings
780.26	780.8	
780.26	789.9	Treatises on recordings
780.28	781	
780.78	780.73	
780.79	780	Financial support
780.89	781.7	
780.93–.99	781.73–.79	Music composed or improvised in specific countries or localities
781.1	780.1	Appreciation
781.2	781	
781.2	781.3	Harmony
781.2	781.4	Counterpoint, Melody
781.2	781.6	Embellishments, Meter, Rhythm
781.3	781.6	
781.4	780.7	Ear training, Eye training, Music reading
781.4	781.6	Performances
781.44–.48	781.6	
781.49	789.9	
781.5	781	
781.5	782.8	Incidental dramatic music
781.5	782.9	Ballet music
781.5	785.3	Program music
781.6	780.43	Art ("Classical") music
781.62	781.7	
781.63–.64	780.42	
781.65	781	
781.66	780.42	
781.7	783	
781.8	781	
782	784	
782.002 6	781.96	Words to be sung or recited
782.1	782	Dramatic music
782.1	782.81	Musical plays, Operettas, Singspiels
782.1	782.9	Masques
782.2	784	
782.2	783	Sacred vocal music
782.2	783.2	Liturgical music
782.2	783.4	Anthems, Cantatas, Motets
782.23	783.3	
782.25	783.6	
782.27	783.9	
782.28	783.6	
782.3	783	
782.32	783.2	
782.4	784	
782.4	782.8	Cantatas
782.4	784.1	Madrigals
782.4	784.3	Song cycles

Edition 12	*Edition 11*	*Notes*
782.42	784.3	
782.42	784.5	Popular songs
782.5–.9	784.1–.2	
783	784	
783	784.9	The voice
783.1	784.1	
784	785	
784.18	785	
784.18	781	Sonata
784.18	781.4	Canon, Fugue
784.18	785.1	Symphony
784.18	785.3	Cassations, Romantic music, Serenade, Symphonic poems, Theme and variations
784.18	785.4	Dance music
784.18	785.5	Overture
784.18	785.8	Suite
784.19	781.91	
784.2	785	
784.2	785.06	Orchestra as type of organization
784.2	785.2	Orchestra with incidental vocal parts
784.2	785.6	Concerto
784.3	785.06	
784.4	785.06	Type of organization
784.4	785.3	Music
784.6	785.06	Type of organization
784.6	785.43	Music
784.7	785.06	Type of organization
784.7	785.3	Music
784.8	785.06	
784.9	785.06	
785	785.06	Chamber music ensembles
785	785.7	Chamber music
786.2–.4	786.1–.4	
786.5	786.5–.8	
786.5	786.9	Electronic organ, Reed organ
786.6	789	
786.7	789.9	
786.8	789	
786.9	789	
787.2	787.1	
787.3–.7	787	
787.8	787	
787.87	787.6	
787.9	787	
788.2–.9	788	

Tables

Use of the Tables

These are auxiliary tables, and are used only in conjunction with the Schedules. In some instances the numbers from one table may be added to those of another table, but in all cases the numbers from one or a combination of tables are to be used only with appropriate numbers from the Schedules.

The dash preceding each number merely shows that the number never stands alone. The dash is omitted when the table number is added to a schedule number to make a complete class number.

Instructions in the use of a particular table precede it. Important supplemental instructions for Tables 1 and 3 are found in the Manual.

A number in square brackets [ ] is not currently in use.

A number in parentheses ( ) is an option to standard usage.

Table 1. Standard Subdivisions

The following notation is never used alone, but may be used as required with any number from the schedules, e.g., workbooks (—076 in this table) in arithmetic (513): 513.076. When adding to a number from the schedules, always insert a decimal point between the third and fourth digits of the complete number.

If at any given number there are special purpose subdivisions having a notation beginning with one 0, use 001–009 for standard subdivisions, e.g., 301–307 is used for sociology, therefore, use 300.1–300.9 for standard subdivisions of social sciences.

Unless other instructions are given, class works to which two or more standard subdivisions are applicable according to the following table of precedence, e.g., periodicals on education in a subject —07 (*not* —05):

Special topics	—04
Persons	—092
Auxiliary techniques and procedures; apparatus, equipment, materials	—028
Education and related topics (*except* —074, —075, —076)	—07
Management	—068
Philosophy and theory	—01
The subject as a profession, occupation, hobby	—023
Commercial miscellany	—029
History and description with respect to kinds of persons	—08
Treatment by specific continents, countries, localities; extraterrestrial worlds	—093-099
Treatment by areas, regions, places in general	—091
Museums, collections, exhibits Collecting	—074
Museum activities and services	—075
Review and exercise	—076
Miscellany (*except* —023, —028, —029)	—02
Organizations	—06
Dictionaries, encyclopedias, concordances	—03
Historical treatment (not limited by area)	—09
Serial publications	—05

See Manual at Table 1

SUMMARY

—01	**Philosophy and theory**
—02	**Miscellany**
—03	**Dictionaries, encyclopedias, concordances**
—04	**Special topics**
—05	**Serial publications**
—06	**Organizations and management**
—07	**Education and related topics**
—08	**History and description with respect to kinds of persons**
—09	**Historical, geographic, persons treatment**

—01 Philosophy and theory

Including computer modeling and simulation, forecasts and forecasting, methodology, scientific and psychological principles, systems, value

Class interdisciplinary works on systems (including computer modeling and simulation) in 003, on philosophy in 100; forecasts and forecasting in specific geographic areas in —09

See Manual at T1—01; T1—01 vs. 302–307 for psychological principles

—(016) Bibliographies, catalogs, indexes

(Optional number; prefer 016)

—02 Miscellany

Use only for topics named here or in subdivisions below

Including synopses, outlines

Works called synopses and outlines that are regular treatises or introductions to a subject are classed in the base number without use of notation from Table 1

Use of this number for manuals discontinued; class in 001–999 without adding notation from Table 1

See Manual at T1—02

—022 Illustrations

Examples: atlases, maps, related forms [*formerly* 912]; charts, designs, diagrams, pictures, plans

Including techniques of drafting illustrations

Class interdisciplinary works on techniques of drafting illustrations in 604.2; interdisciplinary maps and atlases, maps and atlases of geography and travel regardless of area in 912; historical atlases in 911

Audiovisual treatment, humorous cartoons, models and miniatures, statistical graphs are classed in 001–999 without use of notation from Table 1

See Manual at T1—022 vs. 912 for maps and atlases

—023 The subject as a profession, occupation, hobby

Class here vocational guidance, choice of vocation, career opportunities

Class interdisciplinary works on vocational guidance, choice of vocation, career opportunities in 331.7; on hobbies in 790.1

—025 Directories of persons and organizations

Class here directories of public officials and employees of specific occupational categories [*formerly also* 351]; membership lists containing directory information, e.g., employment and education of members

Class directories giving biographical information in —092

See also —029 for directories of products and services, —06 for membership lists not containing directory information

See Manual at T1—06 vs. T1—025; 300 vs. 600: Catalogs and directories

—(026) Law

(Optional number: prefer 340)

—028 Auxiliary techniques and procedures; apparatus, equipment, materials

Examples: maintenance and repair, personal safety and technology of safety, testing and measurement

Use of this number for basic techniques and procedures of the subject (e.g., for how-to books) discontinued; class in 001–999 without adding notation from Table 1

Laboratory manuals relocated to —078

Class interdisciplinary works on safety in 363.1, on personal safety in 613.6, on technology of safety in 620.8, on measurement in 530.8, on testing in 620, on technology of testing and measuring instruments in 681, on maintenance and repair in 620; educational testing in —076; use of apparatus and equipment in study and teaching in —078

For drafting of illustrations, see —022

See Manual at T1—028 for maintenance and repair; 363.1 for safety

—028 5 Data processing Computer applications

Class here data processing in research

Do not use —0285 to indicate that a work is in machine-readable form; class in 001–999 without adding notation from Table 1

Class interdisciplinary works in 004, computer modeling and simulation in —01

See Manual at T1—0285

—029 Commercial miscellany

Examples: advertisements, buyers' guides, consumer reports, evaluation and purchasing manuals, price lists, price trends, product directories, trade catalogs

Including estimates of time, labor, materials

Class here listings of products and services offered for sale, lease, or free distribution

House organs relocated to —05, investment prospectuses to 332.6

Class interdisciplinary commercial miscellany in 380.1029, interdisciplinary evaluation and purchasing manuals in 381.3, catalogs of exhibitions and museum collections in —074, price trends for collectors in —075, catalogs of bibliographic materials in 010, noncurrent offers for sale used primarily to illustrate civilization and customs of an earlier period in 900

See Manual at 300 vs. 600: Catalogs and directories

—03 Dictionaries, encyclopedias, concordances

Class interdisciplinary encyclopedias in 030, interdisciplinary dictionaries in 413

—04 Special topics

Use this subdivision only when it is specifically set forth in the schedules. Add other standard subdivisions —01–09 to it and its subdivisions as required, e.g., technical drawing as a profession 604.2023

—05 Serial publications

Examples: house organs [*formerly* —029], magazines, newspapers, yearbooks

(Option: Class periodicals on all subjects in 050)

Class interdisciplinary serial publications in 050, interdisciplinary newspapers in 071–079; specific kinds of serial publications with the kind, e.g., directories in serial form —025, periodic administrative reports in —06

—06 Organizations and management

Including administrative proceedings and reports, charters, history, membership lists, regulations

Class interdisciplinary organizations in 060, organizations engaged in education and related topics in —07, business enterprises in 338.7, government administrative organizations in 350; directories of organizations, membership lists with directory information in —025, nonadministrative reports and proceedings in 001–999 without adding notation from Table 1

See Manual at T1—06 for organizations; T1—06 vs. T1—025 for directories of organizations

—068 Management

The science and art of conducting organized enterprises and projects

Examples: financial, personnel, production, sales management; initiation of business enterprises

Including personal selling [*formerly* 658.8]

Do not use —068 for management in the sense of carrying out the ordinary activities of a subject, e.g., management of the classroom (when the reference is to teaching) 371.1 (*not* 371.10068)

(Option: Class management of specific enterprises in 658)

Class interdisciplinary works in 658

See Manual at 350–354 vs. 658, T1—068; 647 vs. 647.068, 658.2, T1—068 for management of public households; 658 and T1—068; 658, T1—068 vs. 302.3 for social dynamics of management; 658.8, T1—068 vs. 659 for marketing

—07 Education and related topics

Limited to topics named here or in subdivisions below

Including programmed teaching and learning, programmed texts

Class here study programs, study and teaching, comprehensive works on resources for study and teaching

Do not use for textbooks; class textbooks in 001–999 without adding notation from Table 1

Class interdisciplinary works on education in 370; specific resources for study and teaching with the subject, e.g., directories —025, bibliographies 016, libraries 026

See Manual at T1—07; T1—07 vs. 016, 026 for resources; 407, T1—07 vs. 410.7, 418.007, T4—8007, 401 for study and teaching of language

—071 Schools and courses

Including secondary and higher education; adult education, e.g., correspondence courses, in-service training, residency, workshops

Do not use —071 for financial support; class financial support of schools and courses in 001–999 without adding notation from Table 1

Class management of in-service training and residency in —068, special education in 371.9, elementary education in 372

—074 Museums, collections, exhibits

Class here historical and geographic treatment of museums devoted to a specific subject [*formerly also* 069]; guidebooks, catalogs, lists regardless of whether or not articles are offered for sale

Class interdisciplinary works in 069, comprehensive works on museum science of a subject in —075

−075 Museum activities and services [*formerly* 069] Collecting

Including price trends for collectors

Class here museum science

Class interdisciplinary works on museum activities and services, on museum collecting in 069, on recreational collecting in 790.1; activities and services of or relating to specific museums, collections, exhibits in −074; maintenance and repair of museum objects in −028

−076 Review and exercise

Examples: workbooks with problems, questions, answers; civil service examinations

Including testing, test construction and evaluation

Laboratory manuals for study and teaching relocated to −078

Class review and exercise involving use of apparatus and physical equipment in −078; programmed texts with problems, questions, answers in −07

−078 Use of apparatus and equipment in study and teaching

Class here laboratory manuals [*formerly also* −028, −076], student projects and experiments

Class laboratory manuals for testing in −028, for research in 001–999 without adding notation from Table 1

−079 Competitions, festivals, awards, financial support

Examples: fellowships and scholarships, grants-in-aid, honorary titles, prizes

Including financial support of research

Do not use for description of works that are entered into competitions and festivals, that receive awards, or that result from financial support; class in 001–999 without adding notation from Table 1

Class interdisciplinary works on awards in 929.8

−08 History and description with respect to kinds of persons

Examples: social classes, occupational groups

Unless other instructions are given, class complex subjects with aspects in two or more subdivisions of −08 in the one coming last, e.g., handicapped children −087 (*not* −083)

Class treatment of specific kinds of persons as individuals in −092, e.g., handicapped persons as individuals who have contributed to a subject −092 (*not* −087)

> −081–085 Sex and age groups, relatives

Class comprehensive works; sex and age groups, relatives of specific social, economic, occupational characteristics in −08

—081 Men

Class here males

—082 Women

Class here females

—083 Young people

Including infants

Class here children

—083 5 Young adults

Aged twelve to twenty

Class here comprehensive works on young adults aged twelve to twenty and over twenty

Class young adults over twenty in —084

—084 Persons in specific stages of adulthood

Over twenty years of age

Example: persons in late adulthood

Class comprehensive works on adults in 001–999 without adding notation from Table 1; comprehensive works on young adults, young adults aged twelve to twenty in —0835

—085 Relatives

Examples: brothers, sisters

Class here parents, adoptive and foster parents, stepparents

—087 Handicapped and ill persons

—089 Racial, ethnic, national groups

Class treatment with respect to specific racial, ethnic, national group in places where they predominate in —09; treatment with respect to persons of a specific racial, ethnic, national group having specific sex, age, kinship, handicapped characteristics in —081–087

Comprehensive works on nondominant racial, ethnic, national groups; works on persons of specific racial, ethnic, national groups with specific social, economic, occupational, religious characteristics are classed in —08

See Manual at T1—089 vs. T1—09

—09 Historical, geographic, persons treatment

Class treatment limited by time or place in directories of persons and organizations in —025, in price lists and trade catalogs in —029; historical and geographic treatment of drafting illustrations in —022, of organizations in —06, of museums, collections, exhibits in —074

See Manual at T1—089 vs. T1—09 for racial, ethnic, national groups; T1—09

—091 Treatment by areas, regions, places in general

Add to base number —091 the numbers following —1 in notation 11–19 from Table 2, e.g., Torrid Zone 0913

Class persons regardless of area, region, place in —092; treatment by specific continents, countries, localities in —093–099; history and description with respect to kinds of persons in —08

—092 Persons

Biography, autobiography, description and critical appraisal of work, diaries, reminiscences, correspondence of persons regardless of area, region, place who are part of the subject or who study the subject, e.g., criminals, victims of crime, criminologists

(Option A: Class biography in 920.1–928.9)

(Option B: Class individual biography in 92, or B)

(Option C: Class individual biography of men in 920.71, of women in 920.72)

Class biography, autobiography, diaries, reminiscences, correspondence not clearly related to any specific subject in 920; literary diaries, reminiscences, correspondence in 800; treatment with respect to kinds of persons in —08

Do not use —092 (or 92 or —2 from Table 2 when the standard subdivision has been displaced) under 180–190, 232.9, 759, 809, 810–890

See Manual at T1—092

—093–099 Treatment by specific continents, countries, localities; extraterrestrial worlds

History and description by place, by specific instance of the subject

Add to base number —09 notation 3–9 from Table 2, e.g., the subject in United States 0973, in Brazil 0981, in North America 097

Class persons regardless of continent, country, locality in —092; treatment by areas, regions, places not limited by continent, country, locality in —091; history and description with respect to miscellaneous kinds of persons in —081–087, with respect to specific racial, ethnic, national groups not dominant in their continent, country, locality in —089

See Manual at T1—089 vs. T1—09 for racial, ethnic, national groups

Table 2. Geographic Areas, and Persons

Maps

Use of the Maps

The following outline maps provide a display of key area numbers from Table 2. With the exception of island nations lying beyond the continental maps used, the maps indicate the Dewey Decimal Classification area numbers of members of the United Nations and comparable states. Sub-national areas are shown for the United States, Canada, the British Isles, and Australia.

While DDC area numbers are largely hierarchical, be sure to check Table 2 before using a number for part of a given area. In some instances (as illustrated here with the United States), the numbers for the parts are built on a base other than that of the area as a whole.

Note that certain major regional concepts which do not correspond to delineated areas are listed in the margins.

OCEANS AND CONTINENTS

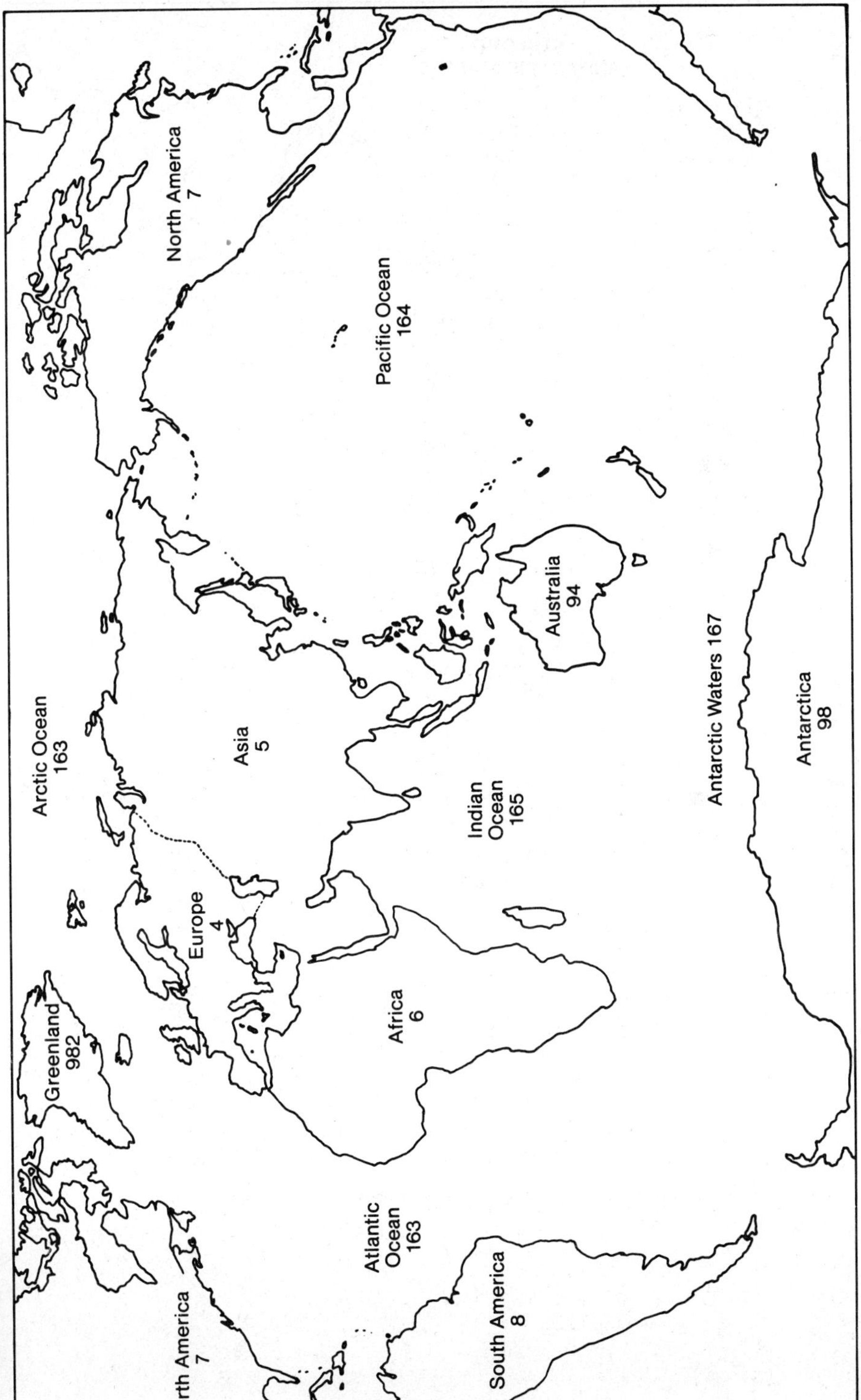

REGIONAL CONCEPTS

4 Western Europe
42 England and Wales
43 Central Europe
47 Eastern Europe
48 Northern Europe, Scandinavia
496 Balkan Peninsula

REGIONAL CONCEPTS

41 British Isles, United Kingdom, Great Britain
411 Scotland, Northern Scotland, Islands Authorities, Scottish Highlands
412 Northeastern Scotland
413 Southeastern Scotland, Central Lowlands
414 Southwestern Scotland
415 Ireland
416 Ulster, Northern Ireland
417 Republic of Ireland (Erie), Connacht
418 Leinster
419 Munster
42 England and Wales, England
421 Greater London
422 Southeastern England, Home Counties, Thames Valley
423 Southwestern England and Channel Islands
424 Midlands, Welsh Marshes, Severn Valley
425 East Midlands, Chilterns, Trent Valley
426 Eastern England, East Anglia
427 Northern England, Northwestern England
428 Northeastern England, Pennines, Yorkshire
429 Wales

ASIA, AUSTRALIA, NEW ZEALAND

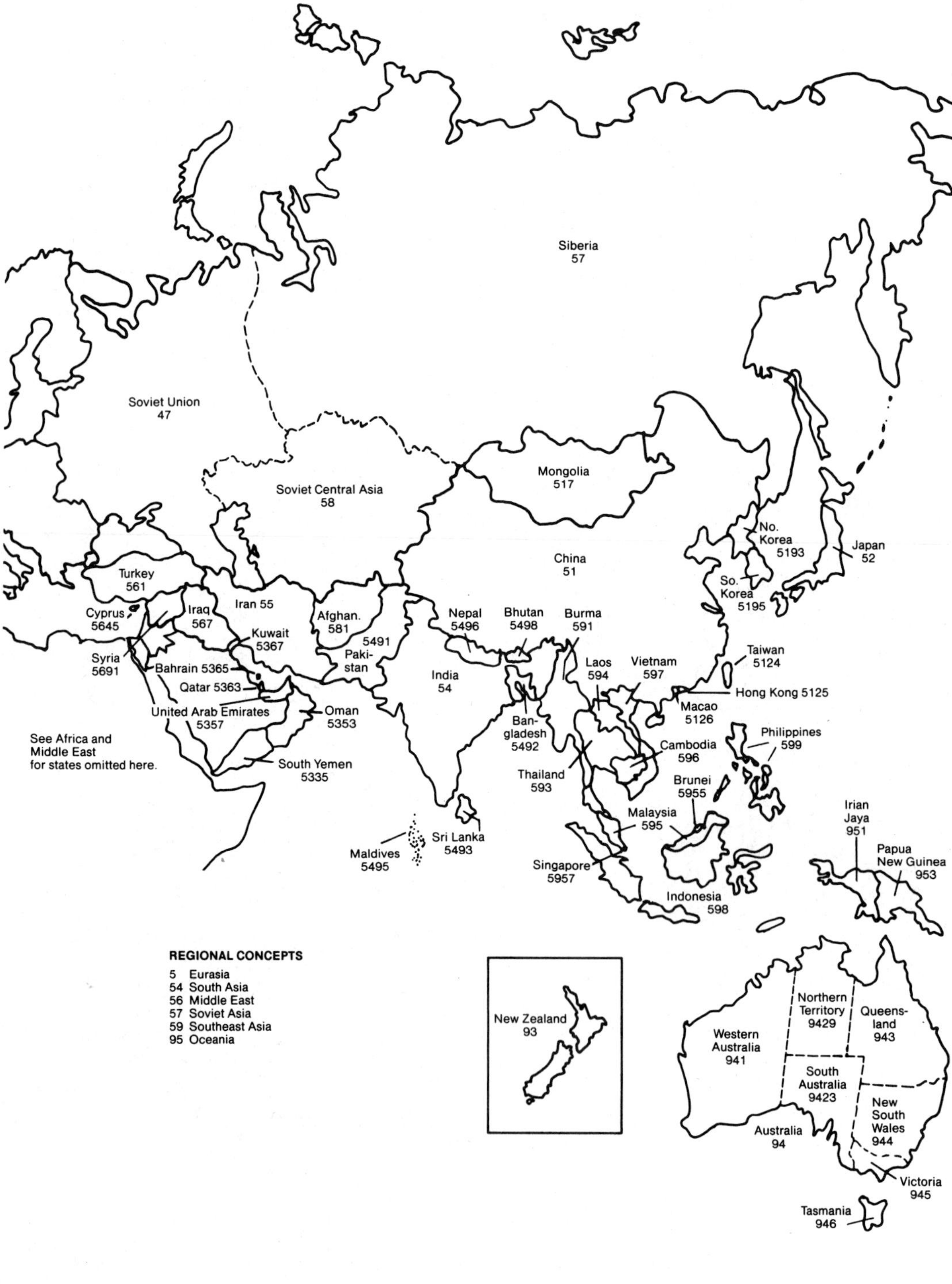

AFRICA AND MIDDLE EAST

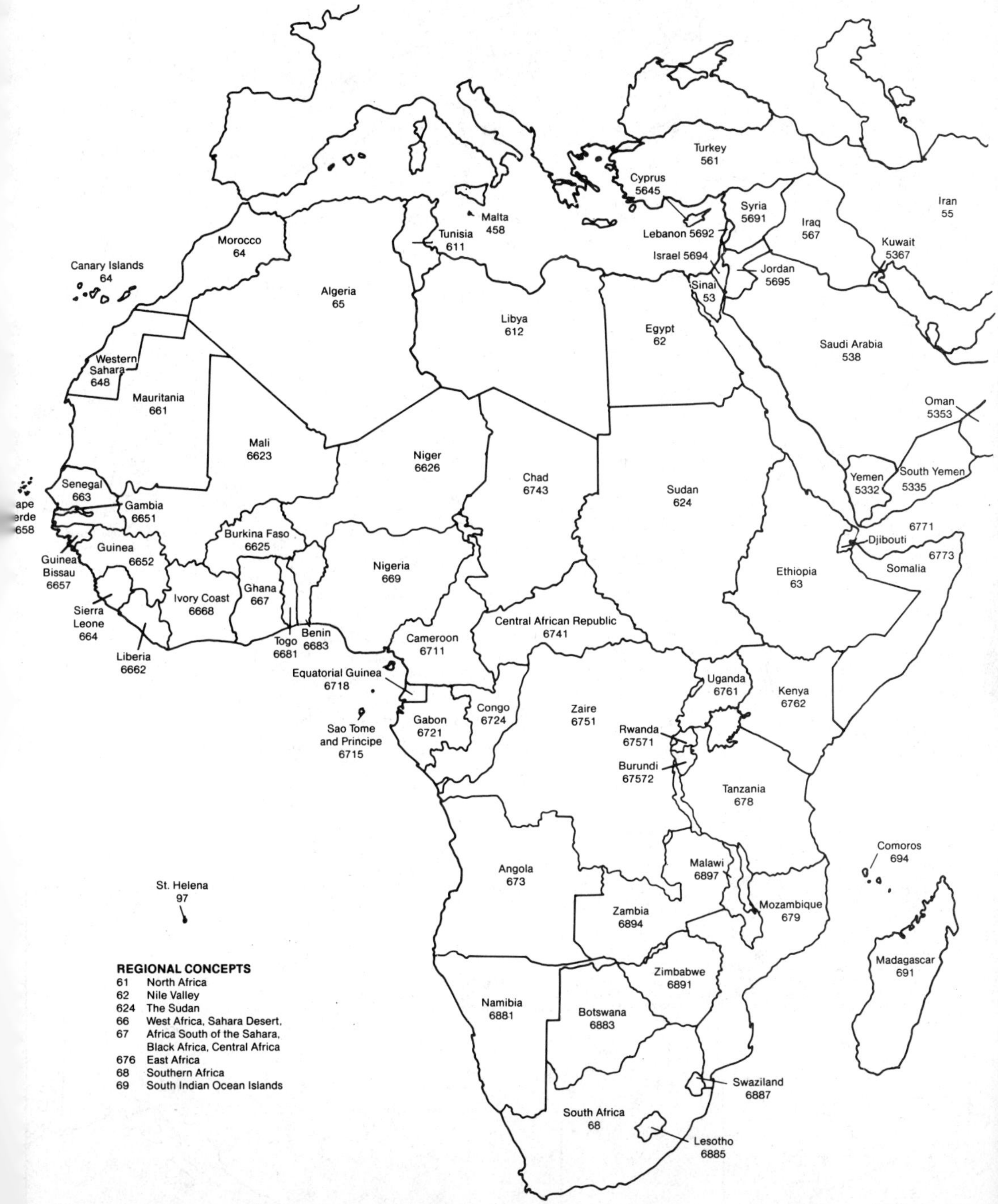

UNITED STATES AND CANADA

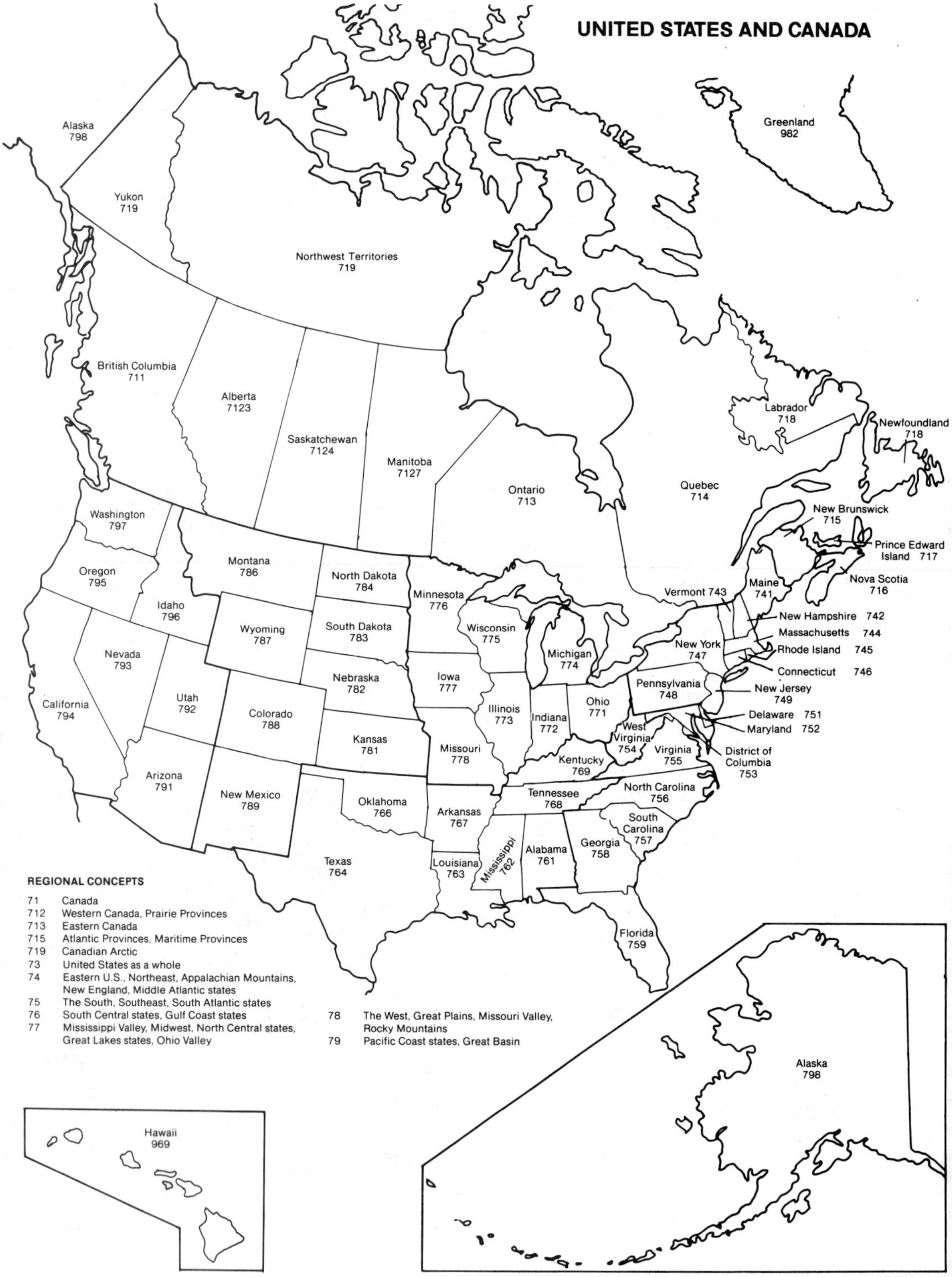

REGIONAL CONCEPTS

71 Canada
712 Western Canada, Prairie Provinces
713 Eastern Canada
715 Atlantic Provinces, Maritime Provinces
719 Canadian Arctic
73 United States as a whole
74 Eastern U.S., Northeast, Appalachian Mountains, New England, Middle Atlantic states
75 The South, Southeast, South Atlantic states
76 South Central states, Gulf Coast states
77 Mississippi Valley, Midwest, North Central states, Great Lakes states, Ohio Valley
78 The West, Great Plains, Missouri Valley, Rocky Mountains
79 Pacific Coast states, Great Basin

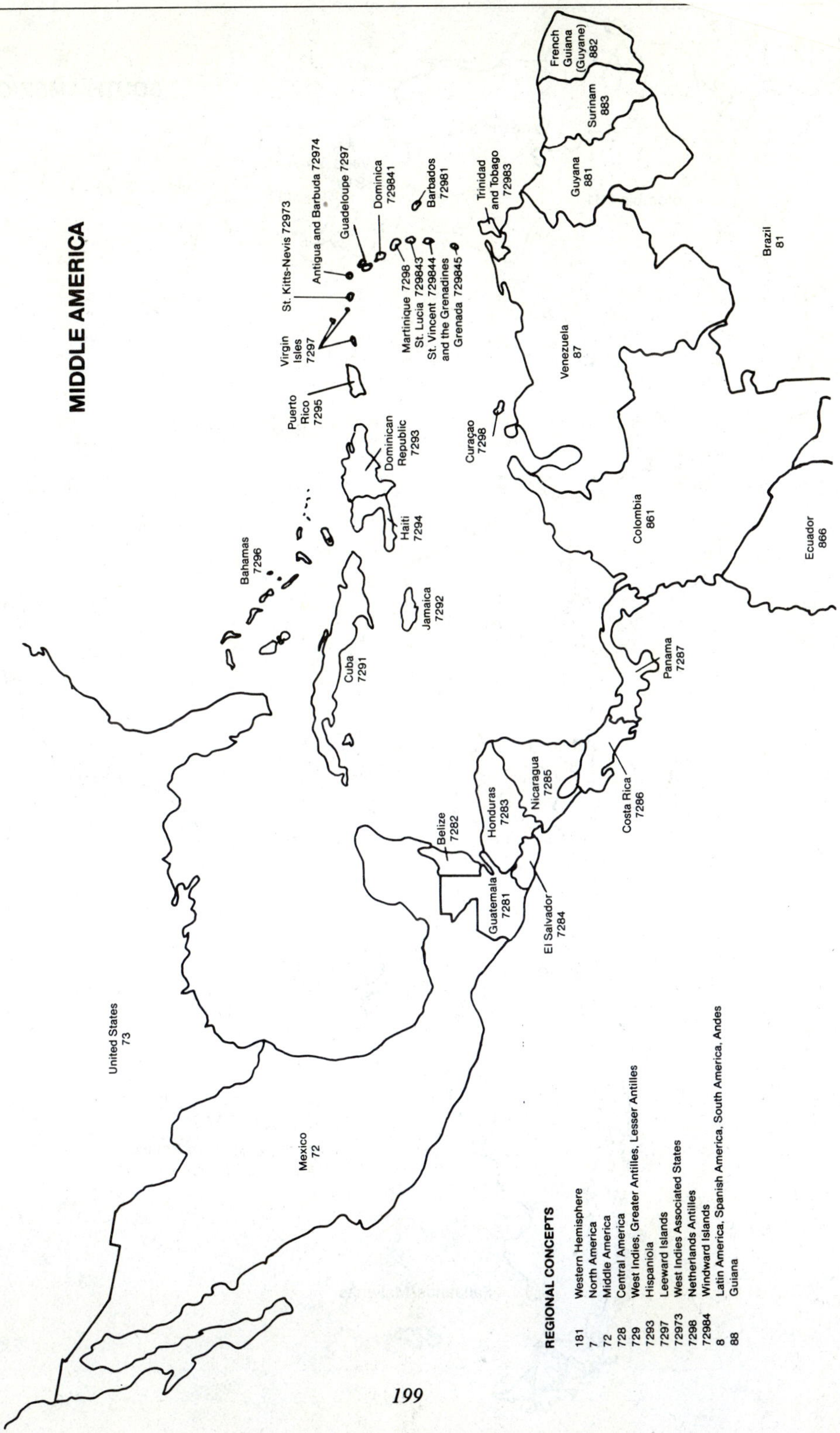
MIDDLE AMERICA
United States 73
Mexico 72
Bahamas 7296
Cuba 7291
Jamaica 7292
Haiti 7294
Dominican Republic 7293
Puerto Rico 7295
Virgin Isles 7297
St. Kitts-Nevis 72973
Antigua and Barbuda 72974
Guadeloupe 7297
Dominica 729841
Barbados 72981
Martinique 7298
St. Lucia 729843
St. Vincent 729844 and the Grenadines
Grenada 729845
Trinidad and Tobago 72983
Curaçao 7298
Belize 7282
Guatemala 7281
Honduras 7283
El Salvador 7284
Nicaragua 7285
Costa Rica 7286
Panama 7287
Colombia 861
Venezuela 87
Ecuador 866
Brazil 81
Guyana 881
Surinam 883
French Guiana (Guyane) 882
REGIONAL CONCEPTS
181 Western Hemisphere
7 North America
72 Middle America
728 Central America
729 West Indies, Greater Antilles, Lesser Antilles
7293 Hispaniola
7297 Leeward Islands
72973 West Indies Associated States
7298 Netherlands Antilles
72984 Windward Islands
8 Latin America, Spanish America, South America, Andes
88 Guiana

SOUTH AMERICA
Venezuela 87
Guyana 881
Surinam 883
French Guiana (Guyane) 882
Colombia 861
Ecuador 866
Peru 85
Brazil 81
Bolivia 84
Chile 83
Paraguay 892
Argentina 82
Uruguay 895
Falklands/Malvinas 97
REGIONAL CONCEPTS
8 Latin America, Spanish America, South America, Andes
88 Guiana

Table 2. Geographic Areas, and Persons

The following notation is never used alone, but may be used as required (either directly when so noted or through the interposition of notation 09 from Table 1) with any number from the schedules, e.g., public libraries (027.4) in Japan (—52 in this table): 027.452; railroad transportation (385) in Japan: 385.0952. When adding to a number from the schedules, always insert a decimal point between the third and fourth digits of the complete number

SUMMARY

—1	**Areas, regions, places in general**
—2	**Persons**
—3	**The ancient world**
—4	**Europe Western Europe**
—5	**Asia Orient Far East**
—6	**Africa**
—7	**North America**
—8	**South America**
—9	**Other parts of world and extraterrestrial worlds Pacific Ocean islands**

—1 Areas, regions, places in general

Not limited by continent, country, locality

Unless other instructions are given, class areas with aspects in two or more subdivisions of this table in the number coming last in the table, e.g., forested valleys in North Temperate Zone —15 (*not* —12 or —14)

Class persons regardless of area, region, place in —2; specific continents, countries, localities in —3–9

See Manual at T2—1; T2—2 vs. T2—1, T2—3–T2—9

—11 **Frigid Zones**

—12 **Temperate Zones (Middle Latitude Zones)**

—13 **Torrid Zone (Tropics)**

—14 **Land and landforms**

Including soil; beaches, caves, coastal regions, continents, islands, mountains, plains, shorelines, steppes, valleys

—15 **Regions by type of vegetation**

Examples: forests, grasslands, deserts

—16 **Air and water**

Including lagoons, inland seas; freshwaters

Class specific inland seas in —4–9

—161 Atmosphere

—162 Oceans and seas

Special oceanographic forms and inland seas are classed in —16

For Atlantic Ocean, see —163; Pacific Ocean, —164; Indian Ocean, —165

See also —182 for the totality of continents facing and islands in major ocean and sea basins

—163 Atlantic Ocean

Including Chesapeake Bay [*formerly also* —755], Arctic Ocean, Baltic Sea, Black Sea, Caribbean Sea, English Channel, Gulf of Mexico, Mediterranean Sea, North Sea

Class Bering Strait, Panama Canal in —164; Atlantic sector of Antarctic waters in —167

See Manual at T2—163 and T2—164, T2—165

—164 Pacific Ocean

Including Arafura Sea, Bering Sea, East China Sea, Java Sea, Panama Canal, Sea of Japan, Sea of Okhotsk, South China Sea

Class Pacific sector of Antarctic waters in —167

See Manual at T2—163 and T2—164, T2—165

—165 Indian Ocean

Including Andaman Sea, Persian Gulf, Red Sea, Suez Canal, Timor Sea

Class Singapore Strait in —164, Indian Ocean sector of Antarctic waters in —167

See Manual at T2—163 and T2—164, T2—165

—167 Antarctic waters

—17 Socioeconomic regions

Including regions where specific racial, ethnic, national groups predominate; where specific languages predominate; where specific religions predominate; nations belonging to specific international organizations, e.g., nations belonging to Organization of Petroleum Exporting Countries

—171 By politial orientation

Examples: noncontiguous empires and political unions, blocs, nonself-governing territories

See also —37 for Roman Empire

—172 By degree of economic development

Examples: regions of high, medium, low development

—173 By concentration of population

Examples: urban, suburban, rural regions

—18 **Other kinds of terrestrial regions**

—181 Hemispheres

—182 Ocean and sea basins

The totality of continents facing and islands in specific major bodies of water, e.g., Atlantic region

Including the Occident

Class ocean and sea waters in —162; zonal, physiographic, socioeconomic regions in a specific ocean or sea basin in —11–17

—19 **Space**

Class extraterrestrial worlds in —99

See Manual at T2—19 vs. T2—99

—2 Persons

Regardless of area, region, place

Class here description and critical appraisal of work, biography, autobiography, diaries, reminiscences, correspondence of persons associated with the subject, e.g., elementary school teachers 372.92

All schedule and Manual notes for notation 092 from Table 1 are applicable here

See Manual at T2—2 vs. T2—1, T2—3–T2—9

> —3–9 Specific continents, countries, localities; extraterrestrial worlds

Class here specific instances of the subject

An area is classed in its present number even if it had a different affiliation at the time under consideration, e.g., Arizona under Mexican sovereignty —791 (*not* —72)

Class comprehensive works in base number; areas, regions, places not limited by continent, country, locality in —1; parts of oceans and non-inland seas limited by country or locality in —16; persons regardless of area, region, place in —2

See Manual at T2—2 vs. T2—1, T2—3–T2—9; T2—3–T2—9; T2—3 vs. T2—4–T2—9

—3 The ancient world

Class a specific part of ancient world not provided for here in —4–9

(Option: Class specific parts in —4–9 as detailed below)

See Manual at T2—3 vs. T2—4–T2—9

—31 **China**

(Option: Class in —51)

—32 Egypt

(Option: Class in —62)

—33 Palestine

Including Israel, Samaria

(Option: Class Palestine, Israel in —5694; the Jordanian part of ancient Palestine, Samaria in —5695)

—34 India

(Option: Class in —54)

—35 Mesopotamia and Iranian Plateau

(Option: Class Iranian Plateau in —55, Mesopotamia in —567)

Class central Asia in —39

—36 Europe north and west of Italian Peninsula

Class here comprehensive works on ancient Europe

(Option: Class in —4)

Class a specific part of ancient Europe not provided for here with the part, e.g., Greece —38

—361 British Isles Northern Britain and Ireland

(Option: Class British Isles in —41, northern Britain in —411, Ireland in —415)

For southern Britain, see —362

—362 Southern Britain England

(Option: Class in —42)

Class comprehensive works on British Isles in —361

—363 Germanic regions

(Option: Class in —43)

For British Isles, see —361

—364 Celtic regions

Class here Gaul

(Option: Class in —44)

For British Isles, see —361

—366 Iberian Penninsula and adjacent islands

(Option: Class in —46)

—37 Italian Peninsula and adjacent territories

Including Etruria, Sicily, Malta, Sardinia, Corsica

Class here Roman Empire

(Option: Class in —45)

Class a specific part of Roman Empire not provided for here with the part, e.g., Britain —361

—38 Greece

Including Macedonia

Class here comprehensive works on Greece and the Roman Empire; the Hellenistic World; southern Europe

(Option: Class ancient Greece in —495, southern Europe in —4)

Class Roman Empire in —37; a specific part of the Hellenistic World, southern Europe not provided for here with the part, e.g., Ptolemaic Egypt —32

For Aegean Islands, Crete, see —39

—39 Other parts of ancient world

Examples: southeastern Europe, including Aegean Islands, Crete, Thrace; Middle East, including Arabia, Asia Minor, Cyprus, Phoenicia, Sinai Peninsula, Syria; Black Sea and Caucasus regions; central Asia; North Africa, including Algerian and Moroccan parts of North Africa, Cush, Ethiopia, Nubia

(Option: Class southeastern Europe in —496; Aegean Islands, Crete in —499; Thrace in —495; Middle East in —56; Asia Minor in —561; Arabia, Sinai Peninsula in —53; Cyprus in —5645; Phoenicia in —5692; Syria in —5691; Black Sea and Caucasus regions in —47; central Asia in —58; North Africa in —61; Algerian part of North Africa in —65; Moroccan part of North Africa in —64; Cush, Ethiopia, Nubia in —625)

For Egypt, see —32; Palestine, —33; Mesopotamia and Iranian Plateau, —35; Greece, —38

> —4–9 The modern world; extraterrestrial worlds

(Option: Class here specific parts of the ancient world; prefer —3)

Class comprehensive works on specific physiographic regions or features extending over more than one country, state or other unit and identified by * with the unit where noted in this table, e.g., Scottish Highlands —411, Appalachian Mountains —74. Class works on a part of such a region or feature with the specific unit where the part is located, e.g., Scottish Highlands in Grampian region —412, Blue Ridge —755

Class comprehensive works in base number

See Manual at T2—3 vs. T2—4–T2—9; T2—4–T2—9

—4 Europe Western Europe

Class here southern Europe

(Option: Class here ancient Europe, western Europe, southern Europe; prefer —36 for ancient Europe, western Europe, —38 for ancient southern Europe)

Class Eurasia in —5

SUMMARY

—41	**British Isles**
—42	**England and Wales**
—43	**Central Europe Germany**
—44	**France and Monaco**
—45	**Italian Peninsula and adjacent islands Italy**
—46	**Iberian Peninsula and adjacent islands Spain**
—47	**Union of Soviet Socialist Republics (Soviet Union) Russia (Russian Soviet Federated Socialist Republic)**
—48	**Scandinavia**
—49	**Other parts of Europe**

—41 British Isles

Class here Great Britain, United Kingdom

(Option: Class here ancient British Isles; prefer —361)

For England and Wales, see —42

—411 Scotland

Including Islands authorities, consisting of Orkney, Shetland, Western Isles (Outer Hebrides); Highland Region, consisting of Badenoch and Strathspey, Caithness, Inverness, Lochaber, Nairn, Ross and Cromarty, Skye and Lochalsh, Sutherland districts

Class here northern Britain, *Scottish Highlands

(Option: Class here ancient northern Britain; prefer —361)

For northeastern Scotland, see —412; southeastern Scotland, —413, southwestern Scotland, —414

—412 Northeastern Scotland

Contains Fife, Grampian, Tayside regions

Including City of Aberdeen, City of Dundee; Angus, Banff and Buchan, Dumfermline, Gordon, Kincardine and Deeside, Kirkcaldy, Moray, North East Fife, Perth and Kinross districts

—413 Southeastern Scotland

Contains Borders, Central, Lothian regions

Including City of Edinburgh; Berwickshire, Clackmannan, East Lothian, Ettrick and Lauderdale, Falkirk, Midlothian, Roxburgh, Stirling, Tweeddale, West Lothian districts; *Forth River

Class here *Cental Lowlands

*Class parts of this physiographic region or feature as instructed under —4–9

—414 Southwestern Scotland

Contains Dumfries and Galloway, Strathclyde Regions

Including City of Glasgow; Annandale and Eskdale, Argyll and Bute, Bearsden and Milngavie, Clydebank, Clydesdale (Lanark), Cumbernauld and Kilsyth, Cumnock and Doon Valley, Cunninghame, Dumbarton, East Kilbride, Eastwood, Hamilton, Inverclyde, Kilmarnock and Loudoun, Kyle and Carrick, Monklands, Motherwell, Nithsdale, Renfrew, Stewartry, Strathkelvin, Wigtown districts; *Clyde River

—415 Ireland

(Option: Class here ancient Ireland; prefer —361)

For divisions of Ireland, see —416–419

> —416–419 Divisions of Ireland

Class comprehensive works in —415

—416 Ulster Northern Ireland

—416 9 Counties of Republic of Ireland in Ulster

Contains Cavan, Donegal, Monaghan

—417 Republic of Ireland (Eire)

Including Connacht, consisting of Galway, Leitrim, Mayo, Roscommon, Sligo counties

Class here *Shannon River

For counties in Ulster, see —4169; Leinster, —418; Munster, —419

—418 Leinster

Contains Carlow, Dublin, Kildare, Kilkenny, Laois, Longford, Louth, Meath, Offaly, Westmeath, Wexford, Wicklow counties

—419 Munster

Contains Clare, Cork, Kerry, Limerick, Tipperary, Waterford counties

—42 England and Wales

(Option: Class here ancient southern Britain, England; prefer —362)

> —421–428 England

Class comprehensive works in —42

—421 Greater London

*Class parts of this physiographic region or feature as instructed under —4–9

—422 Southeastern England

Contains Berkshire, East Sussex, Hampshire, Isle of Wight, Kent, Surrey, West Sussex

Class here Home Counties; *Thames River

Class a specific Home County not provided for here with the Home county, e.g., Hertfordshire —425

For Greater London, see —421

—423 Southwestern England and Channel Islands

Contains Avon, Cornwall, Devon, Dorset, Somerset, Wiltshire

—424 Midlands of England

Contains Gloucestershire, Hereford and Worcester, Shropshire (former Salop), Staffordshire, Warwickshire, West Midlands Metropolitan County

For East Midlands, see —425

—425 East Midlands of England

Contains Bedfordshire, Buckinghamshire, Derbyshire, Hertfordshire, Leicestershire, Lincolnshire, Nottinghamshire, Northamptonshire, Oxfordshire

—426 Eastern England East Anglia

Contains Cambridgeshire, Essex, Norfolk, Suffolk

Class here the *Fens

Class London boroughs created from Essex in —421

—427 Northwestern England and Isle of Man

Contains Cheshire, Cumbria, Greater Manchester Metropolitan County, Lancashire, Merseyside Metropolitan County

Including Lake District

Class here comprehensive works on northern England

For northeastern England, see —428

—428 Northeastern England

Contains Cleveland, Durham, Humberside, North Yorkshire, Northumberland, Tyne and Wear Metropolitan County, South Yorkshire Metropolitan County, West Yorkshire Metropolitan County

Class here the *Pennines

—429 Wales

*Class parts of this physiographic region or feature as instructed under —4–9

—43 Central Europe Germany

Class here Federal Republic of Germany, Holy Roman Empire

(Option: Class here ancient Germanic regions; prefer —363)

Class a specific part of Holy Roman Empire not provided for here with the part, e.g., Lombardy —45

For Switzerland, see —494

—431 East Germany (German Democratic Republic)

Including Berlin

Saxony and Thuringia relocated to —432

—432 Saxony and Thuringia [*formerly* —431]

—436 Austria and Liechtenstein

—436 4 Liechtenstein

—437 Czechoslovakia

—438 Poland

—439 Hungary

—44 France and Monaco

Including Corsica

(Option: Class here ancient Celtic regions, Gaul; prefer —363)

Class a specific overseas department of France with the department, e.g., Martinique —7298

—449 Monaco

—45 Italian Peninsula and adjacent islands Italy

Including Sicily, Sardinia

Class here Apennines

(Option: Class here ancient Italian Peninsula and adjacent islands, Roman Empire; prefer —37)

—454 San Marino

—456 Vatican City

—458 Malta

—46 Iberian Peninsula and adjacent islands Spain

Including Balearic Islands; *Pyrenees Mountains

(Option: Class here ancient Iberian Peninsula and adjacent islands; prefer —366)

For Canary Islands, see —64

—467 Andorra

*Class parts of this physiographic region or feature as instructed under —4–9

—468 Gibraltar

—469 Portugal

Including Madeira, Azores

—47 Union of Soviet Socialist Republics (Soviet Union) Russia (Russian Soviet Federated Socialist Republic)

Including *Caspian Sea

Class here eastern Europe

(Option: Class here ancient Black Sea and Caucasus regions; prefer —39)

For Balkan Peninsula, see —496; Soviet Union in Asia, see —57

—48 Scandinavia

Class here northern Europe

For northwestern islands, see —491

—481 Norway

For divisions of Norway, see —482–484; Jan Mayen Island, Svalbard, —98

> —482–484 Divisions of Norway

Class comprehensive works in —481

—482 Southeastern Norway

Contains Akershus, Aust-Agder, Buskerud, Hedmark, Oppland, Oslo, Ostfold, Telemark, Vest-Agder, Vestfold counties (fylker)

—483 Southwestern Norway

Contains Hordaland, More og Romsdal, Rogaland, Sogn og Fjordane counties (fylker)

—484 Central and northern Norway

Contains Finnmark, Nord-Trondelag, Nordland, Sor-Trondelag, Troms counties (fylker)

—485 Sweden

For divisions of Sweden, see —486–488

> —486–488 Divisions of Sweden

Class comprehensive works in —485

—486 Southern Sweden (Gotaland)

—487 Central Sweden (Svealand)

—488 Northern Sweden (Norrland)

*Class parts of this physiographic region or feature as instructed under —4–9

—489 Denmark and Finland

—489 7 Finland

—49 Other parts of Europe

—491 Northwestern islands

—491 2 Iceland

—491 5 Faeroes

—492 Netherlands (Holland)

Class here comprehensive works on Low Countries, on Benelux countries

For southern Low Countries, see —493

—493 Southern Low Countries Belgium

—493 5 Luxembourg

Grand duchy

—494 Switzerland

Including *Alps

—495 Greece

Including comprehensive works on Thrace

(Option: Class here ancient Greece, Thrace; prefer —38 for ancient Greece, —39 for ancient Thrace)

Class Bulgarian Thrace in —4977

For Turkish Thrace, see —4961; Aegean Islands, —499

—496 Balkan Peninsula

Class here *Danube River

(Option: Class here ancient southeastern Europe; prefer —39)

Class each specific country of Balkan Peninsula not provided for here with the country, e.g., Greece —495

See also —56 for Ottoman Empire

—496 1 Turkey in Europe (Turkish Thrace) [*formerly* —563]

Contains Edirne (Adrianople), Istanbul, Kirklareli, Tekirdag provinces (ilieri); European portion of Canakkale province (ili)

For Asian portion of Istanbul province, see —563

—496 5 Albania

—497 Yugoslavia and Bulgaria

—497 7 Bulgaria

—498 Romania

*Class parts of this physiographic region or feature as instructed under —4–9

—499 Aegean Islands

Including Crete

(Option: Class here ancient Aegean Islands, Crete; prefer —39)

Class Euboea, Kythera in —495; Imbros and Tenedos islands of Turkey in —562

—5 Asia Orient Far East

Class here Eurasia

For Europe, see —4

SUMMARY

—51	**China and adjacent areas**
—52	**Japan**
—53	**Arabian Peninsula and adjacent areas**
—54	**South Asia India**
—55	**Iran**
—56	**Middle East (Near East)**
—57	**Siberia (Asiatic Russia)**
—58	**Central Asia**
—59	**Southeast Asia**

—51 China and adjacent areas

Including Tibet

Class here People's Republic of China

(Option: Class here ancient China; prefer —31)

—512 Taiwan, Hong Kong, Macao

—512 4 Taiwan (Formosa) and adjacent islands

Republic of China (Nationalist China)

—512 5 Hong Kong

British crown colony

—512 6 Macao

Overseas territory of Portugal

—517 Outer Mongolia (Mongolian People's Republic)

Including *Gobi Desert

—519 Korea

—519 3 North Korea (People's Democratic Republic of Korea)

—519 5 South Korea (Republic of Korea)

—52 Japan

*Class parts of this physiographic region or feature as instructed under —4–9

—53 **Arabian Peninsula and adjacent areas**

Including Gaza Strip, Sinai Peninsula

(Option: Class here ancient Arabia, Sinai Peninsula; prefer —39)

—533 Southwestern coast of Arabia

—533 2 Yemen (Yemen Arab Republic)

—533 5 Southern Yemen (People's Democratic Republic of Yemen)

—535 Oman and United Arab Emirates

—535 3 Oman

—535 7 United Arab Emirates

—536 Persian Gulf States

For Oman and United Arab Emirates, see —535

—536 3 Qatar

—536 5 Bahrain

—536 7 Kuwait

—538 Saudi Arabia

—54 **South Asia India**

(Option: Class here ancient India; prefer —34)

For southeast Asia, see —59

—549 Other jurisdictions

Class here Pakistan (West and East, 1947–1971)

—549 1 Pakistan

Former name: West Pakistan

Class here *Indus River

—549 2 Bangladesh

Former name: East Pakistan

Class here comprehensive works on Brahmaputra River

Brahmaputra River in India is classed in —54

—549 3 Sri Lanka

Former name: Ceylon

—549 5 Maldives

—549 6 Nepal

Class here *Himalaya Mountains

*Class parts of this physiographic region or feature as instructed under —4–9

—549 8 Bhutan

—55 Iran

(Option: Class here ancient Iranian Plateau; prefer —35)

—56 Middle East (Near East)

Class here Ottoman Empire

(Option: Class here ancient Middle East; prefer —39)

Class each specific country of Middle East, of Ottoman Empire, not provided for here with the country, e.g., Saudia Arabia —538

—561 Turkey and Cyprus

Class here Asia Minor

(Option: Class here ancient Asia Minor; prefer —39)

For divisions of Turkey and Cyprus, see —562–566

> —562–566 Divisions of Turkey and Cyprus

Class comprehensive works in —561

For Turkey in Europe, see —4961

—562 Western Turkey

Contains Afyon-Karahisar, Aydin, Balikesir, Burdur, Canakkale, Denizli, Izmir (Smyrna), Kutahya, Manisa, Mugla, Usak provinces (illeri)

For European part of Canakkale province, see —4961

—563 North central Turkey

Contains Amasya, Ankara, Bilecik, Bolu, Bursa, Cankiri, Corum, Eskisehir, Kastamonu, Kocaeli, Sakarya, Samsun, Sinop, Yozgat, Zonguldak provinces (illeri); Asian portion of Istanbul province (Ili)

Turkey in Europe (Turkish Thrace) relocated to —4961

—564 South central Turkey and Cyprus

Contains Adana (Seyhan), Antalya, Gaziantep, Hatay (Antakya), Icel, Isparta, Kayseri, Kirsehir, Konya, Nevsehir, Nigde provinces (illeri)

—564 5 Cyprus

Independent island state

(Option: Class here ancient Cyprus; prefer —39)

—565 East central Turkey

Contains Adiyaman, Giresun, Gumusane, Malatya, Maras, Ordu, Sivas, Tokat, Trabzon (Trebizond), Urfa provinces (illeri)

—566 Eastern Turkey

Contains Agri, Artvin (Coruh), Bingol, Bitlis, Diyarbakir, Elazig, Erzincan, Erzurum, Hakkari, Kars, Mardin, Mus, Rize, Siirt, Tunceli, Van provinces (illeri)

Class here comprehensive works on Armenia, on Kurdistan

Class Armenian Soviet Socialist Republic in —47, Iranian Kurdistan in —55, Iraqi Kurdistan in —567

—567 Iraq

Class here Mesopotamia

(Option: Class here ancient Mesopotamia; prefer —35)

—569 Syria, Lebanon, Israel, Jordon

—569 1 Syria

(Option: Class here ancient Syria; prefer —39)

—569 2 Lebanon

(Option: Class here ancient Phoenicia; prefer —39)

—569 4 Palestine Israel

Palestine: area covering Israel, Gaza Strip, and West Bank of Jordan River

Including *Jordan River, *Dead Sea

(Option: Class here ancient Palestine, Israel; prefer —33)

Class West Bank in —5695, Gaza Strip in —53

—569 5 Jordan

(Option: Class here the Jordanian part of ancient Palestine, ancient Samaria; prefer —33)

—57 Siberia (Asiatic Russia)

Class here Soviet Union in Asia

Class Soviet republics of central Asia in —58

—58 Central Asia

Including Kazakh, Kirghiz, Tadzhik, Turkmen, Uzbek Soviet Socialist Republics

(Option: Class here ancient Central Asia; prefer —39)

—581 Afghanistan

—59 Southeast Asia

—591 Burma

—593 Thailand

—594 Laos

*Class parts of this physiographic region or feature as instructed under —4–9

—595 Commonwealth of Nations territories Malaysia

Including Malay Peninsula

For Burma, see —591; Thailand, —593

—595 5 Brunei

—595 7 Singapore

—596 Cambodia (Khmer Republic, Kampuchea)

—597 Vietnam

—598 Indonesia

Including Borneo

Class here Malay Archipelago

Class northern Borneo in —595, Philippines in —599, New Guinea in —95

—599 Philippines

—6 Africa

SUMMARY

—61	**Tunisia and Libya**
—62	**Egypt and Sudan**
—63	**Ethiopia**
—64	**Northwest African coast and offshore islands Morocco**
—65	**Algeria**
—66	**West Africa and offshore islands**
—67	**Central Africa and offshore islands**
—68	**Southern Africa Republic of South Africa**
—69	**South Indian Ocean islands**

—61 Tunisia and Libya

Class here Barbary States, comprehensive works on North Africa

(Option: Class here ancient North Africa; prefer —39)

Class each specific part of North Africa, of Barbary States, not provided for here with the part, e.g., Algeria —65

—611 Tunisia

—612 Libya

—62 Egypt and Sudan

Class here *Nile River

(Option: Class here ancient Egypt; prefer —32)

For Sinai, see —53

—624 Sudan

For provinces of Sudan, see —625–629

*Class parts of this physiographic region or feature as instructed under —4–9

> —625–629 Provinces of Sudan

Class comprehensive works in —624

—625 Eastern [*formerly* —629] and Northern regions of Sudan

Including Nubian Desert

(Option: Class here ancient Cush, Ethiopia, Nubia; prefer —39)

—626 Khartoum province and Central region of Sudan

Class here *Blue Nile River

—627 Darfur region of Sudan

—628 Kordofan region of Sudan

—629 Southern regions

Contains Bahr al Ghazal, Buhayrah, Equatoria, Upper Nile regions

Class here *White Nile River

Eastern region relocated to —625

—63 Ethiopia

Class here Horn of Africa

For Djibouti and Somalia, see —677

—64 Northwest African coast and offshore islands Morocco

Including Canary Islands

(Option: Class here the Moroccan part of ancient North Africa; prefer —39)

—648 Western Sahara

—65 Algeria

(Option: Class here the Algerian part of ancient North Africa; prefer —39)

—66 West Africa and offshore islands

Class here *Sahara Desert

Islands of Gulf of Guinea relocated to —671

—661 Mauritania

—662 Mali, Burkina Faso, Niger

—662 3 Mali

—662 5 Burkina Faso

Former name: Upper Volta

—662 6 Niger

*Class parts of this physiographic region or feature as instructed under —4–9

—663 Senegal

Class here Senegambia

For Gambia, see —6651

—664 Sierra Leone

—665 Gambia, Guinea, Guinea-Bissau, Cape Verde

Class here Upper Guinea area

Class each specific country of Upper Guinea not provided for here with the country, e.g., Sierra Leone —664

—665 1 Gambia

—665 2 Guinea

—665 7 Guinea-Bissau

—665 8 Cape Verde

Class here Cape Verde Islands

—666 Liberia and Ivory Coast

—666 2 Liberia

—666 8 Ivory Coast

—667 Ghana

—668 Togo and Benin

—668 1 Togo

—668 3 Benin

Former name: Dahomey

—669 Nigeria

—67 Central Africa and offshore islands

Class here Black Africa, Sub-Saharan Africa (Africa south of the Sahara)

Class each specific part of Black Africa, of Sub-Saharan Africa not provided for here with the part, e.g., Nigeria —669

—671 Cameroon, Sao Tome and Principe, Equatorial Guinea

Class here Islands of Gulf of Guinea [*formerly* —66], Lower Guinea area

Class each specific country of Lower Guinea not provided for here with the country, e.g., Gabon —6721

—671 1 Cameroon

—671 5 Sao Tome and Principe

—671 8 Equatorial Guinea

—672 Gabon and Republic of the Congo

—672 1 Gabon

—672 4 Republic of the Congo

See also —6751 for Democratic Republic of the Congo (Zaire)

—673 Angola

—674 Central African Republic and Chad

—674 1 Central African Republic

—674 3 Chad

—675 Zaire, Rwanda, Burundi

—675 1 Zaire

Former names: Democratic Republic of the Congo, Belgian Congo

Class here *Congo (Zaire) River

See also —6724 for Republic of the Congo

—675 7 Rwanda and Burundi

Class here former Ruanda-Urundi

—675 71 Rwanda

—675 72 Burundi

—676 Uganda and Kenya

Class here East Africa, *Great Rift Valley

Class a specific part of East Africa not provided for here with the part, e.g., Tanzania —678

—676 1 Uganda

—676 2 Kenya

—677 Djibouti and Somalia

Class here Somaliland

—677 1 Djibouti

—677 3 Somalia

—678 Tanzania

—679 Mozambique

—68 Southern Africa Republic of South Africa

—[681] Botswana, Lesotho, Swaziland

Relocated to —688

*Class parts of this physiographic region or feature as instructed under —4–9

> —682–687 Republic of South Africa

Class comprehensive works in —68

—682 Transvaal

—684 Natal

—685 Orange Free State

—687 Cape of Good Hope

—688 Botswana, Lesotho, Swaziland [*all formerly* —681], Namibia

—688 1 Namibia

—688 3 Botswana

—688 5 Lesotho

—688 7 Swaziland

—689 Zimbabwe, Zambia, Malawi

—689 1 Zimbabwe

Former name: Zimbabwe-Rhodesia

—689 4 Zambia

—689 7 Malawi

—69 South Indian Ocean islands

Including Réunion

—691 Madagascar

—694 Comoros (Federal and Islamic Republic of the Comoros)

—696 Seychelles

—698 Mauritius

—7 North America

Class Western Hemisphere in —181

SUMMARY

—71 Canada
—72 Middle America Mexico
—73 United States
—74 Northeastern United States (New England and Middle Atlantic states)
—75 Southeastern United States (South Atlantic states)
—76 South central United States Gulf Coast states
—77 North central United States Lake states
—78 Western United States
—79 Great Basin and Pacific Slope region of United States Pacific Coast states

—71 Canada

—711 British Columbia

Class here *Rocky Mountains in Canada

—712 Prairie Provinces

Class here western Canada

Class a specific part of western Canada not provided for here with the part, e.g., British Columbia —711

—712 3 Alberta

—712 4 Saskatchewan

—712 7 Manitoba

—713 Ontario

Class here Great Lakes in Canada, eastern Canada

Class a specific part of eastern Canada not provided for here with the part, e.g., Nova Scotia —716

—714 Quebec

Class here *Canadian Shield; *Saint Lawrence River

—715 New Brunswick

Class here Maritime Provinces, Atlantic Provinces

For Nova Scotia, see —716; Prince Edward Island, —717; Newfoundland and Labrador, —718

—716 Nova Scotia

—717 Prince Edward Island

—718 Newfoundland and Labrador, Saint-Pierre and Miquelon

—719 Northern territories

Contains Yukon Territory; Northwest Territories, consisting of Baffin, Fort Smith, Inuvik, Keewatin, Kitikmeot regions

Class here Canadian Arctic

—72 Middle America Mexico

—728 Central America

—728 1 Guatemala

—728 2 Belize

—728 3 Honduras

—728 4 El Salvador

—728 5 Nicaragua

—728 6 Costa Rica

*Class parts of this physiographic region or feature as instructed under —4–9

—728 7 Panama

—729 West Indies (Antilles) and Bermuda

Class here *Caribbean Area

> —729 1–729 5 Greater Antilles

Class comprehensive works in —729

—729 1 Cuba

—729 2 Jamaica and Cayman Islands

—729 3 Dominican Republic

Class here comprehensive works on Hispaniola

For Haiti, see —7294

—729 4 Haiti

—729 5 Puerto Rico

—729 6 Bahama Islands

> —729 7–729 8 Lesser Antilles (Caribbees)

Class comprehensive works in —729

—729 7 Leeward Islands

Including Guadeloupe, Montserrat, Saba, Saint Eustatius, Saint Martin, Virgin Islands

For Dominica, see —729841

—729 73 Anguilla, and Saint Kitts and Nevis

—729 74 Antigua and Barbuda

—729 8 Windward and other southern islands

Including Aruba, Bonaire, Curaçao, Martinique

—729 81 Barbados

—729 83 Trinidad and Tobago

—729 84 Windward Islands

—729 841 Dominica

—729 843 Saint Lucia

—729 844 Saint Vincent and the Grenadines

For Carriacou, see —729845

—729 845 Grenada and Carriacou

*Class parts of this physiographic region or feature as instructed under —4–9

—729 9 Bermuda

—73 United States

For specific states, see —74–79

> **—74–79 Specific states of United States**

Class comprehensive works in —73

For Hawaii, see —969

—74 Northeastern United States (New England and Middle Atlantic states)

Class here United States east of Allegheny Mountains, east of Mississippi River; *Appalachian Mountains; *Connecticut River

For southeastern United States, see —75; south central United States, —76; north central United States, —77

> —741–746 New England

Class comprehensive works in —74

—741 Maine

—742 New Hampshire

—743 Vermont

—744 Massachusetts

—745 Rhode Island

—746 Connecticut

> —747–749 Middle Atlantic states

Class comprehensive works in —74

—747 New York

Including *Lake Ontario

—748 Pennsylvania

—749 New Jersey

—75 Southeastern United States (South Atlantic states)

Class here southern states, *Piedmont, *Atlantic Coastal Plain

For south central United States, see —76

—751 Delaware

*Class parts of this physiographical region or feature as instructed under —4–9

—752 Maryland

Class here *Potomac River

—753 District of Columbia (Washington)

—754 West Virginia

—755 Virginia

Class here *Blue Ridge

Chesapeake Bay relocated to —163

—756 North Carolina

—757 South Carolina

—758 Georgia

—759 Florida

—76 South central United States Gulf Coast states

Class here Old Southwest

> —761-764 Gulf Coast states

Class comprehensive works in —76

For Florida, see —759

—761 Alabama

—762 Mississippi

—763 Louisiana

—764 Texas

Including *Rio Grande

—766 Oklahoma

—767 Arkansas

—768 Tennessee

Class here *Tennessee River and Valley

—769 Kentucky

Comprehensive works on Ohio River relocated to —77

—77 North central United States Lake states

Class here comprehensive works on *Ohio River [*formerly* —769] and Valley, Middle West, *Mississippi River and Valley, *Great Lakes

Class each specific state of Middle West not provided for here with the state, e.g., Kansas —781

*Class parts of this physiographic region or feature as instructed under —4–9

> —771–776 Lake states

Class comprehensive works in —77

For New York, see —747; Pennsylvania, —748

—771 Ohio

Including *Lake Erie

—772 Indiana

—773 Illinois

—774 Michigan

Including *Lake Superior

Class here Lakes *Huron, *Michigan

—775 Wisconsin

—776 Minnesota

—777 Iowa

—778 Missouri

—78 Western United States

Class here the West; *Great Plains; *Rocky Mountains; *Missouri River

For Great Basin and Pacific Slope region, see —79

—781 Kansas

—782 Nebraska

—783 South Dakota

—784 North Dakota

> —786–789 Rocky Mountain states

Class comprehensive works in —78

For Idaho, see —796

—786 Montana

—787 Wyoming

—788 Colorado

—789 New Mexico

—79 Great Basin and Pacific Slope region of United States Pacific Coast states

Class here New Southwest

*Class parts of this physiographic region or feature as instructed under —4–9

—791 Arizona

Including *Colorado River

—792 Utah

—793 Nevada

—794 California

—795 Oregon

Class here Pacific Northwest; *Cascade and *Coast Ranges

For Idaho, see —796; Washington, —797; British Columbia, —711

—796 Idaho

—797 Washington

—798 Alaska

—8 South America

Class here Latin America, Spanish America; the *Andes

For Middle America, see —72

—81 Brazil

Including *Amazon River

—82 Argentina

—83 Chile

—84 Bolivia

—85 Peru

—86 Colombia and Ecuador

—861 Colombia

—866 Ecuador

—87 Venezuela

—88 Guiana

—881 Guyana

Former name: British Guiana

—882 French Guiana (Guyane)

Overseas department of France

—883 Surinam

Former name: Dutch Guiana

*Class parts of this physiographic region or feature as instructed under —4–9

—89 **Paraguay and Uruguay**

—892 Paraguay

—895 Uruguay

—9 Other parts of world and extraterrestrial worlds Pacific Ocean islands

SUMMARY

—93	**New Zealand**
—94	**Australia**
—95	**Melanesia New Guinea**
—96	**Other parts of Pacific Ocean Polynesia**
—97	**Atlantic Ocean islands**
—98	**Arctic islands and Antarctica**
—99	**Extraterrestrial worlds**

> **—93–96 Pacific Ocean islands**

Class comprehensive works in —9; each specific island or group of islands not provided for here with the island or group of islands, e.g., Japan —52

—93 **New Zealand**

Melanesia relocated to —95

—931 Specific islands

Including Antipodes, Auckland, Campbell, Chatham, Pitt

Use of this notation for comprehensive works on New Zealand discontinued; class in 93

—931 2 North Island

—931 5 South Island and Stewart Island

—94 **Australia**

—941 Western Australia

—942 Central Australia

—942 3 South Australia

—942 9 Northern Territory

Class here northern Australia

For Western Australia, see —941; Queensland, —943

—943 Queensland

Including Great Barrier Reef

—944 New South Wales

Class here *Murray River

*Class parts of this physiographic region or feature as instructed under —4–9

—945 Victoria

—946 Tasmania

—947 Australian Capital Territory

—95 Melanesia [*formerly* —93] New Guinea

Class here Oceania

Class Polynesia in —96, Micronesia in —965

> —951-957 New Guinea

Class comprehensive works in —95

—951 Irian Jaya

—953 Papua New Guinea New Guinea region

For Papuan region, see —954; Highlands region, —956; Momase region, —957; Bismarck Archipelago, —958; North Solomons Province, —9592

—954 Papuan region

Contains Central, Gulf, Milne Bay, Northern (Oro), Western (Fly River) provinces; National Capital District

—956 Highlands region

Contains Eastern, Enga, Simbu (Chimbu), Southern Highlands, Western Highlands provinces

—957 Momase (Northern coastal) region

Contains East Sepik, Madang, Morobe, West Sepik provinces

—958 Bismarck Archipelago

Part of Papua New Guinea

Contains East New Britain, Manus, New Ireland, West New Britain provinces

—959 Other parts of Melanesia

—959 2 North Solomons Province

Part of Papua New Guinea

—959 3 Solomon Islands

Independent nation

Former name: British Solomon Islands

—959 5 Vanuatu

Former name: New Hebrides

—959 7 New Caledonia

–96 Other parts of Pacific Ocean Polynesia

–961 Southwest central Pacific Ocean islands, and isolated islands of southeast Pacific Ocean

Including Samoan Islands, Tokelau; Ducie, Easter, Henderson, Oeno, Pitcairn

–961 1 Fiji

–961 2 Tonga

–961 4 Western Samoa

–961 6 Wallis and Futuna Islands

–962 South central Pacific Ocean islands

Including Cook Islands, Tahiti

Class here French Polynesia

For Marquesas, Tuamotu Islands, see –963

–963 Southeast central Pacific Ocean islands

Including Marquesas, Tuamotu Islands

For isolated islands of southeast Pacific Ocean, see –961

–964 Line Islands

Variant name: Equatorial Islands

For Palmyra Island, see –969

–965 West central Pacific Ocean islands (Micronesia)

Class each specific island or group of islands with the island or group of islands, e.g., Marshall Islands –968

–966 Federated States of Micronesia and Republic of Palau

Class here Caroline Islands

–967 Mariana Islands

Class here Commonwealth of the Northern Mariana Islands

–968 Islands of eastern Micronesia

Including Marshall Islands

–968 1 Kiribati

For Line Islands, see –964

–968 2 Tuvalu

–968 5 Nauru

–969 North central Pacific Ocean islands Hawaii

Including Palmyra Island

—97 **Atlantic Ocean islands**

Including Bouvet Island, Falkland Islands, Saint Helena, their dependencies

Class each specific island or group of islands not provided for here with the island or group of islands, e.g., Azores —469

—98 **Arctic islands and Antarctica**

Including Franz Josef Land, Jan Mayen Island, Novaya Zemlya, Severnaya Zemlya, Svalbard (Spitsbergen)

Class each Arctic island or group of islands not provided for here with the island or group of islands, e.g., Baffin region, Canada —719

—982 Greenland

—99 **Extraterrestrial worlds**

Class space in —19

See Manual at T2—19 vs. T2—99

Table 3. Subdivisions for Individual Literatures, for Specific Literary Forms

Notation from Table 3 is never used alone, but may be used as required with the base numbers for individual literatures identified by * under 810–890. It is never used for individual literatures not identified by *; the number for works by or about individual or multiple authors in such literatures ends with the language notation, e.g., works of an author writing in Welsh 891.6

Procedures for building numbers for works by or about more than one author, limited to literatures of specific languages, and for works by individual authors:

1. Look in the schedule 810–890 to find the base number for the language. The base number may be identified in a note, e.g., at 820: "Base number for English: 82"; otherwise, it is the number given for the literature, e.g., Portuguese-language literature 869. If there is a specific literary form, go to step 2; if not, skip to step 4

2. In Table 3 find the subdivision for the literary form, e.g., poetry —1. Add this to the base number, e.g., English poetry 821, Portuguese poetry 869.1. If the work (1) is by an individual author, (2) deals with or falls within a limited time period, or (3) deals with poetry, drama, fiction, or speech of specific media, scopes, kinds, the class number is complete. For other works, go to step 3

3. Go to the subdivisions under the particular form in Table 3, e.g., under —1 for poetry go to —1001–1009. Follow the instructions given there, which will lead to use of the table under —1–8. For example, the number for a collection of English poetry is 821.008

4. If the work is not limited to a specific literary form, consult —01–09 in Table 3, and follow the instructions at the number selected. For example, the number for history and criticism of Swedish literature is 839.709

(Option: Where two or more countries share the same language, either [1] use initial letters to distinguish the separate countries, or [2] for English-language works, use the special number designated for literatures of those countries that are not preferred, e.g., 20th-century drama in English by New Zealand authors NZ822 or 828.99, collections of 20th-century Australian writings in English A820.8 or 828.99. Full instructions appear under 810, 819, 820, 828.99)

See Manual at Table 3; 800: Literary criticism

SUMMARY

−01–09 [Standard subdivisions; collections; history, description, critical appraisal]
−1 Poetry
−2 Drama
−3 Fiction
−4 Essays
−5 Speeches
−6 Letters
−7 Satire and humor
−8 Miscellaneous writings

−01–07 Standard subdivisions

Standard subdivisions are used for general works consisting equally of literary texts and history, description, critical appraisal, e.g., a serial consisting equally of literary texts and history, description, critical appraisal of a variety of literature in English 820.5. Works limited to specific topics are classed in −08

Class collections of literary texts in −08, history, description, critical appraisal in −09

−08 Collections of literary texts

In more than one form by more than one author

Use of this number for general works consisting equally of literary texts and history, description, critical appraisal of a specific literature discontinued; class in the base number for the literature, adding a 0 if necessary to make a three-digit number, e.g., texts and criticism of a variety of literary works in English 820 (*not* 820.8)

Works limited to a specific topic and consisting equally of literary texts and history, description, critical appraisal of a specific literature are classed here, e.g., texts and criticism of English-language literary works about war 820.8

Class collections by individual authors in −1–8; history, description, critical appraisal of a specific literature in −09

−09 History, description, critical appraisal

Of more than one form by more than one author

Class here collected biography

−090 001–090 009 Standard subdivisions

> ## —1–8 Specific forms

Unless other instructions are given, observe the following table of precedence for works combining two or more literary forms, e.g., poetic drama —2 (*not* —1)

Drama	—2
Poetry	—1
Class epigrams in verse in —8	
Fiction	—3
Essays	—4
Speeches	—5
Letters	—6
Miscellaneous writings	—8
Satire and humor	—7

Class collections of satire and humor in two or more literary forms as satire and humor

(Option: Give precedence to satire and humor over all other forms)

When told to add as instructed under —1–8, add as follows:

1–7 Standard subdivisions

Standard subdivisions are used for general works consisting equally of literary texts and history, description, critical appraisal, e.g., a serial consisting equally of literary texts and history, description, critical appraisal of poetry in English 821.005. Works limited to specific topics are classed in 8

Class collections of literary texts in 8, history, description, critical appraisal in 9

8 Collections of literary texts

Use of this notation for general works consisting equally of literary texts and history, description, critical appraisal discontinued; class in the number for the specific form

Works consisting equally of literary texts and history, description, critical appraisal are classed here if limited to specific topics

8001–8007 Standard subdivisions

[8008] With respect to kinds of persons

Do not use; class in 8

[8009] Historical, geographic, persons treatment

Do not use; class in 9

9 History, description, critical appraisal

Class here collected biography

Follow the instructions under 8 for works consisting equally of literary texts and history, description, critical appraisal

901–907 Standard subdivisions

[908] With respect to kinds of persons

Do not use; class in 9

[909] Historical, geographic, persons treatment

Do not use; class in 9

Class comprehensive works on two or more forms in the base number for the individual literature, using notation 01–09 from Table 3 if applicable, adding 0 when required to make a three-figure number, e.g., comprehensive works on English drama and fiction 820

—1 Poetry

See Manual at T3—1 vs. T3—2 for dramatic poetry

—100 1–100 9 Standard subdivisions; collections; history, description, critical appraisal

Add to —100 as instructed under —1–8, e.g., collections of poetry —1008; however, do not add for poetry of specific kinds or periods, e.g., collections of epic poetry, of 20th century poetry —1 (*not* —1008)

—2 Drama

See Manual at T3—1 vs. T3—2 for poetic plays

—200 1–200 9 Standard subdivisions; collections; history, description, critical appraisal

Add to —200 as instructed under —1–8, e.g., collections of drama —2008; however, do not add for drama of specific media, scopes, kinds, periods, e.g., collections of radio plays, of monologues, of farces, of 20th century drama —2 (*not* —2008)

—3 Fiction

Cartoon fiction relocated to 741.5

—300 1–300 9 Standard subdivisions; collections; history, description, critical appraisal

Add to —300 as instructed under —1–8, e.g., collections of fiction —3008; however, do not add for fiction of specific scopes, kinds, periods, e.g., collections of short stories, of science fiction, of 20th century fiction —3 (*not* —3008)

—4 Essays

—400 1–400 9 Standard subdivisions; collections; history, description, critical appraisal

Add to —400 as instructed under —1–8, e.g., collections of essays —4008; however, do not add for essays of specific periods, e.g., collections of 20th century essays —4 (*not* —4008)

—5 Speeches

—500 1–500 9 Standard subdivisions; collections; history, description, critical appraisal

Add to —500 as instructed under —1–8, e.g., collections of speeches —5008; however, do not add for speeches of specific kinds or periods, e.g., collections of debates, of 20th century speeches —5 (*not* —5008)

—6 Letters

See Manual at T3—6

—600 1–600 9 Standard subdivisions; collections; history, description, critical appraisal

Add to —600 as instructed under —1–8, e.g., collections of letters —6008; however, do not add for letters of specific periods, e.g., collections of 20th century letters —6 (*not* —6008)

—7 Satire and humor

Class here parody, collections of humor in various forms to be read for pleasure

Class textbooks and teaching collections showing the development of manifestations of comedy in literature of a specific form with the form, e.g., comedy as an aspect of drama —2008

See Manual at T3—7 vs. T3—8, 001–999

—700 1–700 9 Standard subdivisions; collections; history, description, critical appraisal

Add to —700 as instructed under —1–8, e.g., collections of satire and humor —7008; ; however, do not add for satire and humor of specific periods, e.g., collections of 20th century satire and humor —7 (*not* —7008)

—8 Miscellaneous writings

Examples: anecdotes, diaries, epigrams, graffiti, jokes, journals, quotations, reminiscences, experimental and nonformalized works without identifiable form, prose literature in more than one form

Class a specific identifiable form of literature with the form, e.g., essays —4

See Manual at T3—7 vs. T3—8, 001–999 for jokes and humor; T3—8 for diaries

—800 1–800 9 Standard subdivisions; collections; history, description, critical appraisal

Add to —800 as instructed under —1–8, e.g., critical appraisal of miscellaneous writings from more than one period —8009; however, do not add for miscellaneous writings of specific kinds or periods, e.g., collections of jokes, of reminiscences, of 20th century miscellaneous writings —8 (*not* —8008)

Table 4. Subdivisions of Individual Languages

The following notation is never used alone, but may be used as required with the base numbers for individual languages identified by * as explained under 420–490, e.g., English (base number 42) reading (—84 in this table): 428.4. A point is inserted following the third digit of any number thus constructed that is longer than three digits. Notation from Table 1 is added to the notation in Table 4 when appropriate, e.g., —509 history of grammar, 425.09 history of English grammar

See Manual at 410

SUMMARY

—01–09	**Standard subdivisions**
—1	**Writing systems and phonology of the standard form of the language**
—2	**Etymology of the standard form of the language**
—3	**Dictionaries of the standard form of the language**
—5	**Structural system (Grammar) of the standard form of the language**
—7	**Historical and geographic variations, modern nongeographic variations**
—8	**Standard usage of the language (Prescriptive linguistics) Applied linguistics**

—01 **Philosophy and theory**

Including semantics [*formerly* —2], semiotics

—02 **Miscellany**

—03 **Encyclopedias and concordances**

Do not use for dictionaries; class dictionaries of the standard form of the language in —3, of historical and geographic variations, of modern nongeographic variations in the language in —7

—05–09 **Standard subdivisions**

See Manual at 407, T1—07 vs. 410.7, 418.007, T4—8007, 401 for education and related topics

---

> —1–5 Description and analysis of the standard form of the language

Class comprehensive works in the base number for the language (adding 0 when required to make a three-digit number), e.g., comprehensive works on phonology, etymology, dictionaries, grammar of standard French 440; standard usage, prescriptive and applied linguistics in —8

See Manual at T4—7

—1 Writing systems and phonology of the standard form of the language

Including abbreviations, alphabet, braille, ideographs, intonation, paleography, pronunciation, punctuation, spelling

See also —3 for dictionaries

See Manual at 808.1 vs. 414, T4—1 for prosody

—2 Etymology of the standard form of the language

Including foreign elements

Semantics other than the history of word meanings relocated to —01

—3 Dictionaries of the standard form of the language

Including bilingual dictionaries; specialized dictionaries, e.g., dictionaries of abbreviations

A bilingual dictionary with entry words in only one language is classed with that language, e.g., an English-French dictionary 423. A bilingual dictionary with entry words in both languages is classed with the language in which it will be the more useful; for example, most libraries in English-speaking regions will find English-French, French-English dictionaries most useful classed with French in 443. If classification with either language is equally useful, give priority to the language coming later in the sequence 420–490, e.g., French-German, German-French dictionaries 443

Class etymological dictionaries in —203

See Manual at T4—3 for bilingual dictionaries; T4—3 vs. T4—81

—302 8 Techniques, procedures, apparatus, equipment, materials

Class here lexicography

—5 Structural system (Grammar) of the standard form of the language

Historical and descriptive study of morphology and syntax

Class here comprehensive works on morphology, syntax, and phonology

For phonology, see —1

See also —8 for prescriptive grammar

—7 Historical and geographic variations, modern nongeographic variations

Examples: early forms; dialects, pidgins, creoles; slang

Use notation 7 only for works that stress differences among the forms of a language

Topics classed in —1–5 and —8 when applied to standard forms of the language are classed here when applied to historical and geographic variations, to modern nongeographic variations, e.g., the distinctive grammatical characteristics of a particular dialect

See Manual at T4—7

—8 Standard usage of the language (Prescriptive linguistics) Applied linguistics

General, formal, informal usage

Including translation and interpretation to and from other languages

Class here works for persons learning a second language, works for native speakers who are learning the acceptable patterns of their own language

Class purely descriptive linguistics in —1–5

Topics of —8 applied to historical and geographic variations, to modern nongeographic variations of the language are classed in —7

For dictionaries, see —3; rhetoric, 808

See Manual at 410

—800 1–800 9 Standard subdivisions

See Manual at 407, T1—07 vs. 410.7, 418.007, T4—8007, 401 for education and related topics

—81 **Words**

Meaning, pronunciation, spelling

Class formal presentation of vocabulary in —82, audio-lingual presentation of vocabulary in —83

See Manual at T4—3 vs. T4—81

—82 **Structural approach to expression**

Formal (traditional) presentation of grammar, vocabulary, reading selections

For words, see —81; reading —84

—83 **Audio-lingual approach to expression**

Informal presentation through practice in correct usage

For pronunciation, see —81

—84 **Reading**

Including developmental and remedial reading

For readers, see —86

—86 **Readers**

Graded selections with emphasis on structure and vocabulary as needed

(Option: Class elementary readers in 372.4)

See Manual at T4—86 vs. 001–999 for readers for nonnative speakers

Summaries

First Summary*
The Ten Main Classes

000	**Generalities**
100	**Philosophy & psychology**
200	**Religion**
300	**Social sciences**
400	**Language**
500	**Natural sciences & mathematics**
600	**Technology (Applied sciences)**
700	**The arts**
800	**Literature & rhetoric**
900	**Geography & history**

*Consult schedules for complete and exact headings

Second Summary*
The Hundred Divisions

000 Generalities
010 Bibliography
020 Library & information sciences
030 General encyclopedic works
040
050 General serials & their indexes
060 General organizations & museology
070 News media, journalism, publishing
080 General collections
090 Manuscripts & rare books

100 Philosophy & psychology
110 Metaphysics
120 Epistemology, causation, humankind
130 Paranormal phenomena
140 Specific philosophical schools
150 Psychology
160 Logic
170 Ethics (Moral philosophy)
180 Ancient, medieval, Oriental philosophy
190 Modern Western philosophy

200 Religion
210 Natural theology
220 Bible
230 Christian theology
240 Christian moral & devotional theology
250 Christian orders & local church
260 Christian social theology
270 Christian church history
280 Christian denominations & sects
290 Other & comparative religions

300 Social sciences
310 General statistics
320 Political science
330 Economics
340 Law
350 Public administration
360 Social services; association
370 Education
380 Commerce, communications, transport
390 Customs, etiquette, folklore

400 Language
410 Linguistics
420 English & Old English
430 Germanic languages German
440 Romance languages French
450 Italian, Romanian, Rhaeto-Romanic
460 Spanish & Portuguese languages
470 Italic languages Latin
480 Hellenic languages Classical Greek
490 Other languages

500 Natural sciences & mathematics
510 Mathematics
520 Astronomy & allied sciences
530 Physics
540 Chemistry & allied sciences
550 Earth sciences
560 Paleontology Paleozoology
570 Life sciences
580 Botanical sciences
590 Zoological sciences

600 Technology (Applied sciences)
610 Medical sciences Medicine
620 Engineering & allied operations
630 Agriculture
640 Home economics & family living
650 Management & auxiliary services
660 Chemical engineering
670 Manufacturing
680 Manufacture for specific uses
690 Buildings

700 The arts
710 Civic & landscape art
720 Architecture
730 Plastic arts Sculpture
740 Drawing & decorative arts
750 Painting & paintings
760 Graphic arts Printmaking & prints
770 Photography & photographs
780 Music
790 Recreational & performing arts

800 Literature & rhetoric
810 American literature in English
820 English & Old English literatures
830 Literatures of Germanic languages
840 Literatures of Romance languages
850 Italian, Romanian, Rhaeto-Romanic
860 Spanish & Portuguese literatures
870 Italic literatures Latin
880 Hellenic literatures Classical Greek
890 Literatures of other languages

900 Geography & history
910 Geography & travel
920 Biography, genealogy, insignia
930 History of ancient world
940 General history of Europe
950 General history of Asia Far East
960 General history of Africa
970 General history of North America
980 General history of South America
990 General history of other areas

*Consult schedules for complete and exact headings

Third Summary*

The Thousand Sections

Generalities

000 Generalities
001 Knowledge
002 The book
003 Systems
004 Data processing Computer science
005 Computer programming, programs, data
006 Special computer methods
007
008
009

010 Bibliography
011 Bibliographies
012 Of individuals
013 Of works by specific classes of authors
014 Of anonymous and pseudonymous works
015 Of works from specific places
016 Of works on specific subjects
017 General subject catalogs
018 Catalogs arranged by author & date
019 Dictionary catalogs

020 Library & information sciences
021 Library relationships
022 Administration of the physical plant
023 Personnel administration
024
025 Library operations
026 Libraries for specific subjects
027 General libraries
028 Reading, use of other information media
029

030 General encyclopedic works
031 American
032 In English
033 In other Germanic languages
034 In French, Provençal, Catalan
035 In Italian, Romanian, Rhaeto-Romanic
036 In Spanish & Portuguese
037 In Slavic languages
038 In Scandinavian languages
039 In other languages

040
041
042
043
044
045
046
047
048
049

050 General serials & their indexes
051 American
052 In English
053 In other Germanic languages
054 In French, Provençal, Catalan
055 In Italian, Romanian, Rhaeto-Romanic
056 In Spanish & Portuguese
057 In Slavic languages
058 In Scandinanvian languages
059 In other languages

060 General organizations & museology
061 In North America
062 In British Isles In England
063 In central Europe In Germany
064 In France & Monaco
065 In Italy & adjacent territories
066 In Iberian Peninsula & adjacent islands
067 In eastern Europe In Soviet Union
068 In other areas
069 Museology (Museum science)

070 News media, journalism, publishing
071 In North America
072 In British Isles In England
073 In central Europe In Germany
074 In France & Monaco
075 In Italy & adjacent territories
076 In Iberian Peninsula & adjacent islands
077 In eastern Europe In Soviet Union
078 In Scandinavia
079 In other areas

080 General collections
081 American
082 In English
083 In other Germanic languages
084 In French, Provençal, Catalan
085 In Italian, Romanian, Rhaeto-Romanic
086 In Spanish & Portuguese
087 In Slavic languages
088 In Scandinavian languages
089 In other languages

090 Manuscripts & rare books
091 Manuscripts
092 Block books
093 Incunabula
094 Printed books
095 Books notable for bindings
096 Books notable for illustrations
097 Books notable for ownership or origin
098 Prohibited works, forgeries, hoaxes
099 Books notable for format

*Consult schedules for complete and exact headings

Philosophy and psychology

100 Philosophy & psychology
101 Theory of philosophy
102 Miscellany of philosophy
103 Dictionaries of philosophy
104
105 Serial publications of philosophy
106 Organizations of philosophy
107 Education, research in philosophy
108 Kinds of persons in philosophy
109 Historical treatment of philosophy

110 Metaphysics
111 Ontology
112
113 Cosmology (Philosophy of nature)
114 Space
115 Time
116 Change
117 Structure
118 Force & energy
119 Number & quantity

120 Epistemology, causation, humankind
121 Epistemology (Theory of knowledge)
122 Causation
123 Determinism & indeterminism
124 Teleology
125
126 The self
127 The unconscious & the subconscious
128 Humankind
129 Origin & destiny of individual souls

130 Paranormal phenomena
131 Occult methods for achieving well-being
132
133 Parapsychology & occultism
134
135 Dreams & mysteries
136
137 Divinatory graphology
138 Physiognomy
139 Phrenology

140 Specific philosophical schools
141 Idealism & related systems
142 Critical philosophy
143 Intuitionism & Bergsonism
144 Humanism & related systems
145 Sensationalism
146 Naturalism & related systems
147 Pantheism & related systems
148 Liberalism, eclecticism, traditionalism
149 Other philosophical systems

150 Psychology
151
152 Perception, movement, emotions, drives
153 Mental processes & intelligence
154 Subconscious & altered states
155 Differential & developmental psychology
156 Comparative psychology
157
158 Applied psychology
159

160 Logic
161 Induction
162 Deduction
163
164
165 Fallacies & sources of error
166 Syllogisms
167 Hypotheses
168 Argument & persuasion
169 Analogy

170 Ethics (Moral philosophy)
171 Systems & doctrines
172 Political ethics
173 Ethics of family relationships
174 Economic & professional ethics
175 Ethics of recreation & leisure
176 Ethics of sex & reproduction
177 Ethics of social relations
178 Ethics of consumption
179 Other ethical norms

180 Ancient, medieval, Oriental philosophy
181 Oriental philosophy
182 Pre-Socratic Greek philosophies
183 Sophistic & Socratic philosophies
184 Platonic philosophy
185 Aristotelian philosophy
186 Skeptic and Neoplatonic philosophies
187 Epicurean philosophy
188 Stoic philosophy
189 Medieval Western philosophy

190 Modern Western philosophy
191 United States & Canada
192 British Isles
193 Germany & Austria
194 France
195 Italy
196 Spain & Portugal
197 Soviet Union
198 Scandinavia
199 Other geographical areas

Religion

200	**Religion**
201	Philosophy of Christianity
202	Miscellany of Christianity
203	Dictionaries of Christianity
204	Special topics
205	Serial publications of Christianity
206	Organizations of Christianity
207	Education, research in Christianity
208	Kinds of persons in Christianity
209	History & geography of Christianity
210	**Natural theology**
211	Concepts of God
212	Existence, attributes of God
213	Creation
214	Theodicy
215	Science & religion
216	Good & evil
217	
218	Humankind
219	
220	**Bible**
221	Old Testament
222	Historical books of Old Testament
223	Poetic books of Old Testament
224	Prophetic books of Old Testament
225	New Testament
226	Gospels & Acts
227	Epistles
228	Revelation (Apocalypse)
229	Apocrypha & pseudepigrapha
230	**Christian theology**
231	God
232	Jesus Christ & his family
233	Humankind
234	Salvation (Soteriology) & grace
235	Spiritual beings
236	Eschatology
237	
238	Creeds & catechisms
239	Apologetics & polemics
240	**Christian moral & devotional theology**
241	Moral theology
242	Devotional literature
243	Evangelistic writings for individuals
244	
245	Texts of hymns
246	Use of art in Christianity
247	Church furnishings & articles
248	Christian experience, practice, life
249	Christian observances in family life
250	**Christian orders & local church**
251	Preaching (Homiletics)
252	Texts of sermons
253	Pastoral office (Pastoral theology)
254	Parish government & administration
255	Religious congregations & orders
256	
257	
258	
259	Activities of the local church
260	**Christian social theology**
261	Social theology
262	Ecclesiology
263	Times, places of religious observance
264	Public worship
265	Sacraments, other rites & acts
266	Missions
267	Associations for religious work
268	Religious education
269	Spiritual renewal
270	**Christian church history**
271	Religious orders in church history
272	Persecutions in church history
273	Heresies in church history
274	Christian church in Europe
275	Christian church in Asia
276	Christian church in Africa
277	Christian church in North America
278	Christian church in South America
279	Christian church in other areas
280	**Christian denominations & sects**
281	Early church & Eastern churches
282	Roman Catholic Church
283	Anglican churches
284	Protestants of Continental origin
285	Presbyterian, Reformed, Congregational
286	Baptist, Disciples of Christ, Adventist
287	Methodist & related churches
288	
289	Other denominations & sects
290	**Other & comparative religions**
291	Comparative religion
292	Classical (Greek & Roman) religion
293	Germanic religion
294	Religions of Indic origin
295	Zoroastrianism (Mazdaism, Parseeism)
296	Judaism
297	Islam & religions originating in it
298	
299	Other religions

Social sciences

300	**Social sciences**
301	Sociology & anthropology
302	Social interaction
303	Social processes
304	Factors affecting social behavior
305	Social groups
306	Culture & institutions
307	Communities
308	
309	
310	**General statistics**
311	
312	
313	
314	Of Europe
315	Of Asia
316	Of Africa
317	Of North America
318	Of South America
319	Of other parts of the world
320	**Political science**
321	Systems of governments & states
322	Relation of state to organized groups
323	Civil & political rights
324	The political process
325	International migration & colonization
326	Slavery & emancipation
327	International relations
328	The legislative process
329	
330	**Economics**
331	Labor economics
332	Financial economics
333	Land economics
334	Cooperatives
335	Socialism & related systems
336	Public finance
337	International economics
338	Production
339	Macroeconomics & related topics
340	**Law**
341	International law
342	Constitutional & administrative law
343	Military, tax, trade, industrial law
344	Social, labor, welfare, & related law
345	Criminal law
346	Private law
347	Civil procedure & courts
348	Laws (Statutes), regulations, cases
349	Law of specific jurisdictions & areas
350	**Public administration**
351	Of central governments
352	Of local governments
353	Of U.S. federal & state governments
354	Of specific central governments
355	Military science
356	Foot forces & warfare
357	Mounted forces & warfare
358	Other specialized forces & services
359	Sea (Naval) forces & warfare
360	**Social services; association**
361	General social problems & welfare
362	Social welfare problems & services
363	Other social problems & services
364	Criminology
365	Penal & related institutions
366	Association
367	General clubs
368	Insurance
369	Miscellaneous kinds of associations
370	**Education**
371	School management; special education
372	Elementary education
373	Secondary education
374	Adult education
375	Curriculums
376	Education of women
377	Schools & religion
378	Higher education
379	Government regulation, control, support
380	**Commerce, communications, transport**
381	Internal commerce (Domestic trade)
382	International commerce (Foreign trade)
383	Postal communication
384	Communications Telecommunication
385	Railroad transportation
386	Inland waterway & ferry transportation
387	Water, air, space transportation
388	Transportation Ground transportation
389	Metrology & standardization
390	**Customs, etiquette, folklore**
391	Costume & personal appearance
392	Customs of life cycle & domestic life
393	Death customs
394	General customs
395	Etiquette (Manners)
396	
397	
398	Folklore
399	Customs of war & diplomacy

Language

400	**Language**
401	Philosophy & theory
402	Miscellany
403	Dictionaries & encyclopedias
404	Special topics
405	Serial publications
406	Organizations & management
407	Education, research, related topics
408	With respect to kinds of persons
409	Geographical & persons treatment
410	**Linguistics**
411	Writing systems
412	Etymology
413	Dictionaries
414	Phonology
415	Structural systems (Grammar)
416	
417	Dialectology & historical linguistics
418	Standard usage Applied linguistics
419	Verbal language not spoken or written
420	**English & Old English**
421	English writing system & phonology
422	English etymology
423	English dictionaries
424	
425	English grammar
426	
427	English language variations
428	Standard English usage
429	Old English (Anglo-Saxon)
430	**Germanic languages German**
431	German writing system & phonology
432	German etymology
433	German dictionaries
434	
435	German grammar
436	
437	German language variations
438	Standard German usage
439	Other Germanic languages
440	**Romance languages French**
441	French writing system & phonology
442	French etymology
443	French dictionaries
444	
445	French grammar
446	materials written in Fr.
447	French language variations
448	Standard French usage
449	Provençal & Catalan

450	**Italian, Romanian, Rhaeto-Romanic**
451	Italian writing system & phonology
452	Italian etymology
453	Italian dictionaries
454	
455	Italian grammar
456	
457	Italian language variations
458	Standard Italian usage
459	Romanian & Rhaeto-Romanic
460	**Spanish & Portuguese languages**
461	Spanish writing system & phonology
462	Spanish etymology
463	Spanish dictionaries
464	
465	Spanish grammar
466	
467	Spanish language variations
468	Standard Spanish usage
469	Portuguese
470	**Italic languages Latin**
471	Classical Latin writing & phonology
472	Classical Latin etymology
473	Classical Latin dictionaries
474	
475	Classical Latin grammar
476	
477	Old, Postclassical, Vulgar Latin
478	Classical Latin usage
479	Other Italic languages
480	**Hellenic languages Classical Greek**
481	Classical Greek writing & phonology
482	Classical Greek etymology
483	Classical Greek dictionaries
484	
485	Classical Greek grammar
486	
487	Preclassical & postclassical Greek
488	Classical Greek usage
489	Other Hellenic languages
490	**Other languages**
491	East Indo-European & Celtic languages
492	Afro-Asiatic languages Semitic
493	Non-Semitic Afro-Asiatic languages
494	Ural-Altaic, Paleosiberian, Dravidian
495	Languages of East & Southeast Asia
496	African languages
497	North American native languages
498	South American native languages
499	Miscellaneous languages

Natural sciences and mathematics

500 **Natural sciences & mathematics**
501 Philosophy & theory
502 Miscellany
503 Dictionaries & encyclopedias
504
505 Serial publications
506 Organizations & management
507 Education, research, related topics
508 Natural history
509 Historical, areas, persons treatment

510 **Mathematics**
511 General topics
512 Algebra & number theory
513 Arithmetic
514 Topology
515 Analysis
516 Geometry
517
518
519 Probabilities & applied mathematics

520 **Astronomy & allied sciences**
521 Celestial mechanics
522 Techniques, equipment, materials
523 Specific celestial bodies & phenomena
524
525 Earth (Astronomical geography)
526 Mathematical geography
527 Celestial navigation
528 Ephemerides
529 Chronology

530 **Physics**
531 Classical mechanics Solid mechanics
532 Fluid mechanics Liquid mechanics
533 Gas mechanics
534 Sound & related vibrations
535 Light & related radiations
536 Heat
537 Electricity & electronics
538 Magnetism
539 Modern physics

540 **Chemistry & allied sciences**
541 Physical & theoretical chemistry
542 Techniques, equipment, materials
543 Analytical chemistry
544 Qualitative analysis
545 Quantitative analysis
546 Inorganic chemistry
547 Organic chemistry
548 Crystallography
549 Mineralogy

550 **Earth sciences**
551 Geology, hydrology, meteorology
552 Petrology
553 Economic geology
554 Earth sciences of Europe
555 Earth sciences of Asia
556 Earth sciences of Africa
557 Earth sciences of North America
558 Earth sciences of South America
559 Earth sciences of other areas

560 **Paleontology Paleozoology**
561 Paleobotany
562 Fossil invertebrates
563 Fossil primitive phyla
564 Fossil mollusks & related phyla
565 Other fossil invertebrates
566 Fossil vertebrates
567 Fossil cold-blooded vertebrates
568 Fossil birds
569 Fossil mammals

570 **Life sciences**
571
572 Human races
573 Physical anthropology
574 Biology
575 Evolution & genetics
576 Microbiology
577 General nature of life
578 Microscopy in biology
579 Collection and preservation

580 **Botanical sciences**
581 Botany
582 Seed-bearing plants
583 Dicotyledons
584 Monocotyledons
585 Gymnosperms (Naked-seed plants)
586 Seedless plants
587 Pteridophyta (Vascular seedless plants)
588 Bryophytes
589 Thallophytes & prokaryotes

590 **Zoological sciences**
591 Zoology
592 Invertebrates
593 Protozoa, Echinodermata, related phyla
594 Mollusks & related phyla
595 Other invertebrates
596 Vertebrates
597 Cold-blooded vertebrates
598 Birds
599 Mammals

Technology (Applied sciences)

600 Technology (Applied sciences)
601 Philosophy & theory
602 Miscellany
603 Dictionaries & encyclopedias
604 Special topics
605 Serial publications
606 Organizations
607 Education, research, related topics
608 Invention & patents
609 Historical, areas, persons treatment

610 Medical sciences Medicine
611 Human anatomy, cytology, histology
612 Human physiology
613 Promotion of health
614 Incidence & prevention of disease
615 Pharmacology & therapeutics
616 Diseases
617 Surgery & related medical specialties
618 Gynecology & other medical specialties
619 Experimental medicine

620 Engineering & allied operations
621 Applied physics
622 Mining & related operations
623 Military & nautical engineering
624 Civil engineering
625 Engineering of railroads, roads
626
627 Hydraulic engineering
628 Sanitary & municipal engineering
629 Other branches of engineering

630 Agriculture
631 Techniques, equipment, materials
632 Plant injuries, diseases, pests
633 Field & plantation crops
634 Orchards, fruits, forestry
635 Garden crops (Horticulture)
636 Animal husbandry
637 Processing dairy & related products
638 Insect culture
639 Hunting, fishing, conservation

640 Home economics & family living
641 Food & drink
642 Meals & table service
643 Housing & household equipment
644 Household utilities
645 Household furnishings
646 Sewing, clothing, personal living
647 Management of public households
648 Housekeeping
649 Child rearing & home care of sick

650 Management & auxiliary services
651 Office services
652 Processes of written communication
653 Shorthand
654
655
656
657 Accounting
658 General management
659 Advertising & public relations

660 Chemical engineering
661 Industrial chemicals technology
662 Explosives, fuels technology
663 Beverage technology
664 Food technology
665 Industrial oils, fats, waxes, gases
666 Ceramic & allied technologies
667 Cleaning, color, related technologies
668 Technology of other organic products
669 Metallurgy

670 Manufacturing
671 Metalworking & metal products
672 Iron, steel, other iron alloys
673 Nonferrous metals
674 Lumber processing, wood products, cork
675 Leather & fur processing
676 Pulp & paper technology
677 Textiles
678 Elastomers & elastomer products
679 Other products of specific materials

680 Manufacture for specific uses
681 Precision instruments & other devices
682 Small forge work (Blacksmithing)
683 Hardware & household appliances
684 Furnishings & home workshops
685 Leather, fur, related products
686 Printing & related activities
687 Clothing
688 Other final products & packaging
689

690 Buildings
691 Building materials
692 Auxiliary construction practices
693 Specific materials & purposes
694 Wood construction Carpentry
695 Roof covering
696 Utilities
697 Heating, ventilating, air-conditioning
698 Detail finishing
699

The arts

700 The arts
701 Philosophy & theory
702 Miscellany
703 Dictionaries & encyclopedias
704 Special topics
705 Serial publications
706 Organizations & management
707 Education, research, related topics
708 Galleries, museums, private collections
709 Historical, areas, persons treatment

710 Civic & landscape art
711 Area planning (Civic art)
712 Landscape architecture
713 Landscape architecture of trafficways
714 Water features
715 Woody plants
716 Herbaceous plants
717 Structures
718 Landscape design of cemeteries
719 Natural landscapes

720 Architecture
721 Architectural structure
722 Architecture to ca. 300
723 Architecture from ca. 300 to 1399
724 Architecture from 1400
725 Public structures
726 Buildings for religious purposes
727 Buildings for education & research
728 Residential & related buildings
729 Design & decoration

730 Plastic arts Sculpture
731 Processes, forms, subjects of sculpture
732 Sculpture to ca. 500
733 Greek, Etruscan, Roman sculpture
734 Sculpture from ca. 500 to 1399
735 Sculpture from 1400
736 Carving & carvings
737 Numismatics & sigillography
738 Ceramic arts
739 Art metalwork

740 Drawing & decorative arts
741 Drawing & drawings
742 Perspective
743 Drawing & drawings by subject
744
745 Decorative arts
746 Textile arts
747 Interior decoration
748 Glass
749 Furniture & accessories

750 Painting & paintings
751 Techniques, equipment, forms
752 Color
753 Symbolism, allegory, mythology, legend
754 Genre paintings
755 Religion & religious symbolism
756
757 Human figures & their parts
758 Other subjects
759 Historical, areas, persons treatment

760 Graphic arts Printmaking & prints
761 Relief processes (Block printing)
762
763 Lithographic (Planographic) processes
764 Chromolithography & serigraphy
765 Metal engraving
766 Mezzotinting & related processes
767 Etching & drypoint
768
769 Prints

770 Photography & photographs
771 Techniques, equipment, materials
772 Metallic salt processes
773 Pigment processes of printing
774 Holography
775
776
777
778 Fields & kinds of photography
779 Photographs

780 Music
781 General principles & musical forms
782 Vocal music
783 Music for single voices The voice
784 Instruments & instrumental ensembles
785 Chamber music
786 Keyboard & other instruments
787 Stringed instruments
788 Wind instruments
789

790 Recreational & performing arts
791 Public performances
792 Stage presentations
793 Indoor games & amusements
794 Indoor games of skill
795 Games of chance
796 Athletic & outdoor sports & games
797 Aquatic & air sports
798 Equestrian sports & animal racing
799 Fishing, hunting, shooting

Literature and rhetoric

800 Literature & rhetoric
801 Philosophy & theory
802 Miscellany
803 Dictionaries & encyclopedias
804
805 Serial publications
806 Organizations
807 Education, research, related topics
808 Rhetoric & collections of literature
809 Literary history & criticism

810 American literature in English
811 Poetry
812 Drama
813 Fiction
814 Essays
815 Speeches
816 Letters
817 Satire & humor
818 Miscellaneous writings
819

820 English & Old English literatures
821 English poetry
822 English drama
823 English fiction
824 English essays
825 English speeches
826 English letters
827 English satire & humor
828 English miscellaneous writings
829 Old English (Anglo-Saxon)

830 Literatures of Germanic languages
831 German poetry
832 German drama
833 German fiction
834 German essays
835 German speeches
836 German letters
837 German satire & humor
838 German miscellaneous writings
839 Other Germanic literatures

840 Literatures of Romance languages
841 French poetry
842 French drama
843 French fiction
844 French essays
845 French speeches
846 French letters
847 French satire & humor
848 French miscellaneous writings
849 Provençal & Catalan

850 Italian, Romanian, Rhaeto-Romanic
851 Italian poetry
852 Italian drama
853 Italian fiction
854 Italian essays
855 Italian speeches
856 Italian letters
857 Italian satire & humor
858 Italian miscellaneous writings
859 Romanian & Rhaeto-Romanic

860 Spanish & Portuguese literatures
861 Spanish poetry
862 Spanish drama
863 Spanish fiction
864 Spanish essays
865 Spanish speeches
866 Spanish letters
867 Spanish satire & humor
868 Spanish miscellaneous writings
869 Portuguese

870 Italic literatures Latin
871 Latin poetry
872 Latin dramatic poetry & drama
873 Latin epic poetry & fiction
874 Latin lyric poetry
875 Latin speeches
876 Latin letters
877 Latin satire & humor
878 Latin miscellaneous writings
879 Literatures of other Italic languages

880 Hellenic literatures Classical Greek
881 Classical Greek poetry
882 Classical Greek drama
883 Classical Greek epic poetry & fiction
884 Classical Greek lyric poetry
885 Classical Greek speeches
886 Classical Greek letters
887 Classical Greek satire & humor
888 Classical Greek miscellaneous writings
889 Modern Greek

890 Literatures of other languages
891 East Indo-European & Celtic
892 Afro-Asiatic literatures Semitic
893 Non-Semitic Afro-Asiatic literatures
894 Ural-Altaic, Paleosiberian, Dravidian
895 Literatures of East & Southeast Asia
896 African literatures
897 North American native literatures
898 South American native literatures
899 Other literatures

Geography & history

900 Geography & history
901 Philosophy & theory
902 Miscellany
903 Dictionaries & encyclopedias
904 Collected accounts of events
905 Serial publications
906 Organizations & management
907 Education, research, related topics
908 With respect to kinds of persons
909 World history

910 Geography & travel
911 Historical geography
912 Graphic representations of earth
913 Ancient world
914 Europe
915 Asia
916 Africa
917 North America
918 South America
919 Other areas

920 Biography, genealogy, insignia
921
922
923
924
925
926
927
928
929 Genealogy, names, insignia

930 History of ancient world
931 China
932 Egypt
933 Palestine
934 India
935 Mesopotamia & Iranian Plateau
936 Europe north & west of Italy
937 Italy & adjacent territories
938 Greece
939 Other parts of ancient world

940 General history of Europe
941 British Isles
942 England & Wales
943 Central Europe Germany
944 France & Monaco
945 Italian Peninsula & adjacent islands
946 Iberian Peninsula & adjacent islands
947 Eastern Europe Soviet Union
948 Northern Europe Scandinavia
949 Other parts of Europe

950 General history of Asia Far East
951 China & adjacent areas
952 Japan
953 Arabian Peninsula & adjacent areas
954 South Asia India
955 Iran
956 Middle East (Near East)
957 Siberia (Asiatic Russia)
958 Central Asia
959 Southeast Asia

960 General history of Africa
961 Tunisia & Libya
962 Egypt & Sudan
963 Ethiopia
964 Morocco & Canary Islands
965 Algeria
966 West Africa & offshore islands
967 Central Africa & offshore islands
968 Southern Africa
969 South Indian Ocean islands

970 General history of North America
971 Canada
972 Middle America Mexico
973 United States
974 Northeastern United States
975 Southeastern United States
976 South central United States
977 North central United States
978 Western United States
979 Great Basin & Pacific Slope

980 General history of South America
981 Brazil
982 Argentina
983 Chile
984 Bolivia
985 Peru
986 Colombia & Ecuador
987 Venezuela
988 Guiana
989 Paraguay & Uruguay

990 General history of other areas
991
992
993 New Zealand
994 Australia
995 Melanesia New Guinea
996 Other parts of Pacific Polynesia
997 Atlantic Ocean islands
998 Arctic islands & Antarctica
999 Extraterrestrial worlds

Schedules

Use of the Schedules

Full instructions on the use of the Schedules are found in the Introduction to the Dewey Decimal Classification.

The first three digits of a DDC number are normally found at the top of the page.

A number in square brackets [ ] is not currently in use.

A number in parentheses ( ) is an option to standard usage.

000

000 Generalities

See Manual at 000

SUMMARY

001	**Knowledge**
002	**The book**
003	**Systems**
004	**Data processing Computer science**
005	**Computer programming, programs, data**
006	**Special computer methods**

001 Knowledge

General aspects: history, description, critical appraisal of intellectual activity in general; increase, modification, dissemination of information and understanding

Class here discussion of ideas from many fields

Class epistemology in 121; a compilation of knowledge in a specific form with the form, e.g., encyclopedias 030

See Manual at 500 vs. 001

.01 Theory of knowledge

Class philosophy of knowledge, philosophical works on the theory of knowledge in 121

.1 Intellectual life

Nature and value

For scholarship and learning, see 001.2

See also 900 for broad descriptions of intellectual situations and conditions

.2 Scholarship and learning

Intellectual activity directed toward increasing knowledge

Class methods of study and teaching in 371.3; scholarship and learning in a specific discipline or subject with the discipline or subject, e.g., in the humanities 001.3, in history 900

For research, see 001.4

.3 Humanities

Including the relative value of science versus the humanities

.4 Research

Including descriptive, experimental, historical, statistical methods; support of and incentives for research, e.g., fellowships, grants, prizes

Operations research relocated to 003

Class computer modeling in 003; research and works embodying results of research in a specific discipline or subject with the discipline or subject, e.g., research in linguistics 410; support of and incentives for research in a specific subject or discipline with the discipline or subject, using notation 079 from Table 1, e.g., prizes for research in linguistics 410.79

[.5] Communication

Relocated to 302.2

[.53] Cybernetics and related disciplines

Cybernetics, bionics, decision theory, information theory, perception theory, self-organizing systems relocated to 003; artificial intelligence to 006.3; automata theory to 511.3

[.54] Cryptography

Relocated to 652

[.6] Data processing Computer science

Relocated to 004

.9 Controversial knowledge

Examples: reported phenomena not explained, not fully verified (e.g., abominable snowman, Atlantis, Bermuda Triangle, Loch Ness monster, pyramid power, unidentified flying objects); hoaxes, delusions, superstitions

Including the end of the world

Class here interdisciplinary works on controversial knowledge and paranormal phenomena

Curiosities relocated to 030, Piltdown man hoax to 573.3

Class controversial knowledge concerning a specific discipline or subject with the discipline or subject, e.g., superstitions as a subject of folklore 398, controversial medical remedies 615.8, an alleged conspiracy to assassinate John F. Kennedy 973.922

For paranormal phenomena, see 130

See also 900 for Atlantis as a subject of archaeology

See Manual at 001.9 and 130

002 The book

Class here historical bibliography, interdisciplinary works on the book

Class lists, inventories, catalogs, comprehensive works on historical and analytical bibliography in 010, book publishing in 070.5, social aspects of the book in 302.23, book arts in 686

For rare books, see 090

.029 Commercial miscellany

Class price lists and trade catalogs in 010

.074 Museums, collections, exhibits

Class catalogs and lists in 010

003 Systems

Examples: self-organizing systems [*formerly* 001.53], large-scale systems, linear systems

Including bionics, cybernetics, decision theory, information theory, perception theory [*all formerly* 001.53], coding theory [*formerly* 519.4], theory of communication in systems; interdisciplinary works on forecasting, on control and stability of systems, on computer modeling and simulation, on data processing and computer science applied to systems, on computer implementation of mathematical models of systems

Class here operations research [*formerly* 001.4]; systems theory, analysis, design; models (simulation) applied to real-world systems

Class social aspects of and interdisciplinary works on communication in systems in 302.2; social forecasting in 303.49; automatic control of man-made physical systems in 629.8; systems in a specific subject or discipline with the subject or discipline, using notation 01 from Table 1, e.g., systems theory in the social sciences 300.1

For artificial intelligence, see 006.3

See Manual at 003; 004.2 vs. 003

[.028 5] Data processing Computer applications

Do not use; class in 003

004 Data processing Computer science [*formerly* 001.6]

This schedule (004–006), which replaces that formerly appearing at 001.6, is new

Including online and interactive processing; specific types of computers, processors, computer systems distinguished by their processing modes, e.g., multiprocessors, parallel processors

Class here selection and use of computer hardware; comprehensive works on hardware and programs in electronic data processing; electronic computers; electronic digital computers; computer systems (computers, their peripheral devices, their operating systems); central processing units

Unless other instructions are given, class complex subjects with aspects in two or more subdivisions of 004 in the one coming last, e.g., external storage for microcomputers 004.5 (*not* 004.16)

Class computer modeling and simulation in 003; engineering of computers in 621.39; data processing and computer science applied to a specific subject or discipline with the subject or discipline, using notation 0285 from Table 1, e.g., data processing in banking 332.10285

For computer programming, programs, data, see 005; special computer methods, 006

See also 025.04 for automated information storage and retrieval; 343.09 for computer law; 364.1 for financial and business computer crimes; 371.3 for computer-assisted instruction (CAI); 652.5 for word processing; 658 for data processing in management; 794.8 for computer games

See Manual at 004–006 vs. 621.39; 004 vs. 005

.01 Philosophy and theory

Including computer mathematics [*formerly* 519.4], human-computer interaction, psychological principles and human factors in data processing and computer science

.02 Miscellany

.028 Auxiliary techniques and procedures; apparatus, equipment, materials

Class testing and measurement in 004.2

.1 General works on specific types of computers

Including digital supercomputers, mainframe computers, minicomputers; analog computers

Comprehensive works on minicomputers and microcomputers are classed in 004.16

Specific types of computers, processors, computer systems distinguished by their processing modes, such as multiprocessors, are classed in 004

Class programmable calculators in 510.285

See Manual at 004.1

.16 Digital microcomputers

Including pocket computers capable of manipulating alphabetic as well as numeric data

Class here microprocessors, personal computers, computer systems based on microcomputers, comprehensive works on minicomputers and microcomputers

.165 Specific digital microcomputers

Arrange alphabetically by name of microcomputer or microprocessor, e.g., Apple II®

See Manual at 004.165

.2 **Systems analysis and design, computer architecture**

See Manual at 004.2 vs. 003

.5 **Storage**

.6 **Interfacing and communications**

Equipment and techniques linking computers to peripheral devices or to other computers

Including computer networks

Class here interdisciplinary works on computer communications, on telecommunications

Standard subdivisions are added for either or both of the topics named in the heading

Class data, programs, programming in interfacing and communications in 005.7; economic and related aspects of providing computer communications to the public in 384.3

See Manual at 004.6 and 005.7; 384.3 vs. 004.6 for communications; 621.382 vs. 621.39, 004.6 for communications

.69 Specific kinds of computer communications

Example: videotex

.692 Electronic mail

.693 Electronic bulletin boards

.7 **Peripherals**

Input, output, storage devices that work with a computer but are not part of its central processing unit or internal storage

Examples: printers, terminals, video display screens

Class peripheral storage in 004.5; peripherals devoted to special computer methods in 006, e.g., graphics output devices 006.6

See also 004.6 for communications devices

005 Computer programming, programs, data

Class here text processing

Unless other instructions are given, class complex subjects with aspects in two or more subdivisions of 005 in the one coming last, e.g., microcomputer programs written in a specific programming language 005.362 (*not* 005.13)

Class computer programming, programs, data for special computer methods in 006

See also 652.5 for word processing

See Manual at 004 vs. 005; 005 for text processing

SUMMARY

005.1	**Programming**
.2	**Programming for specific types of computers**
.3	**Programs**
.4	**Systems programming and programs**
.6	**Microprogramming and microprograms**
.7	**Data in computer systems**
.8	**Data security**

> **005.1–005.6 Computer programming and programs**

Class comprehensive works in 005

.1 **Programming**

Including debugging, preparation of software documentation, software maintenance

Class here application programming, software engineering

Special programming techniques (e.g., structured programming) and program design are classed in 005.1, without use of 005.101–005.109; special programming techniques and program design for specific programming languages are classed in 005.13

Class a specific application of programming within computer science with the application in 005.4–006.6

For programming for specific types of computers, see 005.2

See Manual at 005.1 vs. 005.3; 005.1 vs. 510

.101 Philosophy and theory

Do not use notation 01 from Table 1 here or with subdivisions of 005.1 for general discussions of logic in programming

.102 Miscellany

.102 8 Auxiliary techniques and procedures; apparatus, equipment, materials

Class maintenance, repair, measurement, testing, special programming techniques in 005.1

.13 Programming languages

Class here coding of programs

See also 005.4 for job-control languages, for programming-language interpreters and compilers

See Manual at 005.13 for machine and assembly languages

.130 1 Philosophy and theory

Class mathematical principles in 005.13

.2 Programming for specific types of computers

See Manual at 005.13 for machine and assembly languages

.26 Programming for digital microcomputers

Including programming for pocket computers capable of manipulating alphabetic as well as numeric data

Class here programming for microprocessors, for personal computers, for systems based on microcomputers; comprehensive works on programming for minicomputers and microcomputers

.265 Programming for specific microcomputers

Arrange alphabetically by name of microcomputer or microprocessor, e.g., Kaypro II®

See Manual at 004.165

.3 Programs

Software and firmware

Collections of programs, systems of interrelated programs, individual programs having interdisciplinary applications

General aspects: history, description, critical appraisal, selection, use

Class here application programs, electronic spreadsheets, integrated programs, software documentation, comprehensive works on software and firmware

Class programs for a specific application in computer science with the application in 005–006

For firmware, see 005.6

See also 005.1 for preparation of program documentation

See Manual at 005.1 vs. 005.3; 005.3 for programs for specific applications in computer science; 011 vs. 005.3029 for buyers' guides to software

.302 8 Auxiliary techniques and procedures; apparatus, equipment, materials

Class testing, debugging, maintenance of programs in 005.1

.36 Programs for digital microcomputers

Class here programs for microprocessors, for personal computers, for systems based on microcomputers

.362 Programs in specific programming languages

Arrange alphabetically by name of programming language, e.g., BASIC

See Manual at 005.362

.365 Programs for specific microcomputers

Arrange alphabetically by name of microcomputer or microprocessor, e.g., AT&T PC 6300®

See Manual at 004.165

.369 Specific programs

Class here specific computer software systems (organized sets of programs that work together)

Arrange alphabetically by name of program or software system, e.g., Symphony®

See Manual at 005.369

.4 **Systems programming and programs**

Including assemblers, compilers, interpreters, job-control languages, operating systems

Class programming and programs for interfacing and data communications in 005.7, for management of files and databases in 005.74

.6 **Microprogramming and microprograms**

Including firmware viewed as microprograms, firmware development, microcode

Class firmware viewed as hardware in 004

See Manual at 005.6

.7 **Data in computer systems**

Including data communications, interfacing; conversion to machine-readable form, data entry

Data structures are classed in 005.7, without use of 005.701–005.709; data structures in data files and databases are classed in 005.74

For data security, see 005.8

See Manual at 004.6 and 005.7 for data communications, interfacing

.74 Data files and databases

Class here file structures (file organizations), file and database management systems, database design and architecture

Class interdisciplinary works on computer science and information science aspects of databases in 025.04; data files and databases with regard to their subject content with the subject, e.g., encyclopedic databases 030, nonbibliographic medical databases 610

For specific types of data files and databases, see 005.75

See Manual at 005.74

.75 Specific types of data files and databases

Example: relational databases

.8 Data security

Including cryptography used for security in computer systems

Class here access control

Class interdisciplinary works on cryptography in 652

See also 658.4 for data security in management

006 Special computer methods

Not otherwise provided for

Class here programs, programming, selection and use of hardware in relation to special computer methods

Unless other instructions are given, class complex subjects with aspects in two or more subdivisions of 006 in the one coming last, e.g., computer graphics in expert systems 006.6 (*not* 006.3)

See also 004.6 for computer communications; 005.74 for file and database management; 005.8 for data security; 629.8 for special methods in automatic control engineering; 003 for computer modeling and simulation; notation 01 from Table 1 for computer modeling and simulation in a specific discipline or subject

.3 Artificial intelligence [*formerly* 001.53]

Including computer vision, expert systems, machine learning

Class here question-answering systems

See also 006.4 for pattern recognition not used as a tool of artificial intelligence

.4 Computer pattern recognition

Examples: optical pattern recognition, speech recognition

Class pattern recognition as a tool of artificial intelligence in 006.3

.5 Computer sound synthesis

Example: speech synthesis

See also 786.7 for computer music

.6 Computer graphics

Including computer graphics hardware, computer graphics programs and programming

Class here comprehensive works on computer graphics and computer sound synthesis

For computer sound synthesis, see 006.5

See also 760 for computer graphic art

010 Bibliography

History, identification, description of printed, written, audiovisual, machine-readable materials

Preparation and compilation of bibliographies are classed in 010, without use of 010.1–010.9; preparation and compilation of specific kinds of bibliographies are classed with the kind of bibliography in 011–016

Class catalogs and lists of art works with the art, using notation 074 from Table 1, e.g., a catalog of prints 769.074

For historical bibliography, see 002

See also 028.1 for reviews

SUMMARY

010.1–.9 Standard subdivisions
011 Bibliographies
012 Bibliographies and catalogs of individuals
013 Bibliographies and catalogs of works by specific classes of authors
014 Bibliographies and catalogs of anonymous and pseudonymous works
015 Bibliographies and catalogs of works from specific places
016 Bibliographies and catalogs of works on specific subjects or in specific disciplines
017 General subject catalogs
018 Catalogs arranged by author, main entry, date, or register number
019 Dictionary catalogs

[.28] Auxiliary techniques and procedures; apparatus, equipment, materials

Do not use; class in 010

[.74] Collections, guidebooks, catalogs of exhibits

Do not use; class in 011–019

011 Bibliographies

Examples: bibliographies of best books, of computer software, of dissertations and theses

Class here general bibliographies (in any form) in which the items are books or other written or printed works

General bibliographies and catalogs of works published in specific historical periods and general bibliographies of reference books, of free materials, of works published in specific forms (e.g., newspapers, microforms, audiovisual media), of rare books, of reprints, of works in series, of works issued by specific kinds of publishers (e.g., government publications) are all classed in 011, without use of 011.001–011.009; general bibliographies of these kinds of works for specific users are classed in 011.6

General bibliographies of works about serials relocated to 016.05

Catalogs are classed in 012–019 (except for catalogs of works published in specific periods, which are classed in 011)

For bibliographies of individuals, of works by specific classes of authors, of anonymous and pseudonymous works, of works from specific places, of works on specific subjects or in specific disciplines, see 012–016

See also 016.78026 for bibliographies of music scores and discographies of music, 016.79143 for bibliographies of dramatic and entertainment motion pictures and videotapes, 016.912 for bibliographies of maps

See Manual at 011 vs. 005.3029 for machine–readable works, software

.001–.007 Standard subdivisions

.008 Bibliographies with respect to kinds of persons

Class bibliographies of works for specific kinds of users in 011.6

.009 Historical, geographic, persons treatment

Class bibliographies of works published in specific historical periods in 011, bibliographies of works from specific places in 015

.6 *General bibliographies of works for specific kinds of users

.62 *For children and young adults

Class here bibliographies of works for children

.63 *For handicapped users

Examples: braille, large-print publications

Bibliographies of talking and cassette books for blind users are classed in 011

*Do not add notation 091–099 from Table 1 for bibliographies of works from specific places; class in 015

> ## 012–016 Bibliographies and catalogs of individuals, of works by specific classes of authors, of anonymous and pseudonymous works, of works from specific places, of works on specific subjects or in specific disciplines

Unless other instructions are given, observe the following table of precedence, e.g., bibliographies of scientific works published in France by Roman Catholic authors 016.5 (*not* 013 or 015)

Bibliographies and catalogs of works on specific subjects or in specific disciplines	016
Bibliographies and catalogs of individuals	012
Bibliographies and catalogs of anonymous and pseudonymous works	014
Bibliographies and catalogs of works by specific classes of authors	013
Bibliographies and catalogs of works from specific places	015

Class comprehensive works in 011

012 Bibliographies and catalogs of individuals

Works by or about persons not clearly associated with a specific subject

Class here biobibliographies

Class biobibliographies of persons associated with a specific subject with biographies in the subject, e.g., biobibliographies of psychologists 150.92

013 Bibliographies and catalogs of works by specific classes of authors

Works not dealing with a specific subject

Examples: authors resident in specific regions, continents, countries, localities; authors following specific vocations, adherent to specific religions, of specific sexes and ages

For bibliographies and catalogs of individuals, see 012

See also 011 for bibliographies of dissertations and theses

014 Bibliographies and catalogs of anonymous and pseudonymous works

015 Bibliographies and catalogs of works from specific places

Works issued or printed in specific regions, continents, countries, localities, or by specific publishers

Class here sales catalogs of specific college and university presses [*formerly also* 017–019], publishers' catalogs [*formerly also* 070.5029], bibliographies and catalogs of theses and dissertations for degrees awarded at specific institutions and at institutions in specific places

Add to base number 015 notation 1–9 from Table 2, e.g., works issued in Canada 015.71

Class bibliographies and catalogs of works by authors resident in specific regions, continents, countries, localities in 013

016 Bibliographies and catalogs of works on specific subjects or in specific disciplines

In list or essay form

Including indexes [*formerly also* with the subject]

(Option: Class with the specific discipline or subject, using notation 016 from Table 1, e.g., bibliographies of medicine 610.16)

Use 016.0001–016.0009 for standard subdivisions

Add to base number 016 notation 001–999, e.g., general bibliographies of works about serials 016.05 [*formerly* 011], general catalogs of works about serials 016.05 [*formerly* 017–019], bibliographies of philosophy 016.1

Class biobibliographies of persons associated with a specific subject with biographies of the subject, e.g., biobibliographies of psychologists 150.92; bibliographies with abstracts giving substantive information about the subject with the subject, e.g., bibliographies with substantive abstracts about chemistry 540

See also 011 for general bibliographies arranged by subject and general bibliographies of works published in specific forms, e.g., audiovisual materials, computer software, manuscripts, serials; 017–019 for general catalogs arranged by subject and general catalogs of serials; 050 for general indexes of specific serial publications not limited by subject

See Manual at T1—07 vs. 016, 026

> 017–019 General catalogs

Lists of works held in a specific collection or group of collections, or offered for sale by specific organizations other than publishers or at auction, and not restricted to specific subjects, to individuals or specific types of authorship, or to specific places of publication

Class here general catalogs of serials and their indexes, union catalogs

Sales catalogs of specific college and university presses relocated to 015, general catalogs of works about serials to 016.05

Class comprehensive works in 017, general catalogs of works published in specific historical periods in 011, catalogs of individuals, of works by specific classes of authors, of anonymous and pseudonymous works, of works from specific places, of works on specific subjects or in specific disciplines in 012–016

See also 011 for general bibliographies

017 *General subject catalogs

Examples: alphabetically arranged subject catalogs, classified catalogs

Class here comprehensive works on catalogs

Class catalogs on specific subjects in 016; a specific kind of nonsubject catalog with the kind of catalog, e.g., catalogs of works by specific classes of authors 013

018 *Catalogs arranged by author, main entry, date, or register number

019 *Dictionary catalogs

020 Library and information sciences

The science and art utilized in the identification, collection, organization, dissemination, and use of books, other printed and written records, audiovisual and machine-readable materials, information

Class here archival techniques

For bibliography, see 010

See also 003 for information theory, 651.5 for records management as a managerial service

See Manual at 020

*Do not add notation 091–099 from Table 1 for catalogs of works from specific places; class in 015

SUMMARY

[.68] Management

Do not use; class in 025.1

[.75] Book collecting

Do not use; class in 002.075

.9 **Historical, geographic, persons treatment**

Class here comparative librarianship

Class historical and persons treatment of libraries in 027.009, geographic treatment of libraries in 027.01–027.09

021 Relationships of libraries, archives, information centers

Class here libraries, archives, information centers as social forces

Class comprehensive works on libraries, archives, information centers in 027

.2 **Relationships with the community**

Educational, cultural, informational role

Examples: sponsorship of community cultural programs, clearinghouse for information on community action programs

.6 **Cooperation and networks**

Including consortia, centralized systems

Class networks, systems, consortia for specific kinds of libraries in 026–027; specific union catalogs in 017–019; cooperation in and networks, systems, consortia for a specific activity with the activity, e.g., cooperative technical processing 025, cooperative cataloging 025.3, interlibrary loan networks 025.6

Works on bibliographic utilities usually focus on technical processing and are classed in 025

.7 **Promotion of libraries, archives, information centers**

Example: friends-of-the-library organizations

.8 **Relationships with government**

Regardless of governmental level

Examples: relationships with library commissions and governing boards, financial support by government

Including political pressures

022 Administration of physical plant

Including location and site, bookmobiles

Class here maintenance of physical plant

See also 025.8 for physical security of collections, closed versus open stacks; 727 for library architecture

023 Personnel administration

025 Operations of libraries, archives, information centers

Class here documentation (systematic collection, organization, storage, retrieval, dissemination of recorded information)

Technical processes are classed in 025, without use of 025.001–025.009; a specific technical process is classed with the process, e.g., acquisitions 025.2

Use 025.001–025.009 for standard subdivisions

Class comprehensive works on operations in specific kinds of institutions in 026–027

SUMMARY

025.04–.06	**[Automated information storage and retrieval systems]**
.1	**Administration (Management)**
.2	**Collection development and acquisitions**
.3	**Bibliographic analysis and control**
.4	**Subject analysis and control**
.5	**Services to users**
.6	**Circulation services**
.7	**Physical preparation for storage**
.8	**Maintenance and preservation of collections**

.04 Automated information storage and retrieval systems

Class here search and retrieval in automated information storage and retrieval systems; comprehensive works on automated storage, search, retrieval of information; interdisciplinary works on databases

Class computer science aspects of automated information storage and retrieval systems, of databases in 005.74; information storage in 025.3; a specific kind of automated information storage and retrieval system with the kind, e.g., online catalogs 025.3

For automated information storage and retrieval systems devoted to specific disciplines and subjects, see 025.06

See also 658.4 for management use of automated information storage and retrieval systems

See Manual at 005.74

.06 Automated information storage and retrieval systems devoted to specific disciplines and subjects

Example: MEDLARS (Medical Literature Analysis and Retrieval System)

Class here documentation of specific disciplines and subjects

.1 **Administration (Management)**

Including finance, comprehensive works on library user fees; printing, duplication services (reprography)

Publishing by libraries, archives, information centers relocated to 070.5

Class interdisciplinary works on photoduplication in 686.4; user fees for a specific service with the service, e.g., user fees for automated search and retrieval 025.04068; a specific administrative function not provided for here with the function, using notation 068 from Table 1, e.g., administration of cataloging 025.3068

For financial support by government, see 021.8; administration of physical plant, 022; personnel administration, 023

.17 Administration of collections of special materials

Example: audiovisual materials

Class here nonbook materials, comprehensive works on treatment of special materials

Class a specific kind of treatment of special materials with the kind of treatment, e.g., cataloging, classification, indexing of special materials 025.3

.2 **Collection development and acquisitions**

Including selection policies and procedures; collection analysis, evaluation, management; acquisition through purchase, exchange, gift, deposit; weeding; censorship, comprehensive works on library policies and practices relating to intellectual freedom

Class interdisciplinary works on censorship in 363.3

.3 **Bibliographic analysis and control**

Including the catalog and its maintenance, machine-readable catalog record formats, retrospective conversion, filing; descriptive cataloging, name and title authority files; cataloging and classification of special materials, cooperative cataloging and classification, recataloging, reclassification

Class here comprehensive works on cataloging and classification, on indexing, on information storage

For subject analysis and control, see 025.4

See also 025.04 for comprehensive works on information storage and retrieval systems

.4 **Subject analysis and control**

Including subject cataloging, subject indexing; classification, specific classification systems, e.g., Dewey Decimal Classification; assignment of book numbers (shelflisting)

Class classification and subject cataloging of special materials, cooperative classification and subject cataloging, reclassification and subject recataloging in 025.3

.402 8 Abstracting techniques; auxiliary techniques and procedures; apparatus, equipment, materials

Class rhetoric and style in writing abstracts in 808

.5 **Services to users**

Examples: information and referral services, reference services, selective dissemination of information (SDI); library orientation

Including library use studies

Class here comprehensive works on information search and retrieval

Class comprehensive works on the creation and use of information storage and retrieval systems in 025.04, of specific tools for bibliographic control in 025.3; library services to special groups in 027.6; use of books and other media as sources of information in 028.7; a specific service not provided for here with the service, e.g., circulation services 025.6, storytelling for children 027.62

.6 **Circulation services**

Including interlibrary loans, renting materials

Class here document delivery

.7 **Physical preparation for storage**

Example: binding

Including repair and restoration

Class conservation and preservation in 025.8

.8 **Maintenance and preservation of collections**

Including access to collections, closed and open stacks, security against theft and other hazards, taking of inventory, conservation

Class repair and restoration in 025.7

> 026–027 Specific kinds of institutions

Class here specific libraries, archives, informations centers and their collections; systems and networks for specific kinds of institutions; comprehensive works on operations in specific kinds of institutions

Class comprehensive works in 027

See Manual at 026–027 for institutions devoted to specific kinds of special materials

026 Libraries, archives, information centers devoted to specific disciplines and subjects

Class here information organizations and library departments and collections in specific disciplines and subjects; comprehensive works on archives, on special libraries

Class special libraries not devoted to specific disciplines and subjects in 027.6, e.g., general museum libraries, general libraries in newspaper offices, patients' libraries

See Manual at T1—07 vs. 016, 026

.000 1–.000 5 Standard subdivisions

.000 6 Organizations

[.000 68] Management

Do not use; class in 025.1

.000 7–.000 9 Standard subdivisions

027 General libraries, archives, information centers

In the subdivisions of this number, the term *libraries* is used as a short way of saying libraries, archives, information centers, media centers

Class here comprehensive works on libraries, on information centers, on libraries and information centers devoted to special materials

For libraries, archives, information centers devoted to specific disciplines and subjects, see 026

See Manual at 027 for archives

.001–.005 Standard subdivisions

.006 Organizations

[.006 8] Management

Do not use; class in 025.1

.007–.008 Standard subdivisions

.009 Historical and persons treatment

Class geographic treatment in 027.01–027.09

.01–.09 *Geographic treatment

Add to base number 027.0 notation 1–9 from Table 2, e.g., libraries in France 027.044

*Do not add notation 068 from Table 1; class in 025.1

.4 *Public libraries

Institutions that provide free service to all residents of a community, district, region, usually supported in whole or in part from public funds

Class here public library branches, use of bookmobiles (mobile libraries) in public librarianship

Class physical plant management of bookmobiles (mobile libraries) in 022, public library units devoted to specific disciplines and subjects in 026, public library units for special groups and organizations in 027.6

.409 Historical, geographic, persons treatment

Class treatment by specific continents, countries, localities in 027.43–027.49 (*not* 027.4093–027.4099)

.43–.49 *Treatment by specific continents, countries, localities

Add to base number 027.4 notation 3–9 from Table 2, e.g., public libraries in France 027.444

.5 *Government libraries

Class government libraries for special groups in 027.6

See Manual at 027.5 for general government archives

.509 Historical, geographic, persons treatment

Class specific institutions in 027.53–027.59 (*not* 027.5093–027.5099)

.53–.59 *Specific institutions

Add to base number 027.5 notation 3–9 from Table 2 for area served, e.g., Library of Congress 027.573

.6 *Libraries for special groups and organizations

Examples: libraries for persons in late adulthood, for minority groups, for persons with disabilities; patients' libraries; prison libraries; libraries for religious organizations, for nonprofit organizations, for business and industrial organizations Church Libraries

Class here library and information services to special groups and organizations, to socially disadvantaged persons

Class libraries for special groups and organizations but devoted to specific disciplines and subjects, such as medical libraries, in 026

For libraries for educational institutions, see 027.7–027.8

.62 Libraries for children and young adults

Including storytelling

Libraries for children and young adults who are also members of other special groups and organizations, e.g., libraries for children with disabilities, are classed in 027.6

*Do not add notation 068 from Table 1; class in 025.1

> **027.7–027.8 Libraries for educational institutions**

Class here instructional media centers

Class comprehensive works in 027.7; libraries for educational institutions but devoted to specific disciplines and subjects in 026

.7 ***College and university libraries**

Class here comprehensive works on libraries for educational institutions, college and university library branches

Class branches devoted to specific disciplines and subjects in 026, elementary and secondary school libraries in 027.8

.709 Historical, geographic, persons treatment

Class specific institutions in 027.73–027.79 (*not* 027.7093–027.7099)

.73–.79 *Specific institutions

Add to base number 027.7 notation 3–9 from Table 2, e.g., Perkins Library of Duke University 027.7756

.8 ***School libraries**

Libraries in public, private, church-supported elementary and secondary schools

.809 Historica', geographic, persons treatment

Class specific libraries in 027.8

028 Reading and use of other information media

Reading interests and habits, use of books and other media as sources of recreation and self-development are classed in 028, without use of 028.01–028.09; reading interest and habits of children and young adults, use of books and other media as sources of recreation and self-development by chidlren and young adults are classed in 028.5

.1 **Reviews**

Examples: reviews of reference works, of audiovisual materials

Class here general collections of book reviews

Class reviews of computer programs in 005.3029; techniques of reviewing in 808; reviews of works on a specific subject or in a specific discipline with the subject or discipline, e.g., reviews of works on chemistry 540, reviews of entertainment films 791.43, critical appraisal of literature 800

.5 **Reading and use of other information media by children and young adults**

See also 028.1 for reviews of materials for children and young adults

*Do not add notation 068 from Table 1; class in 025.1

.7 **Use of books and other media as sources of information**

Class here use of reference works

For reading and use of other information media by children and young adults, see 028.5

030 General encyclopedic works

Class here general works about curiosities [*formerly also* 001.9], books of miscellaneous facts (e.g., almanacs), encyclopedia yearbooks

.9 **Historical, geographic, persons treatment**

Class historical, geographic, persons treatment of general encyclopedic works in specific languages and language families in 031–039

> **031–039 General encyclopedic works in specific languages and language families**

By language in which originally written

Class here specific encyclopedias and books of miscellaneous facts, works about them

Class comprehensive works in 030

031 American English-language general encyclopedic works

Originating in Western Hemisphere and Hawaii

.02 Books of miscellaneous facts

Examples: almanacs with general information, believe-it-or-not books

Do not use for other types of miscellany; class in 031

032 General encyclopedic works in English

For American English-language general encyclopedic works, see 031

.02 Books of miscellaneous facts

Examples: almanacs with general information, believe-it-or-not books

Do not use for other types of miscellany; class in 032

033 General encyclopedic works in other Germanic languages

Class here comprehensive works on Germanic-language general encyclopedias

Class English-language general encyclopedias in 032, Scandinavian-language general encyclopedias in 038

034 General encyclopedic works in French, Provençal, Catalan

035 General encyclopedic works in Italian, Romanian, Rhaeto-Romanic

036 General encyclopedic works in Spanish and Portuguese

037 General encyclopedic works in Slavic languages

038 General encyclopedic works in Scandinavian languages

039 General encyclopedic works in other languages

050 General serial publications and their indexes

Class here periodicals

(Option: Class here periodicals on all subjects; prefer specific subject, using notation 05 from Table 1, e.g, periodicals on mathematics 510.5)

Class indexes that focus on a specific subject or discipline in general serial publications in 016, e.g., an index to information on medicine in general serial publications 016.61; books of miscellaneous facts (even if published annually, e.g., almanacs), encyclopedia yearbooks in 030; administrative reports and proceedings of general organizations in 060; newspapers in 070

See also 011 for bibliographies of general serial publications, 017–019 for catalogs of general serial publications

.9 Historical, geographic, persons treatment

Class historical, geographic, persons treatment of general serial publications in specific languages and language families, and their indexes in 051–059

> **051–059 General serial publications in specific languages and language families, and their indexes**

By language in which originally written

Class here specific serial publications and works about them

(Option: Arrange general serial publications alphabetically under 050)

Class comprehensive works in 050

051 American English-language general serial publications and their indexes

Originating in Western Hemisphere and Hawaii

052 General serial publications in English and their indexes

For American English-language general serial publications and their indexes, see 051

053 General serial publications in other Germanic languages and their indexes

Class here comprehensive works on general serial publications in Germanic languages and their indexes

Class English-language general serial publications and their indexes in 052, Scandinavian-language general serial publications and their indexes in 058

054 General serial publications in French, Provençal, Catalan and their indexes

055 General serial publications in Italian, Romanian, Rhaeto-Romanic and their indexes

056 General serial publications in Spanish and Portuguese and their indexes

057 General serial publications in Slavic languages and their indexes

058 General serial publications in Scandinavian languages and their indexes

059 General serial publications in other languages and their indexes

060 General organizations and museum science

General organizations: associations, conferences, congresses, foundations, societies whose activity is not limited to a specific field

General aspects: history, charters, regulations, membership lists, administrative reports and proceedings

Class here interdisciplinary works on organizations; on licensing, certification, accreditation by nongovernmental organizations

Class general organizations whose members are political states in 341, e.g., Arab League 341.24; comprehensive works on licensing, certification, accreditation by governmental and nongovernmental bodies in 351.8; organizations devoted to a specific discipline or subject with the discipline or subject, using notation 06 from Table 1, e.g., organizations devoted to library and information sciences 020.6

.4 General rules of order (Parliamentary procedure)

Example: *Robert's Rules of Order*

Do not use standard subdivisions

For rules and procedures of legislative bodies, see 328

See also 658.4 for conduct of meetings of business organizations

.9 Historical and persons treatment

Class geographic treatment of general organizations in 061–068

> **061–068 General organizations**

Class comprehensive works in 060

061 General organizations in North America

Class general organizations in Middle America, in Hawaii in 068

062 General organizations in British Isles In England

063 General organizations in central Europe In Germany

Including general organizations in Austria, Czechoslovakia, Poland, Hungary

Class general organizations in Switzerland in 068

064 General organizations in France and Monaco

065 General organizations in Italy and adjacent territories

066 General organizations in Iberian Peninsula and adjacent islands In Spain

067 General organizations in eastern Europe In Union of Soviet Socialist Republics (Soviet Union)

068 General organizations in other geographic areas

069 Museum science

Including collecting and preparing museum objects, collections and exhibits of museum objects, management of museums, services to patrons

Publishing by museums relocated to 070.5; printing by museums to 686.2; public relations for museums to 659.2; historical and geographic treatment of museums devoted to a specific subject or discipline relocated to the subject or discipline with use of notation 074 from Table 1, e.g., history of an aerospace museum 629.1074; museum activities and services limited to specific subjects or disciplines relocated to the subject or discipline with use of notation 075 from Table 1, e.g., activities and services of an aerospace museum 629.1075

Class collections, guidebooks, catalogs of museums devoted to a specific discipline or subject with the discipline or subject, using notation 074 from Table 1, e.g., museums devoted to mineralogy 549.074

.028 Auxiliary techniques and procedures; apparatus, equipment, materials

Class maintenance and repair of museum objects, prevention of thefts and identification of forgeries in 069

[.068] Management of museums

Do not use; class in 069

.09 Historical, geographic, persons treatment

Class here specific museums not limited to a specific discipline or subject

Historical, geographic, persons treatment of museum buildings is classed in 069

[.1–.5] Museum services, collecting and preparing museum objects, collections and exhibits of museum objects

Numbers discontinued; class in 069

070 Documentary media, educational media, news media; journalism; publishing

SUMMARY

070.01–.09 Standard subdivisions of documentary media, educational media, news media; journalism; publishing
.1–.9 [Documentary media, educational media, news media; journalism; publishing]
071 Journalism and newspapers in North America
072 Journalism and newspapers in British Isles In England
073 Journalism and newspapers in central Europe In Germany
074 Journalism and newspapers in France and Monaco
075 Journalism and newspapers in Italy and adjacent territories
076 Journalism and newspapers in Iberian Peninsula and adjacent islands In Spain
077 Journalism and newspapers in eastern Europe In Union of Soviet Socialist Republics (Soviet Union)
078 Journalism and newspapers in Scandinavia
079 Journalism and newspapers in other geographic areas

.01–.08 Standard subdivisions of documentary media, educational media, news media; journalism; publishing

Standard subdivisions are added for comprehensive treatment; for newspapers and journalism alone

.09 Historical, geographic, persons treatment of documentary media, educational media, news media; journalism; publishing

Class historical and persons treatment of journalism and newspapers in 070.9, geographic treatment of journalism and newspapers in 071–079

.1 Documentary media, educational media, news media

Examples: educational films [*formerly* 791.43]; documentary films, newsreels [*both formerly also* 791.43]; radio news [*formerly also* 791.44]; educational, expository radio programs [*both formerly* 791.44]; television news [*formerly also* 791.45]; educational, expository television programs [*both formerly* 791.45]; newspapers, periodicals

Class here comprehensive works on journalism and production of specific kinds of educational, expository, news media

Class interdisciplinary works on mass media in 302.23; works on motion pictures that are interdisciplinary but lack treatment of sociological aspects in 384; works on radio and television that are interdisciplinary but lack treatment of sociological aspects in 384.54; comprehensive works on documentary, educational, news, and dramatic or entertainment films, radio, television programs in 791.4; specific journalistic activities and types of journalism in 070.4; expository writing and editorial techniques in 808; documentary, educational, news works themselves and discussion of them with the kind of general work or with the subject, e.g., general periodicals 050, recorded television programs on investing 332.6

See also 371.3 for use of motion pictures, radio, television in teaching

.4 Journalism

Collecting, writing, editing information and opinion of current interest for presentation in newspapers, periodicals, films, radio, television

Including radio sports programs [*formerly also* 791.44], television sports programs [*formerly also* 791.45]; journalism directed to special groups, e.g., religious groups, ethnic groups

Class comprehensive works on journalism and information media in 070, journalism of specific kinds of news media in 070.1, school journalism in 371.8, journalistic composition and editorial mechanics in 808

.408 Journalism with respect to groups of persons

Class journalism directed to special groups in 070.4

[.409] Historical, geographic, persons, treatment

Do not use; class historical and persons treatment in 070.9 geographic treatment in 071–079

.5 **Publishing**

Including publishing by libraries, archives, information centers [*formerly* 025.1], by museums [*formerly* 069]; selection and editing of manuscripts, relations with authors, literary agents; kinds of publications, e.g., hardbound and paperback books, serials, maps, music; kinds of publishers, e.g., academic, commercial, governmental publishers

Class here book publishing; publishers regardless of their field of activity; book clubs, e.g., Book-of-the-Month Club®; comprehensive works on publishing and printing

Class editorial techniques in 808

Works on desktop publishing that emphasize typography, such as microcomputer software for typesetting, are classed in 686.2

For printing, see 686.2

See Manual at 808.001–808.7 vs. 070.5 for publishers' relations with authors

.502 9 Commercial miscellany

Publishers' catalogs relocated to 015

.509 Historical, geographic, persons treatment

Class here comprehensive works on specific publishers, using notation from Table 2 for the location of the publisher's main office, e.g., U.S. Government Printing Office 070.509753

.9 **Historical and persons treatment of journalism and newspapers**

Class geographical treatment in 071–079

.92 Persons regardless of area, region, place

> **071–079 Geographic treatment of journalism and newspapers**

Class here specific general newspapers, indexes to them, other works about them

(Option: Arrange newspapers alphabetically under 070)

Class comprehensive works in 070

071 Journalism and newspapers in North America

Class journalism and newspapers in Middle America, in Hawaii in 079

072 Journalism and newspapers in British Isles In England

073 Journalism and newspapers in central Europe In Germany

Including journalism and newspapers in Austria, Czechoslovakia, Poland, Hungary

Class journalism and newspapers in Switzerland in 079

074 Journalism and newspapers in France and Monaco

075 Journalism and newspapers in Italy and adjacent territories

076 Journalism and newspapers in Iberian Peninsula and adjacent islands In Spain

077 Journalism and newspapers in eastern Europe In Union of Soviet Socialist Republics (Soviet Union)

078 Journalism and newspapers in Scandinavia

079 Journalism and newspapers in other geographic areas

080 General collections

Class here addresses, lectures, essays, interviews, graffiti, quotations

Class essays as literary form, collections gathered for their literary quality in 800

See Manual at 080

.9 Historical, geographic, persons treatment

Class historical, geographic, persons treatment of general collections in specific languages and language families in 081–089

> **081–089 General collections in specific languages and language families**

(Option: Arrange collections alphabetically under 080)

Class comprehensive works in 080; collections originally written in two or more languages with the preponderant language or language family; if none is preponderant, but the work appears in one language as a result of translation, class it with the language in which it appears

081 American English-language general collections

Originating in Western Hemisphere and Hawaii

082 General collections in English

For American English-language general collections, see 081

083 General collections in other Germanic languages

Class here comprehensive works on Germanic-language general collections

Class English-language general collections in 082, Scandinavian-language general collections in 088

084 General collections in French, Provençal, Catalan

085 General collections in Italian, Romanian, Rhaeto-Romanic

086 General collections in Spanish and Portuguese

087 General collections in Slavic languages

088 General collections in Scandinavian languages

089 General collections in other languages

090 Manuscripts, rare books, other rare printed materials

General aspects: critical appraisal, description, history

Class interdisciplinary works on books in 002; a manuscript or rare book with its subject, e.g., a book of hours 242; an artistic aspect with the aspect, e.g., illumination 745.6

See also 011 for bibliographies of manuscripts, rare books, other rare printed materials

091 Manuscripts

092 Block books

093 Incunabula

094 Printed books

Examples: early books to 1700; first editions, limited editions, typographic masterpieces

For block books, see 092; incunabula, 093

095 Books notable for bindings

See also 686.3 for bookbinding

096 Books notable for illustrations and materials

Class illustrated manuscripts in 091

097 Books notable for ownership or origin

098 Prohibited works, forgeries, hoaxes

099 Books notable for format

Examples: books of unusual shapes, miniature editions

100

100 Philosophy, parapsychology and occultism, psychology

Class philosophy of a specific discipline or subject with the discipline or subject, using notation 01 from Table 1, e.g., philosophy of history 901

See Manual at 100 for ethics; 100, 109 vs. 190 for philosophy; 100 vs. 200 for philosophy

101–108 Standard subdivisions of philosophy

109 Historical and collected persons treatment of philosophy

Not limited by period or place

Class historical and geographic treatment of philosophy of specific periods and places in 180–190 (*not* 109.1, 109.3–109.9)

See Manual at 100, 109 vs. 190

.2 Collected treatment of persons

Class individual persons in 180–190

110 Metaphysics

For epistemology, causation, humankind, see 120

111 Ontology

Examples: being, essence, existence, substance, nonbeing and nothingness

Including aesthetics

Class aesthetics of a specific subject with the subject, e.g., aesthetics of fine arts 701

113 Cosmology (Philosophy of nature)

Including origin of universe (cosmogony), origin and nature of life, cosmic harmony

Class origin and nature of human life in 128, specific topics of cosmology not provided for here in 114–119; cosmology as a topic in astronomy in 523.1

114 Space

Class here relation of space and matter

115 Time

Including eternity, space and time, space-time, relation of time and motion

For space, see 114

116 Change

Including becoming, cycles, evolution, motion, process

Class relation of time and motion in 115

117 Structure

Including matter, form, order

Class relation of space and matter in 114

118 Force and energy

119 Number and quantity

120 Epistemology, causation, humankind

121 Epistemology (Theory of knowledge)

Including belief and faith; doubt and denial; evidence; meaning, interpretation, hermeneutics; semantics, semiotics as topics in philosophy; worth and theory of values (axiology)

Class here truth

Class knowledge and its extension in 001, logic in 160, reason as a human attribute in 128, religious faith in 200

See also 401 for semantics and semiotics in linguistics

122 Causation

Including chance versus cause

For determinism and indeterminism, see 123; teleology, 124

123 Determinism and indeterminism

Including chance, contingency, fate, freedom, freedom of will, necessity

Class chance versus cause in 122

124 Teleology

126 The self

Class here consciousness and personality

Class the unconscious and the subconscious in 127

127 The unconscious and the subconscious

128 Humankind

Class here human life, philosophical anthropology

Including appetite, imagination, memory, reason, will; death; human action, experience; mind, mind-body relationship; soul

Class reason as an instrument of knowledge in 121, interdisciplinary works on death in 306.9

For freedom of will, see 123; the self, 126; origin and destiny of individual souls, 129; psychology, 150

129 Origin and destiny of individual souls

Including incarnation, reincarnation, immortality

See Manual at 133.9 vs. 129

130 Paranormal phenomena

Class interdisciplinary works on controversial knowledge and paranormal phenomena in 001.9, phenomena of religious experience in 200

See Manual at 001.9 and 130; 130 vs. 133

.1 Philosophy and theory

Do not use here or in any subdivision of 130 for forecasting and forecasts; class comprehensive works on forecasting and forecasts in 133.3; a specific type of forecast with the type, without adding notation 01 from Table 1, e.g., astrological methods of forecasting 133.5

131 Parapsychological and occult techniques for achieving well-being, happiness, success

Class interdisciplinary works on successful living, on management of personal and family living in 646.7; comprehensive works on psychological and parapsychological techniques for achieving personal well-being, happiness, success in 158; specific methods of parapsychology and occultism for achieving well-being with the subject in 130–139, e.g., spells and charms 133.4

133 Parapsychology and occultism

Class here frauds in occultism

Standard subdivisions are added for either or both of the topics named in the heading

For Cabalistic, Hermetic, Rosicrucian traditions, see 135

See Manual at 130 vs. 133; 133 vs. 200

.1 Apparitions

Class here ghosts

Including haunted places

Class comprehensive works on discarnate spirits in 133.9, ghosts as subjects of folklore in 398, folkloristic ghost stories in 398.25, literary accounts of ghosts in 808.8

.3 **Divinatory arts**

Examples: crystal gazing, dowsing, oracles and sibyls, numerology

Class here fortune-telling, symbolism of divinatory arts and objects

For astrology, see 133.5; palmistry, 133.6; dream books, 135; divinatory graphology, 137; physiognomy, 138

See also 003 for interdisciplinary works on forecasting, 291.3 for divination as a religious practice, 303.49 for social forecasting

.4 **Demonology and witchcraft**

Class here the black arts

Including demoniac possession, evil spirits, exorcism, magic, Satanism (devil worship), spells and charms

For divinatory arts, see 133.3

See also 291.2 for religious beliefs about demons; 235 for Christian beliefs; 299 for voodooism, for Satanic cults regarded as religions by their adherents

.5 **Astrology**

.6 **Palmistry**

.8 **Psychic phenomena**

Examples: clairaudience, clairvoyance, precognition, psychokinesis, telepathy

Class here extrasensory perception (ESP); psi phenomena; comprehensive works on psychic communication; comprehensive works on extrasensory perception, spiritualism, and ghosts

Class comprehensive works on divination in 133.3

For ghosts, see 133.1; spiritualism, 133.9

.9 **Spiritualism**

The phenomena and systems of ideas connected with belief in communication with discarnate spirits

Including astral projection, channeling, mediumship; mediumistic phenomena, e.g., table tipping, ectoplasm, spirit photography; nature of spiritual world and life after death; personal recollections of previous incarnations; personal survival; psychic messages (method and content of communications purporting to come from discarnate entities)

Class here necromancy, comprehensive works on discarnate spirits

For ghosts, see 133.1

See Manual at 133.9 vs. 129 for life after death

135 Dreams and mysteries

Including Cabalistic, Hermetic, Rosicrucian traditions; dream books

Class mysteries of magic and witchcraft in 133.4, interdisciplinary works on psychological and parapsychological aspects of dreams in 154.6

See also 001.9 for interdisciplinary works on mysteries in the sense of reported phenomena not explained, not fully verified; 296.1 for Cabala in Judaism

137 Divinatory graphology

Class interdisciplinary works on graphology and use of graphology in analyzing character in 155.2

138 Physiognomy

Class here comprehensive works on determination of character or divination from analysis of physical features

For palmistry, see 133.6; phrenology 139

139 Phrenology

Determination of mental capacities from skull structure

140 Specific philosophical schools and viewpoints

Including the concept of ideology, of a world view, of a system of beliefs

Class comprehensive works on modern Western viewpoints in 190, on modern Western and ancient, medieval, Oriental viewpoints in 100; development, description, critical appraisal, collected writings, biographical treatment of individual philosophers regardless of viewpoint in 180–190; ancient, medieval, Oriental schools in 180; systems and schools of ethics in 171; a specific topic or branch of philosophy treated from a specific philosophical viewpoint with the topic or branch, e.g., existentialist ontology 111, realist epistemology 121; ideologies concerning a specific discipline with the discipline, e.g., political ideologies 320.5

See Manual at 140; 140 vs. 180–190

141 Idealism and related systems and doctrines

Including individualism, modern Platonism and Neoplatonism, personalism, romanticism, spiritualism, subjectivism, transcendentalism

Class ancient Platonism in 184, ancient Neoplatonism in 186

142 Critical philosophy

Including existentialism, Kantianism, neo-Kantianism, phenomenology

Class critical realism in 149

143 Intuitionism and Bergsonism

144 Humanism and related systems and doctrines

Including pragmatism, utilitarianism

145 Sensationalism

146 Naturalism and related systems and doctrines

Including comprehensive works on analytical philosophy, empiricism, evolutionism, materialism, dialectical materialism, positivism, process philosophy

Class philosophic foundations of Marxism in 335.4

See Manual at 146 vs. 335.4 for dialectical materialism

147 Pantheism and related systems and doctrines

Including dualism, monism, pluralism

148 Liberalism, eclecticism, syncretism, traditionalism, dogmatism

149 Other philosophical systems and doctrines

Including fatalism, linguistic philosophies, neo-Aristotelianism, neo-scholasticism, neo-Thomism, nihilism, nominalism, realism, critical realism, optimism, pessimism, rationalism, skepticism, structuralism

Class semantics, semiotics as philosophical topics in 121; comprehensive works on analytical philosophy in 146

See also 302.2 for interdisciplinary works on semiotics, 401 for philosophy of language

150 Psychology

Unless other instructions are given, observe the following table of precedence, e.g., emotions of children 155.4 (*not* 152.4)

[Aptitude and vocational interest tests]	153.9
Comparative psychology	156
Subconscious and altered states and processes	154
Differential and developmental psychology	155
Sensory perception, movement, emotions, physiological drives	152
Conscious mental processes and intelligence (*except* aptitude tests 153.9)	153
Applied psychology	158

Class social psychology in 302; psychological principles (other than the principles of aptitude testing) of a specific discipline or subject with the discipline or subject, using notation 01 from Table 1, e.g., psychological principles of advertising 659.101

Testing for aptitude in a specific discipline or subject is classed in 153.9

See Manual at T1—01 vs. 302–307; 150 vs. 302–307

SUMMARY

150.1–.9	**Standard subdivisions**
152	**Sensory perception, movement, emotions, physiological drives**
153	**Conscious mental processes and intelligence**
154	**Subconscious and altered states and processes**
155	**Differential and developmental psychology**
156	**Comparative psychology**
158	**Applied psychology**

.1 **Philosophy and theory**

.19 Systems, schools, viewpoints

Including Gestalt psychology; functionalism; psychoanalysis, e.g., Freudian, Jungian systems; reductionism, e.g., behaviorism; speculative systems, e.g., existential psychology

See Manual at 150.19 vs. 616.89 for psychoanalytic systems

.8 **History and description with respect to kinds of persons**

Class psychology of specific kinds of persons in 155

.9 **Historical, geographic, persons treatment**

Class the national psychology of specific countries in 155.8

152 Sensory perception, movement, emotions, physiological drives

Former heading: Physiological psychology

Class here comprehensive works on the psychology and neurophysiology of sensory perception, movement, emotions, physiological drives

Class the neurophysiology of sensory perception, movement, emotions, physiological drives in 612.8

See Manual at 152 vs. 612.8

.1 **Sensory perception**

Including senses of hearing, smell, taste, touch; pain, proprioceptive perceptions; biofeedback

See Manual at 152.1 vs. 153.7

.14 Visual perception

Including color, movement, pattern, spatial perception, optical illusions and afterimages

.3 **Movements and motor functions**

Including coordination, habits, handedness and laterality, locomotion, motor learning, reflexes, vocal and graphic expressions

Class here comprehensive works on habits

Class conscious mental habits in 153, meaning of movements (as in body language) in 153.6

See Manual at 152.3 vs. 153.6 for expressive movements

.4 **Emotions and feelings**

Examples: anger, aggressive moods and feelings, embarrassment, envy, fear, guilt, love and affection

Class here affects, attitudes, moods, sentiments; complexes of emotions and feelings

Class character traits such as bashfulness, comprehensive works on psychology of aggression in 155.2, bereavement, loneliness in 155.9, depression in 616.85

.5 **Physiological drives**

Class motivation, comprehensive works on drives in 153.8

.8 **Quantitative threshold, discrimination, reaction-time studies**

Use of this number for quantitative and psychophysical methods applied to other topics discontinued; class in 152

153 Conscious mental processes and intelligence

Class here intellectual processes

Standard subdivisions are added for conscious mental processes

For emotions and feelings, see 152.4

See also 121 for epistemology, 128 for mind-body problem in philosophy

See Manual at 153.4 vs. 153

.028 Auxiliary techniques and procedures; apparatus, equipment, materials

Class testing and measurement in 153.9

.1 **Memory and learning**

Including Pavlovian (classical) conditioning, operant conditioning

Class memory with respect to a specific topic with the topic, e.g., memory and dreams 154.6

See Manual at 153.1 vs. 155.4–155.6 for learning; 153.1 vs. 370.15 for learning

.2 **Formation and association of ideas**

.3 **Imagination and imagery**

Including creativity

Class here daydreams, fantasies, reveries considered as aspects of the imagination

Class comprehensive works on daydreams, fantasies, reveries in 154.3; creativity in a specific field with the field, using notation 01 from Table 1, e.g., creativity in the arts 700.1

.4 **Knowledge (Cognition)**

Including intuition, judgment, problem solving, reasoning, thought and thinking, value

Moral judgment relocated to 155.2

For formation and association of ideas, see 153.2

See Manual at 153.4 vs. 153; 153.4 vs. 160

.402 8 Auxiliary techniques and procedures; apparatus, equipment, materials

Class testing and measurement in 153.9

.6 **Communication**

Including listening; nonverbal communication, e.g., body language

Class here individual aspects of interpersonal communication

Class social psychology of, interdisciplinary works on communication in 302.2; psychology of language and language processing (psycholinguistics) in 401; psychology of reading in 418

See Manual at 152.3 vs. 153.6 for nonverbal communication

.7 **Perceptual processes**

Perceptual apprehension and understanding

Including attention, errors, subliminal perception; perception of space, time, rhythm, movement

For extrasensory perception, see 133.8; sensory perception 152.1

See Manual at 152.1 vs. 153.7

.8 **Will (Volition)**

Including brainwashing, choice, decision, modification of will, persuasion, self-control

Class here intentionality, motivation, comprehensive works on drives

Class physiological drives in 152.5, modification of character and personality in 155.2

.9 **Intelligence and aptitudes**

Including aptitude, intelligence, vocational interest tests and testing

See Manual at 153.9 for aptitude and vocational interest tests

.902 8 Auxiliary techniques and procedures; apparatus, equipment, materials

Class testing and measurement in 153.9

154 Subconscious and altered states and processes

.2 **The subconscious**

.3 **Daydreams, fantasies, reveries**

Class here secondary consciousness

Class daydreams, fantasies, reveries considered as aspects of imagination in 153.3

.4 **Altered states of consciousness**

Including alterations due to use of drugs

.6 Sleep phenomena

Examples: dreams, somnambulism

Class here interdisciplinary works on dreams

Class parapsychological aspects of dreams in 135, physiological aspects of dreams in 612.8

See Manual at 154.6 vs. 612.8

.7 Hypnotism

Class here interdisciplinary works on hypnotism

Class hypnotism as a psychic power in 133.8, medical applications of hypnotism in 615.8

155 Differential and developmental psychology

Unless other instructions are given, observe the following table of precedence, e.g., influence of social environment on children 155.4 (*not* 155.9)

Psychology of specific ages	155.4–.6
Ethnopsychology and national psychology	155.8
Evolutional psychology	155.7
Environmental psychology	155.9
Sex psychology and psychology of the sexes	155.3
Individual psychology	155.2

See Manual at 155

.2 Individual psychology self esteem

Including personality traits and determinants (e.g., moral judgment [*formerly* 153.4], altruism, bashfulness, extroversion, introversion); development and modification of personality; personality appraisals and tests, e.g., graphology, handwriting analysis, Rorschach test; typology, e.g., classification scheme of Jung

Class here the self; character, identity, individuality, personality

.202 8 Auxiliary techniques and procedures; apparatus, equipment, materials

Class testing and measurement in 155.2

.3 Sex psychology and psychology of the sexes

Including erogeneity and libido; masculinity, femininity, bisexuality; sex and personality; sex differences; sexual relations

See Manual at 155.3 vs. 306.7 for sexual relations

> **155.4–155.6 Psychology of specific ages**

Class here developmental psychology

Class comprehensive works in 155, influence of specific situations (e.g., death, accidents) on specific ages and sexes in 155.9

See Manual at 153.1 vs. 155.4–155.6

.4 **Child psychology**

Through age eleven

Class interdisciplinary works on child development in 305.23

See also 649 for child rearing

> **155.42–155.45 Specific groupings**

Observe the following table of precedence, e.g., preschool boys 155.42 (*not* 155.43)

Exceptional children	155.45
Children by status, type, relationships	155.44
Children in specific age groups	155.42
Children by sex	155.43

Class comprehensive works in 155.4

.42 Children in specific age groups

.43 Children by sex

Class here sex psychology of children

.44 Children by status, type, relationships

Examples: adopted, institutionalized children, siblings, twins

Class here psychology of temporary or permanent separation from parents

.45 Exceptional children

Examples: gifted, handicapped children

.5 **Psychology of young adults**

Aged twelve to twenty

Class here comprehensive works on the psychology of young adults aged twelve to twenty and over twenty

Class interdisciplinary works on the development of young adults in 305.23, vocational tests for young adults in 153.9, the psychology of young adults over twenty in 155.6

.6 **Psychology of adults**

See Manual at 155

.67 Persons in late adulthood

.7 **Evolutional psychology**

Evolution of basic human mental and psychological characteristics

Including behavioral genetics

.8 Ethnopsychology and national psychology

Class influence of specific situations (e.g., death, accidents) on specific ethnic and national groups in 155.9

.9 Environmental psychology

Influence and effects of physical and social environments

Including influence and effect of clothing; of community and housing; of deformities, injuries, diseases; of prisons and underground environments; of specific situations, e.g., accidents, disasters, death and dying, reaction to death of others; stress

See Manual at 155.9 vs. 158, 302–307 for influence of social environment

156 Comparative psychology

Comparison of human psychology and the psychology of other organisms; study of other organisms to elucidate human behavior

Class behavior of nonhuman organisms in general in 574.5, behavior of animals in 591.51

[157] Abnormal and clinical psychologies

Relocated to 616.89

✓ 158 Applied psychology

Including cooperation and negotiation, counseling and interviewing, interpersonal relations, leadership, meditation, personal improvement and analysis

Class here application of individual psychology in general; comprehensive works on psychological and parapsychological or occult techniques for achieving personal well-being, happiness, success

Class interdisciplinary works on successful living, on management of personal and family living in 646.7; interdisciplinary works on success in business and other public situations in 650.1; parapsychological and occult techniques for achieving personal well-being, happiness, success in 131; aptitude and vocational interest tests (both general and applied to specific subjects) in 153.9; specific applications of psychology with the application, e.g., educational guidance and counseling 371.4

Application of a specific branch of psychology (other than individual psychology in general 155.2) is classed with the branch, e.g., how to improve one's memory 153.1, how to be creative 153.3

See Manual at 155.9 vs. 158, 302–307 for interpersonal relations

.6 Vocational interests

Class interdisciplinary works on aptitudes in 153.9, on choice of vocation in 331.7

.602 8 Auxiliary techniques and procedures; apparatus, equipment, materials

Class testing and measurement in 153.9

.7 **Industrial psychology**

Works focusing on the psychology of the individual employee in relation to work or taking a broad view that encompasses the concerns of individual employees, union leaders, management

Including job stress, job burnout

Class here psychology of work

Class workaholism as a personality trait in 155.2; industrial psychology applied to a specific subject outside psychology with the subject, using notation 01 from Table 1, e.g., psychological principles of personnel management 658.3001

[159] Other aspects

Number discontinued; class in 150

160 Logic

Class psychology of reasoning in 153.4, symbolic (mathematical) logic in 511.3

See Manual at 153.4 vs. 160

161 Induction

For hypotheses, see 167; analogy, 169

162 Deduction

For syllogisms, see 166

165 Fallacies and sources of error

Examples: contradiction, fiction, paradox

166 Syllogisms

167 Hypotheses

168 Argument and persuasion

169 Analogy

170 Ethics (Moral philosophy)

Class here ethics of specific subjects and disciplines

Class religious ethics in 291.5; ethics of a specific religion with the religion, e.g., Christian moral theology 241

See Manual at 100

.8 **History and description with respect to kinds of persons**

Class ethics of professional and occupational groups in 174, of religious groups in 200

171 Systems and doctrines

Regardless of time or place

Examples: altruism, hedonism, relativism, utilitarianism; systems based on biology, on moral sense, on natural law, on reason, on self-realization, on social factors

Class a specific topic in ethics treated within a specific system with the topic in 172–179

See Manual at 171 for individual moral philosophers

> **172–179 Applied ethics (Social ethics)**

Ethics of specific human qualities, relationships, activities

Class comprehensive works in 170

172 Political ethics

Including duties of citizens, of states and governments, of officeholders and officials; ethics of civil war, espionage, international relations, revolution, weapons testing, war and peace

173 Ethics of family relationships

Examples: ethics of marriage, divorce, separation, parent-child relationships, sibling relationships

Class ethics of sex and reproduction in 176

174 Economic, professional, occupational ethics

Including medical ethics; ethics of gambling business, genetic engineering, human experimentation, industrial espionage

Class here ethics of work

Euthanasia relocated to 179

Class comprehensive works on gambling in 175, experimentation on animals in 179

See Manual at 174 for occupational ethics of clergy

175 Ethics of recreation and leisure

Including betting, human and animal combat, hunting, racing, theatrical performances

Class here sportsmanship, fair play

176 Ethics of sex and reproduction

Including artificial insemination, celibacy, chastity, contraception, embryo transplant, homosexuality, obscenity in art and literature, premarital and extramarital relations, promiscuity, prostitution, surrogate motherhood

Class abortion, obscenity in speech in 179

177 Ethics of social relations

Contains benevolence, charity, conversation, courtesy, courtship, discriminatory practices, flattery, friendship, gossip, hospitality, kindness, liberality, love, lying, personal appearance, philanthropy, politeness, slander, slavery, truthfulness

Class etiquette in 395

178 Ethics of consumption

Examples: abstinence, gluttony, greediness, overindulgence, temperance

Class here ethics of use of natural resources, of wealth

Class environmental, ecological ethics, respect for nature, consumption of meat in 179

179 Other ethical norms

Including euthanasia [*formerly* 174], abortion, capital punishment, genocide, other issues concerning respect for human life; comprehensive works on ethics of violence and nonviolence; environmental ethics; courage, cowardice; profanity; respect for life and nature; treatment of children, of animals; vivisection; vegetarianism; vices and virtues not otherwise provided for

Class here cruelty

Do not use standard subdivisions

Class ethics of violence, of nonviolence in political activity, ethics of war in 172, medical ethics in 174, ethics of contraception in 176

> 180–190 Historical, geographic, persons treatment of philosophy

Class here development, description, critical appraisal, collected writings, biographical treatment of individual philosophers regardless of viewpoint

Do not add notation 092 from Table 1 anywhere in 180–190

Class comprehensive works on geographic treatment in 100, on historical treatment in 109, on collected persons treatment in 109.2; critical appraisal of an individual philosopher's thought on a specific topic with the topic, using notation 092 from Table 1, e.g., critical appraisal of Kant's theory of knowledge 121.092

See Manual at 140 vs. 180–190; 180–190 for works by individual philosophers

180 Ancient, medieval, Oriental philosophy

Do not use standard subdivisions for ancient, medieval, Oriental philosophy

.1–.8 Standard subdivisions of ancient philosophy

.9 Historical and geographic treatment of ancient philosophy

Class treatment of specific schools in 181–188

[.931] Ancient China

Do not use; class in 181

[.934] Ancient India

Do not use; class in 181

[.938] Ancient Greece

Do not use; class in 180

181 Oriental philosophy

Ancient, medieval, modern

Including philosophies based on specific religions of Oriental origin, e.g., on Judaism

Class Christian philosophy in 190

.001–.008 Standard subdivisions

.009 Historical treatment

Class geographic treatment in 181

> **182–188 Ancient Western philosophy**

Class comprehensive works in 180

182 Pre-Socratic Greek philosophies

Examples: Anaxagorean, Democritean, Eleatic, Empedoclean, Heraclitean, Ionic, Pythagorean philosophies

183 Sophistic, Socratic and related Greek philosophies

Including Cynic, Cyrenaic, Elian, Eretrian, Megaric philosophies

184 Platonic philosophy

Class here comprehensive works on ancient and modern Platonism

For modern Platonism, see 141

185 Aristotelian philosophy

Class here comprehensive works on ancient and modern Aristotelianism

For neo-Aristotelianism, see 149

186 Skeptic and Neoplatonic philosophies

Class here comprehensive works on ancient and modern Neoplatonism

For modern Neoplatonism, see 141

187 Epicurean philosophy

188 Stoic philosophy

189 Medieval Western philosophy

Examples: mystic, patristic, Scholastic philosophy

Class here early Christian philosophy

For neo-scholasticism, neo-Thomism, see 149

190 Modern Western philosophy

Class here comprehensive works on Christian philosophy, on modern philosophy, on Western philosophy, on European philosophy

Modern philosophy of areas not provided for in 180 is classed here, even if not in the Western tradition, e.g., North American native philosophy 191.089, traditional African philosophy 199

Class ancient, medieval, Oriental philosophy in 180

See Manual at 100, 109 vs. 190

.9 Historical and geographic treatment

Class treatment by continent, country, locality in 191–199 (*not* 190.94–190.99)

191 United States and Canada

Class here North American philosophy

Class Middle American and Mexican philosophy in 199

192 British Isles

193 Germany and Austria

194 France

195 Italy

196 Spain and Portugal

197 Soviet Union

Finland relocated to 198

198 Scandinavia

Including Finland [*formerly* 197]

199 Other geographic areas

200

200 Religion

Beliefs, attitudes, practices of individuals and groups with respect to the ultimate nature of existences and relationships within the context of revelation, deity, worship

Class here comprehensive works on Christianity

Class comparative religion, works dealing with various religions in 291

See Manual at 100 vs. 200; 133 vs. 200; 200

.1 **Philosophy and theory of religion**

See Manual at 200.1 vs. 210, 291

.2–.6 **Standard subdivisions**

.7 **Education and related topics**

.71 Schools and courses

See also 377 for religious instruction and exercises in nonsectarian schools

.8 **Religion with respect to kinds of persons**

.9 **Historical, geographic, persons treatment of religion**

Class here religious situation and conditions

> **201–209 Standard subdivisions of Christianity**

Class comprehensive works in 200

201 Philosophy and theory of Christianity

Nature, origin, validity of Christian beliefs

Class Christian theology in 230

202–203 Standard subdivisions of Christianity

204 Christian mythology

Class mythology in the Bible in 220.6, Apocrypha and pseudepigrapha in 229

[.01–.09] Standard subdivisions

Use of these numbers discontinued; class in 204

205 Serial publications of Christianity

206 Organizations of Christianity

Class the Christian church in 260

207 Education and related topics of Christianity

Class here Christianity as an academic subject

Comprehensive works on Christian religious education relocated to 268

Class Christian religious education under church auspices at other than the university level in 268

See Manual at 207 vs. 268

[.1] Schools and courses

Do not use; class in 207

[.4–.6] Museums, collections, exhibits; museum activities, collecting; review and exercise

Numbers discontinued; class in 207

[.8–.9] Use of apparatus and equipment in study and teaching; competitions, festivals, awards; financial support of education and related topics

Do not use; class in 207

208 Christianity with respect to kinds of persons

209 Historical, geographic, persons treatment of Christianity and Christian thought

Observe the table of precedence under 230–280

Class historical, geographic, persons treatment of the organized Christian church in 270

See Manual at 209.2 for biography

210 Natural theology

Religious beliefs and attitudes attained through observation and interpretation of evidence in nature, through speculation, through reasoning, but not through revelation

Class a specific topic treated with respect to religions based on revelation or authority in 291, e.g., concepts of God in world religions 291.2; with respect to a specific religion with the religion, e.g., Christian concepts of God 231

See Manual at 200.1 vs. 210, 291

211 Concepts of God

Including agnosticism, anthropomorphism, atheism, deism, dualism, humanism, monotheism, pantheism, polytheism, rationalism, secularism, skepticism

Class here comprehensive works on God, on The Holy

For existence, knowability, attributes of God, see 212

212 Existence, knowability, attributes of God

Including omniscience, proofs

See Manual at 212 vs. 231 for existence of God

213 Creation

Including creation of life and human life, evolution versus creation, evolution as method of creation

See Manual at 231.7 vs. 213, 575 for creationism

214 Theodicy

Vindication of God's justice and goodness in permitting existence of evil and suffering

Including providence

215 Science and religion

Including archaeology, cybernetics, life on other worlds, space flight, technology

Class religion and scientific theories of creation in 213

216 Good and evil

For theodicy, see 214

218 Humankind

Including immortality

Class creation, human evolution in 213

[219] Analogy

Number discontinued; class in 210

220 Bible

Holy Scriptures of Judaism and Christianity

Class Christian Biblical theology in 230, Judaic in 296.3; Biblical precepts in Christian codes of conduct in 241.5, in Judaic codes in 296.3

See Manual at 220 for Biblical theology

SUMMARY

220.01–.09	**Standard subdivisions**
.1–.9	**General topics**
221	**Old Testament**
222	**Historical books of Old Testament**
223	**Poetic books of Old Testament**
224	**Prophetic books of Old Testament**
225	**New Testament**
226	**Gospels and Acts**
227	**Epistles**
228	**Revelation (Apocalypse)**
229	**Apocrypha, pseudepigrapha, intertestamental works**

.01–.02 Standard subdivisions

[.03] Dictionaries, encyclopedias, concordances

Do not use; class dictionaries and encyclopedias in 220.3, concordances in 220.4–220.5

.05–.08 Standard subdivisions

.09 General historical, geographic, persons treatment of the Bible

Class the canon in 220.1; geography, history, chronology, persons of Bible lands in Bible times in 220.9

> **220.1–220.9 General topics**

Class comprehensive works in 220, general topics applied to a specific part of the Bible with the part, e.g., a commentary on Job 223

.1 **Origins and authenticity**

Including canon, inspiration, prophecy and prophecies

Class Christian messianic prophecies in 232, Christian eschatological prophecies in 236, Judaic messianic and eschatological prophecies in 296.3

.3 **Encyclopedias and topical dictionaries**

Class dictionaries of specific texts in 220.4–220.5

> **220.4–220.5 Texts, versions, translations**

Class here critical appraisal of language and style; concordances, indexes, dictionaries of specific texts; complete texts; selections from more than one part; paraphrases

Class comprehensive works in 220.4; texts accompanied by commentaries in 220.7; selections compiled for a specific purpose with the purpose, e.g., selections for daily meditations 242

.4 **Original texts, early versions, early translations**

Examples: Hebrew text, Vulgate

Class here textual (lower) criticism (use of scientific means to ascertain the actual original texts), original texts accompanied by modern translations, comprehensive works on texts and versions

For modern versions and translations, see 220.5

.5 **Modern versions and translations**

In any language

.6 **Interpretation and criticism (Exegesis)**

Including authorship, harmonies, isagogics, symbolism and typology; allegorical, astronomical, mythological, numerical interpretations; mythology in Bible, demythologizing

Class Christian meditations based on Biblical passages and intended for devotional use in 242, Judaic meditations in 296.7; material about the Bible intended for use in preparing Christian sermons in 251, sermons based on Biblical passages in 252; material for preparation of Judaic sermons and text of Judaic sermons in 296.4

For textual (lower) criticism, see 220.4; commentaries, 220.7

See also 808 for the Bible as literature

.7 **Commentaries**

Criticism and interpretation arranged in textual order with or without text

.8 **Nonreligious subjects treated in Bible**

Examples: sciences in Bible, position of women in Bible

Do not use standard subdivisions

Class a religious subject treated in the Bible with the specific religion and topic, e.g., Christian theology 230, Jewish moral virtues based on Old Testament teaching 296.3; geography, history, chronology, persons of Bible lands in Bible times in 220.9

.9 **Geography, history, chronology, persons of Bible lands in Bible times**

Including Bible stories retold

Class general history of areas in the ancient world in 930; an individual person with the part of the Bible in which he is chiefly considered, e.g., Abraham 222

See Manual at 209.2 for Christian biography; 220.9 for Biblical biography

---

> 221–228 Specific parts of Bible

Class comprehensive works in 220

For Apocrypha, see 229

221 Old Testament

Holy Scriptures of Judaism, Old Testament of Christianity

For historical books, see 222; poetic books, 223; prophetic books, 224

[.03] Dictionaries, encyclopedias, concordances

Do not use; class dictionaries and encyclopedias in 221.3, concordances in 221.4–221.5

.09 General historical, geographic, persons treatment of the Old Testament

Class the canon in 221.1; geography, history, chronology, persons of Old Testament lands in Old Testament times in 221.9

.1–.9 **General topics**

Add to base number 221 the numbers following 220 in 220.1–220.9, e.g., commentaries 221.7

See Manual at 209.2 for Christian biography; 220.9 for Biblical biography

222 Historical books of Old Testament

Contains Pentateuch (Torah: Genesis, Exodus, Leviticus, Numbers, Deuteronomy), Joshua (Josue), Judges, Ruth, Samuel, Kings, Chronicles (Paralipomena), Ezra (Esdras 1), Nehemiah (Esdras 2, Nehemias), Esther

(Option: Class here Tobit [Tobias], Judith, deuterocanonical part of Esther; prefer 229)

[.01–.09] Standard subdivisions

Numbers discontinued; class in 222

223 Poetic books of Old Testament

Contains Job, Psalms, Proverbs, Ecclesiastes (Qohelet), Song of Solomon (Canticle of Canticles, Song of Songs)

Class here wisdom literature

(Option: Class here Wisdom of Solomon [Wisdom], Ecclesiasticus [Sirach]; prefer 229)

Class Apocryphal wisdom literature in 229

[.01–.09] Standard subdivisions

Numbers discontinued; class in 223

224 Prophetic books of Old Testament

Contains Isaiah (Isaias), Jeremiah (Jeremias), Lamentations, Ezekiel (Ezechiel), Daniel, Hosea (Osee), Joel, Amos, Obadiah (Abdias), Jonah (Jonas), Micah (Micheas), Nahum, Habakkuk (Habacuc), Zephaniah (Sophonias), Haggai (Aggeus), Zechariah (Zacharias), Malachi (Malachias)

Class here Major Prophets

(Option: Class here Baruch, Song of the Three Children, Susanna, Bel and the Dragon, Maccabees 1 and 2 [Machabees 1 and 2]; prefer 229)

[.01–.09] Standard subdivisions

Numbers discontinued; class in 224

225 New Testament

For Gospels and Acts, see 226; Epistles, 227; Revelation, 228

[.03] Dictionaries, encyclopedias, concordances

Do not use; class dictionaries and encyclopedias in 225.3, concordances in 225.4–225.5

.09 General historical, geographic, persons treatment of the New Testament

Class the canon in 225.1; geography, history, chronology, persons of New Testament lands in New Testament times in 225.9

.1–.9 **General topics**

Add to base number 225 the numbers following 220 in 220.1–220.9, e.g., commentaries 225.7; however, class Jesus Christ, Mary, Joseph, Joachim, Anne, John the Baptist in 232

See Manual at 209.2 for Christian biography; 220.9 for Biblical biography

226 Gospels and Acts

[.01–.09] Standard subdivisions

Numbers discontinued; class in 226

> **226.2–226.5 Specific Gospels**

Class comprehensive works in 226

For miracles, see 226.7; parables, 226.8

.2 **Matthew**

Do not use standard subdivisions

Class Golden Rule as code of conduct in 241.5

For Sermon on the Mount, see 226.9

.3 **Mark**

Do not use standard subdivisions

.4 **Luke**

Do not use standard subdivisions

Class Golden Rule as code of conduct in 241.5

For Sermon on the Mount, see 226.9

.5 **John**

Class here comprehensive works on Johannine literature

Do not use standard subdivisions

For Epistles of John, see 227; Revelation (Apocalypse), 228

.6 **Acts of the Apostles**

Do not use standard subdivisions

.7 **Miracles**

Do not use standard subdivisions

Class miracles in the context of Jesus' life in 232.9

.8 **Parables**

Do not use standard subdivisions

Class parables in the context of Jesus' life in 232.9

.9 **Sermon on the Mount**

Do not use standard subdivisions

227 Epistles

Contains Epistles of Paul to Romans, Corinthians, Galatians, Ephesians, Philippians, Colossians, Thessalonians, Timothy, Titus, Philemon, Hebrews; Epistles of James, Peter, John, Jude

[.01–.09] Standard subdivisions

Numbers discontinued; class in 227

228 Revelation (Apocalypse)

[.01–.09] Standard subdivisions

Numbers discontinued; class in 228

229 Apocrypha, pseudepigrapha, intertestamental works

Apocrypha: works accepted as deuterocanonical in some Bibles

Pseudepigrapha, intertestamental works: works from intertestamental times connected with the Bible but not accepted as canonical

Apocrypha contains Esdras, Tobit (Tobias), Judith, Esther, Wisdom of Solomon (Wisdom), Ecclesiasticus (Sirach), Baruch, Epistle of Jeremiah, Song of the Three Children, Susanna, Bel and the Dragon, Prayer of Manasses, Maccabees (Machabees)

Including pseudo gospels

(Option: Class Tobit [Tobias], Judith, deuterocanonical part of Esther in 222; Wisdom of Solomon [Wisdom], Ecclesiasticus [Sirach] in 223; Baruch, Song of the Three Children, Susanna, Bel and the Dragon, Maccabees 1 and 2 [Machabees 1 and 2] in 224)

Do not use standard subdivisions

> ## 230–280 Christianity

Unless other instructions are given, observe the following table of precedence for the history of Christianity and the Christian church (except for biography, explained in Manual at 209.2), e.g., Jesuit missions 266 (*not* 271); persecution of Jesuits by Elizabeth I 272 (*not* 271 or 274.2):

Specific topics	220–260
Persecutions in general church history	272
Doctrinal controversies and heresies in general church history	273
Religious congregations and orders in church history	271
Denominations and sects of the Christian church	280
Treatment of the Christian church by continent, country, locality	274–279
General historical, geographic, persons treatment of the Christian church	270
Historical, geographic, persons treatment of Christianity and Christian thought	209

Class comprehensive works in 200

For Bible, see 220

See Manual at 209.2 for biography

> ## 230–270 Specific elements of Christianity

Class here specific elements of specific denominations and sects
(Option: Class specific elements of specific denominations and sects in 280)

Class comprehensive works in 200

230 Christian theology Christian doctrinal theology

Class here Biblical theology

Class doctrinal controversies in general church history in 273

For Christian moral and devotional theology, see 240; Christian social and ecclesiastical theology, 260

See Manual at 220 for Biblical theology

SUMMARY

230.01–.09	**Standard subdivisions**
231	**God**
232	**Jesus Christ and his family Christology**
233	**Humankind**
234	**Salvation (Soteriology) and grace**
235	**Spiritual beings**
236	**Eschatology**
238	**Creeds, confessions of faith, covenants, catechisms**
239	**Apologetics and polemics**

.01–.08 Standard subdivisions

.09 Historical, geographic, persons treatment

.092 Theologians

Class here theologians not connected with any specific type of theology

Class theologians who are connected with a specific denomination, Protestant theologians who are not connected with a specific denomination or who are important and influential enough to transcend their own denominations, e.g., Karl Barth, in 230; critical appraisal of an individual theologian's thought on a specific topic with the topic, e.g., on eschatology 236.092

See Manual at 209.2 for biography

> 231–239 Christian doctrinal theology

Class comprehensive works; specific types of Christian doctrinal theology, e.g., evangelical, fundamentalist, liberation theologies; comprehensive works on doctrines of specific denominations and sects in 230

> 231–236 Specific topics in Christian doctrinal theology

Class here specific doctrines of specific denominations and sects

Class comprehensive works in 230

231 God

Including Holy Trinity (God the Father, God the Son, God the Holy Spirit); goodness, justice, love, omnipotence, omnipresence, omniscience, providence, wisdom of God; ways of knowing God, e.g., faith, reason; relation to human experience; non-Trinitarian concepts of God

For Jesus Christ, see 232

See Manual at 212 vs. 231 for existence of God

.7 **Relation to the world**

Including creation [*formerly* 233], covenant relationships, Kingdom of God, miracles, prophecy, revelations, sovereignty

Class here God's relation to individual believers

Class Biblical prophecy and prophecies in 220.1, providence in 231, messianic prophecies in 232, miracles of Jesus in 232.9, miracles associated with Mary in 232.91, creation of humankind in 233, redemption in 234, eschatological prophecies and Kingdom of God to come in 236, divine law in 241, believers' experience of God in 248, God's relation to the church in 262

See Manual at 231.7 vs. 213, 575 for creationism

232 Jesus Christ and his family Christology

Including Christ as Logos (Word of God), as Redeemer; divinity, humanity, incarnation, messiahship of Christ; offices as Prophet, Priest, King; atonement, intercession, resurrection, sacrifice of Christ; typology

Judgment of Christ, Second Coming of Christ relocated to 236

See Manual at 232

.9 **Family and life of Jesus**

Including character, personality, historicity of Jesus; resurrection, appearances, ascension; Joseph, Joachim, Anne, John the Baptist

Class here non-Trinitarian concepts of Jesus

See Manual at 209.2

.900 1–.900 9 Standard subdivisions

.91 Mary, mother of Jesus

Including Immaculate Conception, virginity, assumption (ascent to heaven), sanctity, virtues, spiritual powers, miracles, apparitions of Mary; annunciation to Mary

Class here Mariology

Joseph, Joachim, Anne are classed in 232.9

.92 Infancy of Jesus

Including Holy Family, childhood of Jesus

Joseph is classed in 232.9

For Mary, see 232.91

.96 Passion and death of Jesus

233 Humankind

Including creation, fall, original sin, accountability, guilt; nature as image and likeness of God, as child of God; body, soul, spirit; freedom of choice between good and evil

Comprehensive works on creation relocated to 231.7

Class relation to God in 231.7, salvation in 234, sins in 241

234 Salvation (Soteriology) and grace

Including election, faith, forgiveness, free will, justification, obedience, predestination, reconciliation, redemption, regeneration, repentance, sanctification; gifts of the Holy Spirit, e.g., understanding, wisdom; spiritual gifts, e.g., healing, speaking in tongues; sacraments, e.g., baptism, Lord's Supper, matrimony

Class liturgy and ritual of sacraments in 265

See also 248.2 for religious experience manifesting gifts of the Holy Spirit

235 Spiritual beings

Examples: angels, devils, saints

Class miracles associated with saints in 231.7

For God, see 231; Joseph, Joachim, Anne, John the Baptist, 232.9; Mariology, 232.91

See Manual at 209.2 for biography of saints

236 Eschatology

Including Judgment of Christ, Second Coming of Christ [*both formerly also* 232], antichrist, death, heaven, hell, immortality, life after death, limbos, millennium, probation after death, purgatory, resurrection of the dead

Class here Kingdom of God to come

Class interdisciplinary works on the end of the world in 001.9

238 Creeds, confessions of faith, covenants, catechisms

Class catechetics in 268, creeds and catechisms on a specific doctrine with the doctrine, e.g., attributes of God 231

239 Apologetics and polemics

Apologetics: systematic argumentation in defense of the divine origin and authority of Christianity

Polemics: refutation of alleged errors in other systems

Class apologetics and polemics of a specific denomination in 230; on a specific doctrine with the doctrine, e.g., nature of the church 262; attacks on doctrines of a specific religion with the religion, e.g., attacks on doctrines of Judaism 296.3

See also 273 for doctrinal controversies and heresies in general church history

.001–.009 Standard subdivisions

240 Christian moral and devotional theology

241 Moral theology

Including divine law, sins, vices; virtues, e.g., faith

Class original sin in 233, faith and hope as means of salvation in 234

See Manual at 261.8 vs. 241 for social problems

.5 Codes of conduct

Examples: Golden Rule, Sermon on the Mount, Ten Commandments

Including precepts of church

Class specific moral issues in 241, church law in 262.9

242 Devotional literature

Including prayers and meditations based on passages from Bible

Class here texts of meditations, contemplations, prayers for individuals and families, religious poetry intended for devotional use

Class devotional sermons in 252, devotional literature on a specific subject with the subject, e.g., meditations on God's providence 231

For evangelistic writings, see 243; hymns, 245

243 Evangelistic writings for individuals and families

Works designed to convert readers, promote repentance

Class evangelistic sermons in 252

245 Texts of hymns

For devotional use of individuals and families

Class comprehensive works on texts of hymns in 264, musical scores and parts in 782.27, modern metrical versions of Psalms in 223

246 Use of art in Christianity

Religious meaning, significance, purpose

Examples: icons, symbols; dramatic, musical, rhythmic arts; architecture

Class creation, description, critical appraisal as art in 700

For church furnishings and related articles, see 247

247 Church furnishings and related articles

248 Christian experience, practice, life

See Manual at 209.2 for biography

.06 Organizations

Class here pious societies, e.g., sodalities, confraternities

.2 **Religious experience**

Examples: conversion, moral renewal and commitment, mysticism, speaking in tongues

Class conversion of Christians to another religion with the religion, e.g., conversion of Christians to Judaism 296.7

See also 234 for spiritual gifts

.3 **Worship**

Including contemplation, meditation, prayer

Class here comprehensive works on worship

Class texts of prayers and devotions in 242

For observances in family life, see 249; public worship, 264

.4 **Christian life and practice**

Including asceticism, observance of restrictions and limitations

Class here Christian marriage and family

Guides to Christian life for specific classes of persons who are adherents of specific denominations and sects relocated to 248.8

Class guides to Christian life for specific classes of persons in 248.8

For moral theology, see 241; worship, 248.3

.8 **Guides to Christian life for specific classes of persons**

Examples: guides for boys, mothers, physicians, bereaved persons

Class here guides to Christian life for specific classes of persons who are adherents of specific denominations and sects [*formerly* 248.4]

Including Christian religious training of children in the home [*formerly also* 649]

Class a specific aspect with the aspect, e.g., prayer 248.3

249 Christian observances in family life

Class here family prayer; family observance of religious restrictions, rites, ceremonies

---

> 250–280 Christian church

Class comprehensive works in 260

250 Local Christian church and Christian religious orders

Class here basic Christian communities

Class the local church in overall church organization in 262, public worship in 264, missions in 266, religious training and instructions in 268

[.68] Management

Do not use; class management of local church in 254, of religious congregations and orders in 255

> **251–254 Local church**

Class comprehensive works in 250, special activities of the local church in 259

See Manual at 251–254, 259 vs. 260

251 Preaching (Homiletics)

Including radio and television preaching

Class texts of sermons in 252, pastoral methods in 253

.001–.009 Standard subdivisions

252 Texts of sermons

Class sermons on a specific subject with the subject, e.g., God's providence 231

.001–.009 Standard subdivisions

253 Pastoral office and work (Pastoral theology)

Including professional and personal qualifications; families of clergy; pastoral methods, e.g., telephone in church work

Class here the work of ministers, pastors, priests, rectors, vicars, curates, chaplains, elders, deacons, assistants, laity in relation to the work of the church at the local level

Class education of clergymen in 207; guides to Christian life for secular clergy in 248.8; pastoral methods for service to specific groups in 259; local clergy and laity in relation to the government, organization and nature of the church as a whole, the ordination of women (unless the work treats the ordination of women only in relation to its effect on the local parish) in 262; the role of clergy in religious education in 268

For preaching, see 251; parish government and administration, 254

.092 Persons treatment

Class biography of clergy in the period prior to 1054 in 270.1–270.3, in the period subsequent to 1054 in 280

See Manual at 209.2

.5 Counseling and spiritual direction

Including pastoral psychology

[.7] Pastoral methods

Number discontinued; class in 253

254 Parish government and administration

Including membership, programs; buildings, equipment, grounds

For activities of the local church, see 259

.001–.009 Standard subdivisions

.3 Use of communications media

Including use of audiovisual materials

.4 Public relations and publicity

For use of communications media, see 254.3

.8 Finance

Examples: budget, expenditures, income, methods of raising money

255 Religious congregations and orders

Class here monasticism, comprehensive works on Christian religious congregations and orders

Class guides to Christian life for persons in religious orders in 248.8; specific types of activity of religious congregations and orders with the activity, e.g., sponsoring religious camps 259, missionary work 266

For religious congregations and orders in church organization, see 262; in church history, 271

.001–.009 Standard subdivisions

259 Activities of the local church

Former heading: Parochial activities by parishes and religious orders

Not provided for elsewhere

Examples: recreational and camp programs; programs for children, handicapped people, bereaved people

Class here activities designed to promote religious and social welfare of social groups in community

Class works limited to social welfare work by religious organizations in 361.7

See Manual at 251–254, 259 vs. 260

.08 History and description with respect to kinds of persons

Class students, asocial and antisocial persons in 259

[.083] Young people

Do not use; class in 259

.084 Persons in specific stages of adulthood

Class persons in late adulthood in 259

[.087] Handicapped and ill persons

Do not use; class in 259

260 Christian social and ecclesiastical theology

Institutions, services, observances, disciplines, work of Christianity and Christian church

Class here comprehensive works on Christian church

For local church and religious orders, see 250; denominations and sects, 280

See Manual at 251–254, 259 vs. 260

SUMMARY

260.9	**Historical, geographic, persons treatment**
261	**Social theology and interreligious relations and attitudes**
262	**Ecclesiology**
263	**Days and times of religious observance, holy places**
264	**Public worship**
265	**Sacraments, other rites and acts**
266	**Missions**
267	**Associations for religious work**
268	**Religious education**
269	**Spiritual renewal**

.9 **Historical, geographic, persons treatment**

Class historical, geographic, persons treatment of the Christian church in 270

261 Social theology and interreligious relations and attitudes

Attitude of Christianity and Christian church toward and influence on secular matters, attitude toward other religions, interreligious relations

Class sociology of religion in 306.6

[.1] **Role of Christian church in society**

Number discontinued; class in 261

.2 **Christianity and other systems of belief**

Including Christianity and irreligion

.5 **Christianity and secular disciplines**

Examples: art, literature, philosophy, science

Including attitude toward and use of communications media

Class a specific use of communications media by the church with the use, e.g., television evangelism 269

See Manual at 261.5

.7 **Christianity and political affairs**

Including religious freedom, theocracy

Class here Christianity and civil rights

Class Christianity and international affairs in 261.8

See Manual at 322 vs. 261.7, 291.1

.8 **Christianity and socioeconomic problems**

Including attitude toward and influence on social problems, the economic order, international affairs

Class here comprehensive works on the Christian view of socioeconomic and political affairs

For Christianity and political affairs, see 261.7

See also 361.7 for welfare services of religious organizations

See Manual at 261.8 vs. 241

262 Ecclesiology

Church government, organization, nature

Including governing leaders, e.g., bishops; parishes and religious congregations and orders in church organization; specific forms of church organization, e.g., episcopal; general councils, church and ministerial authority and its denial

Class biography of church leaders in 270, of leaders of specific denominations in 280; government and administration of parishes in 254, of religious congregations and orders in 255; nonlegal decrees of church councils on a specific subject with the subject, e.g., statement of original sin 233

See Manual at 209.2 for biography; 251–254, 259 vs. 260

.001 Philosophy and theory

Including church renewal, ecumenism

Class the history of the ecumenical movement in 270.8

See Manual at 280 vs. 270.8, 262.001 for ecumenism

.002–.005 Standard subdivisions

.006 Organizations and particular aspects of administration

.006 8 Particular aspects of administration

Example: financial administration

Do not use for comprehensive works on management; class in 262

.007–.009 Standard subdivisions

.9 **Church law and discipline**

Including Acts of the Holy See, e.g., encyclicals

Class here canon (ecclesiastical) law

Class civil law relating to church or religious matters in 340; acts of the Holy See on a specific subject with the subject, e.g., on the nature of the church 262

See also 364.1 for offenses against religion as defined and penalized by the state

263 Days and times of religious observance, holy places

Including Sabbath (seventh-day observance), Sunday; church year, saint's days; shrines

Class works treating miracles and the shrines associated with them in 231.7, miracles of Jesus and shrines associated with them in 232.9, miracles associated with Mary and the shrines associated with them in 232.91, pilgrimages in 248.4

See Manual at 394.2 vs. 263, 290 for religious holidays

264 Public worship

Ceremonies, rites, services (liturgy and ritual)

Examples: Eucharist, Holy Communion, Lord's Supper, Mass; music, prayers, scripture readings; creeds and confessions of faith, sermons

Including works limited by denomination or sect about sacraments, other rites and acts [*formerly* 265]

Class comprehensive works on worship in 248.3; works not limited by denomination or sect about sacraments, other rites and acts in 265; texts of creeds and confessions of faith in 238; texts of sermons in 252; Sunday school services in 268; interdisciplinary works on Christian sacred music in 781.7, on sacred vocal music in 782.2, on hymns in 782.27

.001 Philosophy and theory

Class here liturgical renewal

.002–.009 Standard subdivisions

265 Sacraments, other rites and acts

Not limited by denomination or sect

Examples: baptism, ceremonies of joining church, consecrations, dedications, exorcism, foot washing, laying on of hands, love feasts (agapes)

Works limited by denomination or sect about sacraments, other rites and acts relocated to 264

For Eucharist, Holy Communion, Lord's Supper, Mass, see 264

266 Missions

Class here missionary societies, religious aspects of medical missions

Class medical services of medical missions in 362.1

For mission schools, see 377

.001–.008 Standard subdivisions

.009 Historical, geographic, persons treatment

Class here joint and interdenominational missions; foreign missions by continent, country, locality served

Class foreign missions originating in specific continents, countries, localities; historical, geographic, persons treatment of missions of specific denominations and sects in 266

267 Associations for religious work

Including Young Men's and Young Women's Christian Associations

Salvation Army relocated to 287.9

For pious societies, see 248.06; religious congregations and orders, 255; missionary societies, 266

See Manual at 209.2 for biography

268 Religious education

In Sunday schools, church schools, vacation Bible schools, under other church auspices

Class here comprehensive works on Christian religious education [*formerly* 207], catechetics (the science or art devoted to organizing the principles of religious teaching), curriculums

Class religious education at the university level and in secular secondary schools in 207; religion and secular education in 377; textbooks on a specific subject with the subject, e.g., on missions 266

See Manual at 207 vs. 268; 209.2 for biography

[.068] Management

Use of this number discontinued; class in 268

.08 History and description with respect to kinds of persons

Class education of specific groups in 268

269 Spiritual renewal

Including camp meetings, pentecostalism, retreats, revivals; comprehensive works on evangelism, on television evangelism

Class evangelistic writings for individuals and families in 243, texts of evangelistic sermons in 252, Christian attitude toward and use of mass media in 261.5, history of pentecostal movement in 270.8

270 Historical, geographic, persons treatment of organized Christian church (Church history)

Observe table of precedence under 230–280

Class historical, geographic, persons treatment of specific denominations and sects in 280

See Manual at 209.2 for biography

.01–.08 Standard subdivisions

.09 Areas, regions, places in general; persons

[.093–.099] Geographic treatment

Do not use; class in 274–279

> **270.1–270.8 Historical periods**

Class comprehensive works in 270

See Manual at 281 for the early church

.1 Apostolic period to 325

.2 Period of ecumenical councils, 325–787

.3 Periods of struggle between papacy and empire, 787–1054

Including great schism, 1054

.4 Period of papal supremacy, 1054–1200

.5 Late Middle Ages through the Renaissance, 1200–1517

.6 Period of Reformation and Counter-Reformation, 1517–1648

.7 Period from Peace of Westphalia to the French Revolution, 1648–1789

.8 Modern period, 1789–

Including charismatic, ecumenical, pentecostal movements

See Manual at 280 vs. 270.8, 262.001 for ecumenical movement

> **271–273 Special topics of church history**

Class comprehensive works in 270

271 Religious congregations and orders in church history

Class persecutions involving religious congregations and orders in 272, doctrinal controversies and heresies involving congregations and orders in 273

.001–.009 Standard subdivisions

272 Persecutions in general church history

Regardless of denomination

Class here martyrs

Class relation of state to church in 322

273 Doctrinal controversies and heresies in general church history

Examples: Albigensianism, Arianism, Catharism, Christian Gnosticism, Christian Manicheism, Jansenism, modernism, Pietism, Waldensianism

Class comprehensive works and non-Christian Gnosticism, on Christian and non-Christian Manicheism in 299; persecutions resulting from controversies and heresies in 272; churches founded on specific doctrines in 280

See also 239 for apologetics and polemics

274–279 Treatment by continent, country, locality

Add to base number 27 notation 4–9 from Table 2, e.g., Christian church in Europe 274, in France 274.4

Class geographic treatment of a specific subject with the subject, using notation 09 from Table 1, e.g., persecutions in France 272.0944

280 Denominations and sects of the Christian church

Including Protestantism; relations between denominations

Class here general historical and geographic treatment of, comprehensive works on specific denominations and sects and their individual local churches

(Option: Class here specific elements of specific denominations and sects; prefer 230–270)

Class the history of the ecumenical movement in 270.8, persecution of or by specific churches in 272

See also 273 for doctrines of specific churches considered as heresies

See Manual at 209.2 for biography; 280 vs. 270.8, 262.001 for relations between denominations

SUMMARY

280.01–.09 Standard subdivisions
281 Early church and Eastern churches
282 Roman Catholic Church
283 Anglican churches
284 Protestant denominations of Continental origin and related bodies
285 Presbyterian churches, Reformed churches centered in America, Congregational churches
286 Baptist, Disciples of Christ, Adventist churches
287 Methodist churches; churches uniting Methodist and other denominations; Salvation Army
289 Other denominations and sects

.01–.09 Standard subdivisions

281 Early church and Eastern churches

Former heading: Primitive and Oriental churches

Including Coptic, Monophysite, Nestorian churches

Class general history of the early church in 270.1–270.3

See Manual at 281 for the early church

.9 **Eastern Orthodox churches**

.909 Historical, geographic, persons treatment

Use of this number for treatment by continent, country, locality discontinued; class in 281.9

282 Roman Catholic Church

Class here comprehensive works on Roman Catholic Church and Eastern rite churches in communion with Rome

Class Eastern rite churches in communion with Rome in 281, modern schisms in Roman Catholic Church in 284

.09 Historical, geographic, persons treatment

Use of this number for treatment by continent, country, locality discontinued; class in 282

283 Anglican churches

.09 Historical, geographic, persons treatment

Use of this number for treatment by continent, country, locality discontinued; class in 283

284 Protestant denominations of Continental origin and related bodies

Examples: Albigensian, Anabaptist, Arminian, Catharist, Huguenot, Hussite, Moravian, Waldensian churches; modern schisms in Roman Catholic Church, e.g., Jansenism; comprehensive works on Calvinistic churches, on Reformed churches

For Presbyterian churches, Reformed churches centered in America, see 285; Baptist churches, 286; Church of the New Jerusalem, 289.4; Mennonite churches, 289.7

.1 **Lutheran churches**

.109 Historical, geographic, persons treatment

Use of this number for treatment by continent, country, locality discontinued; class in 284.1

285 Presbyterian churches, Reformed churches centered in America, Congregational churches

Including Puritanism

Class United Church of Canada, Uniting Church in Australia in 287.9

.7 **Reformed churches centered in America**

.709 Historical, geographic, persons treatment

Use of this number for treatment by continent, country, locality discontinued; class in 285.7

.8 **Congregationalism**

Class Evangelical and Reformed Church in 285.7; United Church of Canada, Uniting Church in Australia in 287.9

.809 Historical, geographic, persons treatment

Use of this number for treatment by continent, country, locality discontinued; class in 285.8

286 Baptist, Disciples of Christ, Adventist churches

.6 **Disciples of Christ (Campbellites)**

.609 Historical, geographic, persons treatment

Use of this number for treatment by continent, country, locality discontinued; class in 286.6

.7 **Adventist churches**

.709 Historical, geographic, persons treatment

Use of this number for treatment by continent, country, locality discontinued; class in 286.7

287 Methodist churches; churches uniting Methodist and other denominations; Salvation Army

For Evangelical United Brethren Church, see 289.9

.9 **Salvation Army [*formerly* 267]; Churches uniting Methodist and other denominations**

Examples: United Church of Canada, Uniting Church in Australia

[288] Unitarianism, Socinianism, Anti-Trinitarianism

Relocated to 289.1

289 Other denominations and sects

Example: Shakers (United Society of True Believers in Christ's Second Appearing)

.1 **Unitarian and Universalist churches**

Class here Unitarianism, Socinianism, Anti-Trinitarianism [*all formerly* 288]

.109 Historical, geographic, persons treatment

Use of this number for treatment by continent, country, locality discontinued; class in 289.1

(.2) **(Permanently unassigned)**

(Optional number used to provide local emphasis or a shorter number for a specific denomination or sect; prefer the number for the specific denomination or sect in 281–289)

.3 **Latter-Day Saints (Mormons)**

.309 Historical, geographic, persons treatment

Use of this number for treatment by continent, country, locality discontinued; class in 289.3

.4 **Church of the New Jerusalem (Swedenborgianism)**

.409 Historical, geographic, persons treatment

Use of this number for treatment by continent, country, locality discontinued; class in 289.4

.5 **Church of Christ, Scientist (Christian Science)**

.509 Historical, geographic, persons treatment

Use of this number for treatment by continent, country, locality discontinued; class in 289.5

.6 **Society of Friends (Quakers)**

.609 Historical, geographic, persons treatment

Use of this number for treatment by continent, country, locality discontinued; class in 289.6

.7 **Mennonite churches**

Examples: Amish, Church of God in Christ, Hutterian Brethren

.709 Historical, geographic, persons treatment

Use of this number for treatment by continent, country, locality discontinued; class in 289.7

✓ .9 **Others**

Examples: Assemblies of God, Church of the Nazarene, Churches of God, Evangelical United Brethren Church, independent fundamentalist and evangelical churches, Jehovah's Witnesses, New Thought, Pentecostal churches, Unification Church, United Brethren in Christ, Unity School of Christianity

(Option: Class a specific denomination or sect requiring local emphasis in 289.2)

Class nondenominational and interdenominational Christian churces in 280 without subdivision; eclectic New Thought, comprehensive works on New Thought in 299

290 Comparative religion and religions other than Christianity

See Manual at 290; 394.2 vs. 263, 290 for religious holidays

SUMMARY

291 Comparative religion

Including prehistoric religions, religions of nonliterate peoples

Class here works dealing with various religions, with religious topics not applied to specific religions

Class treatment of religious topics with respect to natural theology in 210, with respect to Christianity in 220–280, with respect to a specific religion other than Christianity in 292–299

See Manual at 200.1 vs. 210, 291 for philosophy of religion; 291

.06 Organizations

Class management, religious organizations in 291.6

.07 Education and related topics of religions

Class here education in and teaching of comparative religion, religions as an academic subject

Religious education for the purpose of encouraging believers in religious life and practice, comprehensive works on religious education relocated to 291.7

.09 Historical, geographic, persons treatment

See Manual at 291.09 vs. 294, 299 for religions of Asian origin

.1 **Religious mythology, social theology, interreligious relations and attitudes**

Including attitudes of religions toward secular disciplines, e.g., science; religions and political affairs, socioeconomic problems, international affairs

Class sources of religion in 291.8, welfare work of religious organizations in 361.7; myths on a specific subject with the subject, e.g., creation myths 291.2

See Manual at 322 vs. 261.7, 291.1 for religions and political affairs; 398.2 vs. 291.1 for mythology

.2 **Doctrines**

Including gods and goddesses, nature, persons, images as objects of worship and veneration; humankind, cosmology, creation, eschatology

Class here apologetics, polemics, comprehensive works on theology

For social theology, see 291.1; moral theology, 291.5

.3 **Public worship and other practices**

Including ceremonies, rites; offerings, sacrifices, penances; emblems, symbolism, symbolic objects; sacred places and times; divination, witchcraft

Class pilgrimages and comprehensive works on worship in 291.4; interdisciplinary works on sacred music in 781.7, on sacred vocal music in 782.2

See Manual at 394.2 vs. 263, 290 for religious holidays

.4 **Religious experience, life, practice**

Including religious training of children in the home [*formerly also* 649], asceticism, contemplation, conversion, devotional texts, guides to religious life, meditation, moral renewal and commitment, mysticism, observances of restrictions and limitations, pilgrimages, prayer, worship

For public worship, see 291.3; moral theology, 291.5

.5 **Moral theology**

Including conscience, duties, sins, vices, virtues

.6 **Leaders and organization**

Class laws and decisions in 291.8

See Manual at 291: Biography

.7 **Missions, religious training and education**

Class here religious education for the purpose of encouraging believers in religious life and practice, comprehensive works on religious education [*both formerly also* 291.07]

Use of this number for the concept of religious war discontinued; class in 291

Class education in and teaching of comparative religion, of religions as an academic subject in 291.07

.8 **Sources**

Examples: sacred books and scriptures, oral traditions, laws and decisions

Class civil law relating to religious matters in 340

.9 **Sects and reform movements**

Class specific aspects of sects and reform movements in 291.1–291.8

> **292–299 Religions other than Christianity**

Class comprehensive works in 291

See Manual at 291

292 Classical (Greek and Roman) religion

See also 299 for modern revivals of classical religions

.001–.005 Standard subdivisions

.006 Organizations

Class management, religious organizations in 292.6

.007 Education and related topics

Class here classical religion as an academic subject

Class comprehensive works on religious education, religious education for the purpose of encouraging believers in religious life and practice in 292.7

.008–.009 Standard subdivisions

> **292.07–292.08 By specific culture**

Class comprehensive works in 292, specific elements regardless of culture in 292.1–292.9

.07 Roman religion

.08 Greek religion

.1–.9 Specific elements

Add to base number 292 the numbers following 291 in 291.1–291.9, e.g., mythology 292.1

Class classical religion as an academic subject in 292.007

293 Germanic religion

See also 299 for modern revivals of Germanic religion

.06 Organizations

Use of this number for management, religious organizations discontinued; class in 293

.07 Education and related topics

Class here Germanic religion as an academic subject

Use of this number for religious education for the purpose of encouraging believers in religious life and practice, comprehensive works on religious education discontinued; class in 293

294 Religions of Indic origin

See Manual at 291.09 vs. 294, 299

.3 Buddhism

See Manual at 291

.306 Organizations

Use of this number for management, religious organizations discontinued; class in 294.3

.307 Education and related topics

Class here Buddhism as an academic subject

Use of this number for religious education for the purpose of encouraging believers in religious life and practice, comprehensive works on religious education discontinued; class in 294.3

.4 Jainism

See Manual at 291

.406 Organizations

Use of this number for management, religious organizations discontinued; class in 294.4

.407 Education and related topics

Class here Jainism as an academic subject

Use of this number for religious education for the purpose of encouraging believers in religious life and practice, comprehensive works on religious education discontinued; class in 294.4

.5 Hinduism

Including Vedic literature

Class here Brahmanism

See Manual at 291

.506 Organizations

Use of this number for management, religious organizations discontinued; class in 294.5

.507 Education and related topics

Class here Hinduism as an academic subject

Use of this number for religious education for the purpose of encouraging believers in religious life and practice, comprehensive works on religious education discontinued; class in 294.5

.6 Sikhism

See Manual at 291

.606 Organizations

Use of this number for management, religious organizations discontinued; class in 294.6

.607 Education and related topics

Class here Sikhism as an academic subject

Use of this number for religious education for the purpose of encouraging believers in religious life and practice, comprehensive works on religious education discontinued; class in 294.6

295 Zoroastrianism (Mazdaism, Parseeism)

Class Mithraism in 299

.06 Organizations

Use of this number for management, religious organizations discontinued; class in 295

.07 Education and related topics

Class here Zoroastrianism as an academic subject

Use of this number for religious education for the purpose of encouraging believers in religious life and practice, comprehensive works on religious education discontinued; class in 295

296 Judaism

See Manual at 291

.06 Organizations

Management relocated to 296.6

Class religious organizations in 296.6

.07 Education and related topics

Class here Judaism as an academic subject

Religious education for the purpose of encouraging believers in religious life and practice, comprehensive works on religious education relocated to 296.6

.1 Sources

Including Talmudic literature; Midrash; Cabala; Maimonides, Responsa; Halakah, Aggadah; sources of specific sects and movements, e.g., Qumran community (Dead Sea Scrolls)

Class Judaic theology based on these sources in 296.3, Judaic mystical experience in 296.7, modern Judaic mystical movements in 296.8, pseudepigrapha in Dead Sea Scrolls in 229

For Torah and sacred scripture (Old Testament), see 221

.3 Doctrinal, moral, social theology

Including biblical theology, apologetics, polemics

Class guides to conduct of life in 296.7

See Manual at 220 for Biblical theology

.4 **Traditions, rites, public services**

Description, interpretation, conduct, texts of rites and public services

Including sermons; Sabbath, festivals, holy days, fasts; rites and customs for specific occasions, e.g., bar mitzvah

Class here family celebration and services, hymns, liturgy, music, prayers, responsive reading, symbolism

Class comprehensive works on worship in 296.7; sermons on a specific subject with the subject, e.g., social theology 296.3; musical scores and parts in 781.76

.6 **Leaders, organization, religious education**

Including management [*formerly also* 296.06]; religious education for the purpose of encouraging believers in religious life and practice, comprehensive works on religious education [*both formerly also* 296.07]

Class laws and decisions in 296.1

See Manual at 291: Biography

.7 **Religious experience, life, practice**

Including asceticism, contemplation, conversion, devotional texts, meditation, moral renewal and commitment, mysticism, observance of dietary laws, prayer, worship

Class cabalistic literature in 296.1, public worship, family celebration and services in 296.4, Judaic mystical movements in 296.8

For moral theology, see 296.3

.8 **Sects and movements**

Examples: orthodox, conservative, reform, mystical Judaism

Class specific aspects of sects and movements in 296.1–296.7

297 Islam and religions originating in it

Including Islamic sects; Babism, Bahai Faith; Black Muslim movement, e.g., World Community of al-Islam in the West

Class Sikhism in 294.6

See Manual at 291

.06 Organizations

Use of this number for management, religious organizations discontinued; class in 297

.07 Education and related topics

Class here Islam as an academic subject

Use of this number for religious education for the purpose of encouraging believers in religious life and practice, comprehensive works on religious education discontinued; class in 297

(298) (Permanently unassigned)

(Optional number used to provide local emphasis and a shorter number to a specific religion; prefer the number for the specific religion)

299 Other religions

Examples: anthroposophy, Confucianism, Gnosticism, Manicheism, Mithraism, New Age religions, New Thought, Shintoism, Taoism, theosophy, United Church of Religious Science, Urantia, voodooism; religions originating among Africans and people of African descent; religions of North and South American native origin; religions of other ethnic origin, e.g., ancient Egyptian, Celtic, Polynesian; religions of eclectic and syncretistic origin; modern revivals of long dormant religions

(Option: Class a specific religion requiring local emphasis in 298)

Class Four Books of Confucius in 181, syncretistic religious writings of individuals expressing personal views and not claiming to establish a new religion or to represent an old one in 291

If a religion not named in the schedule claims to be Christian, class it in 289.9 even if it is unorthodox or syncretistic

For Black Muslim movement, see 297

See Manual at 291; 291.09 vs. 294, 299 for religions of East and Southeast Asian origin

300

300 Social sciences

Class here behavioral sciences, social studies

Use 300.1–300.9 for standard subdivisions

Class a specific behavioral science with the science, e.g., psychology 150; military, diplomatic, political, economic, social, welfare aspects of a war with the history of the war, e.g., diplomatic efforts to end the Vietnam War 959.704

For language, see 400; history, 900

See Manual at 300; 300 vs. 600 for technical vs. social considerations of specific topics

SUMMARY

301	**Sociology and anthropology**
302	**Social interaction**
303	**Social processes**
304	**Factors affecting social behavior**
305	**Social groups**
306	**Culture and institutions**
307	**Communities**

301 Sociology and anthropology

Class here interdisciplinary works on society

Class specific topics in sociology or anthropology in 302–307, a specific aspect of society not provided for in 302–307 with the aspect, e.g., social problems and social welfare 361–365, general history 900

For criminal anthropology, see 364.2; educational sociology, 370.19; physical anthropology, 573

See Manual at 301; 301–307 vs. 361–365 for social problems as social phenomena; 361.1 vs. 362, 301 for social problems

.01 Philosophy and theory

Class psychological principles in 302

> ## 302–307 Specific topics in sociology and anthropology

Unless other instructions are given, class complex subjects with aspects in two or more subdivisions of 302–307 in the one coming last in the schedule, e.g., social decay during civil wars 303.6 (*not* 303.45); however, class the effect of one factor on another with the factor affected, e.g., the effect of climate on social change 303.4 (*not* 304.2)

Class comprehensive works in 301

See Manual at T1–01 vs. 302–307 for social psychology; 150 vs. 302–307 for individual vs. group behavior; 155.9 vs. 158, 302–307 for social influences on behavior; 301–307 vs. 361–365 for social problems as social phenomena; 302–307 for an overview of anthropology and sociology; 320 vs. 302–307 for the relationship between political and social behavior

302 Social interaction

Including cooperation, competition; role theory; social dysfunctions, e.g., mass hysteria

Class here social psychology

Class the social psychology of a specific situation with the situation, e.g., of ethnic groups 305.8

See also 155.9 for the psychology of social influences on individuals, 158 for individual aspects of interpersonal relations

.2 Communication

Including body language, nonlinguistic communication, rumor

Class here interdisciplinary works on communication [*formerly* 001.5], mass communication, nonlinguistic communication

Ethnolinguistics, sociolinguistics relocated to 306.4

Class manual language for the hearing-impaired in 419

For conversation, see 302.3; language, 400

.23 Media (Means of communication)

Examples: books, newspapers, motion pictures, radio, television, telephone

Class here mass media

Class effect of media on a subject other than social groups with the subject, e.g., the effect of media on elections 324.7

.230 8 Media (Means of communication) with respect to kinds of persons

Class here the effect of mass media on specific groups [*formerly* 305]

.3 **Social interaction within groups**

Examples: bureaucracy, committees, conversation, gangs, mobs

Class here group decision-making processes

See Manual at 658, T1—068 vs. 302.3 for social vs. managerial aspects of organizational behavior

.4 **Social interaction between groups**

Including ingroups

.5 **Relation of the individual to society**

Including ambition, individualism; alienation, social isolation, aggression; reference groups

See also 155.9 for psychological effects of the social environment upon the individual

303 Social processes

For social interaction, see 302; factors affecting social behavior, 304

.3 **Coordination and control**

Including censorship, coercion, leadership, persuasion, prejudice, propaganda, public opinion, socialization, values

Class here power

Class individual psychology of persuasion in 153.8, coordination and control in and through specific social institutions in 306, socialization by education in 370; public opinion on a specific subject with the subject, e.g., on racial stereotypes 305.8, on the political process 324

.4 **Social change**

Class social changes in a specific aspect of society with the aspect in sociology, e.g., changes in sexual behavior 306.7

.401 Philosophy and theory

Class forecasting and forecasts in 303.49

.44 Growth and development

Including progress, specialization

.45 Deterioration and decay

.48 Causes of change

Examples: contact between cultures, development of science and technology, disasters, social reform

.49 Social forecasts

Class here futurology, social forecasting

Class interdisciplinary works on futurology in 003, forecasting in and forecasts of a specific subject with the subject, using notation 01 from Table 1, e.g., weather in the 21st century 551.601

.490 9 Historical and persons treatment

Class geographic treatment in 303.491–303.499 (*not* 303.49091–303.49099)

.491–.499 Forecasts for specific areas

Add to base number 303.49 notation 1–9 from Table 2, e.g., the United States in the 21st century 303.4973

.6 Conflict

Including civil disobedience and disorder, pacifism, revolution, terrorism, war; conflict resolution

Class interdisciplinary works on war in 355.02, war as a cause of social change in 303.48, prevention of war in 327.1, legal aspects of war in 341.6, the art and science of warfare in 355–359; conflict in a specific area of social relations with the subject in sociology, e.g., racial conflict 305.8; military, diplomatic, political, economic, social, welfare aspects of a specific war with the history of the war, e.g., World War II 940.53

See also 363.3 for the prevention of terrorism

304 Factors affecting social behavior

.2 Human ecology

Including influence of weather and climate; environmental abuse, pollution

Class here human geography

Class interdisciplinary works on pollution in 363.73

See Manual at 363.7 vs. 333.7, 304.2 for environment; 508 vs. 574, 910, 304.2 for ecology of human settlement

.5 Genetic factors

Including sociobiology

.6 Population

Including comprehensive works on statistics of population [*formerly also* 312]; growth, decline; births (fertility), deaths (mortality); family size

Class here demography

Overpopulation relocated to 363.9

Class interdisciplinary works on population control in 363.9

For movement of people, see 304.8

.8 Movement of people

Examples: emigration, immigration

For movement to, from, within communities, see 307.2

.809 Historical, geographic, persons treatment

Internal movement in and emigration from specific areas

Class emigration to specific areas in 304.8

305 Social groups

General aspects: social status, role, interactions, problems of social groups; discrimination against and conflict involving social groups

Class here the culture and institutions of specific groups other than indigenous racial, ethnic, national groups [*formerly also* 306]; equality, inequality; social stratification

Unless other instructions are given, observe the following table of precedence, e.g., young black Roman Catholic middle-class males 305.23 (*not* 305.31, 305.38, 305.5, 305.6, or 305.8)

Persons by physical and mental characteristics	305.9
Age groups	305.2
Groups by sex	305.3–.4
Social classes	305.5
Religious groups	305.6
Language groups	305.7
Racial, ethnic, national groups	305.8
Occupational and miscellaneous groups (*except* persons by physical and mental characteristics)	305.9

The effect of media on specific groups relocated to 302.2308

Class opinions of specific social groups in 303.3; the role of specific groups in specific institutions in 306; specific problems of, welfare services to social groups in 362; a specific aspect of discrimination with the subject, e.g., discrimination in housing 363.5, racial discrimination 305.8

See Manual at 305 vs. 306, 909, 930–990

.2 Age groups

Class here generation gap

For generation gap in families, see 306.874

.23 Young people

Through age 20

Including child development, comprehensive works on young adults

Class here interdisciplinary works on children

Class the psychological development of children in 155.4, of young adults in 155.5; physical development of children, of persons from the beginning of puberty until the attainment of maturity in 612.6; socialization in 303.3; young adults over 20 in 305.24; other aspects of young people with the aspect, e.g., the social welfare of children 362.7

.24 Adults

Class comprehensive works on young adults, young adults aged twelve to twenty in 305.23; adults of specific sexes in 305.3

For late adulthood, see 305.26

.26 Late adulthood

Class the sociology of retirement in 306.3

See also 646.7 for retirement guides

.3 Men and women

Class here interdisciplinary works on sex role, the sexes; adult men and women

Class sex psychology and the psychology of the sexes in 155.3, men and women in late adulthood in 305.26, relations between the sexes and within the sexes in 306.7–306.8; the relation of a specific sex to a specific subject with the subject, using notation 081–082 from Table 1, e.g., women in U.S. history 973.082

For women, see 305.4

.31 Men

Class here interdisciplinary works on men, on males

Class specific aspects of the sociology of men in 305.32–305.38, an aspect not provided for in 305.3 with the aspect, e.g., legal status of men 346.01

> **305.32–305.38 Specific aspects of the sociology of men**

Class comprehensive works in 305.31

.32 Social role and status of men

Class here discrimination against men, men's movements, e.g., men's liberation movement

Class a specific social role of men with the role, e.g., fatherhood 306.874

.33 Men's occupations

.38 Specific kinds of men

Examples: homosexual, Oriental, single men; widowers

Class kinds of men defined by occupation in 305.33

.4 **Women**

Class here interdisciplinary works on women, on females

Class specific aspects of the sociology of women not provided for here with the subject outside sociology, e.g., women's suffrage in 324.6, women's education in 376

.42 Social role and status of women

Class here discrimination against women, women's movements, e.g., women's liberation movement

Class specific social roles of women with the role, e.g., motherhood 306.874

.43 Women's occupations

.48 Specific kinds of women

Examples: Oriental, single women; lesbians, widows

Class kinds of women defined by occupation in 305.43

.5 **Social classes**

Examples: upper, middle, lower classes; white-collar, blue-collar classes; elites, intellectuals, professionals; the poor, homeless persons, tramps

Including social mobility; minority groups in general

Class here class conflict

Use of this number for equality and inequality discontinued; class in 305

Class class conflict from the socialist point of view in 335.4, a specific minority or nondominant group with the kind of group in sociology, e.g., religious minorities 305.6, racial, ethnic, national minorities 305.8

.6 **Religious groups**

Example: the social life of Ohio Roman Catholics

.7 **Language groups**

Example: English-speaking people

.8 Racial, ethnic, national groups

Including ancient Romans, Osco-Umbrians

Class here ethnology, cultural ethnology, ethnography [*all formerly also* 306, 572]; race relations, race discrimination

Except where instructed otherwise, give precedence to ethnic group over nationality, e.g., United States citizens of Irish descent 305.891 (*not* 305.813), British citizens of African descent 305.896 (*not* 305.83)

Except where instructed otherwise, when choosing between two ethnic groups, give precedence to the group for which the notation is different from that of the nationality of the people, e.g., a work treating equally the Hispanic and native American heritage of bicultural Spanish-Quechua mestizos of Peru 305.898 (*not* 305.868)

Except where instructed otherwise, when choosing between two national groups, give precedence to the former or ancestral group, e.g., people from the Soviet Union who have become United States citizens 305.891 (*not* 305.813)

Class unassimilated indigenous racial, ethnic, national groups in 306.08; physical ethnology in 572; a specific aspect of racial, national, ethnic groups with the aspect, e.g., ethnopsychology 155.8

See also 909 for comprehensive history of specific widely distributed racial, ethnic, national groups; 930–990 for history of specific groups in specific continents, countries, localities

.800 1–.800 9 Standard subdivisions

.81 *North Americans

Class Spanish North Americans and specific national groups in Spanish North America in 305.868; national groups of predominantly African descent, e.g., Haitians, in 305.896

For North American native peoples, see 305.897

See Manual at 305.81

.811 Canadians

Including Canadians of British and French origin

.811 001–.811 009 Standard subdivisions

.813 People of the United States ("Americans")

Class here people of the United States of British origin

For African Americans, see 305.896

.813 001–.813 009 Standard subdivisions

*Do not use standard subdivisions

.82 British English

Examples: people of the British Isles, Australians, New Zealanders, South Africans of British origin

Class North Americans of British origin in 305.81; Australian native people, Polynesians in 305.89; Anglo-Indians (Indian citizens of British origin), people of Celtic (e.g., Irish, Scots, Welsh) origin in 305.891; South Africans as a national group in 305.896

.820 01–.820 09 Standard subdivisions

.83 *Germanic (Nordic) people

Examples: Afrikaners, Dutch, Germans

Including comprehensive works on Belgians, Scandinavians, Swiss

Class Walloons and French Swiss in 305.84, Italian and Romansh Swiss in 305.85, Finns and Lapps in 305.894, South Africans as a national group in 305.896

For Anglo-Saxons, see 305.82

.84 *Modern Latin peoples

Including French, Walloons; Catalans

Class Canadians of French origin in 305.811

For Italians, Romanians, related groups, see 305.85; Spanish and Portuguese, 305.86; Basques, 305.89

.85 *Italians, Romanians, related groups

Example: Corsicans

.86 *Spanish and Portuguese

Examples: Spaniards, Brazilians

For Catalans, see 305.84; Basques, 305.89

.868 Spanish Americans

Class here comprehensive works on Latin Americans

Class non-Spanish Latin Americans with their specific ethnic or national affiliation, e.g., Brazilians 305.86, South American native peoples 305.898

.868 001–.868 009 Standard subdivisions

.88 *Greeks and related groups

Including comprehensive works on Cypriots, ancient Greeks and Romans

Class ancient Romans in 305.8, Turkish Cypriots in 305.89, Macedonians in 305.891

*Do not use standard subdivisions

.89 *Other racial, ethnic, national groups

Examples: Australian native peoples; Basques; Dravidians; Malays and related peoples; peoples of North and West Asian origin or situation other than Indo-European and Semitic groups, e.g., Finns, Hungarians, Turks; non-semitic Afro-Asiatic peoples, e.g., Berbers, Hausa

.891 *Other Indo-European peoples

Examples: Celts, e.g., Irish, Scots, Welsh; Indic peoples, e.g., Bengali, Gypsies (Romany people), Hindis; Iranians, e.g., Afghans, Persians; Slavs, e.g., Poles, Russians

Including comprehensive works on people of India, of South Asia

Class ancient Romans, Osco-Umbrians in 305.8; Dravidians, Scytho-Dravidians, Turkic peoples in 305.89; South Asians closely related to Southeast Asian peoples, e.g., Mundas, in 305.895

.892 *Semitic peoples

Examples: Arabs, Ethiopians; Israelis, Jews

Class non-Semitic Afro-Asiatic peoples of Arab countries and Ethiopia, e.g., Berbers, in 305.89; Mauritanians as a national group in 305.896

.895 *East and Southeast Asian peoples; Mundas

Examples: Chinese, Japanese, Koreans, Vietnamese (Annamese); the Bhutia as an ethnic group

Class here comprehensive works on Asian peoples

Class Aeta, Ainu, Andamanese, Malays in 305.89, the Bhutanese as a national group in 305.891; other specific Asian people with the people, e.g., Pakistanis 305.891

.896 *Africans and people of African descent

Examples: African Americans, Haitians, Tanzanians; Bantu, e.g., Zulu, Fulani

Class here African Negro races

Class North Africans, and non-Semitic Afro-Asiatic peoples in 305.89; Arabs and Ethiopians in 305.892

.897 *North American native peoples

Example: Navajo

Including Inuit of Siberia and Greenland

Class here comprehensive works on North and South American native peoples

National groups of modern Central America, e.g., Guatemalans as a national group, are classed in 305.868 even if the majority of their population is of North American native origin

For South American native peoples, see 305.898

*Do not use standard subdivisions

.898 *South American native peoples

Example: Quechua

National groups of modern South America are classed with the group, e.g., Brazilians 305.86, Peruvians 305.868, even if the majority of their population is of South American native origin

.9 **Occupational and miscellaneous groups**

Examples: groups of persons with respect to kinship, marital status, sexual orientation, physical and mental characteristics

Class here occupational mobility

Do not use standard subdivisions

Class men's occupations in 305.33, women's occupations in 305.43, occupational groups considered as a representative of a social class in 305.5

306 Culture and institutions

Culture: the aggregate of a society's beliefs, folkways, mores, science, technology, values, arts

Institutions: patterns of behavior in social relationships

Including subcultures, e.g., counter culture, drug culture

Class here mass culture, cultural and social anthropology

Ethnology, cultural ethnology, ethnography relocated to 305.8

Class cultural exchanges in 303.48, physical anthropology in 573

For customs and folklore, see 390

See Manual at 305 vs. 306, 909, 930–990 for social groups

.08 Indigenous racial, ethnic, national groups

Class here culture and institutions, ethnology, race relations of indigenous groups living in distinct communities not integrated in the economic and social life of a nation

Class culture and institutions of specific groups other than indigenous racial, ethnic, national groups in 305.8

.09 Historical, geographic, persons treatment [*formerly* 909, 930–990]

Class civilization and social conditions of a specific place or group in 909, 930–990

.2 **Political institutions**

Institutions maintaining internal and external peace

See also 320 for political science, 340 for law, 350 for public administration and military science

See Manual at 320 vs. 306.2 for political sociology

*Do not use standard subdivisions

.3 **Economic institutions**

Social arrangements for production, distribution

Including retirement

Class here economic anthropology, sociology of consumption

Class specific occupational groups in 305.9, economic institutions related to housing in 307.3

See also 305.5 for social classes, 330 for economics

.4 **Specific aspects of culture**

Including ethnolinguistics, sociolinguistics [*both formerly* 302.2, 401]; arts, language, recreation, science, technology; bilingualism, biculturalism

Class cultural patterns dealing with death in 306.9, sociology of education in 370.19

See Manual at 401 vs. 412, 415, 306.4 for language

.6 **Religious institutions**

To be classed here, the institutions must be considered from a secular, nonreligious viewpoint

See also 291.1 for social theology, 261 for Christian social theology

.7 **Institutions pertaining to relations of the sexes** sex education

Class here interdisciplinary works on sex, sexual love

Unwed parenthood relocated to 306.85

Class sexual ethics in 176, problems and controversies concerning various sex relations in 363.4, sex offenses and crimes in 364.1, sex customs in 392

For sexual hygiene and techniques, see 613.9

See Manual at 155.3 vs. 306.7 for the psychology of the individual in sexual relations

.73 General sexual relations

Including celibacy, courtship, premarital sexual relations, adultery, extramarital relations

Class here dating

For marriage, see 306.81

.74 Prostitution

See also 363.4 for prostitution as a social problem

.76 Sexual orientation

Including bisexuality, homosexuality, heterosexuality

Class sexual practices in 306.77

.77 Sexual practices 306.7

Incest relocated to 306.877

Class sex techniques in 613.9, sexual practices viewed as treatable disorders in 616.85

.8 Marriage and family

.81 Marriage

Class here interdisciplinary works on marriage

Class mate selection in 306.82; specific aspects of marriage with the aspect, e.g, divorce 306.89, marriage counseling 362.82

For types of marriage, see 306.84

.82 Patterns in mate selection

Class dating patterns in 306.73

.83 Kinship systems

Examples: matrilineal, patrilineal, totemic

.84 Types of marriage

Examples: common-law marriage, mixed marriage, polygamy

Including remarriage

.85 The family

Including unwed parenthood [*formerly* 306.7]

Class here interdisciplinary works on the family

Class a specific aspect of the family with the aspect, e.g., kinship systems 306.83, social services to families 362.82, achieving harmonious family relations 646.7

For intrafamily relationships, see 306.87; alteration of family patterns, 306.88

.87 Intrafamily relationships

Example: in-law relationships

Including birth order

For alteration of family patterns, see 306.88

See also 646.7 for guides to harmonious family relationships

.872 Husband-wife relationship

Class sexual practices in 306.77 306.7

See also 613.9 for sex techniques

.874 Parent-child relationship

grandparents

Examples: adopted children, illegitimacy

Class here the generation gap in families

Class comprehensive works on the generation gap in 305.2

See also 649 for recommended methods of child rearing (parenting)

.875 Sibling relationships

.877 Incest [*formerly* 306.77]

.88 Alteration of family patterns

Examples: desertion, death

For separation and divorce, see 306.89

.89 Separation and divorce

Including shared custody

Class the parent-child relationship in divorced families in 306.874, divorced families with single-parent custody in 306.85

.9 **Institutions pertaining to death**

Class here interdisciplinary works on death

Class specific aspects of death with the aspect, e.g., the psychology of death 155.9

307 Communities

See Manual at 307

.1 **Community planning and development**

See also 711 for the design aspects of city planning

See Manual at 711 vs. 307.1 for city planning

.2 **Population**

Size, composition; movement to, from, within communities

.3 **Community structure**

Including land use, neighborhoods, physical setting, redevelopment, residential patterns, sociology of housing

.7 **Specific kinds of communities**

Class specific aspects of specific kinds of communities in 307.1–307.3

.72 Rural communities

.74 Suburban communities

.740 9 Historical, geographic, persons treatment

Class specific suburban communities in 307.7609

.76 Urban communities

Class here interdisciplinary works on cities

Class suburban communities in 307.74

.760 9 Historical, geographic, persons treatment

Class here specific urban and suburban communities regardless of size or kind

.77 Self-contained communities

Examples: communes

310 General statistics

Collections of quantitative data

Class statistics of a specific subject, other than general statistics of a place, with the subject, e.g., statistics on criminal offenses 364.1

See also 001.4 for analysis and presentation of statistical data

.9 Historical, geographic, persons treatment

Class general statistics by specific continents, countries, localities in modern world in 314–319 (*not* 310.94–310.99)

[312] Statistics of population (Demographic statistics)

Comprehensive works relocated to 304.6; statistics of a specific demographic topic to the topic, e.g., statistics of crimes of violence 364.1

314–319 General statistics by specific continents, countries, localities in modern world

Add to base number 31 notation 4–9 from Table 2, e.g., statistics of France 314.4

Class comprehensive works in 310

320 Political science (Politics and government)

For law, see 340; public administration and military science, 350

See Manual at 320; 320 vs. 302–307; 320 vs. 306.2; 320 vs. 909, 930–990

SUMMARY

320.01–.09 Standard subdivisions
.1–.9 [Structure and functions, ideologies, situation and conditions, related topics]
321 Systems of governments and states
322 Relation of the state to organized groups and their members
323 Civil and political rights
324 The political process
325 International migration and colonization
326 Slavery and emancipation
327 International relations
328 The legislative process

.01 Philosophy and theory

Including nature, legitimacy, role of government [*all formerly* 320.2]; political justice, change, decision making

Class specific theories in the sense of ideologies in 320.5; theories on specific aspects of political science with the aspect, e.g., theories of origin of the state 320.1

.02–.08 Standard subdivisions

.09 Historical, geographic, persons treatment of political science (politics and government) as a discipline

Class historical and geographic treatment of politics and government in 320.9

.092 Political philosophers and scientists

Biography of political thinkers identified with specific ideologies relocated to 320.5

.1 The state

Including sovereignty, territory, theories of origin; geopolitics

Class systems by which states are organized, states with restricted sovereignty in 321; geopolitics in international relations in 327.101, territory in international law in 341.4, history of territorial changes in 911

See Manual at 320

.101 Philosophy and theory

Class theories of origin in 320.1

[.2] Government

Use of this number for comprehensive works on government discontinued; class in 320

Nature, legitimacy, role of government relocated to 320.01

.3 Comparative government

Class comparison of a specific subject with the subject, e.g., comparison of legislatures 328

.4 Structure and functions of government

Class here civics

Branches of government and separation of powers are classed in 320.4, without use of 320.401–320.409; branches of government and separation of powers of a specific area are classed with the area in 320.41–320.49

Relation of local government to higher levels of government relocated to 320.8

Class analysis of systems by which government is structured in 321, systems of relating federal to regional government in 321.02

For comparative government, see 320.3; local government, 320.8; legislative branch, 328; judicial branch 347; executive branch, 350

See Manual at 350–354 vs. 320.4, 320.9

.409 Historical and persons treatment

Class geographic treatment in 320.41–320.49

.41–.49 Geographic treatment

Class here systems of state and government in specific jurisdictions

Add to base number 320.4 notation 1–9 from Table 2, e.g., structure of government in Cuba 320.47291

.5 **Political ideologies**

Examples: anarchism, conservatism, communism, liberalism, nationalism

Including libertarian movement, radicalism, new left; "pan" movements, e.g., Pan-Africanism; racist ideologies, e.g., apartheid

Class here biography of political thinkers identified with specific ideologies [*formerly* 320.092]

Class ideologies respecting a specific aspect of state or government with the aspect, e.g., respecting change in system of government 321.09

See Manual at 320.5 vs. 320.9, 324; 335 vs. 320.5

.8 **Local government**

Class here relation of local governments to higher levels of government [*formerly* 320.4], boundaries, forms, kinds, structure and function

See also 352 for local administration

.9 **Political situation and conditions**

Class here historical and geographic treatment of politics and government; history, description, critical appraisal of political institutions and forms

Class general political history in 900

See Manual at 320; 320 vs. 909, 930–990; 320.5 vs. 320.9, 324; 350–354 vs. 320.4, 320.9

[.901–.909] Standard subdivisions

Numbers discontinued; class in 320.9

.91–.99 Historical, geographic, persons treatment

Add to base number 320.9 notation 1–9 from Table 2, e.g., political conditions in Egypt 320.962

321 Systems of governments and states

Including empires, ideal states, nation states, states with restricted sovereignty, proposed regional and world unions

Class here kinds of states, methods of selection of chief executive

Use 321.001–321.009 for standard subdivisions

Works about "national state" and "nation" in the sense of any sovereign state are classed in 320.1

.02 Federal systems

Including systems of relating federal and regional governments

Class here confederations

Class systems of relating federal and regional governments in specific jurisdictions in 320.4

[.03–.08] Empires, city states, states with restricted sovereignty

Numbers discontinued; class in 321

.09 Change in system of government

Including coup d'etat, revolution

Class interdisciplinary works on revolution in 303.6

[.1–.3] Systems of government among nonliterate peoples, ancient systems of government, feudal system

Numbers discontinued; class in 321

.4 Pure democracy

.5 Elitist systems

Examples: aristocracy, oligarchy, plutocracy, theocracy

Use of this number for autocracy discontinued; class in 321

[.6] Absolute monarchy

Use of this number discontinued; class in 321

.8 Democratic systems

Including cabinet system, limited monarchy, republics

For pure democracy, see 321.4

.9 Authoritarian systems

Including communist and fascist systems

Ancient authoritarian systems, absolute monarchy are classed in 321

For elitist systems, see 321.5

church-state

322 Relation of the state to organized groups and their members

Relation of the state to groups other than political parties

Including religious organizations and groups, labor movements and groups, business and industry, military organizations (armed forces)

Class groups organized for a specific purpose not provided for here with the purpose, e.g., groups organized to promote political rights 323.5

See Manual at 322 vs. 261.7, 291.1 for religion and the state

.4 **Political action groups**

Including pressure groups, reform movements, revolutionary and subversive groups

Class here protest groups; nonelectoral tactics used by political action groups, e.g., civil disobedience, passive resistance; specific kinds of confrontations between such groups and constituted authorities, e.g., riots

Class interdisciplinary works on conflicts and their resolution in 303.6; political action committees (U.S. fund-raising groups) in 324; pressure groups and reform movements with their goal, e.g., suffrage movements 324.6, welfare reform 361.6

See Manual at 361.2 vs. 322.4

323 Civil and political rights

Including citizen participation, repression, resistance to government

Class here relation of the state to its residents; individual freedom, human rights, rights of mankind

Class relation of the state to political parties and related organizations in 324, law of civil rights in 342, welfare aspects of human rights in 361.6; citizen participation in a specific issue with the issue, e.g., participation in control of public education 379.1

For relation of the state to organized groups and their members, see 322

[.08] History and description with respect to kinds of persons

Do not use; class civil and political rights of nondominant aggregates in 323.1, of other social aggregates in 323.3

.1 **Civil rights of nondominant aggregates [*formerly* 323.42], political rights of nondominant aggregates**

Use of this number for comprehensive works on relation of the state to social aggregates discontinued; class in 323

(Option: Class relation of the state to North American native races in 970.5)

Class specific nondominant aggregates other than members of racial, ethnic, national groups in 323.3; specific civil rights of a specific nondominant aggregate in 323.4, specific political rights in 323.5

.109 Historical, geographic, persons treatment

Class treatment by specific continents, countries, localities in 323.1 (*not* 323.1093–323.1099)

.3 **Civil and political rights of other social aggregates**

Other than members of racial, ethnic, national groups

Examples: women, socioeconomic classes

Class a specific civil right of a specific social aggregate in 323.4, specific political rights in 323.5

.4 **Specific civil rights; limitation and suspension of civil rights**

Including freedom of assembly and association; right of petition, right to bear arms, right to life and property

Do not use standard subdivisions; class in 323.01–323.09

Use of this number for comprehensive works on civil rights discontinued; class in 323

.42 Equal protection of laws

Including procedural rights, e.g., trial by jury

Civil rights of nondominant aggregates relocated to 323.1

.44 Freedom of action (Liberty)

Including freedom of conscience and religion, of information, of speech, of the press; right to privacy

Class here intellectual freedom

Class freedom of assembly and association, right of petition in 323.4

.5 **Political rights**

Examples: right to be represented, right to hold office

Voting rights relocated to 324.6

Class freedom of assembly, right of petition in 323.4; exercise of political rights in 324

[.508] History and description with respect to kinds of persons

Do not use; class political rights of nondominant aggregates in 323.1, of other social aggregates in 323.3

.6 **Citizenship and related topics**

Including acquisition of citizenship, aliens, asylum, stateless persons, expatriation and repatriation, passports and visas

324 The political process

Including interest and pressure groups working within the political process

Class here elections

Auxiliary organizations, e.g., youth groups, are classed in 324, without use of 324.01–324.09; auxiliary organizations of specific parties are classed in 324.24–324.29

Class comprehensive works on interest and pressure groups in 322.4

See Manual at 320 vs. 909, 930–990; 320.5 vs. 320.9, 324 for political movements

SUMMARY

.025 Directories of persons and organizations

Class here directories of elected officials [*formerly also* 351]

Class directories of elected officials of specific jurisdictions in 324.9

.09 Historical, geographic, persons treatment

Class historical and geographic treatment of elections in 324.9

.1 **International party organizations, auxiliaries, activities**

Not directly controlled by specific national parties

Class revolutionary and subversive activities of party organizations in 322.4

.2 **Political parties**

Including campaign literature

Finance, platforms, programs, relation of political parties to the state and government are classed in 324.2, without use of 324.201–324.209; finance, platforms, programs, relation of political parties to the state in specific countries in modern world are classed in 324.24–324.29

Class revolutionary and subversive activities in 322.4, auxiliary organizations in 324, international organizations and activities of parties in 324.1, campaign finance in 324.7; campaign literature on a specific subject with the subject, e.g., attacks on United States participation in Vietnamese War 959.704

For nomination of candidates, see 324.5

[.202 3] Politics as a profession

Do not use; class in 324.2

.209 Historical, geographic, persons treatment

Class here treatment of parties in continents and regions of modern world larger than countries [*formerly* 324.24–324.29]

Class treatment in specific countries and parts of countries in modern world in 324.24–324.29 (*not* 324.2094–324.2099)

See Manual at 324.24–324.29 and 324.209

.24–.29 **Parties in specific countries in modern world**

Class here auxiliary organizations and nominations of specific parties

Except where specifically instructed to the contrary below, add to base number 324.2 notation 4–9 from Table 2 for specific country, e.g., parties of France 324.244; however, do not add notation from Table 1 for standard subdivisions

Treatment of parties in continents and regions in modern world larger than countries relocated to 324.209

See Manual at 324.24–324.29 and 324.209

Special developments follow for selected specific countries

.241 Political parties of United Kingdom

Use 324.241001–324.241009 for standard subdivisions

.241 04 Conservative Party

.241 06 Liberal Party

.241 07 Labour Party

.271 Political parties of Canada

Use 324.271001–324.271009 for standard subdivisions

.271 04 Progressive Conservative Party

.271 06 Liberal Party

.271 07 New Democratic Party

.271 1–.271 9 Parties of provinces and territories of Canada

Add to base number 324.271 the numbers following —71 in notation 711–719 from Table 2, e.g., parties in Quebec 324.2714; then add 00 for standard subdivisions, e.g., a periodical on Quebec parties 324.2714005

.273 Political parties of United States

Class parties in specific states and District of Columbia in 324.274–324.279

.273 01–.273 09 Standard subdivisions

.273 2 Historical parties

Parties existing prior to 1945 and no longer in existence

Examples: Federalist, Jeffersonian Republican parties

.273 4 Republican Party

.273 6 Democratic Party

Including Democratic Republican Party

.274–.279 Political parties of states of United States and District of Columbia

Add to base number 324.27 the numbers following —7 in notation 74–79 from Table 2, e.g., parties of California 324.2794; however, do not add notation from Table 1 for standard subdivisions

Class comprehensive works in 324.273, political parties of Hawaii in 324.2969

.294 Political parties in Australia

Use 324.294001–324.294009 for standard subdivisions

Add to base number 324.294 the numbers following —94 in notation 941–947 from Table 2, e.g., parties in New South Wales 324.2944; then add 00 for standard subdivisions, e.g., a periodical on parties in New South Wales 324.2944005

.296 9 Political parties in Hawaii

.5 Nomination of candidates

Examples: by conventions, by primaries

Class here selection of convention delegates, campaigns for nomination

Use 324.5 for works on campaigns for nomination and their results (e.g., delegate counts and primary returns) only if two or more parties are involved. Use 324.24–324.29 if only one party's nomination is involved; 324.9 if both nomination and election campaigns are involved; 930–990 if there is emphasis on the effect of the nomination campaign on general history

Class nominations by specific parties in 324.24–324.29

See also 324.2 for convention finance

.6 Election systems and procedures; suffrage

Including voting rights [*formerly also* 323.5], qualifications for voting; registration of voters; voting procedures, counting and certification of votes, contested elections, election fraud; recall

Class here comprehensive works on systems and procedures for nominations and elections

Class conduct of election campaigns, irregularities in campaign finance in 324.7

For nomination of candidates, see 324.5

See Manual at 324.6 vs. 342 for election procedures and law

.609 Historical, geographic, persons treatment [*all formerly* 324.9]

.7 Conduct of election campaigns

Former heading: Practical politics

Including use and effect of media, campaign finance, citizen participation

Class convention finance in 324.2, conduct of nomination campaigns in 324.5

.9 **Historical and geographic treatment of elections**

Class here campaigns, election returns and results, studies of voting behavior

Add to base number 324.9 notation 1–9 from Table 2, e.g., political campaigns in United Kingdom 324.941; however, do not add notation from Table 1 for standard subdivisions

Historical, geographic, persons treatment of election systems and procedures relocated to 324.609

Class platforms, campaign literature and propaganda, and works about them in 324.2

325 International migration and colonization

Including involuntary population transfer and exchange, political refugees, imperialism

.09 Historical, geographic, persons treatment

Class treatment by specific continents, countries, localities in modern world in 325.4–325.9 (*not* 325.094–325.099)

.4–.9 **International migration to and colonization in specific continents, countries, localities in modern world**

Class here comprehensive works on treatment of international migration and colonization limited by specific places

Add to base number 325 notation 4–9 from Table 2, e.g., migration to Israel 325.5694

Class emigration from, colonization by specific continents, countries, localities; and colonization in specific continents, countries, localities by specific countries in 325

326 Slavery and emancipation

Class interdisciplinary works on slavery in 306.3

327 International relations

Class interdisciplinary works on relations among countries in 303.48, imperialism as national policy in 325, military science in 355; international relations with respect to a specific subject with the subject, e.g., trade relations of Germany 382.0943

See Manual at 341 vs. 327

[.01] Philosophy and theory

Do not use; class in 327.101

.06 Organizations

Class organizations established by two or more governments in 341.2

[.068] Management

Do not use; class in 351.89

.09 Historical, geographic, persons treatment

Class here diplomatic history, international relations of or in specific areas or blocks, e.g., international relations in Middle East 327.0956, foreign relations of Communist bloc 327.09171

Class foreign relations and diplomatic history of specific nations in 327.3–327.9 (*not* 327.093–327.099)

.092 Persons

Class diplomats in 327.2092

.1 General topics of international relations

Examples: international cooperation, alliances and collective security, arms control, disarmament, foreign aid; international conflict, balance of power, boycotts and sanctions, propaganda and war of nerves, spheres of influence, use and threats of force

Class here foreign policy, imperialism in international relations, international politics, power politics

Activities of individuals and of nongovernmental organizations and movements in specific nations to promote international cooperation are classed here, not with foreign relations of specific nations in 327.3–327.9

Class interdisciplinary works on propaganda in 303.3, political propaganda in 320.01; war in 355, general topics other than espionage and subversion pertaining to foreign relations of specific nations in 327.3–327.9

For diplomacy, see 327.2

.101 Philosophy and theory of international relations

Including role and position of small states, economic bases of international relation

Class here geopolitics in international relations, nature of power in international relations

Class comprehensive works on geopolitics in 320.1

.12 Espionage and subversion

Class here interdisciplinary works on espionage, subversion, intelligence gathering

Class relation of the state to internal subversive groups in 322.4, military espionage and subversion in 355.3

.120 9 Historical, geographic, persons treatment

Class here comprehensive works on espionage and subversion in specific nations

Class espionage and subversion by specific nations in 327.123–327.129 (*not* 327.12093–327.12099)

.123–.129 Espionage and subversion by specific nations [*formerly* 327.3–327.9]

Add to base number 327.12 notation 3–9 from Table 2, e.g., espionage by France 327.1244; then add further as follows:
001–008 Standard subdivisions
009 Historical and persons treatment
0092 Persons treatment

.2 **Diplomacy**

Use 327.2 for methods and style of diplomacy (including protocol); 327 for substance and content of diplomatic relations

Class laws and rules governing diplomatic conduct in 341.3; customs of diplomacy in 399

.3–.9 **Foreign relations of specific nations**

Add to base number 327 notation 3–9 from Table 2, e.g., foreign relations of Brazil 327.81; then, for relations between that nation and another nation or region, add 0* and to the result add notation 1–9 from Table 2, e.g., relations between Brazil and France 327.81044, between Brazil and Arab world 327.81017

Give priority in notation to the nation emphasized. If emphasis is equal, give priority to the one coming first in the sequence of area numbers
(Option: Give priority in notation to the nation requiring local emphasis, e.g. libraries in United States class foreign relations between United States and France in 327.73044)

Espionage and subversion by specific nations relocated to 327.123–327.129

328 The legislative process

Class here legislative branch

Rules and procedures of legislative bodies are classed in 328, without use of 328.01–328.09; rules and procedures of legislative committees are classed in 328.3, rules and procedures of specific legislative bodies, in 328.4–328.9

Class comprehensive rules of order in 060.4

See Manual at 320 vs. 909, 930–990 for history of legislative bodies

.09 Historical, geographic, persons treatment

Class legislative process in specific jurisdictions in modern world in 328.4–328.9 (*not* 328.094–328.099)

.2 **Initiative and referendum**

.209 Historical, geographical, persons treatment

Class treatment in specific jurisdictions in modern world in 328.24–328.29 (*not* 328.2094–328.2099)

.24–.29 Treatment in specific jurisdictions in modern world

Add to base number 328.2 notation 4–9 from Table 2, e.g., initiative in California 328.2794

*Add 00 for standard subdivisions; see instructions at beginning of Table 1

.3 **Legislative bodies**

Basis of representation, enactment of legislation, legislative ombudsmen, lobbying; compensation, privileges and immunities, qualifications, terms of members are classed in 328.3, without use of 328.301–328.309; all these topics relating to specific legislative bodies are classed in 328.4–328.9

Class interdisciplinary works on ombudsmen in 351.9, rules in 328

.309 Historical, geographic, persons treatment

Class legislative bodies of a specific jurisdiction in modern world in 328.4–328.9 (*not* 328.3094–328.3099)

.4–.9 **The legislative process in specific jurisdictions in modern world**

Add to base number 328 notation 4–9 from Table 2, e.g., the legislative process in Canada 328.71; use of standard subdivisions discontinued; class in area number for jurisdiction without use of notation from Table 1, e.g., a history of the legislative process in Canada 328.71 (*not* 328.7109)

330 Economics

Unless other instructions are given, observe the following table of precedence, e.g., the role of labor in agricultural production 331.7 (*not* 338.1)

Cooperatives	334
Public finance	336
Labor, financial, land economics	331–333
Production, Commerce (381–382), Transportation (385–388)	338
Macroeconomics and related topics	339
International economics	337
Socialism and related systems	335

Class economics of communications in 384, of transportation in 388

For commerce, see 380.1

See Manual at 650 vs. 330

SUMMARY

330.01–.09 Standard subdivisions
.1–.9 [Systems and theories; economic situation and conditions]
331 Labor economics
332 Financial economics
333 Land economics
334 Cooperatives
335 Socialism and related systems
336 Public finance
337 International economics
338 Production
339 Macroeconomics and related topics

.01 Philosophy

Including econometrics

Class theories in 330.1

.02–.08 Standard subdivisions

.09 Historical, geographic, persons treatment of economics as a discipline

Class economic situation and conditions in 330.9

.1 Systems and theories

Including theories of wealth and property

.12 Systems

Including free enterprise economy (usually synonymous with capitalism), mixed, planned economies

Class laissez-faire economic theory in 330.15, socialism and related systems in 335

.15 Schools of economic thought

Examples: classical economics, Keynesianism

Including laissez-faire economic theory, supply-side economics

Class socialist and related schools in 335

.9 Economic situation and conditions

Class here works describing situation and conditions at both the macroeconomic level (the economy viewed as a whole) and the microeconomic level (level of the individual household or firm)

Class policies to promote economic growth and development in 338.9, macroeconomic policies in 339.5

.91–.99 Geographic treatment (Economic geography)

Add to base number 330.9 notation 1–9 from Table 2, e.g., economic situation and conditions in France 330.944; however, do not add notation from Table 1 for standard subdivisions

---

> 331–333 Labor, financial, land economics

Class comprehensive works on labor, financial, land economics in 330; comprehensive works on labor, capital, land considered as factors of production in 338

331 Labor economics

Class here interdisciplinary works on labor

Industrial relations, including industrial relations in specific industries and occupations and specific groups of industries and occupations, are classed in 331, without use of 331.01–331.09; specific aspects of industrial relations are classed in 331.1–331.6, 331.8

Unless other instructions are given, observe the following table of precedence, e.g., compensation of women 331.4 (*not* 331.2)

Labor force by personal characteristics	331.3–.6
Labor force and market	331.1
Compensation and other conditions of employment	331.2
Labor unions (Trade unions), labor-management (collective) bargaining and disputes	331.8
Labor by industry and occupation	331.7

Class economic conditions of laboring classes in 330.9, full employment policies in 339.5

See also 305.5 for sociology of laboring classes, 306.3 for sociology of labor, 658.3 for comprehensive works on personnel management, 350.1 for personnel management in government

See Manual at 331 vs. 331.8 for industrial relations; 658.3 vs. 331

SUMMARY

331.01–.09 Standard subdivisions
.1 Labor force and market
.2 Compensation and other conditions of employment
.3 Workers of specific age groups
.4 Women workers
.5 Special categories of workers other than by age or sex
.6 Categories of workers by racial, ethnic, national origin
.7 Labor by industry and occupation
.8 Labor unions (Trade unions), labor-management (collective) bargaining and disputes

.01 Philosophy and theory

Including industrial democracy (determination of a company's policies affecting the welfare of its workers by joint action of management and worker representatives)

Class role of labor unions in industrial democracy in 331.88, worker control of industry in 338.6

See also 658.3 for employee representation in management discussed from the managerial viewpoint

.1 **Labor force and market**

Comprehensive works on employment and unemployment are classed in this number; however, works that merely give the number and characteristics of employed and unemployed workers without discussing the labor market are classed in 331.11. If in doubt, prefer 331.1

Class labor force and market in relation to choice of vocation in 331.7

.11 Labor force

All who are employed or available for employment

Including distribution, qualifications, personal characteristics of labor force; labor productivity

Class here human resources, man- and womanpower, labor supply, size of labor force

Class demand for labor, supply related to demand, labor actively employed in 331.12

See also 331.87 for union membership

.12 Labor market

The activities of and opportunities for buying and selling labor

Including demand for labor, job vacancies; government policy on the labor market; labor actively employed; labor mobility (interoccupational and geographic), turnover; placement

Class here supply of labor in relation to demand

For maladjustments in labor market, see 331.13

.13 Maladjustments in labor market

Including unemployment and its prevention and relief; labor shortages and surpluses; discrimination in employment, equal employment opportunity programs

Class discrimination in relation to a specific aspect of industrial relations with the aspect, e.g., discrimination by unions 331.87; a specific measure of prevention or relief with the measure, e.g., economic stabilization 339.5, welfare 362.85

.2 **Compensation and other conditions of employment**

Including factors affecting wages, pay equity; guaranteed-wage plans; comprehensive works on wage-price policy

Collective bargaining on compensation and other conditions of employment is classed in 331.89, but the compensation and other conditions that result from such bargaining are classed here

Class compensation and other conditions of employment in relation to choice of vocation in 331.7, wage-price controls to combat inflation in 332.4, price policy in 338.5, wage-price policy as a factor in economic stabilization in 339.5, guaranteed minimum income (income maintenance) in 362.5

See also 658.3 for compensation and other conditions of employment discussed from the managerial viewpoint

.25 Other conditions of employment

Including veterans' pensions [*formerly* 355.1], other pensions, unemployment compensation, interdisciplinary works on fringe benefits; compressed work week, flexitime, job sharing, overtime work, part-time employment; leave, rest periods; employee discipline; job tenure, seniority rights; interdisciplinary works on vocational training, apprenticeship

Class vocational training conducted as part of the educational system in 370.11

> **331.3–331.6 Labor force by personal characteristics**

Labor force and market, compensation and other conditions of employment, specific industries and occupation, labor unions, labor-management bargaining with respect to workers with specific personal characteristics are classed in 331.3–331.6, without use of notation 01–09 from Table 1

Unless other instructions are given, class complex subjects with aspects in two or more subdivisions of this schedule in the one coming first in the schedule, e.g., young Chinese women 331.3 (*not* 331.4 or 331.6)

Class comprehensive works in 331.11; choice of vocation for persons with specific personal characteristics in 331.7; employment services as a form of social service to persons with specific personal characteristics in 362.6–362.8, e.g., sheltered employment for aged people 362.6

.3 **Workers of specific age groups**

Class apprentices in 331.5

.4 **Women workers**

.5 **Special categories of workers other than by age or sex**

Examples: apprentices; contract, migrant, casual workers; prisoners, ex-offenders; veterans; workers with physical and mental disabilities

Class training of apprentices in 331.25

For categories of workers by racial, ethnic, national origin, see 331.6

.6 **Categories of workers by racial, ethnic, national origin**

Including immigrants

Class migrant workers in 331.5

.7 **Labor by industry and occupation**

Examples: professional, managerial, white-collar, service, industrial, agricultural, unskilled occupations

Including government employment, professional relationships, choice of vocation, interdisciplinary works describing vocations and occupational specialties, interdisciplinary works on career opportunities and vocational counseling

Class studies of vocational interest in 158.6, vocational counseling in schools in 371.4, job hunting in 650.14; a specific element of labor in a specific industry or occupation with the element, e.g., wages 331.2; descriptions of, career opportunities in, choice of vocation with regard to a specific occupation with the occupation, using notation 023 from Table 1, e.g., accounting 657.023

.700 1–.700 9 Standard subdivisions

.8 **Labor unions (Trade unions), labor-management (collective) bargaining and disputes**

Class here interdisciplinary works on labor movements

Class comprehensive works on industrial democracy in 331.01; labor unions and labor-management bargaining in relation to choice of vocation in 331.7; specific aspects of the labor movement with the aspect, e.g., political activities of labor movements 322

See Manual at 331 vs. 331.8 for industrial relations

.87 Labor union organization

Including constitutions, bylaws, rules; levels of organization, e.g., locals, nationals, federations; membership policies, discrimination by unions; officers, elections, conventions; benefits, funds, property

See also 331.88 for comprehensive works about labor unions

.88 Labor unions (Trade unions)

Examples: company, craft, industrial unions

Including open and closed shop, right to work; preferential hiring, sole bargaining rights; control of hiring and layoffs, dues check-off, control of grievance procedures, make-work arrangements (featherbedding)

For labor union organization, see 331.87

See also 322 for political activities of labor unions, 658.3 for the managerial viewpoint on labor unions

.89 Labor-management (Collective) bargaining and disputes

Including organizing, winning recognition, contracts; strikes, picketing, boycotts; lockouts, strikebreaking, yellow-dog contracts; arbitration, conciliation, mediation

332 Financial economics

Capital and international finance are classed in 332, without use of 332.01–332.09; capital and international finance in relation to a specific topic of financial economics are classed with the topic, e.g., the role of banks in international finance 332.1

For public finance, see 336

See Manual at 332 vs. 338, 658.15; 339 vs. 332, 336

.02 Miscellany

.024 Personal finance

Including increasing income, net worth, financial security; planning for retirement; achieving financial independence; estate planning; debt management; coping with depression and inflation

Class management of expenditure in 640; a specific aspect of personal finance not provided for here with the subject, e.g., investment 332.6

See Manual at 332.024 vs. 640

.024 001–.024 007 Standard subdivisions [*formerly* 332.02401–332.02407]

[.024 008] Personal finance with respect to groups of persons

Do not use; class in 332.024

.024 009 Historical, geographic, persons treatment [*formerly* 332.02409]

[.024 01–.024 07] Standard subdivisions

Relocated to 332.024001–332.024007

[.024 08] Personal finance with respect to groups of persons

Number discontinued; class in 332.024

[.024 09] Historical, geographic, persons treatment

Relocated to 332.024009

.06 Organizations

Class financial institutions and their management in 332.1

.1 Banks and banking

Including central, commercial, international banks; savings departments, trust services of commercial banks

Class here government guaranty of deposits; bank failures; comprehensive works on money and banking, on financial institutions and their functions

Class credit unions in 334

For specialized banking institutions, see 332.2; credit and loan institutions, 332.3; money, 332.4; credit, 332.7

See Manual at 332.7 vs. 332.1 for credit

.2 **Specialized banking institutions**

Examples: savings banks, trust companies

Class savings departments and trust services of commercial banks, international banking in 332.1; cooperative banking in 334

For agricultural institutions, see 332.3; investment banks, 332.66

.3 **Credit and loan institutions**

Including agricultural institutions, e.g., land banks; consumer and sales finance organizations; industrial banks; savings and loan associations (building and loan associations, home loan associations, mortgage institutions); credit and loan functions of enterprises whose primary function is not credit and loan, e.g., retail stores, insurance companies; comprehensive works on thrift institutions

Class savings banks in 332.2, credit unions in 334

See also 332.7 for credit

.4 **Money**

Including managed currency [*formerly* 332.5]; devaluation; gold standard, foreign exchange, monetary policy; inflation, stagflation, deflation; wage-price controls to combat inflation

Class comprehensive works on wage-price policy in 331.2; on money and banking, relation of central banks to monetary policy in 332.1; on economic stabilization policies in 339.5; fiscal policy in 336.3, balance of payments in 382

[.409] Historical, geographic, persons treatment

Do not use; class in 332.4

[.5] **Other mediums of exchange**

Use of this number for other mediums of exchange besides managed currency discontinued; class in 332

Managed currency relocated to 332.4

.6 **Investment and investments**

Including brokerage firms, investment counselors, international exchange of securities

Class here investment prospectuses [*formerly also* with the subject with use of notation 029 from Table 1], portfolio analysis and management

Investment for specific purposes (e.g., for tax advantages) is classed in 332.6, without use of 332.601–332.609; investment for specific purposes in relation to other specific aspects of investment is classed with the aspect, e.g., reducing tax liability by investing in municipal bonds 332.63

Class real estate brokerage in 333.33, description and analysis of organizations issuing securities in 338.7–338.8

.601 Philosophy and theory

Class forecasting and forecasts in 332.6

.63 Forms of investment

Examples: stock options, other speculation in specific forms of investment [*both formerly* 332.64]; stocks, bonds, commodities; art, coins; real estate, including mortgages

Class buying and selling procedures in 332.64

See also 332.7 for real estate finance, 333.33 for real estate business, 643 for how to select a home

.64 Exchange of securities and commodities

Including buying and selling of securities and commodities; organization, procedures, activities of organized exchanges, e.g., over-the-counter market

Speculation is included here, but only if multiple forms of investment are involved, e.g., speculation in stocks, bonds, and commodities

Stock options, other speculation in specific forms of investment relocated to 332.63

Brokerage firms, international exchange of securities are classed in 332.6

.66 Investment banks and banking

Investment banking: underwriting and sale of security issues

Class international investment banks and banking in 332.1

.7 Credit

Including agricultural, commercial, mercantile, industrial credit; real estate finance and mortgages; small business loans, personal loans, consumer credit; bankruptcy; checks (cheques), credit cards, money orders

Class credit functions of specific financial institutions in 332.1–332.3, mortgages as an investment in 332.63

For interest and discount, see 332.8

See Manual at 332.7 vs. 332.1

.8 Interest and discount

Including usury

See also 332.63 for interest rate futures

[.9] Counterfeiting, forgery, alteration

Number discontinued; class in 332

333 Land economics

Land: the sum total of natural and man-made resources over which possession of the earth gives control

Including absentee ownership

Land surveys are classed in 333, without use of 333.001–333.009; specific kinds of land surveys are classed with the kind, e.g., land use surveys 333.73

SUMMARY

333.001–.009 Standard subdivisions
.01 Theories
.1 Public ownership and control of land and other natural resources
.2 Ownership and control of land and other natural resources by nongovernmental groups
.3 Individual (Private) ownership and control of land and other natural resources
.5 Rental and leasing of land and other natural resources
.7 Natural resources and energy
.8 Subsurface resources
.9 Other natural resources

.001 Philosophy and theory

Class theories in 333.01

.002–.009 Standard subdivisions

.01 Theories

Example: theory of economic rent

> **333.1–333.5 Ownership and control of land and other natural resources**

Class here ownership and control of specific kinds of natural resources

Class comprehensive works in 333.3

See also 333.7–333.9 for use of land and other natural resources, for control of such usage not stemming from ownership

See Manual at 333.1–333.5 vs. 333.73–333.78; 333.1–333.5 vs. 346.04

.1 Public ownership and control of land and other natural resources

Including nationalization

Public control of privately owned lands and other natural resources relocated to 333.7, comprehensive works on land policy to 333.73

See also 333.2 for ownership and control of land by peoples subordinate to another jurisdiction, 343 for law of public property

.2 Ownership and control of land and other natural resources by nongovernmental groups

Examples: common lands, open-field system

Including enclosure of common lands

For corporate ownership, see 333.3

.3 **Individual (Private) ownership and control of land and other natural resources**

Including corporate ownership, land reform

Class here comprehensive works on land tenure, on ownership and control of land and other natural resources

Use of this number for comprehensive works on ownership and use of land and other natural resources discontinued; class in 333

Development relocated to 333.7

Class absentee ownership in 333, enclosure of common lands in 333.2

For public ownership and control, see 333.1; ownership and control by nongovernmental groups, 333.2

.33 Transfer of possession and right to use

Including sharecropping [*formerly also* 333.5], real estate business and market; value and price, valuation (appraisal), sale and gift of land; rights to use of minerals, water, air space

Class here comprehensive works on real estate business

Class government acquisition and disposal in 333.1, land reform in 333.3, real estate development in 333.7, valuation for tax purposes in 351.72, real estate salesmanship in 658.8

For rental and leasing, see 333.5

See also 332.63 for real estate investment, 332.7 for real estate finance

.5 **Rental and leasing of land and other natural resources**

Including tenancy, landlord-tenant relations; types of rental, e.g., cash rental, share and percentage rental

Sharecropping relocated to 333.33

Class rental and leasing of specific kinds of land and natural resources in 333.33, legal aspects of rental and leasing in 346.04

.7 **Natural resources and energy**

Aspects other than ownership

Class here raw materials; interdisciplinary works on the environment, on waste resources

Development [*formerly also* 333.3], public control of privately owned lands and other natural resources [*formerly* 333.1], other usage control, reclamation, restoration, subsidies, reserves (stock, supply), shortages, requirements (need, demand), consumption (use, utilization), abuse, wastage, impact studies, conservation, protection are all classed in 333.7, without use of 333.701–333.709; these topics in relation to energy or a specific kind of natural resource are classed with energy or the kind of resource in 333.73–333.79, without use of notation 01–09 from Table 1, e.g., land development 333.73, urban real estate development 333.77

Class interdisciplinary works on consumption in 339.4; ownership of land and other natural resources in 333.1–333.5; natural resources other than land in 333.8–333.9; economic geology in 553; other aspects of the environment with the aspect, e.g., environmental protection 363.7

See Manual at 333.7–333.9 for natural resources no longer in their natural state; 363.6 vs. 333.7; 363.7 vs. 333.7, 304.2 for environmentalism

.73 Land

Including kinds of land by physical condition, e.g., arid lands

Class here comprehensive works on land policy [*formerly also* 333.1]

Class kinds of land by use in 333.74–333.78; shorelands and related areas, submerged lands, wetlands in 333.91

See Manual at 333.1–333.5 vs. 333.73–333.78

.74 Pasture (Grazing) lands

See Manual at 333.1–333.5 vs. 333.73–333.78

.75 Forest lands

Class here timber resources

Class parks, recreational and wilderness areas in 333.78; wood as a fuel in 333.95; cut timber as a product in 338.1

See Manual at 333.1–333.5 vs. 333.73–333.78

.76 Rural lands Agricultural lands

Including strip-mined lands

Class rural recreational lands in 333.78

Rural lands of a specific physical condition, if not devoted to a specific use, are classed in 333.73. For example, semiarid lands in general are classed in 333.73; however, semiarid lands devoted to grazing are classed in 333.74

For pasture lands, see 333.74; forest lands, 333.75

See Manual at 333.1–333.5 vs. 333.73–333.78

.77 Urban lands

Examples: commercial, industrial, residential lands; highways and streets

Class urban recreational lands in 333.78

See Manual at 333.1–333.5 vs. 333.73–333.78

.78 Recreational and wilderness areas

Examples: beaches, forests, mountains, parks, rivers

Class wildlife refuges in 333.95

See also 363.6 for park and recreation services

See Manual at 333.1–333.5 vs. 333.73–333.78

.79 Energy

Including electrical utilities [*formerly* 363.6], rural electrification [*formerly* 621.39], electricity; energy from waste materials; energy for specific uses, e.g., for use in transportation

Class here production of energy [*formerly* 338.4], interdisciplinary works on energy

Class extraction of energy resources and comprehensive works on the economics of mineral fuels in 338.2; interdisciplinary works on mineral fuels in 553; specific forms of energy, specific energy resources not provided for here with the form or resource, e.g., fossil fuels, geothermal energy 333.8, wind energy 333.9, hydroelectricity 333.91, biomass as an energy resource 333.95; noneconomic aspects of energy with the aspect, e.g., fuel technology 662

.791 Energy conservation

Do not use standard subdivisions

.792 Solar and nuclear energy

Including electricity derived from solar energy, from nuclear energy

Class distribution of electricity derived from solar energy, from nuclear energy in 333.79; nuclear fuels in 333.8

.8 Subsurface resources

Including supply in storage, shortages, surpluses [*all formerly also* 338.2], requirements (need, demand), consumption (use, utilization), abuse, wastage, impact studies, conservation, protection, control of usage; nuclear fuels, minerals, geothermal energy, electricity derived from geothermal energy, thermal waters

Class here strategic materials

Class electricity derived from fossil fuels, distribution of electricity derived from geothermal energy in 333.79; energy derived from nuclear fuels in 333.792; development of, extraction of subsurface resources and comprehensive works on the economics of subsurface resources in 338.2; supplies of subsurface resources in nature and interdisciplinary works on subsurface resources in 553; interdisciplinary works on metals in 669

For ground water, see 333.91

See Manual at 333.7–333.9 for natural resources no longer in their natural state; 333.8 vs. 338.2, 553 for reserves and demand

.9 Other natural resources

Including wind power

Reserves (stock, supply), shortages, requirements (need, demand), consumption (use, utilization), abuse, wastage, impact studies, development, reclamation, restoration, subsidies, conservation, protection, control of usage are classed in 333.9, without use of 333.901–333.909; these topics in relation to specific natural resources are classed with the resource, without use of notation 01–09 from Table 1, e.g., wildlife conservation 333.95

Class distribution of electricity in 333.79

See Manual at 333.7–333.9 for natural resources no longer in their natural state

.91 Water

Including water requirements and use [*formerly also* 628.1]; groundwater; lakes, rivers, oceans; beaches, coasts; submerged lands, wetlands; hydroelectricity

Class here aquatic resources, comprehensive works on the economics of water resources

Class interdisciplinary works on water in 553.7; recreational use in 333.78; distribution of hydroelectricity in 333.79; a specific aquatic resource with the resource, e.g., minerals 333.8, fish 333.95; a specific aspect of water resources not provided for here with the aspect, e.g., recreational use of water and land adjoining it 333.78, water supply service 363.6

See Manual at 363.6 for water supply and water quality

.910 01–.910 09 Standard subdivisions

.95 Biological resources

Including wood as a fuel, interdisciplinary works on biomass as an energy resource

Class here biosphere, wildlife, wildlife refuges

Class forests, comprehensive works on timber resources in 333.75

334 Cooperatives

Voluntary organizations or enterprises owned by and operated for the benefit of those using the services

Examples: consumer, producer, banking, housing cooperatives

Including benefit societies, credit unions

Class management of consumer cooperatives in 658.8

.06 Organizations and management

Class international organizations in 334

[.091 9] Cooperatives in space

Do not use; class in 334.09

335 Socialism and related systems

Including anarchism, syndicalism; utopian socialism; voluntary anarchist and socialist communities

Class here state socialism, interdisciplinary works on political and economic aspects of socialism and related systems

Class socialism and communism as political ideologies in 320.5; socialist and communist political parties in 324.2; a specific topic of economics treated from a socialist point of view with the subject in economics, e.g., interest 332.8

The term "socialism" is often used in narrow senses to mean communism (335.43) or democratic socialism (335.5)

See Manual at 335 vs. 320.5

.001–.009 Standard subdivisions

.4 Marxian systems

Including dialectical materialism, historical materialism

Class here Marxism

Class democratic Marxian systems in 335.5

See Manual at 146 vs. 335.4 for dialectical materialism

.401 Philosophy and theory

Class philosophical foundations of Marxian systems and general works on theory of Marxian systems in 335.4

.42 Early period

Marxian doctrines and systems characteristic of period before 1917

For democratic socialism, see 335.5

.43 Communism (Marxism-Leninism)

Communism after 1917

Including national variants as schools of thought, e.g., Cuban communism (Castroism); Trotskyite doctrines; comparison of communism with capitalism, with democratic socialism, with other forms of collectivism

Class here Soviet communism

Class communism as a political ideology in 320.5

Use 335.4309 for communism in specific nations viewed as actual economic systems rather than schools of thought, e.g., Cuban communism as an existing system 335.43097291 (but Castroism as a school of thought 335.43)

.430 9 Historical, geographic, persons treatment

Class national variants of communism as schools of thought, e.g., Castroism, Maoism, Titoism, in 335.43

.5 **Democratic socialism**

Marxian and non-Marxian socialism pursued through persuasion and consent of the electorate in a nonauthoritarian state

Use of this number for state socialism discontinued; class in 335

Fabian socialism, Christian socialism, voluntary socialist communities are classed in 335

.6 **Fascism**

Examples: falangism, national socialism

Class fascism as a political ideology in 320.5

336 Public finance

Class here intergovernmental fiscal relations

Finance of associations of sovereign states (e.g., United Nations) and public finance by governmental level (multiple jurisdictions at the same level, e.g., municipal finance in the United States) are classed in 336, without use of 336.001–336.009; specific aspects of finance of associations of sovereign states and public finance by governmental level are classed with the aspect in 336.1–336.3

Class financial administration of governments in 351.72

See Manual at 336 vs. 351.72; 339 vs. 332, 336

.001–.005 Standard subdivisions

.006 Organizations and management

Class finance of associations of sovereign states (e.g., United Nations) in 336

.007–.008 Standard subdivisions

[.009] Historical, geographic, persons treatment

Do not use; class treatment by government level in 336; areas, regions, places in general, persons, ancient world in 336.09; specific continents, countries, localities in modern world in 336.4–336.9

.02 Revenue

Class specific forms of revenue in 336.1–336.2

.09 Historical, geographic, persons treatment

Class treatment by specific continents, countries, localities in modern world in 336.4–336.9

.091 Areas, regions, places in general

.091 7 Socioeconomic regions

Add to base number 336.0917 the numbers following —17 in notation 171–173 from Table 2, e.g., public finance in developing countries 336.09172

.092 Persons

.093 The ancient world

Add to base number 336.093 the numbers following —3 in notation 31–39 from Table 2, e.g., public finance in the Roman Empire 336.0937

> **336.1–336.2 Revenues**

Class comprehensive works in 336.02

.1 **Nontax revenues**

Including revenue from deposits, franchises, investments, lotteries, mineral rights, public industries and services; inter- and intragovernmental revenues, e.g., payments in lieu of taxes, international grants

For public borrowing, see 336.3

.2 **Taxes and taxation**

Examples: customs, estate, excise, gift, inheritance, personal property, sales, value-added taxes

Class here interdisciplinary works on taxes and taxation

Principles of taxation; taxes by governmental level (multiple jurisdictions at the same level); tax reform; provisions that allow tax avoidance, e.g., tax credits, deductions, loopholes; business taxes are all classed in 336.2, without use of 336.2001–336.2009; works on these topics limited to specific kinds of taxes are classed with the kind, e.g., reform of social security taxes 336.249

Class tax law in 343.04, tax administration in 351.72

See Manual at 336.2 vs. 343.04

.200 1–.200 8 Standard subdivisions

.200 9 Historical, geographic, persons treatment

Class treatment by governmental level in 336.2

.22 Real property taxes

Taxes on land, buildings, permanent improvements

Class here rates (United Kingdom), comprehensive works on property taxes

Personal property taxes are classed in 336.2

.24 Income taxes

Including reform of income taxes, provisions that allow avoidance of income taxes (e.g., tax credits), taxes on business income, personal (individual) income taxes

Class here comprehensive works on taxes on personal wealth

Estate, inheritance, gift, personal property taxes are classed in 336.2

For real property taxes, see 336.22

See also 362.5 for negative income tax

.249 Social security taxes

See also 368.4 for social security benefits

.3 **Public borrowing, debt, expenditure**

Including debt repudiation and abrogation, international borrowing, limitation of public indebtedness, public insolvency

Class here fiscal policy, comprehensive works on monetary and fiscal policy

Class investment in government securities in 332.63, use of fiscal and monetary policy in economic stabilization in 339.5

For monetary policy, see 332.4

.4–.9 **Public finance of specific continents, countries, localities in modern world**

Add to base number 336 notation 4–9 from Table 2, e.g., public finance of Australia 336.94

337 International economics

Class here international economic planning; comprehensive works on international economic relations, on international economic cooperation

Class a specific aspect of international economics not provided for here with the aspect, e.g., international (multinational) business enterprises 338.8, foreign trade 382

.09 Historical, geographic, persons treatment

Class foreign economic policies and relations of specific jurisdictions and groups of jurisdictions in 337.3–337.9 (*not* 337.093–337.099)

.1 **Multilateral economic cooperation**

Former heading: Spheres of economic cooperation

Including European Economic Community

Class here economic integration, multilateral agreements and multistate organizations for economic cooperation

Class bilateral economic cooperation in 337.3–337.9, trade agreements in 382

See also 341.2 for interdisciplinary works on international organizations

See Manual at 337.1 vs. 337.3–337.9

.3–.9 **Foreign economic policies and relations of specific jurisdictions and groups of jurisdictions**

Class here bilateral economic cooperation

Add to base number 337 notation 3–9 from Table 2, e.g., economic policy of United Kingdom 337.41; then, for foreign economic relations between two jurisdictions or groups of jurisdictions, add 0* and to the result add notation 1–9 from Table 2, e.g., economic relations between United Kingdom and France 337.41044

Give priority in notation to the jurisdiction or group of jurisdictions emphasized. If the emphasis is equal, give priority to the one coming first in the sequence of area notations

(Option: Give priority in notation to the jurisdiction or group of jurisdictions requiring local emphasis, e.g., libraries in United States class foreign economic relations between United States and France in 337.73044)

Class multilateral economic cooperation in 337.1

See Manual at 337.1 vs. 337.3–337.9 for relations of multistate cooperative organizations

338 Production

Including comprehensive works on commodities and services, on factors of production, on production efficiency (e.g., automation, effect of technological innovations)

Class here comprehensive works on the economic and technical aspects of industry and production, e.g., the economy and technology of the automobile industry 338.4

Entrepreneurship is classed in 338, without use of 338.001–338.009; specific aspects of entrepreneurship are classed with the aspect, e.g., portion of national income distributed to entrepreneurship 339.2

Class specific factors of production in 331–333, economics of cooperative production in 334, production technology in 620–690

See Manual at 332 vs. 338, 658.15 for finance; 363.5, 363.6, 363.8 vs. 338 for housing, public utilities, food

*Add 00 for standard subdivisions; see instructions at beginning of Table 1

SUMMARY

338.001–.009	**Standard subdivisions**
.09	**Historical, geographic, persons treatment of production**
.1	**Agriculture**
.2	**Extraction of minerals**
.3	**Other extractive industries**
.4	**Secondary industries and services**
.5	**General production economics**
.6	**Organization of production**
.7	**Business enterprises and their structure**
.8	**Combinations**
.9	**Economic development and growth**

.001 Philosophy and theory

Class forecasting and forecasts of commodities and services in 338, general production forecasting and forecasts in 338.5

.002–.008 Standard subdivisions

.009 Historical, geographic, persons treatment of general principles and theories

Class historical, geographic, persons treatment of production in 338.09

.09 Historical, geographic, persons treatment of production

Class here existing and potential resources for production, industrial conditions and situation, industrial surveys

Works showing where industry is in fact located are classed here, but works on the rationale for and process of locating industrial organizations are classed in 338.6

Add to base number 338.09 notation 1–9 from Table 2, e.g., industrial surveys of Canada 338.0971

Class a specific resource with the resource, e.g., water for power 333.91

> **338.1–338.4 Specific kinds of industry**

Finance of specific kinds of industries [*formerly also* 338.6]; commodities, services, factors of production, entrepreneurship, production efficiency (e.g., automation, effects of technological innovations) in specific kinds of industry are classed in 338.1–338.4, without use of notation 01–09 from Table 1

Class comprehensive works in 338; cooperatives in specific kinds of industries in 334; organization of production in specific kinds of industries in 338.6; business enterprises other than cooperatives in specific kinds of industries in 338.7–338.8; biographies of entrepreneurs in specific kinds of industries in 338.6–338.8, e.g., biographies of owners of small businesses 338.6, biographies of entrepreneurs in textile manufacturing 338.7; biographies of people known for their contributions in technology in 600, e.g., biographies of mining engineers 622.092

> **338.1–338.3 Primary (Extractive) industries**

Class comprehensive works in 338

.1 **Agriculture**

Including surpluses and shortages of farm products, forecasts and projections of supply and demand, food supply, government farm policies

Class food processing in 338.4, hunger as a social problem in 363.8

See also 334 for agricultural cooperatives

See Manual at 363.8 vs. 338.1 for food supply; 631.5 vs. 338.1 for crop yields

.2 **Extraction of minerals**

Class here extraction of energy resources, comprehensive works on the economics of extraction and processing of minerals and energy resources

Supply in storage, shortages, surpluses relocated to 333.8

Class conservation of mineral and energy resources in 333.7–333.9, processing of minerals and raw materials of energy in 338.4, reserves in nature in 553

See Manual at 333.8 vs. 338.2, 553 for reserves and demand

.3 **Other extractive industries**

Examples: fishing, whaling, hunting, culture of invertebrates and cold-blooded vertebrates

Class insect culture in 338.1

.4 **Secondary industries and services**

Including construction, manufacturing, service industries; professional services; quantities of goods and services produced, shortages, surpluses, stockpiles, forecasts and projections of supply and demand

Production of energy relocated to 333.79

Class financial industries in 332; real estate business in 333.33; insurance industry in 368; commerce, communications, transportation in 380

.5 **General production economics**

Including business cycles, depressions, other economic fluctuations; business forecasting; costs, prices and their determination; law of supply and demand; risk; theories of value

Class here microeconomics (economics of the firm)

Class production economics of specific kinds of industries in 338.1–338.4, effect of money on prices in 332.4, effects of prices on the economy as a whole in 339.4, Marxian labor theory of value in 335.4, economic stabilization in 339.5

For organization of production, see 338.6

.501 Philosophy and theory

Class forecasting and forecasts in 338.5

.6 **Organization of production**

Including competition and restraint; finance; location; specialization, law of comparative advantage; systems of production, e.g., cottage industry, factory system; big business, small business, minority enterprises, private and public enterprise; worker control of industry

Class here organization of production in specific kinds of industries

Finance of specific kinds of industries relocated to 338.1–338.4

Class guild socialism, syndicalism in 335, role of unions in achieving worker control of industry in 331.88; monopoly and monopolies in 338.8; relation of size of enterprise to cost of production in 338.5; specific types of enterprises of specific sizes in 338.7–338.8

For business enterprises and their structure, see 338.7

.7 **Business enterprises and their structure**

Not limited to private or capitalist enterprises

Including formation and dissolution of business enterprises; individual proprietorships, partnerships, corporations; business enterprises in specific industries and groups of industries, specific individual business enterprises, biographies of entrepreneurs in specific fields

Class here interdisciplinary works on business enterprises, on organizations for production

Class financial institutions in 332; real estate business enterprises in 333.33; enterprises engaged in production of energy in 333.79; cooperative enterprises in 334; government corporations as part of the public administrative process in 351.009; insurance companies in 368.006; enterprises engaged in commerce, communications, transportation in 380

For cooperatives, see 334; combinations, 338.8

See Manual at 338.7 for directories and biographies

.8 **Combinations**

Organization and structure for massive production and control of production

Including cartels, holding companies, mergers, trusts; conglomerate combinations; monopolies; multinational enterprises

Class here antitrust policies, economic concentration, comprehensive works on combinations and their practices

To be classed here, works about specific individual enterprises must stress that they are combinations; otherwise, the works are classed in 338.7

Class combinations of financial institutions in 332, combinations of real estate business enterprises in 333.33, of enterprises engaged in energy production in 333.79, of cooperatives in 334, of enterprises in the insurance industry in 368, of enterprises engaged in commerce, communications, transportation in 380; price determination by combinations in 338.5

.9 **Economic development and growth**

Including appropriate technology, science policy; nationalization, subsidies

Class here economic planning, government programs and policies

Class economic development and growth with respect to a specific subject with the subject, e.g., international economic development and growth 337, economic development and growth of specific kinds of industries 338.1–338.4

.900 1–.900 8 Standard subdivisions

.900 9 Historical, geographic, persons treatment

Class treatment by country and locality in 338.93–338.99 (*not* 338.90093–338.90099)

.91 International development and growth

Foreign economic assistance (foreign aid)

Including technical assistance

Class here assistance (aid) by international organizations

Class foreign economic policies and relations of specific jurisdictions and groups of jurisdictions in 337.3–337.9

.93–.99 Economic development and growth in specific continents, countries, localities

Add to base number 338.9 notation 3–9 from Table 2, e.g., economic planning in United Kingdom in 338.941; however, do not add notation from Table 1 for standard subdivisions

339 Macroeconomics and related topics

For economic fluctuations, see 338.5

See Manual at 339 vs. 332, 336

[.01] Philosophy and theory

Do not use; class in 339.3

.2 **Distribution of income and wealth**

Including division among factors of production: land, labor, capital, entrepreneurship, corporate profits; division among families and individuals; consumer income, household income

Standard subdivisions are added for either or both of the topics named in the heading

Class national wealth and income accounts and accounting in 339.3; specific aspects of income distribution in 339.4; transfer payments, redistribution of income in 339.5

.3 **National product, wealth, income accounts and accounting**

Including gross national product (GNP), net national product (NNP), national income (NI), personal income (PI), disposable personal income (DPI)

Class here macroeconomic theory; product, wealth, income accounts and accounting of states, provinces; interdisciplinary works on national product, wealth, income

For distribution of income and wealth, see 339.2; factors affecting national product, wealth, income, 339.4

.309 Historical, geographic, persons treatment

Class product, wealth, income accounts and accounting of specific countries and localities in 339.33–339.39 (*not* 339.3093–339.3099)

.33–.39 Product, wealth, income accounts and accounting of specific countries and localities

Add to base number 339.3 notation 3–9 from Table 2, e.g., gross national product of the United States 339.373

.4 **Factors affecting national product, wealth, income**

Including conservation of national resources; economic causes and economic effects of poverty; income, savings, investment, cost of living, standard of living, consumption, and their interrelationships, e.g., relation of income and consumption; consumption of specific commodities and groups of commodities, interdisciplinary works on consumption

Class social aspects of consumption in 306.3; conservation of natural resources, consumption viewed in light of its effect on the future supply of natural resources and energy in 333.7; consumption as a factor in shortages and surpluses of products in 338; price statistics and indexes in 338.5; government spending in 339.5; works discussing consumption as sales or marketing opportunities (e.g., results of market studies) or as a measure of the volume, value, or kind of trade in 380–382

For economic stabilization, see 339.5

See also 362.5 for social causes and social effects of poverty

.5 **Macroeconomic policy**

Including use of fiscal policy, e.g., income redistribution, government spending, budget surpluses and deficits, taxation; use of monetary policy

Class here economic stabilization and growth, equilibrium, full employment policies, income policies

Class measures to combat inflation in 332.4, to control economic fluctuations in 338.5, to promote growth and development in 338.9

340 Law

Including comparative law, justice, law and society, law reform, legal reasoning, natural law

(Option: Class the law of a specific discipline or subject with the discipline or subject, using notation 026 from Table 1, e.g., education law 370.26)

See Manual at 340; at 363 vs. 340, 350–354 for implementing laws and regulations

SUMMARY

340.02–.09 Standard subdivisions
.5–.9 [Legal systems, conflict of laws]
341 International law
342 Constitutional and administrative law
343 Military, public property, public finance, tax, trade, industrial law
344 Social, labor, welfare, health, safety, education, cultural law
345 Criminal law
346 Private law
347 Civil procedure and courts
348 Laws (Statutes), regulations, cases
349 Law of specific jurisdictions

[.01] Philosophy and theory

Do not use; class in 340

.02 Miscellany

.03 Encyclopedias [*formerly* 348], dictionaries, concordances

.05–.08 Standard subdivisions

.09 Historical, geographic, persons treatment

Class comprehensive works on the law of specific jurisdictions and areas in the modern world in 349, historical and geographic treatment of the law of traditional societies in 340.5

[.093] Treatment by specific jurisdictions and areas in the ancient world

Do not use; class in 340.5

.5 **Legal systems**

History and theory of the law of traditional societies regardless of time or place, ancient and medieval law, civil law systems (systems derived from Roman law), common law, indigenous systems of Oriental law

Class comprehensive works on the law of specific jurisdictions and areas in the modern world in 349; religious laws of a specific religious body with the body, e.g., Christian canon law 262.9; a specific subject in a specific system of law with the subject, e.g., the criminal law of Rome 345.37

See Manual at 340: Civil law

.9 **Conflict of laws**

The body of rules governing choice of jurisdiction in cases in private law which fall under laws of two or more jurisdictions

Class here private international law

Class domestic conflict of laws in 342

See Manual at 340.9

341 International law

The body of rules, principles, and standards to which independent states (nations) are bound by common consent

Class the law of a nation or lesser jurisdiction that carries out the provisions of an international agreement in 342–347

See Manual at 341; 341 vs. 327 for distinguishing international law from international relations

.2 **The world community**

Including world government; dependent states, e.g., colonies; nonself-governing territories; areas having special status in international law, e.g., Antarctica, Berlin

Class public administration of international organizations in 354.1

See Manual at 341.2 for international organizations

> **341.22–341.24 International organizations**

Class here officials and employees of international organizations

Class comprehensive works in 341.2; legal aspects of a specialized international organization with the subject with which it deals in international law, e.g., the World Health Organization 341.7; of a specific activity of an international organization with the subject, e.g., food relief activities of the World Health Organization 363.8

.22 League of Nations

.23 United Nations

[.230 68] Management

Do not use; class in 341.23

.24 Regional associations and organizations

Examples: Arab League, European Community, Organization of American States

.26 States

Including recognition of states and governments, mergers of states

Class here sovereignty

Law regarding semisovereign and dependent states is classed in 341.2

For law regarding relations between states, see 341.3; law regarding jurisdiction of states, 341.4

.3 **Law regarding relations between states**

Including treaties, delegations to international organizations and their staffs

Class diplomacy as an aspect of international relations in 327.2, officials and employees of international organizations in 341.22–341.24, treaties on a specific subject with the subject in international law, e.g., a disarmament treaty between the Soviet Union and the United States 341.7

For jurisdictional relations of states, see 341.4; law regarding disputes and conflicts between states, 341.5; law of international cooperation, 341.7

.4 **Law regarding jurisdiction and jurisdictional relations of states**

Example: jurisdiction over the high seas

Including immigration, nationality, citizenship, extradition, right of asylum

Class private international law in 340.9, law regarding mergers of states in 341.26

.5 **Law of disputes and conflicts between states**

Including international courts and court procedure, role of international organizations and armed forces, role of national courts in adjudicating matters of international law; boycott, sanctions

Class peace conferences in 341.7, disputes on a specific subject with the subject in international law, e.g., jurisdictional disputes 341.4

For law of war, see 341.6

.6 **Law of war**

.7 **Law of international cooperation**

Including defense and security, peace, disarmament; international criminal law

Class international law regarding bodies of water in 341.4, regarding peaceful settlement of international disputes in 341.5; law of war in 341.6

For war crimes, see 341.6

> **342–348 Branches of the law of specific jurisdictions and laws, regulations, cases**

Class comprehensive works in 349

> ## 342–347 Law of specific jurisdictions

Class comprehensive works in 340; comprehensive works on the law of specific jurisdictions in the modern world in 349; general laws, regulations, cases in 348

(Option: Class laws, regulations, cases on specific subjects in 348, courts and procedure in specific fields in 347)

342 Constitutional and administrative law

church/State 322

Including civil service; regulatory agencies and administrative courts, administrative procedure

Class here comprehensive works on public law, on constitutional law

Do not use standard subdivisions

Class the law of government corporations in 346; constitutional provisions and amendments, departments, ministries, regulatory agencies, administrative courts dealing with a specific subject in law with the subject in law, e.g., agencies regulating civil aeronautics 343.09

For international law, see 341; military, public property, public finance, tax, trade, industrial law, 343; social, labor, welfare, health, safety, education, cultural law, 344; criminal law, 345

See Manual at 324.6 vs. 342 for election law; 342 for administrative regulations and agencies

.3–.9 **Constitutional and administrative law of specific jurisdictions**

Add to base number 342 notation 3–9 from Table 2, e.g., constitutional law of the United States 342.73; however, notation from Table 1 for standard subdivisions is not added

343 Military, public property, public finance, tax, trade, industrial law

Including defense law, selective service

Do not use standard subdivisions

Class war claims in 341.6; martial law, law of acquisition and cession of territory in 342; public health and safety law in 344; law of sale, of government securities in 346; comprehensive works on the law of control and use of public and private real property, natural resources law in 346.04; a specific aspect of military, defense law not provided for here with the aspect in law, e.g., civil rights of soldiers 342; of a specific aspect of industrial and trade regulations not provided for here with the aspect in law, e.g., wages 344, regulation of banks 346

.04 Tax law

Class here tax planning, internal revenue law

Class interdisciplinary works on taxes in 336.2, law of tax evasion in 345

For law of specific kinds of taxes, see 343.05–343.06

> **343.05–343.06 Law of specific kinds of taxes**

Class comprehensive works in 343.04, social security taxes in 344

.05 Law of kinds of taxes by base

Examples: customs duties; income, inheritance, property, sales taxes

.06 Law of kinds of taxes by incidence

Examples: on individuals, on business enterprises

Class law of taxes on specific bases regardless of incidence in 343.05

.09 Public utilities law

Examples: communication, transportation law

Class international maritime law in 341.7

.3–.9 Military, public property, public finance, tax, trade, industrial law of specific jurisdictions

Add to base number 343 notation 3–9 from Table 2, e.g., military, tax, industrial law of Canada 343.71, of South American countries 343.8; then add further as follows:

[001–009] Standard subdivisions
Do not use; class in number for the jurisdiction

04–09 Tax law, control of public utilities
Add to 0 the numbers following 343, e.g., transportation law of Canada 343.7109
If the jurisdiction does not have its own number in Table 2, do not add the numbers following 343, e.g., transportation ordinances of Toronto 343.713 (*not* 343.71309)

344 Social, labor, welfare, health, safety, education, cultural law

Including environmental protection, police services

Do not use standard subdivisions

Class law regarding government officials and employees in 342; law regarding military personnel, health and disability benefits for veterans in 343; transportation safety law in 343.09; law of criminal investigation and law enforcement in 345

.3–.9 Social, labor, welfare, health, safety, education, cultural law of specific jurisdictions

Add to base number 344 notation 3–9 from Table 2, e.g., social law of the United States 344.73, of Pennsylvania 344.748; however, notation from Table 1 for standard subdivisions is not added

345 Criminal law

Including criminal courts and trials, juvenile procedure and courts

Do not use standard subdivisions

Class comprehensive works on civil and criminal courts and procedures in 347; interdisciplinary works on criminal justice in 364

See Manual at 345 vs. 346.03

.3–.9 Criminal law of specific jurisdictions and areas

Do not use standard subdivisions

Add to base number 345 notation 3–9 from Table 2, e.g., criminal law of the United States 345.73, of Pennsylvania 345.748; however, notation from Table 1 for standard subdivisions is not added

346 Private law

Including commercial law; agency, contracts, liability; organizations (associations); banking, insurance, securities

Do not use standard subdivisions

Class industrial and trade law in 343; a specific topic in commercial law with the topic, e.g., tax law 343.04; private international law in 340.9; the law of contracts on a specific subject with the subject in law, e.g., law of marriage contracts 346.01; the contract itself with the subject outside law, e.g., defense contracts 351.75, construction contracts 624.068

For the law of criminal liability, see 345

.01 Law of persons and domestic relations

Class law regarding civil rights in 342, law regarding marital property in 346.04

.03 Law of torts (delicts)

Examples: negligence, invasion of privacy, malpractice, libel, product liability

Class torts as crimes in 345, remedies in 347

See Manual at 345 vs. 346.03

.04 Property law

Examples: land, patents

Including real-estate business, rent, zoning

Class here marital property

Class law regarding transfer of property by inheritance in 346.05

For public property law, see 343

.05 Law regarding inheritance, succession, fiduciary trusts, trustees

Including probate law and practice

.3–.9 Private law of specific jurisdictions

Add to base number 346 notation 3–9 from Table 2, e.g., private law of the United States 346.73, of South American countries 346.8; then add further as follows:

[001–009] Standard subdivisions

Do not use; class in number for the jurisdiction

01–05 Persons and domestic relations, torts (delicts), property, inheritance, succession, fiduciary trusts, trustees

Add to 0 the numbers following 346 in 346.01–346.05, e.g., marriage law of New York state 346.74701

If the jurisdiction does not have its own number in Table 2, do not add the numbers following 343, e.g, marriage law of New York City 346.747 (*not* 346.74701)

347 Civil procedure and courts

Including arbitration, evidence, legal aid, remedies

Class here comprehensive works on civil and criminal procedure, judicial branch of government, administration of justice

(Option: Class here courts and procedure in specific fields; prefer the specific field)

Do not use standard subdivisions

Class interdisciplinary works on legal aid in 362.5, law of legal aid in criminal cases in 345; administrative procedure, provisional courts in 342; criminal and juvenile procedure and courts in 345; courts, procedures, trials dealing with a specific subject with the subject in law, e.g., tax courts 343.04; medical jurisprudence, forensic medicine in 614.1

For administrative procedure, see 342

.3–.9 Civil procedure and courts of specific jurisdictions

Do not use standard subdivisions

Add to base number 347 notation 3–9 from Table 2, e.g., civil procedure in the United States 347.73, in Pennsylvania 347.748; however, notation from Table 1 for standard subdivisions is not added

348 Laws (Statutes), regulations, cases

Including codes, digests

(Option: Class here laws, regulations, cases on specific subjects; prefer specific subject in 342–347)

Do not use standard subdivisions

Encyclopedias on law in general relocated to 340.03

Class treatises on the whole law of a specific jurisdiction in 349

.3–.9 Laws (Statutes), regulations, cases of specific jurisdictions

Do not use standard subdivisions

Add to base number 348 notation 3–9 from Table 2, e.g., U.S. Federal Code 348.73, statutes of Pennsylvania 348.748; however, notation from Table 1 for standard subdivisions is not added

349 Law of specific jurisdictions

Comprehensive works on the law of specific jurisdictions in the modern world

Add to base number 349 notation 4–9 from Table 2, e.g., works on the law of the United States 349.73, of Pennsylvania 349.748

Class specific branches of the law of specific jurisdictions in 342–347, original materials on the law of specific jurisdictions in 348

350 Public administration and military science

Class here executive branch of government and its structure, description and administration of government organizations and agencies, comprehensive works on public administration of the three branches of government

Do not use standard subdivisions

Class comprehensive works on structure and function of government or of two or more branches of government, relation of executive branch to other branches in 320.4; public administration of legislative branch in 328.068, of judicial branch in 347

See Manual at 350; 350–354; 350–354 vs. 320.4, 320.9; 350–354 vs. 658, T1—068; 361–365 vs. 350–354; 363 vs. 340, 350–354

SUMMARY

350.003–.9	**Specific aspects of public administration**
351	**Administration of central governments**
352	**Administration of local governments**
353	**Administration of United States federal and state governments**
354	**Administration of specific central governments; international administration**
355	**Military science**
356	**Foot forces and warfare**
357	**Mounted forces and warfare**
358	**Air and other specialized forces and services; engineering and related services**
359	**Sea (Naval) forces and warfare**

.003–.9 Specific aspects of public administration

Add to base number 350 the numbers following 351 in 351.003–351.9, e.g., personnel management 350.1

See Manual at 350.003–350.9 vs. 351

351 Administration of central governments

National and state or provincial governments

Including bureaucracy, lists and directories of officials and employees

Do not use standard subdivisions

Directories of elected officials relocated to 324.025; of public officials and employees in specific occupational categories to the subject with use of notation 025 from Table 1, e.g., of diplomats 327.2025

Class works dealing comprehensively with central and local governments in 350

For specific central governments, see 354

See Manual at 350–354; 350–354 vs. 320.4, 320.9; 350–354 vs. 658, T1—068; 350.003–350.9 vs. 351; 361–365 vs. 350–354; 363 vs. 340, 350–354

SUMMARY

351.003–.009 [Chief executives, cabinets and councils of state, fundamentals of administration, special agencies]
.01–.09 [Specific departments and ministries of cabinet rank, intergovernmental administration]
.1 Personnel management
.3 Civil service examinations
.4 Government work force
.5 Pensions
.6 Civil service system (Merit system)
.7 Property and financial management and related topics; administration of public safety and related fields
.8 Administration of specific fields
.9 Malfunctioning of administration

.003 Chief and deputy chief executives

Use of this number for comprehensive works on executive branch discontinued; class in 351

.004 Cabinets and councils of state

Class here comprehensive works on executive departments and ministries of cabinet rank

Class works dealing comprehensively with structure, agencies, programs, services of central governments in 351; specific departments and ministries of cabinet rank in 351.01–351.08

.007 Fundamentals of public administration

Including leadership, management of executive personnel, organization, oversight, planning, policy making

Class staffing in 351.1, other aspects not provided for here in 351.7

.009 Special agencies

Examples: advisory, independent, quasi-administrative, regulatory agencies; government corporations; special commissions

Class government corporations engaged in finance in 332.1–332.6, in real estate in 333.33, in insurance in 368, in commerce, communications, transportation in 380, in other specific economic fields in 338.7; special agencies dealing with a specific activity with the activity in public administration, e.g., agencies regulating transportation 351.87

> **351.01–351.08 Specific departments and ministries of cabinet rank**

Class comprehensive works in 351.004; a subordinate branch of specific departments or ministries with the branch, e.g., a science bureau 351.85

.01 Foreign relations departments

.02 Finance departments

.03 Home affairs (Interior) departments

.05 Justice departments

.06 Defense departments

.07–.08 Other departments

Add to base number 351.0 the numbers following 351 in 351.7–351.8, e.g., departments of labor 351.083

.09 Intergovernmental administration

Administration of agencies established cooperatively by two or more governments at the same level, of agencies established to deal with affairs of subordinate units

Including administrative relations of state, provincial, local governments to higher levels

Class cooperation among local governments in 352; international administration in 354.1; intergovernmental administration in a specific field of activity with the activity, e.g., fiscal relations between levels 351.72

See also 320.8 for governmental relations between local and higher levels of government

---

> **351.1–351.6 Government service**

Class comprehensive works in 351.1, government service in administration of specific fields in 351.8

.1 **Personnel management**

Class here comprehensive works on government service

Class personnel management in a specific field with the field, using notation 068 from Table 1, e.g., personnel management in labor agencies 351.83068

For management of executive personnel, see 351.007; civil service examinations, 351.3; government work force, 351.4; pensions, 351.5; civil service system, 351.6

.100 1 Philosophy and theory

.100 2 Miscellany

[.100 25] Directories of personnel

Do not use; class in 351

.100 3–.100 9 Standard subdivisions

.3 **Civil service examinations**

Class here review and exercise in public administration

Class examinations on a specific subject with the subject, using notation 076 from Table 1, e.g., accounting 657.076

.4 **Government work force**

History, description, surveys of composition

Class a specific aspect with the aspect, e.g., personnel management 351.1

.5 **Pensions**

See also 331.25 for economic aspects of pensions

.6 **Civil service system (Merit system)**

Class civil service examinations in 351.3

.7 **Property and financial management and related topics; administration of public safety and related fields**

> **351.71–351.72 Property and financial management and related topics**

Class comprehensive works in 351.7; property and financial management and related topics applied to personnel management in 351.1, to administration of specific fields in 351.8

.71 Property and records management and related topics

Including comprehensive works on contracts and contracting, on purchasing

Class interdisciplinary works on archival administration in 025.17; purchase of land for purposes other than direct government use, e.g., for conservation, in 351.82; construction of government buildings in 351.86; contracts and contracting for, procurement of a specific item with the item, e.g., personnel contracts 351.1, defense purchasing 355.6

.72 Financial administration

Example: tax administration

Including budgets and budgeting, administration and use of audits

Financial management of a specific agency or activity relocated to the agency or activity in 351.003–351.9, e.g., of a labor bureau 351.83

Class interdisciplinary works on, and economic aspects of public finance in 336; administration of money and financial institutions in 351.82

See Manual at 336 vs. 351.72

> **351.74–351.78 Administration of public safety and related fields**

Class comprehensive works in 351.75

.74 Police

Including operative management of police agencies

Class administration of traffic control in 351.87

.75 Public safety

Examples: civil defense, disaster and emergency planning; gun control

Including censorship, crowd control

For police, see 351.74; safeguarding public health, 351.77; fire and accident protection, 351.78

See also 323.44 for right to information, 351.9 for denial of right to information in public administration

.76 Factors affecting public morals

Examples: control of gambling, prostitution, alcoholic beverages, drug traffic

See also 351.84 for administration of services to alcoholics, to narcotics addicts

.77 Safeguarding public health

Examples: control of disease and product hazards, waste disposal

Class comprehensive works on administration of public health in 351.84, regulation and control of water supply in 351.87

.78 Fire and accident protection

Class administration of safety measures in a specific field of activity with the field in public administration, using notation 028 from Table 1, e.g., safety administration in public utilities and transportation 351.870028

.8 **Administration of specific fields**

Example: administration of justice

Class here licensing

Class cabinet-level departments in specific fields in 351.01–351.08, administration of courts in 347; management of services in a specific field with the field, e.g., of railway services 385.068

For administration of public safety and related fields, see 351.74–351.78

.81 Human relations, information, related programs

Examples: census taking; civil and human rights programs; birth control and family planning; programs for minorities, for veterans, for women; urban development; immigration and naturalization service

Class informational and research services in a specific field of activity with the field in public administration, e.g., labor information services 351.83; results of information and research services in a subject with the subject, e.g., demographic statistics 304.6

See also 323.44 for freedom of information, 351.75 for censorship, 351.9 for denial of right to information by public administrators

.82 Production, commerce, consumption

Including flood and pollution control, insurance, issue and regulation of money, natural resources and their protection, standardization

Class here economic development, promotion of productivity

Class environmental sanitation and comfort in 351.77; public administration of hunting and fishing for sport in 351.85; provision of housing, public works, e.g., dams, parks, recreation facilities in 351.86; public utilities in 351.87

.83 Labor

Examples: administration of employment services, industrial relations, wages and hours

Including pensions

Class labor relations of governments with their own employees, fringe benefits for government employees in 351.1; pensions for government employees in 351.5; social welfare services to laboring classes in 351.84; labor in a specific occupation, a specific service to laboring classes not provided for here with the subject in public administration, e.g., unemployment insurance 351.82

.84 Social welfare and corrections

Example: health services

Class programs for achieving civil and human rights, family planning in 351.81; health and accident insurance in 351.82; employment services in 351.83

.85 Culture and religion

Examples: education, recreation, science, technology

Class regulation and control of betting and gambling on sporting events in 351.76, of parks in 351.82, of park and recreational public works in 351.86; administration of a specific technology with the technology in public administration, e.g., transportation 351.87

.86 Housing and public works

Construction, maintenance, use

Examples of public works: parks, recreational facilities, roads

Class public administration of urban development in 351.81, of architecture and historic preservation in 351.85

.87 Public utilities and transportation

Examples of public utilities: postal service, telecommunication, water supply

Class environmental impact of utilities, conservation of energy-producing resources, extraction of energy-producing mineral resources in 351.82; construction of dams for water supply, administration of highways, roads, and streets in 351.86

.870 01–.870 09 Standard subdivisions

.89 Foreign affairs

Class foreign affairs department in 351.01, cultural exchanges in 351.85

.9 Malfunctioning of administration

Including conflict of interest, grievances against government investigations, impeachment, interdisciplinary works on ombudsmen

Class malfunctioning of a specific aspect of administration with the aspect, e.g., maladministration in financial administration 351.72

352 Administration of local governments

Do not use standard subdivisions

Class interdisciplinary works on local government in 320.8, local politics in 320, city councils and other local legislative bodies in 328, administrative relations of local governments with higher levels of government in 351.09, port authorities in 351.87, school boards and districts in 379.1

See Manual at 350–354; 350–354 vs. 320.4, 320.9; 350–354 vs. 658, T1—068; 352 for citation order; 361–365 vs. 350–354; 363 vs. 340, 350–354

SUMMARY

352.03–.09	**Treatment by specific continents, countries, localities**
.1	**Property and financial management and related topics**
.2	**Police**
.3	**Fire and accident protection**
.4	**Safeguarding public health**
.5	**Regulation and control of public buildings**
.6	**Environmental sanitation and related activities**
.7	**Housing and public works**
.9	**Miscellaneous fields**

.03–.09 Treatment by specific continents, countries, localities

Class here specific local governments

Add to base number 352.0 notation 3–9 from Table 2, e.g., local governments in Illinois, the government of Chicago 352.0773

.1 **Property and financial management and related topics**

Examples: administration and use of audits, budgets and budgeting, contracts and contracting, records management, purchasing, tax administration

Class fiscal relations between local governments and higher ones in 351.72, property and financial management and related topics applied to administration of specific fields in 352.2–352.9

See also 352.5 for regulation and control of public buildings

---

> **352.2–352.9 Local administration of specific fields**

Class comprehensive works in 352

See Manual at 352.2–352.9

> **352.2–352.4 Police, fire protection, accident prevention, safeguarding public health**

Class comprehensive works in 352.93

.2 **Police**

Including operative management of police agencies

Class traffic control in 352.91

.3 **Fire and accident protection**

Class administration of safety measures in a specific field of activity with the field in local public administration, using notation 028 from Table 1, e.g., safety in construction of public buildings 352.5028

.4 **Safeguarding public health**

Examples: control of disease and product hazards

Class comprehensive works on administration of public health in 352.94

For environmental sanitation and related activities, see 352.6

.5 **Regulation and control of public buildings**

Construction, maintenance, use, disposal

Class procurement of public buildings in 352.1

.6 **Environmental sanitation and related activities**

Examples: water supply, waste control

Class hydroelectric power in 352.91

.7 **Housing and public works**

Construction, maintenance, use

Examples of public works: cemeteries, parks, recreation facilities, streets

Class administration of architecture, historic preservation, urban development in 352.94

For regulation and control of public buildings, see 352.5; environmental sanitation and related activities, 352.6

.9 **Miscellaneous fields**

Limited to fields provided for here and below

Examples: city planning, zoning

Class administration of courts in 347; police administration in 352.2; information services in a specific field of activity with the subject in local public administration, e.g., street maps 352.7

.91 Public utilities and transportation

Examples: electric power and gas

Class administration of streets, roads, highways in 352.7

For water supply, see 352.6

.92 Construction

Class here administration of permits, codes, inspections, standards

Class construction of a specific kind of facility with the facility in local public administration, e.g., housing 352.7

.93 Public safety and related fields

Examples: civil defense; disaster and emergency planning; control of alcoholic beverages and drug traffic, crowds, gambling, guns, prostitution, public gatherings

For police, see 352.2; fire and accident protection, 352.3; safeguarding public health, 352.4

See also 352.94 for services to alcoholics and narcotics addicts

.94 Economic, welfare, cultural activities

Examples: administration of commerce, consumption, labor, urban development; of health services, penal institutions

Including information services

Class relations of governments with their own employees in 352, public works and recreational facilities in 352.7, public utilities and transportation in 352.91, construction in 352.92

353 Administration of United States federal and state governments

(Option: This number may be used to give local emphasis and shorter notation to central governments of a specific country other than United States; in that case, class central governments of United States in 354.73–354.79, 354.969)

Do not use standard subdivisions

Class administration of Confederate States of America in 354.75; of any jurisdiction before it became part of United States in 354, e.g., Texas Republic 354.764

See Manual at 350–354; 350–354 vs. 320.4, 320.9; 350–354 vs. 658, T1—068; 353–354 for citation order; 361–365 vs. 350–354; 363 vs. 340, 350–354

SUMMARY

353.001–.009 [Government service, property and financial management and related topics, administration of specific fields, malfunctioning of administration]
.03–.09 President and vice-president, the cabinet, fundamentals of administration, special agencies
.1 Department of State
.2 Department of the Treasury
.3 Department of the Interior
.4 Post Office Department (1829-1971)
.5 Department of Justice
.6 Department of Defense
.7 Department of the Navy
.8 Other departments
.9 State governments

.001–.008 Government service, property and financial management and related topics, administration of specific fields

Add to base number 353.00 the numbers following 351 in 351.1–351.8, e.g., financial administration 353.0072

Class application of specific concepts covered here to specific federal departments of cabinet rank in 353.1–353.8

.009 Malfunctioning of administration

Including conflict of interest, grievances against the state, investigations, impeachment, ombudsmen

Class malfunctioning of a specific aspect of administration with the aspect, e.g., maladministration in financial management 353.0072

.03–.09 President and vice-president, the cabinet, fundamentals of administration, special agencies

Add to base number 353.0 the numbers following 351.00 in 351.003–351.009, e.g., the cabinet 353.04

Class application of concepts provided for here to government service, property and financial management and related topics, administration of specific fields in 353.001–353.008; to specific federal departments of cabinet rank in 353.1–353.8; to administrative relations between federal and state governments in 353.9

> **353.1–353.8 Specific federal departments of cabinet rank**

Class comprehensive works in 353.04; a specific branch of a specific department with the branch, e.g., a science bureau 353.0085

.1 **Department of State**

.2 **Department of the Treasury**

.3 **Department of the Interior**

.4 **Post Office Department (1829–1971)**

Class United States Postal Service in 353.0087

.5 **Department of Justice**

.6 **Department of Defense**

Class administration of armed forces in 355.6

For Department of the Navy, see 353.7

.62 Department of the Army

.63 Department of the Air Force

.7 **Department of the Navy**

.8 **Other departments**

.81 Department of Agriculture

.82 Department of Commerce

.83 Department of Labor

.84 Department of Health and Human Services, and Department of Education

Class here former Department of Health, Education, and Welfare

.842 Department of Health and Human Services

.844 Department of Education

.85 Department of Housing and Urban Development

.86 Department of Transportation

.87 Department of Energy

.88 Department of Veterans Affairs

.9 State governments

.909 Historical, geographic, persons treatment

Class specific state governments in 353.97–353.99 (*not* 353.9097–353.9099)

.97–.99 Specific states

Add to base number 353.9 notation 7–9 from Table 2, e.g., administration of government of Hawaii 353.9969; then add further as follows:

[0001–0009] Standard subdivisions for administration of specific states
Do not use; class in base number for specific state

001–008 Government service, property and financial management and related topics, administration of specific fields
Add to 00 the numbers following 351 in 351.1–351.8, e.g., financial administration 0072
Class application of concepts covered here to specific departments at council-of-state level in 1–8

009 Malfunctioning of administration
Including conflict of interest, grievances against the state, investigations, impeachment, ombudsmen
Class malfunctioning of a specific aspect of administration with the aspect, e.g., of financial administration 0072

03–09 Governor and lieutenant governor, cabinet and council of state, fundamentals of administration, special agencies
Add to base number 0 the numbers following 351.00 in 351.003–351.009, e.g., council of state 04
Class application of concepts covered here to government service, property and financial management and related topics, administration of specific fields in 001–008; to a specific department at council-of-state level in 1–8; to intergovernmental administration in 9

1 Department of state

2–8 Other specific departments at council-of-state level
Add to base number for the state the numbers following 351.0 in 351.02–351.08, e.g., department of labor 83

9 Intergovernmental administration
Class intergovernmental administration of government service, property and financial management and related topics, administration of specific fields in 001–008; intergovernmental administration of a specific department at council-of-state level in 1–8

Class administration of District of Columbia in 352.0753

354 Administration of specific central governments; international administration

For administration of United States federal and state governments, see 353

See Manual at 350–354; 350–354 vs. 320.4, 320.9; 350–354 vs. 658, T1—068; 353–354 for citation order; 361–365 vs. 350–354; 363 vs. 340, 350–354

.1 International administration

Administration of public international agencies and organizations, e.g., United Nations, Organization of American States

.100 1–.100 9 Standard subdivisions

.3–.9 Specific central governments other than those of United States

(Option: To give local emphasis and a shorter notation to central governments of a specific country other than United States, class central governments of the country in 353; in that case, class central governments of United States in 354.73–79, 354.969)

Add to base number 354 notation 3–9 from Table 2, e.g., administration of government of Germany 354.43; then add further as follows:

[0001–0009] Standard subdivisions for administration of specific governments
Do not use; class in base number for specific jurisdiction

001–008 Government service, property and financial management and related topics, administration of specific fields
Add to 00 the numbers following 351 in 351.1–351.8, e.g., financial administration 0072
Class application of concepts covered here to specific departments of cabinet rank in 06

009 Malfunctioning of administrations
Including conflict of interest, grievances against the state, investigations, impeachment, ombudsmen
Class malfunctioning of a specific aspect of administration with the aspect, e.g., of financial administration 0072

03 Chief and deputy chief executive
Use of this number for comprehensive works on executive branch discontinued; class in base number for specific jurisdiction

04 Cabinet and council of state
Class here comprehensive works on departments and ministries of cabinet rank
Class works dealing comprehensively with structure, agencies, programs, services of the central government in base number for specific jurisdiction
For specific departments and ministries of cabinet rank, see 06

06 Specific departments and ministries of cabinet rank
Add to 06 the numbers following 351.0 in 351.01–351.08, e.g., ministry of foreign affairs 061
Class comprehensive works in 04; a subordinate branch of a specific department or ministry with the branch, e.g., a science bureau 0085

(continued)

.3–.9 Specific central governments other than those of United States (continued)

07 Fundamentals of public administration

Including control, evaluation and reporting, leadership, management of executive personnel, oversight, organization, planning, policy making

Class staffing in 001, other aspects not provided for here in 007

08 Intergovernmental administration

Administration of agencies established cooperatively by two or more governments at the same level, of agencies established to deal with affairs of subordinate levels

Including administrative relations of state, provincial, local governments with higher levels

Class cooperation among local governments in 352; international administration in 354.1; intergovernmental administration in a specific field of activity with the activity, e.g., fiscal relations between levels 0072

See also 320.8 for governmental relations between local and higher government

09 Special agencies

Examples: advisory, autonomous, independent, quasi-administrative, regulatory agencies; government corporations, special commissions

Class special agencies dealing with a specific activity with the activity in public administration, e.g., agencies regulating transportation 0087

355 Military science

Including military aspects of arms control and disarmament, military research and development, military situation and policy

Class here armed forces and services, ground forces and operations

For specific kinds of military forces and warfare, see 356–359

See also 306.2 for sociological aspects of military institutions; 322 for relation of the state to military organizations; 343 for military, defense, and veterans' law

See Manual at 355 vs. 623

SUMMARY

355.001–.009 Standard subdivisions
.02 War and warfare
.1 Military life and customs
.2 Military resources
.3 Organization and personnel of military forces
.4 Military operations
.5 Military training
.6 Military administration
.7 Military installations and reservations
.8 Military equipment and supplies (Matériel)

.001 Philosophy and theory

.002 Miscellany

[.002 8] Auxiliary techniques and procedures; apparatus, equipment, materials

Do not use; class in 355.8

.003–.005 Standard subdivisions

.006 Organizations

[.006 8] Management

Do not use; class in 355.6

.007 Education and related topics

Class reserve training in 355.2, in-service training in 355.5

.007 1 Military schools

See Manual at 355.0071

.008 History and description with respect to kinds of persons

.009 Historical, geographic, persons treatment

Class historical and geographic treatment of specific military establishments in 355.309, military aspects of the history of specific wars in 900

See Manual at 355.0092 vs. 930–990

.02 War and warfare

Including limited and nuclear war; revolutionary warfare; causes of war; antimilitarism, militarism, military-industrial complex; aftermath of war, e.g., reconstruction

Class here conventional warfare, total war

See also 341.6 for law of war

See Manual at 355.4 vs. 355.02 for strategy

.1 Military life and customs

Including ceremonies, colors and standards, discipline and punishment, military housing, military police, morale, promotion, uniforms and medals

Veterans' pensions relocated to 331.25, other veterans' rights and benefits to 362.86

Class administration of military housing in 355.6, quarters for military personnel at military installations in 355.7, issue and use of uniforms in 355.8, war crimes in 364.1

.2 Military resources

Examples: human resources, industrial resources, raw materials

Including draft, draft resisters, mobilization, recruitment, reserve training

.3 **Organization and personnel of military forces**

Including military units, e.g., expeditionary forces, foreign legions, frontier troops, home guards, international forces, mercenary troops, regiments; noncombat services, e.g., chaplain, medical, supply-issuing, unconventional-warfare services; reserves

Administrative services relocated to 355.6

Class interdisciplinary works on espionage and subversion in 327.1; persons treatment of soldiers in 355.0092; promotion and demotion of personnel in 355.1; specific kinds of military units limited to a specific service with the service, e.g., guided-missile units 358.1

.4 **Military operations**

Including camouflage, logistics, military geography, occupation and military government of conquered territory, reconnaissance, tactics, war games

Class here attack and defense operations, strategy

Quelling riots relocated to 363.3

See Manual at 355.4 vs. 355.02 for strategy

.409 Historical and persons treatment

Class geographic treatment in 355.4

.5 **Military training**

Of individuals and units

Examples: basic training, drill, maneuvers, self defense

Class service academies that are universities in 355.0071; reserve training, universal military training in 355.2; training through war games in 355.4

.6 **Military administration**

Examples: financial, housing, personnel, supply administration

Including defense contracts; graves registration, inspection, military postal service

Class here administrative services [*formerly also* 355.3]

Class comprehensive works on military housing in 355.1; organization of military forces, supply-issuing services in 355.3; housing at military installations in 355.7; administration of specific kinds of supplies in 355.8; administration of functions not named here with the function, e.g., training 355.5

.7 **Military installations and reservations**

Including arsenals, barracks, prisoner-of-war camps

Class installations and reservations of a specific military service with the service, e.g., army artillery installations 358

.8 **Military equipment and supplies (Matériel)**

General aspects: development, procurement, issue, operation, use, packing, shipping

Examples: clothing, vehicles, weapons

Class here research and development, administration of specific kinds of equipment and supplies

Class comprehensive works on research and development of supplies in 355, on supply administration in 355.6; mobilization of military resources in 355.2

> **356–359 Specific kinds of military forces and warfare**

General aspects: military life and customs, resources, organization and personnel, operations, training, administration, installations, matériel

Class here history of specific military forces not limited to any one war, services and units dedicated to specific forces, countermeasures against specific forces

Class comprehensive works in 355; history of specific military forces in specific wars in 900; a specific countermeasure with the force wielding it, e.g., coast artillery 358 (*not* 359)

> **356–357 Land forces and warfare**

Class comprehensive works in 355; armored, artillery, biological, chemical, radiological forces and warfare in 358; missile forces and warfare in 358.1

356 Foot forces and warfare

Including commandos, infantry, paratroops, rangers, ski troops

357 Mounted forces and warfare

Including horse and mechanized cavalry, motorcycle troops

Class armored cavalry in 358

358 Air and other specialized forces and warfare; engineering and related services

Examples: coast, field, antiaircraft artillery; armored, space forces; communications, demolition, transportation services; chemical, biological radiological warfare

.1 **Guided missile forces and warfare**

Including antimissile defense, Strategic Defense Initiative (SDI, star wars)

Class here strategic missile forces and warfare, nuclear missile forces and warfare

Do not use standard subdivisions

Class air guided missile forces in 358.4, naval guided missile forces in 359.9; a specific antimissile defense other than surface to air missiles with the defense, e.g., beam weapons 358, air-to-air missiles 358.4

.4 Air forces and warfare

Do not use standard subdivisions

359 Sea (Naval) forces and warfare

.001–.009 Standard subdivisions

As modified under 355.001–355.009

.1–.8 Specific elements of naval forces and warfare

Add to base number 359 the numbers following 355 in 355.1–355.8, e.g., naval operations 359.4

.9 Specialized combat forces; engineering and related forces

Examples: coast guard when under naval or defense forces command, guided missile forces, marines, submarine forces; communications, demolition, transportation services

Class comprehensive works on coast guard in 363.2; chemical, biological, radiological warfare in 358

360 Social problems and services; association

SUMMARY

361	**Social problems and social welfare in general**
362	**Social welfare problems and services**
363	**Other social problems and services**
364	**Criminology**
365	**Penal and related institutions**
366	**Association**
367	**General clubs**
368	**Insurance**
369	**Miscellaneous kinds of associations**

> 361–365 Social problems and services

Class here work and policy of government agencies that enforce the law in matters of social problems and services

Class comprehensive works in 361, insurance in 368; social services in armed forces in 355–359, in specific wars in 900; the internal administration of governmental agencies, including their administrative annual reports, in 350–354; the law itself, draft laws, enforcement by courts in 341–346

See Manual at 301–307 vs. 361–365; 361–365; 361–365 vs. 350–354

361 Social problems and social welfare in general

Social welfare: social assistance, either free or paid for in part or in full by recipients, to enable individuals to cope with situations beyond their individual capacities to overcome

Including material assistance, e.g., financial aid; guidance and related services

Class here comprehensive works on socioeconomic planning and development, on programs and services encompassing several branches of social sciences, on social problems and services

Historical, geographic, persons treatment of social welfare problems and services relocated to 362.9

Class social problems considered purely as social phenomena in 301–307, community planning and development in 307.1, economic planning and development in 338.9, specific problems and services in 362–365, description of present or past social conditions in 306.09; assistance with respect to a specific problem with the problem, e.g., financial aid to persons in late adulthood 362.6

See Manual at 361 vs. 362

.001–.008 Standard subdivisions

[.009] Historical, geographic, persons treatment

Do not use; class in 361.9

.1 **Social problems**

History, description, appraisal of areas and kinds of social breakdown, of problems endemic to human society

Class specific problems in 362–363

See Manual at 361.1 vs 362, 301

.2 **Social action**

Organization, role, description, methods, history

Including planning, international action, protest and dissent, reform movements

Class change as a social phenomenon in 303.4

For social work, see 361.3; governmental action, 361.6; private action, 361.7

See Manual at 361.2 vs. 322.4

.3 **Social work**

Including interviewing, counseling, casework, volunteer social work

For group work, see 361.4

.4 **Group work**

Class counseling in group work in 361.3

.6 **Governmental action**

Including welfare and human rights, welfare state, welfare reform

Class here intergovernmental assistance and planning, governmental international action, interdisciplinary works on government-sponsored socioeconomic planning and development

Class interdisciplinary works on human rights in 323, public social work in 361.3, combined public and private community action in 361.8, management of public agencies regulating social welfare services in 351.84, economics of welfare state in 330.12

See Manual at 361.6 vs. 361.7, 361.8

.7 **Private action**

By individual philanthropists, by religious organizations; by other nonprofit organizations, e.g., CARE; by business organizations, labor unions; by private international organizations, e.g., Red Cross

Class private social work in 361.3, relation of government and private sectors in 361.6, combined public and private community action in 361.8, programs of employers for employees in 658.3

See Manual at 361.6 vs. 361.7, 361.8

.706 8 Management

Including fund raising

.8 **Community action**

Coordination of public and private action to promote welfare of individuals in the community

Class community planning and development in 307.1, governmental community action in 361.6, private community action in 361.7

See Manual at 361.6 vs. 361.7, 361.8

.9 **Historical, geographic, persons treatment**

Add to base number 361.9 notation 1–9 from Table 2, e.g., welfare work in Arizona 361.9791

Class historical, geographic, persons treatment of specific kinds of social action in 361.2–361.8

> ## 362–363 Specific social problems and services

General aspects: social causes and effects; extent, distribution, severity, incidence; control through standards, monitoring, surveillance, reporting, inspection, testing, investigation of specific incidents, certification; preparedness, prevention; remedial measures and forms of assistance, e.g., rescue operations, financial assistance, employment services, residential care, counseling, guidance

Safety measures associated with a specific problem relocated to 363.1

Class comprehensive works in 361, discrimination in 305

For criminology, see 364

See Manual at 364.1 vs. 362–363

362 Social welfare problems and services

Class here social security

Unless other instructions are given, observe the following table of precedence, e.g., mentally ill female veterans 362.2 (*not* 362.86 or 362.83)

Physical illness	362.1
Mental and emotional illnesses and disturbances	362.2
Mental retardation	362.3
Problems of and services to people with physical disabilities	362.4
Victims of political oppression	362.87
Victims of crimes	362.88
Veterans	362.86
Problems of and services to persons in late adulthood	362.6
Problems of and services to young people	362.7
Laboring classes	363.85
Women	362.83
Members of racial, ethnic, national groups	362.84
Problems of and services to the poor	362.5
Families	362.82
Historical, geographic, persons treatment of social welfare problems and services	362.9

To indicate the relation of a specific kind of problem to a specific kind of person, add notation 08 from Table 1 to the number for the problem, e.g., substance abuse among young adults 362.290835

For social security as a form of social insurance, see 368.4

See Manual at 361 vs. 362; 361.1 vs. 362, 301; 364.1 vs. 362–363; 368.4 vs. 362 for social security

SUMMARY

362.1	**Physical illness**
.2	**Mental and emotional illnesses and disturbances**
.3	**Mental retardation**
.4	**Problems of and services to people with physical disabilities**
.5	**Problems of and services to the poor**
.6	**Problems of and services to persons in late adulthood**
.7	**Problems of and services to young people**
.8	**Problems of and services to other groups**
.9	**Historical, geographic, persons treatment of social welfare problems and services**

[.08] Social welfare problems and services with respect to kinds of persons

Do not use; class in 362.1–362.8

[.09] Historical, geographic, persons treatment

Do not use; class in 362.9

> **362.1–362.4 Problems of and services to sick and disabled people**

Including services of general and special hospitals, clinics, sanitariums, dispensaries; extended care facilities, e.g., nursing homes; medical and psychiatric social work; home care, e.g., visiting nurses' services; emergency services, e.g., ambulance services

Class comprehensive works in 362.1; incidence of and public measures to prevent physical diseases in 614.4–614.5

See Manual at 362.1–362.4 vs. 610; 614.4–614.5 vs. 362.1–362.4

.1 **Physical illness**

Including living with a physical illness

Class here interdisciplinary works on illness and disability, on medical care and treatment, on medical missions, on public health

Class problems of and services to persons with a specific physical disability regardless of cause in 362.4; technology of medicine in 610; preventive measures, incidence of disease in 614.4–614.5; religious aspects of medical missions in 266; sociology of medicine, of health, of illness in 306.4; accident and health insurance in 368.3, government-sponsored accident and health insurance in 368.4

For mental and emotional illness, see 362.2; mental retardation, 362.3

See also 649.8 for home care by family members

See Manual at 368.3 vs. 362.1 for health insurance plans

.102 3 Services to physically ill persons as a profession, occupation, hobby

Class here comprehensive works on health occupations peripheral to the medical and paramedical professions

Class specific peripheral professions with the subject, e.g., hospital secretaries 651.3; works covering both the medical and peripheral occupations in 610

.108 Services to specific kinds of physically ill persons

Class services rendered by groups of persons to the physically ill in 362.1, physical illness among groups of persons in 616.008

.108 3 Services to young people

Class services to infants and children up to puberty in 362.1

.108 4 Services to persons in specific stages of adulthood

Class services to persons in late adulthood in 362.1

.2 **Mental and emotional illnesses and disturbances**

Class here mental handicaps that consist of mental retardation combined with mental illness

Class mental retardation in 362.3, life with a psychiatric disorder in 616.890092, institutions for the criminally insane in 365

.29 Substance abuse

Including alcohol, narcotics abuse

Class here drug abuse; interdisciplinary works on substance abuse, addiction, habituation, intoxication, alcoholism

Class subculture of substance abusers in 306; abuse of substances associated with systems other than the nervous system, e.g., food addiction, in 362.1; a specific aspect of substance abuse, drug abuse, alcoholism with the aspect, e.g., drug traffic in 363.4, public drunkenness in 364.1, drug use as a custom in 394.1, medical aspects of substance abuse in 616.86

.3 **Mental retardation**

Class comprehensive works on treatment of mental retardation and mental illness in 362.2, on problems of and services to developmentally disabled people (those who have neurological diseases combined with mental retardation and whose problems exhibit themselves before age 18) in 362.1

.4 **Problems of and services to people with physical disabilities**

Regardless of cause

Including persons with impaired hearing, with impaired vision, with mobility impairment

Class here comprehensive works on problems of and services to people with disabilities, to people with mental and physical disabilities

Class problems of and services to people with mental disabilities in 362.3, comprehensive medical works in 617

.5 **Problems of and services to the poor**

Including legal aid, guaranteed minimum income, negative income tax

Class here services to homeless people

Class aid to families with dependent children (AFDC) in 362.7, housing in 363.5, food programs in 363.8, birth control measures in 363.9, assistance to the poor under social security in 368.4; economic measures to prevent poverty in 339

.6 **Problems of and services to persons in late adulthood**

Class here social gerontology

.7 **Problems of and services to young people**

Through age 17

Including adoption, aid to families with dependent children (AFDC), day care services, foster home care; abused and neglected children, orphans, predelinquents

Class here children

Class families with missing children in 362.82, child abuse as a crime in 364.1, juvenile delinquents in 364.3

.8 **Problems of and services to other groups**

.82 Families

Including abuse within the family, single-parent family, missing children, parental kidnapping

Specific problems not provided for here relocated to the specific problem, e.g., families with alcoholic members 362.29

Class adoption, aid to families with dependent children (AFDC), day care, abused and runaway children in 362.7; abuse as a crime in 364.1

Family welfare when synonymous with general welfare is classed in 362

.83 Women

Including unmarried mothers

Class wife abuse in 362.82, rape in 362.88

.84 Members of racial, ethnic, national groups

.85 Laboring classes

Including migrant workers

.86 Veterans

Class here veterans' rights and benefits [*formerly also* 355.1]

Class veterans pensions in 331.25

.87 Victims of political oppression

.88 Victims of crimes

Example: rape victims

Including crime prevention for the individual

Class here victimology

Class services to abused and neglected children in 362.7, services to abused family members in 362.82, crime prevention for society as a whole in 364.4

.9 **Historical, geographic, persons treatment of social welfare problems and services [*formerly* 361]**

Add to base number 362.9 notation 1–9 from Table 2, e.g., social welfare in France 362.944

Class historical, geographic, persons treatment of specific social problems in 362.1–362.8

363 Other social problems and services

Class here public works

Class communication facilities in 384, transportation facilities in 388

Standard subdivisions are added for comprehensive treatment of environmental and safety problems of society, e.g., assuring a safe and secure environment for Japan 363.0952

See Manual at 363; 363 vs. 340, 350–354; 364.1 vs. 362–363

SUMMARY

363.1	**Public safety programs**
.2	**Police services**
.3	**Other aspects of public safety**
.4	**Controversies related to public morals and customs**
.5	**Housing**
.6	**Public utilities and related services**
.7	**Environmental problems and services**
.8	**Food supply**
.9	**Population problems**

.1 **Public safety programs**

Including alarm and warning systems [*formerly also* 384]

Class here safety measures [*formerly also* with the specific topic in 362–363], interdisciplinary works on safety

Unless other instructions are given, observe the following table of precedence, e.g., use of hazardous materials in health care facilities 363.17 (*not* 363.15)

Hazardous materials	363.17
Hazards in sports and recreation	363.14
Transportation hazards	363.12
Hazardous machinery	363.18
Product hazards	363.19
Domestic hazards	363.13
Hazards in health care facilities	363.15
Occupational and industrial hazards	363.11

Class police services in 363.2, aspects of public safety not provided for here in 363.3; managerial response to safety requirements, comprehensive works on safety management in 658.4, safety management in a specific industry with the industry, using notation 068 from Table 1, e.g., safety management in petroleum industry 665.5068; a specific kind of remedial measure other than rescue operations with the measure, e.g., medical care for the injured 362.1; safety technology of a specific subject with the subject, using notation 028 from Table 1, e.g., safety technology in hydraulic engineering 627.028

See Manual at 363.1

.11 Occupational and industrial hazards

See Manual at 613.6 vs. 363.11

.12 Transportation hazards Shipwrecks 910.4

Class here accidents, fires resulting from accidents

Class transportation fires (e.g., fires caused by deficient electrical wiring in a railroad car) in 363.37

.13 Domestic hazards

.14 Hazards in sports and recreation

.15 Hazards in health care facilities

.17 Hazardous materials

Manufacture, transportation, use

Class here interdisciplinary works on hazardous materials, works on the control of such materials in their ordinary commercial setting (manufacture, sale, commercial and industrial use, disposal)

Class hazardous materials as components of articles that become hazardous products in 363.19, as impurities in the water supply 363.6, as hazardous wastes in 363.72, as environmental pollutants in 363.73

See Manual at 363.17; 363.17 vs. 604.7 for control of hazardous materials

.18 Hazardous machinery

.19 Product hazards

Adulteration, contamination, safety, adequacy, effectiveness of products offered for human consumption and use

Examples: cosmetics, drugs, foods, household appliances, toys

Class here hazards due to containers and applicators that accompany products

.2 Police services

General aspects: duties, functions, activities

Examples: prevention of crime by police [*formerly* 364.4], law enforcement, patrol, surveillance, pursuit, apprehension, detection of crime (criminal investigation); enforcement of civil laws, e.g., traffic control; location of missing persons; auxiliary services, e.g., fingerprint files

Including forensic science (criminalistics), detection of specific types of crime; services of special kinds of security and law enforcement agencies, e.g., coast guards, harbor and border patrols

Class social service functions of police in 362, e.g., counseling of rape victims 362.88; control of violence and terrorism in 363.3, police services in control of factors affecting public morals in 363.4, detection of a specific offense in 364.1, postal inspectors in 383, forensic medicine in 614

[.206 8] Management

Do not use; class in 351.74

.3 Other aspects of public safety

Including control of violence and terrorism, e.g., quelling riots [*formerly also* 355.4], crowd control; censorship; civil defense; control of information, explosives and firearms; disasters, e.g., floods, war

Class civil rights aspects of censorship in 323.44, legal aspects in 342, censorship as an illicit governmental activity in 351.9; gun control as a civil rights issue in 323.4, control of explosives as ordinary hazardous materials in 363.1; epidemics, pandemics in 362.17, prevention of war in 327.1, technology of flood control in 627, disasters treated as historical events in 900, a specific kind of remedial measure other than those applied immediately at the time and site of the disaster with the subject, e.g., medical care for injured 362.1

Specific kinds of disasters resulting from one of the hazards listed at 363.1 are classed in 363.1, e.g., transportation accidents 363.12

See also 303.6 for sociology of war, 362.87 for problems of war refugees when not treated directly in context of the war

See Manual at 363.1

.37 Fire hazards

Class fire fighting and fire safety technology in 628.9

.4 **Controversies related to public morals and customs**

Treated as social problems

Examples: abortion, drug traffic, gambling, homosexuality, obscenity, pornography, pre- and extramartial relations, prostitution, sale of alcoholic beverages

Class interdisciplinary works on homosexuality in 306.76, problems of and services to alcoholics and drug addicts in 362.29, censorship and control of information in 363.3; a controversy treated as a crime, e.g., illegal possession of drugs, in 364.1; a controversy treated other than as a social problem with the aspect of the controversy, e.g., ethic of gambling 174

.5 **Housing**

Including public housing, urban homesteading, discrimination in housing

Class here interdisciplinary works on housing, housing as a social problem

Class a specific aspect of housing with the aspect, e.g., sociological aspects 307.3, economic aspects 333.33

See Manual at 363.5, 363.6, 363.8 vs. 338; 643 vs. 363.5

[.508] Housing of specific kinds of persons

Do not use; class in 363.5

.6 **Public utilities and related services**

Including water and gas supply, park and recreation services, historic preservation

Class here problems of allocation among end users, measures to assure abundance of immediately available supplies and services

Electrical utilities relocated to 333.79

Class park policy and park development in 333.78, flood control in 363.3, communication in 384, transportation in 388, technology of building restoration and preservation in 721.028, recreational centers in 790.06; a specific cultural institution maintained by park and recreation services with the institution, e.g., museums 069, theaters 792

See Manual at 363.5, 363.6, 383.8 vs. 338; 363.6 for water reports; 363.6 vs. 333.7 for public utilities

.7 **Environmental problems and services**

Including disposal of the dead, noise, removal of animal carcasses, interdisciplinary works on pest control

Class here environmental protection; impact of wastes, of pollution, of actions to control waste and pollution

Class interdisciplinary works on the environment in 333.7, on the technology of pest control in 628.9; death customs in 393, technology of disposal of the dead in 614; control of disease-carrying pests in 614.4, of agricultural pests in 632, of household pests in 648; impacts on specific environments or resources with the impact, e.g., economic impact on Rome of a major new water treatment facility 330.945, impact of the same treatment plant on the waters of the Tiber River 333.91; projected impacts with the program or development that is being studied, e.g., projected impact of proposed standards for water pollution 363.73

See Manual at 363.7 vs. 333.7, 304.2

.72 Sanitation problems and services

Including waste disposal and management

See Manual at 628.4 vs. 363.72 for solid wastes

.73 Pollution

Class noise in 363.7, sanitation in 363.72, technology of pollution prevention in 628.5, management responsibilities and measures with respect to protection and preservation of the environment in 658.4

Works that discuss waste and sanitation problems as well as pollution are classed in 363.7

.8 **Food supply**

Including food stamp programs

Class here hunger, famine; interdisciplinary works on food supply, on nutrition

Class economics of food supply in 338.1

See also 362.1 for problems of malnutrition, 614.5 for prevention of malnutrition

See Manual at 363.5, 363.6, 363.8 vs. 338; 363.8 vs. 338.1; 613.2 vs. 641.3, 363.8; 614.5 vs. 363.8 for nutrition surveys

.9 **Population problems**

Including overpopulation [*formerly also* 304.6] and underpopulation, sterilization; interdisciplinary works on eugenics, on birth control, on family planning programs

Class here interdisciplinary works on population problems

Class interdisciplinary works on population in 304.6, on abortion in 363.4; family planning techniques in 613.9; specific manifestations of a population problem with the manifestation, e.g., pressure on food supply leading to famine 363.8; specific aspects of eugenics with the aspect, e.g., civil rights 323.4, eugenic measures to reduce crime 364.4

364 Criminology

Crime and its alleviation

General aspects: extent and incidence of crime

Class here comprehensive works on criminology and criminal law, on criminal justice that includes criminology, police services, and criminal law

Unless other instructions are given, observe the following table of precedence, e.g., punishment of specific types of offenders 364.6 (*not* 364.3)

Penology	364.6
Discharged offenders	364.8
Offenders	364.3
Prevention of crime and delinquency	364.4
Causes of crime and delinquency	364.2
Criminal offenses	364.1
Historical, geographic, persons treatment of crime and its alleviation	364.9

Class social services to victims of crimes and self-protection from criminals in 362.88

For criminal law, see 345

[.08] Treatment with respect to kinds of persons

Do not use; class victimology in 362.88, victims of specific crimes in 364.1, offenders in 364.3

.09 Historical, geographic, persons treatment of criminology as a discipline

Class historical, geographic, persons treatment of crime and its alleviation in 364.9

.1 Criminal offenses

Including organized crime

Class here conspiracy to and incitement to commit an offense, individuals identified with a specific offense or type of offense, investigation of specific crimes, crimes without victims, terrorism as a crime

Class offenses against church law in 262.9; sociology of terrorism in 303.6; child abuse as a social problem in 362.7; abuse within the family as a social problem, parental kidnapping in 362.82; social services aspects of victims of crimes in 362.88; investigation of specific types of offenses in 363.2; a crime as an event in history in 900

See also 341.6 for war crime trials, 363.4 for controversies related to public morals and customs, e.g., drug traffic

See Manual at 364.1 vs. 362–363

[.106] Organizations and management

Do not use; class in 364.1

.2 **Causes of crime and delinquency**

Examples: social factors, e.g., socioeconomic conditions, influence of family; influence of physical environment, e.g., weather; effects of heredity, genetic defects, physical typology; psychological factors

Class here criminal anthropology

Class victimology in 362.88

.3 **Offenders**

Including juvenile delinquents, mentally and emotionally disturbed persons

Class here criminal psychology

Class individuals chiefly identified with a specific offense or type of offense in 364.1; a specific aspect of the justice system for specific types of offenders with the aspect, e.g., determination of sentences for juvenile offenders 364.6, offenders as prisoners in 365

[.308 1–.308 3] Men, women, young people

Do not use; class in 364.3

.308 7 Handicapped and ill persons

Do not use for mentally ill and mentally handicapped persons; class in 364.3

[.308 9] Members of specific racial, ethnic, national groups

Do not use; class in 364.3

.4 **Prevention of crime and delinquency**

What society does to prevent crime

Including counseling, guidance, environmental design; welfare services, e.g., recreational services; identification of potential offenders, e.g., through genetic screening; curfew

Prevention of crime by police relocated to 363.2

Class law enforcement in 363.2; penalties as a deterrent in 364.6; a specific aspect of prevention by a potential victim with the aspect, e.g., what the individual can do 362.88, household security 643

.6 **Penology**

Treatment and punishment of offenders

Including capital punishment, corporal punishment, fines; parole, probation; pardon, amnesty

Class here welfare services to offenders, reform of penal system

Class welfare services to prisoners, reform of penal institutions in 365

For discharged offenders, see 364.8; institutions for correction of offenders, 365

.8 **Discharged offenders**

.9 **Historical, geographic, persons treatment of crime and its alleviation**

Add to base number 364.9 notation 1–9 from Table 2, e.g., persons associated with crime and its alleviation 364.92

Class victims in 362.88, police officers in 363.2092, criminologists in 364.092, offenders associated with specific kinds of crime in 364.1, comprehensive works on offenders in 364.3, penologists in 364.6092

365 Penal and related institutions

Institutions for correction of offenders and for incarceration of other groups considered socially undesirable

Examples: concentration camps, jails, military prisons, penal colonies, penitentiaries, prerelease guidance centers, prison farms, reformatories, work camps; institutions for specific classes of inmates, e.g., criminally insane persons, juveniles, political prisoners

Including prison grounds, buildings, equipment; security, discipline, daily routine within prisons; prison labor; reform of penal institutions

Class here imprisonment and detention

Class parole, probation, indeterminate and suspended sentence, reform of penal system in 364.6, institutions for prisoners of war in 355.1, prison architecture in 725; concentration camps associated with a specific war with the war, e.g., World War II concentration camps 940.53; penal colonies as a part of history of a place in 930–990, e.g., penal colony of Botany Bay a founding settlement of New South Wales 994.4

.068 Management

Class management of plant and equipment in 365

[.09] Historical, geographic, persons treatment

Do not use; class in 365

366 Association

Organizations formed for fraternizing or for mutual assistance

Examples: Benevolent and Protective Order of Elks, Freemasonry, Independent Order of Odd Fellows, Knights of Pythias

Class associations dealing with a specific subject with the subject, using notation 06 from Table 1, e.g., mathematical associations 510.6

For general clubs, see 367; miscellaneous kinds of associations, 369; orders of knighthood, 929.7

See also 200 for religious associations, 368.3 for fraternal insurance

.001–.009 Standard subdivisions

367 General clubs

Examples: social clubs, study clubs

Class here social clubs for specific types of people, e.g., social clubs for actors

Class clubs dealing with a specific subject with the subject, using notation 06 from Table 1, e.g., chess clubs 794.106

[.09] Historical, geographic, persons treatment

Do not use; class in 367

368 Insurance

Including actuarial science, underwriting, claims; conventional comprehensive sales grouping, e.g., automobile, aviation, real property insurance

Class here comprehensive works on risk

Class risk management in 658.15

.001 Philosophy and theory

Class mathematical principles in 368

.002–.005 Standard subdivisions

.006 Organizations and management

Including insurance companies

Class credit and loan functions of insurance companies in 332.3

.007–.008 Standard subdivisions

.009 Historical, geographic, persons treatment

Class treatment by specific continents, countries, localities in modern world in 368

.1 Insurance against damage to and loss of property

Examples: civil commotion, disaster, fire, riot, war risk insurance

Class property damage (liability) insurance with the specific type of liability insurance, e.g., property damage insurance as part of public liability 368.5

For transportation insurance, see 368.2; casualty insurance, 368.5–368.8

.100 1–.100 9 Standard subdivisions

.2 Insurance against damage to and loss of property in transit (Marine insurance, Transportation insurance)

Class here insurance against damage to and loss of instrumentalities of transportation, e.g., trucks

.200 1–.200 9 Standard subdivisions

.3 Insurance against death, old age, illness, injury

Examples: accident, dental, disability income, health, hospital insurance

Including annuities

Class here comprehensive works on insurance for the aged; group, industrial, survivors' insurance

Class comprehensive works on insurance as a fringe benefit in 331.25, personnel administration of insurance in 658.3

For government-sponsored insurance, see 368.4

See Manual at 368.3 vs. 362.1 for health insurance plans

.300 1–.300 9 Standard subdivisions

.4 Government-sponsored insurance

Examples: accident, health, maternity, old-age and survivors, unemployment, workers' compensation insurance; insurance against crimes of violence

Including social security (United States)

Class here social insurance, social security as a form of social insurance

Class workers' compensation (employer liability insurance) in 368.5, government-sponsored bank deposit insurance in 368.8

See also 362.10973 for United States' Medicaid health services, 368.3 for comprehensive works on accident and health insurance

See Manual at 368.4 vs. 362 for social security

.400 1–.400 9 Standard subdivisions

> **368.5–368.8 Insurance against casualties (Casualty insurance)**

Class comprehensive works in 368.5

.5 Liability insurance

Examples: automobile and aviation liability

Including malpractice insurance

Class here comprehensive works on casualty insurance

For glass insurance, see 368.6; insurance against industrial casualties, 368.7; other casualty insurance, 368.8

.500 1–.500 9 Standard subdivisions

.6 Glass insurance

.600 1–.600 9 Standard subdivisions

.7 Insurance against industrial casualties (accidents)

.700 1–.700 9 Standard subdivisions

.8 **Other casualty insurance**

Including business, strike insurance; burglary, robbery, theft insurance; bonds; investment guarantees; bank deposit, credit, mortgage, title insurance

369 Miscellaneous kinds of associations

Including hereditary, military, patriotic societies; nationality clubs

.4 **Young people's societies**

Class a specific aspect of young people's societies with the aspect, e.g., Boy Scout camps 796.54

.42 Boys' societies

For Boy Scouts, see 369.43

.43 Boy Scouts

Including Cub Scouts, Explorers

.46 Girls' societies

For Camp Fire, inc., see 369.47; Explorers, 369.43

.463 Girl Scouts and Girl Guides

.47 Camp Fire, inc.

Former name: Camp Fire Girls

.5 **Service clubs**

Examples: Kiwanis International, Lions International, Rotary International, Zonta International

370 Education

Education is here considered to be a social science—the methods and processes involved in the primary effort outside the home to socialize the young and to prepare them to be independent adults

Class education in the home in 649; comprehensive works on education in a specific subject with the subject, using notation 07 from Table 1, e.g., mathematics education 510.7; education in a specific subject at the elementary level in 372.3–372.8; in special education in 371.9

Unless other instructions are given, observe the following table of precedence, e.g., special education in secondary schools 371.9 (*not* 373.2)

Special education	371.9
Education of women	376
Levels of education and schools	372–374
Higher education	378
School organization and management (*except* 371.9)	371
Government regulation, control, support of education	379
Curriculums	375
Schools and religion	377

SUMMARY

370.1–.9 Standard subdivisions
371 School organization and management; special education
372 Elementary education
373 Secondary education
374 Adult education
375 Curriculums
376 Education of women
377 Schools and religion
378 Higher education
379 Government regulation, control, support of education

.1 **Philosophy, theories, general aspects**

Including philosophical foundations, e.g., idealism, realism, pragmatism

.11 Education for specific objectives

Examples: humanistic, liberal, moral, character, vocational education; education for social responsibility, for creativity, for effective use of leisure

Class vocational secondary schools in 373.246, adult vocational education in 374, vocational schools for a specific subject with the subject, using notation 07 from Table 1, e.g., medical schools 610.71

See also 331.25 for vocational training undertaken by industry

.15 Educational psychology

Including the psychology of learning various specific subjects, psychological effects of education, behavior modification

Class behavior modification for classroom discipline in 371.1; psychology of a specific topic in education with the topic, using notation 01 from Table 1, e.g., the psychology of adult education 374.001

See Manual at 153.1 vs. 370.15 for educational psychology vs. the study of learning

.19 Social aspects of education

Examples: relations between school and society; sociocultural factors affecting education, e.g., racial, ethnic, political factors

Including segregation of racial and ethnic groups, sexism in education; fundamental education (preparation of educationally disadvantaged children and adults for participation in community life); comparative education; intercultural education, e.g., exchange of students and teachers; parent-teacher associations

Class here educational sociology

Class education for social responsibility in 370.11, education of culturally disadvantaged students in 371.96, fundamental education for adults in 374; effects of specific factors on a specific aspect of education with the aspect, e.g., effect on public school finance 379.1

See also 370.11 for basic education

.28 Auxiliary techniques and procedures; apparatus, equipment, materials

Class testing and measurement in 371.2

[.68] Management

Do not use; class in 371.2

.7 **Education, research, related topics**

Including teachers' colleges, practice teaching

Class in-service training of teachers in 371.1; practice teaching at the elementary level in 372.07, in a subject with the subject in 372.3–372.8; practice teaching in a specific subject at the secondary and higher levels with the subject, using notation 07 from Table 1, e.g., practice teaching in mathematics at the secondary level 510.7

[.71] Schools and courses

Do not use; class in 370.7

[.75] Collecting objects

Do not use; class in 370.7

[.76] Review and exercise

Do not use; class in 370.7

[.78] Use of apparatus and equipment in study and teaching

Do not use; class application to education in general in 370.7, to teaching in 371.3078

.8 **History and description with respect to kinds of persons**

Class special education of kinds of persons in 371.9

.82 History and description with respect to women

Class education of women in 376

371 School organization and management; special education

Including student services

Class here public and private schools and school systems; community schools, experimental schools

Do not use standard subdivisions

Class the organization and management of schools at specific levels in 372–374, 378; government regulation, control, support of education in 379; community education in 370.19

> **371.1–371.8 Organization and management**

Class comprehensive works in 371; organization and management of special education in 371.9; at specific levels in 372–374, 378; government regulation, control, support of education in 379

.1 **Teaching and teaching personnel**

Including the relation of teachers to society, e.g., parent-teacher relations, academic freedom; organization of the teaching force, e.g., substitute teaching; evaluation, in-service training; teaching methods, classroom discipline

Class parent-teacher associations in 370.19, professional education of teachers in 370.7, examination and certification of teachers in 379.1

For methods of instruction, see 371.3

.100 1–.100 9 Standard subdivisions

.2 **School administration and management**

Including tuition in private education; accreditation; grouping of pupils for instruction, e.g., on the basis of similar abilities; educational tests and measurements; marking and grading systems; promotion and failure; scholarships; school dropouts, truancy

Class noneducational aspects of intelligence and aptitude tests in 153.9; teaching staff in 371.1; truancy as a disciplinary problem in 371.5; financial administration and tuition of public schools in 379.1; testing in a specific subject in elementary education with the subject in 372.3–372.8, in a specific subject at higher levels with the subject, using notation 076 from Table 1, e.g., testing in chemistry at the secondary level 540.76

For plant management, see 371.6

See Manual at 371.2 vs. 379 for school administration vs. governmental oversight, control, support of education

.200 1–.200 5 Standard subdivisions

.200 6 Organizations and management

[.200 68] Management of schools

Do not use; class in 371.2

.200 7 Education and related topics

Class professional education of school administrators in 370.76

.200 8–.200 9 Standard subdivisions

.3 **Methods of instruction and study**

Including use of audio and visual materials, print media, teaching machines

Class methods used in teaching specific subjects at the elementary level in 372.3–372.8; at a higher level with the subject, using notation 07 from Table 1, e.g., methods used in teaching mathematics 510.7; textbooks on a specific subject with the subject, e.g., history textbooks 900

.302 8 Techniques and procedures

Including lesson plans and planning, methods of study

Class apparatus, equipment, materials in 371.3078

[.302 85] Data processing Computer applications

Do not use; class in 371.3

.307 8 Teaching aids, materials, devices

Including educational technology, educational games, educational toys

Class specific aids in 371.3, an instructional materials center or school resource center in 027.8

.4 **Guidance and counseling**

Educational, vocational, personal

Class choice of vocation in 331.7, student mental health in 371.7, characteristics of a specific occupation with the subject, using notation 023 from Table 1, e.g., teaching as a profession 370.23

[.406 8] Management

Do not use; class in 371.4

.5 **School discipline**

Overseeing student conduct

Including student government

Class classroom discipline in 371.1

See also 371.7 for protection of students from violence

.6 **Physical plant**

Including buildings, grounds; noninstructional facilities, e.g., dormitories

Class here plant management

Class architecture of buildings for educational purposes in 727

.602 8 Auxiliary techniques and procedures; apparatus, equipment, materials

Class maintenance and repair in 371.6

.7 **School health and safety**

Including school lunch and milk programs, birth control programs, sexual hygiene programs

.8 **The student**

General aspects: nonacademic life and welfare

Including student activities, attitudes, behavior, organizations; housing and transportation of students; student activism, protest; Greek-letter societies

Class busing to achieve racial balance in 370.19, counseling in 371.4, school discipline in 371.5

.805 Serial publications

Class here student serials dealing with the school and its activities

Class student periodicals on general subjects in 051–059; school yearbooks for a specific school with the school, student serials on a specific subject with the subject, using notation 05 from Table 1, e.g., student literary periodicals 805

.806 Organizations and management

Class student organizations in 371.8

[.808] History and description with respect to kinds of students

Do not use; class in 371.8

.9 **Special education**

Education employing special curriculums, methods, facilities for exceptional (atypical) students, i.e., students with physical, intellectual, mental, or social differences

Mainstreaming is classed in 371.9, without use of 371.901–371.909; mainstreaming of a specific group is classed with the group in 371.91–371.97

Unless other instructions are given, observe the following table of precedence, e.g., emotionally-disturbed deaf students 371.94 (*not* 371.91)

Gifted students	371.95
Retarded students and slow learners	371.92
Emotionally disturbed students	371.94
Students with physical handicaps	371.91
Socially and culturally disadvantaged students	371.96
Delinquent and problem students	371.93
Students belonging to the upper classes	371.96
Students exceptional because of racial, ethnic, national origin	371.97

Class government regulation, control, support of special education in 379

[.902 8] Auxiliary techniques and procedures; apparatus, equipment, materials

Do not use; class in 371.9

[.906 8] Management

Do not use; class in 371.9

.91 Students with physical handicaps

Examples: blind, partially sighted, hearing-impaired, linguistically handicapped, motor-impaired, brain-damaged students

Class students suffering a disorder because of brain damage with the disorder, e.g., students suffering emotional disorders brought on by brain damage 371.94

.92 Retarded students and slow learners

Class brain-damaged students in 371.91

.93 Delinquent and problem students

Examples: disruptive, hyperactive, maladjusted students

.94 Emotionally disturbed students

Examples: autistic students, mentally ill students

For delinquent and problem students, see 371.93

.95 Gifted students

.96 Students exceptional because of class distinction

Including socially and culturally disadvantaged students, upper class students; compensatory education, teacher corps

Class students socially disadvantaged because of racial, ethnic, national origin in 371.97

.97 Students exceptional because of racial, ethnic, national origin

Class here bilingual education

Do not use standard subdivisions

See also 400 for the study and teaching of languages at secondary and higher levels

---

> **372–374 Levels of education and schools**

Works treating two sublevels of education that are not subdivisions of the same number are classed with the higher level, e.g., kindergarten and first grade 372.24 (*not* 372.21)

Class comprehensive works on education and works dealing comprehensively with elementary and secondary education in 370, on schools in 371, schools and kinds of education covering more than one level with the highest appropriate level, e.g., elementary and middle schools 373.2

For higher education, see 378

372 Elementary education

Class here preschool education, comprehensive works on elementary schools

Class special education at the elementary level in 371.9

[.068] Management

Do not use; class in 372.12

.07 Education and related topics

Class professional education for elementary school teachers in 370.7

.08 History and description with respect to kinds of persons

Class elementary education of kinds of persons in 371.9

[.09] Historical, geographic, persons treatment

Do not use; class in 372.9

.1 Organization and management of elementary schools; curriculums

Class comprehensive works on specific kinds of elementary schools, e.g., private elementary schools, in 372; on specific levels of elementary education in 372.2

[.109] Historical, geographic, persons treatment

Do not use; class in 372.9

.11–.18 Organization and administration

Add to base number 372.1 the numbers following 371 in 371.1–371.8, e.g., marking and grading systems 372.12

.19 Curriculums

Class here comprehensive works on elementary school subjects and courses of study

Class courses of study in specific elementary school subjects in 372.3–372.8

.2 **Levels of elementary education**

Class organization, management, curriculums of a specific level in 372.1, specific schools in 372.93–372.99

.21 Preschool institutions

Examples: nursery school, kindergarten

Class here headstart programs

.24 Specific levels of elementary school

Including primary grades (1–3), intermediate grades (4–6), elementary sections of all-age schools

Class preschools in 372.21

> **372.3–372.8 Specific elementary school subjects**

(Option: Class here elementary textbooks; prefer specific subject, e.g., elementary textbooks on arithmetic 513)

Class comprehensive works in 372.19

.3 **Technology [*formerly* 372.8], science, health**

Including computers, robotics; ecology, environmental studies, nature study; food, diet, hygiene, nutrition; sex education

.4 **Reading**

Including methods of instruction, e.g., word recognition, phonics; remedial reading

(Option: Class here readers; prefer the language in which written, using notation 86 from Table 4, e.g., English language readers 428.6)

See also 371.91 for teaching students with reading disorders, 374 for reading instruction in adult education

.5 **Creative and manual arts**

Including design, drawing, handicrafts, modeling, sculpting, sewing

See also 372.6 for language, literature, theater; 372.87 for music

.6 **Language, literature, theater**

Including composition, grammar, handwriting, penmanship, phonetics, spelling, word study; speech

Class here language arts

Class drama and theater as methods of instruction in 372.13, phonetics in reading in 372.4

For reading, see 372.4

.64 Literature

Including storytelling

Drama is classed in 372.6

.65 Foreign languages

.7 **Mathematics**

.8 **Other studies**

Technology relocated to 372, dance to 372.6

.82 Home economics

Class here family life education

.83 Social studies

For history and geography, see 372.89

.84 Religion

.86 Physical education

Including movement education

.87 Music

.89 History and geography

.9 **Historical, geographic, persons treatment of elementary education**

Add to base number 372.9 notation 1–9 from Table 2, e.g., the elementary schools of Michigan 372.9774

373 Secondary education

Class special education at secondary levels in 371.9

[.068] Management

Do not use; class in 373.12

.07 Education and related topics

Class professional education for secondary school teachers in 370.7

.082 History and description with respect to women

Class secondary education of women in 376

.09 Historical, geographic, persons treatment

Class treatment by specific continents, countries, localities in 373.3–373.9 (*not* 373.093–373.099)

.1 Organization and management of secondary schools; curriculums

Class comprehensive works on specific types and levels in 373.2

.109 Historical, geographic, persons treatment

Class treatment by continent, country, locality in 373.3–373.9 (*not* 373.1093–373.1099)

.11–.18 Organization and management

Add to base number 373.1 the numbers following 371 in 371.1–371.8, e.g., guidance 373.14

.19 Curriculums

Class educational programs of secondary schools offering specific types of curriculums in 373.2; courses of study in a specific subject with the subject, using notation 071 from Table 1, e.g., mathematics curriculum 510.71

.2 Types and levels of secondary education

Examples: middle schools, private high schools

Including work-study programs, apprenticeship training

Class the organization and administration of a specific type or level in 373.11–373.18, curriculums in 373.19, specific schools in 373.3–373.9, continuation schools in 374, schools supported by religious groups in 377; economic aspects of apprenticeship training offered by industry in 331.25, managerial aspects in 658.3

.24 Academic and vocational schools

.246 Vocational schools

Schools that offer both a general education and a vocational program

Class comprehensive works on vocational education in 370.11, vocational training for adults in 374; a vocational school concentrating in a specific subject with the subject, using notation 071 from Table 1, e.g., a secondary school of business and commerce 650.071

.3–.9 Secondary education and schools by specific continents, countries, localities

Add to base number 373 notation 3–9 from Table 2, e.g., the secondary schools of Canada 373.71

374 Adult education

Education outside the regular sequence of schools and courses, offered to and pursued by individuals beyond school-leaving age

Including adult basic education; vocational education; self-development, self-education, programs offered through mass media, community centers for adult education; schools, e.g., correspondence schools, continuation schools

Class here continuing education, lifelong education

Class the educational role of libraries in 021.2; special education of adults in 371.9; libraries and library services in 020; programs leading to a degree, diploma, certificate with the program, e.g., high school equivalency programs 373.2, university extension programs 378

.001–.009 Standard subdivisions

375 Curriculums

Programs of study covering more than one level of education

Including curriculums and courses of study directed toward specific objectives, e.g., environmental studies, ethnic studies

Class curriculums at a specific level with the level, e.g., secondary level 373.19

See Manual at 375 for curriculums at a specific level

.000 1–.000 8 Standard subdivisions

.000 9 Historical periods

Class geographic and persons treatment in 375

376 Education of women

Secondary and higher education

Including coeducation versus separate education for women, convent education, general works on colleges for women

Class elementary education of girls in 372, specific topics in secondary education in 373.1–373.2, specific secondary schools in 373.3–373.9, specific topics in higher education for women in 378, specific colleges for women in 378.4–378.9

See also 370.19 for sexism in education

[.09] Historical, geographic, persons treatment

Do not use; class in 376

377 Schools and religion

Including religious instruction and exercises in public and other nonsectarian schools; monastic and mission schools, other schools supported by religious groups

Class schools for women supported by religious groups in 376; a specific school with its level, e.g., a specific secondary school in Ohio 373.771

378 Higher education

Class special education at higher levels in 371.9, comprehensive works on institutions supported by religious groups in 377, financial administration of publicly supported universities and colleges in 379.1; institutions for the study and teaching of a specific subject with the subject, using notation 07 from Table 1, e.g., courses of study in mathematics 510.7, Christian theological seminaries 207

.001 Philosophy and theory

Class the value of higher education in 378

.002–.005 Standard subdivisions

.006 Organizations and management

[.006 8] Management

Do not use; class in 378.1

.007 Education and related topics

Class the professional education of college and university teachers in 370.7

.007 1 Schools and courses

Do not use for schools and courses in higher education; class in 378.007

.007 9 Competitions, festivals, awards, financial support

Class financial support in 378.3

.008 History and description with respect to kinds of persons

Class special education of persons at the college and university level in 371.9

.008 2 Women

Class higher education of women in 376

.009 Historical, geographic, persons treatment

Class treatment by specific continents, countries, localities in the modern world in 378.4–378.9 (*not* 378.0094–378.0099)

.1 Organization and management; curriculums

Including methods of instruction, college level examination programs

Financial management is classed in 378

.100 1–.100 8 Standard subdivisions

.100 9 Historical, geographic, persons treatment

Class treatment by specific continents, countries, localities in the modern world in 378.4–378.9 (*not* 378.10094–378.10099)

.2 Academic degrees

Including academic costume

.3 **Student finances**

Including college costs; student loans, scholarships, fellowships, employment

Class veterans' education benefits in 362.86; finances of students in a specific field with the field, using notation 071 from Table 1, e.g., for a legal education 340.071

.4–.9 **Higher education and institutions by specific continents, countries, localities in the modern world**

Class here directories

Add to base number 378 notation 4–9 from Table 2, e.g., the University of Michigan 378.774

379 Government regulation, control, support of education

Former heading: Education and the state

Class administration of education departments in 351.85, of cabinet-level departments of education in 351.085

See Manual at 371.2 vs. 379 for school administration vs. governmental oversight, control, support of education

.09 Historical, geographic, persons treatment

Class treatment by specific continents, countries, localities in the modern world in 379.4–379.9 (*not* 379.094–379.099)

.1 **Finance, supervision, control of public education**

Including revenue sources, e.g., tuition, taxes, bonds; school boards and districts; examination, certification, appointment of teachers; supervision of curriculum, courses of study, educational materials, e.g., textbooks; school standards and accreditation

Class personnel management, e.g., evaluation, tenure of teachers in 371.1; financial administration of schools in a specific field with the field, using notation 071 from Table 1, e.g., costs of schools of education 370.71

.2 **Public education and the state**

Including compulsory education, literacy policies

Class here educational policy

Class religion in public education in 377; public regulation, control, support of private education in 379.3

.209 Historical, geographic, persons treatment

Class treatment by specific continents, countries, localities in the modern world in 379.4–379.9 (*not* 379.2094–379.2099)

.3 **Private education and the state**

Including financial assistance

.4–.9 **Government regulation, control, support of public education by specific continents, countries, localities in the modern world**

Add to base number 379 notation 4–9 from Table 2, e.g., regulation of public education in Japan 379.52

380 Commerce, communications, transportation

Use 380.01–380.09 for standard subdivisions

Aside from additions, changes, deletions, exceptions shown under specific entries, add to notation for each term identified by * as follows:

06 Organization and management
Including business organizations, e.g., individual proprietorships, partnerships, companies, public and private corporations, combinations

068 Management
Class here public and private policy, planning, programs, proposals
Do not use for plant management; class in 380–389, without adding from this table

09 Historical, geographic, persons treatment
Class specific business organizations in 06

Class public regulation and control in 351.8

See Manual at 380

SUMMARY

380.1 Commerce (Trade)
381 Internal commerce (Domestic trade)
382 International commerce (Foreign trade)
383 Postal communication
384 Communications Telecommunication
385 Railroad transportation
386 Inland waterway and ferry transportation
387 Water, air, space transportation
388 Transportation Ground transportation
389 Metrology and standardization

.1 ***Commerce (Trade)**

Including commercial policy

Class here marketing, warehousing

Class interdisciplinary works on consumption in 339.4; supply and demand in 338.1–338.5; cooperative marketing in 334; restrictive practices in, business organizations engaged in commerce in 338.6–338.8

For domestic trade, see 381; foreign trade, 382

See Manual at 380.1 vs. 658.8

.102 9 Commercial miscellany

Class here interdisciplinary works on commercial miscellany

Class evaluation and purchasing manuals in 381.3; commercial miscellany respecting specific goods and services with the goods and services, using notation 029 from Table 1, e.g., buyers' guides for tools 621.90029

A noncurrent offer for sale of a broad range of products that is used primarily to illustrate customs of an earlier period is classed in 909 or 930–990

*Add as instructed under 380

[.3] **Communications**

Relocated to 384

[.5] **Transportation**

Relocated to 388

> **381–382 General internal and international commerce (Trade)**

Class here marketing

Class comprehensive works in 380.1; supply and demand in 338.1–338.5; restrictive practices in, business organizations engaged in commerce in 338.6–338.8

381 *Internal commerce (Domestic trade)

Retail and wholesale trade

Including interstate and interregional commerce; garage, yard, apartment sales

.3 **Commercial policy**

Including comprehensive works on evaluation of commodities to be purchased, interdisciplinary evaluation and purchasing manuals, consumer protection

Class here consumer problems and their alleviation, consumerism

Class product hazards in 363.19; evaluation and purchasing guides and consumer education for household and personal products and services in 640.73; evaluation and purchasing manuals for specific products or services with the subject, using notation 029 from Table 1, e.g., manual on evaluating tools 621.90029

Commercial policy with respect to specific kinds of domestic trade, to specific commodities and services, to specific groups of commodities and services is classed in 381

*Add as instructed under 380

382 *International commerce (Foreign trade)

Import and export trade

Including commercial and tariff policy, balance of trade, customs and duties, import quotas; embargoes on, licensing of imports; export controls and restrictions, e.g., licensing, inspection, subsidies; trade agreements, e.g., General Agreement on Tariffs and Trade (GATT), European Economic Community (European Common Market, EEC)

Class here trade between nations and their colonies, protectorates, trusts

Class tax aspects of custom duties in 336.2, international economics in 337

.01 Philosophy and theory

Class theories in 382

[.1–.9] General aspects of international commerce, tariff policy, trade agreements and their implementation

Numbers discontinued; class in 382

> **383–388 Communications and transportation**

General aspects: rates, finance, forms of ownership, public and private policy, activities, services, facilities

Class comprehensive works on communications and transportation, on transportation in 388, on communications in 384

383 Postal communication

Including instantaneous facsimile transmission

Class comprehensive works on communications in 384, on facsimile transmission in 384.1

See also 769.56 for philately

.06 Organizations and management

Class postal organizations in 383

[.09] Historical, geographic, persons treatment

Do not use; class in 383

*Add as instructed under 380

384 *Communications [*formerly* 380.3] *Telecommunication

Example: motion pictures

Alarm and warning systems relocated to 363.1

Class comprehensive works on communications and transportation in 388

For postal communication, see 383

See also 302.2 for sociology of communication

See Manual at 384 vs. 791.4 for motion pictures, radio, television; 621.382 vs. 621.39, 004.6, 384 for digital communications

.1 ***Telegraph**

Including submarine cable telegraph [*formerly* 384.4]; Morse and other code telegraph; printing telegraph (teletype, telex, facsimile, stock tickers)

Class comprehensive works on electronic mail in 384.3, postal facsimile transmission in 383

For radiotelegraph, see 384.5

.102 8 Auxiliary techniques and procedures, materials

Class apparatus and equipment in 384.1

.3 ***Computer communication**

Transfer of computer-based information by any of various media (e.g., coaxial cable or radio waves) from one computer to another or between computers and terminals

Including electronic bulletin boards, electronic mail, teletex; videotex, e.g., teletext, viewdata

Class here links between computers via telephone lines [*formerly* 384.6]; computer communications networks

Class interdisciplinary works on computer communications in 004.6, postal facsimile transmission in 383

See Manual at 384.3 vs. 004.6

.302 85 Data processing Computer applications

Class here computer science applied to economic and related aspects of providing computer communication to the public

[.4] **Submarine cable telegraph**

Relocated to 384.1

*Add as instructed under 380

.5 ***Wireless communication**

Including radiotelegraph, satellite communication; radiotelephone, e.g., citizens band radio, portable telephones

Class a specific form of satellite communication with the subject, e.g., television transmission by satellite 384.55

.54 *Radiobroadcasting

Class here interdisciplinary works on radio- and television broadcasting, public aspects of amateur radio

Class techniques of producing radio programs in 791.44, a specific type of program with the type, e.g., news broadcasts 070.1

Class television broadcasting in 384.55

See Manual at 384 vs. 791.4

.55 *Television

Including general broadcasting (free television), community antenna television (CATV) systems; cable, closed-circuit communication, pay, premium, subscription television; video products, e.g., video cassette recorders (VCR's), videotapes

Class techniques of producing television programs in 791.45; a specific type of television program with the type, e.g., news broadcasts 070.1

See Manual at 384 vs. 791.4

.6 ***Telephone**

Class here comprehensive works on wire and cable communication

Links between computers via telephone lines relocated to 384.3

For telegraph, see 384.1; radiotelephone, 384.5; cable television, 384.55

.602 8 Auxiliary techniques and procedures, materials

Class apparatus and equipment in 384.6

385 *Railroad transportation

Including narrow-gage and monorail railroads; ship railway systems; unitized cargo transportation, e.g., piggyback operations

Class here standard- and broad-gage railroads

Class comprehensive works on transportation, on ground transportation in 388, container-ship operations in 387.5

For local rail transit systems, see 388.4

See Manual at 629.04 vs. 388 for trains

*Add as instructed under 380

386 *Inland waterway and ferry transportation

Transportation via rivers, canals, lakes

Including ports

Class comprehensive works on water transportation in 387, on transportation in 388

See Manual at 386 vs. 387.1 for ports; 629.04 vs. 388 for ships

387 Water, air, space transportation

Class here comprehensive works on water transportation

Class comprehensive works on transportation in 388

For inland waterway and ferry transportation, see 386

See Manual at 629.04 vs. 388 for vehicles

.001–.009 Standard subdivisions of water transportation

Notation from Table 1 as modified under 380, e.g., water transportation business organizations 387.006

.1 Ports

Activities, services, facilities

Including navigational aids, e.g., lighthouses

Class inland ports in 386

See Manual at 386 vs. 387.1

.2 Ships

General aspects: rating, tonnage

Class here economic aspects of ships [*formerly* 387.5]

Class use of ships in specific activities and services in 387.5, in inland waterway transportation in 386

.5 *Ocean (Marine) transportation

Including coastwise and intercoastal routes, salvage

Economic aspects of ships relocated to 387.2

Class seaports in 387.1

For ships, see 387.2

.7 *Air transportation

Including airports and landing fields

.8 *Space transportation

*Add as instructed under 380

388 *Transportation [*formerly* 380.5] *Ground transportation

Passenger and freight services, mass transportation

Class here interdisciplinary works on transportation, comprehensive works on communications and transportation

Class postal transportation in 383, transportation safety in 363.12, transportation security in 363.2, transportation technology in 629.04; services designed to facilitate the use of transportation by the handicapped in 362.4, by the elderly in 362.6

For communications, see 384; railroad transportation, 385; water, air, space transportation, 387

See also 385 for railroads combined with other transportation systems

See Manual at 629.04 vs. 388 for vehicles

.1 ***Roads and highways**

Including bicycle and pedestrian paths

Class highway operations, services, uses in 388.3

For urban roads and streets, see 388.4

.3 ***Vehicular transportation**

Including traffic flow and maintenance, e.g., lighting, traffic control, traffic signs; vehicles (e.g., automobiles, buses, trucks, motorcycles, air-cushion vehicles, off-road vehicles, snowmobiles, wagons, stagecoaches) and their services, terminals, stations, stops

Class air-cushion ships for inland waterways in 386, for ocean transportation in 387.2; urban vehicular transportation in 388.4, police services in traffic control in 363.2

.4 ***Local transportation**

Including vehicular and pedestrian traffic; urban roads and streets, bicycle paths, sidewalks; services of automobiles, buses, trucks; local rail transit systems, e.g., subways, tramways; terminals, stations, stops, parking facilities and their services

Class here urban and suburban transportation, rapid transit, mass transit, commuter services

Class vehicles in 388.3, police services in traffic control in 363.2, a specific aspect of parking with the aspect, e.g., city planning for parking facilities 711

See also 385 for interurban railways

.5 ***Pipeline transportation**

389 Metrology and standardization

Metrology: social use of systems of measurement

Including time systems and standards, e.g., daylight savings time; metric system and its adoption

Class interdisciplinary works on measurement in 530.8

*Add as instructed under 380

390 Customs, etiquette, folklore

Class here folkways

Use 390.001–390.009 for standard subdivisions

Class customs of military life in 355.1

See Manual at 390

SUMMARY

390.01–.09 Standard subdivisions of customs
391 Costume and personal appearance
392 Customs of life cycle and domestic life
393 Death customs
394 General customs
395 Etiquette (Manners)
398 Folklore
399 Customs of war and diplomacy

.01–.07 Standard subdivisions of customs

.08 History and description of customs with respect to kinds of persons

Class customs of persons by economic status, by social class, by occupation in 390

.09 Historical, geographic, persons treatment of customs

> **391–394 Customs**

Class comprehensive works on customs, customs of specific economic, social, occupational classes in 390

For customs of war and diplomacy, see 399

391 Costume and personal appearance

Including hair styles, body contours, use of cosmetics and perfume, personal cleanliness and hygiene, tattooing; interdisciplinary works on jewelry

Class here interdisciplinary works on costume, clothing, fashion

Costumes and clothing associated with a specific occasion relocated to the occasion in 392–394, e.g., wedding apparel 392

Class interdisciplinary works on making jewelry in 739.27; a specific aspect of costume and clothing with the aspect, e.g., military uniforms 355.1, stage costuming 792, clothing construction 646.4

For fashion design, see 746.9

See Manual at 391 vs. 646, 746.9 for costume

.001–.007 Standard subdivisions

.008 History and description with respect to kinds of persons

Class persons by social and economic characteristics, religious groups in 391

[.008 1–.008 4] Sex and age groups

Do not use; class in 391

.009 Historical, geographic, persons treatment

392 Customs of life cycle and domestic life

Examples: customs connected with birth, child rearing, attainment of puberty and majority, courtship, betrothal, weddings, marriage, relations between sexes

Including cooking, furnishings

For death customs, see 393

See also 394.1 for eating and drinking customs

393 Death customs

Including burial, mourning

394 General customs

Including games, dances; official ceremonies and observations; pageants, processions, parades; fairs, customs of chivalry, dueling, suicide

Class pageants, processions, parades associated with a specific activity with the activity, e.g., Thanksgiving Day parade 394.2

See also 355.1 for military ceremonies

See Manual at 394 vs. 791.6 for pageants, processions, parades

.1 Eating, drinking; using drugs

Situations and methods of use, prohibited uses

Including alcoholic beverages; specific meals, e.g., tea

Class here food and meals

.2 Special occasions

Examples: birthdays, carnivals, fast days, festivals, holidays

Class the technology or craft associated with holidays with the technology or craft, e.g., making fireworks 662, decorating Easter eggs 745.594

Pageants, processions, parades, official ceremonies are classed in 394

See Manual at 394.2 vs. 263, 290 for religious occasions

395 Etiquette (Manners)

Prescriptive and practical works on social behavior

Including hospitality and entertainment, social correspondence

Class customs in 391–394, protocol of diplomacy in 327.2, military etiquette in 355.1

See Manual at 395

[.081–.084] With respect to sex and age groups

Do not use; class in 395

398 Folklore

Including origin, role, function of themes and subjects of folklore and superstitions as cultural and social phenomena; chapbooks

See also 291.1 for religious mythology, 800 for literature by identifiable authors, anonymous literary classics

.09 Historical, geographic, persons treatment of sociology of folklore

Class historical, geographic, persons treatment of folk literature in 398.209

✓ .2 **Folk literature** Greek / Roman mythology

Folklore as literature

Class here literary appraisal and criticism, interdisciplinary works on mythology

Class religious mythology in 291.1

For minor forms of folk literature, see 398.6–398.9

See Manual at 398.2; 398.2 vs. 291.1 for mythology; 800 vs. 398.2

.21 Tales and lore of paranatural and legendary beings of human and semihuman form

Examples: centaurs, fairies, giants, mermaids, vampires

Class here fairy tales

Class a specific fairy tale with the subject of the tale, e.g., Puss in Boots 398.24, Cinderella 398.27

See Manual at 398.21 vs. 398.22

.22 Tales and lore of historical and quasi-historical persons and events

Examples: heroes, kings, witches

See Manual at 398.21 vs. 398.22

.23 Tales and lore of places and times

Real and legendary

See also 398.209 for tales originating in specific places

.24 Tales and lore of plants and animals

Real and legendary

See Manual at 800 vs. 591, 636, 398.24 for animals

.25 Ghost stories

.26 Tales and lore involving physical phenomena

Real and legendary

Examples: heavenly bodies, weather, fire, water, minerals

.27 Tales and lore of everyday human life

Examples: birth, love, marriage, death, occupations, recreation, dwellings, food

See Manual at 615.8

> **398.6–398.9 Minor forms of folk literature**

Class here literary appraisal and criticism

Class comprehensive works in 398.2

.6 **Riddles**

Class here interdisciplinary works

Class riddles as recreation in 793.73, as literature in 808.88

.8 **Rhymes and rhyming games**

Examples: counting-out and jump rope rhymes, street cries and songs, tongue twisters

Class here nursery rhymes

.9 **Proverbs**

Class here folk aphorisms

399 Customs of war and diplomacy

Examples: dances, peace pipe, treatment of captives, e.g., scalping

Class cannibalism in 394, protocol of diplomacy in 327.2, customs of military life in 355.1

400

400 Language

Class here interdisciplinary works on language and literature

Bilingualism is classed in 400, without use of 401–409; specific instances of bilingualism are classed in 420–490 with the language dominant in the country in which the linguistic interaction occurs, without use of notation 01–09 from Table 1, e.g., a discussion of Spanish-English bilingualism in the United States 420

Class interdisciplinary works on bilingualism in 306.4; the language of a specific discipline or subject with the discipline or subject, e.g., language of chemistry 540

For literature, see 800; rhetoric, 808

See Manual at 400; 400 vs. 800; 400 vs. 909, 930–990

401 Philosophy and theory

Including semantics [*formerly* 412], language acquisition, psycholinguistics, international and universal languages, semiotics

Sociolinguistics relocated to 306.4

Class ethnolinguistics in 306.4; artificial languages in 499; specific international languages with the language in 420–490, e.g., Latin as a diplomatic language 470

Psychology of bilingualism is classed in 400

See Manual at 401 vs. 412, 415, 306.4 for semantics; 407, T1—07 vs. 410.7, 418.007, T4—8007, 401 for language learning

402 Miscellany

403 Dictionaries, encyclopedias, concordances

Class here dictionaries, encyclopedias, concordances that treat comprehensively both language and literature

Class dictionaries, encyclopedias, concordances of linguistics in 410.3, general polygot dictionaries in 413

405–407 Standard subdivisions

See Manual at 407, T1—07 vs. 410.7, 418.007, T4—8007, 401 for education and related topics

408 Treatment of language with respect to kinds of persons

.9 Treatment of language with respect to specific racial, ethnic, national groups

Class ethnolinguistics in 306.4

409 Geographic and persons treatment

Language history not limited by area relocated to 417

Class specific languages and groups of languages in 420–490

See also 410.9 for geographic and persons treatment of linguistics

410 Linguistics

Science and structure of spoken and written language

Class here comprehensive works on Indo-European languages

Class linguistics of specific languages in 420–490

For specific Indo-European languages, see 420–480

See Manual at 410; 411–418

.1–.9 **Standard subdivisions of linguistics**

Class standard subdivisions of language and languages in 401–409

See Manual at 407, T1—07 vs. 410.7, 418.007, T4—8007, 401 for education and related topics

411 Writing systems

Examples: alphabets, ideographs

Including paleography [*formerly* 417], abbreviations

412 Etymology

Semantics other than the history of word meanings relocated to 401

Class comprehensive works on historical linguistics in 417; specific aspects of etymology with the aspect, e.g., phonetic development of words 414

See Manual at 401 vs. 412, 415, 306.4 for semantics

413 Dictionaries

Including specialized dictionaries, e.g., dictionaries of abbreviations

Class here polyglot dictionaries

.028 Techniques, procedures, apparatus, equipment, materials

Class here lexicography

414 Phonology

Class comprehensive works on phonology and morphology or syntax in 415

See Manual at 808.1 vs. 414, T4—1 for prosody

415 Structural systems (Grammar)

Historical and descriptive study of morphology and syntax

Class here comprehensive works on morphology, syntax, and phonology

For phonology, see 414

See Manual at 401 vs. 412, 415, 306.4 for semantics

417 Dialectology and historical (diachronic) linguistics

Historical (diachronic) linguistics: study of the development of language over time

Including language history not limited by area [*formerly also* 409]

Paleography relocated to 411

Class change in and the history of specific elements of language with the element, e.g., grammar 415

418 Standard usage (Prescriptive linguistics) Applied linguistics

Including interpretation, translation; reading

Class dictionaries and lexicography in 413

.001–.009 Standard subdivisions

See Manual at 407, T1—07 vs. 410.7, 418.007, T4—8007, 401 for education and related topics

419 Structured verbal language other than spoken and written

Class here manual language for the deaf

Class nonlinguistic (nonstructured) communication in 302.2

> ## 420–490 Specific languages

Class here comprehensive works on specific languages and their literatures

Except for additions, changes, deletions, exceptions shown under specific entries, add to base number for each language identified by * notation 01–86 from Table 4, e.g., Portuguese grammar 469.5. The base number is the number given for the language unless the schedule specifies a different number

The numbers used in this schedule for individual languages do not necessarily correspond exactly with those in 810–890

Class comprehensive works in 410

For literatures of specific languages, see 810–890

See Manual at 420–490

> **420–480 Specific Indo-European languages**

Class comprehensive works in 410

For East Indo-European and Celtic languages, see 491

420 *English and Old English (Anglo-Saxon)

Base number for English: 42

Special interpretations of Table 4 for use with English appear below under 427–428

421–425 Description and analysis of standard English

Notation from Table 4

427 Historical and geographic variations, modern nongeographic variations

Including Middle English

For Old English (Anglo-Saxon), see 429

.001–.009 Standard subdivisions

428 Standard English usage (Prescriptive linguistics) Applied linguistics

Class here Basic English

Notation from Table 4

429 Old English (Anglo-Saxon)

See also 427 for Middle English

430 Germanic (Teutonic) languages German

For English and Old English (Anglo-Saxon), see 420

.01–.09 Standard subdivisions of Germanic (Teutonic) languages

> **430.1–438.6 Subdivisions of *German language**

Base number: 43

A special interpretation of Table 4 for use with German appears below under 437

Class comprehensive works in 430

431–435 Description and analysis of standard German

Notation from Table 4

*Add to base number as instructed under 420–490

437 Historical and geographic variations, modern nongeographic variations

Including Yiddish

.001–.009 Standard subdivisions

438 Standard German usage (Prescriptive linguistics) Applied linguistics

Notation from Table 4

439 Other Germanic (Teutonic) languages

.3 Dutch, Flemish, Afrikaans

.7 *Swedish

.8 Danish and Norwegian

440 Romance languages French

For Italian, Romanian, Rhaeto-Romanic, see 450; Spanish and Portuguese, 460

.01–.09 Standard subdivisions of Romance languages

> **440.1–448.6 Subdivisions of *French language**

Base number: 44

Class comprehensive works in 440

441–448 French

Notation from Table 4

449 Provençal and Catalan

450 *Italian, Romanian, Rhaeto-Romanic languages

Base number for Italian: 45

451–458 Italian

Notation from Table 4

459 Romanian and Rhaeto-Romanic

*Add to base number as instructed under 420–490

460 Spanish and Portuguese languages

.01–.09 Standard subdivisions for comprehensive works on Spanish and Portuguese

---

> **460.1–468.6 Subdivisions of *Spanish language**

Base number: 46

Class comprehensive works in 460

461–468 Spanish

Notation from Table 4

469 *Portuguese

470 Italic languages Latin

Class comprehensive works on Latin and Greek in 480

For Romance languages, see 440

See Manual at 470 for Latin

.01–.09 Standard subdivisions of Italic languages

> **470.1–478.6 Subdivisions of *Latin language**

Base number: 47

Special interpretations of Table 4 for use with Latin appear below under 471–478

Class comprehensive works in 470

471–475 Description and analysis of classical Latin

Class here classical revival (medieval and modern) Latin

Notation from Table 4

477 Old (Preclassical), Postclassical, Vulgar Latin

478 Classical Latin usage (Prescriptive linguistics) Applied linguistics

Class here classical revival (medieval and modern) Latin usage

Notation from Table 4

479 Other Italic languages

Including Osco-Umbrian languages

*Add to base number as instructed under 420–490

480 Hellenic languages Classical Greek

Classical Greek: the Greek that flourished between 750 and 350 B.C.

Class here comprehensive works on classical languages

For Latin, see 470

.01–.09 Standard subdivisions of classical languages

.1–.9 Standard subdivisions of Hellenic languages, of classical Greek

---

> **481–488 Subdivisions of *classical, preclassical, postclassical Greek**

Base number: 48

Dialects of classical Greek are classed in the numbers for classical Greek (480.1–485, 488)

Special interpretations of Table 4 for use with Greek appear below under 487

Class comprehensive works in 480

481–485 Description and analysis of classical Greek

Notation from Table 4

487 Preclassical and Postclassical Greek

Examples: Biblical, Byzantine, Koine (Hellenistic) Greek

Class modern Greek in 489

488 Classical Greek usage (Prescriptive linguistics) Applied linguistics

Notation from Table 4

489 Other Hellenic languages

Including modern Greek, e.g., Katharevusa and Demotic

490 Other languages

491 East Indo-European and Celtic languages

Examples: Albanian, Armenian; Baltic languages, e.g., Latvian, Lithuanian; Indic languages, e.g., Bengali, Hindi, Sanskrit; Iranian languages, e.g., Persian

.6 Celtic languages

Examples: Breton, Cornish, Irish and Scottish Gaelic, Welsh (Cymric)

*Add to base number as instructed under 420–490

.7 **East Slavic languages Russian**

Examples: Belorussian, Ukrainian

.700 1–.700 9 Standard subdivisions of East Slavic languages

.701–.786 Subdivisions of *Russian

Base number: 491.7

.8 **Slavic languages**

Examples: Bulgarian, Czech, Polish, Serbo-Croatian, Slovak, Slovenian

Class here Balto-Slavic languages

Class Baltic languages in 491, East Slavic languages in 491.7

492 Afro-Asiatic (Hamito-Semitic) languages Semitic languages

Examples: Arabic, Aramaic, Ethiopic languages

For non-Semitic Afro-Asiatic languages, see 493

.4 **Hebrew**

493 Non-Semitic Afro-Asiatic languages

Former heading: Hamitic and Chad languages

Examples: Berber, Chadic, Coptic, Cushitic, Omotic languages

494 Ural-Altaic, Paleosiberian, Dravidian languages

Examples: Estonian, Finnish, Hungarian, Lapp; Mongolian, Turkish; Tamil, Telugu

495 Languages of East and Southeast Asia Sino-Tibetan languages

Examples: Burmese, Tibetan

Including Munda languages

.1 **Chinese**

.6 **Japanese**

.7 **Korean**

.9 **Annam-Muong, Mon-Khmer, Thai (Tai) languages**

Examples: Austroasiatic languages, e.g., Khmer (Cambodian), Vietnamese; Lao, Thai (Siamese)

Munda languages are classed in 495

496 African languages

Examples: Fulani (Fulah), Ibo (Igbo), Yoruba; Bantu languages, e.g., Swahili, Zulu

For Afro-Asiatic languages, see 492

497 North American native languages

Examples: Inuit, Navajo

Class here comprehensive works on North and South American native languages

For South American native languages, see 498

498 South American native languages

Examples: Guaraní, Quechua

499 Nonaustronesian languages of Oceania, Austronesian languages, miscellaneous languages

Miscellaneous languages limited to Basque, Caucasic, Elamite, Etruscan, Hurrian, artificial languages

Examples: Australian, Malay, Melanesian, Micronesian, Papuan, Polynesian languages

Use of this number for other languages discontinued; class in 490

500

500 Natural sciences and mathematics

Class here comprehensive works on science and technology

Class scientific principles of a subject with the subject, using notation 01 from Table 1, e.g., scientific principles of photography 770.1

Natural history is classed in 508

For applied sciences, see 600

See Manual at 500 vs. 001; 500 vs. 600

.2 Physical sciences

For astronomy and allied sciences, see 520; physics, 530; chemistry, crystallography, mineralogy, 540; earth sciences, 550

See Manual at 530 vs. 500.2

.5 Space sciences

Class astronomy in 520, earth sciences in other worlds in 550; space science aspects of other subjects with the subject, e.g., physical chemistry in space 541.30919

.8 History and description with respect to kinds of persons

Add to base number 500.8 the numbers following −08 in notation 081–089 from Table 1, e.g., women scientists 500.82

501 Philosophy and theory

Class scientific method as a general research technique in 001.4, scientific method applied in natural sciences in 500

502 Miscellany

.8 Auxiliary techniques and procedures; apparatus, equipment, materials

Including interdisciplinary works on microscopes [*formerly* 535], microscopy

Class manufacture of microscopes in 681

503 Dictionaries, encyclopedias, concordances

505 Serial publications

506 Organizations and management

507 Education and related topics

.8 Use of apparatus and equipment in study and teaching

Class here science fair projects, science projects in schools

508 Natural history

Class here description and surveys of phenomena in nature

Do not use for the history and description of the natural sciences and mathematics with respect to groups of persons; class in 500.8

Class the natural history of living organisms in 574

See Manual at 508 vs. 574, 910, 304.2

.09 Historical and persons treatment

Class geographic treatment in 508.3–508.9

.3 Treatment by areas, regions, places in general; by specific continents, countries, localities in the ancient world

Add to base number 508.3 notation 1 or 3 from Table 2, e.g., a natural history of the sea 508.3162, of ancient Greece 508.338

.4–.9 Treatment by specific continents, countries, localities in the modern world; extraterrestrial worlds

Add to base number 508 notation 4–9 from Table 2, e.g., natural history of Brazil 508.81

509 Historical, geographic, persons treatment

Class historical, geographic, persons treatment of natural phenomena in 508

510 Mathematics

See Manual at 005.1 vs. 510 for distinctions regarding algorithms and programming; 510 for branches of mathematics taught in elementary and secondary schools

SUMMARY

510.1	**Philosophy and theory**
511	**General topics**
512	**Algebra and number theory**
513	**Arithmetic**
514	**Topology**
515	**Analysis**
516	**Geometry**
519	**Probabilities and applied mathematics**

.1 Philosophy and theory

Class mathematical logic in 511.3

511 General topics

Including approximations, graph theory, combinatorial analysis, algorithms, mathematical models (simulation)

Class the topics found here applied to a specific branch of mathematics with the branch, e.g., mathematical models of probabilities 519.2

.3 Mathematical (Symbolic) logic

Including automata theory [*formerly also* 001.53], sequential machines [*formerly also* 629.8], Boolean algebra, formal languages, machine theory, recursion theory, set theory, sets

Mathematical modeling is classed in 511

512 Algebra and number theory

Including groups, fields, rings; linear, multilinear algebras

Class here modern algebra (abstract algebra combined with number theory), precalculus

Basic textbooks at the elementary and secondary levels are classed in 512.9

.001–.009 Standard subdivisions

.9 Foundations of algebra

Including theory of equations; matrices, determinants

.900 1–.900 9 Standard subdivisions

513 Arithmetic

Business arithmetic relocated to 650.01

.2 Specific arithmetic operations

Examples: addition, subtraction, multiplication, division; root extraction

Including counting; fractions, percentage; exponents, logarithms

.5 Numeration systems

Examples: binary (base 2), decimal (base 10), sexadecimal (hexadecimal, base 16) systems

514 Topology

Examples: algebraic topology, differential topology

Class here analysis situs

Class topological vector spaces in 515

See also 512 for topological algebras

515 Analysis

Examples: differential and integral calculus and equations, functional analysis

Class here calculus, comprehensive works on the theory of functions

Class applied numerical analysis in 519.4, theory of a specific function or group of functions with the subject, e.g., functions in algebra 512

[.3–.9] **Topics of analysis**

Numbers discontinued; class in 515

516 Geometry

Examples: affine, descriptive, projective geometries

Including geometric constructions and shapes, e.g., angles, arcs, curves, squares

For topology, see 514

.001–.009 Standard subdivisions

.2 **Euclidean geometry**

Including famous geometry problems, e.g., trisecting an angle, squaring the circle

Class a specific type of Euclidean geometry with the type, e.g., Euclidean analytic geometry 516.3

.200 1–.200 9 Standard subdivisions

.22 Plane geometry

.23 Solid geometry

.24 Trigonometry

.3 **Analytic geometries**

Examples: algebraic, differential, integral geometry

Including analytic trigonometry

.9 **Non-Euclidean geometries**

Examples: Bolyai, Lobachevski geometries

Class a specific type of non-Euclidean geometry with the type, e.g., non-Euclidean analytic geometries 516.3

519 Probabilities and applied mathematics

Class a specific application with the application, e.g., game theory in gambling 795.01

.2 **Probabilities**

Including probabilistic processes, e.g., Markov processes; random walks (Monte Carlo method)

Class here random (stochastic) processes, games of chance

Class probabilities applied to statistical mathematics in 519.5

.3 **Game theory**

Class here mathematical optimization

Class control theory in 515, games of chance in 519.2

.4 **Applied numerical analysis**

Coding theory relocated to 003, computer mathematics to 004.01

.5 **Statistical mathematics**

Including the theory of sampling; measures of central tendency, e.g., median, mean; measures of deviation; multivariate analysis; analysis of variance and covariance; regression analysis; statistical inference, e.g., decision theory, hypothesis testing; time-series analysis

Class obtaining, arranging, interpreting statistical data in 001.4

.7 **Programming**

Examples: lincar and nonlinear

Do not use standard subdivisions

.8 **Special topics**

Examples: queuing, quality control

520 Astronomy and allied sciences

See Manual at 520 vs. 523.1 for descriptions of the universe

SUMMARY

.1 **Philosophy and theory**

Class here theoretical astronomy [*formerly* 521]

Class chemical principles in 523, physical principles in 523.01

[.28] Auxiliary techniques and procedures; apparatus, equipment, materials

Do not use; class in 522

> **521–525 Astronomy**

Class comprehensive works in 520, geodetic and positional astronomy in 526

521 Celestial mechanics

Including gravity, orbits

Comprehensive works on theoretical astronomy relocated to 520.1, theoretical astronomy of specific celestial bodies and phenomena relocated to 523

Class celestial mechanics applied to the description of specific celestial bodies and kinds of bodies in 523

522 Techniques, procedures, apparatus, equipment, materials of astronomy

Class here practical astronomy

Class applications to specific celestial bodies and phenomena in 523

[.028] Auxiliary techniques and procedures; apparatus, equipment, materials

Do not use; class in 522

523 Specific celestial bodies and phenomena

Including cosmochemistry, zodiac

Class here the theoretical astronomy of specific celestial bodies and phenomena [*formerly* 521]

Do not use standard subdivisions; class in 520.1–520.9

Use of this number for comprehensive works on descriptive astronomy discontinued; class in 520

Class phenomena of celestial bodies directly comparable to terrestrial phenomena in 550, e.g., structural geology of Mars 551.80999

See also 133.5 for astrology

.01 Astrophysics

For celestial mechanics, see 521

[.02] Cosmochemistry

Number discontinued; class in 523

.1 The universe; space, galaxies, quasars

Including interstellar matter, e.g., diffuse and planetary nebulas

Class here cosmology

See also 523.8 for black holes

See Manual at 520 vs. 523.1; 523.8 vs. 523.1 for stars and galaxies

.2 Solar system

For specific parts, see 523.3–523.7

> **523.3–523.7 Specific parts of the solar system**

Class comprehensive works in 523.2

.3 **Moon**

.4 **Planets**

Class here comprehensive works on planets, satellites, rings

For earth, see 525; satellites and rings, transits, occultations, see 523.9

.5 **Meteoroids, solar wind, zodiacal light**

.6 **Comets**

.7 **Sun**

Class solar wind in 523.5

.8 **Stars**

Including black holes

Class here comprehensive works on stars and galaxies

For galaxies, quasars, see 523.1; sun, 523.7

See Manual at 523.8 vs. 523.1

.802 8 Auxiliary techniques and procedures; apparatus, equipment, materials

Class testing and measurement in 523.8

.9 **Satellites and rings; eclipses, transits, occultations**

For the moon, see 523.3

525 Earth (Astronomical geography)

Including astronomical aspects of seasons

Ocean tides relocated to 551.47

Class interdisciplinary aspects of the seasons in 508

For geodesy, see 526

526 Mathematical geography

Including geodesy

Class here cartography (map making)

Class map-making for a specific purpose with the purpose, e.g., military map-making 623.7

For astronomical geography, see 525

See also 912 for maps, map reading

.022 Illustrations

Including map drawing [*formerly* 526.8]

.3 **Geodetic surveying**

Surveying in which curvature of the earth is considered

[.8] **Map drawing and projections**

Use of this number for map projections discontinued; class in 526

Map drawing relocated to 526.022

.9 **Surveying**

Including photogrammetry

Class here plane surveying (surveying in which curvature of the earth is disregarded)

Class engineering surveys in 622–629

For geodetic surveying, see 526.3

527 Celestial navigation

Class celestial navigation of specific craft with the craft, e.g., of nautical craft 623.8

528 Nautical almanacs

Variant name: astronomical almanacs, ephemerides

Class tables of specific celestial bodies in 523

529 Chronology

Including calendars, horology, intervals of time

Class time systems and standards in 389, instruments for measuring time in 681.1

530 Physics

Class astrophysics in 523.01; physical chemistry in 541.3; general physics of specific elements, compounds, mixtures in 546

See Manual at 530 vs. 500.2; 530 vs. 540 for topics common to physics and chemistry; 621 vs. 530

SUMMARY

530.01–.09	**Standard subdivisions**
.1–.8	**[Theories and mathematical physics, states of matter, testing and measurement]**
531	**Mechanics Solid mechanics**
532	**Fluid mechanics Liquid mechanics**
533	**Gas mechanics (Pneumatics)**
534	**Sound and related vibrations**
535	**Light and related radiations**
536	**Heat**
537	**Electricity and electronics**
538	**Magnetism**
539	**Modern physics**

.01 Philosophy and theory

Class theories and mathematical physics in 530.1

.02 Miscellany

.028 Auxiliary techniques and procedures; apparatus, equipment, materials

Class instrumentation in 530, testing and measurement in 530.8

.03–.09 Standard subdivisions

.1 **Theories and mathematical physics**

Including relativity theory, quantum mechanics (quantum theory), statistical mechanics

Class applications to specific states of matter in 530.4

.4 **States of matter**

Class crystallography in 548

.8 **Testing and measurement**

Including interdisciplinary works on systems of measurement, e.g., metric system

Class here interdisciplinary works on measurement, on mensuration

Class social use of systems of measurement in 389; instrumentation for measurement in 530; measurement theory in 530.1; measurement in a specific subject with the subject, using notation 028 from Table 1, e.g., psychological measurement 150.28

531 Mechanics Solid mechanics

Variant names for mechanics: classical mechanics, continuum mechanics

When "mechanics" is used in its broad meaning, covering both quantum and classical mechanics, it is classed in 530

Including dynamics, energy, gravity, kinematics, kinetics, statics, vibration

Simple machines relocated to 621.8

For fluid mechanics, see 532

532 Fluid mechanics Liquid mechanics

Variant name for liquid mechanics: hydraulics, hydromechanics

For gas mechanics, see 533

.001–.009 Standard subdivisions

533 Gas mechanics (Pneumatics)

Including aerodynamics

534 Sound and related vibrations

Class acoustical properties of states of matter as states in 530.4

.5 **Subsonic and ultrasonic vibrations**

535 Light and related radiations

Class here optics

Microscopes relocated to 502.8

Class optical properties of states of matter as states in 530.4

.01 Spectral regions; philosophy and theory

Including infrared and ultraviolet radiation

.028 Auxiliary techniques and procedures; apparatus, equipment, materials

Class spectroscopy in 535.8

.5 Beams

Including polarization

Lasers relocated to 621.36

.6 Color

.8 Spectroscopy

Class here comprehensive works on spectroscopy in physics

Do not use standard subdivisions

Fiber optics relocated to 621.36

Class interdisciplinary works on spectroscopy in 543; each kind of spectroscopy in physics other than of light and related vibrations with the kind, e.g., microwave spectroscopy 537.5; a specific application with the application, e.g., qualitative analysis 544

536 Heat

Including cryogenics, thermodynamics

Class thermal properties of states of matter as states in 530.4

.01 Philosophy and theory

Class theories in 536

537 Electricity and electronics

Class here electromagnetism

Class electrical and electronic properties of specific states of matter as states in 530.4

For magnetism, see 538

See also 530.1 for electromagnetic theory of matter; 539.2 for electromagnetic spectrum, electromagnetic waves and radiations

.01 Philosophy and theory

Class theories in 537

.5 **Electronics**

Including microwaves, radio waves, photoelectricity

Circuitry relocated to 621.3815

For semiconductors, see 537.6

.6 **Electric currents (Electrodynamics) and thermoelectricity**

Including semiconductors, superconductivity

Alternating current relocated to 621.31

538 Magnetism

Including natural magnets; geomagnetism, e.g., auroras, ionosphere

Artificial magnets relocated to 621.34

Class magnetic properties of specific states of matter as states in 530.4

539 Modern physics

Including the structure of matter, molecular physics

Use 539 for studies of atomic and molecular structure only when made without significant reference to chemical characteristics; prefer 541.2 if there is discussion of chemical phenomena

Class here quantum physics

Class modern physics of a specific subject in physics with the subject, e.g., of light beams 535.5

For quantum mechanics, see 530.1; states of matter, 530.4; electronics, 537.5

.01 Philosophy and theory

Class theories and mathematical physics in 530.1

.2 **Radiations (Radiant energy)**

Class here electromagnetic spectrum, electromagnetic waves and radiations

Class a specific kind of radiation with the kind, e.g., ultraviolet rays 535.01

.7 **Atomic and nuclear physics**

Including ionizing radiations, particle physics

Class electronics of specific particles and radiations in 537.5

Atomic structure is classed in 539

540 Chemistry, crystallography, mineralogy

Standard subdivisions are added for chemistry, crystallography, mineralogy or for chemistry alone

Class cosmochemistry in 523

See Manual at 530 vs. 540 for topics common to physics and chemistry

SUMMARY

540.1–.9	**Standard subdivisions**
541	**Physical and theoretical chemistry**
542	**Techniques, procedures, apparatus, equipment, materials**
543	**Analytical chemistry**
544	**Qualitative analysis**
545	**Quantitative analysis**
546	**Inorganic chemistry**
547	**Organic chemistry**
548	**Crystallography**
549	**Mineralogy**

.1 **Philosophy and theory**

Including ancient and medieval theories, e.g., alchemy

Class physical and theoretical chemistry in 541

.2 **Miscellany**

[.28] Auxiliary techniques and procedures; apparatus, equipment, materials

Do not use; class in 542

> **541–547 Chemistry**

Class comprehensive works in 540

> **541–545 General chemistry**

Inorganic and combined inorganic-organic

Class comprehensive works in 540, general topics of specific inorganic chemicals and groups of chemicals in 546, general topics in organic chemistry in 547

541 Physical and theoretical chemistry

Class physical and theoretical topics of crystals in 548

See Manual at 546 vs. 541

.2 **Theoretical chemistry**

Including atomic and molecular structure, periodic law, stereochemistry

Class chemical crystallography in 548

For radiochemistry, see 541.3

See also 539 for physics of atomic and molecular structure

.3 **Physical chemistry**

Including catalysis, chemical reactions, combustion, electrochemistry, photochemistry, radiochemistry, solution chemistry, surface chemistry

Class chemical physics in 539

Optical activity is classed in 541

542 Techniques, procedures, apparatus, equipment, materials

Class a specific application with the application, e.g., apparatus for chemical analysis 543

543 Analytical chemistry

For qualitative analysis, see 544; quantitative analysis, 545

See Manual at 544–545 vs. 543

.001–.009 Standard subdivisions

544 Qualitative analysis

See Manual at 544–545 vs. 543

.001–.009 Standard subdivisions

545 Quantitative analysis

See Manual at 544–545 vs. 543

.001–.009 Standard subdivisions

546 Inorganic chemistry

Class here physical and theoretical chemistry, analytical chemistry of specific elements, compounds, mixtures; comprehensive works on organic chemistry of specific elements, compounds, mixtures

Class general topics of chemistry applied to inorganic chemistry as a whole in 541–545; organic chemistry of specific elements, compounds, mixtures in 547

See Manual at 546 vs. 541; 546 vs. 549

547 Organic chemistry

Including synthesis and named reactions, e.g., oxidation, polymerization; aliphatic and cyclic compounds

Class here biochemicals when not considered in their biological context

Class interdisciplinary works on biochemicals in 574.19

For biochemistry, see 574.19

.001–.009 Standard subdivisions

.1 **Physical and theoretical organic chemistry**

Class synthesis and named reactions in 547; physical and theoretical chemistry of macromolecular and other organic substances in 547.7–547.8, of organic compounds not provided for in 547.7–547.8 in 547

.3 **Analytical organic chemistry**

Class analytic chemistry of macromolecular and other organic substances in 547.7–547.8; of organic compounds not provided for in 547.7–547.8 in 547

.300 1–.300 9 Standard subdivisions

.7 **Macromolecular and related compounds**

Contains carbohydrates (including gums [*formerly* 547.8], sugars), alkaloids, antibiotics, lipids (including fats), nucleic acids, proteins (including amino acids, enzymes), vitamins

Class here macromolecular chemicals when not considered in their biological context, polymers

Class interdisciplinary works on macromolecular biochemicals in 574.19, fossil substances and comprehensive works on high polymers in 547.8, polymerization as a reaction in 547

.8 **Other organic substances**

Contains fossil substances (including coal, coal tar, petroleum), dyes and pigments, elastomers (including latexes, rubber), comprehensive works on high polymers

Gums relocated to 547.7, plastics to 668.4, man-made fibers to 677

Class synthetic polymers in 668; a specific high polymer not provided for here with the polymer, e.g., cyclic polymers 547, polysaccharides 547.7

548 Crystallography

See Manual at 548 vs. 549

549 Mineralogy

Class crystallography in 548, economic geology in 553

See Manual at 546 vs. 549; 548 vs. 549; 552 vs. 549

.09 Historical and persons treatment

Class geographic distribution of minerals in 549.9

.9 **Geographic distribution of minerals**

Add to base number 549.9 notation 1–9 from Table 2, e.g., minerals of Mexico 549.972

550 Earth sciences

Class here geophysics

Use 550 and its standard subdivisions for works that deal comprehensively with geology, hydrology, and meteorology; for works about geology that deal with all earth sciences. Use 551 and its standard subdivisions for works on geology in the sense limited to properties and phenomena of the solid earth

See Manual at 550 vs. 910 for description of surface features

SUMMARY

.1 **Philosophy and theory**

Chemical principles relocated to 551.9

.9 **Historical, geographic, persons treatment**

Class treatment by continent, country, locality in modern world, extraterrestrial worlds in 554–559 (*not* 550.94–550.99)

551 Geology, hydrology, meteorology

Geology: science that deals with properties and phenomena of the solid earth (lithosphere)

Use 550 and its standard subdivisions for works that deal comprehensively with geology, hydrology, and meteorology; for works about geology that deal with all earth sciences. Use 551 and its standard subdivisions for works on geology in the sense limited to properties and phenomena of the solid earth

For astronomical geography, see 525; geodesy, 526; petrology, 552; economic geology, 553; physical geography, 910

SUMMARY

.01 Philosophy and theory of geology

Chemical principles relocated to 551.9

.02–.08 Standard subdivisions of geology

.09 Historical, geographic, persons treatment of geology

Class treatment by continent, country, locality in modern world, extraterrestrial worlds in 554–559 (*not* 551.094–551.099)

.1 **Gross structure and properties of the earth**

Including plate tectonics (continental drift)

Class structural geology of earth's crust in 551.8

For geomagnetism, see 538

.2 ✓ **Volcanoes, earthquakes, thermal waters and gases**

Class volcanic rocks in 552

See also 363.3 for volcanic and earthquake disasters

.3 **Surface and exogenous processes and their agents**

Including erosion, glaciers, soil formation, weathering, interdisciplinary works on ice

Class a specific aspect of ice with the aspect, e.g., ice manufacture 621.5

.300 1–.300 9 Standard subdivisions

.4 **Geomorphology and hydrosphere**

Including beaches, caves, mountains

Class land formations created by an agent other than water with the agent, e.g., glacial moraines 551.3

.46 Hydrosphere Oceanography

Class here marine science, oceans and seas

Class interdisciplinary works on water in 553.7, ice and geologic work of water in 551.3

For ocean currents, ocean waves, tides, see 551.47; hydrology, 552.48; marine biology, 574.92

See Manual at 551.46 vs. 574.92 for oceanography

.460 01–.460 09 Standard subdivisions

,47 Tides [*formerly also* 525], ocean currents, ocean waves

.470 01–.470 09 Standard subdivisions

.48 Hydrology

Including floods, lakes, ponds, rivers

Class here hydrologic cycle, limnology, water balance

For thermal waters, see 551.2; groundwater, 551.49; hydrometeorology, 551.57

.49 Subsurface water (Groundwater)

Including artesian wells, springs

For thermal waters, see 551.2

.5 **Meteorology**

Including air temperature, lightning, rainbows, wind

Class here atmosphere

Class auroras and other electromagnetic phenomena in 538; micrometeorology, forecasts of specific meteorological phenomena in 551.6

For climatology and weather, see 551.6

See Manual at 551.6 vs. 551.5

.501 Philosophy and theory

Class forecasts and forecasting in 551.6

.55 Atmospheric disturbances and formations

Examples: blizzards, cyclones, hurricanes, tornadoes, typhoons

Class here storms

Class precipitation from storms in 551.57

See also 363.3 for storms as disasters

.57 Hydrometeorology

Including clouds, droughts, frost, rain, snow

.6 **Climatology and weather**

Including forecasting and forecasts, micrometeorology, weather belts, weather lore

See Manual at 551.6 vs. 551.5

.601 Philosophy and theory

Class forecasts and forecasting in 551.6

.609 Historical, geographic, persons treatment of climatology as a discipline

Class geographic treatment of weather in 551.65, of climate in 551.69

.65 Weather forecasts and reports for specific areas [*formerly* 551.69]

Class here forecasts of specific phenomena such as rain for specific areas

Add to base number 551.65 notation 1–9 from Table 2, e.g., forecasts for South Africa 551.6568

.68 Modification and control of weather

.69 Geographic treatment of climate

Add to base number 551.69 notation 1–9 from Table 2, e.g., climate of Australia 551.6994

Weather forecasts and reports for specific areas relocated to 551.65

.7 Historical geology

Class here paleogeography, stratigraphy

Class history of a specific kind of geologic phenomenon with the kind, e.g., Jurassic volcanism 551.2, paleozoic mountain building 551.8

For paleontology, see 560

See Manual at 551.7 vs. 560

.700 1–.700 8 Standard subdivisions

.700 9 Historical, geographic, persons treatment

Class comprehensive works on historical geology of specific continents, countries, localities of modern world and of extraterrestrial worlds in 554–559

.8 Structural geology

Including intrusions, mountain building, stratifications

Class here deformation, tectonics

Class geomorphology of mountains in 551.4; stratifications in specific areas in 554–559, of specific periods in specific areas in 551.7

For plate tectonics (continental drift), see 551.1

.9 Geochemistry

Class here chemical principles of earth sciences [*formerly also* 550.1], of geology [*formerly also* 551.01]

Class chemistry of hydrosphere in 551.46, of atmosphere in 551.5; geochemistry of minerals in 549, of rocks in 552, of useful geologic materials in 553; organic geochemistry in 553.2

552 Petrology

Class here lithology, rocks

Class structural geology in 551.8, economic geology in 553

For mineralogy, see 549

See Manual at 552 vs. 549

.001–.008 Standard subdivisions

.009 Historical, geographic, persons treatment

Class geographic distribution of rocks in 552.09

.09 Geographic distribution of rocks

Add to base number 552.09 notation 1–9 from Table 2, e.g., rocks of Sahara Desert 552.0966

553 Economic geology

Quantitative occurrence and distribution of geological materials of economic utility

Class here interdisciplinary works on nonmetallic materials

Class interdisciplinary works on metals in 669; economic aspects other than reserves of geological materials in 333.7; other specific aspects of geological materials with the aspects, e.g., prospecting 622

See Manual at 333.8 vs. 338.2, 553

.2 Carbonaceous materials

Examples: coal, oil, natural gas

Class here fossil fuels

For diamonds, see 553.8

.3 Iron

.4 Metals and semimetals

For iron, see 553.3

.5 Structural and sculptural stone

Examples: granite, marble

Class petrology of structural and sculptural stone in 552, semiprecious sculptural stone in 553.8

.6 Other economic materials

Examples: abrasives, asbestos, clay, gypsum, lime, mineral fertilizers, sulfur

Class here earthy materials, industrial minerals

Interdisciplinary works on soils relocated to 631.4

Inorganic gases are classed in 553

For gems, see 553.8

.7 Water

Surface and subsurface

Including ice

Class interdisciplinary works on ice in 551.3, on thermal waters in 333.8; geology of thermal waters in 551.2

.8 Gems

Example: diamonds

Class industrial diamonds in 553.6

> **554–559 Earth sciences by continent, country, locality in modern world; extraterrestrial worlds**

Class here geology and geological surveys

Add to base number 55 notation 4–9 from Table 2, e.g., geology of Asia 555, of Japan 555.2

Class comprehensive works on earth sciences in 550, on geology in 551; a specific geological topic (other than historical geology taken as a whole) in a specific region with the subject, e.g., tectonics of Japan 551.80952

554 *Earth sciences of Europe

555 *Earth sciences of Asia

556 *Earth sciences of Africa

557 *Earth sciences of North America

558 *Earth sciences of South America

559 *Earth sciences of other parts of the world and of extraterrestrial worlds

560 Paleontology Paleozoology

Including stratigraphic paleontology, paleobotany, paleozoology; paleoecology

See Manual at 551.7 vs. 560; 560 vs. 575

.9 Historical, geographic, persons treatment of paleontology, of paleozoology

Add to base number 560.9 the numbers following 574.9 in 574.909–574.999, e.g., marine paleontology 560.92

Use 560.9 for persons treatment

561 Paleobotany

Stratigraphic paleobotany is classed in 560

.09 Historical, geographic, persons treatment of paleobotany

Class geographic treatment of fossil plants in 561

> **562–569 Specific animals and groups of animals**

Class here taxonomic paleozoology

Class comprehensive works in 560

*Add as instructed under 554–559

562 Fossil invertebrates

Including conodonts

For fossil Protozoa, Parazoa, Coelenterata, Echinodermata, related phyla, see 563; fossil mollusks and mollusk-like animals, 564; other fossil invertebrates, 565

563 Fossil Protozoa, Parazoa, Coelenterata, Echinodermata, related phyla

Examples: corals, sponges, starfish, unicellular animals

564 Fossil mollusks and mollusk-like animals

Examples: clams, oysters

565 Other fossil invertebrates

Examples: crabs, insects, shrimp

566 Fossil vertebrates

Class here fossil chordates

For fossil cold-blooded vertebrates, see 567; fossil birds, 568; fossil mammals, 569

567 Fossil cold-blooded vertebrates

Including amphibians

Class here fish

.9 Reptiles

Including dinosaurs

568 Fossil birds

569 Fossil mammals

For prehistoric humankind, see 573.3

570 Life sciences

Use 570 by itself only for works including substantial treatment of paleontology; use 574 for general biology

For paleontology, see 560

SUMMARY

572 Human races
573 Physical anthropology
574 Biology
575 Evolution and genetics
576 Microbiology
577 General nature of life
578 Microscopy in biology
579 Collection and preservation of biological specimens

572 Human races

Including causes of physical differences

Class here physical ethnology

Ethnology, cultural ethnology, ethnography relocated to 305.8

.09 Historical, geographic, persons treatment

Class origin of races in 572, geographic distribution of races in 572.9

.9 Geographic distribution of races

Add to base number 572.9 notation 1–9 from Table 2, e.g., races of Asia 572.95

Specific races in a specific place are classed in 572

573 Physical anthropology

Including anthropometry

Class here human biological ecology

Class interdisciplinary works on human ecology in 304.2, comprehensive works on biology of humankind and forebears in 599.9

For human races, see 572

See Manual at 573 vs. 611 for anthropometry

.2 Evolution and genetics of humankind

Including heredity, variation

Class physiology of human genetics in 611

See Manual at 573.2

.3 Prehistoric humankind

Including Piltdown man [*formerly* 001.9]

574 Biology

For evolution, see 575; microbiology, 576; botanical sciences, 580; zoological sciences, 590

See Manual at 508 vs. 574, 910, 304.2

.01 Philosophy and theory

Class general nature of life in 577

.075 Museum activities and services

Class collection and preservation of biological specimens in 579

.09 Historical, geographic, persons treatment of biology

Class geographic treatment of organisms in 574.9

.1 **Physiology**

Class here comprehensive works on anatomy, morphology, physiology

Class pathological physiology in 574.2, physiology of tissues and cells in 574.8

For development and maturation, see 574.3; anatomy and morphology, 574.4, genetics, 575.1

.19 Biophysics and biochemistry

Including interdisciplinary works on biochemicals

Class biochemicals not considered in their biological context in 547, industrial biochemistry in 660; metabolism in 574.1; physics and chemistry of a specific process or part of living organisms with the process or part, e.g., chemistry of cells 574.87

.2 **Pathology**

Including immunity

Class here biological death

Class tissue pathology in 574.8, cell pathology in 574.87

.3 **Development and maturation**

Including aging, embryology, regeneration, sex cells, sex differentiation

Class formation and differentiation of tissues in 574.1

.4 **Anatomy and morphology**

Class comprehensive works on anatomy, physiology, morphology in 574.1; pathological anatomy in 574.2, embryological anatomy in 574.3

.5 **Ecology**

Including food chains, parasitism, predation, rare and endangered species, synecology; specific kinds of environments, e.g., forests, oceans, seashores, tropics

Class here adaptation, behavior, ecosystems, ecological succession

See Manual at 574.5 vs. 574.909–574.92 for ecology of specific kinds of environments

.509 1 Treatment by areas, regions, places in general

Class ecology of specific kinds of environment in 574.5

.6 **Economic biology**

Including beneficial and injurious organisms

.8 **Tissue, cellular, molecular biology**

Class formation and differentiation of tissues in 574.1

.87 Cytology (Cell biology)

Including biological transport, physiological genetics, protoplasm, DNA, RNA

Class comprehensive works on genetics in 575.1

.9 **Geographic treatment of organisms**

See Manual at 508 vs. 574, 910, 304.2

.909 Treatment by areas, regions, places in general

Examples: desert, tropical biology

Class insular biology in 574.9, aquatic biology in 574.92

See Manual at 574.5 vs. 574.909–574.92

.92 Aquatic biology Marine biology

Including freshwater biology

Class here plankton

Class marine biology of, comprehensive works on marine and freshwater biology of specific continents, countries, localities in 574.93–574.99

See Manual at 551.46 vs. 574.92 for marine biology; 574.5 vs. 574.909–574.92

.93–.99 Treatment by specific continents, countries, localities

Class here comprehensive works on marine and freshwater biology of specific continents, countries, localities; marine biology of specific continents, countries, localities

Add to base number 574.9 notation 3–9 from Table 2, e.g., astrobiology 574.999

Class freshwater biology of specific continents, countries, localities in 574.92

575 Evolution and genetics

Including origin and evolution of sexes

Class evolution of a specific process or structure with the process or structure, e.g., evolution of immunity 574.2

For evolution of humankind, see 573.2; of plants, 581.3; of animals, 591.3

See Manual at 231.7 vs. 213, 575; 560 vs. 575; 573.2

.001 Philosophy

Class theory in 575.01

.002–.009 Standard subdivisions

.01 Theories of evolution

Examples: Darwinian, Lamarckian

.1 **Genetics**

Including environmental factors [*formerly* 575.2], population genetics

Class here heredity

For genetics of humankind, see 573.2; physiological genetics, 574.87; variation, 575.2; genetics of plants, 581.1; genetics of animals, 591.1

.2 **Variation**

Example: mutation

Environmental factors relocated to 575.1

576 Microbiology

Including Rickettsiae, viruses

For fungi, see 589.2; algae, 589.3; bacteria, 589.9; Protozoa, 593.1

See Manual at 616 vs. 576

.09 Historical, geographic, persons treatment of microbiology

Class geographic treatment of microbes in 576

577 General nature of life

Origin and beginnings of life, conditions needed for life, differences between living and nonliving substances

578 Microscopy in biology

Regardless of kind of organism

Including slide preparation

Class interdisciplinary works on microscopy in 502.8

579 Collection and preservation of biological specimens

Regardless of kind of organism

580 Botanical sciences

Use 580 by itself only for works involving substantial treatment of paleobotany; use 581 for general botany

For paleobotany, see 561

See Manual at 580–590; 580–590 vs. 630, 641.3

SUMMARY

.74 Museums, collections, exhibits

Including botanical gardens, herbariums

581 Botany

Studies of a particular process or system associated with a specific plant or group of plants are classed with the plant or group, not with the process or system, e.g., genetics of peas 583, not 581.1

Class microscopy regardless of kind of plant in 578, collection and preservation of botanical specimens regardless of kind of plant in 579

For specific plants and groups of plants, see 582–589

See Manual at 581

.074 Museums, collections, exhibits

Class botanical gardens and herbariums in 580.74

.075 Museum activities and services

Class collection and preservation of botanical specimens in 579

.09 Historical, geographic, persons treatment of botany

Class geographic treatment of plants in 581.9

.1 **Physiology of plants**

Including genetics

Class here physiology of agricultural plants, comprehensive works on anatomy, morphology, physiology

Class pathological physiology in 581.2, anatomy and morphology in 581.4, microphysiology in 581.8, physiological genetics in 581.87

For development and maturation, see 581.3

.19 Biophysics and biochemistry

Class physics and chemistry of a specific process or part of plants with the process or part, e.g., chemistry of plant cells 581.87

.2 **Pathology of plants**

Including disease resistance

Class here death

Class tissue pathology in 581.8, cell pathology in 581.87, pathology of agricultural plants in 632

.3 **Development and maturation of plants**

Including evolution, regeneration, sex differentiation

Class formation and differentiation of tissues, genetics in 581.1; evolution of a specific process or structure with the process or structure, e.g., evolution of disease resistance 581.2

.4–.9 **Other general topics in botany**

Add to base number 581 the numbers following 574 in 574.4–574.9, e.g., plants in a marine environment 581.92

.5 Desert plants

> **582–589 Specific plants and group of plants**

Class comprehensive works in 581, microscopy in botany regardless of kind of plant in 578

582 *Seed-bearing plants

Fruit and seeds are classed in 582, without use of 582.001–582.009 or 582.09; fruit and seeds of a specific plant or group of plants are classed with the plant in 582.1–585

For flowering plants, see 583–584; gymnosperms, 585

.001–.006 Standard subdivisions

.007 Education and related topics

.007 4 Museums, collections, exhibits

Class botanical gardens and herbariums of seed-bearing plants in 580.74

.007 5 Museum activities and services

Class collection and preservation of botanical specimens in 579

.008 History and description with respect to kinds of persons

.009 Historical, geographic, persons treatment of the study of seed-bearing plants

Class geographic treatment of seed-bearing plants in 582.09

.09 Geographic treatment of seed-bearing plants

Add to base number 582.09 the numbers following 574.9 in 574.909–574.999, e.g., desert seed-bearing plants 582.0909

*Class collection and preservation of botanical specimens in 579

.1 ***Nontaxonomic groupings**

Examples: herbaceous and woody plants, shrubs, vines

Class specific classes, orders, families, genera, species in 583–585

See also 635.9 for works on special groupings when the emphasis is on plants to be cultivated or appreciated in man-made settings

.13 *Herbaceous flowering plants

Class here wild flowers, comprehensive works on flowering plants

Woody flowering plants are classed in 582.1

For dicotyledons, see 583; monocotyledons, 584

.130 74 Museums, exhibits, collections

Class herbariums and botanical gardens covering flowering plants as a whole in 580.74

.16 *Trees

Class here dendrology

.160 01–.160 08 Standard subdivisions

.160 09 Historical, geographic, persons treatment of dendrology

Class geographic treatment of trees in 582.1609

.160 9 Geographic treatment of trees

Add to base number 582.1609 the numbers following 574.9 in 574.909–574.999, e.g., desert trees 582.160909

> **583–584 Flowering plants**

Class comprehensive works in 582.13

583 *Dicotyledons

Examples: cabbage, cactus, cotton, elm, insectivorous plants, ivy, maple, peas, potatoes, roses

584 *Monocotyledons

Examples: grasses, lilies, orchids, palms

585 *Gymnosperms (Naked-seed plants)

Examples: pines, ginkgo

586 *Seedless plants

For pteridophytes, see 587; bryophytes, 588; thallophytes and prokaryotes, 589

.001–.008 Standard subdivisions

*Class collection and preservation of botanical specimens in 579

.009 Historical, geographic, persons treatment of the study of seedless plants

Class geographic treatment of seedless plants in 586.09

.09 Geographic treatment of seedless plants

Add to base number 586.09 the numbers following 574.9 in 574.909–574.999, e.g., tropical seedless plants 586.0909

587 *Pteridophytes (Vascular seedless plants)

Examples: ferns, club mosses, horsetails, quillworts

588 *Bryophytes

Examples: mosses, hornworts, liverworts

See also 587 for club mosses

589 *Thallophytes and prokaryotes

Class comprehensive works on microorganisms in 576

.1 *Lichens

.2 *Fungi

Examples: molds, mushrooms, yeast

Class here mycology

For lichens, see 589.1

.3 *Algae

Class here phycology

For specific types of algae, see 589.4; lichens, 589.1

.309 Historical, geographic, persons treatment of phycology

Class geographic treatment of algae in 589.39

.39 Geographic treatment of algae

Add to base number 589.39 the numbers following 574.9 in 574.909–574.999, e.g., marine algae 589.392

.4 *Specific types of algae

Examples: diatoms, kelp, seaweed

.9 *Prokaryotes Bacteria

Class here bacteriology

Class blue-green algae in 589.4

For Rickettsiae, viruses, see 576

.900 1–.900 8 Standard subdivisions

*Class collection and preservation of botanical specimens in 579

.900 9 Historical, geographic, persons treatment of prokaryotology, of bacteriology

Class geographic treatment of prokaryotes, of bacteria in 589.909

.909 Geographic treatment of prokaryotes, of bacteria

Add to base number 589.909 the numbers following 574.9 in 574.909–574.999, e.g., tropical bacteria in 589.90909

590 Zoological sciences

Use 590 by itself only for works including substantial treatment of paleozoology; use 591 for general zoology

For paleozoology, see 560

See Manual at 580–590; 580–590 vs. 630, 641.3

SUMMARY

590.74	**Museums, collections, exhibits**
591	**Zoology**
592	**Invertebrates**
593	**Protozoa, Parazoa, Coelenterata, Echinodermata, related phyla**
594	**Mollusks and mollusk-like animals**
595	**Other invertebrates**
596	**Vertebrates**
597	**Cold-blooded vertebrates**
598	**Birds**
599	**Mammals**

.74 Museums, collections, exhibits

Including general zoos, zoos limited to vertebrates, to land vertebrates, to mammals

591 Zoology

Studies of a particular process or system associated with a specific animal or group of animals are classed with the animal or group, not with the process or system, e.g., genetics of fruit flies 595.77, not 591.1

Class microscopy regardless of kind of animal in 578, collection and preservation of zoological specimens regardless of kind of animal in 579

For specific animals and groups of animals, see 592–599

See Manual at 591 vs. 599; 591 vs. 610; 800 vs. 591, 636, 398.24

.074 Museums, collections, exhibits

Class zoos in 590.74

.075 Museums activities and services

Class collection and preservation of zoological specimens regardless of kind of animal in 579

.09 Historical, geographic, persons treatment of zoology

Class geographic treatment of animals in 591.9

.1 **Physiology of animals**

Including genetics

Class here comprehensive works on anatomy, morphology, physiology

Class pathological physiology in 591.2, microphysiology in 591.8, physiological genetics in 591.87, physiology and anatomy of domestic animals in 636.089

For development and maturation, see 591.3; anatomy and morphology, 591.4

.19 Biophysics and biochemistry

Class physics and chemistry of a specific process or part of animals with the process or part, e.g., chemistry of nuclei 591.87

.2 **Pathology of animals**

Including immunity

Class here death

Class tissue pathology in 591.8, cell pathology in 591.87

See Manual at 591.2 vs. 616.07 for immunology

.3 **Development and maturation of animals**

Including evolution, regeneration, sex differentiation

Class formation and differentiation of tissue, genetics in 591.1; evolution of a specific process or structure with the process or structure, e.g., evolution of immunity 591.2

.4 **Anatomy and morphology of animals**

Class comprehensive works on anatomy, morphology, physiology in 591.1; pathological anatomy in 591.2, embryological anatomy in 591.3, microanatomy in 591.8

.5 **Ecology of animals**

Class here adaptations

.51 Habits and behavior of animals

Class specific habits or behavior patterns in 591.52–591.59

See also 156 for comparative psychology

.52 Specific relationships and kinds of environments

Examples: forest, marine, seashore, tropical ecology

Including migration, parasitism, rare and endangered animals, synecology

Class specific adaptations to specific relationships and kinds of environments in 591.53–591.59

> **591.53–591.59 Specific adaptations**

Class comprehensive works in 591.5

.53 Nutritive adaptations

Including food chains, predation

.54 Adaptations to weather, climate, seasons

Example: hibernation

.56 Reproductive and related adaptations

Including courtship, nesting, territoriality

.57 Protective adaptations

Example: camouflage

.59 Communication and production of sound

.6–.9 Other general topics of animals

Add to base number 591 the numbers following 574 in 574.6–574.9, e.g., animal cytology 591.87

> **592–599 Specific animals and groups of animals**

Class comprehensive works in 591, microscopy in zoology regardless of kind of animal in 578

592 *Invertebrates

For Protozoa, Parazoa, Coelenterata, Echinodermata, related phyla, see 593; mollusks and mollusk-like animals, 594; other invertebrates, 595

.001–.008 Standard subdivisions

.009 Historical, geographic, persons treatment of the study of invertebrates

Class geographic treatment of invertebrates in 592.09

.09 Geographic treatment of invertebrates

Add to base number 592.09 the numbers following 574.9 in 574.909–574.999, e.g., marine invertebrates 592.092

593 *Protozoa, Parazoa, Coelenterata, Echinodermata, related phyla

Including Hemichordata, Linguatula

.1 *Protozoa

Example: amoeba

.4 *Parazoa Sponges

.6 *Anthozoa

Example: coral

*Class collection and preservation of zoological specimens in 579

.7 ***Hydrozoa and Scyphozoa**

Class here jellyfish

.8 ***Comb jellies**

.9 ***Echinodermata**

Example: starfish

594 *Mollusks and mollusk-like animals

Examples: clams, octopuses, oysters, snails

.001–.008 Standard subdivisions of mollusks

.009 Historical, geographic, persons treatment of the study of mollusks

Class geographic treatment of mollusks in 594.09

.09 Geographic treatment of mollusks

Add to base number 594.09 the numbers following 574.9 in 574.909–574.999, e.g., freshwater mollusks 594.092

595 *Other invertebrates

Including arthropods, onychophores

.1 ***Worms and related animals**

Including flukes, leeches, water bears

Class here helminthology

.3 ***Crustaceans and chelicerates**

Examples: barnacles, crabs, lobsters, shrimp

For arachnids, see 595.4

.4 ***Arachnids**

Examples: mites, scorpions, spiders, ticks

.6 ***Progoneata**

Examples: centipedes, millipedes

For insects, see 595.7

.7 ***Insects**

Examples: cockroaches, dragonflies, grasshoppers, lice, termites

Class here entomology

.700 1–.700 8 Standard subdivisions

.700 9 Historical, geographic, persons treatment of entomology

Class geographic treatment of insects in 595.709

*Class collection and preservation of zoological specimens in 579

.705 Ecology

Add to base number 595.705 the numbers following 591.5 in 591.51–591.59, e.g., insect communication 595.7059

.709 Geographic treatment of insects

Add to base number 595.709 the numbers following 574.9 in 574.909–574.999, e.g., aquatic insects 505.7092

.76 *Beetles

Including glowworms, weevils

.77 *Diptera and Siphonaptera

Examples: flies, gnats, mosquitoes; fleas

.78 *Lepidoptera

Examples: butterflies, moths

.79 *Hymenoptera

Examples: ants, bees

Class here wasps

596 *Vertebrates

Class here chordates

For cold-blooded vertebrates, see 597; birds, 598; mammals, 599

.001–.006 Standard subdivisions

.007 Education and related topics

.007 4 Museums, collections, exhibits

Class vertebrate zoos in 590.74

.007 5 Museum activities and services

Class collection and preservation of vertebrate specimens in 579

.008 History and description with respect to kinds of persons

.009 Historical, geographic, persons treatment of the study of vertebrates

Class geographic treatment of vertebrates in 596.09

.09 Geographic treatment of vertebrates

Add to base number 596.09 the numbers following 574.9 in 574.909–574.999, e.g., marine vertebrates 596.092

597 *Cold-blooded vertebrates

Class here fish, ichthyology

.001–.008 Standard subdivisions of cold blooded vertebrates, of fish, of ichthyology

*Class collection and preservation of zoological specimens in 579

.009 Historical, geographic, persons treatment of cold-blooded vertebrates, of ichthyology

Class geographic treatment of fish in 597.09

.09 Geographic treatment of fish

Add to base number 597.09 the numbers following 574.9 in 574.909–574.999, e.g., freshwater fish 597.092

.6 ***Amphibians**

Examples: salamanders

Class here herpetology (study of amphibians and reptiles), land vertebrates

For Apoda, see 597.7; Anura, 597.8; reptiles, 597.9; birds, 598; mammals, 599

.7 ***Apoda (Caecilians)**

.8 ***Anura (Salientia)**

Examples: frogs, toads

.9 ***Reptiles**

.92 *Turtles

.95 *Lizards

Examples: chameleons, Gila monsters

Use 597.9 for comprehensive works on lizards and snakes

.96 *Snakes

.98 *Crocodiles and alligators

598 *Birds

Class here ornithology

Class comprehensive works on warm-blooded vertebrates in 599

.07 Education and related topics

Including birdbanding and bird watching

.075 Museum activities and services

Class collection and preservation of ornithological specimens in 579

.09 Historical, geographic, persons treatment of ornithology

Class geographic treatment of birds in 598.29

.2 **Ecology and geographic treatment of birds**

.25 Ecology

Add to base number 598.25 the numbers following 591.5 in 591.51–591.59, e.g., nests 598.256; however, class rare and endangered birds in 598

*Class collection and preservation of zoological specimens in 579

.29 Geographic treatment of birds

Including comprehensive works on land birds, on water birds

Add to base number 598.29 notation 3–9 from Table 2, e.g., birds of Mexico 598.2972

Class specific water birds in 598.3–598.4; specific land birds in 598.5–598.9

> **598.3–598.4 Water birds**

Class comprehensive works in 598.29

.3 ***Charadriiformes, Ciconiiformes, Gruiformes**

Examples: cranes, flamingos, gulls, herons, storks; shore birds, e.g., sandpipers

.4 ***Anseriformes and other water birds**

Examples: albatrosses, ducks, geese, loons, pelicans, penguins, swans

---

> **598.5–598.9 Land birds**

Class comprehensive works in 598.29

.5 ***Palaeognathae**

Examples: kiwis, ostriches

.6 ***Galliformes and Columbiformes**

Examples: chickens, doves, peafowl, pheasants, pigeons, quail, turkeys

.7 ***Coliiformes, Cuculiformes, Piciformes, Psittaciformes, Trogoniformes**

Examples: cuckoos, parakeets, parrots, woodpeckers

.8 ***Perching birds, Apodiformes, Coraciiformes**

Examples: cardinals, crows, hornbills, hummingbirds, kingfishers, larks, robins, sparrows, swifts, thrushes

Class here songbirds

Standard subdivisions are added for perching birds, Apodiformes, Coraciiformes, for perching birds alone

.9 ***Birds of prey, owls, Caprimulgiformes**

Examples: condors, eagles, falcons, hawks, vultures, whippoorwills

*Class collection and preservation of zoological specimens in 579

599 *Mammals

Class here warm-blooded vertebrates

For birds, see 598

See Manual at 591 vs. 599; 591 vs. 610

.001–.006 Standard subdivisions

.007 Education and related topics

.007 4 Museums, collections, exhibits

Class mammalian zoos in 590.74

.007 5 Museum activities and services

Class collection and preservation of mammalian specimens in 579

.008 History and description in respect to kinds of persons

.009 Historical, geographic, persons treatment of the study of mammals

Class geographic treatment of mammals in 599.09

.05 Ecology

Add to base number 599.05 the numbers following 591.5 in 591.51–591.599, e.g., migrations 599.052; however, class rare and endangered mammals in 599

.09 Geographic treatment of mammals

Add to base number 599.09 the numbers following 574.9 in 574.909–574.999, e.g., desert mammals 599.0909; however, class marine mammals in 599.5

.1 *Monotremes

Example: platypuses

.2 *Marsupials

Examples: kangaroos, opossums

.3 *Unguiculata

Examples: anteaters, armadillos, moles, shrews

For bats, see 599.4; primates, 599.8

.32 *Lagomorphs and rodents

Examples: rabbits; mice, porcupines, squirrels

.4 *Bats

.5 *Cetaceans and sirenians

Examples: dolphins, porpoises; sea cows

Class here marine mammals, whales

Class marine carnivores in 599.74

*Class collection and preservation of zoological specimens in 579

.6 ***Paenungulata**

Examples: elephants, hyraxes

For sirenians, see 599.5

.7 ***Ungulates, carnivores, aardvarks**

For Paenungulata, see 599.6

.72 *Odd-toed ungulates

Examples: horses, rhinoceroses, tapirs

.73 *Even-toed ungulates

Examples: buffalo, camels, deer, giraffes, pigs, sheep

.74 *Carnivores

Examples: bears, cats, dogs, otters, raccoons, seals, walruses

.8 ***Primates**

Examples: baboons, monkeys

.88 *Apes

Class here comprehensive works on hominoids

For humankind and forebears, see 599.9

.9 **Humankind and forebears**

Use this number only for works treating both physical anthropology and at least one of the medical sciences (anatomy, physiology, medicine)

For physical anthropology, see 573; medical sciences, 610

*Class collection and preservation of zoological specimens in 579

600

600 Technology (Applied sciences)

Class technology transfer, interdisciplinary works on appropriate technology in 338.9

See also 303.48 for technology as a cause of cultural change, 306.4 for sociology of technology, 338.1–338.4 for economic aspects of industries based on specific technologies

See Manual at 300 vs. 600; 500 vs. 600

601 Philosophy and theory

602 Miscellany

.2 Illustrations

Class techniques of drafting illustrations in 604.2

.9 Commercial miscellany

Class interdisciplinary commercial miscellany in 380.1; commercial miscellany of products and services used in individual and family living in 640.29, of manufactured products in 670.29

603 Dictionaries, encyclopedias, concordances

604 Technical drawing, hazardous materials technology, history and description with respect to kinds of persons

.2 Technical drawing

Class here engineering graphics, techniques of drafting illustrations

Class illustrations of technology in 602.2; techniques of drafting illustrations in a specific subject with the subject, using notation 022 from Table 1, e.g., map drawing 526.022, drafting in electronics 621.381022

For architectural drawing, see 720.28

[.6] Waste technology

Relocated to 628.4

.7 **Hazardous materials technology**

Methods of extracting, manufacturing, processing, utilizing, handling, transporting, storing solids, liquids, gases that are explosive, flammable, corrosive, infectious, radioactive, toxic

Class comprehensive works on and social aspects of hazardous materials safety in 363.17; technology of a specific hazardous material with the technology, e.g., manufacture of explosives 662; safety techniques for a specific use of hazardous materials with the use outside 300, using notation 028 from Table 1, e.g., safety techniques in working with hazardous paving materials 625.8028 (*not* 363.17)

See Manual at 363.17 vs. 604.7; 660 vs. 604.7

.8 **History and description with respect to kinds of persons**

Add to base number 604.8 the numbers following —08 in notation 081–089 from Table 1, e.g., women 604.82

605 Serial publications

606 Organizations

[.8] **Management of technology**

Relocated to 658

607 Education and related topics

Including museums, collections, exhibits and their activities and services; review and exercise

608 Inventions and patents

Do not use for history and description of technology with respect to kinds of persons; class in 604.8

See Manual at 608 vs. 609

[.09] Historical, geographic, persons treatment

Do not use; class in 608.7

.7 **Historical, geographic, persons treatment**

Add to base number 608.7 notation 1–9 from Table 2, e.g., patents from Brazil 608.781

Class history of inventions in 609

609 Historical, geographic, persons treatment

Class here history of inventions, technological aspects of industrial archaeology

Class interdisciplinary works on and economic aspects of industrial archaeology in 338.09, historical aspects of industrial archaeology in 900

See Manual at 608 vs. 609

610 Medical sciences Medicine

Class home care of the sick and infirm in 649.8

Experimental medicine is classed in 619

For veterinary sciences, see 636.089

See Manual at 362.1–362.4 vs. 610; 591 vs. 610; 616 vs. 610

SUMMARY

610.1–.9	**[Standard subdivisions, medical personnel, nursing]**
611	**Human anatomy, cytology (cell biology), histology (tissue biology)**
612	**Human physiology**
613	**Promotion of health**
614	**Forensic medicine, incidence of disease, public preventive medicine**
615	**Pharmacology and therapeutics**
616	**Diseases**
617	**Miscellaneous branches of medicine Surgery**
618	**Other branches of medicine Gynecology and obstetrics**
619	**Experimental medicine**

[.23] Medicine as a profession, occupation, hobby

Do not use; class in 610.69

.28 Auxiliary techniques and procedures; apparatus, equipment, materials

Class here comprehensive works on biomedical engineering, medical instrumentation

Class biological instrumentation in 574.028

.6 Organizations, management, professions

Including group practice

Class economics of group practice in 338.7–338.8

.69 Medical personnel

Including physicians, medical technicians and assistants, medical missionaries; medical relationships

Class medical secretaries in 651.3, medical records librarians in 651.5; medical personnel (other than nurses) of a specific specialty with the specialty, e.g., obstetricians 618.2; critical appraisal and description of work, individual and collected biographies with the specialty, using notation 092 from Table 1, e.g., physicians treating disorders of the eye 617.7092

For nursing personnel, see 610.7306

See Manual at 610.69

.7 **Education, nursing, related topics**

.73 Nursing and services of medical technicians and assistants

Including specialized nursing, e.g., psychiatric nursing

Class here general medical nursing

Class services of medical technicians and assistants as a profession, occupation, hobby in 610.69

See Manual at 610.73 for nursing

.730 1 Philosophy and theory of nursing

.730 2 Miscellany of nursing

[.730 23] Nursing as a profession, occupation, hobby

Do not use; class in 610.7306

.730 3–.730 5 Standard subdivisions of nursing

.730 6 Nursing organizations and personnel

Including professional and practical nurses, attendants, aides, volunteers

Class management of services of nurses in 362.1

.730 7–.730 9 Standard subdivisions of nursing

.9 **Historical, geographic, persons treatment**

See Manual at 610.9 for historical treatment

611 Human anatomy, cytology (cell biology), histology (tissue biology)

Class pathological anatomy in 616.07

See Manual at 573 vs. 611 for human anatomy; 611 vs. 612

.001–.009 Standard subdivisions for human anatomy, cytology, histology; for human anatomy alone

612 Human physiology

Class here comprehensive works on human anatomy and physiology

Biophysics, biochemistry, control processes, tissue and organ culture; physiology of work and sports are all classed in 612, without use of 612.001–612.009; biophysics, biochemistry, control processes, tissue and organ culture; physiology of work and sports in specific body systems and regions are classed with the system or region in 612.1–612.9

Class pathological physiology in 616.07

For human anatomy, cytology (cell biology), histology (tissue biology), see 611

See Manual at 611 vs. 612; 612 vs. 616

.001–.009 Standard subdivisions

.1 **Blood and circulation**

Class bone marrow, lymph and lymphatics, spleen in 612.4; circulation in a specific system or organ with the system or organ, e.g., the brain 612.8

.2 **Respiration**

Including comprehensive works on physiology of the nose

Class physiology of the nose as an olfactory organ in 612.8

.3 **Digestion**

Including metabolism

Class here nutrition

Class dietetics in 613.2; metabolism of drugs in 615, of toxic substances in 615.9; metabolism within a specific function, system, or organ with the function, system, or organ, e.g., the metabolism of plasma 612.1

.4 **Secretion, excretion, related functions**

Including lymphatic, urinary system; hormones

Class here the endocrine system

Class glands and glandular activity in a specific system or organ with the system or organ, e.g., salivary glands 612.3

For mammary glands and lactation, see 612.6

.400 1–.400 9 Standard subdivisions

.6 **Reproduction, development, maturation**

Including mammary glands and lactation; puberty, menopause, aging; comprehensive works on embryology

Class here comprehensive medical works on sex

Class interdisciplinary works on sex in 306.7, comprehensive works on pregnancy and childbirth in 618.2, anatomic embryology in 611, a specific aspect of sex with the aspect, e.g., sexual disorders 616.6; postnatal development of a specific system, organ, region with the system, organ, region, e.g., postnatal development of teeth 612.3

See also 616.07 for death

.600 1–.600 9 Standard subdivisions

.7 **Motor functions and skin (integument), hair, nails**

Including bones, connective tissue, joints, muscles; exercise, rest; voice and speech

Class bone marrow in 612.4; mastoid processes, ossicles in 612.8; muscles of a specific system or organ with the system or organ, e.g., eye muscles 612.8

.8 Nervous functions Sensory functions

Including brain, nerves; ears, eyes; hearing, smell, taste, touch, vision; sleep

Class the psychology of sensory perception, emotions, physiological drives in 152

See Manual at 152 vs. 612.8; 154.6 vs. 612.8 for sleep

613 Promotion of health

Former heading: General and personal hygiene

Including beverages, environmental factors, health resorts, personal cleanliness

Class here measures to promote health and prevent disease taken by the individual and his medical advisers, comprehensive medical works on personal and public measures to promote health and prevent disease

Class public measures to promote health and prevent disease in 614, personal preventive measures applied to specific diseases or groups of diseases in 616–618, personal grooming in 646.7, child rearing in 649

See Manual at 613 vs. 615.8

[.081–.084] Persons of specific sex and age groups

Do not use; class in 613

.2 Dietetics

Including weight gaining and losing programs, vegetarianism

Class comprehensive works on diet and physical fitness in 613.7; beverages in 613; human nutritional requirements considered in relation to physiological processes and the role of nutrients in the body in 612.3; diet therapy in 615.8; dietetics for pregnant women in 618.2; diets to prevent a specific disease with the disease, e.g., diets to prevent arteriosclerosis 616.1

See also 616.3 for conditions resulting from nutritional deficiencies, 641.5 for cooking for preventive and therapeutic diets, 649 for domestic aspects of feeding children

See Manual at 613.2 vs. 641.3, 363.8

.6 Special topics

Including military, occupational health; self-defense; techniques of survival in accidents, disasters, other unfavorable circumstances

Class here personal safety

Class personal safety in a specific field with the field, using notation 028 from Table 1, e.g., personal safety in recreational boating 797.1028

See Manual at 613.6 vs. 363.11 for industrial and occupational health

.7 **Physical fitness**

Including exercise [*formerly also* 796.4], weight lifting for fitness, calisthenics, gymnastic exercises [*all formerly* 796.41]; posture, rest, sleep, physical yoga, health of athletes; comprehensive works on exercise and sports activities for fitness and for improvement in the shape of the body

Class breathing in 613, exercise and sports activities to improve the shape of the body in 646.7, parental supervision of children's exercise and sports activities in 649

See Manual at 613.7 vs. 646.7, 796 for exercise and sports activities

[.708 1–.708 4] Persons of specific sex and age groups

Do not use; class in 613.7

.8 **Substance abuse (Drug abuse)**

Limited to personal preventive aspects

Examples: abuse of cocaine, marijuana, narcotics, stimulants

Class here appeals to the individual to avoid substance abuse for health reasons

Class interdisciplinary works on substance abuse in 362.29, comprehensive medical works on addictive and disorienting drugs in 615, comprehensive medical works on substance abuse as a disease in 616.86

.81 Alcohol

Class here personal aspects of prevention of alcohol abuse

.85 Tobacco

.9 **Birth control and sex hygiene**

Including family planning, manuals of sexual technique

.907 Education and related topics

Class sex education of children in the home in 649

614 Forensic medicine, incidence of disease, public preventive medicine

Former heading: Public health and related topics

Including disposal of the dead

Class social provision for public health services other than those concerned with incidence and prevention of disease in 362.1, public safety programs in 363.1; environmental problems and services, social aspects and services associated with the disposal of the dead in 363.7

.4 **Incidence of and public measures to prevent disease**

Examples of public measures: disinfection, immunization, quarantine

Including health surveys, medical geography; disease carriers and their control

Class here epidemiology

For incidence of and public measures to prevent specific diseases and kinds of diseases, see 614.5

See also 351.77 for premarital examinations and certification, 351.81 for registration and certification of births and deaths

See Manual at 614.4–614.5 vs. 362.1–362.4; 614.4 for epidemiology

.409 Historical, geographic, persons treatment of epidemiology

Class geographical treatment of incidence and distribution of diseases, history of epidemics in 614.4

.5 **Incidence of and public measures to prevent specific diseases and kinds of diseases**

Class incidence of and public measures to prevent mental and emotional illnesses and disturbances in 362.2

See Manual at 614.4–614.5 vs. 362.1–362.4; 614.5 vs. 363.8 for nutrition surveys

615 Pharmacology and therapeutics

Including drugs (materia medica), pharmaceutical chemistry (manufacture, preparation, analysis of drugs), practical pharmacy (preparing prescriptions and dispensing drugs), pharmacodynamics (physiological and therapeutic action of drugs); methods of medication, e.g., oral

See Manual at 615 vs. 616–618 for pharmacodynamics

.5 **Therapeutics**

Including drug therapy, chemotherapy; pediatric and geriatric therapeutics; general therapeutic systems, e.g., chiropractic, osteopathy

Class general therapeutics of a specific drug or group of drugs, methods of medication in 615; therapies applied to specific diseases or groups of diseases in 616–618; a specific aspect of pediatric or geriatric therapeutics with the subject, e.g., acupuncture 615.8

For specific therapies and kinds of therapies, see 615.8; first aid, 616.02

See Manual at 615.5 for general therapeutic systems

.507 Education and related topics

Class here comprehensive works on patient education

Class patient education on a specific topic with the topic, e.g., patient education about diabetes mellitus 616.4

.8 Specific therapies and kinds of therapies

Including hypnotherapy, music, occupational therapy; physical therapies, e.g., electrotherapy, phototherapy, radiotherapy, therapeutic exercises and massage; faith, spiritual healing; acupuncture, folk medicine, patent medicines; quackery

Class comprehensive works on therapies, drug therapy in 615.5; surgery in 617

See Manual at 613 vs. 615.8; 615.8

.9 Toxicology

Sources, composition, physiological effects, tests, detection, antidotes of poisons, e.g., food poisons

Including prevention, diagnosis, treatment of poisoning

Class here poisons and poisoning

Class forensic toxicology in 614, effects of poisons on specific systems and organs in 616–618

.900 1 Philosophy and theory

.900 2 Miscellany

.900 28 Auxiliary techniques and procedures; apparatus, equipment, materials

Class testing and measurement in 615.9

.900 3–.900 9 Standard subdivisions

> **616–618 Diseases, surgery, other branches of medicine**

Medical microbiology, genetic and congenital diseases, symptoms as problems in their own right, causes (etiology) and effects of diseases, preventive measures by the individual and by medical personnel, diagnosis, prognosis, intensive and terminal care, other treatment, rehabilitation are classed in 616–618 without use of notation 01–09 from Table 1

Class comprehensive works in 616, comprehensive works on rehabilitation in 617

See Manual at 615 vs. 616–618 for drug therapy

616 Diseases

Class here internal medicine

Class wounds and injuries, surgical treatment of diseases, diseases by body region, diseases of teeth, eyes, ears in 617; gynecological, obstetrical, pediatric, geriatric diseases in 618

For incidence of and public measures to prevent diseases, see 614.4; therapeutics, 615.5

See Manual at 612 vs. 616; 615 vs. 616–618 for drug therapy; 616 vs. 576 for medical microbiology; 616 vs. 610; 616 vs. 616.07 for clinical medicine; 616 vs. 616.9 for medical microbiology; 617 vs. 616; 617.4 vs. 616; 618.92 vs. 616, 618.3

SUMMARY

616.001–.009 Standard subdivisions
.02–.08 [Domestic medicine, medical emergencies, pathology, psychosomatic medicine]
.1 Diseases of the cardiovascular system
.2 Diseases of the respiratory system
.3 Diseases of the digestive system
.4 Diseases of the blood-forming, lymphatic, glandular systems Diseases of the endocrine system
.5 Diseases of the skin (integument), hair, nails
.6 Diseases of the urogenital system Diseases of the urinary system
.7 Diseases of the musculoskeletal system
.8 Diseases of the nervous system and mental disorders
.9 Other diseases

.001 Philosophy and theory

.002 Miscellany

[.002 3] Work with diseases as a profession, occupation, hobby

Do not use; class in 610.69

.002 8 Auxiliary techniques and procedures; apparatus, equipment, materials

Class testing and measurement in 616.07

.003–.007 Standard subdivisions

.008 History and description with respect to kinds of persons

.008 3 Young people

Class diseases of infants and children up to puberty in 618.92

.008 4 Persons in specific stages of adulthood

Class diseases of persons in late adulthood in 618.97

.009 Historical, geographic, persons treatment

.009 2 Persons

Class life with a physical disease in 362.1, with a mental disorder in 616.890092

.02 Domestic medicine and medical emergencies

Domestic medicine: diagnosis and treatment of ailments without direction of physician

Including first aid, advice on when to go to a doctor

Do not use standard subdivisions

Intensive care is classed in 616

See also 649.8 for home care of the sick and infirm

.07 Pathology

Causes, effects, diagnosis, prognosis

Including death, immunity, comprehensive works on medical radiology

Use for detailed description of diseased conditions, causes and manifestations, diagnostic techniques. For works lacking detail, prefer 616 over 616.07

Use of this number for symptomatology discontinued; class in 616

Failures of immunity, autoimmunity relocated to 616.97

Class interdisciplinary works on human death in 306.9, tissue and cell pathology in 611, forensic pathology in 614, medical microbiology in 616, nonprofessional diagnosis in 616.02

For radiotherapy, see 615.8

See Manual at 591.2 vs. 616.07 for immunology; 616 vs. 616.07 for clinical medicine

.08 Psychosomatic medicine

> **616.1–616.9 Specific diseases**

All notes under 616.02–616.08 are applicable here

Except for additions, changes, deletions, exceptions shown under specific entries, use the following modified standard subdivisions:

001	Philosophy and theory
002	Miscellany
[0023]	The specialty as a profession, occupation, hobby Do not use; class in the number for the disease without adding 0023
0028	Auxiliary techniques and procedures; apparatus, equipment, materials Class testing and measurement in the number for the disease without adding 0028
003–007	Standard subdivisions
008	History and description with respect to kinds of persons
0083	Young people Class diseases of infants and children up to puberty in 618.92
0084	Persons in specific stages of adulthood Class persons in late adulthood in 618.97
009	Historical, geographic, persons treatment
0092	Persons Class life with a physical disease in 362.1, with a mental disorder in 616.890092

Class comprehensive works in 616; comprehensive works on therapy in 615.5, on rehabilitation in 617; public measures for preventing a specific disease in 614.5, social factors contributing to the spread of a disease in 362.1

When a specific type of genetic disease has an indirect etiology, class with the system showing the most visible manifestations, e.g., mental retardation caused by hereditary metabolic disorders 616.85 (*not* 616.3)

\> **616.1–616.8 Diseases of specific systems and organs**

Class comprehensive works in 616, tuberculosis of specific systems and organs in 616.9, diseases of the immune system in 616.97, tumors (neoplasms) of specific systems and organs in 616.99

See Manual at 616.1–616.8

.1 **Diseases of the cardiovascular system**

Including cardiology, hematology

Class diseases of blood-forming system in 616.4; bacterial blood diseases in 616.9; diseases of blood vessels in a specific system or organs with the system or organ, e.g., cerebrovascular diseases 616.8

.100 1–.100 9 Standard subdivisions

As modified under 616.1–616.9

.2 **Diseases of the respiratory system**

Including asthma, common cold, emphysema, hay fever, influenza, pneumonia

Class cardiac asthma in 616.1; pulmonary tuberculosis in 616.9; otorhinolaryngology, comprehensive works on diseases of eyes, ears, nose, throat in 617.5

.200 1–.200 9 Standard subdivisions

As modified under 616.1–616.9

.3 **Diseases of the digestive system**

Including gastroenterology; nutritional and metabolic diseases, e.g., obesity

Class laryngology in 616.2; diabetes in 616.4; appetite and eating disorders as neuroses in 616.85; cholera, dysenteries, typhoid fever in 616.9; allergies of the digestive system in 616.97; oral region in 617.5; diseases of the teeth and gums in 617.6; nutritional and metabolic diseases of a specific system or organ with the system or organ, e.g., metabolic bone diseases 616.7

For endocrinology, see 616.4

See Manual at 616.9 vs. 616.3 for cholera

.300 1–.300 9 Standard subdivisions

As modified under 616.1–616.9

.4 **Diseases of the blood-forming, lymphatic, glandular systems Diseases of the endocrine system**

Including diabetes; diseases of bone marrow, male breast, spleen

Class here endocrinology

Class comprehensive works on diseases of breast in 618.1; anemia in 616.1, endocrinal obesity in 616.3, myxedemia in 616.85, Hodgkin's disease in 616.99; diseases of glands in a specific system or organ with the system or organ, e.g., diseases of female sex glands 618.1

.400 1–.400 9 Standard subdivisions

As modified under 616.1–616.9

.5 Diseases of the skin (integument), hair, nails

Including diseases of sebaceous and sweat glands

Class here dermatology

Class comprehensive works on allergies of the skin in 616.97

For venereal diseases, see 616.95

.500 1–.500 9 Standard subdivisions

As modified under 616.1–616.9

.6 Diseases of the urogenital system Diseases of the urinary system

Including nephrology; comprehensive works on diseases of the genital system; sexual disorders, e.g., infertility

Class here urology

Class comprehensive works on climacteric disorders in 618.1; renal hypertension in 616.1, sexual personality disorders in 616.85, venereal diseases in 616.95; diseases of female genital system, female sexual disorders in 618.1

.600 1–.600 9 Standard subdivisions

As modified under 616.1–616.9

.7 Diseases of the musculoskeletal system

Including neuromuscular diseases; rheumatology, comprehensive works on rheumatism

Class rickets, gout in 616.3; neuromuscular diseases resulting from disorders of the central nervous system in 616.8; treatment of chronic diseases of the skeletal system in 617.3; a specific rheumatic disease with the disease, e.g., rheumatic fever 616.9; diseases of muscles in a specific system or organ, e.g., diseases of heart 616.1

See Manual at 617.3 vs. 616.7, 617.5

.700 1–.700 9 Standard subdivisions

As modified under 616.1–616.9

.8 Diseases of the nervous system and mental disorders

Including cerebral palsy, epilepsy, migraine, poliomyelitis; cerebrovascular diseases, e.g., stroke

Class here neurology, neuropsychiatry

Use 616.8001–616.8009 for standard subdivisions

Class shingles in 616.5; diseases of nerves in a specific system or organ with the system or organ, e.g., neuromuscular diseases 616.7

.801–.809 Standard subdivisions of neurology, of brain diseases

As modified under 616.1–616.9

√.85 Neuroses, disorders of personality and intellect, speech and language disorders

Including amnesia, anorexia nervosa, combat fatigue, depression, hypochondria, hysteria, multiple personality, phobia; homosexuality, kleptomania, sadism, suicidal compulsions; hyperactivity, learning disabilities, mental deficiency; dyslexia, stammering, stuttering

Do not use standard subdivisions

Class substance abuse in 616.86; manic-depressive psychoses in 616.89; neurotic aspects of a specific disease with the disease, e.g., of asthma 616.2

√.86 Substance abuse (Drug abuse)

Examples: abuse of alcohol, cocaine, narcotics, tobacco

Class here addiction, habituation, intoxication

Effect of metallic intoxication on nervous system and mental condition discontinued; class in 616.8

Class interdisciplinary works on substance abuse in 362.29, comprehensive medical works on addictive and disorienting drugs in 615, personal measures to prevent substance abuse in 613.8, food addiction in 616.3

.860 01–.860 09 Standard subdivisions

As modified under 616.1–616.9

.89 Mental disorders

Including psychoanalysis, psychotherapy; psychoses, e.g., paranoia, schizophrenia

Class here abnormal and clinical psychologies [*formerly also* 157], psychiatry

Class puerperal psychoses in 618.7; physical manifestations of mental disorders involving a specific system with the system, e.g., psychosomatic ulcers 616.3

For neuroses, disorders of personality and intellect, see 616.85

See Manual at 150.19 vs. 616.89

.890 01–.890 07 Standard subdivisions

As modified under 616.1–616.9

.890 08 History and description with respect to kinds of persons

.890 083 Young people

Class mental disorders of infants and children up to puberty in 618.92

[.890 083 5] Young adults

Do not use; class in 616.89

.890 084 Persons in specific stages of adulthood

Class mental disorders of persons in late adulthood in 618.97

.890 09 Historical, geographic, persons treatment

.9 Other diseases

Examples: malaria, rabies, rheumatic fever, smallpox, tetanus, tuberculosis; bacterial, parasitic, rickettsial, viral diseases

Including noncommunicable diseases; environmental medicine; specialized medical services, e.g., aerospace, industrial medicine

Communicable diseases not provided elsewhere are classed in 616.9, without use of 616.97001–616.97009; specific kinds are classed with the kind, e.g., communicable diseases of the immune system 616.97

Class parasitic skin diseases in 616.5, injuries from radiation in 617.1; a specific communicable disease not provided for here with the disease, e.g., mumps 616.3; noncommunicable diseases of a specific organ or system with the organ or system, e.g., mental disorders 616.89

See Manual at 616 vs. 616.9 for communicable diseases; 616.9 vs. 616.3 for cholera

.901–.909 Standard subdivisions

As modified under 616.1–616.9

.95 Venereal diseases

Do not use standard subdivisions

Class acquired immune deficiency syndrome (AIDS) in 616.97

.97 Diseases of the immune system

Including failures of immunity, autoimmunity [*formerly* 616.07]; autoimmune diseases; immune deficiency diseases, e.g., AIDS; contact, drug, food allergies; hypersensitivity to physical agents, e.g., heat, sunlight, cold, humidity

Class here comprehensive works on allergies

Class a specific allergy not provided for here with the allergy, e.g., hay fever 616.2

.970 01–.970 09 Standard subdivisions

As modified under 616.1–616.9

.99 Tumors and cancers

Medical and surgical treatment

Example: leukemia

Class here oncology

Do not use standard subdivisions

617 Miscellaneous branches of medicine Surgery

Only those branches named below

Operative surgery is classed in 617, without use of 617.001–617.009; operative surgery of specific systems, organs, regions is classed with the system, organ, region in 617

Except where contrary instructions are given, all notes under 616.02–616.08 are applicable here

Except for additions, changes, deletions, exceptions shown under specific entries, use the following modified standard subdivisions:

001–007 Standard subdivisions
As modified under 616.1–616.9

008 History and description with respect to kinds of persons
Class military surgery in 617.9

0083 Young people
Class dentistry for infants and children in 617.6; surgery for infants and children up to puberty in 617.9; regional medicine, ophthalmology, otology, audiology for infants and children up to puberty in 618.92

0084 Persons in specific stages of adulthood
Class persons in late adulthood in 618.97, except class surgery in 617.9

[009] Historical, geographic, persons treatment
Do not use; class in 09

09 Historical, geographic, persons treatment
Add to 09 notation 1–9 from Table 2, e.g., the subject in India 0954

See Manual at 615 vs. 616–618 for drug therapy; 617 vs. 616; 617.3 vs. 617 for prosthetic equipment and surgical appliances; 618.92 vs. 617 for miscellaneous specialties with respect to children; 618.97 vs. 617 for miscellaneous specialties with respect to persons in late adulthood

.001 Philosophy and theory of surgery

.002 Miscellany of surgery

[.002 3] Surgery as a profession, occupation, hobby

Do not use; class in 617

[.002 8] Auxiliary techniques and procedures; apparatus, equipment, materials

Do not use; class in 617, except class geriatric, pediatric, military, plastic surgery, transplantation of tissue and organs, anesthesiology in 617.9

.003–.007 Standard subdivisions of surgery

.008 History and description of surgery with respect to kinds of persons

Class military personnel in 617.9

.008 3 Young people

Class surgery for infants and children up to puberty in 617.9

.008 4 Persons in specific stages of adulthood

Class persons in late adulthood in 617.9

[.009] Historical, geographic, persons treatment of surgery

Do not use; class in 617.09

.09 Historical, geographic, persons treatment of surgery

Add to base number 617.09 notation 1–9 from Table 2, e.g., collective biographies of surgeons 617.0922

> **617.1–617.5 Surgery**

Class comprehensive works, operative surgery in 617; surgical treatment of tumors in 616.99

For geriatric, pediatric, military, plastic surgery, transplantation of tissue and organs, anesthesiology, see 617.9

.1 **Wounds and injuries**

Examples: burns, dislocations, fractures, sprains

Including sports medicine

Class here traumatology

Use 617.1001–617.1009 for standard subdivisions

Class results of injuries in 617.2; wounds and injuries of specific systems, regions, organs in 617.4–617.5; a specific branch of sports medicine with the branch, e.g., promotion of health of athletes 613.7

.2 **Results of injuries**

Example: shock

See also 617.1 for rehabilitation, rehabilitative therapy

.3 **Orthopedics**

Correction of deformities

Including orthopedic appliances

Class here treatment of chronic diseases of the skeletal system

Class plastic surgery of bones in 617.4, amputations in 617.5

For fractures, see 617.1

See Manual at 617.3 vs. 616.7, 617.5; 617.3 vs. 617 for orthopedic appliances

.300 1 Philosophy and theory

.300 2 Miscellany

.300 28 Auxiliary techniques and procedures; apparatus, equipment, materials

Class orthopedic appliances in 617.3

.300 3–.300 9 Standard subdivisions

\> **617.4–617.5 Surgery by systems and regions**

Class here wounds and injuries of specific systems, regions, organs; surgery of specific organs

Class comprehensive works in 617

.4 **Surgery by systems**

Including cardiovascular, digestive, endocrine, lymphatic, musculoskeletal, nervous, urogenital systems; circumcision, psychosurgery

Class surgery of specific organs of digestive system in 617.5; ophthalmological surgery in 617.7; otological surgery in 617.8; surgery of a specific gland with the gland, e.g., thyroid gland 617.5; surgery of nerves of a specific system or organ with the system or organ, e.g., neurosurgery of the stomach 617.5

For respiratory system, see 617.5

See Manual at 617.4 vs. 616

.5 **Regional medicine Regional surgery**

Including appendectomies, oral surgery, otorhinolaryngology, podiatry, respiratory system; comprehensive works on diseases of eyes, ears, nose, throat

Class ears in 617.8, nonsurgical medicine of specific systems or organs in specific regions in 616

See Manual at 617.3 vs. 616.7, 617.5 for orthopedics; 617.5; 617.5 vs. 617.6 for oral surgery

.6 **Dentistry**

Including cavities, dental diseases, oral surgery, orthodontics, pedodontics; dentures, bridges

See Manual at 617.5 vs. 617.6 for oral surgery

.600 1–.600 8 Standard subdivisions

As modified under 617

.600 9 Historical, geographic, persons treatment

.7 **Ophthalmology**

Treatment of ocular diseases; correction of refractive errors, e.g., astigmatism

Including color blindness, cataracts, glaucoma; optometry; use of eyeglasses, contact lenses

.700 1–.700 8 Standard subdivisions

As modified under 617

.709 Historical, geographic, persons treatment

.8 **Otology and audiology**

Including pathology, medical and surgical treatment of diseases of ears; correction of impaired hearing through fitting and adjusting hearing devices

Class here loss and impairment of function (deafness and hearing impairment)

.800 1–.800 8 Standard subdivisions

As modified under 617

.809 Historical, geographic, persons treatment

.9 **Geriatric, pediatric, military, plastic surgery, transplantation of tissue and organs, anesthesiology**

Do not use standard subdivisions

Class acupuncture as an anesthetic in 615.8; plastic surgery and transplantation of tissue of specific systems, regions, organs in 617.4–617.5; transplantation of specific organs and implantation of artificial substitutes for specific organs in 617.4; geriatric, pediatric, military surgery of a specific organ, system, disorder with the organ, system, disorder, e.g., fractures 617.1

See also 362.1 for tissue and organ banks

618 Other branches of medicine Gynecology and obstetrics

See Manual at 615 vs. 616–618 for drug therapy

.01 Philosophy and theory of gynecology and obstetrics

.02 Miscellany of gynecology and obstetrics

.028 Auxiliary techniques and procedures; apparatus, equipment, materials

Use of this number for testing and measurement discontinued; class in 618

.03–.07 Standard subdivisions of gynecology and obstetrics

.08 History and description of gynecology and obstetrics with respect to kinds of persons

.083 Young people

Class gynecology for girls up to puberty in 618.92

.084 Persons in specific stages of adulthood

Class persons in late adulthood in 618.97

.09 Historical, geographic, persons treatment of gynecology and obstetrics

Class life with a disease in 362.1

> **618.1–618.8 Gynecology and obstetrics**

Medical and surgical

Except where contrary instructions are given, all notes under 616.02–616.08 are applicable here

Class comprehensive works in 618

.1 **Gynecology**

Including artificial insemination, infertility; comprehensive works on diseases of breast, on climacteric disorders

Class male climacteric disorders, comprehensive works on male and female infertility in 616.6; involutional psychoses in 616.89; tumors, cancers of genital tract and breast in 616.99

For diseases of male breast, see 616.4; puerperal diseases, 618.7

.100 1–.100 9 Standard subdivisions

As modified under 616.1–616.9

.2 **Obstetrics**

Including prenatal care, multiple pregnancy

For diseases, disorders, management of pregnancy, childbirth, puerperium, see 618.3–618.8

.200 1–.200 9 Standard subdivisions

As modified under 616.1–616.9

> **618.3–618.8 Diseases, disorders, management of pregnancy, childbirth, puerperium**

Class comprehensive works in 618.2

.3 **Diseases and complications of pregnancy**

Including fetal disorders, miscarriage, perinatal medicine

Class diseases of newborn infants in 618.92

For childbirth, see 618.4

See Manual at 618.92 vs. 616, 618.3 for fetal disorders

.300 1–.300 9 Standard subdivisions

As modified under 616.1–616.9

.4 **Childbirth Labor**

Class a specific aspect not provided for here with the aspect, e.g., obstetrical surgery in 618.8

.5 **Complicated labor**

.6 **Normal puerperium**

Postpartum management and care

.7 **Puerperal diseases**

Including diseases of lactation

.700 1–.700 9 Standard subdivisions

As modified under 616.1–616.9

.8 **Obstetrical surgery**

Including cesarean section

Class embryo transplant ("test-tube baby") in 618.1

.9 **Pediatrics and geriatrics**

.92 Pediatrics

Diseases of infants and children up to puberty

Class pediatric preventive measures in 613; pediatric therapeutics in 615.5; pediatric aspects of wounds and injuries in 617.1, of results of injuries in 617.2; pediatric orthopedics in 617.3; dental diseases of infants and children in 617.6; pediatric surgery in 617.9; perinatal medicine in 618.3; medicine for young people who have reached puberty in 616.00835

See Manual at 618.92 vs. 616, 618.3; 618.92 vs. 617 for regional medicine, ophthalmology, otology, audiology in pediatrics

.920 001–.920 009 Standard subdivisions

As modified under 616.1–616.9

.97 Geriatrics

Diseases of persons in late adulthood

Class geriatric preventive measures in 613; geriatric therapeutics in 615.5; geriatric aspects of wounds and injuries in 617.1, of results of injuries in 617.2; geriatric orthopedics in 617.3; geriatric surgery in 617.9

See Manual at 618.97 vs. 617 for regional medicine, dentistry, ophthalmology, otology, audiology in geriatrics

.970 01–.970 09 Standard subdivisions

As modified under 616.1–616.9

619 Experimental medicine

Study of pathology and treatment of diseases induced in laboratory animals

Class experimental medicine with respect to pharmacology and therapeutics in 615, with respect to specific diseases in 616–618; animal experimentation with respect to anatomy and physiology in 591–599, human experimentation with respect to anatomy and physiology in 611–612

620 Engineering and allied operations

Including computer-aided design (CAD), remote control, interdisciplinary works on maintenance and repair

Class here manufacturing of products of various branches of engineering

Class comprehensive works on manufacturing in 670, on computer-aided design/computer-aided manufacturing (CAD/CAM) in 670.285; maintenance and repair in a specific subject with the subject, using notation 028 from Table 1, e.g., repair of ventilation and air conditioning equipment 697.9028

For chemical engineering, see 660

SUMMARY

620.001–.009 Standard subdivisions
.1–.8 [Engineering mechanics and materials science, sound and related vibrations, mechanical vibration, human-factors and safety engineering]
621 Applied physics
622 Mining engineering and related operations
623 Military and nautical engineering
624 Civil engineering
625 Engineering of railroads, roads, highways
627 Hydraulic engineering
628 Sanitary and municipal engineering Environmental protection engineering
629 Other branches of engineering

.001 Philosophy and theory

Including analysis of large, complex systems [*formerly* 620.7]

Class interdisciplinary works on systems in 003; works covering systems of agriculture, home economics, or management in addition to engineering in 601; design of engineering systems in 620; manufacturing systems in 670.1; physical principles in engineering in 621

.002 Miscellany

.002 8 Auxiliary techniques and procedures; apparatus, equipment, materials

Class maintenance and repair, testing and measurement in 620; safety engineering in 620.8

.003–.008 Standard subdivisions

.009 Historical, geographic, persons treatment

.009 1 Treatment by areas, regions, places in general

Class engineering to overcome problems of specific kinds of geographical environments in 620

.009 2 Persons

Class persons treatment of engineers known primarily as entrepreneurs in 338.7

[.009 99] Engineering in other worlds

Do not use; class in 620

.1 **Engineering mechanics (Applied mechanics) and materials science**

Including applied statics and dynamics of solids, liquids, gases; corrosion, failure, fatigue, strength and other properties of materials; comprehensive works on fluid-power technology

Class comprehensive works on materials, manufacture of materials in 670; steam engineering in 621.1, hydraulic-power technology in 621.2, pneumatic and vacuum technology in 621.5, structural theory in 624.1, hydraulic engineering in 627, aeromechanics of flight in 629.132, air-conditioning engineering in 697.9; manufacturing and chemical properties of specific kinds of materials with the materials, e.g., wood 674

For mechanical vibration, see 620.3

See also 531 for mechanics as a subject in physics, 621.8 for physical principles of machinery

See Manual at 621 vs. 530

.100 1–.100 9 Standard subdivisions of engineering mechanics and materials science, of engineering mechanics alone

.2 **Sound and related vibrations**

Including subsonics, ultrasonics; noise and countermeasures

Class here applied acoustics

Class electroacoustical communications in 621.382; interdisciplinary works on architectural acoustics in 729, engineering works on architectural acoustics in 690

See also 534 for physics of sound

See Manual at 621 vs. 530

.3 **Mechanical vibration**

Class effects of vibrations on materials in 620.1

For sound and related vibrations, see 620.2

[.7] **Engineering of large, complex systems**

Number discontinued; class in 620

Analysis of large, complex systems relocated to 620.001

.8 **Human-factors and safety engineering**

Variant names for human-factors engineering: biotechnology, design anthropometry, ergonomics

Class here engineering of work environment

Environmental health engineering relocated to 628

Class a specific application with the application, e.g., engineering of the home kitchen work environment 643; safety engineering of a specific technology with the technology, using notation 028 from Table 1, e.g., safety in machine engineering 621.8028

621 Applied physics

Mechanical, electrical, electronic, electromagnetic, heat, light, nuclear engineering

Standard subdivisions are added for mechanical engineering

Class engineering mechanics and materials science in 620.1; applied acoustics in 620.2; a specific application with the application, e.g., military engineering 623

See Manual at 621 vs. 530

SUMMARY

.04 Energy and plasma engineering

.042 Energy engineering

Class here engineering of alternative, renewable energy sources

Class interdisciplinary works on energy in 333.79

.044 Plasma engineering

See also 530.4 for plasma as a subject in physics

> **621.1–621.2 Fluid-power technologies**

Class comprehensive works in 620.1

.1 **Steam engineering**

Including engines, boilers, cogeneration of electric power and heat

Class interdisciplinary works on cogeneration of electricity and heat in 333.79

.2 **Hydraulic-power technology**

Examples: hydraulic pumps, waterwheels

Class comprehensive works on pumps in 621.6, hydraulic control in 629.8

.3 **Electric, electronic, magnetic, communications, computer engineering; lighting**

Including superconductivity

Standard subdivisions are added for electromagnetic engineering, for combined electric and electronic engineering, for electrical engineering alone

See also 537 for physics of electricity and electromagnetism

SUMMARY

.302 8 Auxiliary techniques and procedures; apparatus, equipment, materials

Class electrical equipment in 621.31, electrical testing and measurement in 621.37

.31 Generation, modification, storage, transmission of electric power

Including electrical machinery and equipment; batteries, fuel cells, solar cells; power electronics; direct nuclear generation, hydroelectric generation

Class here alternating current [*formerly also* 537.6]

Nuclear steam-powered generation of electricity relocated to 621.48

Class engineering of dams for hydroelectric power in 627; a specific application of electrical machinery with the application, e.g., refrigerators 621.5

For electric motors, see 621.46

.319 Transmission

Including power failure, comprehensive works on electric and electronic circuits and networks

Class here electrification [*formerly* 621.39]

Class interdisciplinary works on electrification, on power failure in 333.79, electronic circuits and networks in 621.3815

For electric power transmission for railroads, see 621.33

.319 01 Philosophy and theory

Class systems in 621.319

.32 Lighting

Including nonelectric lighting, e.g., candles, gas lighting

Class here electric lighting

Class lighting of airports in 629.136

For public lighting, see 628.9

.33 Electric power transmission for railroads

.34 Magnetic engineering

Class here artificial magnets [*formerly also* 538], electromagnets

Class electromagnets as parts of generators in 621.31, of electric motors in 621.46

Use 621.3 for comprehensive works on electromagnetic technology

See also 538 for physics of magnetism

.36 Applied optics and paraphotic engineering

Including lasers [*formerly also* 535.5], fiber optics [*formerly also* 535.8], applied spectroscopy, infrared and ultraviolet technology, integrated optics; technological photography and photo-optics, e.g., holography, optical data processing, remote sensing technology

Class photoelectric and photoelectronic devices in 621.3815, optical communication in 621.382, manufacture of optical instruments in 681, interdisciplinary works on photography in 770

For photogrammetry, see 526.9; lighting, 621.32

See also 535 for optics and light as subjects in physics

See Manual at 778.3 vs. 621.36 for photography

.37 Testing and measurement of electrical quantities

Instruments and their use

Electrical instruments for measuring nonelectrical quantities relocated to 681

Class testing and measurement of a specific apparatus, part, or function with the subject, using notation 028 from Table 1, e.g., testing electromagnets 621.34028

.38 Electronics and communication engineering

SUMMARY

621.380 28	**Auxiliary techniques and procedures; apparatus, equipment, materials**
.381	**Electronics**
.382	**Communications engineering**
.383	**Telegraph**
.384	**Radio and radar**
.385	**Telephone**
.386	**Telephone terminal equipment**
.387	**Telephone transmission and nonterminal equipment**
.388	**Television**
.389	**Sound recording, security, related systems**

.380 28 Auxiliary techniques and procedures; apparatus, equipment, materials

Electroacoustical apparatus and equipment, antennas relocated to 621.382

.381 Electronics

Including microwave electronics, e.g., masers

Class here microelectronics, shortwave and long-wave electronics

Electronic bugging devices relocated to 621.389

Class signal processing, electronic noise and interference in 621.382; a specific application of electronics with the application, e.g., laser technology 621.36, radio engineering 621.384

See also 537.5 for physics aspects, 621.36 for fiber optics

.381 5 Components and circuits

Analysis, design, functions, manufacture

Class here circuitry [*formerly also* 537.5]; analog, digital, integrated, microelectronic, semiconductor, thin-film circuits; circuits and components common to electronics and communications engineering

Including cathode-ray tubes, electric eyes, printed circuits; semiconductors, e.g., transistors

Use of this number for comprehensive works on shortwave and long-wave electronics discontinued; class in 621.381

Class microwave components and circuits in 621.381, components and circuits of a specific branch of communications engineering in 621.383–621.389, very large scale integration in 621.39

.381 502 8 Auxiliary techniques and procedures; apparatus, equipment, materials

Do not use for testing and measurement; class in 621.3815

[.381 9] Computers

Relocated to 621.39

.382 Communications engineering

Including electroacoustical apparatus and equipment, antennas [*all formerly* 621.38028]; laser communications [*formerly* 621.389]; acoustical, electroacoustical, optical communication; satellite communication; facsimile transmission; signal processing; recording devices of two or more communication systems, e.g., discs, tapes

Class here analog, digital, electronic communications; communications systems; telecommunications

Telegraph relocated to 621.383

Class components and circuits common to electronics and communications engineering, e.g., amplifiers, switching circuits, in 621.3815; video recorders in 621.388, audio systems limited to recording and reproduction of sound in 621.389; data communications engineering in 621.39

For specific communications systems, see 621.383–621.389

See Manual at 621.382 vs. 003 for information theory; 621.382 vs. 621.39, 004.6, 384 for digital communications

---

> **621.383–621.389 Specific communications systems**

Class comprehensive works in 621.382

.383 Telegraph [*formerly also* 621.382]

For radiotelegraph, see 621.384

.384 Radio and radar

Including loran, radio control, radiotelegraph

Class here broadcast radio, comprehensive works on radio and television

For television, see 621.388

.384 028 Auxiliary techniques and procedures; apparatus, equipment, materials

Class maintenance and repair of receiving sets in 621.384

.384 1 Amateur (Ham) radio

Do not use standard subdivisions

Use of this number for comprehensive works on radio, on radio and television discontinued; class in 621.384

Mobile and portable radio stations relocated to 621.3845

See Manual at 621.3841 vs. 621.3845

.384 5 Radiotelephone

Including portable radio stations [*formerly* 621.3841], e.g., walkie-talkies; cellular telephones; citizens band radio

Class here mobile radio stations [*formerly* 621.3841], specific instruments and apparatus of radiotelephone [*formerly* 621.3846], comprehensive works on radio transmission in telephone

For radio relays, see 621.387

See Manual at 621.3841 vs. 621.3845 for citizens band radio

[.384 6] Specific instruments and apparatus of radiotelephone

Relocated to 621.3845

.384 8 Radar

.385 Telephone

Class here telephone systems based on wires, cables, lasers, optical fibers

Class cellular telephone systems in 621.3845, data communications engineering in 621.39

For radiotelephone, see 621.3845; telephone equipment and transmission, 621.386–621.387

> 621.386–621.387 Telephone equipment and transmission

Class comprehensive works in 621.385

.386 Telephone terminal equipment

Dialing, transmitting, receiving equipment

.387 Telephone transmission and nonterminal equipment

Including long-distance systems, radio relays, switchboards, transmission lines

Class comprehensive works on radiotelephone and radio relay in 621.3845

.388 Television

Including cameras, video recorders

.388 001 Philosophy and theory

.388 002 Miscellany

.388 002 8 Auxiliary techniques and procedures; apparatus, equipment, materials

Class maintenance and repair of receiving sets in 621.388

.388 003–.388 009 Standard subdivisions

.389 Sound recording, security, related systems

Including electronic bugging devices [*formerly* 621.381], alarms, audiovisual engineering, public address systems, sonar, translating machines

Laser communications relocated to 621.382

Class comprehensive works on acoustical communications, on audio systems covering transmission as well as recording and reproduction in 621.382; telephone message recording in 621.386

✓.39 Computers [*formerly* 621.3819] teaching, software VBC applic.

Class here electronic digital computers, central processing units, computer reliability

Including interfacing and communication devices, e.g., modems; peripherals, e.g., terminals

Use of this number for other branches of electrical engineering, for superconductivity discontinued; class in 621.3

Rural electrification relocated to 333.79, electrification relocated to 621.319, electric heating relocated to 621.402

Class selection and use of computer hardware, works treating both hardware and either programming or programs in 004; computer output printers and microform devices in 681.6; specific applications with the subject, e.g., use of computers to regulate processes automatically 629.8

See Manual at 004–006 vs. 621.39; 621.382 vs. 621.39, 004.6, 384 for digital communications

.4 Heat engineering and prime movers

Including windmills

Class here engines, power plants, propulsion systems

Use 621.4001–621.4009 for standard subdivisions

For steam engineering, see 621.1, hydraulic-power technology, 621.2

.402 Heat engineering

Including electric heating [*formerly* 621.39], combustion, equipment

Class pollution by-products of combustion in 628.5; a kind of heat engineering with the kind, e.g., geothermal engineering in 621.44, heating buildings in 697

For low-temperature technology, see 621.5

See also 536 for physics of heat

.406 Turbines

Class here turbomachines

.43 Internal-combustion engines and propulsion

Examples: diesel, gas-turbine, jet, rocket, spark-ignition engines

Class generation of electricity by internal-combustion engines in 621.31

.44 Geothermal engineering

.46 Electric and related propulsion

Including ion, plasma motors

Class here electric motors

.47 Solar-energy engineering

Including solar engines

Class generation of electricity from solar radiation in 621.31; engineering of secondary sources of solar energy with the secondary source, e.g., wind energy 621.4

.48 Nuclear engineering

Fission and fusion technology

Including nuclear steam-powered generation of electricity [*formerly* 621.31], nuclear reactors and power plants, nuclear propulsion, treatment and disposal of radioactive waste, comprehensive works on radioisotope technology

Class direct nuclear generation of electricity in 621.31; a specific application of radioisotopes with the application, e.g., radioisotope therapy 615.8

See also 539.7 for nuclear physics

.5 Pneumatic, vacuum, low-temperature technologies

Including vacuum pumps [*formerly* 621.6], air compression, ice manufacture, refrigeration, cryogenic engineering

Class pneumatic control in 629.8

For fans, blowers, pumps, see 621.6

See also 533 for vacuum physics, 536 for physics of low temperatures

.6 Fans, blowers, pumps

Vacuum pumps relocated to 621.5

Class hydraulic pumps in 621.2

.8 Machine engineering

Examples: conveying equipment, cranes, derricks, elevators, power shovels

Including simple machines [*formerly also* 531], e.g., pulleys; fasteners, e.g., bolts, nails; friction and lubrication; machine parts, e.g., bearings, gears

Class a specific kind of machinery not provided for here with the kind, e.g., hydraulic machinery 621.2; a specific use of machinery with the use, e.g., gears in clocks 681.1

See also 621.9 for fastening equipment

.801 Philosophy and theory

Class physical principles of machinery in 621.8

.802 Miscellany

.802 8 Auxiliary techniques and procedures; apparatus, equipment, materials

Class maintenance and repair of machinery in 621.8

.9 Tools and fabricating equipment

Examples: fastening equipment, grindstones, lathes, molds,

Including hand, machine tools

Measuring tools relocated to 681

Class a specific use with the use, e.g., lathes in woodworking 684

.900 1–.900 9 Standard subdivisions

622 Mining engineering and related operations

Including in situ processing, ore dressing, prospecting, treasure hunting

Prospecting for water, water extraction relocated to 628.1

Class interdisciplinary works on mine safety in 363.11

See Manual at 622 vs. 669, 662 for ore dressing and in situ processing

.028 Auxiliary techniques and procedures; apparatus, equipment, materials

Class safety measures in 622

623 Military and nautical engineering

Including ballistics, camouflage, demolition, forts, gunnery, mine laying and clearance; military communications, sanitation, transportation technology

See Manual at 355 vs. 623

.4 Ordnance

Including biological and nuclear weapons, missiles, small arms; weaponry of prefirearm origin, e.g., armor, bows and arrows, swords

Class combat ships in 623.8; artistic aspects of arms and armor in 739.7; vehicle-mounted small arms in 623.7

For combat vehicles, see 623.7

.7 **Vehicles**

Support vehicles, combat vehicles and their ordnance

Examples: airplanes, jeeps, tanks, spacecraft

Do not use standard subdivisions

Use of this number for other operations of military engineering discontinued; class in 623

Class railroad rolling stock in 623, ammunition in 623.4, nautical craft in 623.8

See Manual at 629.04 vs. 388

[.74] Vehicles

Use of this number discontinued; class in 623.7

.8 **Nautical engineering and seamanship**

Nautical engineering: engineering of ships and boats and their component parts

Including naval ordnance, shipyards

Class here naval engineering, comprehensive works on military water transportation

Class naval facilities in 623; naval artillery and ammunition in 623.4; harbors, ports, roadsteads in 627; overwater hovercraft in 629.3

See Manual at 629.04 vs. 388

.88 Seamanship

Including marine safety technology, rescue operations, wreckage studies; interdisciplinary works on knotting and splicing

Class safety equipment in 623.8; a specific application of knotting and splicing with the application, e.g., knotting in camping 796.54

For navigation, see 623.89

.880 28 Auxiliary techniques and procedures; apparatus, equipment, materials

Class safety measures in 623.88

.89 Navigation of nautical craft

Selection and determination of course

Including piloting and pilot guides; aids to navigation, e.g., lighthouses

Class navigation procedures to prevent collision and grounding in 623.88

624 Civil engineering

Including bridges

Class here construction engineering

Class specific branches of civil engineering in 625–629, military construction engineering in 623, construction of buildings in 690

See Manual at 624.1 vs. 624; 690 vs. 624

.029 Commercial miscellany

Class estimates of labor, time, materials in 624.1

.068 Management

Including management of production [*formerly also* 658.5]

.1 Structural engineering and underground construction

Including earthquake engineering, engineering geology, excavation, foundations, soil mechanics, tunnels; interdisciplinary works on structural analysis, design, theory

Class subsurface mining in 622, construction of underground waste disposal facilities in 628.4; a specific application of structural engineering with the application, e.g., structural engineering of dams 627; a specific application of structural analysis, design, theory with the application, e.g., structural analysis of aircraft 629.134

See Manual at 624.1 vs. 624

.101 Philosophy and theory

Class structural analysis and design in 624.1

.102 9 Commercial miscellany

Class estimates of labor, time, materials in 624.1

625 Engineering of railroads, roads, highways

General aspects: planning, analysis, design, construction

Class military transportation engineering in 623, bridge engineering in 624, tunnel engineering in 624.1

.1 Railroads

Including monorail railroads, comprehensive works on special-purpose railroads; railroad yards; model railroads and trains

Class electrification of railroads in 621.33

For railroad rolling stock, see 625.2; special-purpose railroads, 625.3–625.6

.100 1 Philosophy and theory

.100 2 Miscellany

.100 28 Auxiliary techniques and procedures; apparatus, equipment, materials

Class maintenance and repair in 625.1

.100 3–.100 9 Standard subdivisions

.2 **Railroad rolling stock**

Examples: freight, passenger-train cars; locomotives

Class rolling stock for special-purpose railways in 625.3–625.6, models in 625.1

See Manual at 629.04 vs. 388

> **625.3–625.6 Special-purpose railroads**

Class here roadbeds, tracks and accessories, rolling stock

Class comprehensive works in 625.1, mine railroads in 622

.3 **Inclined, mountain, ship railroads**

.4 **Rapid transit systems**

Including subways

For surface systems, see 625.6

.5 **Cable and aerial railways**

Class funicular railroads in 625.3

.6 **Surface rail and trolley systems**

Light interurban and local

.7 **Roads**

Including municipal snow and ice removal [*formerly* 628.4], roadside barriers, roadside areas, traffic signs

Class here highways, streets

Class curbs in 625.8, public lighting for roads in 628.9

For artificial road surfaces, see 625.8

.702 8 Auxiliary techniques and procedures; apparatus, equipment, materials

Class maintenance, repair, safety measures in 625.7

.8 **Artificial road surfaces**

General aspects: design, construction, materials

Including driveways, sidewalks

Class here comprehensive works on paving

Class paving surfaces not provided for here with the surface, e.g., airport runways 629.136

.802 8 Auxiliary techniques and procedures; apparatus, equipment, materials

Class maintenance and repair in 625.7

627 Hydraulic engineering

The branch of engineering dealing with utilization and control of natural waters of the earth

Including canals and rivers, dams and reservoirs, dredging, drilling platforms, flood control, harbors and ports, irrigation; navigation aids, e.g., lighthouses; interdisciplinary works on diving; comprehensive work on soil erosion and its control

Class here hydraulic structures, water resources engineering

Subsurface water relocated to 628.1

Class comprehensive works on ocean engineering in 620; use of navigation aids in 623.89; water supply engineering in 628.1; erosion of agricultural soils and its control in 631.4; reclamation of agricultural soils in 631.6, diving sports in 797.2; a specific use of dams and reservoirs with the use, e.g., municipal water supply reservoirs 628.1

628 Sanitary and municipal engineering Environmental protection engineering

Including sewerage and sewage, sanitary engineering for rural and sparsely populated areas

Class here environmental health engineering [*formerly also* 620.8], public sanitation technology

Class interdisciplinary works on environmental protection in 363.7, military sanitary engineering in 623; a specific aspect of municipal engineering not provided for here with the subject, e.g., road and street engineering in 625.7, laying gas pipelines 665.7

For plumbing, see 696

See Manual at 300 vs. 600; 363; 628 for sanitary engineering in rural and sparsely populated areas

.091 73 Treatment in urban and suburban regions

Class treatment in rural regions in 628

.1 Water supply

Including prospecting for water, water extraction [*both formerly also* 622]; subsurface water [*formerly also* 627]; conservation, pollution and treatment, saline water conversion; wells, reservoirs, and their protection

Class here comprehensive works on water supply, sewers, sewage

Water requirements and use relocated to 333.91; comprehensive works on liquid wastes to 628.4

Class interdisciplinary works on water pollution and countermeasures in 363.73; interdisciplinary works on sources, on evaluation of sources in 553.7; economic and social evaluation of adequacy, development requirements, conservation of sources in 333.91; design and construction of dams and reservoirs for water supply in 627; water supply for rural and sparsely-populated areas, sewers, sewage in 628; pollution countermeasures by originating industry with the industry, e.g., engineering control of acid mine drainage by coal companies 622

.3 **Sewage treatment and disposal**

Including sanitary landfills, disposal by conversion into useful products

Class sewage disposal in rural and sparsely-populated areas, sewerage, sewage in 628, industrial waste treatment and disposal by industry in 628.5; creation, treatment, disposal of sewage in a specific technology with the technology, e.g., treatment of food-processing sewage by food processors 664; a specific use of sewage sludge with the use, e.g., use as fertilizer 631.8

See Manual at 363.6

.4 **Waste technology [*formerly also* 604.6], public toilets, street cleaning**

Including comprehensive works on liquid wastes [*formerly* 628.1], solid wastes; sanitary landfills, conversion into useful products

Class here industrial waste treatment and disposal by type of industry [*formerly* 628.5]

Municipal snow and ice removal relocated to 625.7

Class interdisciplinary works on waste in 363.72; waste technology for rural and sparsely populated areas in 628; gaseous wastes, pollution from wastes in 628.5; creation, control, utilization of waste in a specific technology with the technology, e.g., waste control in pulp and paper technology 676, use of scrap metal 669

See Manual at 628.4 vs. 363.72 for specific kinds of solid wastes

.5 **Pollution and industrial sanitation engineering**

Class here industrial pollution

Industrial waste treatment and disposal by type of industry relocated to 628.4

Standard subdivisions may be used for combined treatment of pollution technology and industrial sanitary engineering, or for pollution technology alone

Class interdisciplinary works on pollution in 363.73; treatment and disposal of agricultural waste in 628; water pollution in 628.1; engineering causes of pollution in a specific technology and reengineering a specific technology to control pollution with the technology, e.g., engineering to control pollution in petroleum refineries, 665.5

For noise, see 620.2

.9 **Other branches of sanitary and municipal engineering**

Including comprehensive technical works on fireproofing [*formerly* 693.8]; fire-fighting and fire-safety technology; public lighting; comprehensive works on pest control technology

Class interdisciplinary works on fire hazards and their control in 363.37, on pest control in 363.7; fire-fighting technology for and lighting of airports in 629.136; control of agricultural pests in 632; forest fire technology in 634.9; development of fire resistance in a specific product with the product, e.g., textiles 677, buildings 693.8

629 Other branches of engineering

General aspects: planning, analysis, design, construction, operation

See Manual at 629.04 vs. 388

SUMMARY

629.04	**Transportation engineering**
.1	**Aerospace engineering**
.2	**Motor land vehicles, and cycles**
.3	**Air-cushion vehicles (Ground-effect machines, Hovercraft)**
.4	**Astronautics**
.8	**Automatic control engineering**

.04 Transportation engineering

Including comprehensive works on water transportation engineering, on land transportation engineering; technology of vehicles and other transportation equipment, of trafficways and other transportation facilities; navigation; health and safety engineering

Class military transportation engineering in 623; inland waterways, harbors, ports, roadsteads in 627; operation of transportation equipment for recreational purposes in 796–797; transportation buildings in 690; technical problems peculiar to transportation of a specific commodity with the commodity, e.g., slurry transportation of coal 662.6

For celestial navigation, see 527; nautical engineering and seamanship, 623.8; railroads, roads, highways, 625; aerospace engineering, 629.1; motor land vehicles, and cycles, 629.2; air-cushion vehicles, 629.3; nonmotor land vehicles, 688.6

See Manual at 629.04 vs. 388 for vehicles

.040 28 Auxiliary techniques and procedures; apparatus, equipment, materials

Class safety measures in 629.04

.1 Aerospace engineering

Including portable flight vehicles, e.g., hang gliders

Class hang gliding as a sport in 797.5

For air-cushion vehicles, see 629.3; astronautics, 629.4

.13 Aeronautics

Use 629.13001–629.13009 for standard subdivisions

.130 1 Philosophy and theory of flight

Class aeromechanics of flight, aviation meteorology in 629.132

.130 2–.130 8 Standard subdivisions of flight

.130 9 Historical, geographic, persons treatment of flight

Record of flying activities in all types of aircraft

Class flight guides in 629.132

.130 91 Transoceanic flight

Do not use for other regional treatment; class in 629.1309

.130 92 Fliers

.132 Principles of aerial flight

Including air mechanics, automatic piloting, aviation meteorology, flight guides, navigation, piloting, wreckage studies

Class pilots in 629.13092

See also 629.135 for automatic pilots

.133 Aircraft types

Examples: airplanes, balloons, dirigibles, helicopters, kites and their models and miniatures

Class components and general technique of specific aircraft types in 629.134, hang gliders in 629.1, flying model aircraft in 796.1

.133 028 Auxiliary techniques and procedures; apparatus, equipment, materials

Class maintenance and repair, safety equipment, testing and measurement in 629.134

.134 Aircraft components and general techniques

General aspects: analysis, design, construction

Including comfort and safety equipment, e.g., parachutes

For aircraft instrumentation and systems, see 629.135

.134 028 Auxiliary techniques and procedures; apparatus, equipment, materials

Class maintenance and repair, testing and measurement in 629.134

.135 Aircraft instrumentation and systems

Examples: instruments for navigation, flight operations, power-plant monitoring; electrical, electronic equipment

.136 Airports

Example: heliports

Including air traffic control

.2 Motor land vehicles, and cycles

Including nonsurface motor land vehicles, e.g., ocean-floor vehicles; vehicles for extraterrestrial surfaces, e.g., moon cars

Class here comprehensive works on motor land vehicle and highway safety engineering

Class highway safety engineering in 625.7

For air-cushion vehicles, see 629.3

.202 8 Auxiliary techniques and procedures; apparatus, equipment

Use of this number for materials discontinued; class in 629.2

Class safety engineering of motor land vehicles in 629.2

.22 Types of vehicles

Including off-road vehicles, e.g., all-terrain vehicles, snowmobiles; steam- and electric-powered vehicles; models of all types of vehicles

Class engines in 629.25

Nonsurface motor land vehicles, vehicles for extraterrestrial surface, and design, materials, construction, parts other than engines of specific vehicles are classed in 629.2

.220 28 Auxiliary techniques and procedures; apparatus, equipment, materials

Class testing, measurement, maintenance, repair of all types of vehicles in 629.28

.222 Passenger automobiles

Examples: buses, dune buggies, sport cars, station wagons, taxicabs

Class racing cars in 629.228

.223 Light trucks

Example: pickup trucks

Including customized vans

.224 Trucks (Lorries)

Class here tractor trailers

For light trucks, see 629.223

.225 Work vehicles

Examples: bulldozers, tractors

Class automotive materials-handling equipment in 621.8, steam tractors in 629.22

For trucks, see 629.224

.226 Motorized homes, campers, trailers (caravans)

Class here comprehensive works on recreational vehicles (RVs)

Class construction of towed mobile homes in 690; a specific kind of recreational vehicle not provided for here with the vehicle, e.g., dune buggies 629.222

For tractor trailers, see 629.224

See Manual at 629.226 vs. 643, 690, 728.7 for mobile homes

.227 Cycles

Examples: bicycles, motorcycles

.228 Racing cars

Conventional and converted

Including hot rods, karts

.25 Engines

Including auxiliary systems, e.g., batteries

Do not use standard subdivisions

.28 Tests, driving, maintenance, repairs

Including garages, service stations

Class maintenance and repairs of engines in 629.25, of other specific parts of vehicles in 629.2

.3 Air-cushion vehicles (Ground-effect machines, Hovercraft)

.4 Astronautics

.409 2 Astronautical engineers

Class astronauts in 629.450092

.43 Unmanned flight

Including flight of artificial satellites

Class satellite flight for a specific purpose with the purpose, e.g., weather satellites 551.6

.44 Auxiliary spacecraft

Examples: space laboratories, shuttles, stations

.45 Manned space flight

Including selection and training of astronauts; rescue operations

Class auxiliary spacecraft in 629.44

.450 01–.450 09 Standard subdivisions

.46 Engineering of unmanned spacecraft

Example: artificial satellites

.47 Astronautical engineering

General aspects: analysis, design, construction of spacecraft and their components

Including launch complexes, space suits

Class here comprehensive works on spacecraft

For auxiliary spacecraft, see 629.44; engineering of unmanned spacecraft, 629.46

.8 **Automatic control engineering**

Including robots, servomechanisms, vending machines

Class here automatons that are not computer controlled

Sequential machines relocated to 511

Class a specific application with the application, e.g., numerical control of machine tools 621.9

.801 Philosophy and theory

Class control theory in 629.8

630 Agriculture and related technologies

Class here farming, farms, comprehensive works on plant crops

See also 306.3 for agricultural sociology, 307.72 for rural sociology, 333.76 for agricultural land economics, 338.1 for agricultural economics, 900 for rural conditions and civilization

See Manual at 580–590 vs. 630, 641.3

SUMMARY

630.1–.9	**Standard subdivisions**
631	**Specific techniques; apparatus, equipment, materials**
632	**Plant injuries, diseases, pests**
633	**Field and plantation crops**
634	**Orchards, fruit, forestry**
635	**Garden crops (Horticulture) Vegetables**
636	**Animal husbandry**
637	**Processing dairy and related products**
638	**Insect culture**
639	**Hunting, fishing, conservation, related technologies**

.1 **Philosophy and theory**

Class scientific principles in 630.2

.2 **Miscellany and scientific principles**

Including auxiliary techniques and procedures of agriculture in general [*formerly* 631], comprehensive works on auxiliary techniques and procedures for raising field and plantation crops [*formerly* 633]

Use this number without further subdivision for miscellany provided for in notation 022–029 from Table 1; however, class apparatus, equipment, materials in 631

Agricultural genetics relocated to 631.5

631 Specific techniques; apparatus, equipment, materials

Topics common to plant and animal husbandry or limited to plant culture

Class here comprehensive works on specific techniques, on apparatus, equipment, materials for raising field and plantation crops [*all formerly* 633]

Use of this number for comprehensive works on crops and their production discontinued; class in 630

Auxiliary techniques and procedures of agriculture in general relocated to 630.2

Class techniques, apparatus, equipment, materials of specific plant crops in 633–635; of animal husbandry in 636

For plant injuries, diseases, pests, see 632

.2 **Use of agricultural structures**

Examples: barns, fences, roads

Use of granaries and grain elevators relocated to 633.1, of silos to 633.2

Class housing of domestic animals in 636.08; construction of a specific agricultural structure with the structure, e.g., barns 690

.3 **Use of tools, machinery, apparatus, equipment**

Including workshops

Use of greenhouses relocated to 631.5

Class comprehensive works on manufacture of agricultural tools, machinery, apparatus, equipment in 681; manufacture of a specific article with the article, e.g., manufacture of tractors 629.225; use of a specific kind of tool, machinery, apparatus, equipment with the use, e.g., use of plows 631.5

See also 631.2 for use of agricultural structures

.4 **Soil science**

Including soil erosion, soil surveys, comprehensive works on soil and water conservation

Class here interdisciplinary works on soils [*formerly also* 553.6]

Class soil formation in 551.3, petrology of soils in 552, engineering use of soils in 624.1; comprehensive works on crop rotation, tillage for water conservation in 631.5

For clearing, drainage, revegetation, see 631.6; water conservation, 631.7; use of fertilizers and soil conditioners, 631.8

.401 Philosophy and theory

Class scientific principles in 631.4

[.409] Historical, geographic, persons treatment

Do not use; class in 631.4

.5 **Cultivation and harvesting** Pruning/orchards in 634

Including agricultural genetics [*formerly also* 630.2], use of greenhouses [*formerly also* 631.3], irrigation [*formerly also* 631.7], crop rotation, organic farming, plant propagation, varieties; operations subsequent to harvesting, e.g., grading, storing

Use this number for works on irrigation only when the emphasis is on what is done on the farm, e.g., installation of sprinkler systems

Class comprehensive works on irrigation, works on obtaining irrigation waters from off-farm sources in 627; digging wells in 628.1; sewage irrigation in 628.3; conservation tillage, crop rotation for soil conservation in 631.4; a specific aspect of organic farming with the aspect, e.g., compost 631.8

Most works on greenhouses are limited to gardening and are classed in 635

See Manual at 631.5 vs. 338.1 for crop yields

.6 **Clearing, drainage, revegetation**

Including surface mine reclamation

Class comprehensive works on reclamation and drainage, off-farm reclamation and drainage projects in 627; reforestation in 634.9

.7 **Water conservation**

Irrigation relocated to 631.5

Class tillage for water conservation in 631.5

.8 **Fertilizers and soil conditioners**

Including growth regulators

Class here comprehensive works on agricultural chemicals

Class comprehensive works on soil fertility in 631.4

For pesticides, see 632

See also 668 for manufacture of agricultural chemicals

632 Plant injuries, diseases, pests

Including control methods, pesticides

Class here comprehensive works on injuries, diseases, pests of field and plantation crops [*formerly* 633], pathology of agricultural plants, comprehensive works on plant and animal injuries, diseases, pests

Class pest control services and interdisciplinary works on pests in 363.7; comprehensive works on physiology and pathology of agricultural plants in 581.1; use of agricultural plants in studies of basic pathological processes in 581.2; injuries, diseases, pests of specific crops and groups of crops in 633–635

For veterinary medicine, see 636.089

> **633–635 Specific plant crops**

Class comprehensive works in 631

See Manual at 633–635

633 Field and plantation crops

Large-scale production of crops intended for farm use or industrial processing other than preservation

Comprehensive works on auxiliary techniques and procedures for raising field and plantation crops relocated to 630.2; on specific techniques, on apparatus, equipment, materials for raising field and plantation crops to 631; on injuries, diseases, pests of field and plantation crops to 632; edible roots and tubers to 635

Class truck farming in 635; a specific kind of plantation crop not provided for here with the kind, e.g., plantation fruit crops 634

See Manual at 633–635

.001 Philosophy and theory

.002 Miscellany

[.002 8] Auxiliary techniques and procedures; apparatus, equipment, materials

Do not use; class auxiliary techniques and procedures in 630.2, apparatus, equipment, materials in 631

.003–.009 Standard subdivisions

.1 Cereal grains (Cereals)

Examples: rice, wheat

Including use of granaries and grain elevators [*formerly also* 631.2]

Class cereal crops grown for forage in 633.2

.2 Forage crops

Including comprehensive works on silos [*formerly also* 631.2], pasture and its grasses, cereal grasses

Class here forage grasses

Class use of silos for grain storage in 633.1, forage legumes and other forage crops in 633.3

.200 1–.200 9 Standard subdivisions

.3 Legumes, other forage crops

Example: clover

Class here grain legumes, forage legumes

Class comprehensive works on legumes in 635

.5 **Fiber crops**

Examples: cotton, hemp

Including basketwork plants

.6 **Sugar, syrup, starch crops**

Examples: sugar beets, sweet sorghums, cassava

Standard subdivisions are added for sugar, syrup, starch crops, for sugar crops alone, for syrup crops alone

.7 **Alkaloidal crops**

Examples: coffee, marijuana, tobacco

.8 **Other crops grown for industrial processing**

Examples: oilseed plants; spices; plants grown for dyes, medicine, perfume, rubber

Class poppies in 633.7

634 Orchards, fruit, forestry

Including berries, nuts, olives

Class here comprehensive works on tree crops

Standard subdivisions are added for orchards, fruit, forestry; for orchards alone; for fruit alone

Class trees grown for plantation crops other than fruit in 633, ornamental trees 635.9; melons, tomatoes, peanuts in 635

See Manual at 633–635

.8 **Grapes**

Class here viticulture

.9 **Forestry**

Including forest fire technology, forest products, logging, comprehensive works on lumbering

Class crops grown for rubber in 633.8, sawmill operations in 674

.906 8 Management

Class management of production in 634.9

635 Garden crops (Horticulture) Vegetables

Vegetables: crops grown primarily for human consumption without intermediate processing other than preservation

Including edible roots and tubers [*formerly also* 633], aromatic and sweet herbs, melons, mushrooms, comprehensive works on legumes

Class here home gardening, truck farming

Class legumes as field crops in 633.3, orchards in 634

See Manual at 633–635

√ .9 **Flowers and ornamental plants**

Including houseplants, lawns, trees

Class here floriculture

Class flower arrangement in 745.92

.902 8 Auxiliary techniques and procedures

Class apparatus, equipment, materials in 635.9

636 Animal husbandry

Class culture of nondomesticated animals in 639

See Manual at 800 vs. 591, 636, 398.24

.001 Philosophy and theory

Genetics relocated to 636.08

.002–.009 Standard subdivisions

.08 Production and maintenance, animals for specific purposes, veterinary sciences

Including genetics [*formerly* 636.001], animal hospitals, breeding, feeding, housing

Use 636 for comprehensive works on production and maintenance

.088 Animals for specific purposes

Examples: pets, laboratory animals; animals raised for food, skins, sport, work

Class here production, maintenance, training

Class veterinary sciences of animals for specific purposes in 636.089; anecdotes and reminiscences about and true accounts of a person's pets or favorite animals in 808.88; anecdotes, reminiscences, and accounts in a specific literature with the literature using notation 8 from Table 3; other accounts and stories of pets not intended to illustrate agricultural techniques with the appropriate literary form in 800

See Manual at 800 vs. 591, 636, 398.24 for pets

.089 Veterinary sciences Veterinary medicine

Use 636.08 for animal hospitals and auxiliary care of sick and injured animals

.1 Horses and related animals

Examples: donkeys, mules, zebras

.100 1–.100 9 Standard subdivisions

.2 Ruminants Bovines Cattle

Examples: buffalo, camels, deer, llamas

Including dairy farming, raising cattle for beef

Class milking, processing dairy products in 637

For sheep and goats, see 636.3

.200 1–.200 9 Standard subdivisions

.3 Sheep and goats

.300 1–.300 9 Standard subdivisions for sheep and goats, for sheep alone

.4 Swine

.400 1–.400 9 Standard subdivisions

.5 Poultry Chickens

Examples: ducks, geese, pheasants, turkeys

Class here comprehensive works on raising birds

For birds other than poultry, see 636.6

.500 1–.500 9 Standard subdivisions

.6 Birds other than poultry

Examples: game, ornamental, song birds

Class peafowl, pheasants, comprehensive works on birds in 636.5

.600 1–.600 9 Standard subdivisions

.7 Dogs

.700 1–.700 9 Standard subdivisions

.8 Cats

Including nondomestic cats, e.g., ocelots

.800 1–.800 9 Standard subdivisions

637 Processing dairy and related products

Examples: milk, butter, cheese, eggs

Including manufacture of ice cream, other frozen desserts

Class comprehensive works on dairy farming in 636.2

638 Insect culture

Examples: bees, silkworms

Including honey processing

639 Hunting, fishing, conservation, related technologies

Including aquiculture and mariculture, culture and harvest of invertebrates

Class sport hunting and fishing in 799

For insect culture, see 638

See also 636.088 for fur farming

.091 62 Oceans and seas

Use of this number for aquiculture and mariculture discontinued; class in 639

.2 Commercial fishing, whaling, sealing

Class here works on fisheries encompassing culture as well as capture, on fisheries encompassing invertebrates as well as fish

Class fisheries for invertebrates in 639, culture of fish in 639.3

See also 799.1 for sport fishing

.3 Culture of cold-blooded vertebrates Of fish

Including aquariums, fish hatcheries

.9 Conservation of biological resources

Including control of diseases and predators, habitat improvement, wildlife reserves and refuges

Class here game protection, wildlife conservation

Class interdisciplinary works on conservation of biological resources in 333.95

640 Home economics and family living

Including management of household employees, of money, of time

Class here management of home and personal life, domestic arts and sciences

Class personal health in 613

See Manual at 332.024 vs. 640 for management of household finances

SUMMARY

640.1–.9	**Standard subdivisions**
641	**Food and drink**
642	**Meals and table service**
643	**Housing and household equipment**
644	**Household utilities**
645	**Household furnishings**
646	**Sewing, clothing and accessories, management of personal and family living**
647	**Management of public households (Institutional housekeeping)**
648	**Housekeeping**
649	**Child rearing and home care of sick and infirm**

.28 Auxiliary techniques and procedures; apparatus, equipment, materials

Class maintenance and repair in 643

.29 Commercial miscellany

Class evaluation and purchasing manuals in 640.73

[.68] Household management

Use of this number discontinued; class in 640

.73 Evaluation and purchasing guides

Class here consumer education for home and personal needs

Class interdisciplinary evaluation and purchasing guides and works on consumer education in 381.3; comprehensive works on managing household money in 640; evaluation and purchasing guides for specific products and services with the product or service, using notation 029 from Table 1, e.g., a manual on evaluating automobiles 629.222029

641 Food and drink

For meals and table service, see 642

SUMMARY

641.01	**Philosophy and theory**
.1	**Applied nutrition**
.2	**Beverages (Drinks)**
.3	**Food**
.4	**Food preservation and storage**
.5	**Cooking**
.6	**Cooking specific materials**
.7	**Specific cooking processes and techniques**
.8	**Cooking specific kinds of composite dishes**

.01 Philosophy and theory

Including gastronomy and pleasures of eating

.1 Applied nutrition

Class nutrition in the promotion of health in 613.2; nutritive values of beverages in 641.2, of food in 641.3

.2 **Beverages (Drinks)**

Class here interdisciplinary works on beverages

Class interdisciplinary works on mixed drinks in 641.8; specific nonalcoholic beverages in 641.3; a specific aspect with the aspect, e.g., home preparation 641.8, commercial preparation 663

.3 **Food**

Including interdisciplinary works on specific nonalchoholic beverages

Class here interdisciplinary works on food

Use of this number for comprehensive works on food and beverages discontinued; class in 641

Class interdisciplinary works on composite dishes, including punch, in 641.8; a specific aspect with the subject, e.g., commercial preparation 664

See Manual at 580–590 vs. 630, 641.3; 613.2 vs. 641.3, 363.8

.300 1 Philosophy and theory

.300 2 Miscellany

.300 29 Commercial miscellany

Class evaluation and purchasing manuals in 641.3

.300 3–.300 9 Standard subdivisions

> **641.4–641.8 Food preservation, storage, cooking**

Class comprehensive works in 641.3

.4 **Food preservation and storage**

Including canning, cold storage, drying, pickling, smoking

Class comprehensive works on food preservation in 664

.5 **Cooking**

Preparation of food with and without use of heat

Including cooking leftovers [*formerly* 641.6]

Class menus and meal planning in 642

For cooking specific materials, see 641.6; specific cooking processes and techniques, 641.7; cooking of composite dishes, 641.8

.508 History and description with respect to kind of persons

Class cooking with respect to religious groups in 641.5

[.508 3–.508 4] Persons of specific ages

Do not use; class in 641.5

.508 7 Handicapped persons

Class cooking for sick people in 641.5

.509 Historical, geographic, persons treatment

Class here collections of recipes from specific restaurants

Class cooking characteristic of specific geographic environments in 641.59

.59 Cooking characteristic of specific geographic environments, ethnic cooking

Including international cooking

Class Jewish cooking in 641.5, historical and geographic treatment of general cooking in 641.509; a specific kind of cooking characteristic of specific geographical environments, e.g., French gourmet cooking, in 641.5

.593–.599 Cooking characteristic of specific continents, countries, localities

Add to base number 641.59 notation 3–9 from Table 2, e.g., Mexican cooking 641.5972

Use 641.59 for ethnic cooking of nondominant ethnic groups

See also 641.509 for collections of recipes from specific restaurants

.6 Cooking specific materials

Examples: cooking vegetables

Leftovers relocated to 641.5

Class vegetarian cooking in 641.5, specific kinds of composite dishes featuring specific materials in 641.8

.7 Specific cooking processes and techniques

Examples: baking, barbecuing, broiling, frying, roasting

Including preparation of cold dishes

Class cooking with specific fuels, appliances, utensils, e.g., microwave ovens, outdoor barbecue grills, in 641.5; a specific process applied to specific materials in 641.6, to specific kinds of composite dishes in 641.8

.8 Cooking specific kinds of composite dishes

Examples: appetizers, beverages, breads, casseroles, desserts, salads, sandwiches, stews

Including bartenders' manuals, interdisciplinary works on mixed drinks and punch

Class here interdisciplinary works on specific kinds of composite dishes

Class interdisciplinary works on beverages in 641.2, on specific nonalcoholic beverages other than punch in 641.3

642 Meals and table service

Including catering, menus, picnics, table furnishings and decorations

Class operation of public eating places, catering which includes restaurant operation in 647.95

643 Housing and household equipment

Works for owner-occupants or renters covering activities of members of household

Including selecting, renting, buying, burglarproofing homes; renovation, improvement, remodeling; specific areas and their equipment, e.g., kitchens; appliances and installations; interdisciplinary works on houses

Do not add standard subdivisions for housing

Class economics of house acquisition in 333.33, law of real property in 346.04, household utilities in 644, household furnishings in 645, home construction of articles made of fabric in 646.2, moving in 648, manufacture of household appliances in 683, home workshops in 684, construction of houses in 690, interdisciplinary works on design and construction of houses in 728; appliances and installations for a specific purpose with the purpose, e.g., kitchen stoves 641.5028

See Manual at 629.226 vs. 643, 690, 728.7 for mobile homes; 643 vs. 363.5; 643 vs. 690 for renovation, improvement, remodeling

.028 Auxiliary techniques and procedures; apparatus, equipment, materials

Class maintenance and repair in 643

644 Household utilities

Works for owner-occupants or renters covering activities by members of household

Examples: heating, lighting, water supply

Class lighting fixtures in 645

See Manual at 647 vs. 647.068, 658.2, T1—068

645 Household furnishings

Works for owner-occupants or renters covering activities by members of household

Examples: draperies, floor covering, furniture, lighting fixtures

Class here comprehensive works on household furnishings and interior decoration of residential buildings

Interior decoration of residential buildings relocated to 747

Class home construction of fabric furnishings in 646.2, construction in wood and metal in 684, artistic aspects of furniture and accessories in 749

.029 Commercial miscellany

Class evaluation and purchasing manuals in 645

646 Sewing, clothing and accessories, management of personal and family living

Including comprehensive works on fabrics in the home

Dyeing relocated to 648

Class interdisciplinary works on clothing and accessories in 391; fabrics for a specific use with the use, e.g., use in furnishings 645

For laundry and related operations, see 648

See Manual at 391 vs. 646, 746.9 for clothing

.2 Sewing and related operations

Including construction of home furnishings, reweaving, sewing machines

Class here comprehensive works on mending

Class mending of clothing in 646, clothing construction in 646.4, artistic and decorative aspects of construction of interior furnishings in 746.9

For knitting, crocheting, tatting, see 746.43; embroidery, 746.44

.202 8 Auxiliary techniques and procedures

Use of this number for apparatus discontinued; class in 646

Class sewing machines in 646.2, other equipment and materials in 646

.4 Clothing and accessories construction

Including remodeling

Class here casual clothes, sports clothes

Class mending in 646, construction of boots and shoes in 685, commercial manufacture of clothing in 687, handcrafted costume jewelry in 745.594

For construction of headgear, see 646.5

.400 1–.400 7 Standard subdivisions

[.400 8] Description with respect to kinds of persons

Do not use; class in 646.4

.400 9 Historical, geographic, persons treatment

.5 Construction of headgear

Including millinery

.500 1–.500 7 Standard subdivisions

[.500 8] Description with respect to kinds of persons

Do not use; class in 646.5

.500 9 Historical, geographic, persons treatment

.7 **Management of personal and family living Grooming**

Including charm, dating, mate selection, reducing and massage for appearance, retirement guides, wigs

Class here interdisciplinary works on success, successful living

Class clothing selection and dressing with style in 646, interdisciplinary works on success in business and other public situations in 650.1

For parapsychological and occult means for achieving well-being, happiness, success, see 131; psychological techniques for achieving personal well-being, happiness, success, 158; etiquette (manners), 395; child rearing, 649

See also 362.82 for social services to families, 613.2 for reducing for health, 615.8 for therapeutic massage

See Manual at 613.7 vs. 646.7, 796 for improving appearance

.700 1–.700 7 Standard subdivisions of personal and family living

.700 8 Personal and family living with respect to kinds of persons

.700 84 Persons in specific stages of adulthood

Class personal and family living for persons in late adulthood in 646.7

.700 9 Historical, geographic, persons treatment of personal and family living

.701–.707 Standard subdivisions of grooming

[.708] Grooming with respect to specific kinds of persons

Number discontinued; class in 646.7

.709 Historical, geographic, persons treatment of grooming

647 Management of public households (Institutional housekeeping)

Examples: apartment houses, public housing, hospitals

Including employees

Class comprehensive works on household employees in 640, a specific aspect of public households with the aspect, e.g., laundering 648

See Manual at 647 vs. 647.068, 658.2, T1—068

.068 Management

Class personnel management in 647

See Manual at 647 vs. 647.068, 658.2, T1—068

.9 Multiple dwellings for transients, eating and drinking places

Do not add standard subdivisions

See Manual at 913–919: Guidebooks

.94 Multiple dwellings for transients

.940 9 Historical, geographic, persons treatment

Class treatment by specific continent, country, locality in 647.943–647.949 (*not* 647.94093–647.94099)

.943–.949 Treatment by specific continents, countries, localities

Class here directories; specific kinds of multiple dwellings, e.g., bed and breakfast accommodations, hotels, trailer camps

Add to base number 647.94 notation 3–9 from Table 2, e.g., hotels in Canada 647.9471; however, do not add standard subdivisions for specific kinds of facilities

.95 Eating and drinking places

.950 9 Historical, geographic, persons treatment

Class treatment by specific continents, countries, localities in 647.953–647.959 (*not* 647.95093–647.95099)

.953–.959 Treatment by specific continents, countries, localities

Add to base number 647.95 notation 3–9 from Table 2, e.g., restaurants in Hawaii 647.95969

648 Housekeeping

Including dyeing [*formerly* 646], dishwashing, laundering and related operations, moving, pest control, storage

Class here household sanitation

Class industrial sanitation (sanitation of factories) in 628.5, dry cleaning in 667

See Manual at 647 vs. 647.068, 658.2, T1—068

649 Child rearing and home care of sick and infirm

Including breast feeding, creative activities, training

Religious training of children in the home relocated to 291.4, Christian religious training of children in the home to 248.8

Do not add standard subdivisions for child rearing

Class nutritional aspects of breast feeding in 613.2

.8 Home care of sick and infirm

650 Management and auxiliary services

This division is concerned with the art and science of conducting organized enterprises and with auxiliary skills and operations. The auxiliary skills and operations consist chiefly of communication and record keeping fundamental to management

Class here business

See Manual at 650 vs. 330

SUMMARY

650.01–.09 Standard subdivisions
.1 Personal success in business
651 Office services
652 Processes of written communication
653 Shorthand
657 Accounting
658 General management
659 Advertising and public relations

.01 Philosophy and theory

Including business arithmetic [*formerly* 513]

.02–.09 Standard subdivisions

.1 Personal success in business

Including financial success, personal improvement, success in business relationships

Class interdisciplinary works on success in general, on management of personal and family living in 646.7, success as an executive in 658.4

.14 Success in obtaining jobs and promotions

> **651–657 Auxiliary services**

Class comprehensive works in 650, advertising and public relations in 659

651 Office services

Including description, use, maintenance of office equipment and supplies, e.g., furniture

Class here problems in security and confidentiality

Class procurement of office equipment and supplies in 658.7, a specific type of equipment with its use, e.g., typewriters 652.3

For processes of written communication, see 652; accounting, 657

.028 Auxiliary techniques and procedures; materials

Class apparatus and equipment in 651

[.028 5] Data processing Computer applications

Do not use; class in 651.8

.3 **Office management**

General aspects: planning, organizing, directing, controlling office services

Including role and function of administrative personnel; activities of filers, messengers, receptionists, secretaries, stenographers, switchboard operators, typists

.306 8 Management

Including management of office personnel [*formerly* 658.3]

.5 **Records management**

Including retention, maintenance, final disposition of records; computerization, filing, microreproduction, storage of files

Class creation and transmission of records in 651.7

.7 **Communication Creation and transmission of records**

Examples: correspondence, minutes, reports

Including dictation and use of dictating equipment, mail handling

Style manuals relocated to 808

Class interdisciplinary works on communication in 302.2, records management in 651.5, processes of written communication in 652, managerial communication in 658.4

See Manual at 651.7 vs. 808, 658.4

.8 **Data processing Computer applications**

Use in carrying out office functions

Class interdisciplinary works on data processing in 004; computer applications for a specific office activity with the activity, e.g., computerization of files 651.5, word processing 652.5

652 Processes of written communication

Including interdisciplinary works on cryptography [*formerly* 001.54]; penmanship; duplication of records and duplicating methods, e.g., xerography

Class interdisciplinary works on photoduplication in 686.4, cryptographic techniques used for security in computer systems in 005.8

For shorthand, see 653

See also 745.6 for calligraphy

.3 **Typewriting**

Including typing for specific uses, e.g., medical typewriting

.300 1–.300 9 Standard subdivisions

.5 **Word processing**

653 Shorthand

Machine and handwritten systems

Including abbreviated longhand systems; shorthand for specific uses, e.g., for court reporting

657 Accounting

Including auditing, bookkeeping

See Manual at 657 vs. 658.15

658 General management

The science and art of conducting organized enterprises, projects, activities

Class here management of technology [*formerly also* 606.8]; management of services rendered by nonpublic organizations, whether or not for profit; management of public corporations; management of public agencies that themselves provide direct services (in contrast to public agencies that regulate, support, or control services provided by other organizations)

Management of big enterprises, of enterprises of specific forms of ownership organization (e.g., partnerships, corporations, international enterprises) is classed in 658 without use of 658.001–658.009; specific aspects of management of big enterprises, of enterprises of specific forms of ownership organization are classed in 658.1–658.8

(Option: Including management of enterprises engaged in specific fields of activity, of specific kinds of enterprises; prefer specific subject, with use of notation 068 from Table 1, e.g., management of mines 622.068)

Class sociology of management in 302.3; management of enterprises engaged in specific fields of activity with the field, using notation 068 from Table 1, e.g., management of airlines 387.7068

Control, decision making, information management, internal organization, planning, policy making are classed in 658.4

For public administration, see 350

See also 306.3 for industrial sociology, 330 for economics

See Manual at 350–354 vs. 658, T1—068; 658 and T1—068; 658, T1—068 vs. 302.3; 658.4 vs. 658, 658.1 for organization

SUMMARY

658.001–.009	**Standard subdivisions**
.02	**Small enterprises**
.1	**Organization and finance**
.2	**Plant management**
.3	**Personnel management**
.4	**Executive management**
.5	**Management of production**
.7	**Management of materials**
.8	**Management of distribution (Marketing)**

.001 Philosophy and theory

Class systems in 658.4

.002 Miscellany

[.002 85] Data processing Computer applications

Do not use; class in 658

.003–.009 Standard subdivisions

.02 Small enterprises

Including minority enterprises

Do not use standard subdivisions

Management of enterprises of a specific form of ownership organization regardless of size is classed in 658

.1 **Organization and finance**

Including initiation of business enterprises, e.g., initiation of specific forms of ownership organization such as partnerships, corporations; reorganization, e.g., consolidations, mergers; organization of international enterprises and activities

Class accounting in 657; general management of specific forms of ownership organization in 658; internal organization in 658.4

See Manual at 658.4 vs. 658, 658.1 for organization

.15 Financial management

Procurement and use of funds to establish and operate enterprises

Including management accounting, comprehensive works on capital and its management

Class here financial decision making, financial planning

Class wage and salary administration in 658.3, customer credit management in 658.8

See Manual at 332 vs. 338, 658.15; 657 vs. 658.15; 658.15 and T1—068

.2 **Plant management**

Management of buildings, equipment, facilities, grounds

Including location of plants and warehouses, layout

Class here comprehensive works on energy management

Class office equipment in 651; location of businesses in 658.1; purchase, leasing, rental of plant and equipment in 658.15; specific aspects of energy management with the aspect, e.g., energy management to promote efficiency in production 658.5

See Manual at 647 vs. 647.068, 658.2, T1—068; 658.2 and T1—068

.200 1–.200 9 Standard subdivisions

.3 Personnel management

Procedures for hiring, developing, utilizing the capabilities of employees

Including days and hours of work, leaves of absence; collective bargaining, employee representation in management, labor unions and other employee organizations; health, safety, welfare of employees; wage and salary administration

Management of office personnel relocated to 651.3068

Class interdisciplinary works on industrial safety in 363.11, comprehensive works on safety management in 658.4, industrial relations in 331, industrial democracy in 331.01, clerical techniques used in preparing payroll records in 651.3, payroll accounting procedures in 657, safety of plant and equipment in 658.2, management of executive personnel in 658.4

See also 338.6 for worker control of industry

See Manual at 658.3 and T1—068; 658.3 vs. 331

.300 1–.300 9 Standard subdivisions

.4 Executive management

Role, function, powers, position of top and middle management in planning, organizing, directing, coordinating, reporting, communication

Including business intelligence and security, management of executive personnel, managerial success, project management, social responsibility of management, comprehensive works on safety management

Class interdisciplinary works on safety in 363.1, general success in business in 650.1, mechanics of communication in 651.7, management of small business in 658.02, insurance in 658.1; a specific managerial activity not provided for here with the activity in management, e.g., personnel management 658.3; specific aspects of safety with the aspect, e.g., product safety 658.5

See Manual at 651.7 vs. 808, 658.4 for communication; 658.4 vs. 658, 658.1 for internal organization

.400 1–.400 9 Standard subdivisions

.5 **Management of production**

Planning, organizing, directing, controlling the specific functional activities of the organization

Including automation, modernization; labeling; product control, e.g., inspection, quality control, recall; product planning; research and development (R and D); sequencing, e.g., scheduling; waste control and utilization; work, fatigue, monotony, time and motion studies; interdisciplinary works on packaging; comprehensive works on product development

Class here production management in manufacturing enterprises, comprehensive works on logistics

Management of production in construction enterprises relocated to 624.068

Class comprehensive works on energy management in 658.2; internal transportation (materials handling), physical distribution, packaging for shipment and for storage in 658.7; marketing, market research on new products, use of packaging in sales promotion in 658.8; factory operations engineering in 670.42; packaging technology in 688.8; production management in enterprises engaged in a specific kind of activity other than manufacturing with the activity, using notation 068 from Table 1, e.g., management of agricultural production 630.68

See Manual at 658.5 and T1—068

.500 1–.500 9 Standard subdivisions

.7 **Management of materials**

Including procurement, contracts and their negotiation, vendor selection; internal transportation (materials handling), storage (warehouse management), inventory control (stock control), physical distribution (shipment)

Class here management of supplies

Class management of office supplies in 651; financial control of inventories, procurement of land, buildings, heavy equipment in 658.15, location of warehouses in 658.2

See Manual at 658.7 and T1—068

.8 **Management of distribution (Marketing)**

Goods and services

Including auctions, consumer research, credit management, fairs, franchising, market research and analysis, markets, private sales, sales management and promotion, use of packaging in sales promotion, wholesale and retail marketing

Personal selling of specific goods and services relocated to specific subject with use of notation 068 from Table 1, e.g., personal selling of insurance 368.0068

Class interdisciplinary works on packaging in 658.5, financial aspects of marketing management in 658.15, management of sales personnel in 658.3

For physical distribution, see 658.7; advertising 659.1

See Manual at 380.1 vs. 658.8; 658.8 and T1—068; 658.8, T1—068 vs. 659

.800 1 Philosophy and theory

Class systems in 658.8

.800 2–.800 9 Standard subdivisions

.85 Personal selling (Salesmanship)

Including retail salesmanship

659 Advertising and public relations

Class here publicity

See Manual at 658.8, T1—068 vs. 659

.1 Advertising

Nonpersonal presentation and promotion of ideas, goods, services, paid for by an identified sponsor

Including demonstrations, exhibitions, shows; counter, showcase, wall, window displays; contests, lotteries

Planning, control, managerial organization of advertising; general kinds of advertising, e.g., retail advertising; advertising campaigns; advertising specific kinds of organizations, products, services are all classed in 659.1, without use of 659.101–659.109; these same topics in relation to advertising in printed or related media (e.g., outdoor advertising) or in broadcast media are classed in 659.13–659.14

.13 Advertising in printed and related media

Including directory advertising; direct advertising, e.g., catalogs, circulars, letters; outdoor advertising, e.g., billboards, electric signs; moving displays, e.g., posters on exteriors of moving vehicles

Do not use standard subdivisions

.14 Advertising by broadcast media

Radio and television

Class television selling as a channel of distribution in 658.8

.2 Public relations

Planned and sustained effort to establish and maintain mutual understanding between an organization and its public

Including public relations for museums [*formerly* 069]

Use of this number for publicity discontinued; class in 659

Class public relations in libraries in 021.7, in local Christian churches in 254.4

660 Chemical engineering and related technologies

Including biotechnology, genetic engineering

Class military applications in 623

For pharmaceutical chemistry, see 615; pulp and paper technology, 676; elastomers and elastomer products, 678

See Manual at 660 vs. 604.7 for hazardous chemicals

SUMMARY

660.01–.09 Standard subdivisions
661 Technology of industrial chemicals
662 Technology of explosives, fuels, related products
663 Beverage technology
664 Food technology
665 Technology of industrial oils, fats, waxes, gases
666 Ceramic and allied technologies
667 Cleaning, color, related technologies
668 Technology of other organic products
669 Metallurgy

.01 Philosophy and theory

.02 Miscellany

.028 Auxiliary techniques and procedures

Class apparatus, equipment, materials, safety measures in 660

.03–.09 Standard subdivisions

[.2] **Chemical engineering**

Use of this number discontinued; class in 660

661 Technology of industrial chemicals

Production of chemicals used as raw materials or reagents in manufacture of other products

Including ammonia, cellulose, coal tar; special-purpose chemicals, e.g., photographic chemicals

Petrochemicals in the sense of industrial chemicals produced from petroleum or natural gas, excluding fuels, lubricants, refinery residues, are classed here. Petrochemicals in the sense of all refinery products and by-products of petroleum are classed in 665.5

Class carbon in 662, industrial gases in 665.7, gaseous elements in 665.8

.001–.009 Standard subdivisions

662 Technology of explosives, fuels, related products

Including carbon black, charcoal, coke, fireworks, graphite, matches, synthetic petroleum; wood as a fuel; wastes as fuels, e.g., biomass as fuel

Class interdisciplinary works on energy from waste materials in 333.79, nuclear explosives in 621.48, industrial oils, fats, waxes, gases as fuels in 665

See Manual at 622 vs. 669, 662 for underground fuel processing

.6 Coal

Including treatment, e.g., desulfuration; storage, transportation, distribution; uses as a fuel, as a raw material

Do not use standard subdivisions

Class coke in 662; a specific use of coal with the use, e.g., metallurgical use 669

663 Beverage technology

Commercial preparation, preservation, packaging

Including bottled water

Class interdisciplinary works on beverages in 641.2, household preparation of beverages in 641.8

For milk, see 637

664 Food technology

Commercial preparation, preservation, packaging

Including flavoring aids, e.g., table salt; special-purpose foods and aids, e.g., baby foods, baking powder

Class here comprehensive works on commercial food and beverage technology

Class interdisciplinary works on food in 641.3; household preservation, storage, cookery in 641.4–641.8

For processing dairy and related products, see 637; honey, 638; beverage technology, 663

.001 Philosophy and theory

.002 Miscellany

.002 8 Auxiliary techniques and procedures; apparatus, equipment

Class materials, testing, measurement in 664

.003–.009 Standard subdivisions

665 Technology of industrial oils, fats, waxes, gases

Class here lubricating oils

Class beeswax in 638, turpentine oils in 661, polishing waxes in 667

.5 **Petroleum**

Including asphalt, gasoline, kerosene; refining, storage, transportation, distribution, uses

Class here comprehensive works on petroleum and natural gas

Class synthetic petroleum in 662, a specific use of petroleum with the use, e.g., automobile engine lubricants 629.25

For petrochemicals, see 661; natural gas, 665.7

.502 8 Auxiliary techniques and procedures; apparatus, equipment, materials

Class refinery techniques in 665.5

.7 **Natural gas and manufactured industrial gases**

Including processing, storage, transportation, distribution, uses of natural gas and gases manufactured from coal, coke, petroleum, biological wastes

Class here comprehensive works on industrial gases

Class industrial gases not provided for here in 665.8; a specific use with the use, e.g., heating buildings 697

.8 **Other industrial gases**

Examples: hydrogen, nitrogen, oxygen

For ammonia, see 661

666 Ceramic and allied technologies

Including asbestos, bricks, concrete, enamels, fiber glass, glass, synthetic and artificial gems and minerals; masonry adhesives, e.g., cement, plaster of paris; pottery, e.g., earthenware, stoneware

667 Cleaning, color, related technologies

Including cleaning and bleaching of textiles, leathers, furs, feathers; dyeing and printing; inks, japans, lacquers, paints, polishes, varnishes; coating and coatings

Class household bleaching, cleaning, laundry in 648; a specific application of coating and coatings with the application, e.g., painting automobiles 629.222

See also 668 for detergents and soaps

668 Technology of other organic products

Examples: adhesives, cosmetics, detergents, fertilizers, glue, gums, perfumes, pesticides, resins, soaps, soil conditioners

For masonry adhesives, see 666

.4 **Plastics [*formerly also* 547.8]**

Class plastic fibers and fabrics in 677

[.402 8] Auxiliary techniques and procedures; apparatus, equipment, materials

Do not use; class in 668.4

.9 **Polymers**

Class a specific application with the application, e.g., manufacture of nylon hosiery 687; a specific polymer with the polymer, e.g., plastics 668.4

669 Metallurgy

Including physical and chemical analysis of metals

Class here alloys, interdisciplinary works on metals

Class a specific aspect of metals with the aspect, e.g., mineralogy 549, metalworking and primary metal products 671

See Manual at 622 vs. 669, 662

.028 Specific kinds of techniques and procedures; apparatus, equipment

Example: electrometallurgy

Class materials in 669

670 Manufacturing

General aspects: planning, design, fabrication

Class manufacture of products based on specific branches of engineering in 620, on chemical technologies in 660; military applications in 623; the arts in 700; manufacture of final products for specific uses not provided elsewhere in 680

Unless separate provision is made, class comprehensive works on products made by a specific process with the process, e.g., seasoned wood 674

SUMMARY

670.1–.9	**Standard subdivisions**
671	**Metalworking processes and primary metal products**
672	**Iron, steel, other iron alloys**
673	**Nonferrous metals**
674	**Lumber processing, wood products, cork**
675	**Leather and fur processing**
676	**Pulp and paper technology**
677	**Textiles**
678	**Elastomers and elastomer products**
679	**Other products of specific kinds of materials**

.285 Data processing Computer applications

Class here computer-aided design/computer-aided manufacture (CAD/CAM), comprehensive works on computer use in the management of manufacturing and computer-aided design or computer-aided manufacture

Class computer-aided design (CAD) in 620, computer use in the management of manufacturing in 658, computer-aided manufacture (CAM) in 670.42

See Manual at 670.285 vs. 670.42

.4 **Special topics**

.42 Factory operations engineering

Including inspection technology, machine-shop practice; mechanization and automation of factory operations, e.g., computer-aided manufacture (CAM), robots

Class here shop and assembly-line technology

Class computer-aided design (CAD) in 620, comprehensive works on computer control in 629.8, computer-aided design/computer-aided manufacture (CAD/CAM) in 670.285

For tools and fabricating equipment, see 621.9; packaging technology, 688.8

See Manual at 670.285 vs. 670.42 for flexible manufacturing systems

.420 68 Management

Class management of factory operations in 658.5

.68 Management

Class management of production in 658.5

> **671–679 Manufacture of products from specific materials**

Class here manufacture of primary products

Class comprehensive works in 670; manufacture of ceramic products in 666, of plastic products in 668.4

See Manual at 671–679 vs. 680

671 Metalworking processes and primary metal products

Class metallurgy and interdisciplinary works on metals in 669

For iron, steel, other iron alloys, see 672; nonferrous metals, 673

> **671.2–671.7 Specific metal-working processes**

Class comprehensive works in 671, specific processes applied to specific primary products in 671.8

.2 **Foundry practice (Casting)**

Including patternmaking, moldmaking

See also 671.3 for hot-working operations

.3 **Mechanical working and related processes**

Examples: forging, machining, powder metallurgy, pressing, rolling, stamping; explosive forming

Including cold-working and hot-working operations

.4 **Electroforming of metals**

.5 **Joining and cutting of metals**

Examples: riveting, soldering, welding

Class machining in 671.3

.7 **Finishing and surface treatment of metals**

Examples: deburring, electroplating, polishing

.8 **Primary products**

Examples: cables, cordage, pipes, sheets, strips, tubes, wires

Class here comprehensive works on metal products

Class a specific metal product not provided for here with the product, e.g., metal furniture 684.1

672 Iron, steel, other iron alloys

Metalworking processes and primary products

Add to base number 672 the numbers following 671 in 671.2–671.8, e.g., welding 672.5

Subdivisions are used for any and all of the topics named in the heading

For small forge work, see 682

673 Nonferrous metals

Metalworking processes and primary products

Class here alloys of nonferrous metals

674 Lumber processing, wood products, cork

Examples of wood products: barrels, crates, pallets, spools, toothpicks, woodenware; particle board, plywood, veneers, wood laminates

Including products from wood waste and residues, e.g., excelsior; comprehensive works on wood-using technologies

Use 674.001–674.009 for standard subdivisions

Class a specific product or wood-using technology not provided for here with the product or technology, e.g., wood as a fuel 662, pulp and paper technology 676, wooden furniture 684.1, carpentry 694

.01 Philosophy and theory of lumber technology

.02 Miscellany of lumber technology

.028 Auxiliary techniques and procedures; apparatus, equipment, materials

Class grading lumber in 674

.03–.09 Standard subdivisions of lumber technology

675 Leather and fur processing

Including manufacture of imitation leathers and furs

For leather and fur goods, see 685

676 Pulp and paper technology

Including paperboard containers; products molded from pulp, e.g., pulpboards, fiberboards

Class here comprehensive works on paper and paper products

677 Textiles

Production of fibers, fabrics, cordage

Including chemistry of man-made fibers [*formerly also* 547.8]; blankets, carpets, rugs, tapestries; laces, ropes, string

Class here comprehensive works on manufacture of textiles and clothing

Class dyeing and printing of textiles in 667, manufacture of clothing in 687

.001 Philosophy and theory

.002 Miscellany

[.002 8] Auxiliary techniques and procedures; apparatus, equipment

Do not use; class in 677

.003–.009 Standard subdivisions

678 Elastomers and elastomer products

Including natural and synthetic rubber and latexes

679 Other products of specific kinds of materials

Examples: ivory and feather products, brooms, brushes, mops, cigars, cigarettes

680 Manufacture of products for specific uses

Not provided for elsewhere

General aspects: planning, design, fabrication

Class here interdisciplinary works on handicrafts

Class repairs of household equipment by members of household in 643; artistic handicraft work in 745.5; manufacture of products based on specific branches of engineering with engineering in 620, e.g., military engineering 623, automobile manufacture 629.2; and, except as provided for below, class manufacture of products of specific materials for specific uses in 671–679, e.g., manufacture of steel products 672, but manufacture of steel furniture 684.1

See Manual at 671–679 vs. 680; 680; 745.5 vs. 680 for handicrafts

SUMMARY

681 Precision instruments and other devices

Examples: calculators; cameras, eyeglasses, lenses, telescopes; printing, writing, duplicating machines and equipment; musical instruments

Including testing and measuring instruments, e.g., electrical instruments for measuring nonelectrical quantities [*formerly also* 621.37], measuring tools [*formerly* 621.9]; technological machines, e.g., agricultural machinery

Instruments for measuring time are classed in 681.1

Class instruments for measuring electrical quantities in 621.37, for testing and measuring electronic signals in 621.3815; computers in 621.39, film and other photographic supplies in 661, hand construction of musical instruments in 786–788, wooden pencils in 674; a specific application of testing and measuring instruments with the application, e.g., aircraft instrumentation 629.135

.1 **Instruments for measuring time**

Examples: clocks, watches, sundials, hourglasses

Do not use standard subdivisions

682 Small forge work (Blacksmithing)

Including horseshoeing, production of hand-forged tools and ironwork

683 Hardware and household appliances

Including locksmithing, kitchen utensils

Class here comprehensive works on manufacture of hardware, building materials, other building supplies

Class refrigerators and freezers in 621.5; heating, ventilating, air-conditioning equipment in 697; a specific hardware or building supply product not provided for here with the product, e.g., tools 621.9, bricks 666, paints 667; nonmetallic household utensils and appliances with the material, e.g., woodenware 674

.4 **Small firearms**

Examples: pistols, revolvers, rifles, shotguns

Class here interdisciplinary works on small firearms, on gunsmithing

Class military small arms in 623.4

.400 1 Philosophy and theory

.400 2 Miscellany

.400 28 Auxiliary techniques and procedures; apparatus, equipment, materials

Class maintenance and repair in 683.4

.400 3–.400 9 Standard subdivisions

684 Furnishings and home workshops

Including metalworking, woodworking; fabric furnishings, e.g., draperies, slipcovers

For carpets and rugs, see 677

.001–.009 Standard subdivisions for furnishings and home workshops, for furnishings alone

.1 Furniture

Class camping furniture in 685

.100 1–.100 9 Standard subdivisions

685 Leather and fur goods, and related products

Including saddlery and harness making; leather and fur clothing; footwear and related products, e.g., skates, snowshoes, skis, stilts, crutches, artificial legs; gloves and mittens; luggage; camping equipment, e.g., tents, sleeping bags

Class overshoes in 678, hosiery in 687

686 Printing and related activities

Class here design and manufacture of publications, book arts

Class interdisciplinary works on the book in 002, book illustration in 741.6

.2 Printing

Including printing by museums [*formerly* 069]; typefounding, typesetting; photomechanical printing; nonimpact techniques, e.g., electrophotographic printing, laser printing; works on "desktop publishing" that emphasize typography

Class interdisciplinary works on print media in 302.23, comprehensive works on printing and publishing in 070.5

See also 070.5 for self publishing, 686.4 or electrophotographic processes in photocopying

.209 Historical and geographic treatment

Class invention of printing in 686

.3 Bookbinding

.300 1–.300 9 Standard subdivisions

.4 Photocopying (Photoduplication)

Including blueprinting, microphotography, xerography

Class here interdisciplinary works on photocopying

Class telefax in 621.382

687 Clothing and accessories

Including patternmaking, dressmaking, tailoring; items auxiliary to clothing construction (notions), e.g., buttons, needles, thread

Class interdisciplinary works on clothing and accessories in 391, on clothing construction in 646.4, on making jewelry in 739.27, on making costume jewelry in 688

For leather and fur clothing, footwear, gloves and mittens, see 685

688 Other final products, and packaging technology

Including costume jewelry; smokers' supplies, e.g., pipes; accessories for personal grooming, e.g., combs, razors; interdisciplinary works on models and miniatures

Class interdisciplinary works on handcrafted models and miniatures in 745.592; models and miniatures of a specific object with the subject, e.g., model airplanes 629.133

For cosmetics, see 668; brushes, 679

.6 **Nonmotor land vehicles**

Examples: carriages, carts, wagons, wheelbarrows

For cycles, see 629.2

See Manual at 629.04 vs. 388

.7 **Recreational equipment**

Including interdisciplinary works on mass-produced and handcrafted toys; equipment, not provided for elsewhere, for games and sports, e.g., chessmen, tennis rackets, artificial flies

Class handcrafted toys in 745.592

.8 **Packaging technology**

Materials, equipment, techniques

Class interdisciplinary works on packaging in 658.5; artistic aspects of containers in 700, e.g., vases; manufacture and use of containers made of a specific material with the material, e.g., paper containers 676

690 Buildings

General aspects: planning, analysis, engineering design, construction, destruction of habitable structures and their utilities

Including specific types of buildings, e.g., air terminals, cathedrals, townhouses; specific structural elements, e.g., roofs

Class construction of buildings for defense against military actions (e.g., forts), naval and military air facilities in 623; docks and port buildings in 627; chimneys and fireplaces in 697; home repairs by members of household in 643; interdisciplinary works on design and construction of buildings in 721

See Manual at 629.226 vs. 643, 690, 728.7 for mobile homes; 643 vs. 690 for renovation, improvement, remodeling; 690 vs. 624; 721 vs. 690

.01 Philosophy and theory

.02 Miscellany

.022 Illustrations

Class maps and related forms, plans, diagrams in 692

.028 Auxiliary techniques and procedures; apparatus, equipment

Class maintenance and repair, safety measures in 690; materials in 691

.029 Commercial miscellany

Class estimates of labor, time, materials in 692

.03–.09 Standard subdivisions

691 Building materials

General aspects: selection, preservation, construction properties

Examples: bricks, concrete, plastics, steel, wood; insulating materials

Class construction in a specific type of material in 693

692 Auxiliary construction practices

Including plans, drawings, specifications; estimates of materials, time, labor; contracting

Class application of a specific auxiliary practice to a specific subject with the subject, e.g., estimates for air conditioning 697.9

693 Construction in specific types of materials and for specific purposes

Including construction in masonry, plaster, prefabricated materials; sandwich panels; pneumatic construction

Comprehensive works on construction in all types of materials are classed in 690

For selection, preservation, construction properties of building materials, see 691; wood construction, 694; roof covering, 695

.8 Construction for specific purposes

Examples: fireproofing, insulation, soundproofing; pest-, shock-, lightning-resistant construction; water- and moistureproof construction

Comprehensive technical works on fireproofing relocated to 628.9

694 Wood construction Carpentry

695 Roof covering

Class comprehensive works on roofs as structural elements in 690, wooden roofs in 694

696 Utilities

General aspects: design and installation

Including plumbing, pipe fitting, steam and gas fitting

Class here comprehensive works on energy and environmental engineering of buildings

Class interior electric wiring in 621.319; a specific aspect of energy and environmental engineering with the aspect, e.g., thermal insulation 693.8

For heating, ventilating, air-conditioning engineering, see 697

697 Heating, ventilating, air-conditioning engineering

General aspects: design and installation of systems and components

Including local and central heating

Use 697.0001–697.0009 for standard subdivisions

.001 Philosophy and theory of heating

.002 Miscellany of heating

.002 8 Auxiliary techniques and procedures; apparatus, materials of heating

Class heating equipment in 697

.003–.009 Standard subdivisions of heating

.9 Ventilation and air conditioning

Class heating in 697

698 Detail finishing

Examples: carpeting, finishing woodwork, painting, paperhanging

700

700 The arts Fine and decorative arts

Description, critical appraisal, techniques, procedures, apparatus, equipment, materials of the fine, decorative, literary, performing, recreational arts

Class here conceptual art

For book arts, see 686; literature, 800

See Manual at 700

> **700.1–700.9 Standard subdivisions of the arts**

Use this standard subdivision span for material that includes two or more of the fine and decorative arts and one or more of the other arts, e.g., a work about a painter who is also a sculptor and a poet 700.92. If only one fine or decorative art and one of the other arts is involved, class in the number coming first in the schedule, e.g., a United States painter and poet 759.13

Class comprehensive works in 700

See Manual at 700

.1–.6 Standard subdivisions

.7 Education and related topics of the arts

.74 Museums, collections, exhibits

Notation 074 from Table 1 is never added to the work of an individual artist when the work falls in the number for the individual artist's country (e.g., an exhibition of the work of a Canadian painter 759.11)

.75 Museum activities and services

Notation 075 from Table 1 is never added to the work of an individual artist when the work falls in the number for the individual artist's country (e.g., collecting the work of a Canadian painter 759.11)

.8 The arts with respect to kinds of persons

.9 Historical, geographic, persons treatment

.92 Persons

Class here the works themselves and critical appraisal and description of works of an artist or artists

See Manual at 700.92

701 Philosophy and theory of fine and decorative arts

Including appreciative aspects, e.g., psychology, aesthetics, criticism and appreciation; inherent features, e.g., color, composition, light, perspective, style, time

Class works of critical appraisal in 709

702 Miscellany of fine and decorative arts

.8 Technique, procedures, apparatus, equipment, materials

Including conservation, preservation, restoration, expertizing; testing and measurement; use of artists' models; reproductions, copies, forgeries, alterations; mixed-media and composites, e.g., collage

Class finished works of mixed-media and composite art in 709, two-dimensional mixed-media art or composities in 760, decoupage in 745.54

.9 Commercial miscellany

Class auction and sales catalogs in which an exhibition is involved in 707.4

703 Dictionaries, encyclopedias, concordances of fine and decorative arts

704 Special topics in fine and decorative arts

Including kinds of persons occupied with art, e.g., patrons

Class art dealers in 380.1; the fine and decorative arts of nonliterate peoples in 709.01; description, critical appraisal, works, biography of artists in 709.2

.9 Iconography

Development, description, critical appraisal, works

Including human figures and their parts, nature, still life, architectural subjects, cityscapes, symbolism and allegory, mythology and legend, religion and religious symbolism

Abstractionism relocated to 709.04

Class significance and purpose of art in religion in 291.3, in Christianity in 246, in other religions in 292–299

See Manual at 704.9

705–706 Standard subdivisions of fine and decorative arts

707 Education and related topics of fine and decorative arts

.4 Temporary and traveling collections and exhibits

Class here permanent collections on tour, temporary exhibits of a private collection, auction and sales catalogs in which an exhibition is involved

Do not use for museums and permanent collections and exhibits; class in 708

708 Galleries, museums, private collections of fine and decorative arts

Do not use for history and description of fine and decorative arts with respect to kinds of persons; class in 704

For temporary and traveling collections and exhibits, see 707.4

.001–.008 Standard subdivisions

.009 Historical and persons treatment

Class geographic treatment in 708.1–708.9

> **708.1–708.9 Geographical treatment**

Class here guidebooks and catalogs of specific galleries, museums, private collections

Class comprehensive works in 708

.1 **In North America**

Class galleries, museums, private collections in Middle America in 708.972

.11 Canada

.13–.19 United States

Add to base number 708.1 the numbers following —7 in notation 73–79 from Table 2, e.g., galleries, museums, private collections in Pennsylvania 708.148

Class galleries, museums, private collections in Hawaii in 708.9969

.2 **In British Isles (England, Scotland, Wales, Ireland)**

.3–.8 **In other modern European countries**

Add to base number 708 the numbers following —4 in notation 43–48 from Table 2, e.g., galleries, museums, private collections in France 708.4

Class comprehensive works, and galleries, museums, private collections in other European countries not provided for in notation 43–48 from Table 2 in 708.94, e.g., galleries, museums, private collections in Belgium 708.9493

.9 **In other geographical areas**

Add to base number 708.9 notation 1, 3–9 from Table 2, e.g., comprehensive works on galleries, museums, private collections in Islamic areas 708.917, in European countries 708.94

709 Historical, geographic, persons treatment of fine and decorative arts

Development, description, critical appraisal, works

Class here finished works of experimental and mixed-media art that do not fit easily into a recognized medium

Class two-dimensional experimental and mixed-media art in 760

See Manual at 700

> **709.01–709.05 Periods of development**

Class here schools and styles not limited by country or locality, European art limited by period, school, or style

Class comprehensive works in 709

See Manual at 709.01–709.05 vs. 709.3–709.9

.01 Arts of nonliterate peoples, and earliest times to 499

Arts of nonliterate peoples regardless of place or time, but limited to nonliterate peoples of the past and nonliterate peoples clearly not a part of contemporary society

Including Paleolithic and rock art

.02 500–1499

Including Byzantine, early Christian, Gothic, Renaissance, Romanesque art

Class here medieval art

Class Byzantine, early Christian, Gothic, Renaissance art of any other period with the period, e.g., early Christian art before 500 709.01

.03 1500–

Including art nouveau, baroque art, classical revival, Impressionism, naturalism, realism, rococo art, romanticism

Class art nouveau, naturalism, realism of any other period with the period, e.g., realism of 1900–1990 709.04

For 1900–1999, see 709.04; 2000–2099, 709.05

.04 1900–1999

Including abstractionism [*formerly also* 704.9], art deco, cubism, expressionism, op art, pop art, surrealism

Class here modern art

Class modern art of 1800–1899 in 709.03

.05 2000–2099

.1 **Treatment by areas, regions, places in general**

Class history and description of fine and decorative arts with respect to kinds of persons in 704, art of nonliterate peoples regardless of place in 709.01

.2 **Persons**

Class here description, critical appraisal, biography, works of artists not limited to or chiefly identified with a specific form, e.g., painting, or group of forms, e.g., graphic arts

Class works of more than one artist in the same geographical area in 709.1, 709.3–709.9

.3–.9 **Treatment by specific continents, countries, localities**

Class history and description of fine and decorative arts with respect to kinds of persons in 704; art of nonliterate peoples regardless of place in 709.01; comprehensive works on European art of specific periods in 709.01–709.05 (*not* 709.4), e.g., art of 1800–1899 in Europe 709.03 (*not* 709.4)

See Manual at 709.01–709.05 vs. 709.3–709.9

710 Civic and landscape art

711 Area planning (Civic art)

Design of physical environment for public welfare, convenience, pleasure

Including urban renewal

Class interdisciplinary works on area planning in 307.1, comprehensive works on area planning and architecture in 720

For landscape design, see 712

See Manual at 711 vs. 307.1

.028 Apparatus, equipment, materials

Class auxiliary techniques and procedures in 711

712 Landscape architecture (Landscape design)

Landscaping public, private, semiprivate, institutional parks and grounds

Class engineering aspects of landscape architecture in 624

For specific elements in landscape design, see 714–717; trafficways, 713; cemeteries, 718; natural landscapes, 719

.01 Philosophy and theory

Class aesthetics, style, composition in 712

.028 Apparatus, equipment, materials

Class auxiliary techniques and procedures in 712

713 Landscape architecture of trafficways

> 714–717 Specific elements in landscape design

Class comprehensive works in 712

714 Water features in landscape architecture

Examples: fountains, pools

715 Woody plants in landscape architecture

Nonflowering and flowering trees, shrubs, vines

Including topiary work

Class here comprehensive works on plants in landscape architecture

For comprehensive works on flowering plants in landscape architecture, see 716

716 Herbaceous plants in landscape architecture

Nonflowering and flowering

Including ground cover

Class here comprehensive works on flowering plants in landscape architecture

For flowering woody plants, see 715

717 Structures in landscape architecture

Relationship of buildings, terraces, fences, gates, steps, ornamental accessories to other elements of landscape architecture

718 Landscape architecture of cemeteries

719 Natural landscapes

Including natural monuments; forest and wildlife reserves

Class natural water features in 714

720 Architecture

Class here comprehensive works on architecture and civic and landscape art

For civic and landscape art, see 710

SUMMARY

720.1–.9 [Standard subdivisions]
721 Architectural structure
722 Architecture from earliest times to ca. 300
723 Architecture from ca. 300 to 1399
724 Architecture from 1400
725 Public structures
726 Buildings for religious and related purposes
727 Buildings for educational and research purposes
728 Residential and related buildings
729 Design and decoration of structures and accessories

.22 Illustrations

Including architectural drawings

Class drafting illustrations in 720.28; architectural drawings for a specific type of structure in 725–728, using notation 022 from Table 1

.28 Auxiliary techniques and procedures; apparatus, equipment, materials

Including architectural drawing, remodeling, conservation, preservation, restoration

Class interdisciplinary works on conservation, preservation, restoration in 363.6, architectural drawings in 720.22

See Manual at 930–990: Historic preservation

.8 Architecture with respect to kinds of persons

.84 Persons in specific stages of adulthood

Class persons in late adulthood in 720

[.87] Handicapped and ill persons

Do not use; class in 720

.9 Historical, geographic, persons treatment

Class here Oriental architecture from ca. 300 limited to a specific country or locality [*formerly* 722], schools and styles limited to a specific country or locality, architectural aspects of historic buildings

Class architectural drawings in 720.22, comprehensive works on specific schools and styles not limited to a specific country or locality in 722–724

See Manual at 913–919: Historic sites and buildings

[.93] Ancient world

Do not use; class in 722

.942 English architecture

Class here Elizabethan, Jacobean, Queen Anne architecture [*formerly also* 724]

.946 Spanish architecture

Class here Churrigueresque architecture [*formerly also* 724]

.95 Asia

Class here comprehensive works on Oriental architecture [*formerly* 722]

.97 North America

Class here comprehensive works on ancient American, ancient North American architecture [*formerly also* 722]

.98 South America

Class here comprehensive works on ancient South American architecture [*formerly also* 722]

721 Architectural structure

Examples: foundations, walls, roofs, floors, doors, windows, stairs

Including structures of specific shapes and materials

Class here design [*formerly also* 729] and decoration [*formerly* 729] of, comprehensive works on structural elements; interdisciplinary works on design and construction

Class architectural structure of specific types of structures in 725–728

Works about the architecture of buildings as a whole are classed in 720

For engineering design and construction, see 690; design and decoration, 729; structural engineering, 624.1

See Manual at 721 vs. 690

> 722–724 Architectural schools and styles

Class comprehensive works, schools and styles from ca. 300 limited to a specific country or locality in 720.9; architects of specific schools and styles not limited to a specific type of structure in 720.92; specific types of structures regardless of school or style in 725–728; details of construction of specific schools and styles in 721; design and decoration of structures of specific schools and styles in 729

722 Architecture from earliest times to ca. 300

Examples: Greek and Roman architecture

Comprehensive works on Oriental architecture relocated to 720.95, on Oriental architecture from ca. 300 to 1399 relocated to 723, on Oriental architecture from 1400 relocated to 724; Oriental architecture from ca. 300 limited to a specific country or locality relocated to 720.9; comprehensive works on ancient American, ancient North American architecture relocated to 720.97, on ancient South American architecture relocated to 720.98

723 Architecture from ca. 300 to 1399

Examples: Byzantine, Gothic, Moorish, Romanesque architectures

Class here comprehensive works on Oriental architecture from ca. 300 to 1399 [*formerly* 722]; medieval architecture

[.09] Historical, geographic, persons treatment

Do not use; class architecture from ca. 300 to 1399 limited to a specific country or locality in 720.9, persons treatment in 720.92

724 Architecture from 1400

Examples: baroque, neoclassical, Renaissance, rococo architectures

Class here comprehensive works on Oriental architecture from 1400 [*formerly* 722], modern architecture

Elizabethan, Jacobean, Queen Anne architecture relocated to 720.942, Churrigueresque architecture to 720.946

[.09] Historical, geographic, persons treatment

Do not use; class architecture from 1400 limited to a specific country or locality in 720.9, persons treatment in 720.92

[.9] 1900–

Use of this number discontinued; class in 724

> **725–728 Specific types of structures**

Class here development of architectural schools and styles, comprehensive works on specific structures and their interior design and decorations, interdisciplinary works on design and construction of specific types of structures

Class comprehensive works in 720; engineering design and construction of specific types of habitable structures in 690; structures rehabilitated to a single new use with the new use, e.g., warehouses converted into apartments 728; structures rehabilitated to multiple new uses with the old use, e.g., warehouses converted into retail stores and apartments 725

For structural engineering, see 624.1; interior decoration, 747

725 Public structures

Not used primarily for religious, educational, research, residential purposes

Examples: concert halls, civic centers, factories, hospitals, monuments, office buildings, opera houses, railroad stations, restaurants, shopping malls, stores, theaters; bridges, towers

Class engineering of forts and fortresses in 623, of bridges in 624; comprehensive works on castles in 728.8; memorial buildings for a specific purpose with the purpose, e.g., memorial library buildings 727

726 Buildings for religious and related purposes

Examples: cathedrals, churches, mosques, shrines, synagogues, temples; monasteries, tombs

Including built-in church furniture [*formerly also* 729]

727 Buildings for educational and research purposes

Including college and university buildings, laboratories, library buildings, museums and art galleries

Class here school buildings

728 Residential and related buildings

Including patios, saunas, swimming pools; farm buildings other than human residence, e.g., barns

Examples: houses, apartments, cottages, farmhouses, hotels and motels

Class here domestic architecture, conventional housing

Class official residences in 725, parsonages and episcopal palaces in 726, residential educational buildings (e.g., college dormitories) in 727

[.3] Conventional housing

Use of this number discontinued; class in 728

.7 Vacation houses, cabins, hunting lodges, houseboats, mobile homes

See Manual at 629.226 vs. 643, 690, 728.7 for mobile homes

.8 Large and elaborate private dwellings

Examples: castles, chateaux, palaces, villas

Including comprehensive works on architecture of castles

Class castles as military structures, palaces of rulers in 725

729 Design and decoration of structures and accessories

Including acoustics, lighting, modular design; decoration in specific mediums, e.g., mosaics, sculpture

Class here interior design (the art or practice of planning and supervising the design and execution of architectural interiors and their furnishings)

Design and decoration of structural elements relocated to 721, built-in church furniture to 726

Class design and decoration of structures and accessories of specific types of buildings in 725–728, decoration in a specific medium not in an architectural context with the medium, e.g., sculpture 730

For interior decoration, see 747

See Manual at 729

730 Plastic arts Sculpture

SUMMARY

730.01–.09	**Standard subdivisions of plastic arts**
.1–.9	**Standard subdivisions of sculpture**
731	**Processes, forms, subjects of sculpture**
732	**Sculpture from earliest times to ca. 500, sculpture of nonliterate peoples**
733	**Greek, Etruscan, Roman sculpture**
734	**Sculpture from ca. 500 to 1399**
735	**Sculpture from 1400**
736	**Carving and carvings**
737	**Numismatics and sigillography**
738	**Ceramic arts**
739	**Art metalwork**

.01–.09 Standard subdivisions of plastic arts

> **730.1–730.9 Standard subdivisions of sculpture**

Class comprehensive works in 730

.1 **Philosophy and theory of sculpture**

Including criticism and appreciation

Class works of critical appraisal in 730.9

.2 **Miscellany of sculpture**

[.28] Auxiliary techniques and procedures; apparatus, equipment, materials

Do not use; class in 731.028

.3–.8 **Standard subdivisions of sculpture**

.9 **Historical, geographic, persons treatment of sculpture**

Class here Oriental sculpture from ca. 500 limited to a specific country or locality [*formerly* 732], schools and styles limited to a specific country or locality

Class comprehensive works on specific schools and styles not limited to country or locality in 732–735, sculpture of nonliterate peoples regardless of time or place in 732

.92 Sculptors

Description, critical appraisal, biography of sculptors and their works regardless of process, representation, style or school, period, place

Including works of individual sculptors, of sculptors from several geographical areas

Class sculptors who also work in the other plastic arts in 730.092, works of more than one sculptor in the same geographical area in 730.91, 730.94–730.99, 732–733

[.93] Ancient world

Do not use; class in 732–733

.95 Asia

Class here comprehensive works on Oriental sculpture [*formerly* 732]

> ## 731–735 Sculpture

Class comprehensive works in 730

See Manual at 736–739 vs. 731–735

731 Processes, forms, subjects of sculpture

Including apparatus, equipment, materials; sculpture in relief; sculpture in the round, e.g., busts; mobiles and stabiles; iconography

Class processes, forms, subjects of individual sculptors in 730.92; of specific periods and by specific schools in 732–735; of specific medieval and modern schools limited to a specific country or locality in 730.9

For monumental brasses, see 739.5

.028 Techniques, procedures, apparatus, equipment, materials

Comprehensive works

Class apparatus, equipment, materials in 731, techniques and procedures in 731.4

.4 Techniques and procedures

Including carving, casting, modeling, molding, welding; conservation, preservation, restoration

Class forms and subjects employing specific techniques and procedures in 731

> **732–735 Schools and styles of sculpture**

Class comprehensive works, medieval and modern Western schools and styles limited to a specific country or locality in 730.9; sculptors associated with specific schools and styles in 730.92

732 Sculpture from earliest times to ca. 500, sculpture of nonliterate peoples

Comprehensive works on Oriental sculpture relocated to 730.95, on Oriental sculpture from ca. 500 to 1399 relocated to 734, on Oriental sculpture from 1400 relocated to 735; Oriental sculpture from ca. 500 limited to a specific country or locality relocated to 730.9

For Greek, Etruscan, Roman sculpture, see 733

[.09] Historical, geographic, persons treatment

Do not use; class persons treatment in 730.9, historical, geographic treatment in 732

733 Greek, Etruscan, Roman sculpture

734 Sculpture from ca. 500 to 1399

Examples: Byzantine, Gothic, Romanesque sculpture

Class here comprehensive works on Oriental sculpture from ca. 500 to 1399 [*formerly* 732]; medieval sculpture

Class sculpture from ca. 500 to 1399 limited to a specific country or locality in 730.9

[.09] Historical, geographic, persons treatment

Do not use; class in 730.9

735 Sculpture from 1400

Examples: baroque, Renaissance sculpture

Class here comprehensive works on Oriental sculpture from 1400 [*formerly* 732]; modern sculpture

Class sculpture from 1400 limited to a specific country or locality in 730.9

[.09] Historical, geographic, persons treatment

Do not use; class in 730.9

> **736–739 Other plastic arts**

Processes and products

Class comprehensive works in 730, other plastic arts not provided for here in 745–749

See also 731–735 for sculpture

See Manual at 736–739 vs. 731–735

736 Carving and carvings

Including glyptics, origami, whittling; cameos

Class engraved seals, stamps, signets in 737; setting of precious and semiprecious stones in 739.27

737 Numismatics and sigillography

Including buttons, medals, talismans, tokens; engraved seals, stamps, signets

For paper money, see 769.5

.4 Coins

Class here counterfeit coins

.409 Historical, geographic, persons treatment

Class coins of specific countries in 737.49

.49 Of specific countries

By place of origin

Add to base number 737.49 notation 3–9 from Table 2, e.g., Roman coins minted in Egypt 737.4932

738 Ceramic arts

Class here pottery

Class ceramic sculpture in 731–735

Works about "pottery" in the sense of porcelain and earthenware or stoneware are classed here, in the sense of only porcelain are classed in 738.2

For glass, see 748

[.028] Auxiliary techniques and procedures; apparatus, equipment, materials

Do not use; class in 738.1

.092 Potters

Description, critical appraisal, biography of potters regardless of material or product

Class here ceramic artists

Class enamelers in 738.4092, mosaicists in 738.5092

.1 Techniques, procedures, apparatus, equipment, materials

Class techniques of making specialized products in 738.4–738.8

> **738.2–738.8 Products**

Development, description, critical appraisal, collections of works

Class comprehensive works in 738

.2 Porcelain

Use of this number for comprehensive works on pottery discontinued; class in 738

Class comprehensive works on porcelain, earthenware, stoneware in 738

[.202 8] Auxiliary techniques and procedures; apparatus, equipment, materials

Do not use; class in 738.1

[.209 2] Persons treatment

Do not use; class in 738.092

.3 Earthenware and stoneware

[.302 8] Auxiliary techniques and procedures; apparatus, equipment, materials

Do not use; class in 738.1

[.309 2] Persons treatment

Do not use; class in 738.092

> **738.4–738.8 Specialized products and techniques of making them**

Class comprehensive works in 738

.4 **Enameling and enamels**

Class nielloing in 739

For jewelry, see 739.27

.5 **Mosaics**

Including mosaics used with architecture, e.g., pavements; mosaics applied to portable objects, e.g., mosaic jewelry

Class here mosaic painting, comprehensive works on mosaics in all materials

Class mosaics of a specific material not provided for here with the material, e.g., mosaic glass 748.5

.6 **Ornamental bricks and tiles**

Standard subdivisions are added for bricks and tiles, for bricks alone, and for tiles alone

.8 **Other products**

Examples: candlesticks, figurines, lamps, stoves

739 Art metalwork

Including clocks and watches, clockcases regardless of material

Class clocks as furniture in 749; interdisciplinary works on clocks and watches in 681.1

For numismatics, see 737

[.028] Auxiliary techniques and procedures; apparatus, equipment, materials

Do not use; class in 739

.2 **Work in precious metals**

Including goldsmithing, silversmithing

Class clocks and watches in precious metals in 739

.27 Jewelry

Design of settings, mounting gems, repair work

Class here interdisciplinary works on making fine and costume jewelry

Class interdisciplinary works on jewelry in 391, on making costume jewelry in 688; making handcrafted costume jewelry in 745.594; carving precious and semiprecious stones in 736; jewelry made in a material other than metal with the material, e.g., mosaic jewelry 738.5

[.270 28] Techniques, procedures, apparatus, equipment, materials

Use of this number discontinued; class in 739.27

> **739.4–739.5 Work in base metals**

Class comprehensive works, clocks and watches in base metals in 739

For arms and armor, see 739.7

.4 **Ironwork**

[.402 8] Auxiliary techniques and procedures; apparatus, equipment, materials

Do not use; class in 739.4

[.409] Historical, geographic, persons treatment

Do not use; class in 739.4

.5 **Work in other metals**

Including monumental brasses

.7 **Arms and armor**

Class interdisciplinary works in 623.4

740 Drawing and decorative arts

SUMMARY

741	**Drawing and drawings**
742	**Perspective**
743	**Drawing and drawings by subject**
745	**Decorative arts**
746	**Textile arts and handicrafts**
747	**Interior decoration**
748	**Glass**
749	**Furniture and accessories**

741 Drawing and drawings

Class comprehensive works on drawing and painting in 750, on two-dimensional art in 760

For drawing and drawings by subject, see 743

.01 Philosophy and theory

Including criticism and appreciation

Class works of critical appraisal in 741.09, perspective in 742

[.028] Auxiliary techniques and procedures; apparatus, equipment, materials

Do not use; class in 741.2

.074 Museums and exhibits

Class collections of drawings in 741.9

.09 Historical, geographic, persons treatment

Class collections of drawings of specific periods and places in 741.9

.092 Artists

Description, critical appraisal, biography of artists regardless of medium, process, subject, period, place

Description, critical appraisal, biography of artists working in special applications relocated to 741.5–741.7

Class collections of drawings in 741.9

.2 **Techniques, procedures, apparatus, equipment, materials**

Examples: charcoal, chalk, crayon, pencil, silverpoint; ink with pen, brush, marker; scratchboard, airbrush drawing

Class techniques, procedures, apparatus, equipment, materials used in special applications in 741.5–741.7; used in drawing specific subjects in 743; used by individual artists in 741.092

For perspective, see 742

See also 751.42 for watercolor

> **741.5–741.7 Special applications**

Techniques, procedures, apparatus, equipment, materials, description, critical appraisal, collections

Class here description, critical appraisal, biography of artists working in special applications [*formerly* 741.092]; collections by an individual artist devoted to special applications [*formerly* 741.9]

Class comprehensive works in 741.6

.5 **Cartoons, caricatures, comics**

Including animated cartoons

Class here cartoon fiction [*formerly also* with fiction with use of notation 3 from Table 3], graphic novels (visual novels)

Class comprehensive works on cartoon films in 791.43, photographic techniques in 778.5, cartoons or caricatures whose purpose is to inform or persuade with the subject of the cartoon or caricature, e.g., political cartoons 320

.507 4 Museums and exhibits

Class collections in 741.5

.509 2 Artists

Class collections by individual artists in 741.5

.6 Graphic design, illustration and commercial art

Including match covers [*formerly also* 769.5], advertisements, books and book jackets, calendars, covers for sheet music and recordings, greeting cards, magazines, newspapers, postcards, posters; fashion drawing

Class here comprehensive works on special applications of drawing; on graphic design, illustration, commercial art

Class graphic arts, comprehensive works on two-dimensional art in 760; fashion design in 746.9; posters as a specific form of prints in 769.5; government-issued postcards without illustrations in 769.56; a specific type of illustration, a specific form of graphic design, a specific form of commercial art not provided for here with the subject, e.g., prints 769

See Manual at 800 vs. 741.6 for illustration

[.64–.68] Specific forms

Use of these numbers discontinued; class in 741.6

.7 Silhouettes

Class cut-out silhouettes in 736

.9 Collections of drawings

Regardless of medium or process

Class here exhibition catalogs

Preliminary drawings are classed with the finished work unless they are treated as works of art in their own right

Collections by an individual artist devoted to special applications relocated to 741.5–741.7

Class collections by more than one artist devoted to special applications in 741.5–741.7, collections of drawings by subject not from a specific period or place in 743

.93–.99 Specific continents, countries, localities

Add to base number 741.9 notation 3–9 from Table 2, e.g., collections of drawings from London 741.9421

Collections by individual artists are classed at country level only. Notation 074 from Table 1 for collections is not added. For example, a collection of an individual artist from London is classed in 741.942 (*not* 741.9421, 741.942074)

742 Perspective

Class perspective in drawing specific subjects in 743, in special applications in 741.5–741.7; comprehensive works on perspective in the arts in 701

743 Drawing and drawings by subject

Class artists regardless of subject in 741.092, collections of drawings by subject from a specific period or place in 741.9

For fashion drawing, see 741.6

[.028] Techniques, procedures, apparatus, equipment, materials

Use of this number discontinued; class in 743

745 Decorative arts

Class here folk art

Class decorative arts not provided for here in 736–739, 746–749

.1 Antiques

Class a specific kind of antique with the kind, e.g., brasses 739.5, passenger automobiles 629.222

See Manual at 745.1

.2 Industrial art and design

Creative design of mass-produced commodities

Class design of a specific commodity with the commodity, e.g., automobiles 629.2

.4 Pure and applied design and decoration

Class design in a specific art form with the form, e.g., design in architecture 729

For industrial design, see 745.2

[.409] Historical, geographic, persons treatment

Do not use; class in 745.4

.5 Handicrafts

Creative work done by hand with aid of simple tools or machines

Class home (amateur) workshops in 684, interdisciplinary works on handicrafts in 680

For decorative coloring, see 745.7; floral arts, 745.92

See Manual at 745.5 vs. 680

> **745.51–745.58 In specific materials**

Class comprehensive works in 745.5, specific objects made from specific materials in 745.59, glass handicrafts in 748

For textile handicrafts, see 746

.51 In wood

Examples: inlay trim, marquetry, ornamental woodwork, scrollwork

Including bamboo

Class treen (woodenware) in 674, cabinetmaking in 684, wooden furniture making in 684.1; artistic aspects of furniture, ornamental woodwork in furniture in 749

.53 In leather and fur

Class construction of clothing in 646.4

.54 In paper

Examples: papier mâché, tissue papers, wallpapers

Including decoupage, gift wrapping

Class papier mâché used in sculpture in 731, paper cutting and folding in 736

.55 In shells

.56 In metal

Class art metalwork in 739

.57 In rubber and plastics

.58 From beads, found and other objects

Examples: cattails, scrap, stones, hosiery

Class specific objects made from other objects in 745.59

For bead embroidery, see 746.5

.59 Making specific objects

Class here handicrafts in composite materials

.592 Toys, models, miniatures, related objects

Examples: dolls, stuffed animals, paper airplanes, ships in bottles

Class interdisciplinary works on models and miniatures in 688, on mass-produced and handcrafted toys in 688.7, miniature and model educational exhibits, models for technical and professional use with the subject illustrated, e.g., handcrafted miniature anthropological exhibits 573.074

See Manual at 745.592 for models and miniatures

.593 Useful objects

Examples: candles, decoys, lampshades

Class carved birds not used for hunting in 730

For toys, models, miniatures, related objects, see 745.592

.594 Decorative objects

Examples: artificial flowers, costume jewelry, Easter eggs, greeting cards

Class interdisciplinary works on costume jewelry in 391, on making jewelry in 739.27, on making costume jewelry in 688; arrangement of artificial flowers in 745.92

.6 **Calligraphy, illumination, heraldic design**

Class development, description, critical appraisal of manuscripts in 091, of illustrated books in 096; penmanship in 652, typography in 686.2

See also 741.6 for book illustration

See Manual at 745.6 for illumination

.7 **Decorative coloring**

Examples: gilding, lacquering, painting, stenciling

Class printing, painting, dyeing textiles in 746.6; gilding as an aspect of bookbinding in 686.3, of illumination of manuscripts and books in 745.6

.8 **Panoramas, cycloramas, dioramas**

.9 **Other decorative arts**

.92 Floral arts

Flower arrangement: selection and arrangement of plant materials and appropriate accessories

Class here arrangement of artificial flowers

Class making artificial flowers in 745.594, potted plants as interior decorations in 747

746 Textile arts and handicrafts

Including string art

Class domestic sewing and related operations in 646.2, a specific textile product not provided for here with the product, e.g., stuffed animals 745.592

> **746.1–746.9 Products and processes**

Unless other instructions are given, observe the following table of precedence, e.g., embroidering tapestry 746.3 (*not* 746.44)

Laces and related fabrics	746.2
Pictures, hangings, tapestries	746.3
Rugs and carpets	746.7
Other textile products	746.9
Yarn preparation and weaving	746.1
Needle- and handwork	746.4
Bead embroidery	746.5
Printing, painting, dyeing	746.6

Class comprehensive works in 746, textile manufacturing in 677

.1 **Yarn preparation and weaving**

Including dyeing, spinning

For weaving unaltered vegetable fibers, see 746.41; nonloom weaving, 746.42

.2 **Laces and related fabrics**

Including passementerie, e.g., braids, cords, fringes

For tatting, see 746.43

.3 **Pictures, hangings, tapestries**

[.309] Historical, geographic, persons treatment

Do not use; class in 746.39

.39 Historical, geographic, persons treatment

Add to base number 746.39 notation 1–9 from Table 2, e.g., artists 746.392

.4 **Needle- and handwork**

.41 Weaving, braiding, matting unaltered vegetable fibers

Examples: basketry, raffia work, rushwork

.42 Nonloom weaving and related techniques

Examples: braiding, knotting, macramé, sprang, twining

Class card weaving in 746.1, nonloom weaving of unaltered vegetable fibers in 746.41

.43 Knitting, crocheting, tatting

.44 Embroidery

Including appliqué, bargello, couching, crewelwork, cross-stitch, cutwork, drawn work, hardanger, needlepoint, smocking

.46 Patchwork and quilting

Class quilts in 746.9

.5 **Bead embroidery**

.6 **Printing, painting, dyeing**

Examples: batik, silk-screen printing, tie-dyeing

.7 **Rugs and carpets**

[.709] Historical, geographic, persons treatment

Do not use; class in 746.79

.79 Historical, geographic, persons treatment

Add to base number 746.79 notation 1–9 from Table 2, e.g., carpetmakers 746.792

.9 Other textile products

Examples: costume; interior furnishings (e.g., bedspreads, draperies, quilts, slipcovers, table linens, towels)

Including fashion design

Class interdisciplinary works on clothing in 391, on clothing construction in 646.4

See Manual at 391 vs. 646, 746.9 for costume

747 Interior decoration

Design and decorative treatment with interior furnishings

Including carpets, decorative lighting, draperies, rugs, upholstery, wallpaper; decorating with color and houseplants; decorations for specific occasions, e.g., weddings

Class here interior decoration of residential buildings [*formerly also* 645]

Class textile arts and handicrafts in 746, interior design in 729

For furniture and accessories, see 749

[.09] Historical, geographic, persons treatment

Do not use; class in 747.2

.2 Historical, geographic, persons treatment

Class here artists

Add to base number 747.2 the numbers following 708 in 708.1–708.9, e.g., interior decoration and artists in France 747.24

Individual artists are classed in notation at country level only

.7 Decoration of specific rooms of residential buildings

Specific decorations regardless of room are classed in 747

748 Glass

.092 Persons treatment

Class here glassmakers

The term "glassmakers" when referring only to makers of glassware is classed in 748.29

.2 Glassware

Class here blown, cast, decorated, fashioned, molded, pressed glassware

Class stained glass in 748.5

For methods of decoration, see 748.6; specific articles, 748.8

.202 8 Techniques, procedures, apparatus, equipment, materials

Including glassblowing, bottle and jar cutting

[.209] Historical, geographic, persons treatment

Do not use; class in 748.29

.29 Historical, geographic, persons treatment

Class here glassware makers

Add to base number 748.29 the numbers following 708 in 708.1–708.9, e.g., glassware and glassmakers of Pennsylvania 748.29148

Individual glassmakers are classed in notation at country level only

.5 Stained, painted, leaded, mosaic glass

Standard subdivisions are added for stained glass alone, for painted glass alone, and for leaded glass alone

Class comprehensive works on mosaics in 738.5

For specific articles, see 748.8

[.509] Historical, geographic, persons treatment

Do not use; class in 748.59

.59 Historical, geographic, persons treatment

Class here artists

Add to base number 748.59 the numbers following 708 in 708.1–708.9, e.g., stained glass and artists of France 748.594

Individual artists are classed in notation at country level only

.6 Methods of decoration

Examples: cutting, enameling, engraving, etching, sandblasting

Class methods of decoration of specific articles in 748.8

For painted glass, see 748.5

[.609 2] Persons treatment

Do not use; class in 748.29

.8 Specific articles

Including bottles of artistic interest regardless of use, drinking glasses, mirrors, paperweights

Class manufacture of glass bottles in 666; mirrors as furniture, glass lamps and lighting fixtures in 749

749 Furniture and accessories

Including built-in furniture, fireplaces, lamps, picture frames

For upholstery, see 747; built-in church furniture, 726

[.09] Historical, geographic, persons treatment

Do not use; class in 749.2

.2 **Historical, geographic, persons treatment**

Class here antiques and reproductions, furniture makers

Add to base number 749.2 the numbers following 708 in 708.1–708.9, e.g., English furniture and furniture makers in 749.22

Individual furniture makers are classed in notation at country level only

750 Painting and paintings

Class here comprehensive works on painting and drawing

Unless other instructions are given, observe the following table of precedence, e.g., Canadian painters of portraits 759.11 (*not* 757.0971), portrait painting in Canada 757.0971 (*not* 759.11)

Individual painters and their work	759.1–.9
Techniques, procedures, apparatus, equipment, materials	751.2–.6
Iconography	753–758
Specific forms	751.7
Geographic treatment	759.1–.9
Periods of development	759.01–.07
Color	752

Class comprehensive works on graphic arts, two-dimensional art in 760; painting in a specific decorative art with the art, e.g., illumination of manuscripts and books 745.6

For drawing and drawings, see 741

SUMMARY

750.1–.8	**Standard subdivisions**
751	**Techniques, procedures, apparatus, equipment, materials, forms**
752	**Color**
753	**Symbolism, allegory, mythology, legend**
754	**Genre paintings**
755	**Religion and religious symbolism**
757	**Human figures and their parts**
758	**Other subjects**
759	**Historical, geographic, persons treatment**

.1 **Philosophy and theory**

Including criticism and appreciation

Class works of critical appraisal in 759, color in 752

[.28] Techniques, procedures, apparatus, equipment, materials

Relocated to 751

[.9] **Historical, geographic, persons treatment**

Do not use; class in 759

751 Techniques, procedures, apparatus, equipment, materials [*formerly* 750.28], forms

.2 Materials

Examples: surfaces, pigments, mediums, fixatives, coatings

Class use of materials in specific techniques in 751.4

.3 Apparatus, equipment, artists' models

Class use of apparatus and equipment in specific techniques in 751.4

.4 Techniques and procedures

Including painting with specific mediums, e.g., ink; airbrush painting; collage (with painting as the basic technique)

Class mosaic painting in 738.5

For techniques of reproduction, see 751.5

.42 Watercolor painting

Do not use standard subdivisions

.45 Oil painting

.5 Techniques of reproduction

Execution, identification, determination of authenticity of reproduction, copies, forgeries, alterations

For printmaking and prints, see 760

.6 Conservation, preservation, restoration, routine care

Including expertizing

Class identification of reproductions, copies, forgeries, alterations in 751.5

.7 Specific forms

Examples: frescoes, murals, scene paintings, miniatures

Use of this number for easel paintings discontinued; class in 750

Class miniatures done as illuminations in manuscripts and books in 745.6

See Manual at 745.6 for miniatures

752 Color

Class technology of color in 667, comprehensive works on color in the fine and decorative arts in 701

> 753–758 Iconography

General aspects: development, description, critical appraisal, works regardless of form

Class comprehensive works in 750

See Manual at 753–758

753 Symbolism, allegory, mythology, legend

For religious symbolism, see 755

754 Genre paintings

755 Religion and religious symbolism

[756] Historical events

Relocated to 758

757 Human figures and their parts

Not provided for in 753–755, 758

Class here portraits

758 Other subjects

Including historical events [*formerly* 756]; marine scenes; land-, sea-, and cityscapes; still life; animal and plant life

Class hunting scenes in which animals are not the center of interest with the subject, e.g., hunters 757

759 Historical, geographic, persons treatment

General aspects: development, description, critical appraisal, works

Class exhibitions of paintings not limited by place, period, or subject in 750.74

> 759.01–759.07 Periods of development

Class here schools and styles not limited by country or locality, works on one or two periods of European painting

Class comprehensive works in 759; works on three or more periods of European painting in 759.94; schools associated with a specific locality in 759.1–759.9, e.g., Florentine school of Italian painting 759.5

.01 Nonliterate peoples, and earliest times to 499

Including paintings of nonliterate peoples regardless of time or place

Class paintings of both nonliterate and literate cultures in 759.1–759.9

.02 500–1399

Including Byzantine, early Christian, Gothic, Romanesque painting and paintings

Class here medieval painting and paintings

Class Byzantine, early Christian, Gothic painting and paintings of any other period with the period, e.g., early Christian painting before 500 759.01

.03 1400–1599

Class here Renaissance painting and paintings

Class Renaissance painting and paintings before 1400 in 759.02

.04 1600–1799

Including baroque, rococo painting and paintings

.05 1800–1899

Including art nouveau, impressionism, naturalism, pointillism, realism, romanticism

Class art nouveau, kitsch, naturalism, realism, romanticism of any other period with the period, e.g., art nouveau of 1900–1990 759.06

.06 1900–1999

Including abstractionism, art deco, cubism, expressionism, op art, pop art, surrealism

Class here modern painting

For 1800–1899, see 759.05

.07 2000–2099

> **759.1–759.9 Geographic treatment**

Individual painters are classed at country level

Class comprehensive works in 759, painting and paintings of nonliterate peoples in 759.01, Western painting of one or two specific periods in 759.02–759.07

.1 **North America**

Class painting and paintings of Middle America in 759.972

.11 Canada

.13 United States

Class painting and paintings of specific states in 759.14–759.19

.14–.19 Specific states of United States

Add to base number 759.1 the numbers following —7 in notation 74–79 from Table 2, e.g., painting and paintings of California 759.194

Class individual painters in 759.13, painting and paintings of Hawaii in 759.9969

.2 **British Isles**

.3–.8 **Other European countries**

Add to base number 759 the numbers following —4 in notation 43–48 from Table 2, e.g., painting and paintings of France 759.4

Class comprehensive works, and painting and paintings of other European countries not provided for in notation 43–48 from Table 2 in 759.94, e.g., painting and paintings of Netherlands 759.9492

.9 **Other geographic areas**

.91 Areas, regions, places in general

Add to base number 759.91 the numbers following —1 in notation 11–19 from Table 2, e.g., Western Hemisphere 759.9181

Class individual painters in the notation for their respective countries

.93–.99 Specific continents, countries, localities

Class here painting and paintings of specific periods, e.g., painting and paintings of 1800–1899 in South America 759.98

Add to base number 759.9 notation 3–9 from Table 2, e.g., comprehensive works on painting and paintings of Europe 759.94, Etruscan painting and paintings 759.937

Class works on one or two periods of European painting in 759.02–759.07, e.g., painting and paintings of 1800–1899 in Europe 759.05 (*not* 759.94); individual painters from Soviet Union in 759.7, individual Hawaiian painters in 759.13

760 Graphic arts Printmaking and prints

Graphic arts: any and all nonplastic representation on flat surfaces, including painting, drawing, prints, and photographs

Including rubbings, two-dimensional mixed-media art and composites

Class here two-dimensional art; prints and at least one other of the graphic arts

Class comprehensive works on graphic and plastic arts in 701–709; rubbings used for study and research in a specific field with the field, e.g., rubbings used for study of monumental brasses 739.5

For drawing and drawings, see 741; painting and paintings, 750; photography and photographs, 770; printing, 686.2

SUMMARY

760.01–.09 **Standard subdivisions of graphic arts**
.1–.8 **Standard subdivisions of printmaking and prints**
761 **Relief processes (Block printing)**
763 **Lithographic (Planographic) processes**
764 **Chromolithography and serigraphy**
765 **Metal engraving**
766 **Mezzotinting, aquatinting, related processes**
767 **Etching and drypoint**
769 **Prints**

.01–.09 Standard subdivisions of graphic arts

.1 **Philosophy and theory of printmaking and prints**

Including criticism and appreciation

Class works of critical appraisal in 769.9

.2 **Miscellany of printmaking and prints**

.28 Techniques, procedures, apparatus, equipment, materials

Class techniques, procedures, apparatus, equipment, materials for making specific kinds of prints in 761–767

.3–.6 **Standard subdivisions of printmaking and prints**

.7 **Education and related topics of printmaking and prints**

[.75] Collecting prints

Do not use; class in 769

.8 **History and description of printmaking and prints with respect to kinds of persons**

[.9] **Historical, geographic, persons treatment of printmaking and prints**

Do not use; class in 769.9

> **761–769 Printmaking and prints**

Class comprehensive works in 760

> **761–767 Printmaking**

Fine art of executing a printing block or plate representing a picture or design conceived by the printmaker or copied from another artist's painting or drawing or from a photograph

General aspects: techniques, procedures, equipment, materials

Class comprehensive works in 760.28; techniques, procedures, apparatus, equipment, materials used in reproduction, preservation, rountine care in 769, employed by individual printmakers in 769.92

761 Relief processes (Block printing)

Printing from raised surfaces, e.g., wood, metal, linoleum blocks

763 Lithographic (Planographic) processes

Printing from flat surfaces, e.g., stone, aluminum, zinc

For chromolithography, see 764

764 Chromolithography and serigraphy

Including silk-screen printing

> **765–767 Intaglio processes**

Printing from incised surfaces

Class comprehensive works in 765

765 Metal engraving

Class here comprehensive works on metal relief and metal intaglio processes, on intaglio processes

For relief processes, see 761; mezzotinting and aqautinting, 766; etching and drypoint, 767

766 Mezzotinting, aquatinting, related processes

767 Etching and drypoint

769 Prints

Works produced using a printing block, screen, or plate

General aspects: description, critical appraisal, collections

[.075] Collecting prints

Do not use; class in 769

[.09] Historical, geographic, persons treatment

Do not use; class in 769.9

.5 **Forms of prints**

Examples: paper dolls, paper money, posters; Christmas seals, savings stamps

Match covers relocated to 741.6

Class prints made by an individual printmaker regardless of form in 769.92; comprehensive works on posters in 741.6

Prints other than postage stamps on a specific subject regardless of form are classed in 769

.56 Postage stamps and related devices

Including covers, postal stationery, postmarks, cancellations, cachets

Class here philately

Class stamps other than for prepayment of postage in 769.5

[.560 9] Historical, geographic, persons treatment

Do not use; class in 769.569

.569 Historical, geographic, persons treatment

Add to base number 769.569 notation 1–9 from Table 2, e.g., postage stamps from San Marino 769.569454

.9 **Historical, geographic, persons treatment of printmaking and prints**

Add to base number 769.9 notation 1–9 from Table 2, e.g., printmakers 769.92

Class the history of a specific process with the process, e.g., history of lithography 763.09

See Manual at 769.92 for printmakers

770 Photography and photographs

Class technological photography in 621.36

SUMMARY

770.1–.9	**Standard subdivisions**
771	**Techniques, procedures, apparatus, equipment, materials**
772	**Metallic salt processes**
773	**Pigment processes of printing**
774	**Holography**
778	**Specific fields and special kinds of photography, and related activities**
779	**Photographs**

.2 **Miscellany**

[.28] Techniques, procedures, apparatus, equipment, materials

Do not use for apparatus, equipment, materials; class in 771

Techniques and procedures relocated to 771

.9 **Historical, geographic, persons treatment**

.92 Photographers

Regardless of type of photography; however, class motion-picture photographers in 778.5, television photographers in 778.59092

Class photographs in 779

771 Techniques, procedures [*formerly also* 770.28], apparatus, equipment, materials

Including studios, laboratories, darkrooms

Class here interdisciplinary works on description, use, manufacture of apparatus, equipment, materials

Class techniques, procedures, apparatus, equipment, materials used in special processes in 772–774; in specific fields and special kinds of photography in 778; manufacture of a specific kind of apparatus, equipment, material with the subject, e.g., of cameras 681

.3 **Cameras and accessories**

Including tripods, carrying cases

> **772–774 Special processes**

Techniques, procedures, apparatus, equipment, materials

Class comprehensive works in 771, processing techniques in specific fields and special kinds of photography in 778

For photomechanical printing, see 686.2

772 Metallic salt processes

773 Pigment processes of printing

Class xerography in 686.4

774 Holography

778 Specific fields and special kinds of photography, and related activities

General aspects: techniques, procedures, apparatus, equipment, materials

Class here interdisciplinary works on use and manufacture of apparatus, equipment, materials used in specific fields and special kinds of photography

Class manufacture of a specific kind of apparatus, equipment, materials with the subject, e.g., of cameras 681

.2 **Photographic projection**

Including filmstrips, slides

For stereoscopic projection, see 778.4; motion-picture projection, 778.5

.3 **Special kinds of photography**

Not provided for elsewhere

Examples: photomacrography, photomicrography, telephotography; aerial, close-up, high-speed, infrared, space photography

Class close-up and high-speed motion-picture and television photography, motion-picture photomicrography in 778.5; a specific application of photography with the application, e.g., use of photography in astronomy 522

For technological photography and photo-optics, see 621.36

See also 133.8 for parapsychological aspects of Kirlian photography

See Manual at 778.3 vs. 621.36

.4 **Stereoscopic photography and projection**

Class stereoscopic motion-picture photography and projection in 778.5

.5 **Motion pictures and television photography, and related activities**

Including animated cartoons, motion-picture photography (cinematography) and projection, preservation and storage of motion-picture films

.59 Television photography

Including television recording and recorders

.6 **Color photography and photography of colors**

Class color photomicrography in 778.3, color motion-picture photography in 778.5

.602 8 Auxiliary techniques and procedures; apparatus, equipment, materials

Class processing techniques, procedures, apparatus, equipment, materials in color photography in 778.6

.7 **Photography under specific conditions**

Examples: outdoors, underwater, by artificial light

Including flashbulb photography

Class short-duration flash in high-speed photography in 778.3

For infrared photography, see 778.3

.8 **Special effects and trick photography**

Examples: table-top photography; photography of specters, distortions, multiple images, silhouettes

Class special effects motion-picture photography in 778.5

.9 **Photography of specific subjects**

Class here comprehensive works on techniques of photographing, photographs of, and photographers of a specific subject

Class photographers in 770.92, photography by specific methods regardless of subject in 778.3–778.8

779 Photographs

Class biographies and critical appraisals, which may also contain some photographs, in 770.92

780 Music

This schedule is new and has been prepared with little or no reference to previous editions. Most numbers have been reused with new meanings.

A comparative table giving both old and new numbers for a substantial list of topics and equivalence tables showing the numbers in the old and new schedules appear on pages 171-179 in this edition

(Option: Distinguish scores by prefixing a letter or other symbol to the number for treatises, e.g., music for violin M787.2 or &787.2, and distinguish miniature scores from other scores by a special prefix, e.g., MM787.2; distinguish recordings in a similar manner, e.g., violin recordings R787.2 or MR787.2. Examples in this schedule do not distinguish scores, texts, or recordings)

See Manual at 780

SUMMARY

.1 **Philosophy and theory**

Class scientific principles, theory of music in 781

.15 Analytical guides and program notes

(.16) Bibliographies, catalogs, indexes

(Optional number; prefer 016.78)

(.162) *Bibliographies and catalogs of music literature

(.164) *Bibliographies and catalogs of scores and parts

(.166) *Discographies

Bibliographies and catalogs of music recorded on phonorecords (cylinders, discs, wires, tapes, films)

.2 **Miscellany**

.26 Treatises on music scores, recordings, texts

Including librettos, lyrics, plots

The words must be discussed in a musical context. Thus, if the words are presented as literature, folklore, or religious text, class the work in 800, 398, or 200, respectively

Use this subdivision for texts only for building other numbers; never use it for texts by itself

(Option: Use this number and its subdivisions to distinguish scores and recordings within 780; see details in note under 780)

(Option: Class here law; prefer appropriate subdivisions of 340)

In other parts of the Schedules indicate scores, recordings, texts, and treatises about them by adding 026 from 780.26, e.g., bibliography of musical scores 016.78026, discography of violin music 016.7872026

See also 070.5 for music publishing, 686.2 for music printing, 781.49 for recording of music

See Manual at 780: Standard subdivision 026; 780.26

*(Optional number; prefer 016.78)

.28 Auxiliary procedures; apparatus, equipment, materials

Class techniques of music in 781.4, instruments in 784

See also 780.26 for scores and recordings

.7 Education, performances, related topics

Including use of apparatus and equipment in study and teaching

Class techniques for acquiring musical skills and learning a repertoire in 781.4

.76 Review, exercises, examinations, works for self-instruction

.78 Performances

General aspects: concerts and recitals

Do not use for use of apparatus and equipment in study and teaching; class in 780.7

See also 781.4 for performance techniques

.79 Competitions, festivals, awards, financial support

Class performances at festivals and competitions in 780.78

.8 History and description of music with respect to kinds of persons

.89 Music with respect to specific racial, ethnic, national groups

Class folk music in 781.62

See Manual at 780.89 vs. 781.62

.9 Historical, geographic, persons treatment

General aspects: development, description, critical appraisal

Class critical appraisal in analytical guides and program notes in 780.15

.92 Persons associated with music

Examples: composers, performers, critics

Class here thematic catalogs of individual composers

(Option: Class individual composers in 789)

Class general thematic catalogs in 780

See Manual at 791.092

.94 European music

Use this number only for works that stress that they are discussing the European origin and character of the music in contrast to music from other sources

\> **781–788 Principles, forms, ensembles, voices, instruments**

Class here music of all traditions

(Option: 781–788 may be used for only one tradition of music; in that case, class all other traditions in 789. For example, if it is desired to emphasize Western art music, class it here, and class all other traditions of music in 789, e.g., jazz 789.5; or, if it is desired to emphasize jazz, class it here, and class all other traditions of music in 789, e.g., Western art music 789.8)

Unless other instructions are given, class complex subjects with aspects in two or more subdivisions of 781–788 in the one coming last, e.g., Johann Sebastian Bach's cello sonatas 787.4 (*not* 784.18), rehearsing vocal music 782.044 (*not* 781.44)

Class comprehensive works in 780

781 *General principles and musical forms

Class here music theory

Use the subdivisions of 781 only when the subject is not limited to voice, instrument, or ensemble. If voice, instrument, or ensemble is specified, class with voice, instrument, or ensemble; and then add as instructed. For example, rehearsal of music 781.44, rehearsal of opera (a form for the voice) 782.1

SUMMARY

781.1	**Aesthetics, appreciation, taste**
.2	**Elements of music**
.3	**Composition**
.4	**Techniques of music**
.5	**Kinds of music**
.6	**Traditions of music**
.7	**Sacred music**
.8	**Musical forms**

.1 Aesthetics, appreciation, taste

Do not use standard subdivisions

.2 *Elements of music

Contains harmony, melody, musical sound, texture, time, tonal systems

Including meter, rhythm; pitch, tone color; leitmotif, scales, trills; harmonic rhythm; atonality, twelve-tone system; counterpoint

Class here scientific principles

Class comprehensive works on serialism in 781.3, playing time in 781.4

.3 *Composition

Including arrangement, improvisation, orchestration, serialism

Class atonality in 781.2

[.302 85] Computer composition

Do not use; class 781.3

*Use notation from Table 1 as modified under 780.1–780.9

.4 ***Techniques of music**

Including score reading

Class techniques of composition in 781.3

For improvisation, see 781.3

See also 784.193 for techniques for playing instruments

.44 *Rehearsal and practice

.45 *Conducting

.46 *Interpretation

.47 *Accompaniment

.48 *Breathing and resonance

See also 784.193 for breathing and resonance associated with instrumental performance

.49 *Recording of music

See also 621.389 for sound recording and reproducing equipment, 780.26 for treatises on music recordings

.5 ***Kinds of music**

Contains music for specific times, e.g., evening, harvest; music in specific settings, e.g., street music; music for specific media, e.g., television music; music accompanying public entertainments, e.g., ballet music; program music (music depicting extramusical concepts, e.g., music depicting the sea); music accompanying activities, e.g., inaugurations; music accompanying stages of the life cycle, e.g., weddings; music reflecting other themes and subjects, e.g., military, patriotic, protest music

To be classed here music for specific media must be either background or mood music

Class dramatic vocal music in 782.1; musical forms depicting extramusical concepts (e.g., nocturnes) in 784.18

See also 778.5 for sound synchronization of motion pictures, 778.59 for sound synchronization of television programs

.6 ***Traditions of music**

Works emphasizing a specific tradition

(Option: If 781–788 is used for only one tradition of music, class all other traditions in 789)

*Use notation from Table 1 as modified under 780.1–780.9

.62 Folk music

Music indigenous to the cultural group in which it occurs, usually evolved through aural transmission

See also 780.9 for music of and performed in a specific location

See Manual at 780.89 vs. 781.62; 781.62009 vs. 781.62

.620 01–.620 07 Standard subdivisions

Notation from Table 1 as modified under 780.1–780.9, e.g., performances of folk music 781.620078

.620 08 History and description of folk music with respect to kinds of persons

[.620 089] Treatment with respect to specific racial, ethnic, national groups

Do not use; class in 781.62

.620 09 Historical, geographic, persons treatment

Class geographic treatment of folk music of specific racial, ethnic, national groups in 781.62

See Manual at 781.62009 vs. 781.62

.63 *Popular music

For Western popular music, see 781.64

.64 *Western popular music

Most works on Western popular music are predominantly about popular songs and are classed in 782.42164

For jazz, see 781.65; rock, 781.66

.642 *Country music

Class here bluegrass music

.643 *Blues

Class here rhythm and blues

.644 *Soul

.65 *Jazz

Including swing

.66 *Rock (Rock 'n' roll)

.7 **Sacred music**

Class sacred music accompanying stages of life cycle in 781.5

"Church music" usually means Christian church music and is classed in 781.71

See also 782.2 for sacred vocal music

.700 1–.700 9 Standard subdivisions

Notation from Table 1 as modified under 780.1–780.9, e.g., performances of sacred music 781.70078

*Use notation from Table 1 as modified under 780.1–780.9

.71 Christian sacred music Hymn books

For music of Christian church year, see 781.72

.710 01–.710 09 Standard subdivisions

Notation from Table 1 as modified under 780.1–780.9, e.g., performances of Christian sacred music 781.70078

.72 *Music of Christian church year

.723 *Christmas day

Class here Christmas season

Class Epiphany in 781.72

.727 *Easter Sunday

Class here Eastertide (Easter season)

Class Ascensiontide in 781.72

.76 *Judaic sacred music

.8 *Musical forms

Including da capo, rondo form; chaconne, theme and variations

Class here formal analysis; works that do not specify voice, instrument, or ensemble

Class works for specific voice, instrument, or ensemble with the voice, instrument, or ensemble, e.g., Brahm's Variations on a theme by Schumann 786.2 (*not* 781.8)

For vocal forms, see 782.1–782.4; instrumental forms, 784.18

782 Vocal music

Class orchestral music with vocal parts in 784.2

For music for single voices, see 783

SUMMARY

782.001–.009 Standard subdivisions
.01–.08 [General principles and musical forms]
.1 Dramatic vocal forms Operas
.2 Nondramatic vocal forms
.3 Services (Liturgy and ritual)
.4 Secular forms
.5 Mixed voices
.6 Women's voices
.7 Children's voices
.8 Men's voices
.9 Other types of voices

.001–.009 Standard subdivisions

Notation from Table 1 as modified under 780.1–780.9, e.g., performances of vocal music 782.0078

*Use notation from Table 1 as modified under 780.1–780.9

.01–.07 General principles

Add to base number 782.0 the numbers following 781 in 781.1–781.7, e.g., rehearsing vocal music 782.044

.08 Musical forms

Examples: dance, march, rondo forms

For vocal forms, see 782.1–782.4

> **782.1–782.4 Vocal forms**

Class here treatises about and recordings of vocal forms for specific voices and ensembles

Class comprehensive works in 782

.1 ***Dramatic vocal forms *Operas**

Regardless of type of voice or vocal group

Operas and related forms: musical vocal forms in which the action is predominantly in the music, whether or not dialogue is involved

Examples: musicals, operettas, revues

Class here concert versions

Stage presentations of dramatic vocal forms relocated to 792.5

See Manual at 792.5 vs. 782.1

.109 2 Persons associated with dramatic vocal forms, with operas

Class here biographies of singers known equally well as opera and recital singers, of conductors known primarily as opera conductors

Class biographies of singers known primarily as recital singers in 782.42168092, of conductors known equally well for conducting operas and orchestral music in 784.092

.109 4 European opera

Use this number only for works that stress that they are discussing European opera in contrast to operas from all other sources

.2 ***Nondramatic vocal forms**

Including cantatas, chants, plainsong, sacred vocal music

Class Anglican, Gregorian chant in 782.32; secular cantatas in 782.4

For services, see 782.3; secular forms, 782.4

.23 *Oratorios

Example: passions

*Use notation from Table 1 as modified under 780.1–780.9

.25 *Sacred songs

Example: spirituals

Class here small-scale sacred vocal forms

If the songs are called hymns, class them in 782.27; if called carols, class them in 782.28; otherwise, class them here

Class motets in 782.2

For hymns, see 782.27; carols, 782.28

.27 *Hymns

Class texts of hymns without music in 245, comprehensive works on hymns without music in 264

For carols, see 782.28

.28 *Carols

.3 *Services (Liturgy and ritual)

Musical settings of prescribed texts of specific religions

Including services of specific religions other than Christianity

Class texts used by a specific religion with the religion, e.g., liturgy and ritual of a Christian church 264

.32 *Christian services

Including mass (communion service); morning, evening prayer

.4 *Secular forms

Examples: ballads, madrigals, secular cantatas, song cycles

.42 *Songs

Class here comprehensive works on songs

For sacred songs, see 782.25

.421 General principles of songs

.421 6 Songs of specific traditions of music

.421 62 Folk songs

.421 620 01–.421 620 09 Standard subdivisions

Notation from Table 1 as modified under 780.1–780.9, e.g., performances of folk songs 782.421620078

.421 64 *Western popular songs

For jazz songs, see 782.42165; rock songs, 782.42166

.421 65 *Jazz songs

.421 66 *Rock (Rock 'n' roll) songs

*Use notation from Table 1 as modified under 780.1–780.9

.421 68 *Art songs

Example: lieder

.421 680 92 Persons associated with art songs

Class here biographies of singers known primarily as recital singers

Class biographies of singers known equally well as opera and recital singers in 782.1092

> **782.5–782.9 Vocal executants**

Use 782.5–782.9 for scores and parts of vocal forms for specific vocal ensembles, e.g., scores of pop songs arranged for all male choir 782.8. Use 782.1–782.4 for treatises about and recordings of vocal forms for specific vocal ensembles, e.g., recordings of pop songs by an all male choir 782.42164. Class performance techniques for a specific ensemble or form with the ensemble or form, e.g., conducting choral music 782.5, opera 782.1

Class comprehensive works in 782

.5 ***Mixed voices**

Class here choral music, music intended equally for choral or part-song performance, choral music with solo parts, unison voices

For part songs, see 783.1

> **782.6–782.9 Types of voices**

Class comprehensive works in 782

.6 ***Women's voices**

Examples: soprano, mezzo-soprano, contralto voices

Class here music intended equally for women's or children's voices

Class music for children's voices in 782.7

.7 ***Children's voices**

Class music intended equally for women's or children's voices in 782.6

.8 ***Men's voices**

Examples: countertenor, tenor, baritone, bass voices

.9 ***Other types of voices**

Example: sprechgesang

*Use notation from Table 1 as modified under 780.1–780.9

783 Music for single voices The voice

Use 783 for scores and parts of vocal forms for specific kinds or ensembles of single voice, e.g., scores of rock songs for soprano voice 783.6. Use 782.1–782.4 for treatises about and recordings of vocal forms for specific kinds or ensembles of single voice, e.g., recordings of rock songs sung by a soprano 782.42166. Class performance techniques for a specific kind or ensemble of single voice or for a specific form with the kind, ensemble, or form, e.g., conducting part songs 783.1, opera 782.1

.001–.009 Standard subdivisions

Notation from Table 1 as modified under 780.1–780.9, e.g., performances of music for single voice 783.0078

.1 ***Single voices in combination**

Class here part songs

Class music intended equally for choral or part-song performance in 782.5

\> **783.2–783.9 Solo voices**

Class comprehensive works in 783.2

.2 ***Solo voice**

Class here comprehensive works on types of single voices

Class specific types of single voices in 783.3–783.9

\> **783.3–783.9 Specific types of single voices**

Class comprehensive works in 783.2, single voices in ensembles in 783.1

.3 ***High voice**

Class woman's soprano voice in 783.6; child's soprano voice in 783.7; man's treble, alto, tenor voices in 783.8

.4 ***Middle voice**

Class woman's mezzo-soprano voice in 783.6, child's mezzo-soprano voice in 783.7, baritone voice in 783.8

.5 ***Low voice**

Class woman's contralto voice in 783.6, child's contralto voice in 783.7, bass voice in 783.8

\> **783.6–783.9 Types of voices**

Class comprehensive works in 783

*Use notation from Table 1 as modified under 780.1–780.9

.6 ***Women's voices**

Examples: soprano, mezzo-soprano, contralto voices

Class here music intended equally for women's or children's voices

Class music for children's voices in 783.7

.7 ***Children's voices**

Class music intended equally for women's or children's voices in 783.6

.8 ***Men's voices**

Examples: countertenor, tenor, baritone, bass voices

.9 ***Other types of voice**

Example: sprechgesang

Including voice instruments, e.g., kazoo

> **784–788 Instruments and their music**

Class comprehensive works in 784

784 Instruments and instrumental ensembles and their music

For specific instruments and their music, see 786–788

See also 787 for music for unspecified melody instrument

.01–.09 Standard subdivisions

Notation from Table 1 as modified under 780.1–780.9, e.g., performances 078

.1 **General principles, musical forms, instruments**

.11–.17 General principles

Add to base number 784.1 the numbers following 781 in 781.1–781.7, e.g., performance techniques 784.14

For techniques for playing instruments, see 784.193

.18 *Musical forms

Examples: concerto, fugue, march, overture, sonata, suite, symphony forms; dance forms (including minuet, waltz)

Class comprehensive works on the concerto in 784.2, a specific musical form in relation to an instrument or instrumental ensemble with the instrument or ensemble, e.g., symphony for orchestra 784.2, violin sonata 787.2

*Use notation from Table 1 as modified under 780.1–780.9

.19 Instruments

For specific instruments, see 786–788

.190 28 Auxiliary techniques and procedures

Class description, design, construction, testing, measurement, maintenance, repair in 784.192

[.190 94–.190 99] Historical and geographic treatment by specific continents, countries, localities in modern world

Do not use; class in 784.194–784.199

.192 Specific techniques and procedures

Including description, design, construction, testing, measurement, maintenance, tuning, repair

Class construction by hand in 681.8

.193 *Techniques for playing instruments

Examples: bowing, fingering

Class comprehensive works on techniques of music in 784.14

.194–.199 Geographic treatment

Add to base number 784.19 notation 4–9 from Table 2, e.g., instruments of Germany 784.1943

.2 *Full (Symphony) orchestra

Including concertos

Class here comprehensive works on orchestral combinations, music intended equally for orchestral or chamber performance

For other orchestral combinations, see 784.3–784.9; chamber music, 785

.209 2 Persons associated with full (symphony) orchestras

Class here biographies of conductors known equally well for conducting operas and orchestral music

Class biographies of conductors known primarily as opera conductors in 782.1092

> **784.3–784.9 Other orchestral combinations and band**

Class comprehensive works on orchestral combinations and band, on band in 784; comprehensive works on orchestral combinations in 784.2

.3 *Chamber orchestra

For chamber music, see 785

.4 *Light orchestra

Including dance, school orchestra

Class here salon orchestra

*Use notation from Table 1 as modified under 780.1–780.9

.6 *Keyboard, mechanical, electronic, percussion bands

Including rhythm band

.7 *String orchestra

.8 *Wind band

Band consisting of woodwind instruments, brass instruments, or both

Including marching, military band

For brass band, see 784.9

.9 *Brass band

785 Ensembles with only one instrument per part

Class here chamber music

Class works for solo melody instrument with keyboard or other accompaniment in 786–788

.001–.009 Standard subdivisions

Notation from Table 1 as modified under 780.1–780.9, e.g., performances of chamber music 785.0078

.01–.07 General principles

Add to base number 785.0 the numbers following 781 in 781.1–781.7, e.g., performance techniques 785.04

.08 *Musical forms

.09 †Instruments

Add to base number 785.09 the numbers following 784.19 in 784.192–784.199, e.g., bowing techniques 785.093

*Use notation from Table 1 as modified under 780.1–780.9

†Use notation from Table 1 as modified under 784.19

> **786–788 Specific instruments and their music**

Class here music for solo instrument, music for solo instruments accompanied by one other instrument when accompanying instrument clearly has a subsidiary role

Unless the forerunner of a modern instrument is listed in the schedule, class it with the modern instrument. For example, the shawm, a forerunner of the oboe and an instrument not listed, is classed with the oboe in 788.5; however, the vihuela, the forerunner of the guitar and an instrument listed at 787.8, is classed at 787.8, *not* with the guitar in 787.87

Notation 092 from Table 1 is added for persons associated with an instrument and its music, or with the music for the instrument, e.g., Isaac Stern (a violinist) 787.2092; however, notation 092 from Table 1 is *not* added for persons associated only with the instrument, e.g., Antonio Stradivari (a violin maker) 787.2

Class comprehensive works in 784, chamber music in 785, voice instruments in 783.9

786 *Keyboard, mechanical, electrophonic, percussion instruments

Class here comprehensive works on keyboard instruments, on keyboard stringed instruments; music for unspecified keyboard instrument

> **786.2–786.5 Keyboard instruments**

Class comprehensive works in 786, mechanical keyboard instruments in 786.6, keyboard idiophones in 786.8

> **786.2–786.4 Keyboard stringed instruments**

Class comprehensive works in 786

.2 *Piano

.3 *Clavichord

.4 *Harpsichord

.5 *Keyboard wind instruments *Organ

Class accordion, concertina in 788.8; a keyboard instrument whose sound is generated by conventional means, even though amplified or modified electronically, with the instrument, e.g., electric piano 786.2

See also 786.7 for synthesizer

.6 *Mechanical and aeolian instruments

Aeolian instruments: instruments activated by the blowing of the wind

Examples: carillon, music box, player piano

*Use notation from Table 1 as modified under 780.1–780.9 either for the instrument and its music or for the music itself, not for the instrument alone

.7 ***Electrophones** ***Electronic instruments**

Examples: computer, tape, synthesizer

Including electronic music

Class here music made from electrically produced or manipulated sounds

Class keyboard electrophones in 786.5; a specific electrically amplified or modified standard instrument other than keyboard instruments with the instrument, e.g., electric guitar 787.87

.8 ***Percussion instruments**

Including idiophones (vibrating sonorous solids)

Examples: bells, chimes, cymbals, gong, triangle, West Indian steel drums, xylophone

Class mechanical idiophones in 786.6

For drums, see 786.9; struck stringed instruments, 787.7

.9 ***Drums and devices used for percussion effects**

Examples: bongos, tambourine, timpani; popgun, siren, whip

787 *Stringed instruments *Bowed stringed instruments

Class keyboard stringed instruments in 786, mechanical stringed instruments in 786.6

.2 ***Violin**

Class here comprehensive works on violin family

For viola, see 787.3; cello, 787.4; double bass, 787.5

.3 ***Viola**

.4 ***Cello**

.5 ***Double bass**

.6 ***Other bowed stringed instruments** ***Viol**

For double bass, see 787.5

.7 ***Plectral instruments**

Examples: dulcimer, lyre

Class here zither, comprehensive works on struck stringed instruments

For plectral lute family, see 787.8; harp and musical bow, 787.9

.8 ***Plectral lute family**

Examples: banjo, lute, mandolin, vihuela

.87 *Guitar

.9 ***Harp and musical bow**

*Use notation from Table 1 as modified under 780.1–780.9 either for the instrument and its music or for the music itself, not for the instrument alone

788 *Wind instruments

Class keyboard wind instruments in 786.5, mechanical wind instruments in 786.6

.2 *Woodwind instruments and free aerophones

Free aerophones: aerophones in which the airstream is not directed into or through a cavity or tube but directly into the outer air, or the air remains static and the instrument when moved vibrates through friction with the air, e.g., bull-roarers

For specific woodwind instruments, see 788.3–788.8

\> **788.3–788.8 Specific woodwind instruments**

Class comprehensive works in 788.2

.3 *Flute family

Examples: flute, piccolo, recorder

.4 *Reed instruments

Example: bagpipe

For double-reed instruments, see 788.5; single-reed instruments, 788.6; free reeds, 788.8

.5 *Double-reed instruments

Examples: bassoon, English horn, oboe

For bagpipe, see 788.4

.6 *Single-reed instruments

Example: clarinet

For bagpipe, see 788.4; saxophone, 788.7

.7 *Saxophone

.8 *Free reeds

Examples: accordion, harmonica

.9 *Brass instruments (Lip-reed instruments)

Examples: bugle, cornet, French horn (horn), trombone, trumpet, tuba

*Use notation from Table 1 as modified under 780.1–780.9 either for the instrument and its music or for the music itself, not for the instrument alone

(789) Composers and traditions of music

(Optional number and subdivisions; prefer 780–788)

(Option A: Arrange treatises about all composers at 789 plus an alphabeting mark; then to the result add notation following 78 in 780–788

(Option B: Use 789 and its subdivisions for traditions of music

(If both options are used, class comprehensive works on traditions of music in 789.1)

Unless other instructions are given, class complex subjects with aspects in two or more subdivisions of 789 in the one coming last, e.g., rehearsing folk songs 789.2024214 (*not* 789.20144)

(.1) †General principles of traditions of music

(If both options are used, class here comprehensive works on traditions of music)

Add to base number 789.1 the numbers following 781 in 781.1–781.5, e.g., orchestration in various traditions 789.13

(.2) †Folk music

Music indigenous to the cultural group in which it occurs, usually evolved through aural transmission

(.200 1–.200 7) †Standard subdivisions

Notation from Table 1 as modified under 780.1–780.9, e.g., performances of folk music 789.20078

(.200 8) †History and description of folk music with respect to kinds of persons

[.200 89] Treatment with respect to specific racial, ethnic, national groups

Do not use; class in 789.2

(.200 9) †Historical, geographic, persons treatment

Class geographic treatment of folk music of specific racial, ethnic, national groups in 789.2

(.201) †General principles, stylistic influences of other traditions, musical forms

(.201 1–.201 5) †General principles

Add to base number 789.201 the numbers following 781 in 781.1–781.5, e.g., rehearsing folk music 789.20144

(.201 6) †Stylistic influences of other traditions of music

(.202–.208) †Voices, instruments, ensembles

Add to base number 789.20 the numbers following 78 in 782–788, e.g., folk songs 789.20242

†(Optional number; prefer 781–788)

> **(789.3–789.9) Other traditions of music**

Add to notation for each term identified by * as follows:
001–009 Standard subdivisions
Notation from Table 1 as modified under 780.1–780.9, e.g., performance 0078
01 General principles, stylistic influences of other traditions of music, musical forms
011–015 General principles
Add to 01 the numbers following 781 in 781.1–781.5, e.g., melody 012
016 Stylistic influences of other traditions of music
1 Voices, instruments, ensembles
Add to 1 the numbers following 78 in 782–788, e.g., guitar music 1787

In building numbers, do not add by use of 0 or 1 (alone or in combination) more than once, e.g., history of rock songs 789.61242 (*not* 789.6124209)
(Option: Add as many times as desired)

Class comprehensive works in 789

(.3) †*Popular music

For Western popular music, see 789.4

(.4) †*Western popular music

For jazz, see 789.5; rock, 789.6

(.42) †*Country music

Class here bluegrass music

(.43) †*Blues

Class here rhythm and blues

(.44) †*Soul

(.5) †*Jazz

Including swing

(.6) †*Rock (Rock 'n' roll)

(.8) †*Western art (Classical) music

Class here comprehensive works on art music

For non-Western art music, see 789.9

(.9) †*Non-Western art music

*Add as instructed under 789.3–789.9

†(Optional number; prefer 781–788)

790 Recreational and performing arts

Class here interdisciplinary works on recreation

Class the sociology of recreation in 306.4

For music, see 780

See Manual at 790

SUMMARY

790.01–.09	**Standard subdivisions of recreation**
.1–.2	**[Recreational activities and the performing arts in general]**
791	**Public performances**
792	**Stage presentations**
793	**Indoor games and amusements**
794	**Indoor games of skill**
795	**Games of chance**
796	**Athletic and outdoor sports and games**
797	**Aquatic and air sports**
798	**Equestrian sports and animal racing**
799	**Fishing, hunting, shooting**

.01 Philosophy and theory of recreation

Including influence, psychological principles, effective use of leisure

.02–.05 Standard subdivisions of recreation

.06 Organizations dealing with and management of recreation

Including recreation centers

[.068] Management

Do not use; class in 790.06

.07 Education, research, related topics of recreation

.08 History and description of recreation with respect to groups of persons

Class activities and programs for specific classes of people in 790.1

.09 Historical, geographic, persons treatment of recreation

.1 Recreational activities

Including hobbies, collecting, play with toys

Class a specific activity with the activity, e.g., outdoor sports 796, piano playing 786.2, paper cutting and folding 736; collecting a specific kind of object with the object, using notation 075 from Table 1, e.g., stamp collecting 769.56075; play with a specific toy provided for elsewhere with the toy, e.g., flying model airplanes 796.1

[.101–.109] Standard subdivisions

Do not use; class in 790.01–790.09

.2 **The performing arts in general**

Class a specific art with the art, e.g., motion pictures 791.43, symphony orchestra performance 784.2078

Works that treat only public performances, e.g., stage, radio, television, music, are classed in 791. Works that also include athletic and outdoor sports and games are classed here

791 Public performances

Other than musical, sport, game performances

Including traveling shows, e.g., medicine, minstrel shows

For stage presentations, see 792; magic, 793.8

Class comprehensive works on the performing arts in general in 790.2

See also 780 for musical performances, 793–796 for sport and game performances

.06 Organizations and management

Including amusement parks

[.068] Management

Do not use; class in 791.06

.092 Persons

See Manual at 791.092

.3 **Circuses**

.4 **Motion pictures, radio, television**

Class texts of plays in 800; subject-oriented films and recorded programs themselves with the subject, e.g., flower gardening 635.9

See also 302.23 for social aspects of motion pictures, radio, and television as mass media

See Manual at 384 vs. 791.4

.43 Motion pictures

Class here dramatic films

Educational and documentary films, newsreels relocated to 070.1

Class animation of films in 741.5, photographic aspects of motion pictures in 778.5, made-for-TV movies in 791.45

See also 384 for communication aspects of motion pictures, e.g., programming (scheduling)

See Manual at 791.43 and 791.44, 791.45, 792.9

.430 1 Philosophy, theory, aesthetics

Including theory, technique, history of criticism and appreciation

[.430 2] Miscellany

Do not use; class in 791.43

.430 9 Historical, geographic, persons treatment

Class here description, critical appraisal of specific companies and studios

Class description, critical appraisal of specific films in 791.43

.44 Radio

Class here dramatic programs

Radio educational, expository, news programs relocated to 070.1, radio sports programs to 070.4

See also 384.54 for communication aspects of radio, e.g., programming (scheduling)

See Manual at 791.43 and 791.44, 791.45, 792.9

.440 1 Philosophy, theory, aesthetics

Including theory, technique, history of criticism and appreciation

[.440 2] Miscellany

Do not use; class in 791.44

.440 9 Historical, geographic, persons treatment

Class here description, critical appraisal of specific companies and stations

Class description, critical appraisal of specific programs in 791.44

.45 Television

Class here dramatic and audience programs, use of videotapes

Educational, expository, news television programs relocated to 070.1, television sports programs to 070.4

Class use of videotapes not provided for here with the use, e.g., video recordings of rock music 781.66

See also 384.55 for communication aspects of television, e.g., programming (scheduling)

See Manual at 791.43 and 791.44. 791.45, 792.9

.450 1 Philosophy, theory, aesthetics

Including theory, technique, history of criticism and appreciation

[.450 2] Miscellany

Do not use; class in 791.45

.450 9 Historical, geographic, persons treatment

Class here description, critical appraisal of specific companies, stations, networks

Class description, critical appraisal of specific programs in 791.45

.5 **Puppetry and toy theaters**

Class puppet films in 791.43, texts of plays in 800

.6 **Pageantry**

Examples: festivals, pageants, parades, floats for parades

Including cheerleading

Class circus parades in 791.3

For water pageantry, see 797.2

See Manual at 394 vs. 791.6

.8 **Animal performances**

Examples: bullfights, rodeos

Class circus animal performances in 791.3, equestrian sports and animal racing in 798

792 Stage presentations

Class here theater, dramatic presentation

Class texts of plays in 800

For motion pictures, radio, television, see 791.4; puppetry and toy theaters, 791.5

.01 Philosophy, theory, aesthetics

Including theory, technique, history of criticism and appreciation

[.02] Miscellany

Do not use; class in 792

.09 Historical, geographic, persons treatment

Class here description, critical appraisal of specific theaters and companies

Class specific productions in specific theaters or by specific companies in 792.9

> **792.1–792.8 Specific kinds of performances**

Apply to each subdivision identified by * notation from Table 1 as modified under 792.01–792.09, e.g., appreciation of pantomime 792.301

Class comprehensive works in 792

.1 ***Tragedy and serious drama**

Including historical drama; religious, passion, miracle, mystery, morality plays

*Apply the special meanings of 792.01–792.09 as instructed under 792.1–792.8

.2 ***Comedy and melodrama**

Including modern mystery (suspense) drama

.3 ***Pantomime**

.5 ***Opera**

Class here comprehensive works on stage presentations of dramatic vocal forms [*formerly* 782.1]

For musical plays, see 792.6; variety shows, 792.7

See also 782.1 for comprehensive works on opera

See Manual at 792.5 vs. 782.1

.6 ***Musical plays**

See also 782.1 for comprehensive works on musical plays

See Manual at 792.5 vs. 782.1

.7 ***Variety shows**

Class here burlesque, cabaret, vaudeville, music hall and night club presentations

Including tap dancing [*formerly* 793.3]

Class stage productions in 792.9

See also 791 for minstrel shows and skits

.8 ***Ballet and modern dance**

Including choreography

Class here comprehensive works on dancing, theatrical dancing [*both formerly* 793.3]

Class dancing in musical plays in 792.6

For tap dancing, see 792.7, social, folk, national dancing, 793.3

See Manual at 792.8 vs. 793.3

.809 Historical, geographic, persons treatment

Class here description, critical appraisal of specific theaters and companies

Class specific productions in specific theaters or by specific companies in 792.8

*Apply the special meaning of 792.01–792.09 as instructed under 792.1–792.8

.9 **Stage productions**

General aspects: description, critical appraisal, production scripts and stage guides

Class here description, critical appraisal of specific productions of specific theaters and companies

Class description, critical appraisal, production scripts of operas in 792.5, of musical plays in 792.6, of ballets in 792.8

See Manual at 791.43 and 791.44, 791.45, 792.9

793 Indoor games and amusements

For indoor games of skill, see 794; games of chance, 795

.2 **Parties and entertainments**

Including charades, tableaux

.3 **Social, folk, national dancing**

Examples: ballroom and square dancing

Comprehensive works on dancing, theatrical dancing relocated to 792.8; tap dancing to 792.7

See Manual at 792.8 vs. 793.3

.4 **Games of action**

Examples: blindman's buff, musical chairs

.5 **Forfeit and trick games**

.7 **Games not characterized by action**

Including mathematical games and recreations

For charades and tableaux, see 793.2

.73 Puzzles and puzzle games

Examples: acrostics, anagrams, crossword puzzles, literary recreations, quizzes, riddles; jigsaw puzzles

Class puzzles as formal instructional devices for the teaching of a specific subject with the subject, using notation 07 from Table 1, e.g., puzzles teaching the use of the Bible 220.07

Mathematical games and recreations are classed in 793.7

See also 398.6 for riddles as folk literature

.8 **Magic and related activities**

Examples: scientific recreations, juggling, ventriloquism

Class here conjuring

For card tricks, see 795.4

See also 790.1 for play with scientific toys

.9 Other indoor diversions

Example: war games (battle games)

See also 355.4 for military use of war games, 796.1 for outdoor war games

.93 Adventure games Fantasy games

Examples: Dungeons and Dragons®, RuneQuest®

Class here mystery games, role-playing games

War games (battle games) are classed in 793.9

[.930 285] Data processing Computer applications

Do not use; class in 793.93

794 Indoor games of skill

Class here board games

Class war games in 793.9, adventure, fantasy, mystery games in 793.93, games combining skill and chance in 795

For backgammon, see 795.1

.1 Chess

.2 Checkers (Draughts)

Use of this number for other board games discontinued; class in 794

.3 Darts

.6 Bowling

See also 796.31 for lawn bowling

.7 Ball games

Including billiards, pool (pocket billiards), pinball games

Class athletic ball games, comprehensive works on ball games in 796.3

For bowling, see 794.6

.8 Electronic games Computer games

Class computerized war games (battle games) in 793.9; computerized adventure, fantasy, mystery games in 793.93; computerized forms of a specific indoor game or amusement with the game or amusement in 793–795, using notation 0285 from Table 1, e.g., computerized checkers 794.20285

[.802 85] Data processing Computer applications

Do not use; class in 794.8

795 Games of chance

Class here gambling

Class gambling on a specific activity with the activity, e.g., on horse racing 798.401

See also 364.1 for gambling as a crime

.01 Theory

Including betting systems, probabilities of winning

See also 519.2 for statistical probability in games of chance

.1 **Games with dice**

Examples: backgammon, craps

.2 **Wheel and top games**

Examples: roulette, slot machines

.3 **Games dependent on drawing numbers or counters**

Examples: bingo, dominoes, mah-jongg

.4 **Card games**

Examples: solitaire, twenty-one (blackjack)

Including card tricks

.41 Games based chiefly on skill

Examples: bridge, canasta, pinochle, poker, rummy

796 Athletic and outdoor sports and games

Class computerized athletic and outdoor sports and games in 794.8

For aquatic and air sports, see 797; equestrian sports and animal racing, 798; fishing, hunting, shooting, 799

See Manual at 613.7 vs. 646.7, 796

SUMMARY

796.01–.09	**Standard subdivisions**
.1	**Miscellaneous games**
.2	**Activities and games requiring equipment**
.3	**Ball games**
.4	**Weight lifting, track and field, gymnastics**
.5	**Outdoor life**
.6	**Cycling and related activities**
.7	**Driving motor vehicles**
.8	**Combat sports**
.9	**Ice and snow sports**

.01 Philosophy and theory

Including activities and programs for specific classes of people

.06 Organizations, facilities, management

Including astrodomes, field houses, playgrounds, stadiums

[.068] Management

Do not use; class in 796.06

.07 Study and teaching

Including coaching

.08 History and description of sports and games with respect to groups of persons

Class activities and programs for specific classes of people in 796.01

.1 **Miscellaneous games**

Not provided for elsewhere

Examples: singing and dancing games, leapfrog, hide-and-seek, puss in corner, prisoner's base; play with kites, model airplanes, remote-controlled devices

For activities and games requiring equipment, see 796.2

.2 **Activities and games requiring equipment**

Not provided for elsewhere

Examples: flying discs (Frisbees®), horseshoes, marbles, roller skating, skateboarding, Yo-Yos®

.3 **Ball games**

Class indoor ball games in 794.7

SUMMARY

796.31	**Ball thrown or hit by hand**
.32	**Inflated ball thrown or hit by hand**
.33	**Inflated ball driven by foot**
.34	**Racket games**
.35	**Ball driven by club, mallet, bat**

.31 Ball thrown or hit by hand

Examples: handball, lawn bowling

See also 794.6 for indoor bowling

.32 Inflated ball thrown or hit by hand

Example: netball

.323 Basketball

.323 01–.323 09 Standard subdivisions

Notation from Table 1 as modified under 796.33202–796.33207, e.g., coaching 796.33407

.325 Volleyball

.33 Inflated ball driven by foot

Examples: Australian-rules football, pushball

.332 American football

.332 02 Miscellany

Including official rules, spectators' guides

.332 028 Apparatus, equipment, materials

Examples: balls, goal posts, safety equipment

Class techniques and procedures in 796.332

.332 06 Organizations, facilities, management

Examples: clubs, leagues; grounds and their layout

[.332 068] Management

Do not use; class in 796.33206

.332 07 Study and teaching

Including coaching

.333 Rugby

Class here Union rugby

.333 01–.333 09 Standard subdivisions

Notation from Table 1 as modified under 796.33202–796.33207, e.g., coaching 796.33307

.334 Soccer (Association football)

.334 01–.334 09 Standard subdivisions

Notation from Table 1 as modified under 796.33202–796.33207, e.g., coaching 796.33407

.335 Canadian football

.335 01–.335 09 Standard subdivisions

Notation from Table 1 as modified under 796.33202–796.33207, e.g., coaching 796.33507

.34 Racket games

Examples: court, paddle, table tennis; badminton, lacrosse, rackets, squash

.342 Tennis (Lawn tennis)

.342 01–.342 09 Standard subdivisions

Notation from Table 1 as modified under 796.33202–796.33207, e.g., coaching 796.34207

.35 Ball driven by club, mallet, bat

Examples: croquet, field hockey, polo

See also 796.962 for ice hockey

.352 Golf

.352 01–.352 09 Standard subdivisions

Notation from Table 1 as modified under 796.33202–796.33207, e.g., official rules 796.35202

.357 Baseball

Including softball

.357 01–.357 09 Standard subdivisions

Notation from Table 1 as modified under 796.33202–796.33207, e.g., baseball leagues 796.35706

.358 Cricket

.358 01–.358 09 Standard subdivisions

Notation from Table 1 as modified under 796.33202–796.33207, e.g., equipment 796.358028

.4 Weight lifting, track and field, gymnastics

Exercise relocated to 613.7

.406 Organizations, facilities, management

Including gymnasiums

[.406 8] Management

Do not use; class in 796.406

.407 Study and teaching

Including coaching

.41 Weight lifting

Weight lifting for fitness, calisthenics, gymnastic exercises relocated to 613.7; sports gymnastics to 796.44

.42 Track and field

Class here running

For field events, see 796.43

See also 613.7 for running as an exercise

.420 6 Organizations, facilities, management

Including athletic fields

[.420 68] Management

Do not use; class in 796.42

.43 Jumping, vaulting, throwing

Examples: pole vaulting, shot-putting

Class here field events

See also 796.2 for pitching games, 796.44 for gymnastic vaulting

.44 Sports gymnastics [*formerly* 796.41]

Examples: rhythmic gymnastics, use of horizontal and parallel bars, vaulting

For trapeze work, rope climbing, tightrope walking, see 796.46; acrobatics, tumbling, trampolining, contortion, 796.47

See also 613.7 for gymnastic exercises

.46 Trapeze work, rope climbing, tightrope walking

See also 791.3 for trapeze work and tightrope walking as circus acts

.47 Acrobatics, tumbling, trampolining, contortion

Including floor exercise

See also 791.3 for acrobatics as circus acts

.48 Olympic games

Arrange specific games chronologically

Class paralympics and special olympics in 796.01, a specific activity with the activity, e.g., basketball 796.323, swimming 797.2

For winter Olympic games, see 796.98

.480 93–.480 99 Geographic treatment

Do not use for specific games; class in 796.48

.5 **Outdoor life**

Including walking, backpacking, mountaineering, spelunking, beach activities

Walkers' guides that give only route details are classed here. Guides that also give description of things en route are classed in 914–919

Class a specific activity of outdoor life not provided for here with the activity, e.g., fishing 799.1

.54 Camping

Including woodcraft, campfires

Beach activities are classed in 796.5

.56 Dude ranching and farming

.6 **Cycling and related activities**

Use of wheeled vehicles not driven by motor or animal power

Examples: bicycle touring, land sailing, soap box racing

For roller skating, see 796.2

.7 **Driving motor vehicles**

Racing, driving for pleasure

Including travel for pleasure by mobile home

For snowmobiling, see 796.94

.8 **Combat sports**

Examples: boxing, fencing, wrestling; jujitsu, judo, karate

Class here martial arts

Class combat with animals in 791.8

See also 613.7 for therapeutic exercises related to jujitsu

.9 **Ice and snow sports**

Examples: bobsledding, iceboating, snowshoeing, tobogganing

Class ice fishing in 799.1

See also 796.54 for snow camping, 798 for horse-drawn sleighing

.91 Ice skating

.93 Skiing

Including jumping

.94 Snowmobiling

.96 Ice games

Example: curling

.962 Ice hockey

See also 796.35 for field hockey

.962 01–.962 09 Standard subdivisions

Notation from Table 1 as modified under 796.33202–796.33207, e.g., coaching 796.96207

.98 Winter Olympic games

Arrange specific games chronologically

Class a specific activity with the activity, e.g., skating 796.91

.980 93–.980 99 Geographic treatment

Do not use for specific games; class in 796.98

797 Aquatic and air sports

Class computerized aquatic and air sports in 794.8

> **797.1–797.3 Aquatic sports**

Class comprehensive works in 797

For fishing, see 799.1

.1 **Boating**

Examples: canoeing, rowboating, sailboating, motorboating, yachting, boat racing and regattas

Surfing (Surf riding), water skiing relocated to 797.3

.2 **Swimming and diving**

Including underwater swimming, e.g., skin, scuba diving; springboard and precision diving, water pageantry; water games, e.g., water polo

.200 1–.200 9 Standard subdivisions

.3 **Other aquatic sports**

Examples: surfing (surf riding), water skiing [*both formerly* 797.1], jet skiing, windsurfing (boardsailing, sailboarding)

.5 **Air sports**

Examples: balloon flying, aircraft racing, flying for pleasure, stunt flying, hang gliding, skydiving

798 Equestrian sports and animal racing

Including driving, coaching

Class computerized equestrian sports and animal racing in 794.8, hunting with aid of horses in 799.2

For polo, see 796.35

.2 **Horsemanship**

Including riding, jumping

For horse racing, see 798.4

.4 **Horse racing Flat racing**

Including harness racing, steeplechasing

.400 1–.400 5 Standard subdivisions

.400 6 Organization, facilities, management

Including racetracks

[.400 68] Management

Do not use; class in 798.4

.400 7–.400 9 Standard subdivisions

.401 Betting

Including pari-mutuel

799 Fishing, hunting, shooting

Class computer games based on fishing, hunting, shooting in 794.8

See also 688.7 for the manufacture of both mass-produced and handcrafted equipment

.1 **Fishing**

Class works treating equally commercial and sport fishing in 639.2

.2 **Hunting**

Big and small game

Including falconry

Class here comprehensive works on hunting and shooting sports

Class works treating equally commercial and sport hunting in 639

For shooting other than game, see 799.3

.202 Miscellany

.202 8 Techniques, procedures, apparatus, equipment, materials

Including guns, bows and arrows, boomerangs, spears, nets

[.202 85] Data processing Computer applications

Do not use; class in 799.2

[.209] Historical, geographic, persons treatment

Do not use; class in 799.29

.29 Historical, geographic, persons treatment

Add to base number 799.29 notation 1–9 from Table 2, e.g., hunting in Germany 799.2943

.3 **Shooting other than game**

Examples: archery, skeet shooting, trapshooting

Class ballistic devices in 799.2028

800

800 Literature (Belles-lettres) and rhetoric

Class here works of literature, works about literature

(Option: Class belletristic essays, speeches, letters, satire, humor, quotations, epigrams, anecdotes, diaries, journals, reminiscences on a specific subject with the subject, e.g., essays on architecture 720)

After general topics (800–809) the basic arrangement is literature by language, then literature of each language by form. More detailed instructions are given at the beginning of Table 3

Unless other instructions are given, observe the following table of precedence, e.g., collections of drama written in poetry from more than one literature 808.82 (*not* 808.81)

Drama
Poetry
  Class epigrams in verse with miscellaneous writings
Fiction
Essays
Speeches
Letters
Miscellaneous writings
Satire and humor
  Class here collections of satire and humor in two or more literary forms
  (Option: Give precedence to satire and humor over all other forms)

Class interdisciplinary works on language and literature in 400, interdisciplinary works on the arts in 700, folk literature in 398.2; librettos, poems, words written to be sung or recited with music in 780.26

See Manual at 400 vs. 800; 800; 800 vs. 398.2 for anonymous classics and widely used legendary or historical themes; 800 vs. 591, 636, 398.24 for works about animals; 800 vs. 741.6 for text with illustrations

801 Philosophy and theory

Including aesthetics; theory, technique, history of literary criticism

Class works of critical appraisal in 809

802 Miscellany

803 Dictionaries, encyclopedias, concordances

805 Serial publications

Class collections of literary texts in serial form in 808.80005, history, description, critical appraisal in serial form in 809.005

806 Organizations

807 Education and related topics

808 Rhetoric and collections of literary texts from more than one literature

Rhetoric: the effective use of language

Including professional, technical, expository literature on specific subjects

Style manuals [*formerly* 651.7]; authorship and editorial techniques, e.g., preparation of manuscripts, writing for publication; rhetoric in specific languages are classed in 808, without use of 808.001–808.009; style manuals, authorship and editorial techniques, rhetoric in specific languages for specific literary forms are classed in 808.1–808.7

Class here composition, literary plagiarism

Do not use for history and description of literature and rhetoric with respect to kinds of persons; class history and description of rhetoric with respect to kinds of persons in 808.008, collections of literary texts from more than one literature with respect to kinds of persons in 808.8

Class general treatment of standard usage of language (prescriptive linguistics) in 418; treatment of standard usage in a specific language with the specific language, using notation 8 from Table 4, e.g., English usage 428; theory, technique, history of literary criticism in 801

See also 001.4 for research

See Manual at 651.7 vs. 808, 658.4 for business writing; 808 for readers (textbooks); 808.001–808.7 vs. 070.5 for composition and preparation of manuscripts

.001–.009 Standard subdivisions of rhetoric

.06 Writing children's literature

> **808.1–808.7 Rhetoric in specific literary forms**

Observe table of precedence under 800

Class comprehensive works in 808, specific forms for children in 808.06

.1 **Rhetoric of poetry**

Class here prosody

See Manual at 808.1 vs. 414, T4—1 for prosody

.2 **Rhetoric of drama**

.3 **Rhetoric of fiction**

Including the rhetoric of short stories

Class here the rhetoric of novelettes and novels

.4 **Rhetoric of essays**

.5 Rhetoric of speech

Including public speaking (oratory), e.g., after-dinner, platform, radio speaking; recitation, e.g., reading aloud, storytelling; choral speaking

Class here voice, expression, gesture

For preaching, see 251

.53 Debating and public discussion

.56 Conversation

[.59] Listening

Number discontinued because without meaning in context

.6 Rhetoric of letters

.7 Rhetoric of satire and humor

Including rhetoric of parody

.8 Collections of literary texts from more than one literature

By more than one author

Collections of works not limited to a specific literary form but either limited to a specific period or displaying specific features (displaying specific qualities of style, mood, perspective; displaying specific elements, e.g., stream of consciousness; treating specific themes; emphasizing subjects; or written for and by specific kinds of persons) are classed in 808.8, without use of 808.80001–808.80007. Collections of works limited to a specific literary form and either limited to a specific period or displaying specific features are classed in 808.81–808.88, without adding further from the table under 808.81–808.87

Use of this number for general works consisting equally of literary texts and history, description, critical appraisal of literature discontinued; class in 800

Works consisting equally of literary texts and history, description, critical appraisal of literature are classed in subdivisions of 808.8 if limited to specific topics found in those subdivisions, e.g., texts and criticism of drama 808.82

Class two or more literatures in the same language with the literature of that language

.800 01–.800 07 Standard subdivisions

[.800 08] History and description with respect to kinds of persons

Do not use; class in 808.8

[.800 09] Historical, geographic, persons treatment

Do not use; class in 809

> **808.81–808.88 Collections in specific forms**

Observe table of precedence under 800

Class comprehensive works in 808.8

808.81 Poetry

808.87 Humor, wit

Short Stories 808.83

.81–.87 Collections in specific forms

Add to base number 808.8 the numbers following 808 in 808.1–808.7, e.g., collections of essays 808.84, of debates 808.853; then add further as follows:

001–008 Standard subdivisions [*formerly* 01–08]

009 Geographical treatment [*formerly* 09]

Class historical and persons treatment in the number for the specific form, without adding notation from Table 1

[01–08] Standard subdivisions

Relocated to 001–008

[09] Historical, geographic, persons treatment

Use of this notation for historical and persons treatment discontinued; class in the number for the specific form, without adding from Table 1

Geographic treatment relocated to 009

Quotations

✓ .88 Collections of miscellaneous writings Christian allegory

Examples: anecdotes, diaries, epigrams, graffiti, jokes, journals, quotations, reminiscences, prose literature in more than one form

Do not use standard subdivisions

Class a specific identifiable form of literature with the form, e.g., essays 808.84

809 History, description, critical appraisal of more than one literature

Treating works by more than one author

Class here collected biography

History, description, critical appraisal of works from specific periods are classed in 809, without use of 809.001–809.007; history, description, critical appraisal of works in specific forms from specific periods are classed in 809.1–809.7, without adding further from the table under 808.81–808.87

Class theory, technique, history of literary criticism in 801; two or more literatures in the same language with literature in that language

.001–.007 Standard subdivisions

[.008] History and description with respect to kinds of persons

Do not use; class in 809

[.009] Historical, geographic, persons treatment

Do not use; class in 809

.1–.7 Literature in specific forms

Add to base number 809 the numbers following 808 in 808.1–808.7, e.g., history, description, critical appraisal of poetry 809.1

> 810–890 Literatures of specific languages

Literature is classed by the language in which originally written, regardless of country

(Option: Class translations into a language requiring local emphasis with the literature of that language)

Unless there is a specific provision for a dialect, literature in a dialect is classed with the literature of the basic language

Literature in a pidgin or creole is classed with the source language from which more of its vocabulary comes than from its other source language(s)

Under each literature identified by *, add to designated base number notation 1–8 from Table 3. If the base number is not identified in a note, it is the number given for the literature, e.g., for Swedish 839.7. Full instructions for building numbers are given at the start of Table 3

Class comprehensive works in 800

810 *American literature in English

English-language literature of Western Hemisphere and Hawaii

Base number: 81

(Option: Distinguish literatures of specific countries by initial letters, e.g., literature of Canada C810, of United States U810; or class literatures not requiring local emphasis in 819)

Class comprehensive works on American literature in English and English literature in 820

811–818 Specific forms of American literature in English

Notation from Table 3

(819) American literatures in English not requiring local emphasis

(Optional number; prefer 810–818 for all American literature in English)

Class here English-language literatures of specific American countries other than the country requiring local emphasis, e.g., libraries emphasizing United States literature class here Canadian literature, and libraries emphasizing Canadian literature class here United States literature

*Add to base number as instructed at the beginning of Table 3

See pg 231-235

810 - Am lit collected works
811 Am. poetry
812 Am. Drama ?
813 Am. Short story
814 Humorous/Anecdotal short writing
817 Satire/Humor
818 Essay / Diaries

820 *English and Old English (Anglo-Saxon) literatures

Base number for English: 82

A special number for Shakespeare appears below at 822.3

(Option: Distinguish English-language literatures of specific countries by initial letters, e.g., literature of England E820, of Ireland Ir820 [or, of all British Isles B820], of Australia A820, of India In820; or class literatures not requiring local emphasis in 828.99)

For American literature in English, see 810

821 English poetry

822 English drama

.3 **William Shakespeare**

823–827 Other specific forms of English literature

Notation from Table 3

828 English miscellany

(.99) English-language literatures not requiring local emphasis

(Optional number; prefer 820–828 for all non-American English-language literatures)

Class here English-language literatures of specific non-American countries other than the country requiring local emphasis, e.g., libraries emphasizing British literature may class here Australian, Indian, other literatures, and libraries emphasizing Indian literature may class here British literature

829 Old English (Anglo-Saxon)

830 Literatures of Germanic (Teutonic) languages German literature

For English and Old English (Anglo-Saxon) literatures, see 820

.01–.09 Standard subdivisions of literatures of Germanic (Teutonic) languages

---

\> **830.1–838 Subdivisions of *German literature**

Base number: 83

Class comprehensive works in 830

.1–.9 **Standard subdivisions; collections; history, description, critical appraisal of German literature**

Notation from Table 3

*Add to base number as instructed at the beginning of Table 3

831–838 Specific forms of German literature

Notation from Table 3

839 Other Germanic (Teutonic) literatures

Example: Yiddish

.3 Dutch, Flemish, Afrikaans

.7 *Swedish

.8 Danish and Norwegian

840 Literatures of Romance languages French literature

For literatures of Italian, Romanian, Rhaeto-Romanic languages, see 850; of Spanish and Portuguese languages, 860

.01–.09 Standard subdivisions of literatures of Romance languages

---

> **840.1–848 Subdivisions of *French literature**

Base number: 84

(Option: Distinguish French-language literatures of specific countries by initial letters, e.g., literature of Canada C840, of France F840)

Class comprehensive works in 840, Provençal literature in 849

.1–.9 Standard subdivisions; collections; history, description, critical appraisal of French literature

Notation from Table 3

841–848 Specific forms of French literature

Notation from Table 3

849 Provençal and Catalan

850 Literatures of *Italian, Romanian, Rhaeto-Romanic languages

Base number for Italian: 85

851–858 Specific forms of Italian literature

Notation from Table 3

859 Romanian and Rhaeto-Romanic

860 Literatures of Spanish and Portuguese languages

.01–.09 Standard subdivisions of literatures of Spanish and Portuguese languages

*Add to base number as instructed at the beginning of Table 3

> **860.1–868 Subdivisions of *Spanish literature**

Base number: 86

(Option: Distinguish Spanish-language literatures of specific countries by initial letters, e.g., literature of Chile Ch860, of Colombia Co860, of Mexico M860 [or, of all American countries A860], of Spain S860)

Class comprehensive works in 860

.1–.9 **Standard subdivisions; collections; history, description, critical appraisal of Spanish literature**

Notation from Table 3

861–868 Specific forms of Spanish literature

Notation from Table 3

869 *Portuguese

870 Literatures of Italic languages Latin literature

Class comprehensive works of or on literatures of classical languages in 880

For literatures of Romance languages, see 840

.01–.09 Standard subdivisions of literatures of Italic languages

> **870.1–878 Subdivisions of *Latin literature**

Base number: 87

Special provisions for use with Latin appear below at 871–874

Class comprehensive works in 870

.1–.9 **Standard subdivisions; collections; history, description, critical appraisal of Latin literature**

In more than one form by more than one author

Notation from Table 3

871 Latin poetry

For dramatic poetry, see 872; epic poetry, 873; lyric poetry, 874

872 Latin dramatic poetry and drama

873 Latin epic poetry and fiction

874 Latin lyric poetry

875–878 Other specific forms of Latin literature

Notation from Table 3

*Add to base number as instructed at the beginning of Table 3

879 Literatures of other Italic languages

Example: Osco-Umbrian literatures

880 Literatures of Hellenic languages Classical Greek literature

Class here comprehensive works of or on literatures of classical languages

For Latin literature, see 870

.01–.09 Standard subdivisions of classical literatures

> **880.1–888 Subdivisions of *classical Greek literature**

Base number: 88

Special provisions for use with Greek appear below at 881–884

Class comprehensive works in 880

.1–.9 **Standard subdivisions; collections; history, description, critical appraisal of classical Greek literature**

In more than one form by more than one author

Notation from Table 3

881 Classical Greek poetry

For dramatic poetry, see 882, epic poetry, 883; lyric poetry, 884

882 Classical Greek dramatic poetry and drama

883 Classical Greek epic poetry and fiction

884 Classical Greek lyric poetry

885–888 Other specific forms of classical Greek literature

Notation from Table 3

889 Modern Greek literature

890 Literatures of other languages

891 East Indo-European and Celtic literatures

Examples: Albanian, Armenian; Baltic literatures, e.g., Latvian, Lithuanian; Indic literatures, e.g., Bengali, Hindi, Sanskrit; Iranian literatures, e.g., Persian

.6 **Celtic literatures**

Examples: Breton, Cornish, Irish and Scottish Gaelic, Welsh (Cymric)

*Add to base number as instructed at the beginning of Table 3

.7 **East Slavic literatures Russian**

Examples: Belorussian, Ukrainian

Class comprehensive works on Slavic literatures in 891.8

.700 1–.700 9 Standard subdivisions of East Slavic literatures

.701–.78 Subdivisions of *Russian

Base number: 891.7

.8 **Slavic literatures**

Examples: Bulgarian, Czech, Polish, Serbo-Croatian, Slovak, Slovenian

Class here comprehensive works on literatures of Balto-Slavic languages

Class Baltic literatures in 891, East Slavic literatures in 891.7

892 Afro-Asiatic (Hamito-Semitic) literatures Semitic literatures

Examples: Arabic, Ethiopic literatures

For non-Semitic Afro-Asiatic literatures, see 893

.4 **Hebrew**

893 Non-Semitic Afro-Asiatic literatures

Former heading: Hamitic and Chad literatures

Examples: Berber, Chadic, Coptic literatures

894 Ural-Altaic, Paleosiberian, Dravidian literatures

Examples: Estonian, Finnish, Hungarian, Lapp; Mongolian, Turkish; Tamil, Telugu

895 Literatures of East and Southeast Asia Sino-Tibetan literatures

Examples: Burmese, Tibetan

Including Munda literatures

.1 **Chinese**

.6 **Japanese**

.7 **Korean**

.9 **Annam-Muong, Mon-Khmer, Thai (Tai) literatures**

Examples: Khmer (Cambodian), Vietnamese; Lao, Thai (Siamese)

Munda literatures are classed in 895

896 African literatures

Examples: Fulani (Fulah), Ibo (Igbo), Yoruba; Bantu literatures, e.g., Swahili, Zulu

For Afro-Asiatic literatures, see 892

*Add to base number as instructed at the beginning of Table 3

897 Literatures of North American native languages

Examples: Inuit, Navajo

Class here comprehensive works on literatures of North and South American native languages

For literatures of South American native languages, see 898

898 Literatures of South American native languages

Examples: Guaraní, Quechua

899 Literatures of nonaustronesian languages of Oceania, of Austronesian languages, of miscellaneous languages

Examples: Australian, Basque, Caucasian, Malay, Melanesian, Micronesian, Papuan, Polynesian literatures; literatures in artificial languages, e.g., Esperanto

Use of this number for literatures of other languages discontinued; class in 890

900

900 Geography, history, and auxiliary disciplines

Class here social situations and conditions; general political history; military, diplomatic, political, economic, social, welfare aspects of specific wars

Class historical and geographical treatment of a specific discipline or subject with the discipline or subject, using notation 09 from Table 1, e.g., historical and geographical treatment of natural sciences 509, of economic situations and conditions 330.9, of purely political situations and conditions 320.9, history of military science 355.009

Interdisciplinary works on ancient world, on specific continents, countries, localities are classed in 930–990

See also 303.49 for projected events (future history)

See Manual at 900

.1–.9 **Standard subdivisions of geography and history**

901 Philosophy and theory of history

902 Miscellany of history

Including chronologies

903 Dictionaries, encyclopedias, concordances of history

904 Collected accounts of events

Class here adventure

Class travel in 910; collections limited to a specific period in 909, to a specific area or region in 909, 930–990; history of a specific kind of event with the event, e.g., geological history of earthquakes 551.2

See Manual at 900: Historical events vs. nonhistorical events

905–907 Standard subdivisions of general history

908 History with respect to kinds of persons

[.9] **Racial, ethnic, national groups**

Do not use; class in 909

909 World history

Civilization and events not limited geographically

Including history with respect to racial, ethnic, national groups, e.g., world history of Jews; history of areas, regions, places not limited by continent, country, locality, e.g., history of tropical regions; interdisciplinary works on areas, regions, places in general (other than landforms, oceans, seas)

Interdisciplinary works on historical treatment of culture and institutions relocated to 306.09

Class history of ancient world to ca. 499 in 930; history of specific continents, countries, localities in modern world in 940–990; collected accounts of events not limited by period, area, region, subject in 904; geography of and travel in areas, regions, places in general in 910; interdisciplinary works on land forms, oceans, seas in 551.4

See Manual at 305 vs. 306, 909, 930–990 for history of ethnic groups; 320 vs. 909, 930–990 for political history; 400 vs. 909, 930–990; 910 vs. 909, 930–990

[.001–.008] Standard subdivisions

Do not use; class in 901–908

[.009] Historical treatment

Do not use; class in 900

104 Jewish history

> **909.07–909.08 General historical periods**

Class here general histories covering three or more continents (or three or more countries if not on the same continent)

Class comprehensive works in 909, ancient history in 930

Specific historical periods before 1700 are classed in 909, since 1700 in 909.7–909.8

.07 Ca. 500–1450/1500

Including Crusades

.08 Modern history, 1450/1500–

> **909.7–909.8 Specific historical periods since 1700**

Class comprehensive works in 909

Specific historical periods before 1700 are classed in 909

.7 **18th century, 1700–1799**

.8 **1800–**

.81 19th century, 1800–1899

Class here Industrial Revolution

.82 20th century, 1900–1999

For World War I, see 940.3; World War II, 940.53

.83 21st century, 2000–2099

See also 303.49 for futurology

910 Geography and travel

Including physical geography

Class works on civilization, other than accounts of travel, in 909, in ancient world and specific places in modern world in 930–990; physical geography of ancient world in 913, of specific continents, countries, localities in 913–919, of specific features in 550, e.g., glaciers 551.3; geographical treatment of specific disciplines or subjects with the discipline or subject, e.g., geographical treatment of religion 200.9, of geomorphology 551.409

See Manual at 508 vs. 574, 910, 304.2 for geography; 550 vs. 910 for physical geography; 910 vs. 909, 930–990

(.1) **Topical geography**

(Optional number; prefer specific subject, e.g., economic geography 330.9)

Do not use for philosophy and theory of geography and travel; class in 910

Add to base number 910.1 notation 001–899, e.g., economic geography 910.133; then add 0 and to the result add notation 1–9 from Table 2, e.g., economic geography of British Isles 910.133041

.2 **Miscellany**

Including world travel guides

Class guides to areas, regions, places in general in 910.91, to specific continents, countries, localities in 913–919

.22 Illustrations

Class maps, plans, related forms in 912

.25 Directories of persons and organizations

Class here city directories, telephone books

Class city directories, telephone books of a specific place in 913–919

.3 **Dictionaries, encyclopedias, concordances, gazetteers**

Class here works on place names systematically arranged for ready reference

Class discourses on place names in 910; historical material associated with place names in general in 909, on specific places in 930–990

.4 **Accounts of travel**

Not geographically limited

Including trips around the world, ocean travel, seafaring life, shipwrecks, mutinies; buried treasure, pirates' expeditions

Class travel accounts that emphasize civilization of places visited in 909, travel in specific oceans in 910.9163–910.9167

For discovery and exploration, see 910.9

See also 508 for scientific exploration and travel, 910.2 for world travel guides

.5–.8 **Standard subdivisions**

.9 **Historical, geographic, persons treatment**

Class here discovery, exploration, growth of geographic knowledge

.91 Geography of and travel in areas, regions, places in general

Class interdisciplinary works on landforms, oceans, seas in 551.4; physical geography of areas, regions, places in general in 910

.92 Geographers, travelers, explorers regardless of country of origin

.93–.99 Discovery and exploration by specific countries

Do not use for geography of and travel in specific continents, countries, localities; extraterrestrial worlds; class in 913–919

Add to base number 910.9 notation 3–9 from Table 2 for the country responsible, e.g., explorations by Great Britain 910.941

Class discovery and exploration by a specific country in areas, regions, places in general in 910.91, in specific continents, countries, localities, extraterrestrial worlds in 913–919; periods of discovery and exploration in history in 940–990

911 Historical geography

Growth and changes in political divisions

Class here historical atlases

.09 Historical treatment

Use of this number for geographic and persons treatment discontinued; class in 911

912 Graphic representations of surface of earth and of extraterrestrial worlds

Including map reading

Class here atlases, maps, charts, plans

Atlases, maps, related forms associated with a specific subject relocated to the subject with use of notation 022 from Table 1, e.g., geological maps of Japan 555.2022

Class map drawing in 526.022; historical atlases in 911

See Manual at T1—022 vs. 912

.09 Historical and persons treatment of maps and map making

Use of this number for maps of specific areas, regions, places in general discontinued; class in 912

Maps of specific continents, countries, localities, extraterrestrial worlds relocated to 912.3–912.9

.3–.9 Maps of specific continents, countries, localities, extraterrestrial worlds [*formerly* 912.093–912.099]

Add to base number 912 notation 3–9 from Table 2, e.g., maps of Illinois 912.773

913–919 Geography of and travel in ancient world and specific continents, countries, localities in modern world; extraterrestrial worlds

Add to base number 91 notation 3–9 from Table 2, e.g., geography of England 914.2, of ancient England 913.62; then add further as follows:

001–002 Standard subdivisions [*formerly* 01–02]

003 Dictionaries, encyclopedias, concordances, gazetteers [*formerly* 03]
Class here works on place names systematically arranged for ready reference
Class discourses on place names in 913–919 without adding from this table, historical material associated with place names in 930–990

005–007 Standard subdivisions [*formerly* 05–07]

008 Geography and travel with respect to kinds of persons

[009] Historical, geographic, persons treatment
Do not use; class in 913–919 without adding from this table

[01–02] Standard subdivisions
Relocated to 001–002

[03] Dictionaries, encyclopedias, concordances, gazetteers
Relocated to 003

04 Travel
Class here discovery, exploration; guidebooks
Class guidebooks emphasizing a specific subject with the subject, e.g., guidebook to holy places 263
See Manual at 913–919: Add table: 04

[05–07] Standard subdivisions
Relocated to 005–007

[09] Historical, geographic, persons treatment
Number discontinued; class in 913–919 without adding from this table

Class comprehensive works, geography of and travel in more than one continent in 910; world travel guides in 910.2; historical geography in 911; graphic representations in 912; interdisciplinary works on geography and history of ancient world, of specific continents, countries, localities, travel accounts that emphasize the civilization of country visited in 930–990; archaeology in 930.1; area studies in 940–990

See Manual at 913–919

920 Biography, genealogy, insignia

Class here autobiographies, diaries, reminiscences, correspondence

Class biography of persons associated with a specific discipline or subject with the discipline or subject, using notation 092 from Table 1, e.g., biography of chemists 540.92

(Option: Class individual biography in 92 or B, collected biography in 92 or 920 undivided)

See Manual at T1—092 for biography

.001–.007 Standard subdivisions of biography

.009 General collections of biography by period, region, group

Class collections by specific continents, countries, localities in 920.03–920.09

.009 1 Areas, regions, places in general

.009 2 Racial, ethnic, national groups

.02 General collections of biography

Not limited by period, place, group and not associated with a specific subject

.03–.09 General collections of biography by specific continents, countries, localities

Not associated with a specific subject

Add to base number 920.0 notation 3–9 from Table 2, e.g., collections of biographies of persons resident in England 920.042

Class collections by sex regardless of continent, country, locality in 920.7

> **920.1–928 Biography of specific classes of persons**

(Option A: Use subdivisions identified by *

(Option B: Class individual biography in 92 or B, collected biography in 92 or 920 undivided

(Option C: Class individual biography of men in 920.71, of women in 920.72

(Prefer specific discipline or subject, using notation 092 from Table 1, e.g., collected biography of scientists 509.2)

Class comprehensive works in 920.02

(.1) ***Bibliographers**

(.2) ***Librarians and book collectors**

(.3) ***Encyclopedists**

Class lexicographers in 924

(.4) ***Publishers and booksellers**

(.5) ***Journalists and news commentators**

.7 **Persons by sex**

Class here individual biography of persons not associated with a specific discipline or subject, collected biography of persons by sex

(Option: Class here all individual biography; prefer specific discipline or subject, using notation 092 from Table 1)

.71 Men

.72 Women

(.9) ***Persons associated with other subjects**

Not provided for in 920.1–920.5, 921–928

(921) *Philosophers and psychologists

(922) *Religious leaders, thinkers, workers

(923) *Persons in social sciences

(924) *Philologists and lexicographers

(925) *Scientists

(926) *Persons in technology

(927) *Persons in the arts and recreation

For persons in literature, see 928

*(Optional number; prefer specific subject or discipline, as described under 920.1–928)

(928) *Persons in literature, history, biography, genealogy

Examples: historians, writers and critics of literature

See also 923 for explorers, geographers, pioneers, frontiersmen

929 Genealogy, names, insignia

Including family histories; cemetery records, e.g., epitaphs; genealogical sources, e.g., census records, court records, tax lists, wills

Genealogical sources published by a genealogical organization or by a genealogist are classed here. Sources published by other agencies are classed with the subject of the publication, e.g., United States census records 317.3

Class family histories emphasizing the contributions of the members of the family to a specific occupation with the occupation, e.g., the Rothschilds as a family of bankers 332.1092

.4 Personal names

See also 929.9 for names of houses, pets, ships

.6 Heraldry

Class armorial bearings in 929.8; royal houses, peerage, gentry, orders of knighthood in 929.7

.7 Royal houses, peerage, gentry, orders of knighthood

Class here rank, precedence, titles of honor

Class Christian orders of knighthood in 255, Christian orders of knighthood in church history in 271

.709 Historical and geographic treatment

Class here countries outside Europe

Class historical and geographic treatment by specific countries of Europe in 929.7

.8 Awards, orders, decorations, armorial bearings, autographs

Including coats of arms, crests, seals

Class family coats of arms in 929.6

.9 Forms of insignia and identification

Examples: ownership and service marks; trademarks; national, state, provincial, ship, ownership flags; names of houses, pets, ships

Class military use of flags and banners in 355.1, place names in 910, personal names in 929.4; forms of insignia and identification not provided for here with the form, e.g., coats of arms 929.8; identification marks in a specific subject with the subject, e.g., airline insignia 387.7

*(Optional number; prefer specific subject or discipline, as described under 920.1–928)

\> ## 930–990 History of ancient world; of specific continents, countries, localities; of extraterrestrial worlds

Civilization and events

Class here interdisciplinary works on geography and history of ancient world, of specific continents, countries, localities

Add to base number 9 notation 3–9 from Table 2, e.g., general history of Europe 940, of England 942; then add further as follows:

001–007 Standard subdivisions

008 History with respect to kinds of persons

[0089] Racial, ethnic, national groups

Do not use; class in 930–990 without adding from this table

009 Persons

Description, critical appraisal, biography of persons associated with the history of the continent, country, locality but limited to no specific period

Class historians and historiographers in 930–990 without adding from this table

Persons of a specific period which is set forth in the 930–990 schedules are classed in 01–09, using notation 092 from Table 1; persons of other periods are classed in 930–990 without adding from this table

01–09 Historical periods

Use historical period notation only when it is specifically set forth in the 930–990 schedules, e.g., World War II 940.53, England during Tudor period 942.05

Indigenous groups are classed in the prehistoric period, e.g., Australian native peoples before European settlement 994.01

Class areas, regions, places in general and racial, ethnic, national groups in a specific period in 930–990 without adding from this table

See Manual at 930–990: Add table: 01–09

The schedules that follow do not enumerate all the countries and localities that appear in Table 2; however, the foregoing instructions apply to history of any place in notation 3–9 from Table 2

Interdisciplinary works on historical treatment of culture and institutions relocated to 306.09

Class comprehensive works in 909; geography of ancient world, of specific continents, countries, localities in 913–919; sociology of war in 303.6, of military institutions in 306.2; social factors affecting war, social causes of war in 355.02

See Manual at 305 vs. 306, 909, 930–990 for history of ethnic groups; 320 vs. 909, 930–990 for political history; 355.0092 vs. 930–990 for biography of military personnel; 400 vs. 909, 930–990; 910 vs. 909, 930–990; 930–990

930 General history of ancient world to ca. 499

.01–.09 Standard subdivisions

As modified under 930–990; however, class archaeology in 930.1

.1 **Archaeology**

Study of past civilizations through discovery, collection, interpretation of material remains

Including specific archaeological ages, e.g., Paleolithic (Old Stone) Age

Class here prehistoric archaeology; interdisciplinary works on archaeology

Class archaeology of continents, countries, localities provided for in notation 3 from Table 2 in 931–939; archaeology of modern period, ancient and prehistoric archaeology of continents, countries, localities not provided for in notation 3 from Table 2 in 940–990; archaeology of specific oceans and seas in 909; industrial archaeology in 609

See also 700 for artistic aspects of archaeological objects

> 931–939 Specific places

Class comprehensive works in 930; archaeology of modern period, ancient and prehistoric archaeology of continents, countries, localities not provided for in notation 3 from Table 2 in 940–990; archaeology of specific oceans and seas in 909

931 *China to 420

932 *Egypt to 640

933 *Palestine to 70

See also 220.9 for Biblical archaeology, history of Biblical events

934 *India to 647

935 *Mesopotamia and Iranian Plateau to 637

936 *Europe north and west of Italian peninsula to ca. 499

Class here comprehensive works on ancient Europe

Class a specific part of ancient Europe not provided for here with the part, e.g., Italy 937, Russia 947

937 *Italian Peninsula and adjacent territories to 476

938 *Greece to 323

939 *Other parts of ancient world to ca. 640

Including ancient history of Afghanistan [*formerly also* 958.1]

*Add as instructed under 930–990

> ## 940–990 General history of modern world, of extraterrestrial worlds

Class here area studies; comprehensive works on ancient and modern history of specific continents, countries, localities

Class comprehensive works in 909

For general history of ancient world, see 930

940 General history of Europe Western Europe

SUMMARY

940.01–.09 Standard subdivisions
.1–.5 [Specific periods of European history]
941 British Isles
942 England and Wales
943 Central Europe Germany
944 France and Monaco
945 Italian Peninsula and adjacent islands Italy
946 Iberian Peninsula and adjacent islands Spain
947 Eastern Europe Union of Soviet Socialist Republics (Soviet Union)
948 Scandinavia
949 Other parts of Europe

.01–.09 Standard subdivisions

As modified under 930–990

.1 **Early history to 1453**

Class here Middle Ages, 476–1453

Class ancient history to ca. 499 in 936, comprehensive works on Crusades in 909.07

.2 **1453–**

Including War of the League of Augsburg, 1688–1697; Thirty Years' War, 1618–1648; War of the Spanish Succession, 1701–1714; War of the Austrian Succession, 1740–1748; Seven Years' War, 1756–1763; Napoleonic Wars

Class North American aspects of War of the League of Augsburg, War of the Spanish Succession, War of the Austrian Succession, Seven Years' War in 973.2

For World War I, see 940.3; 1918–   , 940.5

.3 World War I, 1914–1918

Including social, political, economic, diplomatic, history; causes, results; participation of specific countries and groups of countries

Class results in and effects on a specific country with history of the country, e.g., on Germany 943.085

For military history, see 940.4

[.308] World War I with respect to kinds of persons

Do not use; class in 940.3

.4 Military history of World War I

Including strategy, mobilization, racial minorities as troops, repressive measures and atrocities, military participation of specific countries; celebrations, commemorations, memorials, prisoner-of-war camps, medical services, social services, unconventional warfare

.400 1–.400 8 Standard subdivisions

.400 9 Historical, geographic, persons treatment

Class military participation of specific countries, military campaigns, personal narratives in 940.4

.5 1918–

.53 World War II, 1939–1945

Including social, political, economic, diplomatic, history; causes, results; holocaust; participation of specific countries and groups of countries

Class results in and effects on a specific country with history of the country, e.g., on Norway 948.104

For military history, see 940.54

[.530 8] World War II with respect to kinds of persons

Do not use; class in 940.53

.54 Military history of World War II

Including strategy, mobilization, racial minorities as troops, repressive measures and atrocities, military participation of specific countries; celebrations, commemorations, memorials, prisoner-of-war camps, medical services, social services, unconventional warfare

.540 01–.540 08 Standard subdivisions

.540 09 Historical, geographic, persons treatment

Class military participation of specific countries, military campaigns, personal narratives in 940.54

.55 1945–

941 *British Isles

Class here Great Britain, United Kingdom

See Manual at 941

.01 Early history to 1066

Class ancient history to 410 in 936.1

.02–.05 From Norman period through Tudor period, 1066–1603

Add to base number 941.0 the numbers following 942.0 in 942.02–942.05, e.g., Tudor period 941.05

.06 Stuart and Commonwealth periods, 1603–1714

.07 Period of House of Hanover, 1714–1837

Including formation of United Kingdom

.08 Period of Victoria and House of Windsor, 1837–

.081 Reign of Victoria, 1837–1901

Class here 19th century

Class 1800–1837 in 941.07

.082 1901–

For reign of George V, see 941.083; 1936–1945, 941.084; 1945– 941.085

.083 Reign of George V, 1910–1936

.084 1936–1945

Class here reigns of Edward VIII, 1936, and George VI, 1936–1952; period of World War II, 1939–1945

Class reign of George VI during 1945–1952 in 941.085

.085 1945–

Class here reign of Elizabeth II, 1952–

.1 *Scotland

Class northeastern Scotland in 941.2, southeastern Scotland in 941.3, southwestern Scotland in 941.4

.101 Early history to 1057

Class ancient history to 410 in 936.1

.102 1057–1314

Including Battle of Bannockburn, 1314

.103 1314–1424

.104 Reigns of James I-James V, 1424–1542

*Add as instructed under 930–990

.105 Reformation period, 1542–1603

Class here 16th century

Class 1500–1542 in 941.104

.106–.108 From personal union with England to present time, 1603–

Add to base number 941.10 the numbers following 941.0 in 941.06–941.08, e.g., reign of George V 941.1083

.5 *Ireland

.501 Early history to 1086

Class ancient history to 410 in 936.1

.502 1086–1171

.503 Under House of Plantagenet, 1171–1399

.504 Under Houses of Lancaster and York, 1399–1485

.505 Under Tudors, 1485–1603

.506 Under Stuarts, 1603–1691

.507 1691–1799

.508 1800–

.508 1 1800–1899

.508 2 1900–

.508 24 1970–

.6 *Ulster Northern Ireland

.601–.607 Early history to 1800

Add to base number 941.60 the numbers following 941.50 in 941.501–941.507, e.g., period under Tudors 941.605

.608 1800–

.608 1 1800–1899

.608 2 1900–

.608 24 1969–

.7 *Republic of Ireland

Class Leinster in 941.8, Munster in 941.9

.701–.707 Early history to 1800

Add to base number 941.70 the numbers following 941.50 in 941.501–941.507, e.g., period under Tudors 941.705

*Add as instructed under 930–990

.708 1800–

.708 1 1800–1899

.708 2 1900–

Including period as Irish Free State, 1922–1937; as Eire, 1937–1949

.708 24 1970–

942 *England and Wales

See Manual at 941

.01 Early history to 1066

Class ancient history to 410 in 936.2

.02 Norman period, 1066–1154

Including Battle of Hastings, 1066

Class here 12th century

Class 1154–1199 in 942.03

.03 Period of House of Plantagenet, 1154–1399

.04 Period of Houses of Lancaster and York, 1399–1485

Class here Wars of the Roses, 1455–1485

.05 Tudor period, 1485–1603

.06–.08 From Stuart and Commonwealth periods to present time, 1603–

Add to base number 942.0 the numbers following 941.0 in 941.06–941.08, e.g., Commonwealth 942.06

.9 *Wales

.901–.908 Historical periods

Add to base number 942.90 the numbers following 942.0 in 942.01–942.08, e.g., Wales during the Wars of the Roses 942.904

943 Central Europe Germany

Class ancient history of Germany in 936.3

.000 1–.000 9 Standard subdivisions of Central Europe

As modified under 930–990

.001–.009 Standard subdivisions of Germany

As modified under 930–990

.08 Germany since 1866

.085 Period of Weimar Republic, 1918–1933

*Add as instructed under 930–990

.086 Period of Third Reich, 1933–1945

.087 1945–

Class here Federal Republic, 1949– , comprehensive works on Federal and Democratic Republics

Class German Democratic Republic in 943.1087

.1 *Northeastern Germany

.108 1866–

.108 5 Period of Weimar Republic, 1918–1933

.108 6 Period of Third Reich, 1933–1945

.108 7 German Democratic Republic, 1949–

Class here East Germany, 1945–

.6 *Austria and Liechtenstein

Class ancient history to 481 in 936.3

.605 Austria since 1919

.7 *Czechoslovakia

.704 1945–

.8 *Poland

.805 1939–

.9 *Hungary

.905 1918–

944 *France and Monaco

Including Hundred Years' War, 1337–1453

Class ancient history to 486 in 936.4

> **944.04–944.08 France since 1789**

Class comprehensive works in 944

.04 Revolutionary period, 1789–1804

*Add as instructed under 930–990

.05 Period of First Empire, 1804–1815

Class here reign of Napoleon I, 1804–1814

Class Napoleonic Wars in 940.2

.06 Period of restoration, 1815–1848

Class here 19th century

Class a specific part of 19th century not provided for here with the part, e.g., Second Empire 944.07

.07 Period of Second Republic and Second Empire (period of Napoleon III), 1848–1870

.08 1870–

.081 Period of Third Republic, 1870–1945

.082 Period of Fourth Republic, 1945–1958

.083 Period of Fifth Republic, 1958–

945 *Italian Peninsula and adjacent islands Italy

Class ancient history to 476 in 937

.09 Italy since 1900

Use of this number for 1870–1900 discontinued; class in 945

.091 Reign of Victor Emmanuel III, 1900–1946

Class here Fascist period

.092 Period of Republic, 1946–

946 Iberian Peninsula and adjacent islands Spain

Class ancient history to 415 in 936.6

.000 1–.000 9 Standard subdivisions of Iberian Peninsula and adjacent islands

As modified under 930–990

.001–.009 Standard subdivisions of Spain

As modified under 930–990

.08 Spain since 1931

Class here 20th century

Use of this number for 1868–1931 discontinued; class in 946

.081 Period of Second Republic, 1931–1939

Class here Civil War, 1936–1939

.082 Period of Francisco Franco, 1939–1975

.083 Reign of Juan Carlos I, 1975–

*Add as instructed under 930–990

.9 *Portugal

Class ancient history to 415 in 936.6

.904 1910–

947 Eastern Europe Union of Soviet Socialist Republics (Soviet Union)

.000 1–.000 9 Standard subdivisions of eastern Europe

As modified under 930–990

.001–.009 Standard subdivisions of Russia

As modified under 930–990

.08 Russia since 1855

.084 1917–

Class here Communist period; Union of Soviet Socialist Republics, 1923–

For 1953– , see 947.085

.085 1953–

948 *Scandinavia

Class here northern Europe

.08 1905–

.1 *Norway

Class ancient history to 481 in 936.3, southeastern Norway in 948.2, southwestern Norway in 948.3, central and northern Norway in 948.4

.104 1905–

.5 *Sweden

Class ancient history to 481 in 936.3, southern Sweden in 948.6, central Sweden in 948.7, northern Sweden in 948.8

.505 1905–

.9 Denmark and Finland

Class ancient history of Denmark to 481 in 936.3

.900 1–.900 9 Standard subdivisions for Denmark

As modified under 930–990

.905 Denmark since 1906

.97 *Finland

.970 3 1917–

*Add as instructed under 930–990

949 Other parts of Europe

.1 ***Northwestern islands**

.12 *Iceland

.120 5 1940–

.2 ***Netherlands (Holland)**

Class ancient history to 481 in 936.3

.207 1901–

.3 **Southern Low Countries Belgium**

Class ancient history of Belgium to 486 in 936.4

.300 01–.300 09 Standard subdivisions of southern Low Countries

As modified under 930–990

.300 1–.300 9 Standard subdivisions of Belgium

As modified under 930–990

.304 Belgium since 1909

.35 *Luxembourg

Class ancient history to 486 in 936.4

.350 4 1890–

.4 ***Switzerland**

Class ancient history to 486 in 936.4

.407 1945–

.5 ***Greece**

Class here Byzantine Empire

Class ancient history to 323 in 938

.507 1924–

.6 ***Balkan Peninsula**

Including Balkan Wars, 1912–1913

.65 *Albania

Class ancient history to 323 in 938

.650 3 1946–

.7 **Yugoslavia and Bulgaria**

Class ancient history of Yugoslavia to ca. 640 in 939

.700 01–.700 09 Standard subdivisions of Yugoslavia and Bulgaria

As modified under 930–990

*Add as instructed under 930–990

.700 1–.700 9 Standard subdivisions of Yugoslavia

As modified under 930–990

.702 Yugoslavia since 1918

.77 *Bulgaria

Class ancient history to ca. 640 in 939

.770 3 Period of People's Republic, 1946–

.8 *Romania

Class ancient history to ca. 640 in 939

.803 Period of People's Republic, 1947–

.9 *Aegean Islands

Class ancient history to 323 in 939

.907 1924–

950 General history of Asia Orient Far East

SUMMARY

950.01–.09	**Standard subdivisions**
.4	**Asia since 1905**
951	**China and adjacent areas**
952	**Japan**
953	**Arabian Peninsula and adjacent areas**
954	**South Asia India**
955	**Iran**
956	**Middle East (Near East)**
957	**Siberia (Asiatic Russia)**
958	**Central Asia**
959	**Southeast Asia**

.01–.09 Standard subdivisions

As modified under 930–990

.4 Asia since 1905

951 China and adjacent areas

Class ancient history to 420 in 931

.000 1–.000 9 Standard subdivisions of China and adjacent areas

As modified under 930–990

.001–.009 Standard subdivisions of China

As modified under 930–990

.04 Period of Republic, 1912–1949

*Add as instructed under 930–99

.05 Period of People's Republic, 1949–

Class here 20th century

Class 1900–1912 in 951, 1912–1949 in 951.04

.2 *Taiwan, Hong Kong, Macao

.25 *Hong Kong

.250 5 1945–

.9 *Korea

.904 1945–

.93 *North Korea

.930 4 1945–

.95 *South Korea

.950 4 1945–

952 *Japan

.03 1868–1945

.04 1945–

953 *Arabian Peninsula and adjacent areas

Class ancient history to 622 in 939

.05 1926–

.8 *Saudi Arabia

Class ancient history to 622 in 939

.805 1926–

954 *South Asia India

Class ancient history of India to 647 in 934

> **954.02–954.05 Historical periods of India**

Class comprehensive works in 954

.02 647–1785

.03 Period of British rule, 1785–1947

.04 1947–1971

.05 1971–

*Add as instructed under 930–990

.9 **Other jurisdictions**

Class here *Pakistan (West and East, 1947–1971)

.902 647–1785

.903 Period of British rule, 1785–1947

.904 1947–1971

.905 1971–

.91 *Pakistan

.910 2 647–1785

.910 3 Period of British rule, 1785–1947

.910 4 Period of union of West and East Pakistan, 1947–1971

.910 5 1971–

.92 *Bangladesh

.920 2 647–1785

.920 3 Period of British rule, 1785–1947

.920 4 Period of union of West and East Pakistan, 1947–1971

.920 5 1971–

.93 *Sri Lanka

.930 3 1948–

955 *Iran

Class ancient history to 637 in 935

.05 1906–

Including Iraqi-Iranian Conflict, 1980–

956 *Middle East (Near East)

Class ancient history to ca. 640 in 939

.04 1945–1980

Including Israel-Arab War, 1948–1949; Sinai Campaign, 1956; Israel-Arab War, 1967 (Six Days' War); Israel-Arab War, 1973 (Yom Kippur War)

.05 1980–

Including Israel-Lebanon-Syria Conflict, 1982–1985

.1 **Turkey and Cyprus**

Class divisions of Turkey and Cyprus in 956.2–956.6

.100 01–.100 09 Standard subdivisions of Turkey and Cyprus

As modified under 930–990

*Add as instructed under 930–990

.100 1–.100 9 Standard subdivisions of Turkey

As modified under 930–990

.103 Turkey since 1950

.4 *South central Turkey and Cyprus

Class ancient history to ca. 640 in 939

.45 *Cyprus

Class ancient history to ca. 640 in 939

.450 4 1960–

.7 *Iraq

Class ancient history to 637 in 935

.704 1920–

.9 *Eastern Mediterranean Region

.91 *Syria

Class ancient history to ca. 640 in 939

.910 4 1920–

Class Israel-Arab wars of 1948–1949, 1967, and 1973, in 956.04; Israel-Lebanon-Syria Conflict, 1982–1985, in 956.05

.92 *Lebanon

Class ancient history to ca. 640 in 939

.920 4 1926–

Class Israel-Arab War, 1948–1949, in 956.04; Israel-Lebanon-Syria Conflict, 1982–1985, in 956.05

.94 *Palestine Israel

Class ancient history to 70 in 933, ancient Edom in 939

See also 909 for world history of Jews

.940 5 1948–

Class Israel-Arab wars of 1948–1949, 1967, and 1973, Sinai Campaign, 1956, in 956.04; Israel-Lebanon-Syria Conflict, 1982–1985, in 956.05

.95 *Jordan

Class ancient history to 70 in 933; ancient Moab, Petra in 939

.950 4 1923–

Class Israel-Arab wars of 1948–1949 and 1967 in 956.04

957 *Siberia (Asiatic Russia)

.08 1855–

*Add as instructed under 930–990

958 *Central Asia

Class early history to ca. 640 in 939

.1 *Afghanistan

Ancient history to ca. 640 relocated to 639

.104 1919–

959 *Southeast Asia

.05 1900–

.1 *Burma

.105 1948–

.3 *Thailand

.304 1910–

.4 *Laos

.404 1949–

Class here 20th century

Class military operations in Laos during Vietnamese War in 959.704

1900–1949 is classed in 959.4

.5 *Commonwealth of Nations territories Malaysia

.505 Malaysia since 1963

Class here 20th century

1900–1963 is classed in 959.5

.55 *Brunei

.550 5 1946–

Class here 20th century

1900–1946 is classed in 959.55

.57 *Singapore

.570 5 Periods of federation with Malaysia, 1963–1965, and separate nationhood, 1965–

Class here 20th century

1900–1963 is classed in 959.57

*Add as instructed under 930–990

.6 ***Cambodia (Khmer Republic, Kampuchea)**

.604 1949–

Class here 20th century

Class military operations in Cambodia during Vietnamese War in 959.704

1900–1949 is classed in 959.6

.7 ***Vietnam**

.704 1949–

Including Vietnamese War, 1961–1975

.8 ***Indonesia**

.803 Period of Republic, 1945–

Class here 20th century

1900–1945 is classed in 959.8

.9 ***Philippines**

.904 Period of Republic, 1946–

960 General history of Africa

SUMMARY

960.01–.09	**Standard subdivisions**
.3	**Africa since 1885**
961	**Tunisia and Libya**
962	**Egypt and Sudan**
963	**Ethiopia**
964	**Northwest African coast and offshore islands Morocco**
965	**Algeria**
966	**West Africa and offshore islands**
967	**Central Africa and offshore islands**
968	**Southern Africa Republic of South Africa**
969	**South Indian Ocean islands**

.01–.09 Standard subdivisions

As modified under 930–990

.3 **Africa since 1885**

961 *Tunisia and Libya

Class here North Africa

Class ancient history to ca. 640 in 939

.04 1950–

.1 ***Tunisia**

Class ancient history to 647 in 939

.105 1956–

*Add as instructed under 930–990

.2 ***Libya**

Class ancient history to 644 in 939

.204 1952–

962 Egypt and Sudan

Class ancient history to 640 in 932

.000 1–.000 9 Standard subdivisions of Egypt and Sudan

As modified under 930–990

.001–.009 Standard subdivisions of Egypt

As modified under 930–990

.05 Egypt sinee 1922

Class Israel-Arab wars of 1948–1949, 1967, and 1973, Sinai Campaign, 1956, in 956.04

.4 ***Sudan**

Class parts of Sudan in 962.5–962.9

.404 1956–

963 *Ethiopia

See also 939 for ancient Ethiopia (a part of what is now modern Sudan, not modern Ethiopia)

.07 1974–

964 Northwest African coast and offshore islands Morocco

Class ancient history of Morocco to 647 in 939

.000 1–.000 9 Standard subdivisions of northwest African coast and offshore islands

As modified under 930–990

.001–.009 Standard subdivisions of Morocco

As modified under 930–990

.05 Morocco since 1956

965 *Algeria

Class ancient history to 647 in 939

.05 1962–

966 *West Africa and offshore islands

.03 1885–

.1 ***Mauritania**

.105 1960–

*Add as instructed under 930–990

.2 ***Mali, Burkina Faso, Niger**

.203 1960–

.23 *Mali

.230 5 1960–

.25 *Burkina Faso

.250 5 1960–

.26 *Niger

.260 5 1960–

.3 ***Senegal**

.305 1960–

Including Confederation of Senegambia, 1982–

Class Gambian part of Senegambia in 966.5103

.4 ***Sierra Leone**

.404 1961–

.5 ***Gambia, Guinea, Guinea-Bissau, Cape Verde**

.51 *Gambia

.510 3 1965–

Including period as a part of Senegambia, 1982–

.52 *Guinea

.520 5 1958–

.57 *Guinea-Bissau

.570 3 1974–

.58 *Cape Verde

.580 3 1975–

.6 **Liberia and Ivory Coast**

.62 *Liberia

.620 3 1945–

.68 *Ivory Coast

.680 5 1960–

.7 ***Ghana**

See also 966.1 for Ghana Empire

.705 1957–

*Add as instructed under 930–990

.8 **Togo and Benin**

.81 *Togo

.810 4 1960–

.83 *Benin

Former name: Dahomey

See also 966.9 for kingdom of Benin

.830 5 1960–

.9 ***Nigeria**

.905 1960–

967 *Central Africa and offshore islands

.03 1885–

.1 ***Cameroon, Sao Tome and Principe, Equatorial Guinea**

.11 *Cameroon

.110 4 1960–

.15 *Sao Tome and Principe

.150 2 Period of Republic, 1975–

.18 *Equatorial Guinea

.180 3 1968–

.2 ***Gabon and Republic of the Congo**

.205 1959–

.21 *Gabon

.210 4 1960–

.24 *Republic of the Congo

.240 5 1960–

.3 ***Angola**

.304 1975–

.4 ***Central African Republic and Chad**

.41 *Central African Republic

.410 5 1960–

.43 *Chad

.430 4 1960–

*Add as instructed under 930–990

.5 **Zaire, Rwanda, Burundi**

.51 *Zaire

.510 3 1960–

.57 *Rwanda and Burundi

Class here former Ruanda-Urundi

.570 4 1962–

.571 *Rwanda

.571 04 1962–

.572 *Burundi

.572 04 1962–

.6 ***Uganda and Kenya**

.604 1961–

.61 *Uganda

.610 4 1962–

.62 *Kenya

.620 4 1963–

.7 ***Djibouti and Somalia**

Class here Somaliland

.71 *Djibouti

.710 4 1977–

.73 *Somalia

.730 5 1960–

.8 ***Tanzania**

.804 Period as United Republic, 1964–

.9 ***Mozambique**

.905 1975–

968 *Southern Africa Republic of South Africa

> **968.02–968.06 Historical periods of Republic of South Africa**

Class comprehensive works in 968

.02 Early history to 1488

.03 Period of European exploration and settlement, 1488–1814

.04 1814–1910

*Add as instructed under 930–990

.05 Period of Union, 1910–1961

.06 Period as Republic, 1961–

[.1] **Botswana, Lesotho, Swaziland**

Relocated to 968.8

.8 ***Botswana, Lesotho, Swaziland [*all formerly* 968.1], Namibia**

.803 1885–

.81 *Namibia

.810 3 South African period, 1915–

.83 *Botswana

.830 3 1966–

.85 *Lesotho

.850 3 1966–

.87 *Swaziland

.870 3 1968–

.9 ***Zimbabwe, Zambia, Malawi**

.904 1964–

.91 *Zimbabwe

.910 5 Period as Republic of Zimbabwe, 1980–

.94 *Zambia

.940 4 Period as Republic of Zambia, 1964–

.97 *Malawi

.970 4 1964–

969 *South Indian Ocean islands

.1 ***Madagascar**

.105 1960–

970 General history of North America

SUMMARY

970.001–.009	**Standard subdivisions**	
.01–.05	**Historical periods**	
971	**Canada**	
972	**Middle America**	**Mexico**
973	**United States**	
974-979	**Specific states of United States**	

.001–.003 Standard subdivisions

*Add as instructed under 930–990

.004 North American native peoples

(Option: Class North American native peoples in North America in 970.1, specific native peoples in 970.3)

Specific native peoples in a specific place relocated to the place in 971–979, e.g., the Hopi in Arizona 979.1004

See Manual at 970.004

.005–.007 Standard subdivisions

.008 History with respect to kinds of persons

[.008 9] Racial, ethnic, national groups

Do not use; class in 970; however, class North American native peoples in 970.004

.009 Persons

Description, critical appraisal, biography of persons associated with the history of North America but limited to no specific period

Class historians and historiographers in 970; persons of a specific period in 970.01–970.05, using notation 092 from Table 1

> **970.01–970.05 Historical periods**

Class comprehensive works in 970

.01 Early history to 1599

.02 1600–1699

.03 1700–1799

.04 1800–1899

.05 1900–

.051 1900–1918

Class here period of World War 1, 1914–1918

.052 1918–1945

Class here period of World War 2, 1939–1945

.053 1945–

(.1) North American native peoples **Indians of North America**

(Optional number; prefer 970.004)

Class special topics in 970.3–970.5

(.3) **Specific native peoples**

(Optional number; prefer 971–979 with use of subdivision 004 from table under 971–979, e.g., the Hopi in Arizona 979.1004)

Class government relations with specific native peoples in 970.5

(.4) **Native peoples in specific places in North America**

(Optional number; prefer 971–979 with use of subdivision 004 from table under 971–979, e.g., native peoples in United States 973.04, in Arizona 979.1004)

Add to base number 970.4 the numbers following —7 in notation 71–79 from Table 2, e.g., Indians in Arizona 970.491

Class government relations in specific places in 970.5, specific native peoples in specific places in 970.3

(.5) **Government relations with North American native peoples**

History and policy

(Optional number; prefer 323.1 for comprehensive works; a specific subject with the subject, e.g., Black Hawk War 973.5)

> **971–979 Countries and localities**

Add to base number 97 the number following —7 in notation 71–79 from Table 2, e.g., general history of Canada 971, of Quebec 971.4; then add further as follows (observing variant instructions for 973):

001–003 Standard subdivisions

004 North American native peoples [*formerly* 970.004]
(Option: Class specific native peoples in 970.3, native peoples in specific places in North America in 970.4)

005–007 Standard subdivisions

008 History with respect to kinds of persons

[0089] Racial, ethnic, national groups
Do not use; class in 971–979 without adding from this table; however, class North American native peoples in 004

009 Persons
Description, critical appraisal, biography of persons associated with the history of the continent, country, locality but limited to no specific period
Class historians and historiographers in 971–979 without adding from this table
Persons of a specific period which is set forth in the 971–979 schedules are classed in 01–09, using notation 092 from Table 1; persons of other periods are classed in 971–979 without adding from this table

(continued)

> ## 971–979 Countries and localities (continued)

01–09 Historical periods

Use historical period notation only when it is specifically set forth in the 971–979 schedules, e.g., period of 1791–1841 in Canadian history 971.03

Indigenous groups are classed in the prehistoric period, e.g., Canadian native peoples before European settlement 971.01

Class areas, regions, places in general and racial, ethnic, national groups other than North American native peoples in a specific period in 971–979 without adding from this table; North American native peoples in a specific period in 004

See Manual at 930–990: Add table: 01–09

Class comprehensive works in 970

See Manual at 305 vs. 306, 909, 930–990 for history of ethnic groups; 320 vs. 909, 930–990 for political history; 355.009 vs. 930–990 for biography of military personnel; 400 vs. 909, 930–990; 910 vs. 909, 930–990; 930–990

971 *Canada

.01 Early history to 1763

(Option: Class here North American aspects of War of the League of Augsburg, War of the Spanish Succession, War of the Austrian Succession, Seven Years' War; prefer 973.2)

Class comprehensive works on War of the League of Augsburg, War of the Spanish Succession, War of the Austrian Succession, Seven Years' War in 940.2; North American aspects of War of the League of Augsburg, War of the Spanish Succession, War of the Austrian Succession, Seven Years' War in 973.2

.02 Period of early British rule, 1763–1791

.03 Period of Upper and Lower Canada, 1791–1841

(Option: Class here War of 1812; prefer 973.5)

.04 Period of Province of Canada, 1841–1867

.05 Period of Dominion of Canada, 1867–

For 1911– , see 971.06

.06 1911–

.061 1911–1921

.062 1921–1935

.063 1935–1957

.064 1957–

*Add as instructed under 971–979

972 Middle America Mexico

.000 1–.000 9 Standard subdivisions of Middle America

As modified under 971–979

.001–.009 Standard subdivisions of Mexico

As modified under 971–979

.08 Mexico since 1867

> **972.8–972.9 Other parts of Middle America**

Class comprehensive works in 972

.8 *Central America

.805 1900–

.81 *Guatemala

.810 5 1871–

.82 *Belize

.820 5 1964–

.83 *Honduras

.830 5 1838–

.84 *El Salvador

.840 5 1859–

.85 *Nicaragua

.850 5 1893–

.86 *Costa Rica

.860 5 1948–

.87 *Panama

.870 5 1903–

✓ **.9 *West Indies (Antilles) and Bermuda**

Class here Caribbean Area

.905 1902–

.91 *Cuba

.910 6 1899–

Class here period of Republic, 1902–

.92 *Jamaica and Cayman Islands

.920 6 Jamaica since 1962

*Add as instructed under 971–979

.93 *Dominican Republic

.930 5 1902–

.94 *Haiti

.940 7 1957–

.95 *Puerto Rico

.950 5 1900–

.983 *Trinidad and Tobago

.983 04 1962–

973 United States

For specific states, see 974–979

.01–.09 Standard subdivisions

Add to base number 973.0 the numbers following 00 in notation 001–009 from table under 971–979, e.g., periodicals on United States history 973.05

.1 Early history to 1607

.2 Colonial period, 1607–1775

Including King William's War (North American aspects of War of the League of Augsburg), 1688–1697; Queen Anne's War (North American aspects of War of the Spanish Succession), 1701–1714; King George's War (North American aspects of War of the Austrian Succession), 1740–1748; French and Indian War (North American aspects of Seven Years' War), 1756–1763

(Option: Class North American aspects of War of the League of Augsburg, War of the Spanish Succession, War of the Austrian Succession, Seven Years' War in 971.01)

Class comprehensive works on War of the League of Augsburg, War of the Spanish Succession, War of the Austrian Succession, Seven Years' War in 940.2

.3 Periods of Revolution and Confederation, 1775–1789

Including social, political, economic, diplomatic, military history; causes, results; celebrations, commemorations, memorials, prisons, health services, secret service and spies, propaganda

.4 Constitutional period, 1789–1809

Including Tripolitan War, 1801–1805

.5 1809–1845

Including War of 1812; War with Algiers, 1815

Class here 19th century

(Option: Class War of 1812 in 971.03)

Class a specific part of 19th century not provided for here with the part, e.g., Civil War 973.7

*Add as instructed under 971–979

.6 **1845–1861**

Including Mexican War, 1845–1848

.7 **Administration of Abraham Lincoln, 1861–1865 Civil War**

Including social, political, economic, diplomatic, military history; causes, results; celebrations, commemorations, memorials, prisons, health services, social services, secret service and spies, propaganda

[.708] Civil War with respect to kinds of persons

Do not use; class in 973.7

.709 2 Persons

Class personal narratives in 973.7

.8 **Reconstruction period, 1865–1901**

Including Spanish-American War, 1898

.9 **1901–**

.91 1901–1953

.917 Administration of Franklin Delano Roosevelt, 1933–1945

.918 Administration of Harry S Truman, 1945–1953

.92 1953–

.921 Administration of Dwight David Eisenhower, 1953–1961

.922 Administration of John Fitzgerald Kennedy, 1961–1963

.923 Administration of Lyndon Baines Johnson, 1963–1969

.924 Administration of Richard Milhous Nixon, 1969–1974

.925 Administration of Gerald Rudolph Ford, 1974–1977

.926 Administration of Jimmy (James Earl) Carter, 1977–1981

.927 Administration of Ronald Reagan, 1981–1989

.928 Administration of George Bush, 1989–

974–979 Specific states of United States

Add to base number 97 the numbers following –7 in notation 74–79 from Table 2, e.g., Arizona 979.1; then add as instructed under 971–979, e.g., Indians of Arizona 979.1004

Class comprehensive works in 973

For Hawaii, see 996.9

975.3 Wash, D.C.

979.1 Grand Canyon, ARIZ.

976.4 Alamo, Texas

980 General history of South America

Class here Latin America, Spanish America

For Middle America, see 972

.001–.009 Standard subdivisions

As modified under 930–990

.03 South America since 1830

981 *Brazil

.06 1930–

Class here 20th century

1901–1930 is classed in 981

982 *Argentina

.06 1910–

983 *Chile

.06 1861–

Including War of the Pacific, 1879–1883

984 *Bolivia

For War of the Pacific, see 983.06

.05 1899–

985 *Peru

.06 1867–

For War of the Pacific, see 983.06

986 *Colombia and Ecuador

.1 *Colombia

.106 1863–

.6 *Ecuador

.607 1896–

987 *Venezuela √

.06 1830–

988 *Guiana

.03 1945–

Class here 20th century

1901–1945 is classed in 988

*Add as instructed under 930–990

989 Paraguay and Uruguay

.2 ***Paraguay**

.207 1902–

.5 ***Uruguay**

.506 1886–

990 General history of other parts of world, of extraterrestrial worlds Pacific Ocean islands

.01–.09 Standard subdivisions of Pacific Ocean islands

As modified under 930–990

993 *New Zealand

Melanesia relocated to 995

> 993.01–993.03 Historical periods [*formerly* 993.101–993.103]

Class comprehensive works in 993

.01 Early history to 1840

Including history of Maoris before European settlement, of European settlers

.02 Colonial period, 1840–1908

.03 Dominion period, 1908–

.1 **Specific islands**

Use of this number for comprehensive works on New Zealand discontinued; class in 993

[.101–.103] Historical periods

Relocated to 993.01–993.03

994 *Australia

.01 Early history to 1788

.02 Period of settlement and growth, 1788–1851

.03 Period of development of self government, 1851–1901

.04 Period of Commonwealth, 1901–

For 1945–1966, see 994.05; 1966– , 994.06

.05 1945–1966

.06 1966–

*Add as instructed under 930–990

995 *Melanesia [*formerly also* 993] New Guinea

Class here Oceania

Class Polynesia in 996

.3 *Papua New Guinea New Guinea region

Class Papuan region in 995.4, Highlands region in 995.6, Momase region in 995.7, Bismarck Archipelago in 995.8, North Solomons Province in 995.92

.305 1975–

996 *Other parts of Pacific Polynesia

.001–.009 Standard subdivisions of Polynesia

As modified under 930–990

.9 North central Pacific Hawaii

.900 01–.900 09 Standard subdivisions of north central Pacific

As modified under 930–990

.900 1–.900 9 Standard subdivisions of Hawaii

As modified under 930–990

997 *Atlantic Ocean islands

Class each specific island or group of islands not provided for here with the island or group of islands, e.g., Azores 946.9

998 *Arctic islands and Antartica

999 Extraterrestrial worlds

Class here speculation on and the search for intelligent life on other worlds

Do not add from table under 930–990

*Add as instructed under 930–990

Relative Index

Use of the Relative Index

Full instructions on the use of the Relative Index are found in the Introduction to the Dewey Decimal Classification.

Alphabeting is word by word. A hyphenated word is filed as two words. Abbreviations are filed as spelled.

Digits are printed in groups of three purely for ease in reading and copying. The spaces are not part of the numbers, and the groups are not related to the segmentation shown in DDC numbers on Library of Congress cataloging records.

The abbreviations used in this index are:

T1	Table 1 Standard Subdivisions
T2	Table 2 Geographic Areas, and Persons
T3	Table 3 Subdivisions for Individual Literatures, for Specific Literary Forms
T4	Table 4 Subdivisions of Individual Languages

B.C.	Before Christ
Colo.	Colorado
D.C.	District of Columbia
Dept.	Department
Md.	Maryland
Mich.	Michigan
N.S.W.	New South Wales
N.W.T.	Northwest Territories
N.Y.	New York
N.Z.	New Zealand
Nfld.	Newfoundland
Ont.	Ontario
Qld.	Queensland
R.S.F.S.R.	Russian Soviet Federated Socialist Republic
S. Aust.	South Australia
S.S.R.	Soviet Socialist Republic
U.S.	United States of America
Va.	Virginia

A

(continued)

B

E

(continued)

H

J

(continued)

M

(continued)

N

P

(continued)

(continued)

(continued)

T

U

V

X

Y

The 12th Abridged Edition of the Dewey Decimal Classification was designed by Lisa Hanifan of Albany, New York. The book was composed in Times Roman and Helvetica by Inforonics, Inc. of Littleton, Massachusetts and by Word Management Corporation of Albany, New York. The book was printed and bound by Hamilton Printing Company of Rensselaer, New York.